Injury Prevention for Children and Adolescents

Research, Practice, and Advocacy

Editor

Karen DeSafey Liller, PhD

American Public Health Association

American Public Health Association
800 I Street, NW
Washington, DC 20001–3710
www.apha.org

Cover photgraphs by Ryan McVay/Getty Images, Doug Menuez/Getty Images, SW Productions/Getty Images, PhotoLink/Getty Images, and S. Wanke/PhotoLink/Getty Images.

Georges C. Benjamin, MD, FACP
Executive Director

Publications Board Liaison: Linda Degutis

Printed and bound in the United States of America
Set In: New Baskerville and Gill Sans
Interior Design and Typesetting: Susan Westrate
Cover Design: Irma Rodenhuis
Printing and Binding by Victor Graphics, Inc., Baltimore, MD

ISBN 0-87553-068-0
1200M 11/05

Dedication

This book is especially dedicated to the children and families profiled in the chapters and to all children so that they can live in a world free from needless injury. I also dedicate this book to my husband Dave and our children, Matthew and Rebecca, who selflessly endured my long hours of work, and to my parents who provided a safe and loving environment so my sisters and I could thrive and reach our life goals.

My thanks go to all the chapter authors, the APHA Publications Board, and my injury prevention colleagues worldwide whose exemplary work has truly touched the lives of children.

Table of Contents

Foreword

Over the past fifty years, we have seen progress in the field of injury prevention and intervention, particularly in the area of motor vehicle occupant protection and the development of safety standards for products that are used by infants and young children. This is the result of multiple disciplines working together to document the problem through epidemiological research; to propose solutions through engineering and environmental strategies; to advocate for change in policy and standards; and to evaluate the effectiveness of innovations and programs once they have been put into place. Progress has been made in the treatment of injuries, through improvements in emergency medical service systems, trauma system organization, resuscitation, hospital care and rehabilitation, with special attention paid to the unique needs of children.

Despite the progress that has been made, we still have a long way to go in decreasing morbidity and mortality due to injury in children and adolescents. Injury remains the leading cause of death and disability for children and adolescents, yet the emphasis on injury prevention and interventions, as well as funding for injury research lags far behind that of other diseases that have lower mortality and morbidity rates. Budget issues result in cuts in funding for prevention programs and community based interventions. Inadequate insurance coverage or lack of coverage has an impact on preventive care, acute care and rehabilitation. Decreasing funding for program evaluation and research decreases the likelihood of advances in the field. Advocacy for injury related efforts is challenging, due to the nature of injuries themselves, and a general sense that injuries are "accidents" that happen to someone else's child.

Dr. Liller and the chapter authors have worked to put a face on the problem of injury in children and adolescents, and have clearly highlighted the importance of a multidisciplinary and multi-strategy approach to this problem. They document the evidence base for various types of injury events that occur in this age group, highlight effective strategies, and describe successful advocacy efforts. The book provides a framework for practitioners, program planners and evaluators and injury researchers that is both complementary to other work in this area, and fills in some gaps. This book represents the work of numerous experts in the field of injury prevention and intervention, and Dr. Liller and her co-authors are to be congratulated for their success in highlighting not just the scientific aspects of injury, but linking the science to the reality of injury in children and adolescents.

Linda C. Degutis, DrPH, MSN
Associate Professor of Surgery (Emergency
Medicine) and Public Health
Yale University

Prologue

David Sleet, PhD,[1] Stephanie Bryn, MPH,[2]
and Angela Mickalide, PhD, CHES[3]

Injuries are probably the most under-recognized public health problem facing the nation today. About 20 children die every day from a preventable injury—more than die from all diseases combined. One in four children annually will be injured severely enough to miss school or require medical attention or bed rest. For every child injury death, there are approximately 19 hospitalizations, 233 hospital emergency visits, and 450 doctor visits.

Today we recognize that childhood injuries, like the diseases that once killed them, are predictable, preventable and controllable using a public health approach that includes injury surveillance, risk factor identification, intervention development and implementation and dissemination of effective strategies. Public health leadership is critical to these efforts.

The U.S. Centers for Disease Control and Prevention (CDC) began studying home and recreational injuries in the early 1970s and violence prevention in 1983. From these early activities grew a national program to reduce injury, disability, death, and costs associated with injuries outside the workplace. In June 1992, CDC established the National Center for Injury Prevention and Control (NCIPC). As the lead federal agency for injury prevention, NCIPC works closely with other federal agencies; national, state, and local organizations; state and local health departments; and research institutions to reduce fatal and non-fatal injuries, disabilities, and costs related to unintentional injuries violence, and suicide (http://www.cdc.gov/injury).

Safe Kids Worldwide is the first and only national non-profit organization dedicated solely to the prevention of unintentional childhood injury (http://www.safekids.org/tier3_cd.cfm?content_item_id=440&folder_id=362). Children's National Medical Center and Founding Sponsor (http://www.safekids.org/tier3_cd.cfm?content_item_id=442&folder_id=362).

---

1 National Center for Injury Prevention and Control at the Centers for Disease Control and Prevention
2 Maternal and Child Health Bureau, Health Resources Services Administration
3 Home Safety Council and formerly SAFE KIDS

Johnson & Johnson launched the Safe Kids Campaign in 1987. Today, there are more than 300 state and local Safe Kids Worldwide coalitions in all 50 states, the District of Columbia, and Puerto Rico. As well, Safe Kids Worldwide operates in 7 other countries as part of a global effort to reduce unintentional injuries to children. Safe Kids Worldwide's aim is to stimulate changes in attitudes, behavior and the environment. From its inception, the Campaign has relied on developing injury prevention strategies that work in the real world—conducting public outreach and awareness campaigns, stimulating hands-on grassroots activity and working to make injury prevention a public policy priority. The proven science of injury prevention and control underpins all Safe Kids Worldwide initiatives.

The Maternal and Child Health Bureau (MCHB) of the Health Resources and Services Administration (HRSA), Department of Health and Human Services (DHHS) has the primary responsibility for promoting and improving the health of our nation's women, children and families. They provide national leadership to improve the physical and mental health, safety and well-being of all of the nation's women, infants, children, adolescents, and their families, including fathers and children with special health care needs. MCHB funds are used to develop and support systems and programs that address specific health and safety issues such as emergency medical services for children, infant mortality, injury prevention, nutrition, oral health, poison control, traumatic brain injury, universal newborn screening and women's health.

CDC, HRSA, and Safe Kids Worldwide support comprehensive injury control efforts to reduce injuries to children. By working together, public agencies and private organizations have demonstrated we can make progress against childhood injuries -as much as a 26% reduction in the past 10 years. Public health can be used to encourage individual behavior change, for example placing children in the back seat of a vehicle, properly restrained, and it can be a major contributor to changing social norms, for example decreasing public acceptance of child maltreatment. Public health can also contribute to policy change that saves lives, such as regulations for the manufacture of childproof cigarette lighters, or child endangerment statutes that make alcohol-impaired driving with a child passenger aboard a legal offense. These kinds of injury prevention successes result when public health works with those in law enforcement, product safety, and advocacy to protect those who cannot protect themselves.

Our agencies are making large national investments in preventing injuries to children whether through motor vehicle safety research, smoke alarm distribution and fire safety education programs, emergency medical services for children, or anti-bullying programs in schools. Our challenge is to ensure that these resource investments are used wisely. For example, we still need well-designed research on theory-based interventions for children and their parents, and more program evaluation to determine "what works" for childhood injury prevention in the community.

We are committed to lowering the rates of unintentional injury and violence, but we recognize the injury crisis cannot be solved by public health alone. In order to address the problem comprehensively in the US, we need parents, educators, and child-serving agencies to assist. We also need to involve engineers, pediatricians, developmental psychologists, playground and pool manufacturers, city planners, and architects to take an interest in our work and contribute to solutions.

Injuries to children do not occur in isolation. Individual behavioral factors, the quality of environments where children spend their time, and the involvement of caring, responsible adults are important determinants of injury. In regards to child development, we think it is important to bear in mind that taking risks is an important part of growing up. Risk taking can enhance learning by providing children an opportunity to test their limits and increase their adaptation to their environment. The goal of promoting safety and security is not to eliminate all risk, but to minimize, manage and control risk exposure and outcomes.

During the past four decades, the United States has made remarkable progress in reducing the number of people seriously injured and killed, especially from motor vehicle crashes, and we have already surpassed several of the *Healthy People 2010* injury prevention objectives, but we must do more. Theory-based approaches to injury prevention must be further developed and applied. Common risk factors for both unintentional and violence-related injuries will continue to emerge and must be addressed in community-based programs. Health promotion strategies can be helpful as part of a comprehensive approach in the future and we must learn how best to disseminate those interventions found effective.

Individuals, families, communities, schools and other social institutions will be important partners in creating a "culture of safety" for children and youth in the future. To this end, injury prevention and safety promotion is everybody's business. It is our hope that Dr Liller's book will inspire others to join the injury prevention crusade, for there is much left to do. What better future can we offer our children than to grow and thrive without the threat of injury and violence.

Editor and Chapter Authors with Biographies

Editor

Karen D. Liller, PhD, is a Professor of Public Health and Associate Dean for Academic Affairs at the University of South Florida College of Public Health in Tampa, FL. Dr. Liller has over 17 years of experience in children's injury prevention. She has been the recipient of several federal and state grant awards, has developed many injury prevention and programs, serves on several national and state injury prevention boards and groups and successfully advocated for injury prevention legislation. She has published extensively in the field covering such injury areas as the integration of unintentional and intentional injury prevention efforts, the evaluation of several school-based injury prevention programs, farm injuries and deaths, bicycle injuries, issues related to violence, and the importance of child death review teams.

University of South Florida
College of Public Health
13201 Bruce B. Downs Blvd.
Tampa, FL 33612
Phone: 813-974-6685
FAX: 813-974-6616

Prologue

David A. Sleet, PhD, is the Associate Director for Science, Division of Unintentional Injury Prevention at the CDC's National Center for Injury Prevention and Control. He is the senior advisor to the division on matters of science and policy. Before joining the CDC, Dr. Sleet taught and conducted research in injury prevention and public health at San Diego State University, California.

National Center for Injury Prevention and Control (NCIPC)
Centers for Disease Control and Prevention (CDC)
4770 Buford Highway, NE, K-63
Atlanta, GA 30341-3724

CAPT Stephanie Bryn, Director of Injury and Violence Prevention Programs for the Health Resources and Services Administration's Maternal and Child Health Bureau plays a critical role in HRSA's mission by facilitating technical assistance and education/training to states, organizations and others through a network of national resource centers referred to as the Children's Safety Network (CSN) and by providing vision and leadership for injury and violence prevention programming.

Maternal and Child Health Bureau
Injury and Violence Prevention Programs
5600 Fishers Lane
Rm. 18A-39, Parklawn Bldg
Rockville, MD 20857
Phone: 301-443-6091
Fax: 301-443-1296

Angela Denise Mickalide, PhD, CHES, is the Director of Education and Outreach for the Home Safety Council, headquartered in Washington, DC For 15 years prior, she served as the Program Director of the National SAFE KIDS Campaign, the only nationwide, non-profit organization to prevent unintentional injuries among children ages 14 and under.

Director, Education and Outreach
Home Safety Council
1725 Eye Street, NW
Suite 300
Washington, DC 20006

Chapter 1: Applying a Developmental and Ecological Framework to Injury and Violence Prevention

James A. Mercy, PhD
David A. Sleet, PhD
Lynda Doll, PhD

National Center for Injury Prevention and Control (NCIPC)
Centers for Disease Control and Prevention (CDC)
Mailstop K60
4770 Buford Highway, NE
Atlanta, GA 30341-3724.
E-mail: jam2@cdc.gov

Chapter 2: Cost of Children's Injuries and the Value of Prevention

Ted Miller, PhD, and Eduard Zaloshnja, PhD, are economists at the Pacific Institute for Research and Evaluation, 11710 Beltsville Drive, #300, Calverton MD 20705.

Eric Finkelstein, PhD, is an economist with Research Triangle Institute, Center for Economic Research, 3040 Conrwallis Road, Research Triangle Park, NC 27709.

Delia Hendrie is a Lecturer in Health Economics, Graduate Diplomate in Road Safety, and doctoral candidate at the School of Population Health, The University of Western Australia, Nedlands, WA 6907 Australia.

Chapter 3: Hazards Associated with Common Nursery Products

Carol Pollack-Nelson, PhD, is a human factors psychologist, having worked in the field of consumer safety since 1982. From 1988 through 1993, she was employed by the U.S. Consumer Product Safety Commission (CPSC) in the Human Factors Division. For the past 11 years, she has worked independently as a human factors consultant in Rockville, MD. Her practice includes consultation to industry, trade associations, and to the CPSC on variety of issues relating to consumer products including age grading and safety analyses of toy premiums. In addition, she serves as a consultant and expert witness in litigation throughout the country relating to human factors and product-related injuries. Dr. Pollack-Nelson has published research studies and presented her findings on a range of product safety issues including: supervision of young children, facial suction suffocation hazard to infants, fall and suffocation injuries involving infant seats and carriers, and playground injuries and fatalities.

Independent Safety Consulting
13713 Valley Drive
Rockville, MD 20850
(301) 340-2912

Dorothy Ann Drago, MA, MPH, has over 25 years of experience in the field of safety, having worked at the US Consumer Product Safety Commission for nearly 10 years, and having worked as a private safety consultant for the last 18 years, with a focus on infants and children. Her work experience is supplemented by her academic credentials, including an MPH with focus on Injury Prevention and Control from Johns Hopkins University (1995). She is familiar with injury data, injury epidemiology, and intervention/prevention strategies. She has published in peer-reviewed journals, including Injury Control & Safety Promotion (2002), Pediatrics (1999 and 2005), and Archives of Pediatrics & Adolescent Medicine (1997). She is currently working on a book to be published in 2006 by The Johns Hopkins University Press entitled The Daily Routine—Making it Safe for Infants, Toddlers, and Pre-Schoolers.

She actively and voluntarily participates in the development of ASTM safety standards for consumer products, especially those intended for children. She has volunteered her time to teach and promote safety at SAFE KIDS events, local adult-education programs, and parents' groups.

127 Harrison Ave
Wakefield, MA 01880-4383

Chapter 4: Preventing Motor Vehicle Crashes and Injuries among Children and Adolescents

Bruce Simons-Morton, EdD, MPH, is Chief of the Prevention Research Branch in the Division of Epidemiology, Statistics, and Prevention Research at the National Institute of Child Health and Human Development, NIH, where he directs a program of research on child and adolescent health behavior. Dr. Simons-Morton's research on teen driving has focused on the nature of teen driving risks, the benefits and status of parental limits on teen driving privileges, and evaluation of the effects of the Checkpoints Program on parental management of newly licensed teens.

Chief, Prevention Research Branch
6100 Executive Blvd 7B13M
9200 Wisconsin Ave
Bethesda, MD 20892-7510

Angela Mickalide, PhD, CHES

Erik C.B. Olsen is currently an Intramural Research Training Award Postdoctoral Fellow of the Prevention Research Branch in the Division of Epidemiology, Statistics, and Prevention Research at the National Institute of Child Health and Human Development, NIH. He serves as a co-investigator for research efforts preventing motor vehicle crashes among young drivers, with an emphasis on novice (teen) drivers. Dr. Olsen was educated at Virginia Tech, San Jose State University, and California State University, Long Beach. Previously he was a summer Research Fellow at the Liberty Mutual Research Institute for Safety and was a Graduate Research Assistant at the Virginia Tech Transportation Institute, where he conducted and assisted with both test-track and on-road behavioral research. Dr. Olsen has authored or co-authored over 20 publications including journal articles, proceedings papers, and technical reports

Chapter 5: Home Injuries

Eileen M. McDonald, MS, is assistant scientist and core faculty of the Center for Injury Research and Policy at the Johns Hopkins Bloomberg School of Public Health. She is the program director of the Children's Safety Center and her health education work is directed toward reducing unintentional childhood injury.

Deborah Girasek, PhD, MPH, Johns Hopkins Bloomberg School of Public Health

Andrea Carlson Gielen, ScD, ScM, CHES, is professor and deputy director of the Center for Injury Research and Policy at the Johns Hopkins Bloomberg School of Public Health. Her research focuses on the application of behavioral sciences and health education to injury prevention programs for children and women.

Chapter 6: Adolescent Employment: Relationships to Injury and Violence

Carol W. Runyan, PhD, is Director of the University of North Carolina Injury Prevention Research Center, and is a Univeristy of North Carolina–Chapel Hill Professor of Health Behavior and Health Education and of Pediatrics. She has led research on injury in young workers for over a decade.

University of North Carolina
Injury Prevention Research Center

Bank of America, Suite 500, CB 7505
Chapel Hill, NC 27599-7505

Michael D. Schulman, PhD, is Alumni Distinguished Graduate Professor and Professor of Sociology and Anthropology at North Carolina State University. His scholarly work addresses various aspects of labor sociology, including a longstanding focus on the working conditions of young workers.

Department of Sociology and Anthropology
North Carolina State University
Box 8107
Raleigh, NC 27695-8107

Myduc L. Ta, MPH is a doctoral student in the Department of Epidemiology at the University of North Carolina-Chapel Hill School of Public Health. She is specializing in occupational injury epidemiology.

Department of Epidemiology
University of North Carolina at Chapel Hill
CB #7435
Chapel Hill, NC 27599-7435

Chapter 7: Injuries in the School Environment

Ellen Schmidt, MS, OTR, is a Senior Project Director at the Education Development Center (EDC) and is the National Outreach Coordinator for the National Injury and Violence Prevention Resource Center—Children's Safety Network (CSN). Over the past seven years, she has been the lead for school-related injury prevention.

Education Development Center
National Injury and Violence Prevention Resource Center
Children's Safety Network
1000 Potomac Street, NW, Suite 350
Washington, DC 20007
Phone: (202) 572-3734
Fax: (202) 572-3795
Web: www.ChildrensSafetyNetwork.org

Abbey Mahady is completing her MPH in Maternal and Child Health from the George Washington University, School of Public Health and Health Services. Abbey has a background in children's health and health communication, and is currently working as a research assistant at the Education Development Center, Inc., in Washington, DC.

CAPT Stephanie Bryn

Chapter 8: Childhood Agricultural Injuries

Barbara C. Lee is a senior scientist with the Marshfield Clinic Research Foundation where she directs the National Farm Medicine Center as well as the National Children's Center for Rural and Agricultural Health and Safety, funded by the National Institute for Occupational Safety and Health.

Barbara Marlenga is a Research Scientist with the National Farm Medicine Center. She received her PhD in Nursing from the University of Wisconsin-Milwaukee with a minor in rural sociology from the University of Wisconsin–Madison. She was Principal Investigator of two NIOSH-funded studies evaluating the *North American Guidelines for Children's Agricultural Tasks.* Dr. Marlenga is currently working on two NIOSH funded policy evaluation studies: *Removing the Family Farm Exemption from the Hazardous Occupations Order for Agriculture: Impact on Injury,* and *Evaluation of a policy (Wisconsin Act 455) to Reduce Youth Tractor Crashes on Public Roads.*

National Children's Center for Rural
   and Agricultural Health and Safety
National Farm Medicine Center
Marshfield Clinic Research Foundation
1000 N. Oak Ave.
Marshfield, WI 54449

Chapter 9: Sports and Recreational Injuries

Gitanjali Saluja, PhD, MA, is a Research Fellow at the National Institute of Child Health and Human Development, part of the National Institutes of Health. Much of her research focuses on the epidemiology and prevention of child and adolescent injuries, particularly drowning. She is also interested in parent and child behaviors as they relate to health and injury.

Division of Epidemiology, Statistics and Prevention Research
National Institute of Child Health and Human Development
National Institutes of Health
U.S. Department of Health and Human Services
6100 Executive Blvd
Room 7B03 MSC 7510
Bethesda, MD 20892-7510
Phone: (301) 435-6917
Fax: (301) 402-2084
Email: salujag@mail.nih.gov

Steve Marshall, PhD, is an Assistant Professor of Epidemiology and Orthopedics at the University of North Carolina at Chapel Hill. He is closely associated with the University of North Carolina Injury Prevention Research Center. He has been involved in researching and preventing sports and recreational injuries for over a decade and has authored or co-authored over 80 papers related to injury prevention.

CB#7435, Dept. Epidemiology
McGarvan-Greenberg Hall
SPH, UNC-CH, NC 27599-7435
Phone: (919) 966-1320
Fax: (919) 966-2089
E-mail: smarshal@email.unc.edu

Julie Gilchrist, MD, joined the US Public Health Service in 1997 at CDC's Injury Center. As a pediatrician with undergraduate degrees in Sports Medicine and Human Physiology, she leads CDC research and programs in sports and recreation-related injury prevention. In addition, she continues CDC's efforts in other areas affecting children such as drowning, dog bites, playground injuries, poisoning, and choking.

LCDR, United States Public Health Service
Medical Epidemiologist
National Center for Injury Prevention & Control
Centers for Disease Control & Prevention
4770 Buford Hwy NE, Mailstop K63
Atlanta, GA 30341
Phone: (770) 488-1178
Fax: (770) 488-1317
E-mail: jgilchrist1@cdc.gov

Tom Schroeder, MS, has been at the Consumer Product Safety Commission since 1995 where he is the senior statistician overseeing the statistical design and quality control of the National Electronic Surveillance System (NEISS). He became the Division Director of Data Systems in October, 2004.

US Consumer Product Safety Commission
4330 East West Highway
Bethesda, MD 20814
Phone: (301) 504-0539 x1179
Fax: (301) 504-0038
Email: TSchroeder@cpsc.gov

Chapter 10: Water-Related Injuries of Children and Adolescents

Linda Quan, MD, is Professor of Pediatrics at the University of Washington School of Medicine and a Pediatric Emergency Medicine physician at Children's Hospital, Seattle, WA. Her research has focused on drowning, drowning prevention, and resuscitation of children and adolescents. Recently, she was on the Task Force of the World Congress on Drowning held in Amsterdam, 2002.

Karen D. Liller, PhD, USF College of Public Health (See Editor Bio)

Elizabeth "Tizzy" Bennett, MPH, CHES, is the Health Education Manager at Children's Hospital and Regional Medical Center in Seattle Washington and a clinical instructor in the School of Public Health and Community Medicine at the University of Washington. She has worked in injury prevention for over 20 years, spearheading the hospital's Stay on Top of It Drowning Prevention campaign and the Washington State Drowning Prevention Network. She chairs the Washington State SAFE KIDS coalition and recently completed work as the community campaign section editor for the Handbook on Drowning.

Chapter 11: Child Abuse and Neglect

David DiLillo, PhD, is an associate professor of clinical psychology at the University of Nebraska–Lincoln. His research interests lie in the areas of family violence and marital and couple relations. He is particularly interested in the long-term impact of child maltreatment. Recently, Dr. DiLillo has begun a NIMH-funded project exploring associations between childhood abuse history and adult marital and parent-child functioning. Dr. DiLillo has also conducted research on the causes and consequences of unintentional injury.

Michelle Fortier, MA, received her Bachelor of Arts degree in Psychology from the University of California, Riverside in 1997. She was awarded a Master of Arts in Psychology from San Diego State University in 2000, while researching mediating factors of the relationship between early family environment and adult psychopathology. Currently, Michelle is pursuing her doctorate in clinical psychology at the University of Nebraska–Lincoln. At UNL, Michelle has specialized in child and family psychology and is currently examining processes by which child maltreatment impacts adult functioning.

Andrea R. Perry received a bachelor of science degree in psychology from Middle Tennessee State University in 2002. She currently is enrolled in the doctoral program in Clinical Psychology at the University of Nebraska–Lincoln, where she completed a master's degree in 2004. Andrea's research interests include child maltreatment, adult couple relationships, and processes that mediate relations among these constructs (e.g., adult attachment).

Department of Psychology
238 Burnett Hall
University of Nebraska–Lincoln
Lincoln, NE 68588-0308

Chapter 12: Firearm Injuries

Shannon Frattaroli, PhD, MPH, is on the faculty of The Johns Hopkins Bloomberg School of Public Health where she is affiliated with the Center Injury Research and Policy. Her research interests include understanding the role of policy in improving the health of populations, with particular attention to the effects of injury and alcohol prevention policies, the implementation of public health policies and programs, and the role of advocacy and communities in the policy and intervention processes. She uses both qualitative and quantitative approaches toward those ends.

Sara B. Johnson, MPH, is a doctoral candidate at the Johns Hopkins Bloomberg School of Public Health. Her research interest is in injury and violence prevention in adolescence, particularly how developmental processes in adolescence affect injury risk and intervention strategies.

Stephen P. Teret, JD, MPH, is Professor of Health Policy and Management and Director of the Johns Hopkins Center for Law and the Public's Health. Professor Teret holds joint faculty appointments in Pediatrics and in Emergency Medicine at the Johns Hopkins School of Medicine, and is Adjunct Professor of Health Law at the Georgetown University Law Center.

Professor Teret has worked as a poverty lawyer and a trial lawyer in New York. Since 1979, he has been a full-time faculty member at the Johns Hopkins School of Public Health. His work includes research, teaching and public service in the areas of injury prevention and health law. Professor Teret's work has also focused on the understanding and prevention of violence, with an emphasis on gun policy.

The Johns Hopkins School of Public Health
624 North Broadway
Baltimore, MD 21205

Chapter 13: Youth Suicide

Lloyd Potter, PhD, is a Distinguished Scholar at Education Development Center, the Director for a National Suicide Prevention Resource Center (SPRC), and the Director of Children's Safety Network (CSN). His work focuses on working with state and local practitioner efforts to develop and implement suicide, violence, and unintentional injury prevention efforts.

Education Development Center
Health and Human Development Programs
55 Chapel Street
Newton, MA 02458-1060

Appendix I: Selected Historic Time Line for Injury Prevention and Control

Les Fisher, MPH, is a 40-year seasoned veteran NY state government researcher, practitioner and educator who has directly established a dozen new national and state injury prevention laws or regulations; served on numerous national advisory panels, and as a resource expert, consultant and conference speaker; as principle investigator for various national grants and contracts and published some 35 professional journals. Presently, he is a safety/management consultant and archivist for the Injury Control and Emergency Health Services Section of the American Public Health Association.

97 Union Avenue South
Delmar NY, 12054
Phone: (518) 439-0326

Introduction

Karen D. Liller*

It is difficult to imagine that in the United States of America, the most prosperous nation in the world, children and adolescents continue to be harmed and die from needless injuries. However, the reality of the situation is that the National Center for Injury Prevention and Control of the Centers for Disease Control and Prevention reports that over 14 000 children and adolescents, ages 0–18, were killed in 2002 as a result of injury and over 9 million suffered nonfatal injuries during 2003. It is well known that injuries are the leading cause of death for children between the ages of 0–4 and continue to be a leading cause of death throughout childhood and adolescence.[1] Leading causes of injury and death for children and adolescents are motor vehicle, fire, falls, poisonings, drownings, and violence. While this book focuses on injuries among children and adolescents in the United States, we are very cognizant that a great amount of injury morbidity and mortality takes place outside of the United States—largely in developing nations. As we make our advancements in the United States, it is hoped that we can tailor our successful interventions to assist other nations throughout the world. It is known that the World Health Organization is planning multiple strategies to address children's injury prevention, including the development of a world report on child injury prevention.

The chapters in this book take a detailed look at child and adolescent injuries, incorporating research, practice, and advocacy with recommendations for future work. Each chapter provides an account of a child/adolescent's particular injury; the injury's pertinent risk factors; up-to-date research findings and how research has led to successful action and practice; the importance of the role of advocacy; and future research, practice, and advocacy efforts. Many of the chapters include resources for further information and Appendix II includes information on resources and funding agencies. It is important for the readers to understand that each of the chapter authors used various reference sources to report morbidity, mortality, and other information pertaining to specific injuries and age groups. Therefore, when citing data from the text, the source needs to be noted. Also, children enter adolescence at different points in time. We considered

* University of South Florida, College of Public Health.

adolescence the time between the onset of puberty and full maturity. A brief synopsis of what you as readers will find in each of the chapters is as follows:

In Chapter 1, Mercy, Sleet, and Doll review a developmental and ecological framework to injury and violence prevention, whereby the importance of a child and adolescent's developmental stage and ecology including personal, familial, community, organizational, and socio-cultural factors, play a huge role in recommendations for injury prevention. Viewing injury prevention in this regard suggests that if interventions are developmentally appropriate and include ecological contexts, injury prevention behavior changes will hopefully remain for a lifetime.

An extremely important factor related to child and adolescent injury is cost and value of prevention. Miller and colleagues in Chapter 2 utilize analyses of national and state data sets to present data on frequency, severity, costs, and quality of life losses associated with childhood injury in the year 2000. Childhood injuries in 2000 resulted in an estimated $24 billion dollars in lifetime medical spending and $82 billion in present and future work losses. An even more surprising figure is that these injuries imposed quality of life losses equivalent to 75 000 child and adolescent deaths. This chapter clearly shows that governments, managed care companies, and third party payers have a vested financial interest in assuring children's safety. However, many proven interventions are not universally implemented. Miller and colleagues also show that the cost-effectiveness of child and adolescent injury prevention strategies reviewed in this chapters are comparable or often *better* than the cost-effectiveness of several other widely implemented child and adolescent illness prevention measures.

It is appropriate that a chapter be included in this text that focuses on our youngest population—those infants and children who use nursery products. This becomes even more appropriate in the light of the company GRACO recently being fined millions of dollars due to faulty nursery products. Pollack-Nelson and Drago take a detailed look in Chapter 3 at nursery product injuries and their standards and regulations beginning with the story of Daniel Keysar, who was strangled to death when a portable crib in which he was sleeping collapsed across his neck. This tragedy led his parents to develop the organization, Kids In Danger, that works today to remove dangerous products from the marketplace. The chapter authors advocate for people to become involved in grass-roots efforts such as regularly checking the Consumer Product Safety Commission website for product recalls, reporting dangerous products to the Commission, petitioning the Commission to remedy a product, or becoming a consumer member of the American Society of Testing and Materials subcommittee. Research efforts need to continue to promote safer product standards and making recalled product information more accessible and available. A very helpful table showing the standards for nursery products is also provided.

The leading cause of injury death for children and adolescents is motor-vehicle-related. After reporting an all-to-common scenario of the death of a teenager (Alicia) due to a motor vehicle crash, Simons-Morton, Mickalide, and Olsen review in Chapter 4 the statistics surrounding these injuries, the pertinent risk factors, and comprehensive injury prevention approaches, including technology and legislation. The authors continue their discussion with information about protecting young children from motor vehicle crashes, followed by a detailed account of the prevention of motor vehicle crashes among young drivers. Highlighted in this section is the role of graduated driver licensing. The chapter concludes with a call for advocacy.

Young children spend much of their time in the home environment and this setting creates the opportunity for injuries to occur. McDonald, Girasek, and Gielen in Chapter 5 report in detail information pertaining to choking/suffocation, fire and burns, poisoning, falls, and animal bites. This information includes background statistics, risk factors, prevention and advocacy efforts, and related research. Interspersed throughout the chapter are stories of children who have suffered from these injuries. The information on animal bites is very important as these types of injuries continue to be a great public health concern. As for the future, the authors point to the need for more research done on what constitutes "adequate supervision" of children, the importance of improved data surveillance measures, and the continued efforts of organizations such as the Home Safety Council and the American Public Health Association, to advocate for child and adolescent injury prevention and control through resources for practitioners and researchers.

Chapter 6 by Runyan, Schulman, and Ta focuses on adolescent employment. It provides information not only on the settings, risk factors, and dangers of teen employment, but also the important role work plays in the life course perspective. The chapter begins with vignettes of real teens who were injured on the job to bring home the risks associated with adolescent employment. The information provided by the authors clearly shows that teens who work often receive little safety training and poor supervision. Not only are more safety interventions needed (both in the workplace and in schools), but these need to be evaluated for efficacy. There is a strong role for parents to become more involved in determining the safety of their teen's work environment. Community coalitions should be involved with adolescent work safety issues and advocate for safe environments and enforcement of regulations. This chapter concludes with very useful resources for further information.

In Chapter 7, Schmidt, Mahady, and Bryn detail injuries that occur in school and include information on playground and violence-related school injuries. The issue of school bullying has taken on growing importance in the past few years. The chapter begins with case profiles of school injuries. The role of the community and public health, and the availability of a multitude of federal and organizational resources are highlighted. Future steps that focus on the recognition that a non-injured child can learn better in school, the improvement of reporting mechanisms, evaluation of programs, social climate and physical environment changes, policy revisions, and others are provided.

Many children in the United States not only work in agricultural settings but also live in this environment, increasing their potential for injuries. Lee and Marlenga in Chapter 8 begin the agricultural injuries chapter with several actual child profiles reported in newspapers. As stated by the authors, these are "just a sampling of the tragedies that occur on farms and ranches across the U.S." The authors go on to report that "The fatalities have striking similarities, such as siblings working together, inadequate adult supervision, and farm machinery designed for adults who willingly choose to work in one of our nation's most dangerous occupations. Beyond the news clippings, is the unreported psychological, social and financial toll that often reaps a devastating impact on survivors, especially parents."

Included in this chapter is information on morbidity and mortality, risk factors, research and interventions related to the National Institute of Occupational Safety and Health (NIOSH) initiatives, the role of the National Guidelines for Children's Agricultural Tasks (NAGCAT), the need for advocacy, and future recommendations including enhanced partnerships with agricultural organizations and businesses.

Chapter 9 focuses on child and adolescent sport and recreational injuries. Saluja, Marshall, Gilchrist, and Schroeder begin by describing the story of Brandon Schultz, who suffered second impact syndrome while playing a varsity football game. This chapter details leading child and adolescent sport injuries in the United States, including team sports (basketball, football, baseball/softball, soccer, hockey, and cheerleading) and individual sports (playground, bicycle, skiing/snowboarding, trampolines, all terrain vehicles, in-line skating/roller sports). Research and effective interventions are highlighted in addition to those groups and organizations who advocate for safer sports and recreational activities. With these groups and parent involvement, advocacy can be enhanced thereby decreasing the number of these injuries.

Because drownings are the second major cause of unintentional injury death in children less than 15 years, Chapter 10 has been devoted to water-related injuries. Quan, Liller, and Bennett begin the chapter with the heartbreaking account of Preston Thomas de Ibern's death due to a near-drowning that was written by his mother, Carole Y. de Ibern. This story of Preston's life and death not only brings a "face" to this injury but details the common risk factors, sequelae, the long fight to survive, and the importance of advocacy efforts to pass pool safety legislation. The chapter continues with information pertaining to morbidity and mortality, risk factors including diseases such as epilepsy, current research and prevention efforts, important recommendations for further research, guidelines for practice, and advocacy. The chapter ends with information about personal watercraft injuries as these injuries are becoming more and more important as the sales of personal watercrafts increase.

The last three chapters of the text focus on violence-related injuries. These chapters have been grouped together based on the theme of violence and not because many of the interventions and research recommendations provided in the previous chapters do not pertain also to these injuries. Although some individuals in the injury prevention field divide injuries into unintentional (done without harmful intent) and violence (done with harmful intent), there are many common risk factors related to both of these categories and artificial divisions only separate those individuals and organizations who work in these areas. If risk factors such as poverty, lack of social support, and behavioral issues such as substance abuse are ameliorated, both unintentional and violence-related injuries should decrease.

In Chapter 11, DiLillo, Fortier, and Perry address child abuse and neglect. The chapter begins with the tragic story of Diana N. Molina, who died at the hands of an abusive father while her mother, filled with fear and helplessness, did not know how to prevent the abuse from occurring in the home. The reason cited for the final beating that lead to Diana's death was due urinating in her crib and not alerting her parents this occurred. This chapter continues with a detailed review of morbidity/mortality and risk factor information, definitions, up-to-date research findings and prevention approaches, treatment mechanisms (both child and family (multisystemic focused), and the crucial role for advocacy efforts. Recommendations for the future include the need for more comprehensive etiological models of child abuse and neglect, reaching out to older victims with practice interventions, and advocating with empirical data rather than emotions only.

In Chapter 12, Frattaroli, Johnson, and Teret address firearm injuries. The lead-in to this chapter is the story of Anthony who believed that his father's semi-automatic pistol was not loaded when he pointed and fired it at his best friend Eric, who later died from the injuries. Anthony and Eric were simply playing and Anthony thought the gun was safe since he removed the magazine or clip that held the ammunition. However, a round remained in the chamber. This chapter continues with a detailed examination of the nature of firearm injury in the United States, morbidity, cost figures, and risk factors. Current research, education, and advocacy efforts are highlighted, in addition to future recommendations which include research focused on changing social norms about the acceptance of violence, adolescent development research, policy implementation, surveillance, and better advocacy and practice initiatives to maximize impact. The authors highlight the need for injury prevention researchers, practitioners, and advocates to work collaboratively at the federal, state, and local levels to bring together effective change.

Finally, chapter 13 by Potter focuses on the important topic of youth suicide and covers risk and protective factors, current research, prevention, and intervention strategies (including use of medications and screening issues), and the need for better research, practice, and advocacy so that we have quality data and scientific information to develop and evaluate interventions. It is also important to begin studying youth violence utilizing a comprehensive framework so that we may address multiple types of violence among youth through our efforts. As the author states, "Efficiency and efficacy of prevention efforts might enhance our ability to reduce perpetration of multiple types of violence impacting youth while other prevention strategies may need to focus on a particular type of violence and the groups at greatest risk."

The chapter appendices that follow provide further information about milestones in injury prevention and control throughout the decades, many of which are related to children and adolescents, resources (funding, organizational, journals, books, listservs, etc.), and injury data charts from the National Center for Injury Prevention and Control. All of this information should help in research, practice, and advocacy efforts.

The purpose of this text is to reach not only academicians and students but practitioners as well. My work in children's injury prevention spans 17 years and I continue to observe a division between these groups that often hampers meaningful collaborations. Through this text, it is hoped that researchers and practitioners can come together and sit at one planning table and put their expertise to work. No one group can do it alone.

Over at least the last two decades, the Haddon Matrix and Countermeasures, which emphasize the host, agent (usually a type of energy such as mechanical, thermal, chemical, radiation, electrical or the absence of essentials such as oxygen or heat that exceed the body's ability to withstand), the vehicle or vector for the agent, and physical and sociocultural environment factors, have been used to help guide the development of injury interventions.[2] The Unified Framework that incorporates the Public Health Approach of surveillance, risk factor identification, intervention evaluation, and intervention implementation with the Haddon Matrix has also been proposed as a useful guide for prevention efforts.[3] It is also important to not lose sight of the role of behavior and the importance of behavior change strategies in our efforts.

The injuries discussed in this book are more than statistics, research designs, policy statements, legislation, and program development activities. They are about people—children and adolescents—who look to adults for protection. That is why each chapter contains stories related to a particular child (a face of injury) who has suffered from some or all of the injuries discussed in the chapter. As you read, please do not lose site of that child or story because it helps bring you back to the realization that every number, research endeavor, prevention project, or outreach effort, is about a real person—a real "face." I hope you enjoy and learn a great deal from the content that lies ahead.

References

1. National Center for Injury Prevention and Control. Available at http://www.cdc.gov/ncipc/. Accessed December 28, 2004.

2. National Committee for Injury Prevention and Control. Oxford University Press; 1989.

3. Lett, R., Kobusingye, O., and Sethi, D. A unified framework for injury control: The public health approach and Haddon's Matrix combined. *Injury Control and Safety Promotion*, 9, 199-205, 2002.

Applying a Developmental and Ecological Framework to Injury and Violence Prevention[1]

James A. Mercy, David A. Sleet, and Lynda Doll

njuries, regardless of their cause, profoundly impact healthy physical and emotional development during childhood and adolescence. In every industrialized country, injury is the leading killer of children, accounting for almost 40% of all deaths among children ages one to 14 (United Nations Foundation, pp 5). In the United States, about 20 children die every day from an injury, more than from all other diseases or conditions combined (Sleet, Schieber, and Dellinger p 185). For each injury death to children less than 20 years of age, there are approximately 16 hospitalizations and 562 children treated and released from emergency departments (Centers for Disease Control and Prevention [CDC]–a). In 2000, injuries requiring medical attention in the United States affected more than 44 million people and cost $117 billion annually for medical care (Finkelstein, Fiebelkorn, Corso and Binder 2–3). Injuries also are one of the primary causes of death and disability to children in the developing world (Krug; McQueen, McKenna and Sleet).

Injuries can have serious long-term consequences for the healthy development of children and adults. For example, the accumulated scientific evidence shows very clearly that exposure to child maltreatment and other forms of violence during childhood is associated with risk factors and risk-taking behaviors later in life (eg, depression, smoking, high-risk sexual behaviors, unintended pregnancy, and substance use) as well as leading causes of death, disease, and disability (eg, heart disease, cancer, suicide, and sexually transmitted diseases) (Felitti et al; Anda et al; Dietz et al; Hillis,

1   This paper is adapted, in part, from: Mercy, J.A., Sleet, D.A., Doll, L.S. (2003). Applying a developmental approach to injury prevention. *American Journal of Health Education* (Supplement) 34(5):6-12 (by permission of the *American Journal of Health Education* and the American Association for Health Education: Reston, Virginia).

James A. Mercy, David A. Sleet, and Lynda Doll are with the National Center for Injury Prevention and Control (NCIPC), Centers for Disease Control and Prevention (CDC), Mailstop K60, 4770 Buford Highway, NE, Atlanta, GA 30341-3724. E-mail: jam2@cdc.gov).

Anda, Felitti, Nordenberg and Marchbanks; Hillis, Anda, Felitti, and Marchbanks; Dube et al; Koenig, Doll, O'Leary and Pequagnat). It is unknown how many adults still suffer from injuries they received during childhood, but it is likely that childhood injuries can have lifelong impact on health and development by causing permanent physical disabilities, or long-term cognitive or psychological damage (eg, traumatic brain injury) (Sleet and Mercy; Zaff, J.F. et al). One follow-back survey of adults found that 62% of men and 26% of women reported at least one hospitalized injury since age 16, with 3.2% of these causing permanent physical disability (Barker, Power and Roberts, p 157).

The purpose of this chapter is to describe injury risk and prevention strategies across the developmental stages and ecological contexts of childhood and adolescence. We frame our discussion within an ecological model that emphasizes, for each developmental stage, the multiple levels of influence (ie, family/peer, community, and social-cultural context) on both the causes and approaches for preventing injury risk. We emphasize social influences, though we also provide examples of physical settings (eg, home, school, workplaces) that can be both sites where injuries occur as well as locations for injury prevention messages.

Injury, Human Development, and Ecology

Pediatric and developmental psychologists have long recognized the importance of children's developmental stages when considering adaptations to disease and health status (Fuemmeler). Changes in injury patterns, including likely causes, settings, and individuals' abilities to respond to risks, are closely related to developmental changes over the life course (Dahlberg and Potter; Mercy, Sleet and Doll; Williams, Guerra and Elliott; Zuckerman and Duby). Growth in infancy and early childhood is characterized by relatively rapid changes in height, weight, and physiological functioning, increasing mastery of perceptual, cognitive, and motor skills, and exploration of the physical and social environment (Alexander and Roberts). Children gradually encounter more and different injury risks (eg, toxic substances, playground equipment, motor vehicles) at the same time they are developing the perceptual and cognitive abilities to evaluate these risks and the motor skills to avoid them. Hazard-free environments and caregiver supervision are critical for avoiding unintentional injuries during this period. The social and emotional environment during infancy and childhood also play an important role in the achievement of health and well being over a lifetime. As noted above, early exposure to physical, emotional, or sexual abuse is strongly related to aggressive and violent behaviors, as well as many health threats including sexual revictimization, early pregnancy, multiple sexual partners, depression, and a variety of chronic diseases. On the other hand, parenting styles that emphasize the construction of positive self-identity, opportunities for children to explore their social and physical environment, gradual training for independence, and academic achievement may buffer a child against a variety of health risks, including injuries (Bigner).

As older children and adolescents grow they become increasingly capable of abstract thinking, problem solving, and an extended time perspective, and thus are more likely to comprehend risks and evaluate their long-term consequences (Crockett and Petersen). They gradually take on more responsibility for personal decision-making and more responsibility for self-protection from injury. At the same time, opportunities for physical and social independence, and risk taking increase with age. Risk taking, a normal part of childhood and adolescence, can enhance learning by providing opportunities to test limits and increase adaptation to a range of environments. However, these opportunities are often accompanied by exposure to increasingly risky behavior and risky environments [eg, youth violence, underage drinking and driving] (National Research Council and Institute of Medicine), and potentially dangerous sports (Kontos) which may in turn be accompanied by increased rates of injuries and deaths.

Figure 1 shows death rates for major causes of injury from birth to age 21. Death rates are higher for unintentional than violence-related injuries at every age, and the u-shaped death rate curves by cause of death parallel one another. They show dramatically high injury death rates in young children, followed by a drop in middle childhood, then a sharp rise in late childhood and early adolescence that continues through late adolescence and early adulthood. The pattern in age-specific risks of nonfatal injuries treated in emergency departments is somewhat different then that for fatalities. As for fatalities, rates of nonfatal unintentional injuries are higher at every age then those for violence-related injuries. The u-shaped pattern is

Figure 1

Injury fatality rates by single year of age and manner of death, United States, 2001

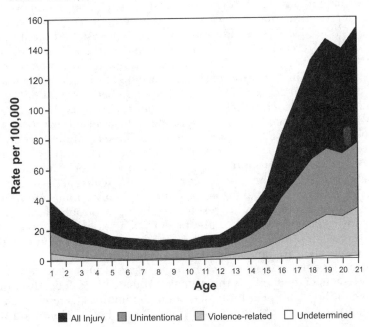

similar for nonfatal unintentional injuries to that for fatalities with the exception that rates among children less then 1 year of age are lower then those for 1 year olds and then after peaking at age 18, rates level off until age 21. In addition, the u-shaped curve found for those between 1 and 17 years of age is less pronounced then that for fatalities (CDC–a). Age-specific patterns for nonfatal violence-related injuries, however, have a less consistent pattern, but in general, increase with age, peaking at age 21.

The circumstances under which injuries occur over the life course change, as well. During infancy and middle childhood, violence-related injuries are primarily caused by child maltreatment at the hand of parents or caretakers, but as children enter adolescence, injuries from peer to peer violence and suicidal behavior predominate (Lung and Daro; Dahlberg; CDC–a). Similarly as children age and grow, unintentional injuries change from those determined and controlled by the physical or social environment (eg, drownings and ingestion of toxic substances) to those determined and controlled by individual behaviors (eg, sports, biking, and pedestrian injuries). However, even for teens and adults, the environment plays an important part in overall risk potential, making the management of environmental risks important throughout the lifecycle. Just as individual factors like physical size, cognitive ability, perceptual integration, personal independence, and risk taking are related to injury risk and prevention, so are the ecological contexts of children and adolescents.

Ecological frameworks propose that behavior is a function of multiple sources of influence including intra- and intra personal, familial, community, organizational, and socio-cultural (Bronfenbrenner). As children grow and develop, the ecological contexts that affect them change with development as do exposure to a variety of physical environments (eg, home, streets, playgrounds, pools) and products (eg, cribs, toys, bicycles, weapons) that influence risk. Social relationships with family members and peers undergo substantial change as children develop. For example, the nature and intensity of parental supervision changes, as children are perceived to be more competent and independent. Moreover, the potential influence of peers on behavior in adolescence is much more intense then at earlier ages. As children grow older and become more independent and mobile, they are also exposed to an increasing number of community contexts such as schools, churches, neighborhoods, and workplaces. These influences have important implications for both the level and nature of risk for unintentional and violence-related injuries. These community contexts also have implications for exposure to physical contexts and products that influence risk (eg, playground equipment at schools, motor vehicles and weapons in streets and other public areas). The socio-cultural environment includes such things as social norms or values (eg, norms that support violence as an acceptable way to resolve conflict), economic and social inequalities, and the presence or absence of public policies that are relevant to the risk for unintentional injury and violence (eg, laws requiring the use of child safety seats, booster seats, and safety belts).

According to the ecological model in Figure 2, from infancy through early adolescence, the family is the primary influence on safety. Also influential in childhood are peer influences and communities' actions, such as policies and structural changes. During infancy and early childhood the social and cultural context (eg, social norms, state and national laws requiring safe behaviors) affects the safety of children primarily through its influence on parents and caretakers. Moving into and through adolescence, peers and the social/cultural context have even greater influence, although characteristics of the family and community remain essential to ensure safety.

Linking Injury Prevention with Human Development and Ecological Context

Table 1 presents a matrix of injury prevention strategies by developmental stage (ie, infancy, childhood, adolescence) and by ecological context towards which the intervention is directed (ie, family/peers, community, social-cultural). Some interventions influence injury risk across several developmental periods (eg, parent training or traffic calming measures on the roads). Other interventions may be relevant in more than one physical setting and developmental stage (eg, policies against bullying in schools and communities or rules governing sports participation). The matrix reinforces the idea that what is ultimately needed to promote safety is a continuum of effective programs and services across the developmental spectrum that addresses salient ecological contexts.

Infant and toddler years (ages 0–3)

The safety of infants and toddlers is dependent primarily upon two factors: an appropriately safe home and community environment, and adequate parenting. Prevention of injuries to infants and toddlers can be achieved through a variety of means. These include modifying the home and community environment to increase safety, enhancing the child-rearing and supervision skills of new parents through home visitation and other strategies

---

Figure 2

Ecological model of life course development* by level of influence and developmental stage

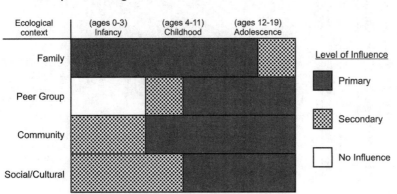

* Adapted from Williams, Guerra, and Elliott, 1997.

Table 1

Prevention Strategies by Developmental Stage (Infancy through Adolescence) and Ecological Context

Ecological Context	Developmental Stage		
	Infant and Toddler Years (ages 0–3)	Childhood (ages 4–11)	Adolescence (ages 12–19)
Family/Peer	• Provide home visitation services to high-risk families • Train new parents in child-rearing skills • Increase access to prenatal and postnatal services • Avoid infant walkers • Use stair gates • Use approved child safety seats • Reduce hot water heater temperatures • Remove home hazards • Avoid dog breed likely to bite • Provide screens or grills on upstairs windows • Reduce access to poisons • Install working smoke alarms • Install 4-sided fencing on pools	• Provide parents with training in child-rearing skills • Use bicycle helmets • Use child safety seats, booster seats and seat belts • Monitor pedestrian crossing • Keep guns unloaded and locked	• Support home-school partnership programs to promote parental involvement • Provide parents with training in child-rearing skills • Provide therapeutic foster care for high-risk youth • Install and test smoke alarms on all floors • Wear safety belts • Enforce zero tolerance alcohol policies • Support graduated licensing programs
Community	• Inspect and modify school and daycare playground hazards	• Provide social development training in anger management, social skills, and problem-solving • Provide preschool enrichment programs (eg, Head Start) • Provide bullying prevention programs • Provide school policies to prevent injuries • Use protective equipment in sports • Institute traffic calming	• Provide mentoring for high-risk youth • Provide education to promote healthy relations with the opposite sex and decrease dating violence • Provide social development training in anger management, social skills, and problem-solving • Develop and enforce school safety policies • Insist on using protective gear in sports

Table 1 continued

Community (continued)	• Provide safe pedestrian and bike paths • Dial 911 access and child training	• Create safe havens for children on high-risk routes to and from school • Provide after-school and recreational programs to extend adult supervision • Train health care professionals in identification and referral of high-risk youth • Separate bicyclists from motorists
Social-Cultural	• Adopt and enforce child safety seat laws • Ban baby walkers • Provide adequate levels of funding for child protective services • Reduce levels of media violence • Develop a "culture of safety" • Educate drivers to share the road	• Deconcentrate lower-income housing • Reduce levels of media violence • Promote pro-social norms through public information campaigns • Provide educational incentives for at-risk, disadvantaged high school students • Enforce laws prohibiting illegal transfers of guns to youth • Support bicycle and motorcycle helmet laws • Support restrictions on access to alcohol

(Tertinger, Greene and Lutzker; Hawkins, Von Cleve and Catalano; Patterson, Capaldi and Bank; Krugman; Olds et al; DiGuiseppi and Roberts; U.S. Department of Health and Human Services), improving safety in day care environments, particularly on the playground (Briss et al), and adopting and/or enforcing laws that protect infants and toddlers from harm. Examples of effective laws include those that address pool fencing, infant and child safety seats, child resistant packaging to prevent poisoning, safe cribs to prevent strangulation, sleepwear regulations for burn prevention, and the safety of baby walkers (Sleet, Schieber and Gilchrist; Grossman).

Childhood (ages 4–11)

During childhood, the family remains the most influential social influence though peers, the community, and the broader social/cultural context gradually take on greater significance. Involvement by parents, teachers, and community members in supervision of children and in providing positive role models for safety behaviors and nonviolent social relationships is critical during this developmental stage (Roberts and Peterson; Peterson and Roberts; Peterson, Ewigman and Kivlahan). As children grow older, however, they increasingly become involved in carrying out safety guidelines for their own self protection and thus initiating safe or risky behaviors that parents and other adults have taught or modeled (Schieber and Thompson). For example, at this stage the use of protective gear in sports and recreational activities (eg, bicycle helmets, shin guards, and face masks) becomes increasingly important and some approaches for modifying individual child behaviors have been found to be effective (Peterson; Jones, Kazdin and Haney), as well as laws and regulations (Schieber, Gilchrist and Sleet).

Although childhood is a period of relatively low injury risk compared to infancy and adolescence, behavior patterns established during this stage can influence injury risk at later stages of life. Prevention programs at this stage not only focus on self-protection from injury, but also prevention of children's violent behavior towards others. For example, early educational enrichment programs (eg, Head Start) and social development programs that improve children's social skills with peers have been found to have both short and long-term effects on the prevention of violent behavior (Richards and Dodge; Berrueta-Clement, Schweinhart, Barnett, Epstein and Weikart; Lally, Mangione and Honig; Schweinhart, Barnes and Weikart; Guerra and Williams; Kellermann, Fuqua-Whitley, Rivara and Mercy; Hawkins et al; U.S. Department of Health and Human Services). Also important are the structural characteristics of the neighborhood and community that make it safer for children, such as the presence of "safe houses," sidewalks and signalized intersections, safe playgrounds, and bike paths and venues for participating in safe recreational activities (Fuemmeler). These can all affect the likelihood of injury to children.

Adolescence (ages 12–19)

Achieving safety from unintentional injuries for adolescents includes many of the same features, such as parental involvement and policy changes, as in earlier stages of life. Graduated licensing programs for teen drivers are a recent example. Graduated licensing systems are a way of managing driving experience and exposure of new teen drivers through driving restrictions that are gradually lifted with time and experience (National Safety Council). Parental involvement in administering and monitoring the teen "graduated licensing" provision of state laws has been shown to change teen driving behavior and injury risk on the road (Simons-Morton and Hartos). Injury risk in motor vehicle travel also can be reduced through laws, policies, and environmental modifications such as zero tolerance alcohol laws, minimum drinking age laws, lowering legal limits on blood alcohol levels to 0.08 g/dL, and primary safety belt use laws (Shults et al; CDC–b). Strategies that encourage individual behavior change become particularly salient during this developmental stage. Effective interventions have been developed for use in this population (Towner, Simpson and Jarvis; Thornton et al) including techniques to increase use of safety belts (Streff and Geller), reduce youth violence (U.S. Department of Health and Human Services), modify bullying (Olweus, Limber and Mihalic), change drivers' attitudes toward speeding (Parker), increase bicycle helmet use (Schneider, Ituarte and Stokols), and prevent school-associated unintentional injuries and violence (CDC–c). Although safety (or risk reduction) devices and behaviors related to their use are likely to result in decreased injury, teenagers have among the lowest rates of behavioral safety compliance. Greater emphasis needs to be placed on obtaining and maintaining safety-related behaviors in adolescents. Interventions that focus on increasing use of safety devices by teens and those that induce or reward safe behaviors will also help. Fostering linkages with supportive community-based services such as schools, clinics, and health departments will be necessary to nurture safety-promoting behavior and social norms (McGinnis, Williams-Russo and Knickman).

The social and cultural context in which adolescents reside also has important influences on their involvement in violent behavior. For example, studies of efforts to reduce the concentration of poverty through rental voucher programs have found that these programs improve the safety of adolescents by reducing their involvement in and exposure to violence (CDC–d; Ludwig, Duncan and Hirschfield). At the same time, however, as adolescents mature, more intensive personalized interventions may be necessary to reduce the chances of adolescents engaging in violent behavior. For example, mentoring programs that match youth (particularly youth growing up in a single parent family or in adverse situations) with a non-familial caring adult, and therapy for families experiencing high levels of conflict and behavioral problems have been found to be effective in reducing child behavior problems and violence (Mihalic and Grotpeter; Grossman and Garry; Hazelrigg, Cooper and Borduin; Shadish).

Conclusion

Models and research on human development and social ecology describe the fluidity and overlapping nature of the various levels of influence on injury risk and safety over the life course (Williams, Guerra, and Elliott). Fuemmeler (409) describes such a framework as "transdisciplinary, incorporating input from social ecology, systems therapy, behavioral theory, developmental research, and social epidemiology." An understanding of the individual influences (and interactions) of biology, psychology, and sociology on development and behavior is a necessary prerequisite to assessing risk of injury. Human development and ecological approaches also inform efforts to tailor specific injury and violence prevention programs to the cognitive and physical skills of children and adolescents and to the social worlds in which they live.

These same models and research also can inform broader decision-making on the combination of prevention programs that are needed to reduce effectively the injury and violent behavior. These models suggest that developmentally appropriate interventions conducted over several stages and across ecological contexts may be more likely to motivate and sustain injury prevention behavior change across a lifetime than a single intervention or a single policy change. For example, sequential and complementary, developmentally appropriate interventions may be particularly important for preventing violence and assuring adherence to safety guidelines for pedestrian safety and drowning. An important implication of a developmental perspective is that interventions at early stages of development may play an important role in preventing injury at later stages of development. For example, given the link between child maltreatment and suicidal behavior, the successful prevention of child maltreatment may prevent injuries from suicidal behavior during adolescence and adulthood (Wolfe). Similarly, simultaneous interventions across multiple ecological contexts may be essential to reduce other risks (eg, multi-level interventions to reduce teen drinking and driving or provide parenting skills). Research by Holder and colleagues supports this view, showing that multi-level interventions that simultaneously addressed social and structural contexts of alcohol use were associated with reductions in high alcohol consumption and alcohol-related injuries resulting from motor vehicle crashes and assaults. Komro et al's work also demonstrates that alcohol use among young adolescents could be modified by using multi-component community wide strategies to change the personal, social and environmental factors contributing to adolescent drinking.

Families, communities, schools, workplaces, and other social institutions are important partners in creating a "culture of safety" for children and youth. Further, promoting safety in many settings across the stages of development will increase the chances for the healthy development of children and adolescents. Practitioners are encouraged to take every available opportunity to use evidence-based prevention strategies in applying this developmental and ecological approach.

References

1. Alexander, K. and M. C. Roberts. Unintentional injuries in childhood and adolescence. *Health and Behaviour in Childhood and Adolescence.* Eds. L. L. Hayman, M. M. Mahon, and J. R. Turner. New York: Springer, 2002.
2. Anda, R. F., J. B. Croft, V. J. Felitti, D. Nordenberg, W. H. Giles, D. F. Williamson, et al. Adverse childhood experiences and smoking during adolescence and adulthood. *Journal of the American Medical Association* 282 (1999): 1652-1658.
3. Barker, M., C. Power, and I. Roberts. Injuries and the risk of disability in teenagers and young adults. *Archives of Diseases in Childhood* 75.2 (1996): 156-158.
4. Berrueta-Clement, J. R., L. J. Schweinhart, W. S. Barnett, A. S. Epstein, and D. P. Weikart. *Changed Lives: The Effects of the Perry Preschool Program on Youth through age 19.* Ypsilanti, MI: High/Scope Press, 1984.

5. Bigner, J. J. *Human Development: A Life-span Approach.* New York: Collier Mac-Millan, 1983.

6. Briss, P. A., J. J. Sacks, D. G. Addiss, M. Kresnow, and J. O'Neil. A nationwide study of the risk of injury associated with day care centers. *Pediatrics* 94.3 (1994): 364-368.

7. Bronfenbrenner, U. Ecological systems theory. *Six Theories of Child Development.* Ed. R. Vasta. London: Jessica Kingsley, 1992.187-250.

8. Centers for Disease Control and Prevention (CDC)–a. Web-based Injury Statistics Query and Reporting System (WISQARS) [Online]. National Center for Injury Prevention and Control, Centers for Disease Control and Prevention (producer). (2004): Available from: www.cdc.gov/ncipc/wisqars.

9. CDC–b. Motor-vehicle occupant injuries: Strategies for increasing use of child safety seats, increasing use of safety belts, and reducing alcohol-impaired driving. *Morbidity and Mortality Weekly Report* 50.RR-7 (2001): 1-16.

10. CDC–c. School health guidelines to prevent unintentional injuries and violence. *Morbidity and Mortality Weekly Report,* Recommendations and Reports 50.RR-22 (2001): 1-73.

11. CDC–d. Community interventions to promote healthy social environments: Early childhood development and family housing. *Morbidity and Mortality Weekly Recommendations and Reports* 51.RR-1 (2002): 1-8.

12. Crockett, L. J. and A. C. Petersen. Adolescent development: health risks and opportunities for health promotion. *Promoting the Health of Adolecents.* Eds. S. G. Millstein, A. C. Petersen, E. O. Nightingale. New York: Oxford, 1993.

13. Dahlberg, L.L. Youth violence in the United States: Major trends, risk factors, and prevention approaches. *American Journal of Preventive Medicine* 14.4 (1998): 259-272.

14. Dahlberg, L.L. and L. B. Potter. Youth violence: Developmental Pathways and Prevention Challenges. *American Journal of Preventive Medicine* 20 (2001): 3-14.

15. Dietz, P. M., A. M. Spitz, R. F. Anda, D. F. Williamson, P. M. McMahon, J. S. Santelli et al. Unintended pregnancy among adult women exposed to abuse or household dysfunction during their childhood. *Journal of the American Medical Association* 282 (1999): 1359-1364.

16. DiGuiseppi, C. and I. Roberts. Individual level injury prevention strategies in the clinical setting. *The Future of Children* 10 (2000): 53-82.

17. Dube, S. R., R. F. Anda, V. J. Felitti, D. Chapman, D. F. Williamson, and W. H. Giles. Childhood abuse, household dysfunction, and the risk of attempted suicide throughout the life span. *Journal of the American Medical Association* 286 (2001): 3089-3096.

18. Felitti, V. J., R. F. Anda, D. Nordenberg, D. F. Williamson, A. M. Spitz, V. Edwards et al. The relationship of adult health status to childhood abuse and household dysfunction. *American Journal of Preventive Medicine* 14 (1998): 245-258.

19. Finkelstein, E. A., I. C. Fiebelkorn, P. S. Corso, and S. C. Binder. Medical expenditures attributable to injuries—United States, 2000. *Morbidity and Mortality Weekly Report* 53.1 (2004):1-4.

20. Fuemmeler, B. F. Bridging disciplines: An introduction to the special issue on public health and pediatric psychology. *Journal of Pediatric Psychology* 29.6 (2004):405-414.

21. Grossman, D.C. The history of injury control and the epidemiology of child and adolescent injuries. *The Future of Children* 10 (2000): 23-52.

22. Grossman, J. B. and E. M. Garry. Mentoring—A proven delinquency prevention strategy. *Juvenile Justice Bulletin.* Washington, DC: United States Department of Justice, 1997.

23. Guerra, N. G. and K. R. Williams. *A Program Planning Guide for Youth Violence*

Prevention: A Risk Focused Approach. Boulder, CO: Center for the Study and Prevention of Violence, 1996.

24. Hawkins, J. D., E. Von Cleve, and R. F. Catalano. Reducing early childhood aggression: Results of a primary prevention program. *Journal of the American Academy of Child and Adolescent Psychiatry* 30 (1991): 208-217.

25. Hawkins, J. D., R. F. Catalano, R. Kosterman, R. Abbott, and K. G. Hill. Preventing adolescent health-risk behaviors by strengthening protection during childhood. *Archives of Pediatrics & Adolescent Medicine* 153 (1999): 226-234.

26. Hazelrigg, M. D., H. M. Cooper, and C. M. Borduin. Evaluating the effectiveness of family therapies: An integrative review and analysis. *Psychological Bulletin* 101 (1987): 428-442.

27. Hillis, S. D., R. F. Anda, V. J. Felitti, D. Nordenberg, and P. A. Marchbanks. Adverse childhood experiences and sexually transmitted diseases in men and women: A retrospective study. *Pediatrics* 106.1 (2000): E11.

28. Hillis, S. D., R. F. Anda, V. J. Felitti, and P. A. Marchbanks. Adverse childhood experiences and sexual risk behaviors in women: A retrospective cohort study. *Family Planning Perspectives* 33 (2001): 206-211.

29. Holder, H. D., P. J. Gruenewald, W. R. Ponicki, et al. Effect of community-based interventions on high-risk drinking and alcohol-related injuries. *Journal of the American Medical Association* 284 (2000): 2341-2347.

30. Jones, R. T., A. E. Kazdin, and J. I. Haney. Social validation and training of emergency fire safety skills for potential injury prevention and lifesaving. *Journal of Applied Behavior Analysis* 14 (1981): 245-260.

31. Kellermann, A. L., D. S. Fuqua-Whitley, F. P. Rivara, and J. A. Mercy. Preventing youth violence: What works? *Annual Review of Public Health* 19 (1998): 271-292.

32. Koenig, L., L. Doll, A. O'Leary, and W. Pequagnat. *Childhood Sexual Abuse and Adult Sexual Risk.* Washington: APA Books, 2004.

33. Komro, K. A, C. L. Perry, C. L. Williams, M. P. Stigler, K. Farakhsh, and S. Veblen-Mortenson. How did Project Northland reduce alcohol use among young adolescents? Analysis of mediating variables. *Health Education Research: Theory and Practice* 16.1 (2001): 59-70.

34. Kontos, A. P. Perceived Risk, Risk Taking, estimation of ability and injury among adolescent sport participants. *Journal of Pediatric Psychology* 29.6 (2004): 447-456.

35. Krug, E. (Ed.). *Injury: A Leading Cause of the Global Burden of Disease.* Document # WHO/HSC/PVI/99.11. Geneva, Switzerland: World Health Organization, 1999.

36. Krugman, R. D. Universal home visiting: A recommendation from the U.S. Advisory Board on Child Abuse and Neglect. *The Future of Children* 3 (1993): 184-191.

37. Lally, J. R., P. L. Mangione, and A. S. Honig. The Syracuse University Family Development Research Project: Long-range impact of an early intervention with low-income children and their families. *Annual Advances in Applied Developmental Psychology: Parent Education as an Early Childhood Intervention.* Ed. D. R. Powell. Norwood, NJ: Ablex, 1988.

38. Ludwig, J., G. J. Duncan, and P. Hirschfield. Urban poverty and juvenile crime: evidence from a randomized housing-mobility experiment. *Quarterly Journal of Economics*, 16 (2001): 655-680.

39. Lung, C. T. and D. Daro. *Current Trends in Child Abuse Reporting and Fatalities: The Results of the 1995 Annual Fifty State Survey.* Chicago: National Committee to Prevent Child Abuse, 1996.

40. McGinnis, J. M., P. Williams-Russo, and J. R. Knickman. The case for more active policy attention to health promotion. *Health Affair* 21.2 (2002): 78-93.

41. McQueen, D. V., M. T. McKenna, and D. A. Sleet. Chronic Diseases and Injury. *International Public Health: Diseases, Programs, Systems, and Policies.* Eds. M. H.

Merson, R. E. Black, A. J. Mills. Gaithersburg, MD, 2001. 293-330.

42. Mercy, J. A., D. A. Sleet, and L. S. Doll. Applying a developmental approach to injury prevention. *American Journal of Health Education* (Supplement) 34.5 (2003):6-12.

43. Mihalic, S. F. and J. K. Grotpeter. *Blueprints for Violence Prevention: Big Brothers/Big Sisters of America, Book Two.* Boulder, CO: Center for the Study and Prevention of Violence, 1997.

44. National Research Council and Institute of Medicine. Reducing underage drinking: A collective responsibility. Committee on Developing a Strategy to Reduce and Prevent Underage Drinking. Eds. R. J. Bonnie and M. E. O'Connell. Board on Children, Youth, and Families, Division of Behavioral and Social Sciences and Education. Washington: The National Academies Press, 2003.

45. National Safety Council. Graduated driver licensing. *Journal of Safety Research* (Supplement), 34.1 (2003); 1-125.

46. Olds, D. L., C. R. Henderson, K. Cole, J. Eckenrode, H. Kitzman, D. Luckey, L. Pettitt, K. Sidora, P. Morris, and J. Powers. Long-term effects of nurse home visitation on children's criminal and antisocial behavior: 15-year follow-up of a randomized controlled trial. *Journal of the American Medical Association* 280 (1998): 1238-1244.

47. Olweus, D., S. Limber, and S. F. Mihalic. *Blueprints for violence prevention: Book nine: Bullying Prevention Program.* Boulder, CO: Center for the Study and Prevention of Violence, 1999.

48. Parker, D. Changing drivers' attitudes to speeding: Using the theory of planned behavior. *Changing Health Behavior.* Eds. D. Rutter and L. Quine. Philadelphia: Open University Press, 2002.138-152.

49. Patterson, G. R., D. Capaldi, and L. Bank. An early starter model for predicting delinquency. *The Development and Treatment of Childhood Aggression.* Eds. D. J. Pepler and K. H. Rubin. Hillsdale, NJ: Lawrence Erlbaum, 1991.139-168.

50. Peterson, L. The "Safe at home" game: Training comprehensive safety skills to latchkey children. *Behavior Modification* 8 (1984): 474-494.

51. Peterson, L. and M. C. Roberts. Compliance, misdirection and effective prevention of children's injuries. *American Psychologist* 23 (1992): 375-387.

52. Peterson, L., B. Ewigman, and C. Kivlahan. Judgments regarding appropriate child supervision to prevent injury: The role of environmental risk and child age. *Child Development* 64 (1993): 934-950.

53. Richards, B. A. and K. A. Dodge. Social maladjustment and problem solving in school-aged children. *Journal of Consultative Clinical Psychology* 50 (1982): 226-233.

54. Roberts, M. C. and L. Peterson. *Prevention of Problems in Childhood.* New York, NY, 1984.

55. Schieber, R. S. and N. Thompson. Developmental risk factors for childhood pedestrian injuries. *Injury Prevention,* 2 (1996): 228-236.

56. Schieber, R. S., J. Gilchrist, and D. A. Sleet. Legislative and regulatory strategies to reduce childhood unintentional injuries. *The Future of Children* 10.1 (2000): 111-136.

57. Schneider, M. L., P. Ituarte, and D. Stokols. Evaluation of a community bicycle helmet promotion campaign: What works and why. *American Journal of Health Promotion* 7.4 (1993): 281-287.

58. Schweinhart, L. J., H. V. Barnes, and D. P. Weikart. *Significant Benefits: The High/Scope Perry Preschool Project Study through Age 27.* Ypsilanti, MI: High/Scope Press, 1993.

59. Shadish, W. R. "Do family and marital psychotherapies change what people do? A meta-analysis of behavior outcomes. *Meta-analysis for Explanation: A Casebook.*

Eds. T. D. Cook, H. Cooper, D. S. Cordray, H. Hartmann, L. V. Hedges, and R. J. Light. New York: Russell Sage Foundation, 1992.

60. Shults, R. A., R. W. Elder, D. A. Sleet, J. L. Nichols, M. O. Alao, V. G. Carande-Kulis, S. Zaza, D. M. Sosin, R. S. Thompson, and Task Force on Community Preventive Services. Reviews of evidence regarding interventions to reduce alcohol-impaired driving. *American Journal of Preventive Medicine*, 21.4S (2001): 66-89.

61. Simons-Morton, B. and J. Hartos. How well do parents manage young driver crash risk? *Journal of Safety Research* 34 (2003): 91-97.

62. Sleet, D. A. and J. A. Mercy. Promotion of safety, security, and well-being. *Well-being: Positive development across the life course*. Eds. M. H. Bornstein, L. Davidson, C. L. M. Keyes, K. A. Moore, and The Center for Child Well-being. Mahwah, NJ: Erlbaum, 2003. 81-97.

63. Sleet, D. A., R. A. Schieber, and A. Dellinger. Childhood injuries. *The Encyclopedia of Public Health, Vol. 1*. Ed. L. Breslow. New York: Macmillan Reference USA, 2002,184-87.

64. Sleet, D. A., R. A. Schieber, and J. Gilchrist. Health promotion policy and politics: Lessons from childhood injury prevention. *Health Promotion Practice* 4(2) (2003): 103-108.

65. Streff, F. M. and E. S. Geller. Strategies for motivating safety belt use: the application of applied behavior analysis. *Health Education Research* 1986:1:47-59.

66. Tertinger, D. A., B. F. Green, and J. R. Lutzker. Home Safety: Development and validation of one component of an ecobehavioral treatment program for abused and neglected children. *Journal of Applied Behavior Analysis* 17 (1984): 154-174.

67. Thornton, T. N., C. A. Craft, L. L. Dahlberg, B. S. Lynch, and K. Baer, eds. *Best Practices of Youth Violence Prevention: A Sourcebook for Community Action*. Atlanta: Centers for Disease Control and Prevention, National Center for Injury Prevention and Control, 2000.

68. Towner, E. M. L., G. Simpson, and S. Jarvis. Preventing unintentional injuries in children and youth. *Effective Health Care* 2.5 (1996): 1-16.

69. United Nations Foundation. *Injuries: OECD Could Prevent 12,000 Child Deaths Per Year: Report*. UNICEF Innocenti Research Center, United Nations Foundation UNWire, 6 Feb. 2001.

70. U.S. Department of Health and Human Services. *Youth Violence: A Report of the Surgeon General*. Rockville, MD: U.S. Department of Health and Human Services, Centers for Disease Control and Prevention, National Center for Injury Prevention and Control; Substance Abuse and Mental Health Services Administration, Center for Mental Health Services; and National Institutes of Health, National Institute of Mental Health, 2001.

71. Williams, K. R., N. G. Guerra, and D. S. Elliott. *Human Development and Violence Prevention: A Focus on Youth*. Boulder, CO: University of Colorado, Center for the Study and Prevention of Violence, Institute of Behavioral Science, 1997.

72. Wolfe, D. A. *Child Abuse: Implications for Child Development and Psychopathology, 2nd ed.* Thousand Oaks, CA: Sage, 1999.

73. Zaff, J. F., D. C. Smith, M. F. Rogers, C. H. Leavitt, T. G. Halle, and M. H. Bornstein. Holistic well-being and the developing child. *Well-being: Positive Development Across the Life Course*. Eds. M. H. Bornstein, L. Davidson, C. L. M. Keyes, K. A. Moore, and The Center for Child Well-being. Mahwah, NJ: Erlbaum, 2003. 23-32.

74. Zuckerman, B. S. and J. C. Duby. Developmental approach to injury prevention. *Pediatric Clinics of North America* 32 (1985): 17-29.

CHAPTER 2

The Cost of Child and Adolescent Injuries and the Savings from Prevention

Ted R. Miller, A. Eric Finkelstein,
Eduard Zaloshnja, and Delia Hendrie

Cost of illness data are useful in comparing magnitudes of various health problems, assessing risks, setting research priorities, and selecting interventions that most efficiently reduce health burdens. Using analyses of national and state data sets, this chapter presents data on the frequency, costs, and quality of life losses associated with child and adolescent injury in 2000. The frequency, severity, and costs of injury—unintentional and intentional—make it a leading child and adolescent health problem. Child and adolescent injuries in 2000 resulted in an estimated $24 billion in lifetime medical spending and $82 billion in present and future work losses, including caregiver losses. These injuries killed almost 18 000 children and left 160 000 with permanent work-related disabilities. Since Medicaid and other government sources paid for 29% of the days children spent in hospitals due to injury, the government has a financial interest in, and arguably a responsibility for assuring the safety of disadvantaged children.

Many proven child safety interventions cost less than the medical and other resource costs they save. Thus, governments, managed care companies, and third party payers could save money by increasing the routine use of selected child safety measures such as child safety seats, booster seats, bicycle helmets, smoke alarms, and aggression replacement training or

Ted Miller and Eduard Zaloshnja are PhD economists at the Pacific Institute for Research and Evaluation, 11710 Beltsville Drive, #300, Calverton MD 20705. Eric Finkelstein is a PhD economist with Research Triangle Institute, Center for Economics Research, 3040 Cornwallis Road, Research Triangle Park, NC 27709. Delia Hendrie is a lecturer in Health Economics, Graduate Diplomate in Road Safety, and doctoral candidate at the School of Population Health, The University of Western Australia, Nedlands WA 6907 Australia.

This paper is adapted, in part, from: Miller TR, Romano EO, Spicer RS. (2000). The Cost of Unintentional Childhood Injuries and the Value of Prevention, *The Future of Children*, 10:1, 137-163 (by permission of the David and Lucile Packard Foundation: Los Altos, CA).

functional family therapy for juvenile offenders. Yet these and other proven injury prevention interventions are not universally implemented. Possible barriers to adoption include, among others, that savings may be split across multiple payers, the payback period may be too long, safety device subsidizers would have to subsidize parents who would buy the devices anyway as well as parents who would not, and intervention may be a risky departure from proven practice or prove politically difficult.

Introduction

Injury is a common and costly childhood affliction, accounting for approximately 15% of medical spending among those ages 1–19 years.[1] Indeed, for children and adolescents 5–19 years of age, injury rivals the common cold in frequency.[2] Injuries, however, are much more likely than colds to have lasting effects. Injury has long been the leading mechanism of death among those ages 1–19.[3] In 2000, almost 18 000 children and adolescents were killed by injuries. Another 160 000 children and adolescents were permanently disabled as a result of an injury.[*]

Coupled with its high death rate, the frequency and severity of nonfatal injury make it a costly childhood health problem. Quantifying the costs associated with childhood injuries is important. Cost estimates translate different injuries—deaths, broken legs, dog bites, even rapes—to a common metric, and allow injuries to be compared with other prevalent health conditions. This makes cost data a useful element in gauging the relative size of various problems, assessing risks, setting research priorities, and selecting interventions that most efficiently reduce the burden of injury. For example, injury costs by diagnosis can inform a decision between spending a playground improvement budget to fix swings (estimated to prevent 7 broken arms at a total medical cost of $14 300) or to fix slides (estimated to prevent 2 broken legs at a total medical cost of $11 200). Measuring the benefit of interventions in dollars also helps planners and evaluators to estimate the "net cost" of a safety investment (ie, the total cost of the investment minus the benefits accrued). On a broader scale, comparably measured costs of injury and illness provide insight into the relative magnitude of these problems and inform resource allocation. Finally, cost data can be used for advocacy purposes, by conveying risk reductions in a way that captures the attention of politicians, the media, and the public. For example, a car safety seat give-away program targeting Medicaid recipients may reduce an infant's risk of death by 1% and yield net government savings of $15 per seat.[4] While both risk reduction and government savings are important, communicating the benefit in monetary terms may be more informative for policy makers concerned with overall state or federal budgets.

The widely quoted report, *Cost of Injury in the United States, 1989: A Report to Congress,*[3] estimated medical spending and other costs resulting from child and adolescent injuries using data from the mid-1980s. This report provided cost of injury estimates that helped draw recognition to the role of injury as a major public health threat. It did not differentiate injuries by intent, however, combining unintentional injuries with intentional harm,

---

[*] This estimate comes from the analyses reported in this chapter.

such as child abuse and homicide. It omitted sexual assault. Its age categories for children and adolescents were coarse: 0–4, 5–14, and 15–24. It also grouped costs by only seven mechanisms—burns, drownings, falls, firearms, motor vehicles, poisonings, and other. These groupings fail to distinguish among important sub-categories of motor vehicle injuries (occupant, pedestrian, and bicycle) and do not capture other important injury categories, such as being struck by or against an object as often occurs in contact sports and physical assaults or when a falling object hits someone.

Since the mid-1980s, substantial efforts have been made to decrease the prevalence of injuries through informational campaigns (eg, home safety checklists, child seat installation checkpoints), intervention with high-risk youth (eg, youth substance abuse and violence prevention, family therapy for violent youth), legislation (eg, seat belt laws, zero alcohol tolerance for drivers under 21, child bicycle helmet laws), law enforcement (eg, intensive sobriety checkpoints, underage drinking law enforcement), and technological improvements (eg, airbags, booster seats). Additionally, advances in acute care have increased injury survival and case management has reduced hospitalization frequency and duration, thus changing costs of care. It is unclear how these changes have affected prevalence or costs.

Four subsequent studies provided a fragmented update on child and adolescent injury costs. Miller, Cohen and Wiersema[5] estimated costs of violence against children and youth ages 0–17 for 1987–1990. Miller et al[6] updated the mid-80s estimates in the 1989 report with estimates for 1995 and added estimated costs for cut/pierce injuries and sexual assault, as well as a table by intent. For some injury mechanisms, however, they merely inflated costs from the 1989 study and adjusted them to account for fatality trends. Danseco et al[7] estimated injury costs at ages 0–19 for 1987–1994, with breakdowns by demographics and by place of occurrence, but not by mechanism or intent. Miller, Romano and Spicer[1] estimated injury costs at ages 0–19 for 1996 and added detail about sub-categories, but only for unintentional injury. None of these studies gave the full picture.

This chapter defines the costs associated with child and adolescent injuries and briefly reviews the concepts used in estimating injury costs. It then reports estimates of the lifetime costs of childhood injury in the year 2000 that are based on more recent, mechanism-specific, and child-specific data than were previously available. This information allows us to assess the trend since 1985 and compare the costs of injuries and other child and adolescent health problems. To more fully address the issue of injury's priority in child preventive health, the chapter closes with a review of cost-effectiveness estimates for selected child and adolescent injury prevention interventions and comparisons with similar estimates for other child and adolescent health measures.

Injury Costs and Quality of Life Losses
Defining Costs

Injuries among children and adolescents impose a financial burden on many segments of society. Parents and health insurers, for example, assume responsibility for a myriad of medically related expenses due to injury. Parents may be forced to stay home from work to care for an injured child, affecting both the family's income and their employer's profit. Children and adolescents disabled from an injury may be unable to work in the future. Deciding which of these costs to include in cost-of-injury estimates is critical, because the decision can influence the estimated monetary burden of injuries by orders of magnitude. As recommended by the Panel on Cost-Effectiveness in Health and Medicine,[8] we adopt a *societal perspective* that attempts to estimate all costs associated with child and adolescent injuries—costs to victims, families, government, insurers, and taxpayers. Other perspectives would constrain the analysis to, for example, government expenditures or health care payer expenditures, which include only a subset of total injury costs.

We separate injury costs into resource and productivity costs. *Resource costs* are associated with caring for injury victims and managing the aftermath of injury incidents. Medical costs dominate them. *Productivity costs* value wage work and housework that children and adolescents will be unable to do because of their injury, as well as the work that parents or other adults forego to care for injured children. Box 1 more fully describes the cost-of-injury concepts used in this chapter.

Because injuries sustained during childhood and adolescence may impact the productivity (and quality of life) of both children and their caregivers over time, accounting for losses to both parties is critical. For example, an employed adolescent temporarily disabled from an injury may lose wages in the near term. Likewise, an injury that keeps a child or adolescent home from school for a few days may force a parent to stay home to act as a caregiver. Since injuries are relatively frequent among children, total work losses by adult family members while caring for injured children and youth also are a major cost. Of course, the most extreme impact on productivity occurs when a child or adolescent is killed or permanently disabled by an injury. In such instances, a lifetime of work is lost.

Defining Quality of Life Losses

This chapter primarily focuses on *resource and work loss costs* associated with child and adolescent injuries. However, these costs do not fully capture the burden of these injuries. Injuries also reduce the quality of life of children and families. Losing a child unnecessarily to injury can cause a lifetime of mental anguish. Children and youth who are permanently disabled by injury may experience lifelong pain, or suffer permanent loss of motor or cognitive functioning. To capture these less quantifiable consequences of child and adolescent injuries, we report quality of life losses, valued in nonmonetary terms as *quality-adjusted life years* (QALYs) (See Box 2). Both monetary costs and quality of life measures should be considered when allocating resources, and both should be incorporated into cost-effectiveness analyses that weigh "net costs" against quality of life improvements.

Estimating Costs and Quality of Life Losses

The next two sections report findings from an analysis that estimated the incidence and present and future costs of child injuries (including poisonings and medically treated child neglect) that occurred during 2000. We included injuries that affected children and youth ages 0–19 years and resulted in a physician office visit, a hospital outpatient visit, an emergency

Box 1: Cost-of-Injury Concepts

Incidence-based vs. Prevalence-based Costs

Incidence-based costs: are the present value of the lifetime costs that may result from injuries that occur during a single year. For example, the incidence-based cost of head injuries in 2000 estimates total lifetime costs associated with all head injuries that occurred in 2000. Incidence-based costs measure the total savings over one's lifetime that prevention could yield and are the appropriate costs for cost-effectiveness analysis. **Present value** shows the amount that would be invested today to pay future costs when they come due. It is computed using a **discount rate**, essentially an inflation-free interest rate. We discount because (1) money deposited today will earn interest, so less than $1 needs to be deposited today to pay $1 in the future and (2) the future is uncertain; in 10 years, we may be able to regrow injured nerve tissue, ending the quality of life loss from an injury, or a catastrophe could shorten average lifespan, unexpectedly truncating lives and with them the losses caused by permanently disabling prior injury. This paper uses the 3% discount rate recommended by the Panel on Cost-Effectiveness in Health and Medicine.[8]

Prevalence-based costs: measure all injury-related expenses during one year, regardless of when the injury occurred. For example, the prevalence-based cost of head injuries in 2000 measures the total health care spending on head injuries during 2000, including spending on victims injured many years earlier. Prevalence-based costs are needed to project health care spending and evaluate cost controls.

Resource vs. Productivity Costs

Resource costs are broken down into medical costs and other resource costs. Productivity costs include immediate and future work losses due to a childhood injury.

Medical costs: include emergency medical services, physician, hospital, rehabilitation, prescription, and related treatment costs, as well as ancillary costs for crutches, physical therapy, etc., and coroner/medical examiner expenses for fatalities. Except for victims of interpersonal violence, lack of data forced us to omit the costs of mental health care for the injured and their family and friends traumatized by an injury incident.

Other resource costs: include police, child welfare, and fire department costs; costs of processing compensation for injury losses through litigation, insurance, or public programs like Medicaid, food stamps and Supplemental Security Income; plus the travel delay for uninjured travelers that results from transportation crashes and the injuries they cause. We excluded other resource costs from our costs per injury.

Work loss costs: include victims' lost wages and the value of lost household work and fringe benefits. Work losses by family and friends who care for injured children and adolescents also are included. We excluded productivity losses of employers of injured adolescents (eg, investigating an injury at work, shuffling schedules or hiring and training a replacement for a youth who misses work due to injury) and of parents who are temporarily or permanently diverted from work when their offspring suffer disabling injuries.

Box 2: Quality-Adjusted Life Years

Estimating quality-adjusted life years (QALYs) is one way to value the good health lost to an individual who suffers a health problem, is disabled, or dies prematurely. A QALY is a measure based on individual preferences for states of health that assigns a value of "1" to a year of perfect health and "0" to death.[8] QALY losses are affected by the duration and severity of a health problem. To estimate QALY losses, years of potential life lost to a fatal injury are added to the number of years spent with an injury-related disability times a "weighting factor" that represents the severity of the disability.[†] Such "weighting factors" can be estimated by using rating scales,[9] or by using trade-off methods that elicit individual preferences between death and various health states.[10,11]

We based our QALY loss estimates on physician ratings of the functional losses resulting from injury by diagnosis that are routinely used in regulatory analysis by the National Highway Traffic Safety Administration.[12] The ratings, although the best available, are not fully validated and more than 20 years old. Thus, our QALY loss estimates only indicate the order of magnitude of the losses.

For sexual assault, we instead used QALY estimates derived from jury awards for non-economic damages by Miller, Cohen, and Wiersema.[5] The estimates from Miller, Cohen, and Wiersema[5] are consistent with the QALYs we used for physical injury. Had we used their QALY estimates for physical assault, our QALY loss per physical assault would have been 0.169 instead of 0.163, a 3.7% difference.

---

† Following the recommendations of the Panel on Cost-Effectiveness in Health and Medicine,[8] QALY losses in future years are discounted to present value at a 3% discount rate as they are summed.

department visit, a hospitalization, or a death. Based on youth and provider survey data, we also included interpersonal violence that resulted in a mental health care visit.‡ Cost-of-injury estimates were computed by multiplying the *number* of injury victims in 2000—stratified by age group, sex, place of treatment/survival, and mechanism—times the corresponding *costs* per victim (in 2000 dollars). Data for these estimates were extracted from the literature and 11 national and 3 state data sets.

We report total and per-injury costs and QALY losses by age group, sex, intent, mechanism, and cost category. We discuss the QALY losses more selectively due to space limitations and the greater uncertainty surrounding these estimates. The Appendix more fully describes the methods used to estimate injury frequencies, costs, and QALY losses.

---

‡ We lacked the data needed to include other injuries treated only in the mental health care system, but except possibly for suicide acts, as documented below, the literature on untreated post-traumatic stress disorder following childhood injury suggests those cases are rare.

Incidence

Almost 18 000 children and youth ages 0–19 died and 17 million were medically treated due to injuries in 2000. Almost 250 000 survivors were admitted to hospitals (as the left side of Table 1 shows). The right side of Table 1 shows injury rates per 10 000 children and youth in the non-institutionalized US population. In 2000, 21% of US children and youth had medically treated injuries. The injury rate at ages 0–9 combined was 70% of the rate at ages 10–19 combined. The lowest injury rate was at ages 5–9.

The left panel in Table 2 shows injury incidence by intent (ie, unintentional, suicide act, assault, undetermined, or legal/military action) and mechanism (the process causing the injury, eg, cut/pierce, poisoning, submersion). The overwhelming majority of child and adolescent injuries (89%) were unintentional. Sexual assaults accounted for 6% of cases, physical assaults for 4%, and suicide acts and cases with undetermined intent account for about 0.5% each. Assaults rose in importance at ages 15–19, accounting for 17% of the injuries.

Variations in the leading mechanisms across age groups suggest it may be appropriate to target select prevention practices to specific ages. Among unintentional injuries, the leading mechanisms were falls (28% of all injuries) and struck by/against (22%). The pattern was markedly different at ages 15–19 than younger ages, with falls dropping from 33% to 15%, motor vehicle occupant injuries rising from 4% to 15%, overexertion injuries rising from 5% to 12%, bites and stings dropping from 9% to 2%, and struck by/against injuries rising slightly from 21% to 24%. Burns, poisonings, and submersions primarily occurred at ages 0–4 and unintentional firearm injuries (including b-b gun injuries) and struck by/against injuries at ages 10–14. Pedalcyclist injuries peaked at ages 5–9 and 10–14, while motor vehicle occupant injuries started rising at ages 10–14. The incidence of falls declined more than 600 000 cases (more than 50%) between ages 10–14 and 15–19.

In terms of frequency, poisonings dominated the suicide acts and sexual assaults dominated the assaults. Physical assault injuries most often resulted from being struck by another person or a weapon or pushed into something. Most injuries of undetermined intent lacked external cause codes in the source data, and consequently lacked data on both intent and mechanism.

Boys were 1.2 times as likely as girls to have medically treated injuries, as the right panel in Table 2 shows. Their excess risk was highest at ages 0–4 and lowest at ages 15–19. Boys were the victims in only 15% (0.18/1.18) of child sexual assaults. They were half as likely as girls to have fatal or medically treated suicide acts, but 1.3 times as likely to suffer physical assaults or unintentional injuries. Their risks were especially high for all types of firearm injuries, 5 to 15 times the risks for girls. Their pedalcycle and unintentional suffocation risks also were substantially elevated, as were their burn risks at ages 0–4 and 15–19. Girls generally were at higher risk of bites and stings, motor vehicle occupant injury at ages 10–14 and 15–19, and overexertion injuries at ages 0–4 and 5–9 (although some of these differences may not be statistically significant). Boys 5–9 and 10–14 were at the greatest added risk of assault compared to girls. Physical assault rates equalized at ages 15–19, perhaps due to dating violence. Some of the risk differentials reflect differences between boys and girls in terms of activities and behavior. Others are hard to explain and warrant exploration.

Table 1

Incidence and Rates per 10,000 Residents of Fatal and Medically Treated Injury Cases, by Age Group and Gender, 0–19, United States, 2000

	INCIDENCE					RATE PER 10,000 RESIDENTS				
	0–4	5–9	10–14	15–19	Total	0–4	5–9	10–14	15–19	Total
TOTAL										
Fatal	3532	1561	2 180	10 505	17 778	1.8	0.8	1.1	5.2	2.2
Admitted	47 200	37 200	51 300	112 600	248 300	25	18	25	56	31
Not Admitted	3 437 900	3 261 600	4 728 500	4 441 000	15 869 000	1793	1587	2303	2196	1972
Mental Health Only	26 500	160 000	350 600	464 200	1 001 300	14	78	171	230	124
Total	3 515 100	3 460 400	5 132 600	5 028 300	17 136 400	1833	1684	2500	2487	2129
MALE										
Fatal	2059	923	1 474	7891	12 347	2.1	0.9	1.4	7.6	3.0
Admitted	27 300	23 200	33 400	70 000	153 900	28	22	32	67	37
Not Admitted	2 067 800	1 814 000	2 759 400	2 577 200	9 218 400	2108	1724	2623	2480	2235
Mental Health Only	8 800	40 200	81 200	31 600	161 800	9	38	77	30	39
Total	2 106 000	1 878 300	2 875 500	2 686 700	9 546 500	2147	1785	2733	2586	2315
FEMALE										
Fatal	1473	638	706	2614	5431	1.6	0.6	0.7	2.7	1.4
Admitted	19 900	14 000	17 900	42 600	94 400	21	14	18	43	24
Not Admitted	1 370 100	1 447 600	1 969 100	1 863 800	6 650 600	1463	1444	1968	1896	1695
Mental Health Only	17 700	119 800	269 400	432 600	839 500	19	119	269	440	214
Total	1 409 200	1 582 000	2 257 100	2 341 600	7 589 900	1505	1578	2255	2382	1935

Note: Totals and rates were computed prior to rounding.

Table 2

Injury Incidence and Relative Risk by Gender, by Age Group and Mechanism, Ages 0-19, United States, 2000

	Incidence					Relative Risk, Male Rate/Female Rate				
	0-4	5-9	10-14	15-19	Total	0-4	5-9	10-14	15-19	Total
UNINTENTIONAL										
Cut/pierce	127 428	166 324	301 375	295 522	890 649	1.70	1.64	2.65	1.36	1.80
Submersion	3209	864	573	747	5393	1.73	2.06	0.98	2.31	1.73
Fall	1 375 414	1 052 670	1 221 752	603 439	4 253 275	1.36	1.25	1.34	1.21	1.30
Burn	138 887	27 649	22 833	100 902	290 271	1.87	0.90	1.05	4.48	2.13
Firearm	499	1913	18 765	7644	28 821	2.42	5.95	24.55	10.87	15.01
Motor Vehicle Occupant	89 041	83 191	219 624	596 883	988 739	2.06	1.06	0.43	0.78	0.77
Pedalcyclist	36 281	200 948	171 248	75 538	484 015	2.50	1.77	3.65	8.56	2.78
Pedestrian	8363	17 140	28 370	19 910	73 783	1.59	1.71	0.83	1.22	1.16
Bites and stings	436 957	312 100	304 213	99 917	1 153 187	0.78	1.03	0.59	0.70	0.77
Overexertion	77 099	102 444	335 912	488 193	1 003 648	0.76	0.64	1.33	1.99	1.43
Poisoning	170 430	103 766	55 267	61 281	390 744	1.10	1.42	2.66	0.91	1.28
Struck by/against	501 879	624 122	1 265 662	990 638	3 382 301	1.84	1.38	2.57	1.47	1.83
Suffocation	66 059	2277	1660	1250	71 246	8.52	1.74	2.84	2.88	7.33
Other specified	225 157	292 636	269 962	307 009	1 094 764	1.27	1.14	0.37	1.71	1.00
Unspecified	143 525	209 640	363 156	406 378	1 122 699					
TOTAL	3 400 228	3 197 684	4 580 372	4 055 251	15 233 535	1.42	1.17	1.34	1.37	1.33
SUICIDE										
Cut/pierce		140	1891	12 663	14 694			0.09	0.59	0.51
Firearm		6	239	1156	1401			7.17	7.80	7.70
Poisoning		404	10 465	39 004	49 873			0.21	0.43	0.38
Suffocation		16	399	676	1091			7.30	4.43	5.30
Other specified		216	1748	4673	6637			0.79	1.23	1.16
Unspecified		121	38	181	340					
TOTAL		903	14 780	58 353	74 036		1.16	0.29	0.55	0.49

continued

Table 2 (continued)

	Incidence					Relative Risk, Male Rate/Female Rate				
	0–4	5–9	10–14	15–19	Total	0–4	5–9	10–14	15–19	Total
ASSAULT										
Cut/pierce	452	2898	6268	22 931	32 549	0.81	1.46	1.46	2.30	1.98
Firearm	146	543	2048	10 505	13 242	2.44	1.91	1.56	9.22	5.43
Struck by/against	32 885	66 147	147 007	310 678	556 717	0.87	1.64	1.85	1.23	1.39
Suffocation	53	14	418	208	693	0.92	0.95	2.08	2.13	1.93
Sexual only	26 496	159 917	350 659	464 263	1 001 335	0.47	0.32	0.29	0.07	0.18
Other specified	6983	31 479	13 649	17 655	69 766	1.68	11.36	1.46	0.72	2.30
Unspecified	826	315	556	40 023	41 720					
TOTAL	67 841	261 313	520 605	866 263	1 716 022	0.75	0.73	0.56	0.37	0.48
UNDETERMINED *	46 817	298	15 176	38 507	100 798				0.74	1.57
LEGAL/MILITARY	236	121	1607	9976	11 940			8.09	5.13	4.52
GRAND TOTAL	3 515 122	3 460 319	5 132 540	5 028 350	17 136 331	1.43	1.13	1.21	1.09	1.20

* = 74% of the cases of undetermined intent have unspecified mechanisms as well.

Warning: We did not test if the relative risks differed significantly from 1.0.

Table 3

Costs of Injury, Total and per Child, by Cost Category and Age Group, Ages 0–19, United States, 2000

	TOTAL COST (Millions of 2000 dollars)					COST PER CHILD (Dollars)				
	0–4	5–9	10–14	15–19	Total	0–4	5–9	10–14	15–19	Total
Medical	4051	4285	6850	9248	24 433	$211	$209	$334	$457	$304
Wage Work*	12 794	10 620	17 830	25 813	67 057	$667	$517	$869	$1277	$833
Household Work	2533	2359	3604	6297	14 792	$132	$115	$176	$311	$184
Total		19 378	17 263	28 283	41 357	106 282	$1010	$841	$1379	$2045	$1321

* = For children under 15, includes parental work loss and child work loss to permanent disability and death.

Child and Adolescent Injury Costs

The estimated lifetime medical and productivity costs of injuries experienced by U.S. children and youth ages 0–19 years during 2000 totaled $106 billion (Table 3). The bulk of this financial burden (77%) resulted from future work losses experienced by injured children and youth and current work losses by their caregivers. Current and future losses of earnings and fringe benefits accounted for 63% ($67.1 billion) of the total lifetime childhood injury costs. Household work loses accounted for 14% ($14.8 billion). Medical costs made up the remainder, accounting for 23% ($24.4 billion) of lifetime costs. Thus, although injuries may be viewed appropriately as a *health* problem, from a cost perspective, injuries are even more an *economic* problem. Each year injuries kill or disable almost 180 000 otherwise healthy children and youth before they have a chance to enter the workforce and maximally contribute to society. The current workforce is affected, too, as many adult caregivers are forced to stay home to tend to injured offspring.

Injuries in 2000 cost an average of $1320 per U.S. resident ages 0–19 (as shown in the right panel of Table 3). Averaged across injured and uninjured children and youth, medical spending on injury averaged $300 per "child." Future work losses and parental work losses due to injury averaged $1020 per child. By comparison, a middle-income household with two parents spent $590 per child on clothing and $1590 per child on food in 2000 (Figure 1).[13]

Figure 1

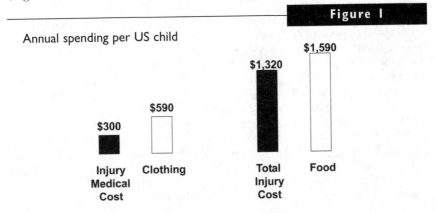

Annual spending per US child

$1,590 Food
$1,320 Total Injury Cost
$590 Clothing
$300 Injury Medical Cost

Costs by Injury Severity

Table 4 differentiates costs between fatalities, hospital-admitted survivors, and other medically treated survivors. The most severe child and adolescent injuries, those that result in death, disproportionately contributed to lifetime injury costs. Fatal injuries represented 0.1% of all child and adolescent injuries in 2000, but produced 23% of injury-related costs. By contrast, the least severe injuries, non-fatal injuries where the child was not hospitalized, accounted for 93% of all child and adolescent injuries, yet produced only 55% of the estimated lifetime costs. Thus, although the very rare injury fatalities contributed disproportionately to the financial burden of child and adolescent injuries, the most common and least severe injuries still accounted for more than half of total injury costs.

The severity of child and adolescent injuries also affected the relative contribution of medical costs versus productivity losses to total injury costs. Medical spending accounted for 93% of the cost of sexual assaults that require only mental health treatment. In contrast, when a child or adolescent suffered a medically treated non-fatal injury, caregiver work losses typically cost much more than medical treatment. Although hospital care is expensive, medical costs still accounted for a smaller proportion of hospitalized injury costs (21%) than work loss of caregivers and permanently disabled children and youth (79%). For children and youth killed as a result of an injury, the overwhelming cost (99%) was the future work that they will never do. Medical costs accounted for less than 1% of the total injury costs for these victims.

Per injured child, costs averaged $6200 including $1430 in medical spending and $4770 in work losses. Costs averaged $1.35 million per fatality, $71 900 per hospital-admitted injury, $3700 per injury treated without hospitalization, and $5670 per sexual assault injury resulting in only mental health treatment.

Costs by Age

As children grow, their motor skills and cognitive skills develop and their environment changes. Therefore, their injury risks shift. Critical milestones that affect injury risk may include starting to crawl, walk, attend school, ride a bicycle, drink alcohol, and drive a car, as well as developing an ability to recognize and make decisions about dangerous situations. Thus, injury rates, mechanisms, and severity vary with age.

We examined injury rates and costs in five-year age groups. Adolescents ages 15–19 experienced higher rates of injuries that were fatal or required hospitalization compared with children in younger age groups (see Table 1). Similarly, injury costs were higher among adolescents than among children of other ages. We estimated the total lifetime medical and productivity costs of injuries that teenagers 15–19 years old experienced in 2000 at $41 billion (Table 3). Among younger and school-aged children, costs were considerably less ($19 billion among 0–4 year olds; $17 billion among 5–9 year olds; $28 billion among 10–14 year olds). Adolescents also had higher lifetime costs per child due to injury ($2040 per injury) (but slightly lower average costs compared to the $2240 average for young adults ages 20–24).

The higher total injury costs among adolescents reflected the greater absolute number of hospitalized and fatal injuries that occurred in this age

Table 4

Total and Unit Costs and QALY Losses of Injury by Severity, Ages 0–19, United States, 2000

	TOTAL COST (millions of 2000 $)					COST/CASE (2000 $)				
	Medical	Wage Work	House Work	Total	TOTAL QALYs	Medical	Wage Work	House Work	Total	QALYs/Case
Fatal	134	19 615	4322	24 071	501 434	$7548	$1 103 316	$243 131	$1 353 996	28.2
Admitted	3698	11 779	2371	17 848	386 293	$14 894	$47 440	$9548	$71 882	1.6
Not Admitted	15 308	35 662	7712	58 683	593 165	$965	$2247	$486	$3698	0.04
Mental Health	5293	317	70	5679	666 140	$5286	$316	$70	$5672	0.67
Total	24 433	67 373	14 475	106 282	2 147 033	$1426	$3913	$863	$6202	0.13

group. More than 10 500 adolescents ages 15–19 years died from injuries that occurred in 2000—more than the number of deaths from injuries among all children ages 0–14 years combined (7273 deaths). The higher number of adolescent fatalities translated into higher total injury costs in this age group, since youth who were killed lost a lifetime of future work. The mechanisms of injuries sustained by adolescents also tended to result in the most costly injuries per victim. For example, as shown in Table 5, intentional firearm injuries and suffocation (suicide or assault) were among the most costly mechanisms of child and adolescent injury per victim. Although rare, these injuries occurred much more frequently among adolescents than children in any other age group (Table 2). The injury surge in adolescence probably resulted from increased exposure to risk, with 30% of ninth through twelfth grade students binge drinking and many starting to drive (estimated from the 2001 Youth Risk Behavior Surveillance Survey).

Costs by Intent

Unintentional injury costs were the dominant factor in child and adolescent injury. They accounted for 93% of injury costs at ages 0–4, 90% at ages 5–9, and 87% at ages 10–14, but only 71% at ages 15–19. Unintentional injury costs rose rapidly starting at ages 10–14, increasing almost $9 billion (57%) over their costs at ages 5-9 ($15.5 billion, from Table 5). They increased again, by $5 billion, at ages 15–19.

In adolescence, intentional injury costs tripled. They jumped from $3.7 billion at ages 10–14 to $11.5 billion and accounted for 28% of injury costs at ages 15–19. Suicide acts accounted for 7% ($2.8 billion), physical assaults[§] for 15% ($6.0 billion), and sexual assaults for 6% ($2.6 billion). The data suggest that effective violence prevention programs targeting adolescents should be a priority and might offer significant savings.

Costs by Mechanism of Injury

Five primary mechanisms of unintentional injury accounted for almost 75% of total lifetime unintentional injury costs among children and youth ages 0–19 years. As shown in the left-hand columns in Table 5, these mechanisms included falls; occupant injury in motor vehicle crashes; pedestrian and pedalcyclist injury combined; being struck by/against an object or person; and overexertion injuries (eg, strains, sprains, and muscle tears). These five mechanisms of unintentional injuries contributed substantially to overall injury costs because the combination of the *frequency* of the injury in the population and *average cost per victim* was exceedingly high. The relative importance of frequency versus cost per case, however, varied by type of injury. For example, although falls were relatively low in cost ($5600 per victim as shown in the right-hand columns in Table 5), they were the most prevalent injuries. As a result, they were the largest contributor to total child and adolescent unintentional injury costs (Table 2). In contrast, although motor vehicle crashes that injured children and adolescents occurred much less frequently than falls, the resulting injuries were often severe and costly (averaging $16 100 per victim). It was primarily the severity of such injuries that made motor vehicle crashes the second leading con-

---

§ Physical assaults are computed as total assaults minus sexual assaults.

Table 5

Total and Unit Costs of Injury by Age Group and Mechanism, Ages 0–19, United States, 2000

	TOTAL COST (Millions of 2000 dollars)					COST PER INJURY CASE (Dollars)				
	0–4	5–9	10–14	15–19	Total	0–4	5–9	10–14	15–19	Total
UNINTENTIONAL										
Cut/pierce	360	450	658	709	2,177	$2826	$2706	$2183	$2398	$2444
Submersion	824	315	303	663	2,105	$256 679	$364 789	$528 958	$886 949	$390 229
Fall	6821	6563	6947	3318	23 649	$4959	$6235	$5686	$5498	$5560
Burn	965	392	220	579	2157	$6949	$14 186	$9631	$5742	$7430
Firearm	31	35	127	333	527	$63 124	$18 276	$6793	$43 536	$18 275
Motor-Vehicle Occupant	1377	1027	1853	11 665	15 922	$15 465	$12 341	$8437	$19 543	$16 103
Pedalcyclist	136	1028	1404	773	3341	$3752	$5116	$8198	$10 229	$6902
Pedestrian	442	520	529	825	2316	$52 899	$30 327	$18 637	$41 439	$31 389
Bites and stings	694	460	640	365	2159	$1589	$1473	$2104	$3658	$1873
Overexertion	358	317	1904	1345	3923	$4646	$3090	$5667	$2755	$3909
Poisoning	244	107	87	620	1058	$1434	$1027	$1569	$10 117	$2707
Struck by/against	2750	2025	6400	4366	15 540	$5479	$3244	$5056	$4407	$4594
Suffocation	847	69	121	123	1160	$12 822	$30 272	$72 942	$98 249	$16 279
Other specified	1173	1282	1518	2206	6179	$5210	$4380	$5624	$7185	$5644
TOTAL	17 945	15 572	24 497	29 465	87 479	$5278	$4870	$5348	$7266	$5743
SUICIDE										
Cut/pierce			32	154	189			$16 853	$12 146	$12 829
Firearm			159	1418	1577			$664 328	$1 226 274	$1 125 393
Poisoning			52	275	330			$5013	$7047	$6612
Suffocation		12	251	802	1065		$727 018	$629 280	$1 186 438	$975 937
Other specified			20	178	201			$11 408	$38 184	$30 299
TOTAL		20	517	2839	3376		$22 482	$34 974	$48 644	$45 508

continued

Table 5 (continued)

	TOTAL COST (Millions of 2000 dollars)					COST PER INJURY CASE (Dollars)				
	0–4	5–9	10–14	15–19	Total	0–4	5–9	10–14	15–19	Total
ASSAULT										
Cut/pierce	26	34	70	462	591	$56 719	$11 685	$11 161	$20 134	$18 162
Firearm	49	69	241	2899	3259	$336 915	$127 869	$117 784	$275 935	$246 077
Sexual only*	151	914	1985	2629	5679	$5714	$5714	$5662	$5662	$5672
Struck by/against	212	424	676	2025	3336	$6436	$6408	$4598	$6518	$5993
Suffocation	51	15	24	57	146	$957 802	$1 039 716	$57 027	$273 572	$210 765
Other specified	453	162	140	237	992	$64 876	$5160	$10 255	$13 417	$14 223
TOTAL	1208	1639	3167	8650	14 663	$17 803	$6273	$6082	$9985	$8545
UNDETERMINED	224	32	90	318	665	$4801	$106 350	$5958	$8271	$6604
LEGAL/MILITARY				85	99				$8542	$8276
GRAND TOTAL	19 378	17 263	28 283	41 357	106 282	$5513	$4989	$5511	$8225	$6202

* 2 male and 56 female rape-murders are classified by the mechanism causing death.

A few numbers were deleted because they were based on less than 5 cases. Estimates less than $50 million generally are based on relatively small samples and should be used with caution.

tributor to total unintentional injury costs among children and youth. Injury prevention efforts ideally would include a mix of interventions that greatly reduce the prevalence of less costly injuries and ones that more modestly reduce severe injuries.

The relative cost per injury case varied greatly across mechanisms (the right panel in Table 5). The data fell into two clusters, with costs per case either above $200 000 or below $35 000. Suicide acts with a firearm or by suffocation/hanging were most costly at $1 125 000 and $976 000 per case respectively, including medical and work loss costs. Drowning or submersion caused the most expensive unintentional injuries at $390 000 per case. Among assaults, the most costly involved firearms ($246 000) or suffocation ($211 000). Although high-cost mechanisms occurred less frequently among children and adolescents than most injury mechanisms, the severity of the injuries and the long-term disability and deaths that often resulted made them extremely expensive when they did occur. The last 3 columns in Table 6 illustrate this clearly, showing that fatality probabilities exceeded 13% (130 per thousand) for every high-cost category but fell below 1.5% (15 per thousand) for every remaining injury category.

Unintentional pedestrian injuries and all categories of intentionally self-inflicted injuries involved either a hospital admission or death in at least 10% of cases. The admitted suicide acts, however, tended to involve short hospital stays which may result more from the need to provide temporary protection from repeat injury than from treatment of physical effects. Indeed, many were coded as psychiatric admissions.

The most costly unintentional injury mechanisms were fairly consistent across the child and adolescent age categories, although their relative importance differed (Table 5). Through age 14 years, falls were the most costly mechanism of unintentional injury, struck by/against was second, and motor vehicle occupant injury was third or fourth. Among 15–19 year olds, however, motor vehicle crashes and struck by/against displaced falls as the most costly injury mechanisms. Some mechanisms only showed up as leading contributors for one or two age groups. Burns, suffocation, and drowning/submersion were the fourth through sixth leading mechanisms of injury costs at ages 0–4 years, but not a leading mechanism at other ages. Pedalcyclist injury tied for third place at ages 5–9 and was in fifth place at ages 10–14. Overexertion injury was in the top five at ages 10–14 and 15–19. Pedestrian injury was in fifth place at ages 5–9 and again at ages 15–19.

A more detailed breakdown of injuries by mechanism and by age group (results available upon request) revealed that the nature of fall risks varied by age. Falls caused an estimated 25% of injuries at ages 0–4, 5–9, and 10–14 and 15% of injuries at ages 15–19, resulting in an estimated 27% of lifetime unintentional childhood injury costs. They accounted for 34% of costs from ages 0–4, 41% from ages 5-9, 24% from ages 10–14, and 13% from ages 15–19. From ages 0–4, the largest factors were falls from furniture, stairs, and slipping. At ages 5–9, fall risks shifted to playgrounds, trees, and slipping incidents, then at ages 10–14 to pedalcycles, slipping, and sports. Even though total falls dropped precipitately after age 14, falls in sports (and related overexertion and striking injuries) remained important through age 19. Although Rice et al[3] identified falls as a major childhood injury risk factor in 1985, few effective approaches, with notable exceptions of window guards, stair gates, improved stairway design, and protective sporting gear like helmets and kneepads, have been developed to prevent them. The high frequency and cost of fall injuries in 2000 strongly supports the need to identify cost-effective strategies to reduce the incidence of falls among children.

Motor vehicles and other vehicles ranging from pedalcycles to trains to jet-skis pose risks to child and adolescent passengers and pedestrians. Bicycles are typically the first vehicles that children drive. From ages 5–14, pedestrian and pedalcycle injuries together outranked injuries to motor vehicle occupants in cost. Motor vehicle crash costs increased steadily throughout childhood and took a noticeable leap when girls ages 10–19 and boys ages 15–19 began riding with friends and siblings and subsequently reached driving age. The rise in motor vehicle injury costs for girls ages 10–14 is a target for exploration and intervention. We speculate it occurred because socializing with older teenagers who have cars may be more common among girls. Crashes imposed by far the largest injury costs for adolescents ages 15–19, comprising 28% of total injury costs for this age group.

Unintentional struck by/against injuries are an ill-defined mix that includes sports injuries, people hit by falling objects, people bumping into furniture and closing doors on fingers, and people tripping and striking hard objects as they land, among other things. Better epidemiology is needed to understand this injury mechanism. It accounted for 15% of total costs and 21% of injuries, but only 1% of fatalities and 7% of hospital admissions. Although it is a major contributor to child and adolescent injury costs, outside of sports, we know too little about it to develop preventive interventions.

Quality of Life Losses

Injuries among children impose more than monetary costs on society. They reduce the quality of life among injured children and their families. We measured those losses in units of quality-adjusted life years (QALYs). A QALY is a year of healthy life and functioning. (See Box 2.) The QALY losses were estimated from physicians' estimates by diagnosis of the effects that a childhood injury has on mobility, cognition, bending/grasping/lifting, sensory function, pain, and appearance (eg, scarring or prostheses), as well as on ability to work, plus the value people place on those functional losses. In total, children and adolescents fatally and non-fatally injured in 2000 lost the equivalent of 2.1 million years of life (Table 4), a loss comparable to 75,000 child and adolescent deaths.[1]

The quality-adjusted life years (QALYs) lost were concentrated in three groups of injuries. Injury fatalities accounted for 23% of quality-adjusted life years lost, even though only 0.1% of all childhood injuries in 2000 resulted in death (table not shown). Hospital admissions were 1.5% of cases but accounted for 18% of QALYs lost. Another 28% of the QALYs lost were associated with medically treated non-fatal injuries that did not require hospitalization. The losses for these injuries resulted from short-term disability and from long-term disability that arose when complications developed or

---

[1] To compute the number of equivalent deaths, we divided the QALY loss by 29, which is the present value (at a 3% discount rate) of the 66 years of life that the average 11-year-old child has remaining.

a non-fatal injury like a facial laceration or arm fracture scarred a child or permanently restricted range of motion.

Sexual assault accounted for 31% of all QALY losses (Figure 2). It resulted in substantial economic and personal losses, It was responsible for 30% to 40% of girls' QALY losses in every age group from 5–19 and for about 16% of boys' QALY losses at ages 5–9 and 10–14. The average sexual assault victim's loss was 0.67 quality-adjusted life years. Policy discussion and preventive effort on this dominating problem is too modest. Child and adolescent sexual assault is a national tragedy. We should do more.

Similar to the patterns observed for injury frequency and costs across age groups, total estimated QALY losses were highest among adolescents ages 15–19 years (853 000 QALYs, a loss comparable to 30 700 child deaths), and lowest among children ages 0–4 years (357 000 QALYs, a loss comparable to 11 900 child deaths). The number of children in each five-year age group was similar. The differences in QALY losses resulted from the same injury frequency and severity differences that caused teenagers to have higher resource and productivity loss costs.

Because children develop rapidly early in life, the 0–4 age group lumps evolving risks. Therefore, we examined QALY losses by detailed mechanism and individual year of age (table not shown). For infants, the largest losses came from suffocation, other breathing threats including submersion, assaults and other maltreatment, and falls from beds, falls on stairs, and falls of unspecified nature. Fatalities dominated QALY loss at this age. Drownings, house fires, assaults, and falls were the largest threats at ages 1–2. Motor vehicle pedestrian and occupant incidents also began to emerge as risks by age 2, a pattern that strengthened at ages 3–4.

Choosing a Burden Measure to Guide Resource Allocation

Decisions on how to allocate injury surveillance, research and prevention resources among injury mechanisms should be made with full information on the societal burden imposed by each injury mechanism. The gold standard measures, because they capture the burden most completely, are total costs and QALY losses. Ideally, the easiest comparisons would result if these measures were combined into a single comprehensive measure, but the methods currently available to combine them are controversial.[14-17] Furthermore, these measures rarely are available below the national level, but

Figure 2

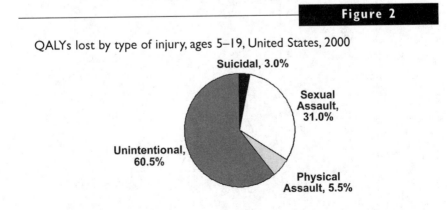

QALYs lost by type of injury, ages 5–19, United States, 2000

Suicidal, 3.0%

Sexual Assault, 31.0%

Unintentional, 60.5%

Physical Assault, 5.5%

Table 6

QALYs Lost per Year by Age Group and per Case, Plus Other Severity Measures, by Mechanism, Ages 0–19, United States, 2000

	TOTAL QALYs LOST					QALYs Lost per Case	Total Medical (Millions of 2000 $)	Fatals per 1000 Cases	Fatal or Admitted per 1000 Cases	Fatalities
	0–4	5–9	10–14	15–19	Total					
UNINTENTIONAL										
Cut/pierce	1336	1036	2707	2899	7978	0.01	697	0.007	8	6
Submersion	17 267	5985	5019	10 545	38 815	7.20	39	246.8	580	1331
Fall	155 755	115 481	102 903	48 095	422 236	0.10	4827	0.04	12	184
Burn	11 837	6046	3062	3077	24 021	0.08	397	2.4	23	685
Firearm	765	747	1799	5162	8473	0.29	58	6.7	79	193
Motor Vehicle Occupant	35 703	23 840	30 915	202 713	293 172	0.30	2401	6.7	46	6589
Pedalcyclist	4310	21 721	19 668	8662	54 360	0.11	631	0.5	24	227
Pedestrian	12 298	12 898	10 204	13 279	48 679	0.66	344	14.2	139	1047
Bites and stings	959	978	1370	3311	6618	0.01	610	0.2	6	200
Overexertion	1013	1406	29 210	13 266	44 896	0.04	1233	0.001	4	1
Poisoning	1794	666	903	9729	13 092	0.03	295	1.1	32	442
Struck by/against	10 651	18 562	56 313	33 979	119 506	0.04	3039	0.03	5	108
Suffocation	20 444	1326	2076	1982	25 828	0.36	52	12.1	43	865
Other specified	15 063	15 707	21 866	53 472	106 109	0.10	1298	0.5	21	516
TOTAL	305 133	241 521	316 607	432 547	1 295 808	0.09	16 887	0.8	14	12 532

SUICIDE										
Cut/pierce			94	607	709	0.05	28	0.4	261	6
Firearm			3137	24789	27929	19.93	13	718.8	827	1007
Poisoning		203	518	3550	4068	0.08	131	2.5	471	126
Suffocation			4754	14134	19092	17.50	6	632.4	806	690
Other specified			220	3061	3321	0.50	17	14.2	119	94
TOTAL		253	8754	46314	55321	0.75	197	26.0	408	1930
ASSAULT										
Cut/pierce	636	455	928	8822	10841	0.33	99	6.4	90	208
Firearm	1374	1701	4851	51210	59135	4.47	202	134.2	500	1777
Sexual only*	21380	129037	221915	293809	666140	0.67	5293	0*	0*	*
Struck by/against	1310	1662	1824	7675	12471	0.02	1319	0.1	8	41
Suffocation	1565	383	548	1183	3678	5.31	2	181.8	215	126
Other specified	12349	1572	1669	3164	18755	0.27	231	7.1	39	493
TOTAL	46313	135283	232405	368692	782692	0.46	7245	1.7	11	2999
UNDETERMINED	5520	690	1543	4256	12009	0.12	89	2.9	49	287
LEGAL/MILITARY	690			1063	1203	0.10	15 .	2.5	8	30
GRAND TOTAL	356974	377754	559433	852871	2147033	0.13	24433	1.0	16	17778

* 2 male and 56 female rape-murders are classified by the mechanism causing death.
A few numbers were deleted because they were based on less than 5 cases. Estimates less than 1000 QALYs generally are based on relatively small samples and should be used with caution.

resource allocation decisions often must be made locally. Comparing the injury mechanisms that create the largest burden according to different measures is helpful in understanding the relative degree of resource misallocation that is likely to result if local decision makers base policies on different second-best measures.

Tables 5 and 6 display a range of measures that could be used to set prevention priorities. Sexual assault dominated QALY loss to child and adolescent injury. It cost only slightly fewer QALYs than unintentional falls and motor vehicle occupant injuries combined. The three leading mechanisms contributing to medical and productivity costs and the next three contributors to QALY loss were identical (Table 6)—unintentional falls, motor vehicle occupant injuries, and injuries from being struck by or against an object. Because their fatality rate was low, struck by/against injuries, nevertheless, were a far larger contributor to total costs than to QALY losses. Notable incongruities between total costs and total QALY losses also arose for unintentional cut/pierce injuries, unintentional bites and stings, and firearm suicide acts. Again, high or low fatality rates for these mechanisms drove the differentials. Priority decisions about these injuries may be clearer if a dollar value is placed on the QALYs.

Because mortality data by injury mechanism have been readily available at the state and county levels for decades, fatal counts traditionally have been used in injury priority-setting. The fatal burden ranking differed markedly from rankings based on the gold standard measures (total costs and QALYs). Fatal counts, however, differed only modestly in rank ordering from three other measures: QALYs lost per case (except for sexual assaults), total cost per case, and fatalities per thousand medically attended or fatal injury cases. Fatalities and these related burden and severity measures are unwise choices to guide resource allocation and program planning.

Counts of live hospital discharges for injury (Table 6) or the sum of discharges and fatalities (data not shown) yielded rankings that more closely matched the rankings on the gold standard measures than fatality counts did. However, they undervalued the total burden of sexual assault. The magnitude of sexual assault was only identified by measures that incorporated total QALY losses or by a total medical cost measure. For other mechanisms, live discharge counts tracked total medical costs reasonably closely, although firearm suicide acts were a much more important contributor to discharges than to medical costs. Summed counts of hospital discharges and fatalities also tracked reasonably well with total costs, though poorly with total QALYs lost. When available, hospital discharge data are much better guides for local planning than fatality data.

Rankings for suicide acts based on incidence measures differed markedly from rankings based on costs or QALYs. The cost and QALY measures raised the importance of suicide acts involving firearms or suffocation and lowered the emphasis on poisoning suicide acts (which ranked third as a cause of admission but 23nd as a factor in total costs or QALY losses). These biases need to be factored into suicide prevention decision-making that is based on incidence measures.

Table 7 combines the QALY and cost measures by placing a dollar value on a QALY. Although monetized QALYs have been criticized for methodological reasons,[15,17] we attached a monetary value to the QALY estimates to

Table 7

Comprehensive Costs of Injury Including Monetized QALYs, by Age Group and Mechanism, Total and for Females, Ages 0–19, United States, 2000

	TOTAL COST (Millions of 2000 dollars)					TOTAL FOR FEMALES (Millions of Dollars)					%
	0–4	5–9	10–14	15–19	Total	0–4	5–9	10–14	15–19	Total	Female
UNINTENTIONAL											
Cut/pierce	492	552	925	995	2965	174	216	195	210	794	27%
Submersion	2531	907	799	1705	5941	878	282	192	151	1503	25%
Fall	22218	17979	17119	8072	65388	9295	7850	7262	1992	26399	40%
Burn	2135	990	523	884	4531	827	408	229	190	1654	36%
Firearm	107	109	305	843	1364	36	16	28	87	167	12%
Motor Vehicle Occupant	4906	3383	4909	31703	44902	1546	1531	2128	10719	15923	35%
Pedalcyclist	562	3175	3348	1629	8714	64	1459	577	114	2213	25%
Pedestrian	1658	1795	1537	2138	7128	586	587	545	600	2318	33%
Bites and stings	789	556	775	693	2814	440	267	310	214	1231	44%
Overexertion	458	456	4791	2656	8361	253	271	484	868	1876	22%
Poisoning	422	172	176	1582	2352	165	65	71	349	652	28%
Struck by/against	3803	3860	11966	7725	27353	1190	1736	1546	2296	6769	25%
Suffocation	2868	200	326	319	3713	1112	77	47	54	1289	35%
Other specified	2662	2834	3680	7492	16668	824	1181	1334	1661	5001	30%
TOTAL	45611	36969	51180	68434	202194	18046	17854	17504	20813	74216	37%
SUICIDE											
Cut/pierce			41	214	259			27	87	116	45%
Firearm			469	3868	4337			81	413	494	11%
Poisoning			104	626	732			62	263	327	45%
Suffocation			721	2199	2952			132	392	528	18%
Other specified		32	42	481	529				111	125	24%
TOTAL		45	1377	7388	8809			318	1280	1605	18%

continued

Table 7 (continued)

	TOTAL COST (Millions of 2000 dollars)					TOTAL FOR FEMALES (Millions of Dollars)					%
	0–4	5–9	10–14	15–19	Total	0–4	5–9	10–14	15–19	Total	Female
ASSAULT											
Cut/pierce	88	79	162	1334	1663	38	31	65	249	383	23%
Firearm	185	238	721	7961	9104	59	97	126	782	1064	12%
Sexual only *	2265	13 669	23 922	31 672	71 528	1514	10 237	18 380	29 513	59 644	83%
Struck by/against	341	588	856	2784	4569	97	84	165	680	1026	22%
Suffocation	206	52	78	174	510	103	27	47	134	311	61%
Other specified	1674	318	305	550	2846	663	103	115	214	1095	38%
TOTAL	4759	14 944	26 044	44 474	90 220	2891	10 608	18 942	31 853	64 293	71%
UNDETERMINED	770	100	243	739	1852	246	26	41	195	508	27%
LEGAL/MILITARY				190	218					11	5%
GRAND TOTAL	51 141	52 059	78 867	121 225	303 293	21 184	28 497	36 805	54 147	140 633	46%

* 2 male and 56 female rape-murders are classified by the mechanism causing death.

Note: Cost for Male equals Total Cost minus Cost for Females.

A few numbers were deleted because they were based on less than 5 cases. Estimates less than $100 million generally are based on relatively small samples and should be used with caution.

allow for a better understanding of relative burden of QALYs vis a vis total medical and productivity losses. The dollar value was derived in the same controversial way that the US Department of Transportation and the US Food and Drug Administration, as well as a variety of peer-reviewed publications,[18-22] derive it. They divide the value of a statistical life (the amount that a group of people are collectively willing to pay—and actually do pay—to save one life) by the present value of the expected number of years of life saved. We used a conservative value of statistical life of $3.4 million (in 2000 dollars), which derives from a systematic review[23] and is used in regulatory analyses at the US Department of Transportation and US Department of Justice. The corresponding value per QALY, net of the value of productivity, is $98 851.

The monetized QALYs reveal that QALY losses accounted for two thirds of total childhood injury costs. Although much of the preceding discussion focused on quantifying the economic burden of injuries, this finding reveals that the non-economic burden, including pain and suffering, is what truly drives the burden. Clearly, these non-economic factors need to be considered when allocating scarce healthcare resources toward injury prevention activities. For example, for sexual assault, 92% of the total burden results from QALY losses. Sexual assaults account for 7% of female injury costs at ages 0–4, 36% at ages 5–9, 50% at ages 10–14, and 54% at ages 15–19.

Summary of Cost and Quality of Life Losses

We estimate that injuries in 2000 to US children and youth ages 0–19 years imposed $106 billion in lifetime medical and productivity costs and cost 2.1 million quality-adjusted years of life. They left almost 18 000 children and youth dead and 160 000 with permanent disabilities that restricted their ability to work and reduced their quality of life. Costs per injured person ages 0–19 averaged $6200. Costs per injury were higher at ages 15–19 than at younger ages, suggesting adolescents' injuries were more severe. Although unintentional falls, motor vehicle crashes, and injuries resulting from striking by/against people or objects dominated the costs, sexual assaults were the leading cause of QALY loss. Injury costs rose as children passed age 10 and especially age 15. Beginning at age 10, violence (assaults and suicide acts) emerged as a major cost factor. The limitations of these estimates are discussed in the methods appendix.

Trend Over Time

The medically treated or fatal injury rate per 100 000 children and youth ages 0–19 declined 26% between 1985 and 2000 (from 26 600 per 100 000 to 20 100 per 100 000).** The decline was fairly uniform across ages, with injury rates in 2000 22% lower than in 1985 at ages 0–4, 31% lower at ages 5–14, and 28% lower at ages 15–19.

The important question is why injury rates declined. To gain insight, we probed the trend by cause. Injury rates declined for most of the causes Rice

---

** To compare with 1985 injury rates from Rice et al,[3] we reran their non-admitted injury counts from the 1984–86 National Health Interview Survey, excluding cases that were not medically treated.

Figure 3

Injury rates by cause in 1985 vs 2000, ages 0–19

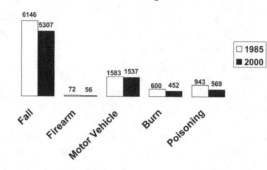

et al[3] analyzed (Figure 3). They fell by 25% for burns, 14% for falls, 22% for firearm injuries, 40% for poisoning, and 29% for other non-motor-vehicle injuries. One major factor was the implementation of 21-minimum drinking age laws in 19 states in 1986–88.[24] The largest declines were for burns and poisonings, both areas where the Nation mounted aggressive intervention campaigns in the 15-year interval. In fire and burn prevention, the US Consumer Product Safety Commission mandated that cigarette lighters have "childproof" dual catches, cigarette smoking declined, smoke alarms continued to spread, building codes gradually shifted homes away from dual-faucet plumbing, and use of electric rather than flammable-fuel home heating rose dramatically between 1980 and 2000 (from 18% to 30% of all homes).[25,††] Poisoning measures included expanded coverage by poison control centers, which triage poisoning treatment, allowing many exposures to be handled without outside medical intervention; sustained media-based parent education about safe storage; and increased unit dose packaging—for example of iron supplements starting in 1997.[26] In contrast to a 47% decline through age 14, the medically treated poisoning rate rose by 5% at ages 15–19, possibly suggesting a lack of progress in reducing suicide acts and drug overdoses. The decline in firearm injuries probably resulted in part from laws and education campaigns that have promoted safe firearm storage in homes with children.[27]

There was one glaring exception. The motor vehicle injury rate was virtually unchanged between 1985 and 2000. The critical factor was exposure. Daily miles of travel rose by 50% at ages 0–15 (from 16.2 miles to 24.5 miles) from 1983 to 2001,[28] with an even larger rise at ages 16–20 (from 22.2 to 38.1 miles). Overall, motor vehicle injuries per mile traveled dropped by more than 36%. Important factors in this gain included numerous state safety laws, among them zero alcohol tolerance for youth, a .08 maximum blood alcohol level for all drivers, graduated licensing with a driving curfew, the 21-minimum drinking age, and safety belt use mandates, as well as the increased presence of airbags. Repeal of the 55 mile-per-hour national speed limit had an offsetting effect.

---

†† See Table 8 for estimates of the savings from these and other measures listed here.

Implications of Injury Costs for Investing in Safety Behaviors and Practices

The first part of this chapter examined the lifetime costs and quality of life losses associated with child and adolescent injuries that occurred during 2000. The following sections explore the implications of these costs for decisions about policy investments in safety behaviors and practices. We examine how the medical costs and lost productivity of child and adolescent injuries compare with the costs of other child and adolescent health problems, with emphasis on a payer's perspective. That analysis points to the government as a major player in child and adolescent injury prevention and control. Funding priorities should be influenced by the relative magnitude of the burden of child and adolescent injuries compared with illnesses and how much of the burden is financed by the public sector. Our research raises the question of whether the level of government funding for injury prevention is consistent with the magnitude of the problem. A second, and arguably more important factor in determining appropriate resource allocation concerns the percent of the burden that could be eliminated through allocation of additional resources. The last part of this chapter considers that issue.

Comparing Costs and Sources of Payment for Childhood Injury and Illness

The estimated medical costs of child and adolescent injury exceed the costs associated with low birth weight, an important health problem afflicting children in the United States.[f] The annual productivity losses are comparable to those resulting from high school drop-out.[29] In 2000, child and adolescent injuries accounted for 11% of hospital discharges, 42% of non-admitted emergency department visits, and 11% of physician office visits.[‡‡]

Excluding uncomplicated live birth and well-care visits, injury was responsible for 12.9% of medical spending for ages 0–19 in 2000. Our analysis of 2000 Medical Expenditure Panel Survey (MEPS) data shows it ranked second in spending behind asthma (13.5%). As Figure 4 shows, injury accounted for more medical spending for ages 0–19 than all non-respiratory infectious diseases combined (10.9%).

In terms of lost productivity, child and adolescent injuries are almost twice as costly as child and adolescent illnesses. In 2000, 45% of all deaths and related future work loss costs among children and youth ages 1–19 resulted from unintentional injury, 18.5% resulted from intentional injury, and only 36.5% resulted from illness.

Given the tremendous financial burden of child and adolescent injuries, in terms of both medical and future productivity costs, continued investment in effective injury prevention makes sense. Who should invest in prevention, however, largely depends on who pays the costs associated with child and adolescent injuries. The remainder of this section describes the payment sources for injury-related medical costs and lost productivity costs.

---

‡‡ The visit counts come from the NAMCS, NHAMCS, and HCUP-NIS incidence data sets used to estimate injury incidence.

Figure 4

Medical spending by condition, ages 0–19, United States, 2000

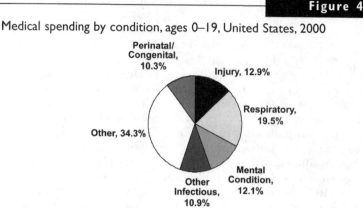

Source: MEPS 2000 on-line analysis system.

Payment Sources for Medical Costs

Private insurers paid most of the medical bill for child and adolescent injury. Health and auto insurers combined paid 80% of the bill in 2000, according to MEPS. Government paid 10% of the bill and the remaining 10% was paid by uninsured families. The government's Medicaid and Child Health Insurance programs paid a larger share of the hospital bills. Private insurers paid for 75% of the days children and youth spent in hospitals due to injury and government sources paid for another 14%, with the uninsured responsible for the remainder.[1]

Payment Sources for Lost Productivity

Work loss costs fall heavily on victims and their families, with modest contributions from property-casualty insurance and public welfare programs including Supplemental Security Income and food stamps. Government loses the associated income taxes. Presumably property-casualty insurance (Workers' Compensation or auto insurance) partially covers work loss costs for the 5% of adolescent injury victims whose medical costs it pays. The financial burden of short-term work losses by parents of injured children and youth fall on parents and their employers.

How Cost-Effective are Child and Adolescent Injury Prevention Strategies?

Estimating the cost-effectiveness of injury prevention strategies relative to the cost-effectiveness of efforts aimed at mitigating other child and adolescent health problems is useful to inform decisions about the allocation of scarce resources. For example, the costs and outcomes of one intervention (eg, child safety seat use) can be compared with the costs and outcomes of another intervention (eg, immunizations or drug abuse prevention) when the outcomes measured are the same. In health-related studies, the outcome most frequently considered is good health measured in QALYs. Decision-makers may decide to invest only in interventions which cost less than a specified amount per QALY saved. Alternatively, they may decide to invest in one intervention over another because it has a more favorable cost-effectiveness ratio (ie, the cost per QALY is lower).

Drawing primarily on three related systematic reviews,[18,19,30] this section summarizes the cost-effectiveness and return on investment of a diversity of child, adolescent and all-age injury prevention measures that published studies have demonstrated to be effective. Table 8 summarizes results for 11 categories of injury prevention measures, with most of the measures targeting road crashes, youth violence, or substance abuse and the injuries it causes. These areas have the richest literature with respect to the cost-effectiveness of select interventions. All the analyses reported in Table 8 use a 2.5% or 3% discount rate and take a societal perspective. They use the status quo as a comparator group unless otherwise indicated. The estimates assume that program effectiveness levels observed in demonstration programs would decline by 25% in replication. The estimates for unintentional injury and suicide all were recomputed for the systematic reviews using the same QALY loss estimates used in this chapter, except that the losses for physical assaults come from the same source we used for sexual assaults, Miller, Cohen, and Wiersema.[5] The benefit-cost analyses in Table 8 monetized QALYs with the method used to construct Table 7. Since Table 8 is in 2002 dollars, the estimated number of QALYs saved by any prevention measure can be computed by dividing its quality of life cost saving estimate from Table 8 by $110 403.[§§] Again, we emphasize that the QALY estimates are rough and that monetizing them is controversial.

The cost-effectiveness of the injury prevention strategies is compared with published cost-effectiveness estimates for measures that address other important neonatal and childhood problems, including drug and alcohol abuse, smoking, various vaccinations, nutritional additives, phenylketonuria screening, and neonatal intensive care. The data presented here suggest that many child and adolescent injury prevention strategies have similar cost-effectiveness ratios compared with other well-accepted strategies to prevent child and adolescent illnesses.

Many measures in Table 8 appear cost-effective and some even offer the potential for long term savings. If the medical and other resource costs saved by an intervention exceed its implementation and maintenance costs, the intervention offers *net cost savings* (cost/QALY < $0 in Table 8). Society as a whole will save money if the program is implemented, although the savings may be spread across many payers. Consistent with the literature,[31] we label measures that offer net cost savings or cost less than $50 000 per QALY as cost-effective.[18] Even counting the value of the QALYs saved, some interventions, although effective, do not offer a positive return on investment. Their benefit-cost ratio is less than 1.0. Other interventions work but may not offer a high enough return to merit widespread adoption.

Cost Savings Estimates for Injury Interventions

This section discusses the injury interventions by topic. Fuller descriptions and citations for most of the measures appear in the systematic reviews.[18,30,32]

---

§§ This value is the same as the $98 851 used in Table 7, but inflated from 2000 dollars to 2002 dollars.

Table 8

Unit Costs, Cost Savings, and Costs/QALY Saved for Childhood/General Injury Prevention Measures, Child Development and Substance Abuse Prevention Measures that Indirectly Target Injury, and Selected Other Child Preventive Health Measures (in 2002 dollars, computed at a 3% discount rate)

	Unit Cost	Medical Cost Savings	Productivity and Other Savings	QALY Savings (a)	Benefit-Cost Ratio	Cost/ QALY (a)
1. ROAD SAFETY AND PERSONAL PROTECTION						
Child Safety Seat Law, Ages 0–4	$49/new user	$120	$430	$1200	37	<$0
Child Safety Seat Distribution, Ages 0–4	$45/seat provided	$120	$430	$1200	40	<$0
Child Seat Misuse Check-up	$60/seat checked	$530	$2000	$300	85	<$0
Booster Seat Law, Ages 4–7	$33/new user	$280	$640	$1100	61	<$0
Pass/Upgrade Safety Belt Law	$275/new user	$220	$1500	$3200	18	<$0
Enhanced Belt Law Enforcement	$260/new user	$220	$1500	$3200	19	<$0
Motorcycle Helmet Law	$1200/new user	$190	$1400	$2300	3.2	$29 000
Child Bicycle Helmet Law	$11/new user	$43	$130	$350	48	<$0
Wear a Helmet Riding an All-Terrain Vehicle	$120/helmet	$9	$110	$350	4.0	$33 000
Provisional Licensing + Midnight Driving Curfew	$68/driver	$34	$200	$320	8.1	<$0
Change Driving Curfew to 10 PM	$130/driver	$20	$120	$190	2.6	$31 000
55 Mile/Hour Speed Limit	$7/added travel hour	$1	$11	$16	4.2	$18 000
Child Pedestrian Safety Program	$1600/school	$780	$3600	$10 300	9.0	$1700
2. IMPAIRED DRIVING PREVENTION						
.08% Driver Blood Alcohol Limit	$2.90/driver	$3	$16	$26	15	<$0
Zero Alcohol Tolerance, Drivers Under 21	$31/driver	$48	$250	$480	25	<$0
Sobriety Checkpoints	$8800/checkpoint	$4200	$18 000	$44 000	7.6	<$0
Administrative License Revocation (ALR)	$2850/ALR	$2900	$13 000	$33 000	17	<$0
ALR with Per Se Law	$2700/ALR	$3500	$16 000	$39 000	22	<$0
Alcohol-Testing Ignition Interlock	$1000/vehicle	$230	$2200	$3900	6.5	<$0

3. FIRE PREVENTION AND CONTROL						
Childproof Lighter (product standard)	$.036/lighter	$0.30	$1.10	$1.50	73	<$0
Less Porous "Fire-safe" Cigarette Paper	$.0001/pack	$0.004	$0.007	$0.05	607	<$0
Pass Smoke Alarm Law	$33/new user[c]	$19	$220	$640	26	<$0
4. OTHER TARGETED INJURY PREVENTION						
Harlem Hospital Child Injury Prevention Program (Community-based)	$16/child	$38	$0	$0	2.5	<$0
American Academy of Pediatrics TIPP Injury Prevention Counseling, Ages 0–4	$10/child	$7	$16	$63	8.6	$2800
Youth Suicide Prevention, Native America	$160/youth	$34	$900	$5300	39	$850
Winter Coats that Float Drowning Prevention, Native Alaska	$0.10/person	$0	$52	$150	2045	<$0
5. NON-OFFENDER VIOLENCE PREVENTION PROGRAMS (also address substance abuse risk, suicide, etc.)						
Perry Preschool and Home Visits	$14 700/child	$1,400	$40 000	$39 000	5.5	<$0
Rochester 2-Yr Nurse Home Visits	$7800/child	$1,100	$19 000	$22 000	5.4	<$0
Syracuse 5-Yr Home Visits	$47 900/child	$850	$25 000	$23 000	1.02	$150 000
Parent Training	$3400/child	$500	$3000	$11 000	4.4	$23 000
Big Brothers/Big Sisters Mentoring	$4000/child	$150	$3900	$2900	6.5	$32 000
Graduation Incentives	$19 400/child	$310	$4000	$5400	0.5	$315 000
6. YOUTH OFFENDER PROGRAMS WITH MULTI-RISK ORIENTATION (address interpersonal violence, suicide, substance abuse, etc.)						
Multi-Systemic Therapy	$4800/client	$5100	$109 000	$93 000	43	<$0
Functional Family Therapy	$2200/client	$1900	$40 000	$34 000	35	<$0
Treatment Foster Care	$2000/client	$3700	$78 000	$66 000	73	<$0
Drug Courts	$2100/client	$200	$5600	$9600	4.6	<$0

continued

Table 8 (continued)

	Unit Cost	Medical Cost Savings	Productivity and Other Savings	QALY Savings (a)	Benefit-Cost Ratio	Cost/QALY (a)
7. NARROWLY TARGETED CRIME PREVENTION AND YOUTH OFFENDER PROGRAMS (address interpersonal violence only)						
Monitored Burglar and Fire Alarms	$740/home/year	$1.30	$400	$400	1.1	$98 000
Youth Offender Aggression Replacement Training	$420/client	$1100	$23 000	$19 000	101	<$0
Lansing Adolescent Diversion	$1600/client	$1500	$38 000	$30 000	44	<$0
Intensive Probation Supervision, Youth	$1600/client	$200	$4000	$3600	5.0	<$0
Scaring Young Offenders Straight	>$0	$0	$0	$0	0	Infinite
Young Offender Boot Camp	-$2100/client	-$630	-$13 000	-$11 000	0.08	Infinite
8. YOUTH DEVELOPMENT THROUGH INTEGRATED FAMILY OR COMMUNITY AND SCHOOL PROGRAMS (reduce injury related to substance abuse and other violent behavior)						
Across Ages	$1750/pupil	$190	$730	$1380	1.3	$105 000
CASAstart	$5650/pupil	$390	$1770	$2950	0.9	$163 000
Child Development Project	$230/pupil	$120	$550	$840	6.5	<$0
Good Behavior Game	$61/pupil	$30	$510	$1480	33	$2100
Guiding Good Choices (aka Preparing for the Drug-Free Years)	$710/family	$170	$880	$1340	3.3	$16 000
Skills, Opportunities and Recognition (SOAR aka Seattle Social Development Program)	$3200/child	$600	$7600	$11 000	5.9	<$0
Social Competence Promotion	$350/pupil	$210	$730	$1460	6.8	$630
Strengthening Families	$880/family	$530	$3100	$5970	11	<$0
9. ENVIRONMENTAL ALCOHOL INTERVENTIONS (reduce alcohol-related injury)						
21 Minimum Legal Drinking Age	$160/youth 18–20	$34	$190	$360	3.6	$18 000
20% Alcohol Tax	$9/drinker/year	$4	$30	$50	9.3	<$0
30% Alcohol Tax	$17/drinker/year	$5	$38	$66	6.4	$6800
Mandatory Server Training	$40/driver	$9	$56	$95	3.8	$16 000
Enforce Serving Intoxicated Patron Law	$0.30/driver	$3	$10	$13	84	<$0

10. SCHOOL-BASED LIFE SKILLS (prevent substance abuse and related injury)

Adolescent Transitions	$800/pupil	$340	$2300	$5860	11	$5100
All Stars	$140/pupil	$176	$1230	$3090	32	<$0
DARE Drug Abuse Resistance Education	$100/pupil	$0	$0	$0	0.0	Infinite
Family Matters	$160/family	$170	$1210	$3090	28	<$0
Keepin' It Real	$130/pupil	$220	$990	$2210	27	<$0
Life Skills Training	$220/pupil	$110	$1230	$3010	19	$990
Project Alert	$120/pupil	$53	$360	$380	6.9	<$0
Project Northland	$400/pupil	$240	$1880	$4390	16	<$0
Project STAR (aka Midwest Prevention Program)	$400/pupil	$160	$1300	$2650	10	$2200
Project TND (Toward No Drugs)	$180/pupil	$51	$350	$370	4.3	$8500
STARS for Families	$120/pupil	$69	$160	$230	3.8	<$0

11. POST-EVENT INJURY CONTROL

Poison Control Center Services	$36/call	$250	$0	$0	6.8	<$0
Triaged Regional Trauma System Services	$1,450/admission	$1,800	$420	$1900	2.7	<$0
Tetanus-Diptheria-Pertussis Vaccine, Ages 0–6	$56/child				27	<$0
Tetanus-Diptheria-Pertussis Vaccine, Ages 10–19	$37/child					<$0

12. TOBACCO PREVENTION AND CONTROL

Know Your Body	$140/pupil	$80	$1070	$3860	37	$1700
MN Smoking Prevention Program	$95/pupil	$73	$360	$3640	52	$620
Project TNT (Toward No Tobacco)	$180/pupil	$40	$160	$1970	15	$7300
Youth Anti-smoking Mass Media Campaign	$370/pupil	$57	$480	$2830	10	$11000
Stop Smoking Mass Media Campaign	$1100/quitter	$1000	$18000	$51000	66	$52
Reduce Cessation Program Prices	$220/quitter	$1000	$18000	$51000	320	<$0
Brief Tobacco Counseling	$5600/quitter	$1000	$18000	$51000	13	$9100
Add Nicotine Patch	$4000/quitter	$1000	$18000	$51000	17	$6000
Instead Add Nicotine Gum	$7100/quitter	$1000	$18000	$51000	9.9	$12000
Group Intensive Tobacco Counseling	$1900/quitter	$1000	$18000	$51000	35	$1900
Add Nicotine Patch	$2200/quitter	$1000	$18000	$51000	31	$2400
Instead Add Nicotine Gum	$4300/quitter	$1000	$18000	$51000	16	$6500

Table 8 (continued)

	Unit Cost	Medical Cost Savings	Productivity and Other Savings	QALY Savings (a)	Benefit-Cost Ratio	Cost/QALY (a)
13. OTHER CHILD PREVENTIVE HEALTH						
Hepatitis B Vaccination of Newborns[42]						
Pneumococcal Vaccination of Infants	$232/person					$3900–$61 000
Varicella Vaccination, 18 months[65]	$35/person					$7000
Measles/Mumps/Rubella Immunization[45]	$44/person				5.4	<$0
Hepatitis A Vaccination of College Freshmen[41]	$43/person				26	<$0
Screening + Human Papilloma Vaccination, Females Age 12[41]	$400/person					<$0
Meningococcal Vaccination, Ages 11–17	$83/person					$14 000–$24 000
Cereal Fortification with Folic Acid to Improve Pregnancy Outcomes[43]						$74 000
Water Fluoridation[65]						<$0
Phenylketonuria Screening of Newborns[45]						<$0
Neo-natal Intensive Care, weight 500–999 grams[44]						<$0
Neo-natal Intensive Care, weight 1000–1499 grams[44]						$26 000
						$15 000

(a) Cost/QALY=QALYs saved/(intervention cost − resource cost savings).

(b) To determine the number of QALYs saved, divide the QALY savings by $110 403. Total savings are the sum of the Medical Cost, Productivity and QALY savings. The benefit-cost ratio equals total savings divided by the unit cost.

(c) Includes 2 alarms per home.

Source: Miller and Hendrie[19] or price-adjusted from Miller and Levy[18] unless another citation is shown.

Road Safety

The road safety category encompasses motor vehicle, pedalcyclist, pedestrian, and all-terrain vehicle safety. Of 13 interventions in this area, the literature review reveals that eight offer net cost savings. That means the medical and other resource costs they save exceed the intervention cost. Child occupant protection and bicycle helmet laws pay for themselves, as does provisional or graduated driver licensing with a midnight driving curfew and passenger restrictions for novice drivers.

Impaired Driving

Such measures as zero alcohol tolerance for drivers under the legal drinking age and blood alcohol limits for other drivers may reduce alcohol consumption and associated harms including crime, high-risk sex, and suicide acts. However, only their impact on impaired driving has been evaluated.[19] Even with that narrow evaluation, all six impaired driving measures in Table 8 offer net cost savings. These interventions have both a specific deterrence effect and a general deterrence effect. Sobriety checkpoints, for example, apprehend some impaired drivers who would otherwise have crashed, but fear of getting caught in sobriety checkpoints also deters people from driving after drinking. Typically this general deterrence effect dominates.[33]

Fire Prevention and Control

National adoption of childproof cigarette lighters already is providing net cost savings and reducing smoking-related injuries. Less porous cigarette paper will self-extinguish if left to smolder, thus reducing deadly cigarette fires, many of which also involve alcohol.[34] Smoke alarm laws and voluntary smoke alarm purchases address these risks and broader fire risks. The literature reviewed suggests that both a mandated shift to less porous paper and an alarm law would offer net cost savings.

Other Targeted Injury Prevention

The Harlem Hospital Childhood Injury Prevention Program organized a community response to unintentional childhood injury in a low income neighborhood. It adopted approaches ranging from traffic calming to school playground renovation by local residents to after-school programs. This program, which offers net cost savings, has been replicated by Children's Hospitals in several cities.

Evaluation of physician counseling by pediatricians through the American Academy of Pediatrics' TIPP injury prevention program suggests that it produces good health at a cost of $2800 per quality-adjusted life year.[35] The only economic analyses of suicide and drowning prevention that we found were for programs in Native American communities.[36] The programs were cost effective in these settings.

Violence Prevention

Non-Offender Violence Prevention Programs

Some violence prevention measures try to prevent children from becoming troubled. They try to address the root causes of crime, and potentially also could reduce multiple risky behaviors associated with injury including binge drinking and drug abuse. Except for home visitation programs for infants and toddlers, however, these measures have been evaluated solely in terms of their impact on violence or crime more broadly. That makes their costs/QALY conservative. Two of the six listed programs in Table 8 targeting non-offenders offer net cost savings, but two others are not cost-effective. Intensive home visitation, possibly coupled with pre-school enrichment, can reduce infant/toddler abuse and a range of problems as the targeted low-income toddlers reach adolescence and adulthood. But the return on these costly investments takes decades and has not always appeared. That makes them difficult to recommend when resources are tight. Integrated youth development programs (discussed below) may be more cost-effective.

Youth Offender Programs with Multi-Risk Orientation

The four youth offender programs identified all intensively treat troubled youth ages 12–17 and yield net cost savings. These interventions address the causes of delinquency and related substance abuse. They seek to improve family and school/community functioning. Multi-systemic therapy costs more per youth than functional family therapy or treatment foster care, but also has a greater impact on problem behaviors. Treatment foster care also appears cost-effective, but in addition to financial resources, it requires trained, dedicated foster parents for each child.

Narrowly Targeted Crime Prevention and Youth Offender Programs

Three of the narrowly targeted crime prevention measures assessed are not cost-effective and three offer net cost savings. Intensive probation supervision for young offenders yields net cost savings primarily because it is less expensive than incarceration, not because it improves outcomes. Only two measures in this group are strong candidates for widespread implementation: aggression replacement training and diversion of low-risk first offenders from juvenile court to a service-oriented system. These interventions are less costly than the multi-risk approaches to violence prevention, but they also yield narrower benefits.

Youth Development through Integrated Family or Community and School Programs

Eight youth development programs integrate family, community, and school efforts to strengthen families or adolescents; evaluations suggest they may reduce violence and delay initiation of alcohol, tobacco, or other drug use. Reduced alcohol use should reduce impaired driving, interpersonal violence, suicide acts, and unintentional falls, burns, drownings, and pedestrian injuries. The youth development programs are comprehensive and often expensive. Meta-analysis[32,37] suggests the greatest impacts on alcohol initiation, and consequently on injury, will result from the Strengthening Families Program (16.7%), followed by Social Competence Promotion (10.8%), SOAR (8.1%, plus a direct violence reduction), and Guiding Good Choices (also known as Preparing for the Drug-Free Years— 7.9%). The Good Behavior Game improves classroom order in the short term and appears to reduce violence in the long run.[38] The proven benefits of CASAstart are smaller than its costs. Across Ages offers a minimal proven return. Some of these interventions—the Strengthening Families Program, Guiding Good Choices, and the Good Behavior Game—have been replicated successfully. Others are one-time demonstrations, so their effectiveness is especially uncertain.

Substance Abuse Prevention

Environmental Alcohol Interventions

Two of the five environmental alcohol interventions in Table 8 offer net cost savings. Raising alcohol excise taxes to 20% of the pre-tax selling price is cost-effective, especially against alcohol-related youth injury, but politically difficult. The review suggests that the national 21-minimum drinking age reduces the number of adolescent injuries. Passing and enforcing laws against serving intoxicated (and underage) patrons, and training servers to recognize impairment and terminate service without excessive confrontation may be cost-effective strategies to reduce adolescent injuries, but need wider evaluation before moving to national implementation.

School-based Life Skills Programs

Six of the 11 school-based life skills training programs offer net cost savings, and five more cost less than $10 000 per QALY saved. The greatest effects on alcohol initiation, and thus on injury, have been achieved with Adolescent Transitions (13.7%), followed by STARS (7.9%), All Stars (6.7%), Project Northland (6.6%), and Family Matters (6.6%). One of the programs analyzed, the original Drug Abuse Resistance Education or DARE program is not cost-effective.

Post-Event Injury Control Through Medical Intervention

Health services improve trauma outcomes. Establishing regional hospital specialties in trauma care, then triaging serious injuries to these hospitals, raises the costs of initial treatment but improves survival and ultimately reduces the medical care costs required to achieve maximum medical recovery.[39] Regional or phone-in poison control centers advise on poisoning response 24-hours a day. They greatly reduce poisoning treatment costs and may improve outcomes by advising on whether treatment is needed, supervising home treatment of minor poisonings without more costly medical intervention, more quickly linking serious cases to appropriate treatment, and providing toxicological consultation to hospital staff.[40] Tetanus-diptheria-pertussis vaccination reduces possible bacterial complications of wounds.[41] This combination vaccination protects against three diverse conditions, only one of which is associated with injury. The vaccines were combined to reduce delivery costs. The measures discussed in this paragraph all offer net cost savings.

Comparison with the Cost-Effectiveness of Other Child and Adolescent Health Risks

To further interpret the cost-effectiveness analyses of child and adolescent injury prevention efforts, we examined similar estimates of cost per QALY saved for other neonatal and child health risks (categories 12 and 13 in Table 8). These examples were selected because the cost-effectiveness studies (1) were of good quality, (2) used a 3% discount rate (which makes them comparable to the injury cost-effectiveness estimates) or could readily be recomputed at that discount rate (because discounting only was needed to compute the QALYs lost to mortality), and (3) represented diverse approaches to child and adolescent risk reduction.[42-45] Tobacco prevention and cessation programs (category 12) had low costs per QALY saved. The health effects they addressed were far enough in the future, however, that they rarely achieved net cost savings, although their costs/QALY saved were reasonably low. Of the remaining measures (category 13), 43% offered net cost savings including measles-mumps-rubella vaccination, Hepatitis A vaccination of college freshmen, cereal fortification with folic acid, water fluoridation, and newborn screening for phenylketonuria. Assorted vaccinations and neonatal intensive care were less cost-effective but within the common $50 000 per QALY implementation threshold.

Summary of Cost-Effectiveness Estimates

This section summarized the cost-effectiveness of child and adolescent injury prevention interventions in the literature and compared the results to other child and adolescent interventions. Twenty-one of 25 unintentional injury prevention measures (84% of measures in categories 1–4 of Table 8) and 9 of 16 child and adolescent intentional injury prevention measures (56% of measures in categories 5–7) offered net cost savings, as did all four injury control measures (category 11). Of the 25 youth substance abuse prevention measures, 11 (44% of measures in categories 8–10) offered net cost savings. These 25 measures often reduce youth alcohol use and related injuries.

The cost-effectiveness of child and adolescent unintentional injury prevention strategies reviewed here is comparable to or better than the cost-effectiveness of several other widely implemented child and adolescent illness prevention measures. Only one of 12 tobacco prevention and control programs (8%) offered net cost savings, as did 5 of the other 12 child and adolescent health interventions (42%). These findings should be interpreted cautiously since the studies are not completely comparable, especially in their methods for estimating QALY savings, and standard errors are not available to gauge the reliability of the estimates.

Despite the substantial uncertainty about the cost-effectiveness estimates reported here, these findings suggest that society may benefit from the implementation of many child and adolescent safety measures and more widespread use of these measures may be warranted. Third party payers—such as managed care organizations, other health insurers, and auto insurers—may save money by advocating for, subsidizing, or paying to promote routine use of some safety measures, such as child safety seats, booster seats, and smoke alarms. Yet these and other proven injury prevention interventions are not universally implemented.

Many barriers hamper adoption. Among them:

- Savings may be split across multiple payers. Even interventions that would save government more than they cost may be difficult to implement if the savings are split across insular departments or multiple levels of government.

- The payback period may be too long. Governments concerned with annual budgets sometimes demand even shorter payback periods than the private sector.
- The expected return is uncertain and situational. The estimates shown are averages. They will vary with local risk levels and prevention efforts.
- Health care payers may be intimidated by prevention. They know how to profit by managing and predicting treatment costs, but tread risky ground when investing in and trying to manage the unfamiliar area of prevention.
- Safety device subsidizers would have to subsidize parents who would buy the devices anyway, as well as parents who would not. That can dilute their return on investment.
- Affordability is an issue. Low-income families may not be willing or able to purchase safety equipment (eg, child safety seats, bicycle helmets, etc) that protects their children against injuries, and related financial and functional losses. Absent government and charitable intervention, therefore, children from low-income families may be at greater risk for injuries.[46]
- Intervention may be politically difficult. Interference with the personal freedoms of adults is unacceptable in some political circles. Moreover, legislation often imposes discomfort and inconvenience costs for new safety device users, mobility loss costs when legal driving conditions are restricted, or delay costs at enforcement checkpoints. And some interventions may not be culturally acceptable.
- Investment dollars are scarce. Although injury prevention may be an inexpensive way to buy good health, financially pressed investors may hesitate to pay to achieve gains in quality of life, even for children. Additionally, even if injury prevention produces good health at a lower price than existing health interventions, unless resources are growing, increasing injury prevention requires shrinking those entrenched interests.

Policymakers selecting injury prevention interventions should apply a series of filters. The estimates in this chapter provide the first filter, allowing elimination of interventions that offer a questionable return on investment. This financial information also should be used to guide choices between interventions that score comparably on other criteria. Additional filters might include political feasibility, local priorities, appropriateness for the target population, aggregate impact on the injury problem, affordability, unmeasured spillover benefits (eg, shifting drinking to residential settings may reduce impaired driving and barroom brawling but also could increase domestic violence; a designated driver or free taxi home may dangerously increase intoxication levels), immediacy of the impacts (weeks versus years), and reductions in effectiveness due to prior or planned implementation of measures with overlapping impacts.

Many other injury prevention measures merit careful evaluation, and, if effective, cost-effectiveness analyses. Among others, possible candidates include youth suicide prevention; readily grasped, small-diameter handrails without sharp edges; window guards; pool fencing ordinances; learn-to-swim programs; and home safety inspections that incorporate low-tech interventions like childproof cabinet latches and plastic plug covers for electric outlets. Particularly for safety measures that are expensive, widespread adoption should be informed by cost-effectiveness analyses.

Conclusions

In 2000, injuries were by far the most prevalent and expensive health risk faced by children and adolescents ages 1–19 years. Child and adolescent injuries that occurred in 2000 resulted in $26 billion in lifetime medical spending and $82 billion in present and future work losses. Injuries permanently disabled 160 000 children and youth; they cost the same number of QALYs as 75 000 child and adolescent deaths would cost. In aggregate, the most costly risks were falls, motor vehicle crashes, and incidents where someone unintentionally was struck by or struck against an object. Despite their relatively small numbers, deaths and hospitalized injuries accounted for 40% of the costs and QALY losses. Sexual assaults accounted for 31% of the QALY losses.

Most injuries are, in theory, preventable, and proven strategies exist to reduce the injury toll. Indeed, the child and adolescent injury toll declined 26% between 1985 and 2000. Moreover, from a societal perspective, the cost of preventing injuries often is less than the cost of treating them. The studies reviewed reveal that providing child safety seats, booster seats, and bicycle helmets to infants and children enrolled in Medicaid would save tax dollars. Equipping homes with working smoke alarms and intensive sobriety and belt use checkpoints would reduce insurance bills. Further restricting child gun access would reduce firearm injuries.[27] Aggression replacement training and functional family therapy for youthful offenders are saving taxpayers money in Washington state and could elsewhere. Yet these and other proven injury prevention interventions often are not widely implemented, and injury remains the leading cause of child and adolescent death from ages 1–19.

Although the data and methods we used to quantify the burden have many limitations, this chapter presents policy makers with the clearest picture available of the economic and non-economic burden of child and adolescent injuries and compares this burden to that of other child and adolescent problems. It also presents the most promising strategies for reducing this burden. As a result, this chapter provides a roadmap that can be used when determining how best to allocate scarce healthcare resources in efforts to improve the health of children and youth in this country.

Appendix: Methods of Estimating Incidence-Based Childhood Injury Costs and Quality of Life Losses

The incidence-based costs reported estimate the present value of all expected costs over the child's lifespan. The present value of future costs depends on how many years in the future the costs are borne and on the discount rate.

Estimating the costs and quality of life losses associated with child and adolescent injuries required separately estimating the frequency of injuries, the present and future costs (medical and productivity) of the injuries, and the quality-adjusted life years (QALYs) lost due to injury.

The sub-sections below summarize the data sources and limitations of the methods used to estimate each component of injury frequency, cost, and quality of life losses in this analysis. Details on the methods used to estimate incidence, medical costs, and productivity losses are being published as a book.[47] The book excludes sexual assault.

Estimating Injury Occurrence

Injury Frequency, Diagnosis, Mechanism, and Intent

Fatal injury counts came from the 2000 National Vital Statistics System (NVSS) fatality census,[48] with supplemental information about on-the-road crash deaths from the Fatality Analysis Reporting System (FARS) census of deaths involving motor vehicles on public roads. We used the 2000 Healthcare Cost and Utilization Project—Nationwide Inpatient Sample (HCUP-NIS) data file to estimate hospitalized nonfatal injury episodes. HCUP-2000 contains data on 8 million inpatient stays from 1000 hospitals.[49] We removed readmissions from the HCUP-NIS counts using readmission rates by primary diagnosis group derived from pooled 1997–1998 hospital discharge census data for Maryland, Vermont, and New Jersey—a choice driven by necessity; no other readily accessible data exist about readmission rates. HCUP-NIS identifies mechanisms for 83% of injury incidents. Under the assumption that these cases were representative, we inferred missing external cause codes by applying the mechanism distribution by age group, sex, and primary diagnosis for cases with known mechanism.

We estimated injury survivors treated in the Emergency Department (ED) and released from the 2001 National Electronic Injury Surveillance System—All Injury Program (AIP),[49] which details all injuries at a national probability sample of 66 hospitals. We validated the NEISS counts against counts from the 1999–2000 National Hospital Ambulatory Medical Care Survey (NHAMCS), which surveys a representative sample of 500 EDs.[50] The comparison revealed the AIP incidence and NHAMCS ED visit counts agree to within 2.5%, suggesting the NEISS-AIP counts are sound incidence estimates. We estimated the number of injuries resulting in medical treatment without hospitalization or ED treatment from parallel provider surveys in the NHAMCS family, the 1999–2000 National Ambulatory Medical Care Survey (NAMCS) of office visits and the 1999–2000 NHAMCS hospital outpatient department sample.[50]

NHAMCS and NAMCS detail injury mechanism and diagnoses but count visits, not incidents. Thus, NAMCS might report three office visits that resulted from a single dog bite. To estimate incident counts, we compared these data with data from data sets that counted incidents but had other information gaps that precluded their use as the primary incidence data sets. We compared the outpatient and office visit counts with incidence and visit counts by broad mechanism from the 1999 Medical Expenditure Panel Survey (MEPS).[51] MEPS tracks all health care for a national sample of non-institutionalized residents over a two-year period. The comparison confirmed that the other data sets include many follow-up visits. We reduced the NHAMCS and NAMCS visit counts to match the MEPS victim counts by sex within each five-year age group. We first removed NHAMCS and NAMCS cases within each age-sex strata where mechanism information was missing or coded as 'unspecified' (approximately 19% of cases from each file). Next, within the seven broad mechanism categories in MEPS, we multiplied the weights of all remaining visits within each strata times the ratio of the MEPS victim count to the NHAMCS or NAMCS visit count. This procedure reduced the weighted NHAMCS and NAMCS counts by age group, sex and broad mechanism so that they matched the corresponding MEPS incidence estimates.

Sexual assault incidence, net of cases that also involved physical assault, came from the 1995 National Survey of Adolescents in the United States.[52] From the survey data on victimization history, we reconstructed the percentage of children and youth who were sexually assaulted by age and sex and removed those cases that also involved medically treated physical assault. We applied the percentages to U.S. resident population counts for 2000 to estimate the number of children sexually assaulted. Mental health provider survey data suggest that virtually all victims of child sexual assault and sexual abuse eventually will receive mental health treatment to deal with their victimization.[53]

These data sets provide nationally representative estimates, but have methodological limitations that may lead to an undercounting or overcounting of injuries. For example, HCUP-NIS does not clearly distinguish initial hospitalizations from transfers and follow-up hospitalizations, so some injuries may have been counted more than once, even though we tried to remove transfers and follow-ups from the analyses. Basing our count of poisonings treated in doctors' offices on MEPS self-report rather than diagnosis codes caused us to classify 90 000 poisonings in other mechanism categories. (Classifying these cases as poisonings would mean poisonings in the 0–14 age groups fell by 53% rather than 71% between 1985 and 2000. The count for ages 15–19 would not change).

Estimating Injury Costs

We estimated lifetime costs that result from a fatal or nonfatal injury. The costs fit into two categories: (1) medical and (2) work loss. We discounted future costs (and QALYs) to present value at a 3% discount rate and defined costs from a societal perspective that includes all costs—costs to victims, families, government, insurers, and taxpayers. Estimates were price-adjusted to 2000 dollars using the Employment Cost Index and Consumer Price Indices by medical care component (eg, hospital). Mental health care costs for sexual and physical assault/abuse by age group came from Cohen and Miller[53] and Miller et al[5] as did associated, largely treatment-related parental work losses for sexual assault. These studies derived their mental health care costs from a survey of providers that collected the number of visits per episode of care by crime type, as well as average payments per visit. All other costs were estimated using the methods employed by the CDC in updating the 1989 report.[3] These methods are documented in detail elsewhere.[47]

Medical Costs

In summary, by diagnosis group, we used HCUP-NIS charge data adjusted with cost-to-charge ratios developed for use with HCUP-NIS by AHRQ, data from MEDSTAT's MarketScan database on the ratio of professional fee payments to hospital payments, inpatient rehabilitation cost estimates from Miller et al,[54] 1999 National Nursing Home Survey data on nursing home payments for patients who were discharged to nursing homes according to HCUP/NIS, and MEPS data (five longitudinal interviews over a two-year period) about other post-discharge costs. Combining these estimates, we derived short-to-medium-term medical costs (on average, through month 18 post-injury) for injuries resulting in hospitalizations with live discharges. We used MEPS data to quantify short-to-medium-term unit medical costs for injuries not requiring a hospitalization. To compute lifetime costs, we divided the estimates by the percentage of lifetime medical costs that occur in the first 18 months by diagnosis group and whether hospital-admitted. The lifetime percentages were computed from 1979–1988 National Council on Compensation Insurance Detailed Claims Information (DCI) data on more than 450 000 injury victims.[10] Although these data are old, more recent data on this percentage were not available. Moreover, the DCI and MEPS showed similar percentages of costs in months 0–6 versus 7–18, which suggests the aged DCI percentages remain reasonably accurate.

For fatalities, we obtained the distribution of place of injury death by mechanism and age group from 2000 NVSS data. We computed costs separately for six different places of death (death-on-scene, death-on-arrival to the hospital, death at the emergency department, death at the hospital after inpatient admission, death at home, and death at a nursing home). The medical costs incurred, depending on place of death, include coroner/medical examiner, emergency and/or non-emergency medical transport, emergency department treatment, inpatient hospitalization, and nursing home care.

Productivity Costs

Productivity cost estimates paralleled the CPSC injury cost model[55] where those estimates were tailored to children. Work loss and QALY loss per injury by diagnosis and age/gender adapt published estimates[55,56] by substituting a refined cost per day of household work lost from Haddix et al.[57] For non-fatal injuries, the work loss cost is the sum of the lifetime loss due to permanent disability (averaged across permanently disabling and non-disabling cases), plus the loss due to temporary disability. We assumed the lower-earning parent would stay home with an injured child on each day that an adult suffering a comparable injury would have been unable to work. For fatal injuries, the work loss cost is the present value of expected lifetime earnings, fringe benefits, and household work. The work loss days are built from 1993 Bureau of Labor Statistics data on days lost per injury with work loss; 1986–1992 National Health Interview Survey data on the probability an injury to an employed person will cause work loss; and DCI data on the percentage of injuries that result in permanent total and permanent partial disability, as well as the percentage of earning power lost for partial disabilities.

Limitations of the Incidence and Cost Estimates

This chapter provides up-to-date and comprehensive estimates of the incidence and cost of childhood injuries in the United States. The estimates are gleaned from myriad data sources; their limitations unavoidably apply to our estimates. For example, our physician's office visit count is limited to the civilian non-institutionalized population. Although we used the best data available, some of our sources are old, some extrapolate values for children from data on working age populations, some are based on non-representative samples, and all are subject to reporting and measurement error. Some data sets lacked complete coding information and required imputation of missing data. These factors may have incorporated significant bias into the cost estimates. Our approach was designed to minimize the potential bias. However, more current and nationally representative data would have been preferable.

Especially our tables that break the data into detailed categories are challenged by small samples of cases. The detailed estimates have great uncertainty. Readers are cautioned that the actual incidence and costs for any given injury mechanism category could be substantially higher or lower than the estimates reported here. Moreover, because we used multiple data sets and assumptions to generate estimates, we could not compute standard errors.

This chapter excludes many injuries and does not capture all the costs of the injuries it does include. It excludes injuries treated only by dentists, chiropractors, acupuncturists, and other alternative medicine healers, as well as injuries that, although potentially severe, did not receive medical attention. It focuses on medical and work loss costs. It excludes other resource costs (eg, for property damage, police services, fire services, victim services, cost recovery through tort litigation, and adjudication and sanctioning for criminal behavior). It also ignores post-traumatic stress disorder (PTSD) associated with unintentional injury. Three studies[58-60] found that at least 25% of samples of children hospitalized for injury suffered diagnostic PTSD. These children, however, rarely were treated for even persistent symptoms. For lack of data, we excluded the costs and QALY losses resulting from their PTSD.

Our tables report intent as recorded by the medical system. Comparison of our estimates for ages 15–24 (which includes cases not shown in this chapter) with contemporaneous 1999–2000 data from the National Crime Victimization Survey suggests the medical system captured cases not requiring hospitalization well, including child physical abuse and domestic violence. It recorded 135,000 more treated assaults than the NCVS. Unlike the non-hospitalized cases, where the Federal government asks and sometimes pays a sample of providers to code intent, the hospital counts come from administrative data systems. They capture only 60% of the 46 000–49 000 hospitalizations estimated from NCVS data for ages 15–24. Correcting this coding shift from assault to unintentional (or very rarely, to undetermined) would raise our physical assault incidence estimate by only 3% but raise physical assault costs by 10% and the associated medical by 22%. Additionally, our medically treated physical assault estimates assume that all mental health treatment was for victims who also were medically treated. Although this procedure captures total medical costs of assault correctly, it undercounts medically treated physical assaults, omitting ones treated only by mental health providers.

Although the hospitalization and mental health cost estimates used in this analysis are age-specific, other data are not. Specifically, the permanent disability cost estimates associated with productivity account for the longer lifespan of children, but are not child-specific in other respects. Work loss cost estimates in this analysis have other drawbacks too. Because women and minorities are paid less than white males for comparable work, productivity costs undervalue their lives.[3] For example, using a 3% discount rate, at age 7 the present value of lifetime wage and household work loss resulting from the death of a girl is $949 000 compared to $1 363 000 for the death of a boy. Because children's earnings are in the future, their present value also is less than the present value earnings losses of young adults, even though more years of future work are lost.[3] Some of the minor cost contributors in this analysis, notably coroner costs, also have limitations, in that data used to estimate them are 10–20 years old. Inflating these old estimates to current dollars may introduce some inaccuracy, but they contribute too little to total costs to justify the expense of collecting new estimates.

For all these reasons, our estimates should be interpreted with caution. They are, however, the best available estimates of childhood injury incidence and costs in the United States today. Future studies will improve upon the methodology and results.

Estimating Lost Quality of Life: Methods and Limitations

Quality of life losses were estimated as the present value of the sum of years of potential life lost to fatal injury, plus the quality-adjusted life year (QALY) losses resulting from nonfatal injury. For each death and for paralyzing injuries that shorten the life span, the years of life lost were estimated from a life expectancy table.[61,62] QALY loss per child sexual assault came from Miller et al.[5] For QALY losses associated with physical injury that caused temporary or permanent disability, estimates by injury diagnosis and victim age were taken from a previous study.[10] Although that study's estimates are routinely used in regulatory analysis by the National Highway Traffic Safety Administration, they rely on physician ratings of functional outcomes in the 1980s which were never fully validated. The estimates combined physician ratings of the impact of injuries over time on ability to think, see, walk, etc, and on pain,[9,10] with diagnosis-specific National Council on Compensation Insurance data on the probability that injury would permanently reduce earning capacity or prevent the victim from working and on the percentage earnings reduction.[63] The rating scales used were not tailored to children, although the physicians were asked to rate probable impairment levels and durations separately for children. The estimated impairment impacts were translated into QALY losses using a systematic review of survey data that weighed the relative importance which respondents' placed on different dimensions of impact.[10] Most of these weights were specific to a child and adolescent population, but reflect the views of adults rather than children of the value of temporary and permanent functional losses by children. The uncertainty in our QALY loss estimates, nevertheless, is quite large.

For sexual assault, we started with the non-monetary losses per rape and per sexual abuse case that Miller, Cohen, and Wiersema[5] derived from 361 jury verdicts for sexual assault, most of them against bars that served drunken patrons, public places with unsafe parking lots, improperly secured hotels, or employers that poorly screened or supervised staff who were working with children. We summed the average non-economic loss and wage loss per sexual assault. We divided the sum by the amount Cohen and Miller[38] estimate juries were willing to award for a lifetime of QALY loss. They derived that estimate from regressions on jury awards for physical assault and the QALY loss estimates by diagnosis used in the present chapter. This calculation showed that the mean loss for all sexual assaults was 2.36% of lifetime QALYs, with slightly higher percentage losses when the victims were children under age 11. By comparison, had we used survey-based estimates of what people are willing to pay to reduce their risk of a rape or a homicide,[64] the lifetime loss would have been 2.44% of QALYs. Thus, our estimates are conservative. Multiplying the percentage loss times the present value of lifetime QALYs implicit in the willingness to award estimate, the estimated loss is 0.807 QALYs per sexual assault victim under age 10 and 0.633 QALYs per sexual assault victim above this age.

Acknowledgment

The research reported here was supported in part by a contract from the National Center for Injury Prevention and Control, Centers for Disease Control and Prevention, National Institute on Mental Health grant number R01 MH60622, and a Children's Safety Network contract from the Maternal and Child Health Bureau, Health Resources and Services Administration. Participating in the International Collaborative Effort on Injury Statistics, sponsored by the National Center for Health Statistics with funding from the National Institute of Child Health and Development, also contributed critically to this research. We thank Ian Fiebelkorn at RTI and Bruce Lawrence at PIRE for their assistance in computing the numbers reported here. We are especially grateful to our Project Officer at CDC, Phaedra Corso, for her insightful advice, her comments, and her hard work helping us to develop and document the medical and work loss cost estimates for physical injury presented in the first half of this chapter. The sexual assault estimates, QALY-related work and cost savings analyses were not funded by CDC. Nothing in this chapter should be construed as the official position of the funding agencies.

References

1. Miller TR, Romano ED, Spicer RS. The cost of childhood unintentional injuries and the value of prevention. *The Future of Children*. 2000;10(1):137–163.
2. Bureau of the Census. *Statistical Abstract of the United States 1997 (117th edition)*. Washington, DC: U.S. Government Printing Office; 1997. Table 217.
3. Rice DP, MacKenzie EJ, Jones AS, et al. *Cost of injury in the United States: A report to Congress*. San Francisco, CA: Institute for Health & Aging, University of California, and Injury Prevention Center, The Johns Hopkins University; 1989.
4. Miller TR, Demes J, Bovbjerg R. Child seats: How large are the benefits and who should pay? *Child occupant protection*. Malvern, PA: Society for Automotive Engineers; 1993:81–90.
5. Miller TR, Cohen MA, Wiersema B. *Victim costs and consequences—A new look*. Washington, DC: National Institute of Justice; 1996. NIJ Research Report NCJ 155281 & U.S. GPO: 1996—495-037/20041.
6. Miller TR, Covington K, Jensen A. Costs of injury by major cause, United States,

1995: Cobbling together estimates. In: Mulder S, van Beeck EF, eds. *Measuring the burden of injuries (Proceedings of a conference in Noordwijkerhout, Netherlands, May 13-15, 1998)*. Amsterdam, Netherlands: European Consumer Safety Association; 1999:23–40.

7. Danseco ER, Miller TR, Spicer R. Incidence and costs of 1987–1994 childhood injuries: Demographic breakdowns. Pediatrics. 2000;105(2):e27–34 (electronic pages), http://www.pediatrics.org/cgi/content/full/105/102/e127.

8. Gold MR, Siegel JE, Russell LB, Weinstein MC, eds. *Cost-effectiveness in Health and Medicine*. New York, NY: Oxford University Press; 1996.

9. Hirsch A, Eppinger R, Shame T, et al. *Impairment scaling from the abbreviated injury scale*. Washington, DC: National Highway Traffic Safety Administration; 1983.

10. Miller TR, Pindus NM, Douglass JB, Rossman SB. *Nonfatal injury costs and consequences: A data book*. Washington, DC: The Urban Institute Press; 1995.

11. Drummond MF, O'Brien B, Stoddart GL, Torrance GW. *Methods for the economic evaluation of health care programmes*. 2nd ed. Oxford: Oxford University Press; 1997.

12. Blincoe L, Seay A, Zaloshnja E, et al. *The economic impact of motor vehicle crashes, 2000*. Washington, DC: U.S. Department of Transportation, National Highway Traffic Safety Administration; May 2002. DOT HS 809 446.

13. Lino M. *Expenditures on children by families, 2000 annual report*. Washington, DC: U.S. Department of Agriculture, Center for Nutrition Policy and Promotion; 2001. Miscellaneous Publication No. 1528-2000.

14. Miller TR. Assessing the burden of injury: Progress and pitfalls. In: Mohan D, Tiwari G, eds. *Injury Prevention and Control*. New York, NY: Taylor & Francis; 2000:49–70.

15. Kenkel DS. Using estimates of the value of a statistical life in evaluating regulatory effects. In: Kuckler F, ed. *Valuing the Health Benefits of Food Safety: A Proceedings*. Miscellaneous Publication 1570 ed. Washington, DC: U.S. Department of Agriculture; 2001.

16. Sunstein CR. *Lives, life-years and willingness to pay*. Washington, DC: AEI-Brookings Joint Center for Regulatory Studies; 2003.

17. Krupnick AJ. *Valuing health outcomes: Policy choices and technical issues*. Washington, DC: Resources for the Future; 2004.

18. Miller TR, Levy DT. Cost-outcome analysis in injury prevention and control: Eighty-four recent estimates for the United States. *Med Care*. 2000;38(6): 562–582.

19. Miller T, Hendrie D. How should governments spend the drug prevention dollar: A buyer's guide. In: T. Stockwell, P. Gruenewald, J. Toumbourou, Loxley W, eds. *Preventing Harmful Substance Use: The Evidence Base for Policy and Practice*. West Sussex: John Wiley & Sons; 2005:415–431.

20. Cutler DM, Richardson E. The value of health: 1970–1990. *Am Econ Rev*. 1998;88(2):97–100.

21. French MT, Mauskopf JA, Teague JL, Roland J. Estimating the dollar value of health outcomes from drug abuse interventions. *Med Care*. 1996;34(9):890–910.

22. Tolley G, Kenkel D, Fabian R, eds. *Valuing health for policy: An economic approach*. Chicago, IL: The University of Chicago Press; 1994.

23. Miller TR. The plausible range for the value of life: Red herrings among the mackerels. *J Forensic Econ*. 1990;3(3):17–39.

24. Alcohol Policies Project. Fact sheet: Lowering the minimum drinking age is a bad idea. *Advocacy for the Prevention of Alcohol Problems, Center for Science in the Public Interest* [Online]. Available at: http://www.cspinet.org/booze/mlpafact.htm. Accessed June 7, 2005.

25. U.S. Census Bureau. Historical Census of Housing Tables, House Heating Fuel. *U.S. Census Bureau, Housing and Household Economic Statistics Division* [Online]. December 2, 2004. Available at: http://www.census.gov/hhes/www/housing/census/historic/fuels.html. Accessed June 7, 2005.

26. Tenenbein M. Unit-dose packaging of iron supplements and reduction of iron poisoning in young children. *Arch Pediatr Adolesc Med.* 2005;159:557–560.

27. Grossman DC, Mueller BA, Riedy C, et al. Gun storage practices and risk of youth suicide and unintentional firearm injuries. *JAMA.* 2005;293(6):707–714.

28. Hu PS, Reuscher TR. *Summary of travel trends, 2001 National Household Travel Survey.* Washington, DC: Federal Highway Administration; 2004.

29. Biglan A, Brennan PA, Foster SL, et al. *Helping adolescents at risk: Prevention of multiple problem behaviors.* New York: Guilford Press; 2004.

30. Miller T, Hendrie D. *Cost and benefit analyses of substance abuse prevention interventions.* Rockville, MD: Westat; 2005, in press. Final Report to the Center for Substance Abuse Prevention.

31. Owens DK. Interpretation of cost-effectiveness analyses [Editorial]. *Journal of General Internal Medicine.* 1998;13:716–717.

32. Aos S, Lieb R, Mayfield J, Miller M, Pennucci A. *Benefits and costs of prevention and early intervention programs for youth.* Olympia, WA: Washington State Institute for Public Policy; 2004.

33. Hingson R, Howland J. Use of laws to deter drinking and driving. *Alcohol Health Res World.* 1990;14:36–43.

34. Istre GR, McCoy MA, Osborn L, Barnard JJ, Bolton A. Deaths and injuries from house fires. *N Eng J Med.* 2001;344(25):1911–1916.

35. Miller TR, Galbraith MS. Injury prevention counseling by pediatricians: A benefit-cost comparison. *Pediatrics.* 1995;96(1):1–4.

36. Zaloshnja E, Miller TR, Galbraith MS, et al. Reducing injuries among Native Americans: Five cost-outcome analyses. *Accid Anal Prev.* 2003;35(5):631–639.

37. Hansen WB, Derzon JH, Dusenbury L. *Analysis of magnitude of effects of substance abuse prevention programs included in the National Registry of Effective Programs through 2003: A core components analysis.* Washington, DC: Internal document prepared at the request of the Center for Substance Abuse Prevention, Substance Abuse and Mental Health Services Administration; 2004.

38. Substance Abuse and Mental Health Services Administration. Model programs: Good behavior game. *Substance Abuse and Mental Health Services Administration.* Available at: http://modelprograms.samhsa.gov/textonly_cf.cfm?page=effective&pkProgramID=84. Accessed May 8, 2005.

39. Miller TR, Levy D. The effect of regional trauma care systems on costs. *Arch Surg.* 1995;130(2):188–193.

40. Institute of Medicine–Committee on Poison Prevention and Control. *Forging a poison prevention and control system.* Washington, DC: National Academies Press; 2004.

41. Ortega-Sanchez I, the Working Group on Leading Economic Issues on New Vaccines for Adolescents. *An inquiry into the projected cost-effectiveness of new vaccines and other health interventions for adolescents.* Atlanta, GA: Centers for Disease Control and Prevention; 2005.

42. Graham JD, Corso PS, Morris JM, Segui-Gomez M, Weinstein MC. Evaluating the cost-effectiveness of clinical and public health measures. *Annu Rev Public Health.* 1998;9:125–152. Used estimates for hepatitis vaccination and cigarette sales to minors from comparably computed costs per QALY saved at a 3% discount rate.

43. Kelly AE, Haddix AC, Scanlon KS, Helmick CG, Mulinare J. Cost-effectiveness of strategies to prevent neural tube defects. In: Gold MR, Siegel JE, Russell LB,

Weinstein MC, eds. *Cost-effectiveness in health and medicine*. New York: Oxford University Press; 1996:313–348. Note 4. Estimated cost per QALY saved from cereal fortification at a 3% discount rate.

44. Boyle MH, Torrance GW, Sinclair JC, Horwood SP. Economic evaluation of neonatal intensive care of very-low-birth-weight infants. *N Eng J Med*. 1983;308(22): 1330–1337. Estimated cost per QALY saved of neonatal intensive care was at a 5% discount rate. The estimate in Table 8 was recomputed at a 3% discount rate and omitted expected earnings gains (an indirect cost) from the calculation of net costs to avoid double counting. This estimate unavoidably reflects 1978 treatment capabilities so it may not measure current cost-effectiveness very accurately.

45. Tengs TO, Adams ME, Pliskin JS, et al. Five hundred life-saving interventions and their cost-effectiveness. *Risk Anal*. 1995;15:369–390. Used measles immunization and phenylketonuria (PKU) screening estimates of costs per life year saved computed at a 5% discount rate. Estimates were recomputed using a 3% discount rate.

46. For example, low income parents are less likely to own a child safety seat than other parents, but those who do own child safety seats use them at the same rate as other parents. Mayer M, LeClere FB. *Injury prevention measures in households with children in the United States, 1990*. Hyattsville, MD: Vital and Health Statistics of the Centers for Disease Control and Prevention, National Center for Health Statistics; 1990. Advance Data No. 250.

47. Finkelstein EA, Corso PC, Miller TR. *Incidence and economic burden of injuries in the United States, 2000*. New York: Oxford University Press; 2005, in press.

48. National Center for Health Statistics. Mortality Data, Multiple Cause-of-Death Public-Use Data Files, 2000. *U.S. Department of Health and Human Services, Centers for Disease Control and Prevention, National Center for Health Statistics*. Available at: http://www.cdc.gov/nchs/products/elec_prods/subject/mortmcd.htm. Accessed January, 2004.

49. National Center for Injury Prevention and Control. National electronic injury surveillance system all-injury profile. *Centers for Disease Control and Prevention, National Center for Injury Prevention and Control*. Available at: http://www.cdc. gov/ncipc/wisqars/nonfatal/datasources.htm. Accessed June, 2004.

50. National Center for Health Statistics. Ambulatory Health Care Data. *U.S. Department of Health and Human Services, Centers for Disease Control and Prevention, National Center for Health Statistics*. Available at: http://www.cdc.gov/nchs/about/major/ahcd/ahcd1.htm. Accessed January, 2004.

51. Agency for Healthcare Research and Quality. Medical Expenditure Panel Survey. *Department of Health and Human Services, Rockville, MD*. Available at: http://www.meps.ahrq.gov/. Accessed Jan 21, 2005.

52. *National Survey of Adolescents in the United States, 1995* [computer program]. Version ICPSR. Charlestown, SC [Ann Arbor, MI]: Medical University of South Carolina, 1999 [Inter-university Consortium for Political and Social Research {distributor}, 2000]; 2000.

53. Cohen MA, Miller TR. The cost of mental health care for victims of crime. *Journal of Interpersonal Violence*. 1998;13(1):93–110.

54. Miller TR, Langston EA, Lawrence BA, et al. *Rehabilitation costs and long term consequences of motor vehicle injury*. Calverton, MD: Pacific Institute for Research and Evaluation; 2004. Final report to National Highway Traffic Safety Administration.

55. Miller TR, Lawrence B, Jensen A, et al. *Estimating the cost to society of consumer product injuries: The revised injury cost model*. Bethesda, MD: U.S. Consumer Product Safety Commission; 1998.

56. Zaloshnja E, Spicer R, Romano E, Miller T. Does using AIS85 costs with AIS90

data create serious errors? *45th Annual Proceedings of the Association for the Advancement of Automotive Medicine, San Antonio, Texas, September 24-26, 2001.* Barrington, IL: Association for the Advancement of Automotive Medicine (AAAM); 2001.

57. Haddix AC, Teutsch SM, Corso PS. *Prevention effectiveness: A guide to decision analysis and economic evaluation.* Second ed. New York: Oxford University Press; 2003.

58. de Vries AP, Kassam-Adams N, Cnaan A, Sherman-Slate E, Gallagher PR, Winston FK. Looking beyond the physical injury: Posttraumatic stress disorder in children and parents after pediatric traffic injury. *Pediatrics.* 1999;104(6): 1293–1299.

59. Daviss WB, Mooney D, Racusin R, Ford JD, Fleischer A, McHugo GJ. Predicting posttraumatic stress after hospitalization for pediatric injury. *J Am Acad Child Adoles Psychiat.* 2000;39(5):576–583.

60. Schreier H, Ladakakos C, Morabito D, Chapman L, Knudson MM. Posttraumatic stress symptoms in children after mild to moderate pediatric trauma: A longitudinal examination of symptom prevalence, correlates, and parent-child symptom reporting. *J Trauma.* 2005;58(2):353–363.

61. Arias E. United States life tables, 2000. *National Vital Statistics Reports.* 2003;51(3):(PHS) 2003-1120.

62. Berkowitz M, Harvey C, Greene CG, Wilson SE. *Economic consequences of traumatic spinal cord injury.* New York: Demos Publishers; 1992.

63. National Council on Compensation Insurance. *Detailed claims information special tabulation.* Boca Raton, FL: NCCI; 1998.

64. Cohen MA, Rust R, Steen S, Tidd S. Willingness-to-pay for crime control programs. *Criminology.* 2004;42(1):86–106.

65. Goldsmith LJ, Hutchison B, Hurley J. *Economic evaluation across the four faces of prevention.* Hamilton, Ontario: Centre for Health Economics and Policy Analysis, McMaster University; 2004.

CHAPTER 3

Hazards Associated with Common Nursery Products

Carol Pollack-Nelson, Ph.D.[*] and Dorothy Drago, MA, MPH

On May 12, 1998, 16-month-old Daniel Keysar was strangled to death when a portable crib, in which he was placed for a nap, collapsed across his neck. Danny died at the home of his childcare provider, in her portable, foldable crib. When she checked on Danny, she found he was trapped by the neck in the "V" of the cribs' folded rails. Danny's mother was unaware of the situation as she drove from work to pick up her son at the end of the day. She was greeted by police at the door of the daycare, where she learned of her son's death.

Shortly thereafter, Danny's parents, University of Chicago professors Linda Ginzel and Boaz Keysar, discovered that the portable crib in which Danny died had been recalled in 1993 after three children had died in these cribs. Since the recall, other children have died in these same cribs which remained in the hands of consumers who were unaware of the recall. Danny was the crib's fifth victim.

Mobilizing their grief into a movement of positive change, Danny's parents founded an organization, Kids In Danger, that works to reform the juvenile product system so that potentially dangerous products never reach the marketplace. KID also works to educate and alert consumers and day care providers of recalled products.

Product Safety

According to the Consumer Product Safety Commission (CPSC or "the Commission"), deaths, injuries and property damage from consumer product-related incidents cost the nation more than $700 billion annually. In 2003, an estimated 60 700 children aged five and younger were treated for injuries associated with nursery in emergency departments throughout the US.[1] The CPSC is the government agency responsible for overseeing the safety of consumer products, including nursery items. The Commission is an independent federal regulatory agency that was created in 1972 by

---

* Independent Safety Consulting, Rockville, Maryland.

Congress under the Consumer Product Safety Act. The agency's mission is to protect the public from unreasonable risks of serious injury or death involving a wide variety of consumer products. To accomplish its mission, the Commission collects data and information relating to injury and death associated with 15 000 different consumer products.

The CPSC maintains four different databases: the National Electronic Injury Surveillance System; Reported Incidents; Death Certificates; and In-Depth Investigations. A description of these data bases is presented below.

1. *The National Electronic Injury Surveillance System (NEISS)*—The NEISS system is comprised of a sample of approximately 100 hospital emergency departments that are statistically representative of hospital emergency rooms nationwide. These emergency departments record data (in accordance with a CPSC coding manual) pertaining to presenting cases which involve consumer products. This data is transmitted to the CPSC once a day. CPSC uses these data to estimate the number of injuries occurring nationwide which are associated with a particular category of consumer product. A NEISS record includes product code(s), treatment date, age, gender, diagnosis, body part injured, disposition (eg released, hospitalized, etc.), location (eg school, home, etc.), and a comment (brief description of the event). NEISS data cited throughout this paper are available from the US Consumer Product Safety Commission.

2. *Death Certificate File (DTHS)*—In cases where a death was associated with a consumer product, CPSC purchases the death certificates from the state health departments. A DTHS record includes date of death, age, gender, race, external cause of death (E-Code), product code(s), location, lot number, and brief description of the circumstances of the death.

3. *Injury/Potential Injury Incident File (IPII)*—This database of reported incidents contains summaries of Hotline reports, product-related newspaper accounts, reports from medical examiners, letters to CPSC, and referrals from other government agencies. An IPII record includes product code(s), incident date; age, gender, hazard, disposition (eg released, hospitalized, etc.), city and state, and a brief description of the event.

4. *In-Depth Investigations (INDP) File*—This file contains summaries of follow-up investigations of certain cases originally reported through one of the other databases. Based on victim/witness on-site or phone interviews, the reports provide details about incident sequence, human behavior, and product involvement.

In addition to these four data bases, the CPSC maintains a website, www.cpsc.gov, that provides valuable hazard information, including up-to-date recall notices. Also available on the website are annual updates for the estimated numbers of emergency department treated injuries associated with different types of nursery products.

Based on the data it collects, the agency, when deemed appropriate, takes action. The Commission has the authority to pursue a variety of options to address hazards: (1) it can develop mandatory standards; (2) it can work with industry to develop voluntary standards; (3) it can "defer" to an existing voluntary standard, lending it the status of a quasi-mandatory standard; (4) it can ban products from the marketplace; or (5) it can require that products be recalled and "fixed" so they no longer pose a hazard.

The work of the Commission appears to have had a dramatic effect on consumer product injuries and fatalities. In 2000, the CPSC released a report stating that US hospital emergency room-treated injuries associated with nursery products had dropped almost 20 percent from 1995 to 1999.[2] This marked the first decrease in nursery product injuries to children under 5 years since the CPSC first began keeping such records in 1973. It was noted that the downward trend was largely due to the dramatic reduction in injuries associated with baby walkers; new requirements prevent walkers from fitting through doorways or toppling down stairs. Additionally, changes to other nursery products—including cribs, play yards, high chairs, and strollers—as a result of mandatory and voluntary standards were credited with this reduction. Since 1999, the number of hospital emergency room visits by children under 5 associated with nursery products has actually increased, though this increase is not statistically significant.[1,3]

Nursery Product Safety

The word "nursery" conjures up an image of a peaceful environment for an infant or toddler. However, as in Danny's case that is not always the reality. Each year thousands of children are injured, some fatally, on nursery products. Consumers are often surprised by dangerous nursery products and many consumers expect that products intended for use by a baby are tested and their safety assured. However, there is no pre-market safety clearance procedure for nursery products (or any other consumer products) in the US. There are mandatory standards, promulgated by the Commission, for cribs but not for other nursery products. All cribs sold in the United States must meet the mandatory requirements. There are voluntary industry standards, usually developed with input from CPSC, for most nursery products (see table). Thus, companies that market nursery products must have cribs tested for compliance with the CPSC mandatory regulation, and may have other nursery products tested for compliance with the relevant voluntary industry standards.

While standards are an important method for bolstering product safety, they do not eliminate all hazards. Standards typically attempt to address the most frequent and serious hazards associated with a product, but other risks may not be addressed. Furthermore, test methodologies do not cover all types of use patterns. Another limitation of standards is the time needed before a standard is issued. Standard development can take years, particularly in cases of mandatory standards where industry is not fully supportive of the regulation. The long time needed for CPSC mandatory standards is largely due to required public comment periods which may involve the submission of written comments and/or public hearings on a matter.

In most instances, industry members develop standards through a voluntary standards process, such as that established under the auspices of ASTM, formerly the American Society for Testing and Materials. This process may be initiated by industry members or at the urging of the CPSC. A voluntary standard may be processed much more quickly than a mandatory standard, thereby greatly reducing the amount of time required to see design changes occur in the marketplace.

Table

Regulations and Standards for Nursery Products

Nursery Product	Regulations and Standards (M= mandatory; otherwise, voluntary)	Year Originally Approved	Current Version Published	Key Provisions Relevant to Salient Hazards
Bassinets	ASTM F 2194	2002	2002	• precludes unintentional collapse • precludes tip-over • limits mattress thickness • limits space between mattress and sidewall
Bath Seats	ASTM F 1967	1999	2003	• precludes suction cups from detaching from tub • precludes suction cups from detaching from seat • limits size of leg openings • ensures stability • warns about drowning potential
Bedding (infant)	ASTM F 1917	1999	2000	• limits string lengths to preclude strangulation • ensures bumper guards be secured in all corners • warns about suffocation on pillows • warns about strangulation on wall hangings, sheets
Bouncer Seats	ASTM F 2167	2001	2002	• requires waist and crotch restraint • precludes tip-over • precludes significant slippage on a surface
Carriers (hand held)	ASTM F 2050	2000	2001	• precludes handle breakage or unlatching • precludes significant slippage on a surface
Carriers (worn)	ASTM F 2236	2003	2003	• limits size of leg openings • precludes fasteners breaking or disengaging • precludes seam separation • preclude slippage of adjustable straps • must support test weight
Changing Tables	ASTM F 2388	2004	2004	• must provide a barrier • precludes entrapment

Regulations and Standards for Nursery Products (continued)

Nursery Product	Regulations and Standards (M= mandatory; otherwise, voluntary)	Year Originally Approved	Current Version Published	Key Provisions Relevant to Salient Hazards
Cribs (full size)	16CFR1508 (M)	1973	1982	• defines dimensions of crib and mattress • limits inter-slat spacing • prescribes hardware • precludes head entrapment in cut-outs
Cribs (non full size)	16CFR1509 (M)	1976	1982	• defines dimensions of crib and mattress • limits inter-slat spacing • prescribes hardware • precludes head entrapment in cut-outs
Cribs (full size)	ASTM F 1169	1988	2003	• precludes mattress support detachment from crib • minimizes component separation spacing • limits cornerpost extensions • precludes drop-side latches from failing • precludes detachment of teething rail • warns about suffocation and strangulation hazards
Cribs (non-full size)	ASTM F 1822	1988	2003	• precludes mattress support detachment from crib • minimizes component separation spacing • limits cornerpost extensions • precludes drop-side latches from failing • precludes detachment of teething rail • precludes detachment or deformation of mesh • warns about suffocation and strangulation hazards
Crib corner-posts	ASTM F 966	1990	2000	• limits cornerpost extensions
Gates and Enclosures	ASTM F 1004	1986	2002	• precludes passage of lower body through openings • precludes positional strangulation in openings

(continued)

Regulations and Standards for Nursery Products (continued)

Nursery Product	Regulations and Standards (M= mandatory; otherwise, voluntary)	Year Originally Approved	Current Version Published	Key Provisions Relevant to Salient Hazards
Gates and Enclosures	ASTM F 1004	1986	2002	• ensures gate will resist push out force • prescribes gate height
High Chairs	ASTM F 404	1975	1999	• requires waist and crotch restraint • limits size of leg openings • precludes unintentional tray detachment • ensures overall chair stability • ensures overall chair integrity • warns that restraint must be used • warns that tray is not substitute for restraint
Playpens	ASTM F 406	1977	2002	• precludes unintentional folding • precludes "V" formation collapse • ensures automatic latches/locking devices • precludes finger/button mesh-entrapment • precludes body entrapment in mesh-sided pens
Swings (infant)	ASTM F 2088	2001	2003	• requires waist and crotch restraint • limits incline angle to <5 degrees • precludes tip-over • precludes unintentional folding • precludes hardware detachment due to vibration
Strollers	ASTM F 833	1983	2001	• ensures adequate brake performance • precludes tip-over • precludes unintentional collapse/folding • requires waist and crotch restraint • precludes pinch/scissor/shear injury • precludes lower torso entrapment in leg openings

Nursery Product Injury and Fatality Data

While mandatory and voluntary standards have led to a decline in nursery product injuries and fatalities, incidents do still occur. This chapter examines 10 common nursery items and the injury and fatality data associated with each. The data cited in this chapter were obtained from the National Injury Information Clearinghouse at the CPSC. CPSC's data are available to anyone upon request. Depending on the type and extent of request, there may or may not be a charge for the data. Typically, data are purged of manufacturer and brand names.

For the purposes of this chapter, records from the death certificate database (DTHS), incident investigations database (INDP) and reported incidents database (IPII) for the period 1999–2003 were reviewed; NEISS records from 2002 and 2003 were reviewed, as well as CPSC summary data for those years.[1-3] In addition, the CPSC website was searched for recalls.

Bassinets and cradles

Bassinets and cradles are used for very young infants, typically to about five months of age, who often sleep the night in them. A typical bassinet is a basket-like container on free-standing legs with wheels. Bassinets make it convenient to push an infant from room to room. Cradles typically have a stationary frame, but rock side-to-side or front-to-back.

The most severe injury outcome associated with these products is suffocation death, usually by entrapment between the mattress and side wall in a bassinet and by positional asphyxia in a cradle that comes to rest at an angle, rather than level. Other severe injuries are associated with product collapse or tip-over. Minor to moderate injuries are associated with sharp points, sharp edges, or splinters.

At least 50 bassinet/cradle deaths were reported to the CPSC between 1999 and 2003. Of those, only one appeared to be directly related to product failure (a bassinet collapsed); a few were related to a combination bassinet/playpen product that posed an entrapment hazard and which was eventually recalled; most of the others were related to bedding in the bassinet/cradle, such as pillows, comforters, and blankets. Positional asphyxia, with the baby either face-down or between the bassinet/cradle mattress and side wall, was reported with less frequency.

About 500 to 700 bassinet and cradle-related injuries are treated yearly in emergency departments. Infants six months old and younger make up the majority of cases, with head injuries common. Some examples of scenarios include: bassinet overturned by sibling or family dog; baby fell out of bassinet; and bassinet leg collapsed.

Infants who use bassinets and cradles are very young and still have not developed the ability to roll over, or to hold the head erect for any substantial length of time. Beal et al[4] studied 11 infants aged between 44 and 82 days old in various positions and in various angles in rocking cradles as related to the potential for asphyxiation. They found that when an infant is placed face-down on a horizontal surface, he/she naturally extends the neck slightly and pivots the head to a side to free the nose and mouth for breathing. This motion is readily accomplished and suffocation is not likely. However, they found that when the infant's face was against the cradle bars or when an infant was placed in a rocking cradle that came to rest at an angle equal to or greater than 10 degrees, the infant could not pivot the head, and remained face-down. Often an arm extended between the cradle side/bars, or got trapped between the side/bars and the body. Being wedged like that, the infant could not turn its head against gravity to get a clear airway. If the infant tried to bring both hands up beside the head, he/she ended up with an extended trapped arm and a flexed free arm. Even if the infant was successful at turning the head away from the bars, the asymmetric tonic neck reflex returned the head to a face down position. An infant in such a position gets stressed and begins to cry and fuss. The moisture generated makes the mattress surface less permeable to air.[5] Repeated attempts to lift the head free lead to exhaustion; the circumstances favorable for suffocation are in place.

The pattern of suffocation described by Beal et al[4] was evidenced in a cradle sold in the US between 1990 and 1992 and recalled in 1992. The product was a motorized cradle (part of a combination swing and cradle product) that swung head-to-foot, but came to rest at an angle. Babies were found pushed down in one corner of the cradle. At the time of the recall, there were at least four incidents of partial or total suffocation associated with the product. In this case, the failure of the cradle to come to rest level was due to a poor design. Other defects that could cause the same result include a missing locking pin, or excessive tilt.

Cradles or bassinets have been recently recalled for other causes of suffocation as well. In 2000, a bassinet was recalled because infants could become trapped between the side and mattress. A three-month old boy suffocated and three other infants were not seriously injured. A multi-use product that combined a bassinet, changing table and playpen was recalled in 1998 because the bassinet could have loose mesh, creating a pocket near the floorboard. Four babies were known to have gotten their head caught. This hazard pattern mimics the suffocation hazard associated with mesh playpens.

Bassinets recalled for other reasons include a portable bassinet recalled in 2001 because of a finger-pinching hazard in moving parts, and a product that converted between a carrier and a bassinet recalled in 2000 because when used as a carrier, the handle disengaged, flipping the baby out.

Assuming the new ASTM standard[6] ensures safer future bassinets and cradles, at least two messages still need to be reinforced: get bedding (blankets, pillows, etc) out of the product; and find out if your product has been recalled. Products like bassinets and cradles, which have relatively long lives, can be responsible for deaths and injuries long after they have been recalled. For example, a one-month-old boy in Burlington, Iowa, died in the bassinet portion of a playpen that had been recalled two years earlier because the bassinet portion had a loose mesh side, which created an entrapment hazard.

Bath Rings or Seats

Bath seats (also called "bath rings") are plastic devices used to support an infant during bathing. Bath rings/seats are typically attached to the tub surface by means of suction cups. Most bath seats are recommended for children beginning at 6 months of age, the age at which the average infant can sit unsupported.[7] The upper age limit for using a bath ring depends on the particular product (eg, its size) and is normally stated on the packaging. However, it has been suggested that consumers cease using bath rings when a child reaches 8 or 9 months, the time at which an infant can pull to a stand, since infants who try to get out of the bath ring may be at risk for drowning.[8]

While there are relatively minor injuries reported on bath rings (eg, laceration, pinching, bruising), drowning is the major hazard pattern associated with these products. In 2003, the CPSC was notified of 12 infant fatalities resulting from drowning in a baby bath ring or bath seat. Given the narrow age when these are used, that number can be considered significant. Victims ranged in age between 5 and 12 months. The mean age was 8.75 months. There was an equal number of male and female victims.

In nearly all of the drowning incidents reported to the Commission, a lapse in supervision was noted. In most cases, the parent or caregiver had reportedly left the bathroom where the baby was bathing. Oftentimes, the baby had been left in the bath seat with an older sibling in the tub. Parents typically reported that they had only left the bathroom for a few minutes— to get a towel or to answer the phone. However, because drowning can occur in as little as 3–5 minutes and in as little as an inch of water,[9] even a few minutes away can prove fatal.

Researchers have suggested that some parents erroneously believe that children who can sit unassisted and pull themselves up will be capable of lifting their heads out of water or otherwise saving themselves from drowning.[10,11] As the incident data demonstrate, infants and toddlers are not necessarily capable of lifting their heads and chests out of the water, particularly when a bath seat is involved since it may trap the baby's legs or chest.

Another erroneous belief apparently held by some parents is that an older child is capable of "watching" the infant in the tub.[12] In Rauschwalbe, Brenner and Smith's[8] parental survey about bath rings, some respondents reported feeling more comfortable leaving a child unattended "for a moment in the bath" if the infant was contained in a bath seat, or if there was an older child present. However, as the data demonstrate, older siblings may not recognize the risk or be capable of responding to and rescuing a drowning baby.[13]

Drowning incidents involving bath rings and bath seats demonstrate that older children cannot be relied upon to protect an infant from drowning. A typical example of such a scenario occurred in Vintondale, PA in 2003. A mother reportedly left a healthy one-year-old baby girl with her two-year-old brother, alone in the bathtub. Although the infant was initially placed in the seat, she apparently got out of the seat and was discovered by her mother lying in the water. In another case in Des Moines, IA, a 12-month-old female was found by her father floating in the water. The child was left by her father who had left her in a baby bath seat with her 3-year-old sister also in the tub. This baby died 38 days later.

Drowning incidents associated with bath rings and bath seats typically result from one of three major hazard patterns: (1) tip over where the suction cups of the bath seat/ring unexpectedly release, causing the baby and the bath seat/ring to tip over in the water; (2) entrapment where the baby slips between the legs of the bath ring and becomes entrapped, under water; and (3) the baby attempting to climb out of the bath seat or tub.

Reducing the likelihood of injuries and fatalities associated with bath rings requires effort by both consumers and manufacturers. Parents must maintain continuous supervision when a bath seat is being used. Manufacturers are advised to adhere to the voluntary standard for Bath Seats and Bath Rings.[14] This standard covers a wide range of hazard patterns, including specifications for stability and restraints. Consumers are advised to purchase only bath seats that meet the ASTM standard (see markings on the product package for the ASTM seal).

Suction cup release is a serious hazard associated with bath seats. In 2003, one company re-issued an earlier recall due to suction cup failure on its bath rings. The company had received four reports of infants tipping over after the suction cups separated from the seat. Fortunately, none of the incidents resulted in injury.

To ensure that a particular bath seat's suction cups work effectively on a given tub surface, consumers are advised to check the hold of the suction cups prior to each use. After filling the tub with a few inches of water—that is all that is needed to bathe a baby—consumers should pull up on each of the legs of the bath ring to make certain that the suction cups are firmly adhered to the tub surface. Suction cups will not adhere to textured, ridged or appliqued surfaces. They also will not stick to scratched, chipped or repainted tub surfaces.

To prevent a drowning due to a defective bath ring, a baby submerging underneath a bath ring, or the baby attempting to climb out of a bath seat or ring, constant and direct supervision is required. Yet parents continue to leave the bathroom while their infants are in the tub. It seems that there is a lack of understanding of the hazards associated with these products. A bath ring that appears secure gives parents the impression that it will retain the infant in an upright position. However, as the data show, that is not always the case. Leaving an infant in a bath seat for a few minutes, even when in the company of an older sibling, can be a fatal mistake.

Carriers and Seats (excluding car seats)

Parents have a wide range of baby carriers and infant seats to choose from today. Some carriers are worn by the parent, either as a front-carrier or a backpack. Others are hand-held carriers or bouncy seats that provide a place for the baby to sit independent from the parent. Carriers of all kinds are typically used for infants and in some cases for toddlers. The intended age depends on the individual product and the age range specified.

Each year, the Consumer Product Safety Commission is notified of injuries and in some cases deaths occurring while baby carriers and seats are in use. The CPSC estimated that there were more than 3600 baby seat and carrier injuries nationwide in 2003. Additionally, there were an estimated 1400 baby bouncer injuries that year.

The major cause of injury associated with infant seats and carriers is falls. Both front and back carriers can pose a risk of falls if the infant slips through the leg holes or is able to push up (in the case of back carriers) and topple out of the top of the carrier. Back and front carriers have been the subject of six recalls in the last five years. Two of these recalls involved soft carriers and both were due to the potential for a baby to fall through the leg openings. The four recalls affecting back carriers were due to the harness failing to keep the baby inside the carrier. This allowed infants to fall out (either through the leg holes or out the top of the carrier).

Parents are advised to use only carriers that are matched to the infant's size and weight and should try the carrier out with the baby in it and check to make sure that the leg openings are small enough to prevent the baby from slipping through.[9] Also, with back carriers, it is important to make sure that the baby is restrained and that he or she sits far enough down in the seat to reduce the likelihood that he or she will topple out of the top.

Hand-held baby carriers and bouncer seats have also been associated with infant fall injuries. In some cases, the baby's fall is actually the result of the parent falling or tripping while transporting the infant in the carrier or seat. Many times, however, a baby falls out of a carrier that was placed on an elevated surface. Parents often place a baby in a carrier on an elevated surface where they are working (eg, kitchen table, counter, dining room table, washing machine) in order to stay engaged with the baby while doing chores. A combination of factors—the bouncing or rocking feature of the seat, the baby's movements, and placement on an elevated surface—come together to pose a very serious fall risk that typically results in injuries to the head and face. Babies who are secured in restraints may flip off of an elevated surface with the seat. Unrestrained babies may be ejected out of the seat and onto the floor.

A 2000 study of hazard patterns associated with infant seats and carriers revealed that more than a third were attributable to falls from elevated surfaces in the home.[15] Another 10% resulted from falls from elevated surfaces outside the home (eg, shopping or baggage carts). In an effort to address this hazard pattern, an ASTM standard[16] was drafted specifying a performance requirement for slip resistance. It appears that this standard may be having an effect, since falls from elevated surfaces (both inside and outside of the home) had declined to about 20% of the 2003 NEISS data for baby carriers. [It should be noted, however, that this may be an underestimate as it is based only on reports that specified an elevated surface. Many more falls to tile and wood floors were reported in the NEISS data for 2003, but were not counted if they did not specifically mention an elevated surface].

Like carrier seats, bouncer seats are also likely to be placed on elevated surfaces and are susceptible to pitching the baby to the floor. Falling from an elevated surface is the predominant hazard pattern found in the 2003 NEISS data. Of the 1400 estimated bouncy seat injuries that year, 68% specifically mentioned that the bouncer seat fell off of an elevated surface. ASTM Standard 2167[17] addresses a number of hazards including falls from elevated surfaces (as well as disassembly, collapse and stability). Due to the recency of the standard, coupled with the fact that bouncer seats may be used over a number of years with different children, more time is needed to determine if it will effectively mitigate the fall hazard.

Falls from baby seats and carriers occur in ways other than from elevated surfaces. One key hazard pattern noted during the early part of this decade was a large number of falls associated with defective carrying handles. In the past 5 years, hand-held carriers have been the subject of six recalls, all relating to the handles releasing, moving, or breaking which allowed the infant to fall out. The ASTM standard for hand-held infant carriers[16] includes performance requirements for carrying handle integrity. It appears that this standard, along with recalls and attention to the hazard, is having some effect as this hazard pattern was not overly represented in the 2003 NEISS data.

One of the most serious risks posed by infant carriers and bouncer seats is positional asphyxiation. This hazard has been reported to occur in various types of baby seats and carriers when the baby's air supply is restricted due to his or her position within the carrier. For example, one 5-week old female being carried in a cloth infant carrier was found to be unresponsive and not breathing when her mother checked on her after about 20 minutes. The infant died two days later. Positional asphyxia has been reported in slings and portable carriers as well. Parents are advised to check the position of their baby to ensure that the face is clear and the head is not bent forward. Also, parents are advised to make sure that their baby meets the age and weight requirements specified on the product. Infants who are younger than the specified age may not possess the neck strength to support the head and prevent positional asphyxiation.

Another serious risk posed by carriers and bouncer seats is the potential for them to overturn when placed on plush surfaces, resulting in suffocation. Some parents place infant seats and carriers on plush surfaces such as beds or water beds under the mistaken impression that such surfaces provide a soft landing in the event that the seat overturns. Such surfaces can present a risk of suffocation due to the limited air flow. Young infants are unable to lift their heads sufficiently to clear the bedding and suffocate.

A study of this hazard pattern from 1990 through 1997 revealed that there were 16 suffocation deaths resulting from a seat overturning onto a plush surface.[15] It was suggested that parents may not recognize the hazards associated with this common placement scenario for infant seats and carriers. Such incidents continue to occur today. Fatality data from 1999 through 2003 revealed five overturn suffocation incidents.

The last significant hazard pattern associated with infant seat and carrier fatalities is entanglement in restraint straps. The ASTM standard for hand-held carriers[16] specifies that a restraint system shall be provided to secure the child. However, infant movement in the seat may cause entanglement. In the last five years (1999 through 2003), seven strap entanglement fatalities were reported to the CPSC. Victims ranged in age from one month to one year. The hazard pattern differed depending on the age of the victim. For the newborn infants, entanglement results when the infant slips down in the seat, causing the neck to get caught in the restraint. For older infants, it is not clear how they become entangled in the straps, but this may result from more intentional movement in the seat.

Changing Tables

Changing tables are a basic nursery accessory found in many homes with infants. These products can be used from birth through about 3 years, depending on the weight specifications of the particular product. In 2003, the CPSC NEISS system received 93 reports of injuries to children aged 4 and younger associated with changing tables. There were an estimated 1800 changing table injuries nationwide that year. This number is substantially lower than the national estimate in 2000, which was 3170.[3]

Despite this reduction in changing table injuries, falls remain the predominant hazard pattern, representing 98% of estimated injuries in 2003.

Most falls associated with changing tables occurred when the child tumbled off of the table and onto the floor. In some cases, this happened when the parent left the baby's side—even if only momentarily (eg, to get a diaper). In other cases, the fall occurred when the infant or toddler suddenly squirmed away from the parent's control. Using a safety restraint can lessen the chances of a fall. However, even when straps are in use, parents must attend to their child closely since straps may not adequately restrain the child and also, straps may pose an entanglement hazard.

Aside from falls due to an active or unattended baby, falls can also occur if the changing table is defective and breaks. In 2001, a changing table was recalled due to the possibility that it could fall apart and cause the infant to fall. In 2003, the CPSC investigated four incidents in which children were injured after the changing table platform broke. Such cases resulted in contusion and fracture injuries, and in some cases, head injuries.

Another hazard pattern associated with changing tables involves entrapment in the structure of the changing table. While fatalities are relatively uncommon with changing tables—only 2 were reported to the Commission between 1999 and 2003—both were the result of an infant's head becoming entrapped in openings in a changing table (eg, in the frame or railing). In one incident, a 10-month-old boy died after his head became wedged between the space of a wooden changing table's shelf and its guard rail. The other incident involved entrapment between the end of a changing table and the side of a playpen.

Some entrapment incidents associated with changing tables are not fatal, however, they can be quite painful to the infant. In Cranford, New Jersey, a 9.5 month-old female suffered a fractured right tibia when her lower leg got caught in the horizontal front rail of a baby changing table. The injury occurred after the mother had changed the child, and was attempting to pick her up. Finger pinch is another cause of injuries associated with changing tables that have hinged doors. In 2002, one manufacturer recalled its changing tables after learning that a child's finger could become trapped inside spaces between parts of the hinges, causing finger crush or pinching to occur while the door is closing.

In an effort to prevent injuries and fatalities associated with changing tables, ASTM published F 2388, Standard Consumer Safety Specification for Baby Changing Tables for Domestic Use in July, 2004.[18] The standard includes performance requirements and test methods for changing tables marketed to consumers with children weighing up to 30 lbs. The standard addresses: (1) falls from changing tables, (2) the failure of structural or mechanical components, (3) instability and (4) entrapment in openings in the table structure.

Cribs

Cribs constitute the sleeping environment for infants and young children, usually to the age of about three years. Cribs are about 28 by 52 inches, with a rail height of about 26 inches when measured from the top of the rail in its highest position to the top of the mattress support in its lowest position. Mattresses should not exceed 6 inches in thickness.

There have been mandatory standards in place for full size and non-full size cribs since the 1970s.[19,20] The standards set requirements for side rail height, slat spacing, type of hardware, locking dropsides, surface finishing, mattress size and thickness, and assembly instructions. In 1982, the Commission amended the rules to address the hazard of head and neck entrapment in head/footboard cutouts. According to the new sections a head-form probe is placed in any partially bounded opening along the upper edges of the crib end or side panel, then rotated to evaluate the potential for entrapment.

In 1988, ASTM supplemented the mandatory requirements by addressing failure of mattress supports, failure of glued or bolted connections, failure of dropside latches, and dislodgement of teething rails.[21] Similar hazards were addressed for non-full size cribs.[22] The hazard presented by tall finials was addressed by an ASTM standard in 1990.[23] Tall finials (corner posts) acted as clothing or necklace catch points. When children attempted to climb out of a crib, or lean over a finial, the loose clothing or necklace would catch on the finial, create a noose, and strangle the child. The standard limits the height of any finial to 0.06 inches above the upper edge of an end or side panel, unless the corner post extends 16 inches above the uppermost surface of the side rail in its highest position.

Because bedding has been involved in crib suffocation and strangulation incidents, ASTM published a standard for infant bedding and related accessories.[24] It addresses strangulation hazards presented by decorative ribbons, bumper guard ties, wall hangings, fitted sheets, and unraveling threads. The standard also has labeling requirements for infant bedding items. Decorative pillows are required to carry a label informing of the suffocation potential and advising against the use of a pillow in the crib. Fitted crib sheets must be labeled to remind users that the sheet must fit securely to avoid entanglement or strangulation.

In spite of the federal mandatory standard and the ASTM standards, there were an estimated 10 000 crib-related injuries treated in emergency departments in 2003.[1] Infants 7 to 18 months (n~6000), followed by two year olds (n~2000) experienced the highest incidence of crib-related injuries. Contusions, abrasions, and internal injury occurred most frequently, with the head and face the most common sites. Fractures were twice as common among two year olds as among the younger ages. Injuries tended to be associated with falling out of the crib.

From 1999–2001, cribs represented the leading nursery product associated with infant fatalities. About 32% of deaths reported on nursery products during that time period involved cribs. In the five-year period 1999–2003 there were at least 70 deaths involving entrapment, primarily between the crib mattress and side rail, and at least 70 deaths involving bedding (pillows, blankets, quilts, comforters, sheets). Nearly all victims were under ten months old. Where entrapment occurred, hardware (side rail bolts or mattress supports) was missing or loose, allowing a larger than normal space to be created between the frame and mattress. For example, a nine month old Gabbs, NV baby girl asphyxiated when she became entrapped between her crib mattress and side rail. The side rail was not properly attached to the crib frame, so it created a larger than intended space. In other instances, slats were missing or incorrect crib assembly had occurred. Some cribs were very old. Sometimes, a second, smaller mattress or cushion was placed on top of the crib's mattress, creating a space large enough for entrapment.

Where bedding was involved in deaths, infants had gotten tangled in the bedding, pulled it up over their faces, or were face down in the bedding. As with bassinets/cradles, it seems that the message about the hazard of soft bedding, pillows, and sheets needs to be made more effectively.

In at least ten instances, infants died (by compression asphyxia) after climbing out of the crib and getting trapped between the crib and the wall or other furniture.

Several crib deaths which may in fact be mechanical suffocations still get classified as SIDS. These two mechanisms of death essentially present the same at autopsy. Efforts need to be focused on on-site investigation and reenactment of such deaths to minimize the likelihood that they will be erroneously classified as SIDS.

During the years a child uses a crib, much physical development occurs. Children are at risk for different types of injury and death depending on where they are in terms of growth and development. Young infants three to six months old, who do not have well-developed muscle and movement control, are at highest risk for crib-related suffocation deaths simply because they cannot move out of harm's way by themselves. Their heads are relatively larger than at any other age, and the neck muscles are weaker. The smaller bifrontal diameter (compared to the bitemporal diameter) gives the head a wedge-shape and makes it more likely to fit into a small space and remain entrapped.[25]

The most common pattern of death was asphyxiation associated with entrapment between the mattress and crib frame. Cribs that meet the standard should not have a hazardous space in this area. One must conclude that the crib either originally did not comply with the standard, or that the crib's integrity had been compromised by loss or loosening of hardware, or by use of an ill-fitting mattress. Even while these factors are not present in new, complying cribs, they can and do develop over time and with use. For this reason, old, pre-standard, hand-me-down cribs and used cribs purchased at yard sales remain hazardous. Giving periodic notice of this hazard may be the only way to address this issue. Parents need to be reminded to check a used crib for structural integrity.

As infants get older, injuries associated with climbing out of the crib become more common than entrapment and suffocation. Studies done by Ridenour[26,27] point out that the side rails height requirements in the mandatory standard were based on static anthropometry, that is, physical height. Ridenour videotaped 48 children aged 17 to 32 months as they climbed out of cribs. Most children tended to move to a corner before climbing out, placing one hand on the side rail and one on an end, then lifting a foot over. [This corner approach explains why tall finials could pose a catch point hazard.] Ten percent of children climbed out over the side rail. Ridenour noted that, given the typical crib mattress thickness of six inches, the standard allows for a crib rail to be 20 inches above the mattress surface. She compared the net twenty inches in accessible rail height to a recommendation that children be removed from a crib to a toddler bed when the side rail height is less than 75% of the standing height (based on ASTM F 1004-02a, appendix X1.2.5.2). Twenty inches is seventy-five percent of 26.66 inches, which is nearly 8 ½ inches less than 35 inches, the recommended standing height for removal of a child from the crib to a bed. She claimed there is no acceptable rationale for these numbers. She studied the appropriateness of side rails 26, 30, 35, and 39 inches to prevent climbing over the side. The ability to climb out of the crib was not a function of age, since some children 13 to 34 months old could climb out while others could not. The height range of children who could climb out was reported as 30 to 40 inches, indicating the inadequacy of the 35-inch guide for removal to a toddler bed. She emphasized the need to apply motor development research to the design and evaluation of products for infants and children.

Changing the mandatory standard with regard to the 35-inch height would probably be unlikely simply because the process of changing existing regulations is cumbersome and time-consuming. Crib manufacturers could suggest moving children to a bed when the child reaches 35 inches or "is able to climb out of the crib." Some parents lower a crib rail to in fact make climbing out more safe by effectively lowering the fall height. Recognizing that a "counterintuitive" measure like reducing the height of a barrier may be the best solution helps professionals to remember to consider all possible solutions in seeking successful interventions.

From January, 1999 through March, 2004 ten recalls, involving about 453 000 cribs, were conducted by manufacturers in conjunction with the CPSC. In most cases, the underlying problems became evidenced without injury or death, but for one of the products there had been reported one entrapped infant who survived unharmed and ten who had fallen out of the crib without serious injury. Four of the recalls were related to slats loosening or falling out, creating an entrapment space; five of the recalls were related to hardware failure, creating an entrapment hazard, a pinch hazard, or a fall hazard; and one recall was related to violation of the standard's head/foot board cut out requirements.

Gates and Enclosures

Gates and enclosures serve as barriers to keep young children out of certain areas or to keep them confined in a limited space. They are typically used for children 6 to 24 months old. A common use for gates is to block the top of stairs. Historically, head entrapment in diamond- and V-shaped openings of accordion-style gates or enclosures was the major hazard. Head entrapment following a foot-first entry was also reported in the injury data. In 1986, ASTM published a standard[28] to address head entrapment and the ability of the gate to resist "push-out" force exerted by a child. The standard was revised in 2002.

The CPSC estimates that there were 1800 injuries relating to gates and barriers involving children under 5 years of age in 2003. Most of the injuries were sustained by children 7 to 23 months old, corresponding to the primary intended users' ages. Most of the injuries were contusions, abrasions, or internal injury to the head. At the time of injury, children were attempting to climb over the gate, or pushed/pulled the gate down. In some cases, the child then fell down stairs, as did a two-year-old girl who she was able to push through a baby gate. In some of these cases, children were able to defeat latches; in other cases, the latch mechanism was not working properly.

Only two deaths involving baby gates were reported in the five-year period 1999–2003. One was reported as compression asphyxia, the child entrapped between the gate and a playpen; the other was reported as positional asphyxia, the child wedged next to a gate.

Most toddlers have a natural inclination to climb. Climbing is a skill that most children develop before 2 years of age. A gate is a natural challenge to this budding motor skill, so it is foreseeable that children would attempt to scale a barrier. The introduction to the ASTM standard for gates and enclosures indicates that among the injuries CPSC identified were those associated with children attempting to climb up and over gates. Yet the standard appears not to have addressed that hazard pattern. The standard limits the size of completely bounded openings to essentially less than 3 inches by 5.5 inches (the size of the small torso probe) to prevent entrapment. But such openings could function as foot/hand holds for climbing. The fifth percentile foot breadth of 13–18-month-olds was reported as 1.57 inches; the 95th percentile foot breadth of 19 to 24-month-olds as was reported as 2.36 inches.[29] While the strangulation and entrapment hazards have been successfully addressed by the standard, perhaps there needs to be attention given to eliminating the potential for climbing on gates.

The few recalls (one in 1999 and one in 2001) that occurred were due to mounting hardware failure or locking mechanism failure.

High Chairs

High chairs are freestanding chairs that elevate the child to a standard dining table height to facilitate eating or feeding. They are intended for infants who can sit by their own coordination, usually around age eight to nine months, and for children up to three years of age.

Historically, high chair injuries occurred when children fell out of the chair, and deaths occurred when children slipped under the tray table and either were strangled by the safety belt or suffered compression asphyxia by the tray. For example, a two-year-old girl slid down in her high chair so that her neck became wedged by the tray; she died of airway compression. Falls were associated with children not being strapped into the chair. Those children were able to stand on the chair seat and fall over a side. Head and face injuries were most common.

In 1975, the first ASTM standard for high chairs was published.[30] The current version of the standard was published in 1999. Two key portions of the standard address restraints and tray performance.

There were an estimated 9200 emergency department treated injuries associated with high chairs in 2003. Most injuries involved children aged 7 to 23 months, and occurred when the child fell out of or off the chair. The head and face were most often injured, suggesting the fall was head-first. Few injuries required hospitalization. For the 12 to 23 month age group, females were injured about twice as frequently as were males, an unusual pattern.

At least fifteen deaths were reported between 1999 and 2003. Most were asphyxiation by entrapment involving the tray. One case involved an armrest; a few involved strangulation in the restraint. One death was the result of tip-over and subsequent forehead impact.

Based on the pattern of injuries, one can only conclude that either restraints are not used or they are not effective. In spite of the ASTM standard's requirement that the chair carry a warning indicating that the tray table is not designed to hold the child in the chair, consumers may incorrectly regard the tray table as a barrier to the child's getting out, and thus believe that the restraint is unnecessary. Erring in this regard can have serious effects because some children are able to defeat the tray table's latching mechanism. The other possibilities that allow children to get out of the chair are that the chair is too old to have a restraint system, or that the restraint requires too much of a effort to fasten, that is, high compliance cost. Yet another possibility is that the restraint is used, but the child is nonetheless able to disengage it or wiggle out.

The ASTM standard requires horizontal and vertical pull tests on a restrained CAMI dummy, but the actual motion of a child struggling to get out might be different, rendering the test method meaningless. As Ridenour studied the manner in which children climbed out of cribs, perhaps a similar observational study of children climbing out of high chairs would be useful.

Overall, there have been very few high chair recalls. Recent recalls (2000 and forward) have involved structural problems, like legs or seats detaching from the frame. The last recall for a defective [crotch] restraint was in 1997, and before that in 1993.

Infant swings (Portable Baby Swings for Home Use)

Infant swings are used to calm a crying baby and to otherwise free up a care giver's hands. In 2003, CPSC was notified of 44 injuries reported through the NEISS system. Based on this data, the CPSC estimated that there were almost 1200 infant swing injuries nationwide that year.

Three-quarters of all infant swing injuries reported through the NEISS system in 2003 resulted from the baby falling out of the swing. About 25% of these fall incidents resulted when an older sibling—typically a preschooler—attempted to remove the baby from the swing. In other cases, the fall resulted from the swing being knocked over or as a result of structural failure which caused the swing to come apart and/or the infant to fall to the ground. One Green Bay, WI parent reported that her 3 month-old daughter suffered contusions and abrasions after the swing she was in fell apart. According to the CPSC Incident Investigation, one of the swing's arms suddenly let loose from the side of the swing where it was attached. The infant fell to the floor, while still remaining strapped into the swings restraint belt. Other swing injuries reported to the CPSC involve fingers being pinched or smashed, bumps on the head, lacerations, and contusions.

Infant fatalities have also been reported in baby swings. From 1999 through 2003, there were 13 baby swing deaths reported to the CPSC. Most of these resulted from either the baby becoming entangled in the straps of the swing, or from positional asphyxiation. Both of these hazard patterns result from a combination of the swing's movement and movements of the baby, which result in the baby's position shifting from how he or she was originally placed in the swing. This shift can prove fatal if the baby slips down and becomes entangled in the restraint, or if the baby's neck becomes compressed, causing positional asphyxia. Due to the fact that parents may not remain with the baby the entire time he or she is in the swing—particularly once he or she falls asleep—the parent may not be present at the time of danger.

Of the 13 fatalities reported to the Commission from 1999 through 2003, eight were due to restraint entanglement. In some cases, the infant slipped down or maneuvered out of the position in which he or she was originally placed in the swing. For example, a 6-month-old baby girl died of asphyxia and was found hanging in an infant swing seat by the strap. She had been placed in an infant swing to sleep, but apparently slid down. Similarly, a 3-month-old Topeka infant was found unresponsive in a baby swing. A buckled seat restraint belt was at his neck and both of his legs were through the hole that was designed for his left leg.

Positional asphyxiation caused by wedging or inadequate head support was reported in the remaining five fatalities. Two of these incidents were due to suffocation or wedging. A 4 month-old female was found slumped face forward and unresponsive in a swing. A 24-day-old infant died from postural asphyxia due to being in a baby swing. After being in the swing for several hours, her mother found her blue and unresponsive. Factors including (1) the swing design and movement, (2) baby's age and ability to keep his head upright, (3) baby's position inside the swing, and (4) the baby's being able to maneuver inside the swing contributed to this hazard.

ASTM Standard F2088,[31] originally drafted in 2001 and updated in 2003, was developed to reduce hazards associated with infant swings. Though this voluntary standard is likely to reduce swing injuries and fatalities, one can expect a lag time before observing injury reduction. This is because consumers often use older-model swings acquired for children born previously, or they buy swings second-hand. Swings that fail to comply with the standard, or that comply but still pose a risk of injury, may be recalled. In the last five years, five infant swings were recalled. Three addressed a design defect that could cause an infant to fall from the swing. The other two recalls related to the potential for strangulation in the restraints of older-model swings.

Playpens

Playpens or portable play yards are enclosures intended to provide a sleep or play environment for a child less than 35 inches in height, that is, essentially the same age child for whom a crib is intended. An ASTM standard for playpens was first published in 1977[32] and was directed at hazard patterns that included climbing out of the playpen, falls onto playpen parts, and finger pinching/shearing as a result of scissor action. As injury patterns changed with the introduction of new product designs, later versions of the standard addressed: the size of mesh holes [for finger and button entrapment, the latter resulting in hanging]; body entrapment in pockets formed in drop-side mesh playpens resulting in positional asphyxia; and head/neck entrapment in collapsed top rail V-shaped hinges resulting in positional asphyxia. The latest version of the standard was published in 2004. This constant review and revision of standards is necessary and poignantly highlighted by a combination playpen product new to the market in 2001. The product was a playpen that also incorporated a changing table and/or bassinet. The product posed a new hazard, not addressed by the standard. A 13-month-old girl died when she was trapped by the neck between the underside of the changing table portion and the top rail of the playpen. The product was recalled in 2003.

In 2003, there were an estimated 1600 emergency department treated injuries associated with playpens. As with cribs, most were related to the child's climbing out of the playpen, and most involved the head or face. The highest frequency of injuries was among 7 through 18 month olds, followed by two year olds. When deaths occurred, they were due to suffocation by wedging, positional asphyxia, or entanglement with bedclothes.

Between 1999 and 2003 there were at least 52 playpen-related deaths reported to the CPSC. The majority of deaths were due to either positional asphyxia or obstruction of the nose/mouth. Most positional asphyxia deaths were associated with wedging between the playpen mattress and sidewall; less often, positional asphyxia death was due to the neck resting on a rail or in a V-shaped rail opening created by a collapsed playpen. Obstruction of the nose/mouth was associated with bedding (quilts, blankets, pillows, etc.). In two unusual entrapment circumstances, a parent had covered the playpen with plywood or other wooden structure to keep the child from climbing out. Those two children died by compression asphyxia when they were trapped between the playpen and the wooden cover. A similar kind of entrapment was reported with a combination playpen/changing table product, where the child was trapped between the rail and the raised changing table portion of the playpen. There were also a few deaths that occurred as a result of the child's climbing out of the playpen and getting trapped between the playpen and other furniture or the wall.

Exploring their surroundings is a primary function for young children. It is understandable that they do not like to be limited or restrained, because it interferes with their goal to discover and experience. Hence, it is not surprising that children attempt to climb out of playpens just as they attempt to climb out of cribs and over gates. Since playpens have the same height requirements as cribs, Ridenour's observational studies and recommendations for higher side rail height, as described in the section on cribs, could be applied to playpens.

Because playpens can have a long life, associated hazards can remain in consumers' homes and day care centers for many years. This trend is reflected in deaths and injuries that occur with recalled products. For example, in 1996 the CPSC issued a recall of a playpen because the top rail collapsed, creating a V-shaped entrapment area. The recall was re-issued in 2004, following the death of an 18-month-old Fairfax County, VA boy. In another case, a 2001 recall was a renewed effort, following a death in Longview, WA, to find playpens that had been recalled in 1995. The company offered a new playpen in exchange for turning in a recalled product. Several brands of playpens were recalled in 2002, after originally being recalled in 1998, for the strangulation hazard presented by protruding rivets. Cloths or strings at the neck could catch on the rivets (the same way tall finials caught clothing) leading to hanging/strangulation deaths. Playpens manufactured as long ago as 1960 and 1976 were subject to the recall.

Strollers and Carriages

Baby strollers are a staple for most parents with young children. Today's strollers are associated with fewer injuries than in years past, however, that is not to say that such injuries do not occur with frequency. In 2003, 416 stroller-related injuries involving children aged 0–4 years were reported to the CPSC through the NEISS system. Nationwide, the CPSC estimates that there were more than 10 700 such injuries that year. (This is down from about 15 000 such injuries in 2000).

Stroller injuries decline as the child ages. Nonetheless, across age groups, the most common hazard pattern involves the child falling or climbing out of the stroller. Oftentimes this is due to their not being restrained, or because the child managed to get out of the restraint by unbuckling or wiggling out of it. Injuries to the head, neck and face are typical from stroller falls. Most are treatable contusions, abrasions and lacerations. Some are more serious fractures or internal injuries.

Stroller deaths are not common. There were five death reports reported to the Commission from 1999 to 2003. Information about the hazard pattern was provided in only two of the incidents. Both were due to mechanical asphyxiation or suffocation. In one case, the victim's head lodged between the tray and seat. In another, the infant slipped through the leg hole. The child's head became caught in the opening. This is due to the strangulation hazard posed if an infant slips through a leg hole opening. This hazard pattern occurs when infants move ("creep") down in a stroller and work their way into a leg hole when the stroller is in a reclined position. The leg opening would allow passage of the infant's body but not the head. As such, strangulation in the leg opening occurred. ASTM Standard F833[33] is intended to mitigate such injuries and fatalities.

While the ASTM standard is intended to prevent injuries by designing safety into the stroller, recalls issued by manufacturers and the CPSC are intended to prevent injuries after the product is already on the market. From 1999 to 2003, there were seven stroller recalls. In four cases, the recall was due to the potential for the stroller to collapse. The other recalls were due to the potential for (1) wheels to break; (2) brakes to fail; and (3) a lock mechanism on a jogging stroller to break and create a pinch point.

To prevent injuries and fatalities, consumers are urged to directly supervise their child while in a stroller or carriage. This is particularly important on older-model strollers and carriages that do not have some of the protections built into them that will be present on products manufactured after the standard went into effect. Specifically, the restraints on older-model strollers may consist only of a waist strap. Infants can slip down (when awake or asleep) and become caught at the neck in the strap. As mentioned above, infants can also slip down (when awake or asleep) and become caught in a leg opening. Therefore, constant supervision—particularly of a sleeping infant—is crucial.

The Role of Supervision in Injury Prevention

Product-related injuries may be due to a number of factors including: product design, child's age and personality, the play environment, and the presence of others in the play environment. Another factor—one that is widely cited in incident reports—is the lack of appropriate supervision. While "appropriate" supervision may not prevent injuries from occurring, it can produce a rapid response to an injury, thereby mitigating its effects.

Defining the adequacy of supervision is difficult to do since there are many ways of conceptualizing supervisory behaviors. Saluja et al[34] propose a theory of supervision that provides a template for investigating the relationship between supervision and injury risk. According to their model, supervision is evaluated on three dimensions: attention, proximity, and continuity. As these variables increase, so does supervision.

The research on supervision demonstrates that supervision practices vary as a child gets older. Peterson et al[35] found that for young children and high hazard situations, parents, medical professionals, and social workers agree that vigilant supervision is needed. However, they observed greater variability as children get older and the environment less hazardous.

Pollack-Nelson and Drago[36] studied supervision of parents with children aged 2 through 6 years. Results were consistent with the Peterson et al's findings. In particular, parents professed greater supervision of younger children. For example, when children are playing out of sight, most parents with 2- and 3-year-old children reported checking on them every 5–15 minutes. Whereas, most parents with 4- and 5-year-old children reported checking on those children every 15–30 minutes and those with children over 5 years of age reported checking in about 30 minutes to an hour.

While parents reported checking on their young children with some frequency, as noted above, a contradiction in behavior and perceived risk was noted in the study. About three-quarters of respondents stated that their children get up in the morning before they do. Yet, the overwhelming majority (95%) perceived that this posed no or slight risk to their child. This may be due to the perception that their home is relatively safe, whether or not it actually is. Eighty percent of respondents reported that their homes were moderately to very "child-proof." Yet, the only "child-proofing" measures taken with some frequency were the use of outlet covers, locks on cabinets and drawers, and baby gates. Further, with the exception of outlet covers, these other safety measures were employed by only about one-third of respondents. Thus, the perception of safety may not be objectively correct and may exceed the actual level of safety in the home.

Advocacy/Practice/Future Research

As the data demonstrate, children continue to be injured and killed while using nursery products, despite work of the CPSC and the development of mandatory and voluntary standards for these items. This is likely due to a combination of the limited staff and funding of the Commission compared with the billions of consumer products that flood the marketplace each year. The CPSC employs fewer than 500 people and was funded at under $60 million in 2004.

There are a number of different means by which individual consumers and professionals in the field of consumer health and safety can be involved and have an impact on the safety of nursery products including (1) working with established advocacy groups; (2) becoming involved at a grass-roots level; and (3) conducting and publishing research in this area.

Advocacy Groups

Advocates for consumer safety play a critical complementary role. A number of advocacy groups work to identify and publicize hazards associated with consumer products. These groups often petition the CPSC to take action to ban, recall, or draft standards for products of concern. Below is a description of three such advocacy organizations.

Consumer Federation of America (CFA)

The Consumer Federation of America is the nation's largest consumer advocacy organization, representing over 280 state, local, and national consumer organizations. A non-profit organization, started in 1968, CFA works to advance pro-consumer policy on a variety of issues—including those relating to consumer products—before the Congress, White House, regulatory agencies, and courts. CFA also researches consumer issues, publishing their findings in order to assist consumer advocates, policy makers, and the general public.

CFA has been active in a number of areas relating to nursery products. For example, in 2000, CFA joined with other advocacy groups to petition the CPSC to ban bath rings. The following year, CFA launched a comprehensive internet website focusing on children's safety and health. This website includes all recalls of products intended for children from 1990 to present. In 2004, the CFA joined with the Danny Foundation (see below) to support the introduction of The Infant Crib Safety Act (S. 2016/H.R. 3371) which would make mandatory and voluntary standards applicable to the sale or use of secondhand cribs. Currently, these standards only apply to new cribs.

The Danny Foundation*

The Danny Foundation is a non-profit organization dedicated to protecting babies from preventable injuries and deaths associated with unsafe cribs, other children's products and sleep environments. The organization is named for Danny Lineweaver, a 23-month-old who suffered permanent brain damage after his shirt became entangled on the corner post extension of his crib.

The Danny Foundation is dedicated to educating the public about crib dangers. The work of the Foundation led to a change in the height of crib corner posts. Currently, the allowable height for crib corner posts is $\frac{1}{16}$ inch (per the ASTM standard for crib cornerpost extensions). In 2001, the Danny Foundation initiated a program, Project Safe Crib, to assist low-income families by removing dangerous cribs and educating parents and care givers about safe sleeping environments. Since the project was started, over 800 safe cribs have been distributed and 85 unsafe cribs removed from homes.

Kids In Danger (KID)

Kids In Danger (KID) is another nonprofit organization dedicated to protecting children by improving children's product safety. KID was founded in 1998 by the parents of 16-month-old Danny Keysar who died in his Chicago childcare home when a portable crib collapsed around his neck. Although the portable crib had been recalled five years earlier, word of its danger had not reached Danny's parents, caregiver, or a state inspector who visited the home just eight days before Danny's death. See the case study in the introduction to this chapter for more information regarding Danny's death.

KID is an advocacy group that seeks to protect children from dangerous

---

* In 2005, the Danny Foundation closed its doors. When the foundation started its program in 1986, there were an estimated 100 to 200 baby deaths per year involving cribs. Today, that number has been reduced to about 15 per year nationwide.

products. In 1999, KID worked with state legislators to have the Children's Product Safety Act enacted, making it illegal to sell or lease recalled or dangerous children's products or to use those products in licensed childcare facilities. KID sponsors a number of outreach programs to further their objectives. For example, the Health Care Providers Outreach Program educates health care providers and parents about dangerous and recalled children's products. Also, the Teach Early Safety Testing (TEST) program encourages designers and engineers to incorporate safety and testing into product development.

Grass-Roots Efforts

Despite the work of the Commission and advocacy groups, the safety of a nursery is not assured. Consumers must be advocates for their own children's safety. Here are some actions that can be taken:

- Report injuries and safety concerns about products to the CPSC. The web site (www.cpsc.gov) makes it easy to fill out and submit a form, or call the Hotline at 1-800-638-2772 (1-800-638-CPSC).
- Check the CPSC web site and www.recalls.gov regularly for recalls. Create you own recall network among parents of young children.
- Encourage your neighborhood groups, like Safe Kids, Boys and Girls Clubs, Meals on Wheels, etc., to join in CPSC's new Neighborhood Safety Network, a grass-roots effort to distribute monthly e-mail lists with safety and recall information. The goal is to reach in particular the elderly, urban and rural low-income families and minorities. See CPSC's web site for details.
- Petition the CPSC to remedy a product. Anyone can petition the agency. A petition is a formal request to the agency seeking either rulemaking for a product, revision of an existing rule, or a product ban. The petition should identify the consumer product for which a safety rule or change is sought, along with the basis for the request. This may include personal experience or published research findings. The petition should describe the specific risk of injury including data on severity and likelihood of injury, along with possible reasons for the injury potential (eg, product defect, design flaw, unintentional misuse). For more information on how to file a petition, see the CPSC web site.
- Become a consumer member of an ASTM subcommittee and take part in the development of standards. ASTM International is one of the largest voluntary standards development organizations in the world. ASTM Committee F15 has jurisdiction over general products, chemical specialties, and end use products (typically consumer products). Committee F15 on Consumer Products maintains 77 standards, including those referenced in this chapter. Standards are drafted by subcommittees that are comprised of industry and consumer representatives. Most subcommittees have openings for consumer members and in many cases will pay the expenses of consumers so that they can travel to attend the meetings. For more information on joining ASTM as an Affiliate member, go to ASTM's website, www.astm.org.
- Read and follow product instructions for use, paying special attention to age grading, warnings and maintenance issues.

- Inspect nursery products for continued integrity throughout the life of the product.

Conduct Research

Practitioners and researchers can partner and awaken the public to product safety issues when they publish their findings. Moreover, published works can prompt the development of new standards or cause industry, advocacy groups, and the CPSC to revisit and update existing standards. For example, following a study on fall and suffocation incidents in infant seats published in 2000,[15] the Commission worked with ASTM to revise the standard to include provisions aimed at reducing the likelihood of tip over. Using free and available data from the CPSC, researchers are encouraged to investigate product safety issues and publish their findings.

Concluding Comments

Finding a way to make recalled information more widely known and with less effort exerted will be important for preventing tragic and unnecessary nursery product–related deaths and injuries. Though many homes have computers, one must visit the site(s) regularly to stay informed. Radio, television and newspapers may need to do more with community service announcements/ads to reduce the "cost" of actively seeking out that information. Consumers can advocate for establishing a regular site (for example a weekly newspaper column, or a particular radio/television timeslot) for recall information. Increasing knowledge and awareness will be key to future reduction in injury burden.

References

1. McDonald J. Nursery product-related injury estimate for CY 2003. CPSC: Internal memorandum, November 22, 2004.
2. Consumer Product Safety Commission (CPSC). *Nursery Products Report.* September 2000.
3. Consumer Product Safety Commission, *Nursery Products-Related Injury Estimate for CY 2000.* November 20, 2001.
4. Beal SM, More L, Collett M, Montgomery B, Sprod C, Beal A. The danger of freely rocking cradles. *J. Paediatr Child Health.* 1995;31:38-40.
5. Emery JL, Thornton JA. Effects of obstruction to respiration in infants, with particular reference to mattresses, pillows, and their coverings. *Bri Med J.* 1968; 3:209-213.
6. ASTM Standard F 2194, *Standard Consumer Safety Specification for Bassinets and Cradles,* ASTM International.
7. Needleman RD. Growth and Development. In: Behrman RE, Kliegman RM, Arvin AM, Eds. *Nelson Textbook of Pediatrics.* 15th ed. Philadelphia, PA: WB Saunders Company; 1996.
8. Rauchschwalbe R, Brenner, RA, Smith GS. The role of bathtub seats and rings in infant drowning deaths. *Pediatrics.* 1997; 100e1.
9. Consumer Product Safety Commission. *The Safe Nursery.* 2002.
10. Pearn JH, Brown J, Wong R, Bart R. Bathtub drownings: Report of seven cases. *Pediatrics.* 1979;64:68-70.
11. O'Carroll PW, Alkon E, Weiss B. Drowning mortality in Los Angeles County, 1976 to 1984. *JAMA* 1988;260:380–383.

12. Jensen LR, Williams SC, Thurman DJ, Keller PA. Submersion injuries in children younger than 5 years in urban Utah. *West J Med.* 1992; 157:641-644.

13. Thompson KM. The Role of Bath Seats in Unintentional Infant Bathtub Drowning Deaths. *Medscape General Medicine.* March 26, 2003.

14. ASTM F1967, *Standard Consumer Safety Specification for Infant Bath Seats,* ASTM International.

15. Pollack-Nelson C. Injuries associated with in-home use of infant seats and baby carriers. Pediatric Emergency Care. 2000:16:77-79.

16. ASTM F 2050, *Standard Consumer Safety Specification for Hand-Held Infant Carriers,* ASTM International.

17. ASTM Standard F 2167, *Standard Consumer Safety Specification for Infant Bouncer Seats,* ASTM International.

18. ASTM Standard F 2388, *Standard Consumer Safety Specification for Baby Changing Tables for Domestic Use,* ASTM International.

19. 16 CFR 1508, Requirements for Full-Size Baby Cribs, 38 FR 32129, Nov 21, 1973.

20. 16 CFR 1509, Requirements for Non-Full-Size Baby Cribs, 41 FR 6240, Feb. 12, 1976.

21. ASTM Standard F 1169, *Standard Specification for Full-Size Baby Crib,* ASTM International.

22. ASTM Standard F 1822, *Standard Consumer Safety Specification For Non-Full-Size Baby Cribs,* ASTM International.

23. ASTM Standard F 966, *Consumer Safety Specification for Full-Size and Non-Full-Size Baby Crib Corner Post Extensions,* ASTM International.

24. ASTM Standard F 1917, *Standard Consumer Safety Performance Specification for Infant Bedding and Related Accessories,* ASTM International.

25. Byard RW, Bourne AJ, Beal SM. Mesh-sided cots—yet another potentially dangerous infant sleeping environment. *Forensic Sci Internat.* 1996;83:105-9.

26. Ridenour MV. How do children climb out of cribs? *Percep Motor Skills.* 2002;95:363-366.

27. Ridenour MV. Age, side height, and spindle shape of the crib in climbing over the side. *Percep Motor Skills.* 1997;85:667-674.

28. ASTM Standard F 1004, *Standard Consumer Safety Specification for Expansion Gates and Expandable Enclosures,* ASTM International.

29. Snyder RG, Spencer ML, Owings CL, Schneider LW. Physical Characteristics of children as related to death and injury for consumer product safety design. 1975. Contract FDA 72-70, Report No. UM-HSRI-BI-75-5.

30. ASTM Standard F 404, *Standard Consumer Safety Specification for High Chairs,* ASTM International.

31. ASTM Standard F 2088, *Standard Consumer Safety Specification for Infant Swings.* ASTM International.

32. ASTM Standard F 406, *Standard Consumer Safety Specification for Non-Full-Size Baby Cribs/Play Yards.* ASTM International.

33. ASTM Standard F 833, *Standard Consumer Safety Performance Specification for Carriages and Strollers.* ASTM International.

34. Saluja G, Brenner R, Morrongiello B, Haynie D, Rivera M, Cheng TL. The role of supervision in child injury risk: definition, conceptual and measurement issues. *Injury Control and Safety Promotion.* 2004;11:17-22.

35. Peterson L, Ewigman B, Kivlahan C. Judgements regarding appropriate child supervision to prevent injury: The role of environmental risk and child age. *Child Development.* 1993;64:934-950.

36. Pollack-Nelson C. and Drago D. Supervision of children aged two through six years. *Injury Control and Safety Promotion,* 2002;9:121-126.

CHAPTER 4

Preventing Motor Vehicle Crashes and Injuries Among Children and Adolescents

Bruce G. Simons-Morton,[1] Angela D. Mickalide,[2] and Erik C. B. Olsen[3]

Alicia, a 16-year old junior at a Maryland high school, died when another teenager lost control of the car in which she was a passenger. Her father's lament: "My daughter, Alicia, 16, died recently in a motor vehicle accident. She was a passenger in a car driven by a 16-year-old who lost control while speeding. The car went off the road and hit a utility pole, killing my daughter on impact. The police report is not official, but contributing factors were: speeding, not paying attention, driver inexperience." (*Washington Post*, Nov. 13, 2004)

Sadly, motor vehicle crashes take the lives of innocent children and adolescents daily in the US. In the case described above, the teenage girl was a passenger when a teenage driver lost control of the car. Crash rates for teenage drivers are highly elevated compared with older drivers and both drivers and passengers are at risk. Similarly, children not correctly secured in car seats or booster seats are at great risk of injury or death in motor vehicle crashes. Many of these injuries could be prevented through the combination of strict policies, improved technology, enhanced enforcement, and effective education.

Introduction

The United States is highly dependent on motor vehicles and has a long and romantic history with cars and trucks, despite their long-standing and substantial contribution to national injury and death tolls. Given that the country is geographically large and relatively wealthy, the United States has

1   Chief, Prevention Research Branch Division of Epidemiology, Statistics, and Prevention Research National Institute of Child Health and Human Development
2   Home Safety Council
3   Postdoctoral Fellow , Prevention Research Branch Division of Epidemiology, Statistics, and Prevention Research National Institute of Child Health and Human Development

developed a greater reliance on motor vehicle transportation than almost any other nation. Possibly, only Australia and Canada would be even remotely similar in this regard. Given our great reliance on motor vehicles, it is not surprising that the US leads the world in annual miles driven per driver. Currently the US ranks among the nations with the highest rates of injury and death due to motor vehicle crashes (MVCs) with over 40 000 fatalities and 3 million injuries annually (Sleet and Branche, 2004). While MVCs is one of the leading causes of death for every age group in the United States, it is the leading cause of death and disability among children and adolescents (Anderson et al, 2004).

Prevalence

In the United States, MVCs represent 27% of deaths for all causes, and 41% of unintentional injury deaths, as indicated in Figure 1. MVC's represent the single greatest cause of U.S. deaths for those aged 1 to 19 years (CDC, 2004a). While MVCs stand out as a major cause of death among children and adolescents partly because death rates among children, at least after the first year of life, are relatively low, the high rates are, nonetheless, dramatic. Shown in Figure 2 are percentages of MVC deaths in each of several age groups. Note that deaths increase with age through the late teens and then decline dramatically into late adulthood. The pattern is identical for males and females, although males are generally at somewhat higher risk. While deaths due to MVC per mile driven are similar for major race categories during childhood, the population rate for Blacks is nearly three times that of whites and the rate for Hispanics is nearly double (Baker et al, 1998). Similar patterns exist for children aged 13 to 19, with somewhat higher death rates for Hispanics and Blacks compared to Whites (Baker et al, 1998). The primary reason for the higher death rates for Hispanics and

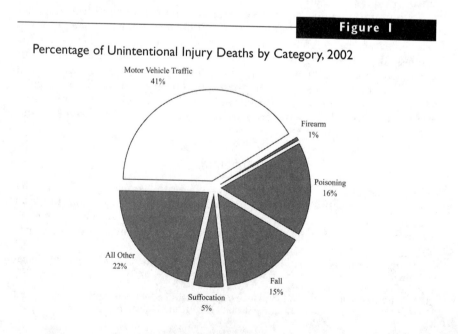

Figure 1

Percentage of Unintentional Injury Deaths by Category, 2002

Motor Vehicle Traffic 41%

Firearm 1%

Poisoning 16%

All Other 22%

Fall 15%

Suffocation 5%

Blacks is probably the lower rate of child restraints and safety belt use among these populations, exacerbated by socioeconomic status, parental education and income, vehicle type, and road-conditions (Baker et al, 1998; Grossman, 2000).

The best MVC data is on fatalities because a national reporting system is in place, the Fatal Accident Reporting System, or FARS. However, non-fatal crashes are more common and account for substantial cost and misery. Annually, 3.5 million Americans suffer nonfatal motor vehicle-related injuries, causing about 4 million emergency department visits and 500 000 hospitalizations (CDC, 2002). As shown in Figure 3, pre-adolescent children and adolescents are at particularly elevated risk for non-fatal motor vehicle collision injuries compared with adults. As indicated, injuries increase dramatically during the teen years and decline gradually over time. Non-fatal injuries are highest in the 15–19 year age group and remain particularly elevated through at least age 25, when they begin a gradual decline over the period of several decades. Non-fatal injuries are generally higher for females than males, probably because males tend to be involved in crashes involving high speeds, which are more likely to be fatal. While the severity of many MVC injuries are modest and transitory, about 10% of injuries among children are disabling; (NHTSA, 2004a). In addition to physical trauma, motor vehicle injuries can have long-term effects on mental health (Aiko et al, 1999).

Teenagers are at notably elevated risk for crashes compared with older drivers. When crash involvement is evaluated by miles traveled, number of licensed drivers, and per population, teenage drivers emerge as the highest risk group (Williams, 2003). Males aged 16–21 comprise the group with the highest number of fatalities, with an annual average of 4578 fatalities per year over the past 30 years (NHTSA, 2004b). In general, males are at

Figure 2

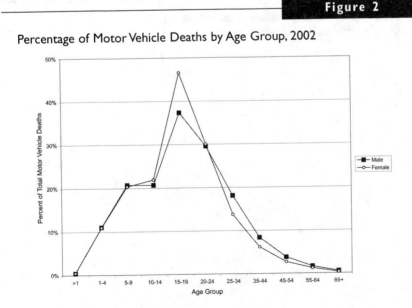

Percentage of Motor Vehicle Deaths by Age Group, 2002

greater risk than females, but teenage girls are at much elevated risk compared with older females. Sixteen year olds in particular are at elevated risk for crashes and fatal crashes per million miles driven (McCartt, Shabanova, Leaf, 2003).

By all measures children and adolescents are at great risk for MVC injury and death. Despite a 40 percent decline in the motor vehicle occupant death rate from 1987 to 2001 (National Safe Kids Campaign, 2004a), over 1500 child occupants between 0 and 14 years old die in motor vehicle crashes annually (NHTSA, 2003a) and an estimated 220 000 children are injured (NHTSA, 2004c). Over the same period, 8278 drivers 15–20 years old were involved in fatal crashes, including 3827 deaths for this age group (NHTSA, 2003b).

While young drivers are at elevated risk for MVCs, teen passengers, pedestrians, and bicyclists are also at risk. Passenger deaths increase substantially from about age 13 until about age 20, due presumably to increased riding with young drivers (Williams, 2003; Chen, Elliott, Durbin, Winston, 2005). About 40% of the MVC deaths of 16–19 year-olds are sustained by passengers, about half of these among 16 year olds (Williams, 2003). Motor vehicles also present substantial risk to pedestrians and bicyclists, many of whom are children and adolescents. In 2003, 4749 pedestrians and 622 cyclists died in motor vehicle crashes (about 13% of all MVC deaths) (NHTSA, 2004d). Among pedestrians involved in serious traffic crashes, 17 percent of those killed and 7% of those injured were under age 16 (NHTSA, 2004d). Of cyclists injured in traffic crashes at least 17 000 (37%) were under age 16. Annually, over 300 000 children under age 16 suffer motor vehicle-related pedestrian and cyclist injuries (NHTSA, 2004e).

Figure 3

Percentage of Total Nonfatal Motor Vehicle Injuries, 2003, Male, Female, and Both Genders

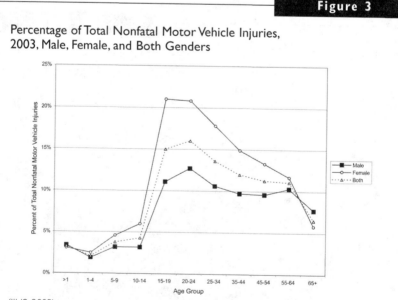

(IIHS, 2005)

Fortunately, pedestrian and cyclist deaths and injuries among children have declined steadily in recent decades, at least in part because children walk less and therefore are less exposed to traffic (National SAFE KIDS Campaign, 1999), as illustrated by Figure 4.

Factors Associated with MVCs

The causes of MVCs are complex. The glut of vehicles, high traffic density, and complex roadways all contribute to the problem. Also, modern vehicles are powerful and fast, posing new risks, despite advances in safety features. The variability in size and weight of vehicles vary substantially, greatly increasing the likelihood of injury in the case of multiple-vehicle crashes (Dewar, 2002; IIHS, 1998; Thomas and Frampton, 2002). Specific driving conditions play a role. For example, crashes are more likely in inclement weather (NHTSA, 2001) and at night (NHTSA, 2001). Driver behavior is often associated with crashes. Notably, speeding is a major cause of crashes (Chiloutakus et al, 2002) and speed contributes to the severity of resultant injuries (NHTSA, 2001; Navon, 2003). Reckless driving is implicated in some crashes and a small proportion of reckless drivers may account for a disproportionate number of such crashes (Chiloutakus et al, 2002). Certainly, alcohol is an important risk factor for MVCs, particularly crashes involving serious injury and death (NHTSA, 2001, p. 56–57; Hingston and Winter, 2004). Drivers and passengers engage in a myriad of activities ranging from cell phone use to personal grooming that can provide substantial distraction and crash risk (Stutts et al, 2003). Driver sleepiness is a factor in MVC, but the extent of its contribution to the prevalence and severity of crashes is not known (Connor et al, 2000). Injuries are much more likely and severe in MVCs when passengers are unrestrained (NHTSA, 2001. p. 39).

Figure 4

Percentage of Motor Vehicle Deaths Among Children <13 Years Old as Passengers, Pedestrians, and Bicyclists (1975-2003)

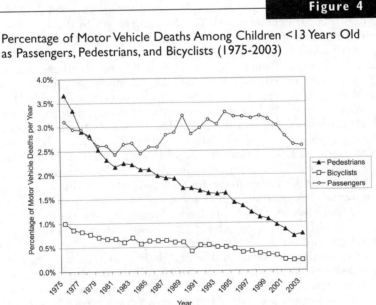

After a long and steep ascent throughout most of the 20th century, death and injury due to MVCs have been on the decline for several decades, despite continued increases in average miles driven. Notably, advances in technology and policy have had a substantial impact on road safety. For example, improvements in child passenger protection and other safety devices have greatly improved the survivability of serious crashes. Nevertheless, MVC injuries remain a major public health problem and children and adolescents are among those at greatest risk. Because the causes of MVC are complex, only a comprehensive approach to prevention and control is likely to be effective. Fortunately, a range of effective safety options are available that could save lives and prevent serious injuries due to MVCs. Notably, great advances have been made in technology and a range of innovations in regulation, policy, and practices are available that have promise for reducing MVC injuries. What is needed is sufficient public will to foster their adoption, implementation, and enforcement. Children and adolescents cannot serve as their own advocates in this regard. The adoption of a comprehensive range of solutions to the problem of MVC injuries is needed and public health professionals and informed citizens must advocate for their adoption and implementation (Gielen, 2002). In this chapter, we describe the range of possible solutions and then, first for child occupants and then for teen drivers, we describe the unique risk of MVC injuries to which these population groups are exposed and describe the most effective approaches to preventing future MVC injuries and deaths.

Comprehensive Approaches

As with so many areas of prevention in general and injury prevention in particular, MVC injuries are multi-causal and, therefore, may require comprehensive, inter-related approaches that would form a sort of ecology of prevention. Recent declines in MVC injury and death in the US, despite continued increases in the amount of motor vehicle travel, have been due to combinations of innovations of various sorts and not due to any single advance. As shown in Figure 5, technology, policy, enforcement, and personal behavior are important aspects or components of prevention. While each of these components is independently important, none is fully adequate to protect safety and each interacts with the others. Indeed, these various innovations are highly inter-related and inter-dependent. Policies, technology, enforcement, and behavior influence each other in dynamic ways. For example, both education and enforcement practices are known to increase behavioral adherence with safety belt laws (Dinh-Zarr et al, 2001). Safety belts have been in use for decades, but the technology continues to improve and soon cars will be equipped with belts that provide pretensioners that eliminate slack, are better integrated into the seat, secure over both shoulders and across the chest and waist to better secure shoulders and hips, and are generally more secure and require less of the user. While the technologies of road and vehicle design have advanced rapidly to reduce crash and injury risks, most policy and technology advances are designed to facilitate safety behavior, but depend in part on the elective behavior of the population. Speed limits are designed to balance safety and traffic efficiency, but drivers can elect how fast they go under various conditions. Drivers can set their vehicles automatic speed control, but drivers select the speed. Safety belts protect passengers but only when they are secured. Laws requiring safety belts increase their use (Beck et al, 2004) and strong enforcement increases use and reduces fatalities (Calkins and Zlatoper, 2001). Clearly, the available crash prevention options are highly inter-related.

In the following pages we describe some of the modern advances in road and vehicle design and advances in automotive and road safety technology as a backdrop for more detailed discussions of the inter-relationships of technology, policy, enforcement, and behavior with respect to child and adolescent transportation safety. It appears that we may be at the dawning stage of technological advances that will make motor vehicle transportation increasingly safer. Vehicles may become much smarter, with advanced computer, laser, and other systems that can warn drivers when they are at risk of a crash or otherwise deviate from normal driving. Incremental advances can be expected in vehicle designs and crash protection that will improve safety outcomes in case of a crash. Also, licensing and other policies related to driving are undergoing fundamental changes that may reduce driving risks, particularly among vulnerable age groups and high-risk drivers. Moreover, research on driving risks and behavior is also advancing rapidly, providing new insights into how best to foster safe driving behavior. For example, interlock systems are available to prevent inebriated drivers from starting their vehicles (CDC, 2001) and electronic devices for monitoring risky driving behavior such as rapid starting and stopping are now available (Knipling, 2005). Nevertheless, motor vehicles are likely to remain one of the nation's most important causes of injury and death for many years. Children and adolescents experience unique and profound MVC risks, about which there a great deal is now known and about which much can be done.

However, change does not occur without a great deal of concerted effort. The safety of children and adolescent depends on concerned adults who advocate on their behalf. Advocacy for the latest safety technology, the most enlightened policies, and the best educational programs is needed at local, state, and national levels if reductions in child and adolescent injuries due to motor vehicle crashes are to be reduced. In the following pages we describe the nature of the problem and potential solutions and then return to the issue of advocacy.

Technology

Despite the ever-increasing numbers of vehicles and average annual miles driven per driver, road safety has improved in important ways and U.S. deaths due to MVC have declined from 54 589 in 1974 to 42 643 in 2003 (NHTSA, 2004b, 2004f). Shown in Figure 6 is the absolute number of MVC fatalities in the U.S. over the past century, showing the great increase from the advent of driving until the 1970s and a gradual and modest decline thereafter. When overall miles driven are taken into account, as shown in Figure 7, the rates of MVC fatalities per annual vehicle miles traveled (VMT) have increased, but have declined per 100 million VMT. Logically, the overall number of deaths is largely a product of exposure, with a greater number of miles driven associated with a greater number of fatal crashes. However, when average exposure is controlled, fatalities are shown to have declined per exposure. The reduction in MVC-related fatalities per 100 million VMT is due to a variety of improvements in vehicle design and technology, roadway design, traffic and licensing regulations, and enforcement. This section will provide an overview of some of the most important technological advances.

Roadway Safety

Roadway safety has improved over the years, despite increased traffic and speed, through the gradual improvement of road construction, separation of traffic, and signage (Graham et al, 1967; Wendling, 1996). Divided highways and the movement toward clear roadsides, where trees, signs, poles, and the like were moved away from the road, have reduced serious crashes (American Association of State Highway and Transportation Officials, 2002). According to the Roadway Safety Guide (RSF, 2004) installation of rumble strips along the roadside have reduced run-off-the-road crashes by 60% and restoring surface friction by timely removal of ice and snow reduces injury crashes by 20% during winter months and by 88% right after a storm. The Roadway Safety Guide also reports that further reductions in the number of roadway collisions are possible through the following low-cost solutions: (1) realigning roadways and removing roadside obstacles can reduce fatalities by 66%; (2) constructing dedicated turning lanes and traffic channelization at high-risk intersections can reduce fatalities by 47%; and (3) improving motorist information through improved signage and pavement markings can reduce fatalities by up to 39% (RSF, 2004). Additional research by the National Cooperative Highway Research Program (NCHRP) of the Transportation Research Board (TRB) is underway that would provide practical guidance for state and local highway agen-

Figure 5

Inter-related components of motor vehicle injury control.

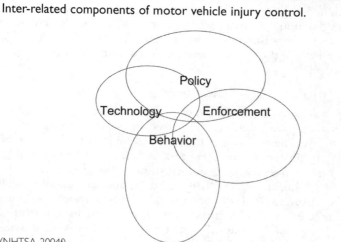

(NHTSA, 2004f)

cies to reduce fatalities. Thus far, 13 design documents have been published, known as NCHRP Report 500, covering relevant topics such as hazardous trees, intersections, horizontal curves, utility poles, and work zones (TRB, 2004). Accordingly, substantial improvements in road design can be expected in the coming years, but improvements may be impeded to some extent by cost and the ever increasing amount of traffic.

Vehicle Design

Fortunately, modern vehicles are better designed for safety than ever before and gradual improvements in vehicle safety can be expected over the coming decade. Improvements in vehicle safety, of course, may be mitigated by other vehicle characteristics. For example, in general, modern vehicles can accelerate faster and attain higher speeds than ever before. Also, the disparity in size between the many small cars and newly dominant large vehicles on the road poses new risks. Not only are injury claims more substantial for people in small cars, but fatality rates are up to 7 times more likely in a small 2-ton vehicle in a collision with a larger 4-ton vehicle (Dewar, 2002). Notably, the recent increase in the number of trucks, vans, and sports utility vehicles (SUVs) on public roadways has made driving a passenger car a disadvantage in some cases (Dewar, 2002; IIHS, 1998; Thomas and Frampton, 2002). Nonetheless, new designs for passenger vehicles large and small allow for better crash prevention and passenger protection. Overall vehicle crash worthiness seems to have improved over the years, although there is great variability in the crash worthiness of vehicles as assessed by an assortment of methods including crash tests using crash test dummies and analysis of accident data based on real-world events (Ford, 2004). Antilock braking systems (ABS), now standard are most new vehicles, help prevent skidding in rapid-stopping situations, especially on slippery surfaces (Dewar, 2002). A host of vehicle design improvements provide increased passenger safety. For exam-

Figure 6

Number of Motor Vehicle Fatalities per Year from 1899 to 2003

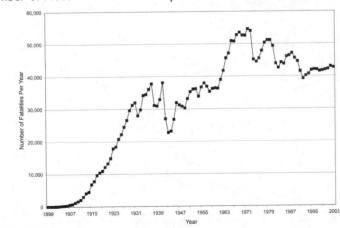

(NHTSA, 2004f)

ple, most modern vehicles have energy absorbing frame structures or crush zones that collapse upon contact to absorb crash energy, thereby reducing the forces transmitted to vehicle occupants (Mahmood and Fileta, 2004). In addition, all new vehicles sold in the United States must include safety features designed to further protect the driver and passengers. These features include penetration-resistant windshields, energy-absorbing dashboards and knee bolsters, as well as steering wheel columns designed to collapse upon contact, reducing the likelihood a secondary impact following a collision (Chou, 2004). Recent developments, such as electronic stability control (ESC), intelligent cruise control, back-up alarms, improved mirrors, and the introduction of video technology into vehicles, hold promise for improving vehicle safety as well (Papeilis et al, 2004). In the not too distant future in-vehicle warning systems, including collision, navigation, rollover, and other warning systems, may become standard (Dewar, 2002).

Passenger Protection

The most important safety innovations, of course, have been those that keep the passenger in the vehicle and safe from secondary impact. While the initial impact in a crash may be the primary cause of injury, secondary impact where passengers then come into contact with hard vehicle surfaces or are thrown from the vehicle, greatly increase the likelihood and severity of injury (Stevens, 2003; Chou, 2004). Safety belts and supplemental air bag restraint systems are among the great advances in automotive safety and substantial research attests to their safety benefits (Chou, 2004; NHTSA, 2004a). The technology of safety restraint devices and systems continues to evolve and

Figure 7

Motor-Vehicle-Related Deaths (Fatality Rate) Per Million Vehicle Miles Traveled (VMT) and Annual VMT, by Year, 1921-2003

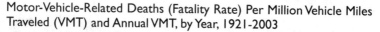

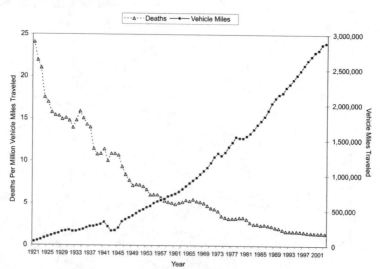

improve, for example with the introduction of side airbags, the advent of 3-point and 4-point safety belts, and improvements in child protective devices (Braver and Kyrychenko, 2003; CarTrackers.com, 2000; Edgerton et al, 2004; Kahane, 2000; Weber, 2000). Because safety belts and child protective devices such as car and booster seats are not entirely passive and require action on the part of passengers, they aptly illustrate the important relationship between technology, education, policy, enforcement, and safety behavior.

Legislation an Policy

Without legislative and regulatory requirements, many important automotive safety advances would probably not be in place. Safety belt and airbag technologies were available long before they were included in vehicles. These technologies became generally available only when federally mandated (O'Neil, 2002; Wendling, 1996). Safety belt and car safety seat use, of course, require the active participation of the passenger, despite advances that have reduced the complexity and inconvenience of their use. Use rates increase substantially when laws are passed requiring them (Beck, Mack, Shults, and Beck 2004) and improve with enforcement and education (Dinh-Zarr et al, 2001). Nevertheless, while safety belt use has increased dramatically during the past several decades, there remains room for improvements, particularly among minority populations and young drivers and passengers (Beck et al, 2004). Indeed, for most types of traffic injuries, morbidity and mortality are higher among lower socioeconomic groups, particularly among children (Laflamme and Diderichsen, 2000). Overall, car safety seat use with small children up to age 2 is estimated to be over 95% but child restraint use for 3 to 8 year olds is less than 65% (Winston et al, 2004). However, child safety restraint use is lower among lower income and minority populations (Piani and Schoenborn, 1993). For example, the rates of using a car safety seat immediately after birth for families with incomes less than $10 000 was only 79%, compared with 97% for families with incomes of $50 000 or more. Likewise, one study found that the likelihood that children would be transported in a car seat immediately after birth was 92% for Whites, 85% for Blacks, and 74% for Hispanics (Pianl, and Schoenborn, 1993). A more recent study reported that Hispanics are less likely to place their child in the rear seat, a location that is associated with fewer injuries and fatalities for child occupants (Greenberg-Seth et al, 2004). It is likely that booster seat use is also lower among children of lower socioeconomic status, in part because there are costs involved and children may be transported in a variety of vehicles and drivers.

Between 1977 and 1985, all 50 states and the District of Columbia and all U.S. territories passed child passenger safety laws. Yet these laws varied dramatically in their age requirements, exemptions, enforcement procedures, and penalties. In 2001, the National SAFE KIDS Campaign rated states on the quality of their child occupant protection laws in relation to a model law. Most states received low grades of "D" or "F" and no state was found to provide full protection for child passengers ages 15 and under (Ross et al, 2001). In the ensuing three years, 49 states either introduced a bill or passed legislation to more adequately protect children traveling in motor vehicles (Ross et al, 2004). Yet for children to be fully protected, more states need to include booster seat provisions in their laws. In addition, use rates might increase in states that enact primary enforcement safety belt laws allowing police officers to write tickets for unrestrained passengers even when the car has not been stopped for another violation (eg, speeding, drunk driving).

Like safety belt use and child occupant protection, driver-licensing practices are largely a state responsibility. The long-standing tradition has been for states to allow licensure at relatively young ages, usually 16, compared for example with most European countries where it is uncommon to allow licensure before the age of 18. The tradition of many U.S. states to allow early licensure after completion of a driver education course has gradually been eliminated. However, given the high crash rates among teen drivers, licensure policies have changed dramatically in recent decades. Most states have adopted some form of graduate driver licensing (GDL) policy that includes three stages rather than the traditional two stages (permit then licensure). GDL provides for an extended learner's permit period, often 4 months or longer rather than the meager two weeks many states once required. GDL also provides for a provisional license, usually in effect until age 18, that provides modest restrictions on high risk driving conditions, particularly late night driving. Some states have also adopted restrictions on teen passengers and most GDL policies include a zero blood alcohol requirement for novice drivers. The several statewide evaluations that have been conducted have demonstrated substantial reductions in teen crash rates and fatalities (Shope et al, 2001; Foss et al, 2001). The nature of the effects of GDL on crashes has been debated. The obvious and certain effect of these policies has been to reduce exposure. While the primary goal of GDL is to reduce the exposure of newly licensed to high risk driving conditions, a great deal of the beneficial effects may be due to the incidental delay in the age of licensure (McKnight and Peck, 2002). Because the actual restrictions on teen drivers are modest and enforcement is passive (Foss and Goodwin, 2003), a secondary effect may be to empower parents to restrict their teens from high risk driving (Simons-Morton and Hartos, 2002a). Nevertheless, there is no debate about the importance and effectiveness of GDL as a policy initiative for reducing MVCs among young drivers.

Protecting Young Children From MVC Injuries

Young children are particularly vulnerable in motor vehicle crashes, however, appropriate child restraint provides considerable protection. When correctly installed and used in motor vehicles, child safety seats can dramatically decrease morbidity and mortality rates among children (Zaza et al, 2001). Child safety seats have been shown to reduce the risk of death by 71 percent among infants and 54 percent among children ages 1 to 4, as well as to diminish hospitalizations by 69 percent among children ages 4 and under (NHTSA, 1996). In 2003, of 471 MVC fatalities among children under 5 years of age, 167 (35%) were totally unrestrained (NHTSA, 2004c). From 1975 through 2003, the federal government estimates that the lives of 7020 children were saved by the use of child restraint systems (NHTSA, 2004c). In addition, an estimated 182 000 serious injuries could be prevented annually if all children ages 14 and under were consistently and correctly restrained when they rode in motor vehicles (NHTSA, 2001).

Child Protective Devices and Practices

The key to the protection of passengers of any age is to keep them from being thrown from the vehicle, abused by the initial impact, or encountering secondary impact. The idea is to secure passengers in place so that in crashes they remain in the vehicle and suffer least from the force between (1) the vehicle and the initial object it strikes; (2) the passenger's body and the interior of the vehicle; and (3) the passenger's organs and the inside of the body itself (Stevens, 2003). For a variety of reasons, including the fact that it is further away from the usual point of contact in most crashes and has relatively fewer hard surfaces than the front seat, the back seat is much safer than the front (CDC, 2002; Winston et al, 2001). Therefore, infants and young children should always be properly restrained and ride in the back of the vehicle (American Academy of Pediatrics, 2005; NSKC, 2005). For maximum protection, infants should ride in the back in rear-facing safety seats at least until they are 12 months old and 20 pounds. Children, who are at least 1 year old and weigh 20 to 40 pounds and can no longer ride rear-facing, should ride in forward-facing child safety seats. Children over 40 pounds should be correctly secured in belt-positioning booster seats or other appropriate child restraints until the adult lap and shoulder belts fit correctly (around age 8). Adult safety belts do not adequately protect children under age 8 from injury in a crash, so they should ride secured in belt-positioning booster seats. Installing children in booster seats with proper belt-positioning rather than transferring small children to adult safety belts can reduce young children's injury risk due to MVC's by as much as 59 percent (Durbin et al, 2003). However, it is estimated that 62 percent of children ages 4 to 8 ride improperly restrained in adult safety belts (Winston et al, 2004). The improper use of safety restraints can result in a distinct set of injuries, typically of the trunk and head (Decina and Lococo, 2004; Stevens, 2003).

The decision about when to transition a child to a booster seat from a car seat is a difficult one for many parents. However, it appears that a growing percentage of parents are beginning to use belt-positioning booster seats as the best way to protect their toddlers. While less than 5% of children were restrained in belt-positioning booster seats in 1999 (Arbogast et al, 2001), a recent report indicated that that 19% of parents of children who should be restrained in booster seats reported using them (Durbin et al, 2003). While booster seat use may be on the rise, it remains quite low, with only 16 percent of 4-year-olds, 13 percent of 5-year-olds, and 4 percent of 6- and 7-year-olds using them regularly (Durbin et al, 2003). A great deal more needs to be learned about the extent to which risk may be greater among certain populations and how best to improve the successful transition from car safety seats to booster seats.

Risks of Riding Unrestrained and Improperly Restrained

While young children (aged 0–7) have the highest rates of restraint use (NHTSA, 2004c), misuse is common (NHTSA, 2000), and approximately 14 percent of children ages 14 and under ride completely unrestrained (Cody et al, 2002). While this represents a substantial improvement over the past several decades, restraint remains particularly low among lower income populations (Vivoda, Eby, and Kostyniuk, 2004; Lerner et al, 2001).

This failure to buckle up is particularly disheartening given the great safety benefits of child protective devices. Notably, half of children ages 14 and under who died in motor vehicle crashes in 2002 were not appropriately secured by safety restraints at the time of the collision (NHTSA, 2003a). Also, child restraint use is lower among drivers who have been drinking, essentially doubling the risk to child passengers because they are less likely to be restrained when riding with an impaired driver (Quinlan, 2000). An estimated 20% of crashes in which children are injured are alcohol related (NHTSA, 2003a).

Incorrect use of child safety seats is widespread. Most studies indicate that four out of five child safety seats are misused in some way. National SAFE KIDS analyses of nearly 38 000 observed restraints revealed that 81.6 percent were used incorrectly, with an average of three errors per restraint (Cody et al, 2004). The highest misuse rates involve errors that are potentially the most injurious, including the safety belt not holding the car seat tightly in the vehicle and the harness straps not holding the child tightly in the car seat. Many parents are unaware that have installed and used their child safety seats incorrectly. Parents and others who care for children are not entirely to blame. Until recently there was little standardization for car and booster seats, making their use difficult even for the most dedicated users. Many parents have found it difficult to correctly secure the seat to the vehicle and adequately secure the child in the seat. Adding to the difficulties of installation, many children are routinely transported in a myriad of vehicles, requiring tedious effort in taking the car or booster seat out of one vehicle and tediously securing it in another. Modern seats are easier to use and offer some level of standardization for installation and securing.

As with other safety measures, child car and booster seat use is highly dependent on technology, policy, enforcement, and education. Recent regulations have improved the quality of child safety seats and seats are now better developed, improving ease of correct use (NHTSA, 2002; NHTSA, 2004g). In addition, some of the most recent passenger vehicles provide convenient latches that are more convenient and less prone to error when securing and tightening seats to the vehicle (NHTSA, 2002). For example, LATCH (Lower Anchors and Tethers for Children) is a new system that allows LATCH-equipped child safety seats to be fastened to anchors where the vehicle's seat cushions meet.

Primary enforcement laws are in place in all 50 states requiring the use of federally-approved child restraint devices, but the laws vary widely in terms of their application to child characteristics, enforcement, and penalties imposed for failing to follow the law (Zaza et al, 2001). Enhanced enforcement and education campaigns appear to be effective at increasing use and decreasing incorrect use of child safety seats by 4%–21% (Zaza et al, 2001).

The distribution of free seats accompanied by educational training has been proven to dramatically increase the use of booster seats among children ages 4 to 6 (Apsler, 2003). The use of child safety seats is generally lower among low-income families, who may have limited access to affordable seats. However, among low-income families who own a safety seat, an estimated 95% of them use them (Zaza et al, 2001). It is likely that the strategy of providing free or inexpensive seats to low-income families would increase use as well (Zaza et al, 2001). Still, a great deal more needs to be learned about how best to increase the use of child restraints.

According to the National SAFE KIDS Campaign (NSKC, 2004b), 22 states and the District of Columbia have improved their laws to require older children to ride in booster seats. Interestingly, it appears that adoption of a primary seat belt law for adults seems to have an influence on child restraint use rates (NHTSA, 1998). In Louisiana, seat belt use rates in 1994 were 50% and child restraint use rates were 45%. However, after primary seat belt use laws were put in effect for adults seat belt use increased to 68% and child restraint use rates increased to 82% in 1997. Notably, these changes in the child restraint use rate were without any change in the state's child passenger safety law (NHTSA, 1998)! Further, child occupant protection and safety belt legislation has been shown to increase restraint use and 90% of Americans report favoring stronger enforcement of laws that require all children to be buckled up (NSKC, 2004b).

Preventing MVCs Among Young Drivers

MVC rates are particularly elevated for young drivers and passengers and remain so into the 4th decade of life (see Figure 2). Teenagers are more likely to die or be injured as a result of motor vehicle crashes than for any other cause (CDC, 1999; Cvijanovich et al, 2001; Ulmer, Williams, Preusser, 1997). Today, it is clearly understood that driving among teenagers and young adults is a major public health problem greatly in need of address from multiple perspectives. While teen drivers benefit from advances in road designs just as do adult drivers, they are young and inexperienced, tend to drive smaller and older vehicles with fewer safety features, are least likely to wear seat belts (Williams, Rappold, and Ferguson, 2002), and may be highly likely to use electronic devices and engage in other distracting activities while driving (Stutts et al, 2003). Recent recognition of the high crash rates of newly licensed drivers has lead to changes in the driver licensing policies in many states and a model policy called graduated driver licensing (GDL) has been developed (IIHS, 1999). GDL is an extremely important policy initiative that has been demonstrated to reduce statewide crashes and fatalities in this age group (Shope et al, 2001; Foss et al, 2001). However, the provisions of GDL in most states place limited restrictions on novice drivers, enforcement is lax (Foss and Goodwin, 2003), and parents remain the primary guardians of novice teen driving (Simons-Morton and Hartos, 2002).

Risk Factors

Most authorities attribute the elevated risks of teen driving to young age, inexperience, and risk taking behavior (Williams and Ferguson, 2002). Teenagers are uniquely at risk when first licensed (McCartt et al, 2003). In their first year of driving, 16-year-old drivers are nearly four times more likely to crash per mile driven than drivers in their 20s (Mayhew et al, 2003; Williams, Preusser, Ulmer, Weinstein, 1995). The first several hundred miles of independent driving are particularly risky (McCartt et al, 2003). However, the conditions under which driving occurs is also important. Notably, the risk of a crash is greatest during the first months following licensure and throughout adolescence while carrying teen passengers and driving at night (Doherty, 1998; Williams, Rappold, and Ferguson, 2002; Chen et al, 2000). In addition, teenagers have the lowest rates of safety belt use (Williams, Rappold, and Ferguson, 2002), may be more likely than other drivers to drive in a risky and aggressive manner (McKenna et al, 1998; NHTSA, 2000), and are particularly susceptible to traffic accidents involving alcohol (Zador et al, 2000).

Inexperience and Young Age

Driving a motor vehicle is a complex task requiring the integration of psychomotor, perceptual, and cognitive skills and it can take several years before full proficiency is developed (Mayhew and Simpson, 1995). So driving seems to improve with experience (see figure 2), however, the more one drives, regardless of age or driving performance, the greater one's inherent risk for a crash. Therefore, the best way of reducing crash risk is to reduce exposure. For adolescents, this is best done by delaying licensure (McKnight and Peck, 2002) and for a period after licensure, limiting driving under the highest risk conditions (Simons-Morton and Hartos, 2003b).

Crash rates are particularly elevated early in licensure (Mayhew, Simpson, Pak, 2003; McCartt, Shabanova, Leaf, 2003). McCartt et al (2003) demonstrated that crash rates are about 12 times higher during the first weeks after licensure than among experienced drivers. Crash rates then decline rapidly over the first 6 months and 1000 miles of driving experience to a level that is about twice that of older drivers and then remain more or less at this elevated level until the mid 20s. The very high crash rate immediately after licensure and rapid decline over a several month period suggests that substantial learning occurs during the initial months of unsupervised, independent driving. Stated differently, this finding indicates that driving inexperience is a cause of crashes. Curiously, the amount of practice driving reported prior to licensure does not seem to influence crash rates after licensure (McCartt et al, 2003), suggesting that independent driving may be very different than supervised practice driving or, possibly, that the amount of practice driving teens obtain varies by their driving aptitude. That is, the teens that get the most supervised practice driving may be those that have greater difficulty learning to manage the vehicle. In any case, regardless of the amount of practice, once teens get licensed they are at great risk of having a crash, and nearly half of newly-licensed drivers experience a reportable crash in their first year of licensure (McCartt et al, 2003). While many of these crashes do not involve personal injury, they do reflect the high risk of novice teen driving.

Getting licensed at a younger age increases crash risks and also increases teen's exposure to crash risks, at least to the extent they would drive during this period beyond the amount they would ride with other teen drivers (McKnight and Peck, 2002). However, the age of licensure has not been shown to be as important as driving experience. For example, in New Jersey, where teens cannot get licensed until age 17, crash rates during the first year of licensure are about the same as in states where teens can be licensed at age 16 (Williams et al, 1983). Nevertheless, delaying licensure by an average of even a few months could provide important protective effects against teen crashes (McKnight and Peck, 2002). Taking into account the increased maturity associated with a single year of adolescent development (Arnett, Irwin, and Halper-Felsher, 2002), delaying licensure can only be a good thing with respect to safety. Nevertheless, newly-licensed teens of any age experience a period of elevated crash risk (McCartt et al, 2003; Ferguson et al, 1996).

Fortunately, newly licensed teen drivers tend not to drive as much as more experienced drivers, but the amount teens drive increases the longer the teen has been licensed, with a substantial increase in crashes and injuries. As noted, crash rates are highest during the initial months of licensure, but decline (per miles driven) after about 6 months and 1000 miles to a level that remains somewhat elevated compared with older drivers. This is why insurance rates are so high for young drivers and do not decline until drivers are well into their 20s. While inexperience accounts for a substantial portion of teen drivers' elevated crash risk, road conditions such as nighttime driving and teen passengers, and risk taking significantly increase driving risk (Simons-Morton, Hartos et al, 2003; Williams and Ferguson, 2002).

Nighttime Driving

Compared to adults, adolescents actually drive less overall, but they drive disproportionately more at night and have a much higher nighttime crash rate (Farrow, 1987; Williams, Rappold, and Ferguson, 2002). Shown in Figure 8, fatal crashes are higher for young drivers at night, particularly during the very late night and early morning hours, a risk that declines with age. Nighttime driving increases both the likelihood of teens of having a crash and the severity of crashes (Farrow, 1987; Williams, Rappold, and Ferguson, 2002).

Teen Passengers

Crash risks increase exponentially for each additional teen passenger (Chen et al, 2000). In a survey asking teenagers to describe their dangerous driving situations during the past 6 months, 85 percent of the reported incidents involved one or more teen passengers (Farrow, 1987). As shown in Figure 9, a monotonic increase in crash rate is observed for each additional teen passenger for drivers ages 16–17 and 18–19, but the rates are highest for the youngest age group. This is in contrast to adult drivers, for whom additional passengers pose little increased crash risk, as indicated in Figure 8.

The presence of other teens in the car may influence teen drivers to take risks or become distracted. Teenagers in general may be more susceptible to distraction by the behavior of other teens and newly-licensed, novice drivers may be particularly susceptible. It may also be that teen passengers when riding with another teen engage in particularly distracting behaviors that make driving more difficult. In any case, it seems that teen drivers tend to engage in somewhat more risky driving behavior in the presence of teen passengers than adults. McKenna et al (1998) conducted a study in England (where the minimum age for obtaining a drivers license is 18 and most do not obtain licenses before age 20) in which observers, stationed unobtrusively along side a road with a 30 MPH speed limit, videotaped vehicles and measured vehicle speed with a radar gun. Males, but not female drivers, were found to drive faster in the presence of a male passenger than in the presence of a female passenger. Both males and females allowed less frontal headway in the presence of a male passenger than in the presence of a female passenger or no passengers. Simons-Morton and Lerner (2004) conducted a similar study in the US designed to examine teen passenger effects on 16–18 year old drivers. Vehicles and the age (adult or teen) and sex of the drivers and passengers were observed at the end of the school day while exiting high school parking lots and again once they emerged onto a nearby road where they could merge with general traffic and get up to speed. On average, teen drivers drove faster and allowed less frontal gap when carrying teen passengers than teens driving alone or general traffic. This effect was greater for male drivers carrying a male passenger than carrying a female passenger and greater than female drivers with male or female passengers. These findings are consistent with the hypothesis that teen passengers alter teen driving behavior, although much remains to be learned about this phenomenon.

Risk Taking

Driving performance is highly variable. Under similar circumstances, some drive faster or slower than others, allow greater or lesser headway with the vehicle in front, change lanes more or less rapidly, and pay more or less attention to the road and the drivers around them. In short, some drivers take more risks than others and probably have different perceptions about how risky various maneuvers might be for them. Consistent with all that known about adolescent development (Arnett, 1992), adolescents tend to engage in more risky driving behavior than adults (Jonah, 1986; Wasielewski, 1984; McKenna et al, 1998). Compared with older drivers, younger

Figure 8

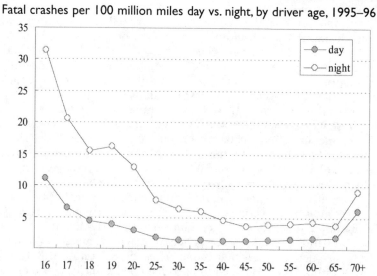

Fatal crashes per 100 million miles day vs. night, by driver age, 1995–96

Fatal Accident Reporting System (FARS) and National Personal Transportation Systems (NPTS)

people are more likely to drive at excessive speeds, follow too closely, violate traffic signs and signals, overtake other vehicles in a risky manner, allow too little time to merge, and fail to yield to pedestrians (Romanowicz, Gebers, 1990; Jonah, 1986; Hartos et al, 2000; Williams, 1998; McKnight and McKnight, 2003; Williams, 2003). In general, adolescent males tend to engage in more risky driving than females (Jonah, 1986; Hartos et al 2000). Driving too fast is particularly associated with youthfulness. During the early months of licensure, driver inattention and error, along with speed and other risky behavior are implicated in non-fatal crashes (McKnight and McKnight, 2003). Notably, in the studies just described by Mckenna et al, (1998) and Simons-Morton and Lerner (2005) teenaged younger drivers drove faster and allowed less frontal headway than general traffic (which was exacerbated in the presence of a front seat male passenger). Not surprisingly, excessive speed is cited as a factor in a higher proportion of teen crashes (Williams, Preusser, Ulmer, Weinstein, 1995; Ulmer, Williams, Preusser, 1997).

In some cases, risky driving may reflect deliberate thrill-seeking, while, in other cases it can merely reflect lack the recognition (due to inexperience) and perception (due to young age or inexperience) that the behavior is risky, or a combination of the two (McKnight and McKnight, 2003). Risky driving behavior and inexperience factors can interact, where risky driving leads young people into hazardous situations and inexperience makes it more difficult for them to cope with such situations safely. There is some evidence that young drivers who participate in advanced driving courses where they are taught evasive maneuvers, such as skid control, have higher crash rates thereafter than teens not exposed to the course (Gregersen, 1996). Of course, this may be due in part to selection, where

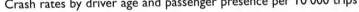

Figure 9

Crash rates by driver age and passenger presence per 10 000 trips

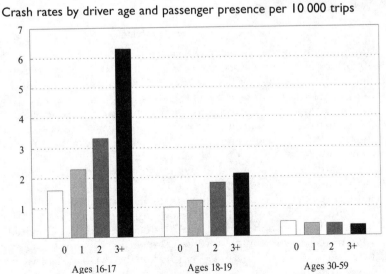

NPTS and the National Automotive Sampling System General Estimates System (NASS/GES)

teens who are greater risk takers are more likely to enroll in such courses. Nevertheless, in general it seems clear that adolescents drive in a manner that increases crash risks. However, it is not clear how much this behavior has to do with learning to drive safely, perceptions about risk, and actual sensation seeking. Moreover, while risky driving behavior is particularly dangerous among less experience drivers, the behavior and associated risks persist into young adulthood, particularly among males.

Safety Belts

Seat belts are an effective protective device, but teenagers are less likely to use seat belts than older drivers (Williams, Rappold, and Ferguson, 2002), greatly increasing their risk of injury in a crash. Sadly, safety belt use is lower under the influence of alcohol, when the risk of crash is greatly increased (Schechtman, Shinar, and Compton, 1999).

Alcohol

While drinking and driving among adolescents remains an important problem, national rates have declined significantly from the mid-1980s (O'Malley, Johnston, 1999). Moreover, most teen crashes do not involve alcohol, although, alcohol is involved in 21 percent of fatal crashes among drivers aged 15 to 20 (Chen et al 2000). Drinking may be particularly problematic for teens because inexperienced drinkers may be highly susceptible to the intoxicating effects of alcohol, even at low doses, and inexperienced drivers may not be safe behind the while to begin with. Also, alcohol may interact with the tendency of younger drivers to speed and engage in risky driving behaviors that increase the risk of a crash (Smith, 1994). Moreover, drinking and driving is more likely late at night and in the presence of teen passengers, both significant risk factors (Williams and Lund, 1986; Farrow, 1987; Williams et al, 1995).

Licensing Policy and Practice

Licensing policy is variable from state to state (Williams, Weinberg, Fields, et al, 1996) and crash rates vary according to licensing policy (Ferguson, Leaf, Williams, Preusser, 1996). In particular, the earlier the age of licensure, the greater the crash rate for the age group (Ferguson et al, 1996), which is not surprising because getting licensed increases adolescents' exposure to driving. The minimum age for getting a license is 16 in most states, but it is 15 in a few states and 17 in New Jersey (Williams et al, 1996). Most teens get licensed within a year of eligibility, although rural and suburban youth are licensed sooner and at younger ages than urban youth and upper SES youth are licensed younger and earlier after eligible than lower SES youth (Preusser, Ferguson, Williams, Leaf, and Farmer, 1998). Substantial attention has been paid to licensure policy over the years. A landmark paper by Leon Robertson in the 1970s documented that policies that allowed teens to become eligible for licensure earlier by completing driver education courses actually increased crash rates by exposing teens to the risk of a crash earlier than they would be otherwise (Robertson and Zador, 1978). As noted, early licensure increases risk (Ferguson et al, 1996) partly allowing earlier exposure to driving risks (McKnight and Peck, 2002), but also to an unknown amount due to younger drivers being less mature.

Driver education is an important part of driver licensing, but numerous studies have failed to document protective effects of these programs (Mayhew et al, 2002). This is not surprising given that most of the curriculum is devoted to teaching about driving rules so that teens can pass the test for their learner's permit. Most states require driver education programs to provide only a few hours of behind the wheel training, just enough to help the young driver manage the vehicle. Too little professional instruction time behind the wheel is available to allow for mastery of various driving conditions and safe driving practices. For the most part supervised practice driving is left to parents who may not be particularly well prepared for the task or effective. However, little is known about how much supervised practice parents provide and the nature of this experience.

Graduated Driver Licensing (GDL) has emerged as a solution to the dilemma that on-road driving by beginners is both necessary and risky (Williams and Ferguson, 2002). The goal of GDL is to manage exposure to risk, keeping beginners out of higher risk situations while they are learning. Thus, beginners go through licensure stages that vary by amount of crash risk involved, starting with the lowest risk. Learning drivers typically are required to spend an extended period of time, sometimes as much as six months and 50 hours or more, practicing while supervised by a parent or other licensed adult so that they gain experience in a wide range of driving situations prior to getting a license. In states with GDL policies, teenagers graduate to a provisional license with which they can drive without adult supervision, but are restricted for a period of time from driving under the highest risk driving activities such as driving at night and with other teen passengers in the car. Only after a period of time and presumable substantial experience driving only under lower risk conditions can beginners graduate to a fully unrestricted license. Unrestricted licensure usually occurs at age 18, finally allowing teenagers so licensed to drive anywhere, anytime, with whomever they choose. The aim of the provisional driver licensing period is not to reduce the quantity of driving, but to reduce exposure to the higher risk driving conditions while the teenager gains experience and presumably improves driving skills. Of course, in allowing some types of driving but not others, graduated licensing represents a compromise between safety and mobility.

It makes eminent sense to have a staged approached to licensure as offered by GDL. This approach allows for a relatively prolonged period for acquiring complex skills that take time to develop in an attempt to minimizing the danger that learning errors will lead to crashes and injuries. It is no different in principle from mastering other skills where performance errors can have serious consequences, eg, rock climbing or airplane piloting where people are taught such skills under supervised conditions, initial experience is limited to lower risk settings, and greater privileges are allowed with increased experience. Graduated licensing addresses the crash risks of teenage drivers by delaying higher risk driving until teenagers are both more experienced and more mature (McKnight, Peck, 2002).

Research indicates that certain components and consequences of GDL programs, including the extended period of supervised practice driving during the learner's permit phase, increased supervised driving prior to licensure, delayed ages at permit and provisional licensure, and nighttime driving curfews, have resulted in reductions in violations and crashes among teenagers (Foss et al, 2001; Shope et al, 2001). However, the characteristics of GDL programs vary from state to state and few jurisdictions have all the elements of an optimal program as identified by the Insurance Institute for Highway Safety (1999). Presumably, states with more of the specified provisions would be most effective in reducing teen crashes. However, enforcement of GDL provisions is problematic and lax (Foss and Goodwin, 2003). Police have other important business to attend to late at night and in any case it would hardly be fair for police to stop without provocation young looking drivers out after midnight. Hence, the most important effect of GDL may be to enhance and support parents' efforts to moderate teen driving (Beck et al, 2002; Simons-Morton and Hartos, 2002).

Parental Management of Novice Teen Driving

With or without GDL programs, parents are in a prime position to restrict novice young drivers to less risky driving conditions and to manage teen driving, at least during the first year or so of driving. Parents are involved in their teenagers' driving from the beginning, teaching them to drive, governing their access to vehicles, and setting rules (Simons-Morton et al, 2002a). Interestingly, Hartos et al (2001) found that teens who reported parental restrictions during the early months after licensure reported less risky driving behavior during the first year of driving. In one study, violations were four times more likely and crashes were seven times more likely among adolescents with lenient driving restrictions (Hartos et al, 2001). Hence, parental restrictions may not only reduce exposure to high risk driving conditions during the early stages of driving, but also influence driving behavior thereafter (Hartos et al, 2001). While most parents restrict the driving privileges of their newly-licensed teens, the restrictions tend not to be very strict, focus on responsibility (letting parents know where the teen is with the car and when they will return) and not on risk conditions such as the number of teens passengers and nighttime curfew, and tend not to remain in effect for long (Hartos et al, 2002). Moreover, most rules and consequences are verbal and informal (Hartos et al, 2002), and therefore subject to selective recall and disputes. The challenge is to increase the proportion of parents who manage their teens' early driving experiences and the extent of parental management.

Simons-Morton and colleagues have shown that parental management of novice teen drivers can be increased through conventional behavioral intervention. In one study, Connecticut families were recruited at the time the teens obtained a learners permit and randomized to an intervention or comparison group. Over the next several months, the intervention group received a video and persuasive newsletters designed to increase perceptions of risk and efficacy and outcome expectations for adopting a parent-teen driving agreement, which they received at the time the teen became eligible for a license. On the same schedule the comparison group received materials related to driving, but not to driving risk. As administered, the Checkpoints Program was relatively passive, but resulted in significant treatment group differences through 12 months post-licensure (Simons-Morton et al, 2003; Simons-Morton et al, 2005). The best predictor of later driving limits was initial driving limits. A similar intervention was implemented at the time of licensure in one Maryland Motor Vehicle Administration licensing office. Weeks were randomized to intervention or comparison and during the intervention weeks families waiting to complete the licensure forms were recruited, viewed the video, provided the Checkpoints Parent-Teen Driving Agreement, and encouraged by a research assistant to adopt and maintain the agreement. Surprisingly, this very brief intervention occurring at the last moment before licensure had about the same initial (Simons-Morton et al, 2003) and nearly as lasting effects (Simons-Morton et al, 2004) as the Connecticut Checkpoints Program that was designed to prepare teens and parents for restrictions at licensure and consisted of a more extensive and prolonged, if more passive intervention (eg, the persuasive materials were not accompanied by any personal admonition). Because Maryland is a GDL state and Connecticut is not, it would be interesting to determine the relative effectiveness of The Checkpoints Program in each state. An intervention such as Checkpoints designed to increase parental management of teen driving would be expected to be more effective under GDL than not. Because the administration of the Checkpoints Program varied considerably in the two states a direct comparison is not possible. However, Hartos et al, (2004 or 2005) found that (untreated) parents in Maryland, a state with GDL, imposed somewhat greater restrictions on their newly-licensed teens than did parents in Connecticut, a state without GDL. Also, Beck et al (2003) found that parents in Maryland imposed somewhat greater restrictions on their newly licensed teens after state adoption of a more strict form of GDL. This provides evidence that one of the effects of GDL may be to shift public norms about teen licensing, encouraging parents to adopt restrictions, and providing them with some legislative teeth for requiring teens to at least comply with GDL restrictions on late night driving and the like (Simons-Morton et al 2002b, 2003a, 2003b).

A Call for Advocacy

Motor vehicle crashes are a leading cause of death during childhood and adolescence. Young children are at particular risk unless they are correctly restrained. Novice teen drivers and their teen passengers are at highly elevated crah and injury risk. In general passenger safety has improved for most groups, given advances in technology and policy, but many children could be saved from injury and death if they were correctly restrained and teenagers remain the highest risk group. The following areas of improvement would make the most difference with respect to the protection of children and adolescents: (1) increase the percentage of children and adolescents who are correctly restrained while riding in vehicles; (2) adopt strict GDL policies that would delay the age of licensure and restrict the driving conditions for novice teen drivers; (3) increase parental management of novice teen drivers leading to reduced exposure of novice drivers to high risk driving conditions; and (4) reduce incidence of drinking and driving (CDC, 2001; Simons-Morton and Hartos, 2003b).

The theme of this chapter is that advances in child and teen occupant protection depend on the inter-relationships of technology, policy, enforcement, and behavior. Children and adolescents can be expected to benefit from improvements in road and vehicle technology, but additional improvements in child safety will require advances in policy, enforcement, and education. Technology related to transportation safety is advancing rapidly, including road and vehicle designs, crash warning and avoidance systems, passive and active occupant protection designs and devices. Over time, there has been a distinct trend toward transportation safety policies that favor the use of protective devices and staged licensure and discourage drinking and driving. While primary enforcement of these policies might improve compliance, this raises legitimate concerns about civil liberties. Ultimately, a large part of motor vehicle safety depends on behavior. However, individual behavior can be inconsistent, thoughtless, and self destructive. What is needed, really, is a shift in social norms, where responsible transportation safety behavior is part of the culture and not an elective individual behavior. The idea is to make it socially standard to use child safety seats, wear safety belts, delay licensure, and restrict the driving privileges of novice teen drivers. Individuals should be able to exercise considerable personal agency with respect to many aspects of transportation, but the use of passenger protective devices and the age of licensure eligibility should not be personal decisions. Social norms are certainly no easier to manage than individual behavior, but policy, enforcement, and education can go a long way toward fostering a social climate that supports responsible transportation safety behavior.

While improvement in the rates of child and adolescent MVC injuries is possible, it is hardly assured. Only concerted advocacy on the part of concerned citizens and public health, transportation, and injury prevention professionals can assure improvements (Gielen, 2002; Altman, Balcazar, Fawcett, Seekins, Young, 1994). Better policies are available than are in place, enforcement is lax or non-existent, and appropriate transportation safety behavior is not uniform or adequate in all population sectors. Indeed, there does not seem to be full public awareness that the safest possible transportation environment for children and adults is not yet in place. Advocacy for appropriate transportation safety technology, policies, and practices is the responsibility of all people concerned about child health. Advocacy is a broad umbrella that includes a range of skills and activities that can be used to create a shift in public opinion and mobilize resources and forces needed to foster change (Wallack, Dorfman, Jernigan, and Themba, 1993, p. 27). A number of organizations provide guidance on advocacy relevant to injury prevention, including the American Public Health Association, the National Center for Injury Prevention and Control of the Centers for Disease Control and Prevention, and the National SAFE KID Program. Effective advocacy for transportation safety requires additional research, substantial public education, and direct action applied in a concerted and lasting fashion (Altman et al, 1994).

References

1. Shaffer, R. Grieving father wants laws changed. *Washington Post.* November 14, 2004: C02. Available at: http://www.washingtonpost.com/wp-dyn/articles/A48448-2004Nov13.html. Accessed February 8, 2005.
2. Sleet DA, Branche CM. Road Safety is No Accident. *Journal of Safety Research.*

2004; 35:173-74. Available at http://www.thecommunityguide.org/mvoi/mvoi-JSR-35-2-173-174.pdf. Accessed March 2, 2005.

3. Anderson RN, Miniño AM, Fingerhut LA, Warner M, Heinen MA. Deaths: Injuries, 2001. Center for Disease Control and Prevention. National Vital Statistics Reports. June 2, 2004; 52(21). Available at: http://www.cdc.gov/nchs/data/nvsr/nvsr52/nvsr52_21acc.pdf. Accessed February 2, 2005.

4. Centers for Disease Control and Prevention. Web-based Injury Statistics Query and Reporting System (WISQARS), Leading Causes of Death Reports, 1999-2002. National Center for Injury Prevention and Control. 2004a. Available at: http://webapp.cdc.gov/sasweb/ncipc/leadcaus10.html. Accessed January 17, 2005.

5. Baker SP, Braver ER, Chen L-H, Pantula JF, Massie D. Motor Vehicle Occupant Deaths Among Hispanic and Black Children and Teenagers. Archives of Pediatrics & Adolescent Medicine. 1998; 152:1209-12. Available at: http://arch pedi.ama-assn.org/cgi/reprint/152/12/1209.pdf. Accessed January 17, 2005.

6. Grossman DC. The History of Injury Control and the Epidemiology of Child and Adolescent Injuries. The Future of Children: Unintentional Injuries in Childhood. 2000; 10 (1):23-52. Available at: http://www.futureofchildren.org/usr_doc/vol10no1Art2.pdf. Accessed January 17, 2005.

7. Centers for Disease Control and Prevention. CDC Injury Research Agenda. National Center for Injury Prevention and Control. June 2002. Available at: http://www.cdc.gov/ncipc/pub-res/research_agenda/. Accessed January 17, 2005.

8. National Highway Traffic Safety Administration. Traffic Safety Facts 2003: A Compilation of Motor Vehicle Crash Data from the Fatality Analysis Reporting System and the General Estimates System Early Edition. DOT HS 809 775. National Center for Statistics & Analysis U.S. Department of Transportation. Washington D.C. 2004a. Available at: http://www-nrd.nhtsa.dot.gov/pdf/nrd-30/NCSA/TSFAnn/2003/TSF2003-Early.htm. Accessed January 17, 2005.

9. Aiko PJV, Kassam-Adams N, Cnaan A, Slate-Sherman E, Gallagher PR, Winston FK. Looking Beyond the Physical Injury: Post-Traumatic Stress Disorder in Children and Parents After Pediatric Traffic Injury. Pediatrics. 1999; 104 (6):1293-99.

10. Williams AF. Teenage drivers: Patterns of risk. Journal of Safety Research. 2003; 34 (1):5-15.

11. National Highway Traffic Safety Administration. National Center for Statistics and Analysis. Motor Vehicle Traffic Fatalities. U.S. Department of Transportation. Washington, D.C.: 2004b. Generated August 11, 2004 by Khorrami Babak (Babak.Khorrami@nhtsa.dot.gov), Information Services Branch.

12. McCartt AT, Shabanova VI, Leaf WA. Driving Experience, Crashes, and Traffic Citations of Teenage Beginning Drivers. Accident Analysis and Prevention. 2003; 35 (3):311-20.

13. National SAFE KIDS Campaign. Childhood Injury Fact Sheet. Washington, D.C.: National SAFE KIDS Campaign. 2004. Available at: http://www.usa.safe kids.org/tier3_cd.cfm?folder_id=540&content_item_id=1213. Accessed October 13, 2005.

14. National Highway Traffic Safety Administration, National Center for Statistics & Analysis. Traffic Safety Facts 2002: Children. U.S. Department of Transportation. Washington, D.C. 2003a. Available at: http://www-nrd.nhtsa.dot.gov/pdf/nrd-30/NCSA/TSF2002/2002chdfacts.pdf. Accessed January 17, 2005.

15. National Highway Traffic Safety Administration, National Center for Statistics and Analysis. Traffic Safety Facts 2003: Children. U.S. Department of Transportation. Washington D.C. 2004c. Available at: http://www-nrd.nhtsa.dot.gov/pdf/nrd-30/NCSA/TSF2003/809762.pdf. Accessed January 17, 2005.

16. National Highway Traffic Safety Administration, National Center for Statistics and Analysis. Traffic Safety Facts 2002: Young Drivers. U.S. Department of Transportation. Washington D.C. 2003b. Available at: http://www-nrd.nhtsa. dot.gov/pdf/nrd-30/NCSA/TSF2002/2002ydrfacts.pdf. Accessed January 17, 2005.

17. Chen IG, Elliott MR, Durbin DR, Winston FK. Teen Drivers and the Risk of Injury to Child Passengers in Motor Vehicle Crashes. *Injury Prevention.* 2005; 11: 12-17.

18. National Highway Traffic Safety Administration, National Center for Statistics and Analysis Traffic Safety Facts 2003: Pedestrians. U.S. Department of Transportation. Washington D.C. 2004d. Available at: http://www-nrd.nhtsa.dot. gov/pdf/nrd-30/NCSA/TSF2003/809769.pdf. Accessed January 17, 2005.

19. National Highway Traffic Safety Administration, National Center for Statistics and Analysis. Traffic Safety Facts 2003: Pedacyclists. U.S. Department of Transportation. Washington D.C. 2004e. Available at: http://www-nrd.nhtsa.dot. gov/pdf/nrd-30/NCSA/TSF2003/809768.pdf. Accessed January 17, 2005.

20. National SAFE KIDS Campaign. Firehouse & Safe Kids Pedestrian Injury. Washington, D.C.: National SAFE KIDS Campaign, 1999. Available at: http:// www.firehouse.com/safekids/factsheets/ped_inj.html. Accessed January 17, 2005.

21. Dewar, R.E. *Vehicle Design. Human Factors in Traffic Safety.* Eds. R. E. Dewar and P.L. Olson. Tuscon, AZ: Lawyers & Judges, 2002.

22. Insurance Institute for Highway Safety. Crash Compatibility: How Vehicle Weight, Type Affect Outcomes. Status Report. February 14, 1998; 33(1). Arlington, VA: Insurance Institute for Highway Safety. Available at: http:// www.hwysafety.org/sr/pdfs/sr3301.pdf. Accessed January 17, 2005.

23. Thomas P, Frampton RJ. Car Size in UK Crashes—The Effects of User Characteristics, Impact Configuration and the Patterns of Injury. *Journal of Traffic Injury Prevention.* 2002;3(4): 275-282.

24. National Highway Traffic Safety Administration, National Center for Statistics and Analysis. Traffic Safety Facts 2000. U.S. Department of Transportation. Washington D.C. 2001.

25. Evans L. *Traffic Safety.* Bloomfield, MI: Science Serving Society. 2004:209-216.

26. Navon D. The paradox of driving speed: two adverse effects on highway accident rate. *Accident Analysis and Prevention.* 2003; 35(3):361–367.

27. Hingston R, Winter M. Epidemiology and Consequences of Drinking and Driving. *Alcohol Research & Health.* 2003; 27(1):63-78.

28. Stutts J, Feaganes J, Rodgman E, et al. Distraction in everyday driving. Prepared for the AAA Foundation for Traffic Safety, Washington, D.C. 2003. Available at: http://www.hsrc.unc.edu/pdf/distraction2003.pdf. Accessed January 7, 2005.

29. Connor J, Whitlock G, Norton R, Jackson R. The role of driver sleepiness in car crashes: a systematic review epidemiological studies. *Accident Analysis and Prevention.* 2001; 33(1): 31–41.

30. Gielen AC. *Injury and Violence Prevention: A Primer.* Patient Education & Counseling. 2002;46: 163-168.

31. Dinh-Zarr TB, Sleet DA, Shults RA, Zaza S, Elder RW, Nichols JL et al. Reviews of Evidence Regarding Interventions To Increase the Use of Safety Belts. *American Journal of Preventive Medicine.* 2001; 21(4 Suppl):48-65.

32. Beck LF, Mack KA, Shults RA. Impact of Primary Laws on Adult Use of Safety Belts—United States, 2002. *JAMA.* 2004;291(19): 2310-11.

33. Calkins LN, Zlatoper TJ. The Effects of Mandatory Seat Belt Laws on Motor Vehicle Fatalities in the United States. *Social Science Quarterly.* 2001; 82(4): 716-32.

34. Centers for Disease Control and Prevention, Task Force on Community Preventive Services. Recommendations for reduce injuries to motor vehicle occupants: increasing child safety seat use, increasing safety belt use, and reducing alcohol-impaired driving. *American Journal of Preventive Medicine.* November 2001; 21(4 Suppl):16-22.

35. Knipling R. Should teenage drivers be electronically monitored? Workshop presented at the 84th Annual Meeting of the Transportation Research Board, Washington DC, January 9-13, 2005.

36. National Highway Traffic Safety Administration. National Center for Statistics and Analysis. Motor Vehicle Traffic Fatalities. U.S. Department of Transportation. 2004f. Washington, D.C. Provided August 5, 2004 by K. Lyn Cianflocco (NCSA.WebMaster@nhtsa.dot.gov), Information Services Branch.

37. Graham MD, Burnett WC, Gibson JL, Freer RH. New Highway Barriers: The Practical Application of Theoretical Design. *Highway Research Record.* 1967;174. Highway Research Board.

38. Wendling WH. Roadside Safety Milestones. 1996 Semisesquicentennial Transportation Conference. Iowa State University. 1996. Available at: http://www. ctre.iastate.edu/pubs/semisesq/session1/wendling/index.htm. Accessed January 17, 2005.

39. American Association of State Highway and Transportation Officials. AASHTO Roadside Design Guide. 3rd ed. Document Number AASHTO RSDG-3. Washington, D.C. 2002.

40. Roadway Safety Foundation. Roadway Safety Guide. Washington, D.C. 2004. Available at: http://www.roadwaysafety.org/toc.html. Accessed January 17, 2005.

41. Transportation Research Board. National Cooperative Highway Research Program Report 500: Guidance for Implementation of the AASHTO Strategic Highway Safety Plan. Washington, D.C. 2004. Available at: http://www4. nationalacademies.org/trb/crp.nsf/All+Projects/NCHRP+17-18(3). Accessed January 17, 2005.

42. Ford Motor Company. Corporate citizenship report 2003-2004: Safety ratings systems. 2004. Available at: http://www.ford.com/en/company/about/ corporateCitizenship/report/principlesSafetyVehicleDoingSystems.htm. Accessed January 17, 2005.

43. Mahmood HF, Fileta BB. Design of Vehicle Structures for Crash Energy Management. Eds. P. Prasad and J.E. Belwafa. Vehicle Crashworthiness and Occupant Protection. Southfield, MI: American Iron and Steel Institute. 2004. Available at: http://www.autosteel.org/AM/Template.cfm?Section=Home& TEMPLATE=/CM/ContentDisplay.cfm&CONTENTID=5944. Accessed January 17, 2005.

44. Chou CC. Fundamental Principles for Vehicle/Occupant Systems Analysis. Eds. P. Prasad and J.E. Belwafa. Vehicle Crashworthiness and Occupant Protection. Southfield, MI: American Iron and Steel Institute. 2004. Available at: http://www.autosteel.org/AM/Template.cfm?Section=Home&TEMPLATE= /CM/ContentDisplay.cfm&CONTENTID=5944. Accessed January 17, 2005.

45. Papelis, Y.E., T. Brown, G. Watson, D. Holtz, and P. Weidong. Study of ESC Assisted Driver Performance Using a Driving Simulator. Iowa City, IA: National Advanced Driving Simulator, 2004. Available at: http://www.esceducation. org/downloads/University_of_Iowa_ESC_Study.pdf>.

46. Stevens, S. L. Developing Guidelines for Designing Child Safety Printed Educational Materials: A User-Centered Approach (Dissertation). Virginia Tech, Blacksburg, VA (2003). Available at: http://scholar.lib.vt.edu/theses/available/ etd-04152003-194333/.

47. Braver, E.R., and S.Y. Kyrychenko. Efficacy of Side Airbags in Reducing Driver Deaths in Driver-Side Collisions. Arlington, VA: Insurance Institute for High-

way Safety, 2003. Available at: http://www.autoalliance.org/archives/sideair bags.pdf.

48. CarTrackers.com. The Next Belt for Passenger Safety: 4—Point Seat Belt Design. (2000). Available at: http://www.cartrackers.com/Buyers_Guide/Consumer_ Advice/Safety/PID.6499.27301969101.1.html>.

49. Edgerton, E. A., K.M. Orzechowski, and M.R. Eichelberger. (2004). Not All Child Safety Seats Are Created Equal: The Potential Dangers of Shield Booster Seats. *Pediatrics*, 113.3 (2004).

50. Kahane, C.J. Fatality Reduction by Safety Belts for Front-Seat Occupants of Cars and Light Trucks. National Highway Traffic Safety Administration, Washington, D.C., 2000. Available at: http://www.nhtsa.dot.gov/cars/rules/ regrev/evaluate/pdf/809199.pdf.

51. Weber, K. Crash Protection for Child Passengers. UMTRI Research Review 31.3 (July-September). University of Michigan Transportation Research Institute, Ann Arbor, Michigan, 2000. Available at: http://www.umtri.umich. edu/library/pdf/rr31_3.pdf.

52. O'Neil, B. Accidents: Highway Safety and William Haddon, Jr. Contingencies. (American Academy of Actuaries), 2002.

53. Laflamme, L., and F. Diderichsen. (2000), Social Differences in Traffic Injury Risks in Childhood and Youth—A Literature Review and a Research Agenda. *Injury Prevention* 6 (2000):293-98.

54. Winston F.K., I.G. Chen, M.R. Elliott, K. B. Arbogast, and D.R. Durbin. Recent trends in child restraint practices in the United States. *Pediatrics* 113.5 (2004): e458-e464.

55. Piani, A.L., and C.A. Schoenborn. (1993). Health Promotion and Disease Prevention: United States, 1990. National Center for Health Statistics. Vital and Health Statistics 10.185 (1993). Available at: http://www.cdc.gov/nchs/data/ series/sr_10/sr10_185.pdf.

56. Greenberg-Seth, J., D. Hemenway, S. Susan, S.S. Gallagher, K.S. Lissy, and J.B. Ross. Factors Associated with Rear Seating of Children in Motor Vehicles: A Study in Two Low-Income, Predominantly Hispanic Communities. *Accident Analysis and Prevention* 36 (2004): 621-26.

57. Ross T.C., A.D. Mickalide, A.R. Korn et. al. Child passengers at risk in America: a national rating of child occupant protection laws. Washington, DC: National SAFE KIDS Campaign, February 2001.

58. Ross T.C., J.M. Colella, A.D. Mickalide AD, et. al. Closing the gaps across the map: a progress report on SAFE KIDS' efforts to improve child occupant protection laws. Washington, DC: National SAFE KIDS Campaign, February 2004.

59. Shope J.T., L.J. Molnar, M.R. Elliott et al. Graduated driver licensing in Michigan: early impact on motor vehicle crashes among 16-year-old drivers. *JAMA* 286 (2001): 1593-8.

60. Foss, R.D., J.R. Feaganes, and E.A. Rodgman. Initial Effects of Graduated Driving Licensing on 16-Year-Old Driver Crashes in North Carolina. *JAMA* 286 (2001):1588-92.

61. McKnight, A.J. and R.C. Peck. Graduate Driver Licensing: What Works? *Injury Prevention* 8(II) (2002):ii32-ii38.

62. Foss, R., and A. Goodwin. Enhancing the Effectiveness of Graduated Driver Licensing Legislation. *Journal of Safety Research* 34:1 (2003): 79-84.

63. Simons-Morton B.G., and J. Hartos. How Well Do Parents Manage Young Driver Crash Risks? *Journal of Safety Research* 34 (2003a): 91-97.

64. Zaza, S., D.A. Sleet, R.S. Thompson, D.M. Sosin, J.C. Bolen, and the Task Force on Community Preventive Services. Reviews of evidence regarding interventions to increase use of child safety seats. *American Journal of Preventive Medicine*

21.4S (2001): 31-47.

65. National Highway Traffic Safety Administration and National Center for Statistics and Analysis, Research and Development. Revised Estimates of Child Restraint Effectiveness. Washington D.C.: U.S. Department of Transportation, 1996.

66. Winston, F.K., D.R., Durbin, M.J., Kallan, and M. R. Elliott. Rear seating and risk of injury to child occupants by vehicle type. *Annual Proceedings of the Association for the Advancement of Automotive Medicine.* 45 (2001): 51–60.

67. American Academy of Pediatrics. Car Safety Seats: A Guide for Families. 2005. Available at: http://www.aap.org/family/carseatguide.htm. Accessed October 21, 2005.

68. National SAFE KIDS Campaign. Kids Buckle Up: Frequently Asked Child Passenger Safety Questions. Washington, D.C.: National SAFE Kids Campaign, 2005. Available at: http://www.safekids.org/content_documents/Public_FAQ-Final.pdf.pdf.

69. Durbin, D.R., M.R. Elliot, and F.K. Winston. Belt-Positioning Booster Seats and Reduction in Risk of Injury Among Children in Vehicle Crashes. *JAMA.* 2003; 289(21): 2835-40.

70. Decina, L.E., and K.H. Lococo. Misuse of Child Restraints. Washington, D.C.: National Highway Traffic Safety Administration, 2003. Available at: http://www.nhtsa.dot.gov/people/injury/research/Misuse/images/misusescreen.pdf.

71. Arbogast, K.B., E.K. Moll, S.D. Morris, and F.K. Winston. Child Occupant Protection: A Summary of Current Safety Recommendations. *Primary Care Update for OB/GYNS* 8.4 (2001): 141-48.

72. National Highway Traffic Safety Administration. Standardized Child Passenger Safety Training Program Participant Manual, 2000. DOT HS 366 R2/00:D-1. United States Department of Transportation, Washington, DC.

73. Cody, B.E., A.D. Mickalide, H.A. Paul, and J.M. Colella. Child Passengers at Risk in America: A National Study of Restraint Use. Washington, D.C: National SAFE KIDS Campaign, 2002.

74. Vivoda J.W., D.W. Eby, and L. P. Kostyniuk. Differences in safety belt use by race. *Accident Analysis and Prevention* 36.6 (2004): 2004.

75. Lerner E.B., D.V.K. Jehle, A.J. IV, Billittie, R.M. Moscati, C.M. Connery, and G. Stiller. The Influence of Demographic Factors on Seatbelt Use by Adults Injured in Motor Vehicle Crashes. *Accident Analysis and Prevention* 33.5 (2001): 659-62.

76. Quinlan K.P., et. al. Characteristics of child passenger deaths and injuries involving drinking drivers. *JAMA* 283.17 (2000): 2249-52.

77. Cody B.E., A.D. Mickalide, and Colella J. Patterns of Incorrect Child Restraint Use, 2001-2002. (Unpublished data). Washington, DC: National SAFE KIDS, 2004.

78. National Highway Traffic Safety Administration. LATCH Makes Child Safety Seat Installation As Easy As 1,2,3. Washington, D.C.: U.S. Department of Transportation, 2002. Available at: http://www.nhtsa.dot.gov/CPS/LATCH/LATCH_PDFs/LATCHeasy. pdf.

79. National Highway Traffic Safety Administration. *2004 Child Safety Seat Ease of Use Ratings.* Washington, D.C. 27 July (2004g). Available at: http://www.nhtsa.dot.gov/CPS/CSSRating/Index.cfm>.

80. Apsler, R., S.W. Formica, and A.F. Rosenthal. Increases in Booster Seat Use among Children of Low Income Families and Variation with Age. *Injury Prevention* 9.4 (2003): 322-25.

81. National SAFE KIDS Campaign. Motor Vehicle Occupant Injury Fact Sheet. Washington D.C.: National SAFE KIDS Campaign, 2004b. Available at: http://

www.safekids. org/tier3_cd.cfm?folder_id=540&content_item_id=1133>.

82. National Highway Traffic Safety Administration. Seat Belts Save Lives: Section IV, Successful Examples. Washington D.C.: U.S. Department of Transportation, 1998. Available at: <http://www.nhtsa.dot.gov/people/injury/airbags/Archive-04/Seatbelt/doomed/Examples>.

83. Centers for Disease Control and Prevention. Motor Vehicle Safety-A 20th Century Public Health Achievement. *Morbidity and Mortality Weekly* 48 (1999): 369-74.

84. Cvijanovich, N.Z., L.J. Cook, M.N. Mann, et al. A Population-Based Study of Crashes Involving 16- and 17-Year-Old Drivers: The Potential Benefit of Graduated Driver Licensing Restrictions. *Pediatrics* 107 (2001): 632-37.

85. Ulmer RG, A. F. Williams, and D.F Preusser. Crash involvements of 16-year-old drivers. *Journal of Safety Research* 28 (1997): 97-103.

86. Williams, A. F., V. Rappold, S.A. Ferguson et al. Seat belt use by high school students. Arlington, VA: *Insurance Institute for Highway Safety* (2002).

87. Insurance Institute for Highway Safety. Recommendations for an ideal graduated licensing law. Status Report 1999. Arlington, VA: *Insurance Institute for Highway Safety* 34 (1999): 6.

88. Williams, A. F. and S.A. Ferguson. Rational for graduated licensing and the risks it should address. *Injury Prevention* (2002) 8.suppl II: ii9-ii13.

89. Mayhew, D.R., H.M. Simpson, and A. Pak. Changes in Collision Rates among Novice Drivers During the First Months of Driving. *Accident Analysis & Prevention* 35.5 (2003): 683-91.

90. Williams, A. F., D.F., Preusser, R.G., Ulmer, and H.B. Weinstein. Characteristics of fatal crashes of 16-year-old-drivers: implications for licensure policies. *Journal of Public Health Policy* 16 (1995): 347-60.

91. Doherty, S.T., J.C. Andrey, and C. MacGregor. The Situational Risks of Young Drivers: The Influence of Passengers, Time of Day and Day of Week on Accident Rates. *Accident Analysis and Prevention* 30.1 (1998): 45-52.

92. Chen L, S.P. Baker, E.R. Braver, and G. Li. Carrying Passengers as a Risk Factor for Crashes Fatal to 16- and 17-Year-Old Drivers. *JAMA* 283.12 (2000): 1578-618.

93. McKenna, F.P., A.E. Waylen, and M. E. Burkes. *Male and Female Drivers: How Different Are They?* AA Foundation for Road Safety Research, 1998.

94. Zador P.L., S.A. Krawchuk, and R.B. Voas. Alcohol-related relative risk of driver fatalities and river involvement in fatal crashes in relation to driver age and gender: an update using 1996 data. *Journal of Studies of Alcohol* 61 (2000): 387-395.

95. Mayhew, D.R. and H.M. Simpson. *The Role of Driving Experience: Implications for the Training and Licensing of New Drivers.* Ottawa, Ontario: Traffic Injury Research Foundation, 1995.

96. Simons-Morton B.G., and J.L. Hartos. Improving the effectiveness of counter measures to motor vehicle crashes among young drivers. *Journal of Health Education* 34.5 (2003b):S57-S61.

97. Williams, A.F., R.S., Karpf, and P. L. Zador. Variations in minimum licensing age and fatal motor vehicle crashes. *American Journal of Public Health* 73 (1983): 1401-02.

98. Arnett J.J. Developmental sources of crash risk in young drivers *Inj. Prev.,* Sep 2002; 8: 17 - 23.

99. Ferguson, S.A., W.A. Leaf, A.F. Williams, et al. Differences in Young Driver Crash Involvement in States with Varying Licensure Practices. *Accident Analysis and Prevention.* 28 (1996):171-80.

100. Farrow, J.A. Young Driver Risk Taking: A Description of Dangerous Driving Situations Among 16- to 19-Year-Old Drivers. *International Journal of Addictions*

22 (1987):1255-67.

101. Simons-Morton, B., Lerner, N. Singer, J. The observed effects of teenage passengers on the risky driving behavior of teenage drivers. *Accident Analysis and Prevention.* 2005, 37 (6), 973-982.

102. Arnett, J. (1992). Reckless behavior in adolescence: A developmental perspective. *Developmental Review,* Vol 12(4), 339-373.

103. Jonah, B.A. Accident Risk and Risk-Taking Behavior Among Young Drivers. *Accident Analysis and Prevention* 18 (1986):225-71.

104. Wasielewski P. Speed as a measure of driver risk: observed speeds versus driver and vehicle characteristics. *Accident Analysis & Prevention,* 16 (1984): 89-103.

105. Romanowicz, P.A., and M.A. Gebers. Teen and senior drivers. Sacramento, CA: California Department of Motor Vehicles, 1990.

106. Hartos, J.L., P. Eitel, D.L. Haynie, B.G. Simons-Morton. Can I Take the Car? Relations Among Parenting Practices and Adolescent Problem Driving Practices. *Journal of Adolescent Research,* 15.3 (2000):352-67.

107. Williams, A. F. Risky driving behavior among adolescents. Ed. R. Jessor R. *New Perspective on Adolescent Risk Behavior.* Cambridge, MA, Cambridge University Press, 1998: 221-237.

108. McKnight, A.J. and A.S. McKnight. Young Novice Drivers: Careless or Clueless? *Accident Analyses and Prevention* 35.6 (2003): 921-23.

109. Gregersen, N.P. (1996). Young drivers' overestimation of their own skill: an experiment on the relation between training strategy and skill. *Accident Analysis and Prevention,* 28 (2), 243-250.

110. Schechtman E, Shinar D, Compton RC. The relationship between drinking habits and safe driving behaviors Transportation Research Part F: Traffic Psychology and Behaviour. March 1999; 2 (1): 15-26

111. O'Malley, P.M. and Johnston, L.D. (1999). Drinking and driving among US high school seniors, 1984-1997. *AJPH* 89, 678-684.

112. Smith, M. F. Research Agenda For An Improved Novice Driver Education Program Report To Congress DOT-HS-808-161. National Highway Traffic Safety Administration, Washington, D.C. (1994, May 31) Available at: http://www.nhtsa.dot.gov/people/injury/research/pub/drive-ed.pdf>

113. Williams, A. F., & Lund A.K. Drinking and driving among high school students. *International Journal of the Addictions* 21 (1986): 643-55.

114. Williams, A. F., K. Weinberg, M. Fields, S. A. and Ferguson. Current requirements for getting a driver's license in the United States. *Journal of Safety Research* (1996) 27: 93-101.

115. Preusser D.F., S. A. Ferguson, A. F. Williams, W.A. Leaf, and C.M. Farmer. Teenage driver licensure rates in four states. *Journal of Safety Research,* 29.2 (1998):97-105.

116. Robertson, L. S., and P. L. Zador. Driver education and fatal crash involvement of teenaged drivers. *American Journal of Public Health* 68 (1978): 959–65.

117. Mayhew, D.R. and H.M. Simpson. The Safety Value of Driver Education and Training. *Injury Prevention* 8(II) (2002):ii3-ii8.

118. Beck, K. H., J., Hartos, and B.G., Simons-Morton. Parental influence on adolescent driving and motor vehicle crash risk. *Health Education and Behavior,* 29.1 (2002): 71-82.

119. Simons-Morton B.G., J. Hartos, and D. Haynie. Application of Authoritative Parenting to Adolescent Health Behavior. Eds. R. DiClemente, R. Crosby, and M. Kegler M. *Emerging Theories and Models in Health Promotion Research and Practice: Strategies for Improving Practice* 2002. San Francisco: Jossey-Bass Publishers, 2002a.

120. Hartos, J.L., P. Eitel, and B.G. Simons-Morton. Do Parent-Imposed Delayed

Licensure and Restricted Driving Reduce Risky Driving Behaviors Among Newly-Licensed Teens? *Prevention Science* 2.2 (2001): 111-20.

121. Hartos, J.L., P. Eitel, and B.G. Simons-Morton. Parenting Practices and Adolescent Risky Driving Behaviors: A Three-Month Prospective Study. *Health Education and Behavior* 29.2 (2002):194-206.

122. Simons-Morton B.G., J. Hartos J, and K. Beck. The Persistence of Effects of a Brief Intervention On Parental Restrictions of Teen Driving Privileges. *Injury Prevention* 9 (2003b): 142-146.

123. Simons-Morton, B.G., J. Hartos, W.A. Leaf, and D. Preusser. The Persistence of Effects of The Checkpoints Program on Parental Restrictions of Teen Driving Privileges. *American Journal of Public Health* (2005).

124. Simons-Morton B.G., J. L., Hartos, and K. Beck. Increased Parent Limits on Teen Driving: Positive Effects from a Brief Intervention Administered at the Motor Vehicle Administration. *Prevention Science* 5.2 (2004): 101-11.

125. Hartos, J.L., T. Shattuck, B.G. Simons-Morton, and K.H. Beck. An In-Depth Look at Parent-Imposed Driving Rules. *Journal of Safety Research.* 2004;35(5):547-55.

126. Hartos, J.L., B.G. Simons-Morton, K.H. Beck, and W.A. Leaf. Parent-Imposed Limits on High-Risk Adolescent Driving: Are They Stricter with Graduated Driver Licensing? *Accident Analysis and Prevention.* May, 2005;37(3):557-62.

127. Beck KH, Shattuck T, Raleigh R, Hartos J. Does Graduated Licensing Empower Parents to Place Greater Restrictions on Their Newly Licensed Teens' Driving? Health Education & Behavior. 2003; 30(6): 695-708.

128. Simons-Morton B.G., J. Hartos J, and W.A. Leaf. Promoting Parental Management of Teen Driving though Persuasion: Impact of the Checkpoints Program on Immediate Outcomes. *Injury Prevention,* 8 (II) (2002b): 24-38.

129. Wallack, L, L. Dorfman, D. Jernigan, and M. Themba. *Media Advocacy and Public Health.* Newbury Park, CA: Sage, 1993.

130. Altman, D.G., F.E. Balcazar, S.G. Fawcett, T.M. Seekins, and J.Q. Young. *Public Health Advocacy: Creating Community Change to Improve Health.* Palo Alto, CA: Stanford Center for Research in Disease Prevention, 1994.

CHAPTER 5

Home Injuries

Eileen M. McDonald, MS,[1]
Deborah C. Girasek, PhD, MPH,[2]*
Andrea Carlson Gielen, ScD, ScM, CHES[1]

We like to think of our home as a retreat; somewhere to unwind, recharge, and most of all—be with our family. It's unsettling to realize, then, that home is also the place where most fatal injuries to infants and toddlers occur. This makes sense though considering that before they enter school, a majority of young children spend their days at their home or that of a caregiver. Older children are most likely to be injured at home during after school hours. With so many parents working outside of the home nowadays, the Census Bureau reports that nearly 7 million school age children are left home alone on a regular basis. It is perhaps not surprising then that more than 4 million children under the age of 19 visit emergency departments for the treatment of home injuries each year,[1] and more than 2500 in this same age group die as a result of injuries sustained in the home.[2]

Children younger than 15 are considered one of two high-risk age groups for unintentional injuries in the home; adults over the age of 70 comprise the other high-risk group. Among children 0 to 14 years old, the leading causes of home injury death are fire/burns, choking/suffocation, drowning/submersion, firearms and poisonings (see Table 1). As children approach adulthood, their risk of dying from injuries suffered at home generally declines, although the risk of unintentional poisoning rises dramatically. Males throughout their lifespan are at higher risk of death from home injury compared to females.

For every home injury death among children younger than 15, there are almost 1500 nonfatal home injuries.[2] Of injuries that result in visits to the emergency department, children ages 0 to 14 experience a higher rate of serious nonfatal home injury than any other age group. Falls are the leading cause of these nonfatal injuries (see Table 2).[3]

* The views expressed are those of the author, who was not writing as a representative of any government agency.
1 Johns Hopkins Bloomberg School of Public Health
2 Uniformed Services University of the Health Sciences

Table 1

Unintentional Home Injury Deaths Involving Children.

Leading Causes of Death, Ranked by Rate (per 100 000 persons), U.S., 1992–1999.

RANK	<1	1–4	5–9	10–14	TOTAL <15
1	Choking/ Suffocation	Fire/burn	Fire/burn	Fire/burn	Fire/burn
2	Fire/burn	Drowning/ Submersion	Drowning/ Submersion	Firearm	Choking/ Suffocation
3	Drowning/ Submersion	Choking/ Suffocation	Choking/ Suffocation	Choking/ Suffocation	Drowning/ Submersion
4	Fall* Poisoning*	Fall	Firearm	Poisoning	Firearm
5	—	Struck by/ Against	Fall	Drowning/ Submersion	Poisoning

From the Home Safety Council, 2004
* Tied as fourth leading cause

This chapter will touch on many of the major threats that children and adolescents face at home: fire/burns, poisoning, falls, choking/suffocation. We will also cover dog bites, which are the third leading cause of children's emergency hospital admissions in the United States.[4] Drowning, nursery products, playground equipment, firearms and violence will be addressed in other chapters.

Each section is organized to give readers a sense of why we have included the topic: its importance, how such injuries occur, what is known about high risk populations and circumstances, as well as what can be done to prevent each type of injury. There are also stories about children, true stories of children who were hurt or killed in their homes. It is important to remember that the statistics in this book represent real families, like that of a 10-year-old from Minnesota who died in the few minutes it took his parents to go pick up his brother. The boy fell as he was riding his bike out of the garage. This is not a tale about wearing bike helmets or checking twice

Table 2

Nonfatal Unintentional Home Injury Resulting in Emergency Department Visits and Involving Children.

Leading Causes of Injury, Ranked by Rate (per 100 000 persons), U.S., 1993–2000.

RANK	<1	1–4	5–9	10–14	TOTAL <15
1	Fall	Fall	Fall	Fall	Fall
2	Struck by/ Against	Struck by/ Against	Struck by/ Against	Struck by/ Against	Struck by/ Against
3	Miscellaneous	Miscellaneous	Cut/pierce	Cut/pierce	Cut/pierce
4	Fire/Burn	Cut/pierce	Miscellaneous	Miscellaneous	Miscellaneous
5	Unspecified	Natural/ Environmental	Natural/ Environmental	Natural/ Environmental	Natural/ Environmental

From the Home Safety Council, 2004

before crossing the street though. David[†] had pushed the automatic garage door opener on his way out of the garage. When his bike fell, the heavy door came down on his throat, entrapping him.[5] Garage doors can come down with three hundred pounds of force. In Canada, it took five people to lift a garage door off one 5-year-old, who was suffocated in the process.[6]

Such tragedies evoke calls for safer products, better supervision, government regulation, and public education. Each of these remedies has a role to play in reducing child home injuries. We will share success stories as well: describing programs that have been documented as effective, and advocacy efforts that have brought about important social change.

Our goal was to work from an evidence base in pulling together the material that follows, but we frequently call for more research or better data. That holds true for home injuries in particular, because a large proportion of injuries are reported to public health authorities with no information about the location of the accident. Therefore we may assume that many estimates of home injuries are underreports of the true scale of the problem. As yet, there is not even one standard definition of what constitutes a "home," for the purposes of scientific research. So while the field of injury prevention and control continues to advocate for more systematically collected and better quality data, some progress is being made to reduce the burden of home injury, as reflected in the information in the pages that follow.

Fire and Burn Injuries

Section Goals

This section focuses on fire and burn injuries, with special attention to residential fires as they are the most common source of burn injuries in children. In addition to outlining the various mechanisms of fire and burn injuries, the section also highlights available countermeasures to prevent or minimize them. Finally, the section ends with a brief review of current research and effective advocacy efforts aimed at reducing fire and burn injuries.

Problem Description

Why are fire and burn injuries important?

Newspaper articles like the one below are not uncommon and tell of the continuing toll wrought by fire and burns injuries. For those lucky enough to survive such events, recovery is often painful, extensive and costly. Treatment for burns has "long been recognized as among the most painful and devastating injuries human beings can sustain and survive."[7]

In 2002, fire departments across the country responded to 401 000 home fires, which took the lives of an estimated 2670 people (not including firefighters) and injured another 14 050.[8] This same year, residential fires caused property damage in excess of $6.1 billion.[9]

Home fires constitute the lion's share of fatal fire and burn events. Cigarettes are responsible for 65% of deaths in fatal home fires in the United States.[10] Children as young as 2 years old have caused home fires

---

† While the injury stories included in this chapter actually happened, the names of the children involved have been changed.

Three Children Die in City Rowhouse Fire:
Woman, 45, injured in leap from second-story window;
No smoke detector found in home.

A baby, a toddler, and a 4-year-old were killed in a fire that ripped through an East Baltimore rowhouse early yesterday, the latest fatalities in a year that has seen a marked increase in city fire deaths.... A 45-year-old woman... was injured after jumping from a second-story window to escape the fire. She suffered a broken femur and back injures.... [A] city Fire Department spokesman said the cause of the one-alarm fire is under investigation. Firefighters could not find a smoke detector in the two-story home. – Baltimore Sun, 3/15/04

---

playing with matches and lighters,[11] products that have been identified as a significant contributor to the fire burden both nationally and internation-ally.[12] Other products ubiquitous to the home environment also either cause fires or can produce burn injuries themselves. These common house-hold items include: wax- and oil-burning candles, stoves and microwave ovens, wood burning stoves and fireplaces,[13] hair curling irons,[14] and elec-trical wires and sockets. Children have been burned by hot grease from cooking.[15] Water and other liquids that reach temperatures above 125 degrees (F) can burn a child in less than one minute.[16] Steam, a common inhalation treatment for upper respiratory tract infections in children, has been implicated in child burn injuries[17] but may not be considered risky by parents, especially if they are following a physician's advice.

Adult caretakers of children may fail to recognize the risks associated with a variety of other products used in and around the home. For example, children have experienced friction burns from treadmills[18] and electrical burns from placing metal chopsticks in electric sockets.[19] Improper use of batteries—either recharging the wrong battery, mixing batteries, or putting batteries in backwards—causes batteries to overheat and rupture. The Consumer Product Safety Commission (CPSC) estimates that 740 children under the age of 16 have been treated in hospital emergency rooms for bat-tery-related chemical burns.[20] More than 4100 children under the age of 15 were treated in hospital emergency departments for firework-related injuries in 2003.[21]

What are fire and burn injuries?

In general, injuries occur to the body when a threshold for absorbing some type of energy is exceeded; this is the case with fire and burn injuries. Different types of energy can be implicated in burn injuries and include thermal (heat), electrical or chemical energy. When thermal energy is in the form of a liquid or steam and it results in an injury, this is usually referred to as a scald burn. Most (69%) fire-related deaths are caused by inhaling the toxic gases produced as fires develop and spread; an addition-al 15% of fire-related deaths are caused by burns.[22,23] Regardless of energy type, burn injuries can be classified either by the percentage of body surface involved (eg, 10%, 45%) or the depth of the skin involved (eg, first-degree through fourth-degree burns). The depth of the burn depends upon the temperature and duration of the heat applied as well as upon characteristics of the skin.

Morbidity and mortality data

Substantial gains have been realized in protecting children from fire- and burn-related deaths. Child mortality rates from fire and burn injuries have declined steadily for the past 20 years. For children ages 1 to 4, death rates per 100 000 have dipped to a low of 1.7 in 2001 compared to 6.1 in 1980 for the same age group. The death rate for older children (5 to 14 years of age) in 2001 was 0.7.[24] While progress has been made, these rates translated into 532 children under the age of 15 who died from fire- and burn-related injuries in the United States in 2001.[25] During the same year, 120 967 children under the age of 15 suffered nonfatal, unintentional fire and burn injuries. More than half of these events occurred among children ages 1 to 4 years old. Among infants (children less than one-year old), fire and burn injuries rank third among the top ten injury events. For both morbidity and mortality, children between the ages of 1 to 4 are particularly susceptible to fire and burn injuries.[26]

Child characteristics linked to fire and burn injuries

Sociodemographic characteristics of the child. A variety of sociodemographic characteristics have been linked to fire deaths. According to the CDC,[26] children younger than 5 years, poor Americans, and persons living in rural areas, are at increased risk for home fire fatalities. Young children may be at increased risk due to their propensity to "play with fire" coupled with their lack of ability to "react appropriately and plan escape."[27] Young children are also at increased fire-death risk because they may need to depend on others for escape. In general, younger children have faster metabolic rates and are less able to physically endure the toxic products of combustion compared to adults. The increased risk for poor Americans and persons living in rural areas may be related to issues of housing quality, heating sources, and access by fire fighters in the event of a fire.

Children's behaviors. Istre and colleagues[28] report that children who engage in "fireplay" (ie, playing with any type of combustible material) are at increased risk for fire and burn injuries. Another study found that children with attention deficit/hyperactivity disorder (ADHD) are at increased risk for burn injuries perhaps due to their compromised impulse control.[29]

Anatomy of the skin. The skin is the largest organ of the body and serves as the first line of defense against trauma and infection. The skin is composed of two main layers—the epidermis and the dermis. Located under the dermis is subcutaneous tissue, such as fat and sweat glands. Muscle and bone reside below that. First-degree burns involve only the epidermis; second-degree burns affect both the epidermis and dermis, and so on. Because the epidermis varies in thickness across the body (eg, thickest on upper back and thinnest on the eyelids), a burn of the same temperature will affect various parts of the body differently.[16] In general, children's skin is thinner than adults and is therefore more susceptible to injury at lower temperatures and more serious injury at higher temperatures compared to adults.

Other characteristics linked to fire and burn injuries

Water temperature. A factor affecting the rate of scald burn is the temperature of the water. Water at 120 degrees (F) will burn a child's skin in 3 minutes compared to 5 minutes for the skin of an adult. Water ten degrees hotter (130 degrees F) will burn a child's skin in about 15 seconds; while water at 140 degrees (F) will burn a child's skin in only 2 ½ seconds.[30]

Parental factors. In a review of the literature regarding parental factors linked to unintentional burn risk, Joseph and colleagues[31] reported an association between child's burn risk and parent's level of education, income, employment status, and marital status, among other variables. At the same time, the authors acknowledge a variety of methodological limitations of the studies reviewed (over-reliance on self-report, single informants, etc) that may minimize these associations and calls for improved methodological approaches to better understand the link between child's burn risk and parental factors.

Alcohol consumption. Although not associated with scald burn risk, alcohol consumption has been linked to an increased risk for fire burn injuries.[32] In a meta-analysis synthesizing U.S. medical examiner studies of non-traffic fatalities at least some of which were home fire deaths, Smith and colleagues found that unintentional injury deaths were tested for alcohol involvement in 84% of cases; among these, 31% of the accident victims were determined to be intoxicated.[33] However, the authors could not report on the role of alcohol in child-related fatalities due to the inconsistent reporting of age across the 65 studies examined in the meta-analysis. In a review of alcohol's contribution to alcohol and fire casualties, the U.S. Fire Administration reported that 15% of children less than 15 years old "died in fires where the surviving adult was impaired by alcohol."[34]

Housing conditions. A variety of factors related specifically to the physical qualities of the home have been linked to injury and include the age of the house and owner occupancy, with older homes[35] and those inhabited by tenants at increased risk for fire and burn injuries.[36] Older homes may be less likely to be in compliance with building codes and inadequate or deferred maintenance can be a problem with rental properties.

Prevention Strategies

Perhaps the best thing we can do to protect our families and ourselves from fire injuries is to ensure that there are working smoke alarms in our homes. The presence of smoke alarms is reported in 95% of homes in the United States and recommendations call for at least one working smoke alarm on each level and in each sleeping area.[37] Smoke detectors have been repeatedly found to be effective, reliable, and inexpensive early warning devices.[38] Compared to homes without smoke alarms, homes with smoke alarms have almost half as many fire-related deaths.[39] The NFPA[37] reports that homes with smoke alarms, regardless of whether they are working, have a mortality rate that is between 40–50% less than the rate for homes without smoke alarms. In fact, the majority of deaths due to house fires occur in the 5% of homes with no smoke alarms. The one situation in which smoke alarms appear to offer no protection from injury or death is during "fireplay" events involving children.[28]

Knowing what to do in the event of a residential fire is another recommended prevention strategy; however, only 16% of residents of homes with smoke alarms have planned and practiced a fire escape plan for themselves or their family.[40] Holmes[41] and Hillman[42] were successful in teaching fire escape skills to children between 7 and 10 years old, but additional research is needed to determine if such skills are protective for burn injuries.

Scald burn prevention skills can be taught to parents and caregivers of young children. In a pilot study that used public health nurse home visits to observe parents' current practices and teach scald burn prevention techniques, Corrarino and colleagues[43] found significant differences four weeks after the intervention. Parents were more likely ($p < .001$) to be practicing more scald burn prevention behaviors, such as reducing water heater temperature to 120°F and removing tablecloths from kitchen tables to avoid inadvertent spills of hot liquids. Passive prevention techniques, such as requiring water heaters to be preset by manufacturers at safe temperatures, play an important role in preventing children from unintentional scald burns.[44] However, preset temperature settings do not completely eliminate the threat of scald burns so interventions that combine education with passive techniques are necessary.

Recent Research Findings

The benefit of smoke alarms cannot be overstated. However, they do emit nuisance alarms, which have been identified as the main reason why their owners disable smoke alarms. A nuisance alarm occurs when the alarm is inadvertently activated without the presence of a real fire. Steam from a hot shower or bath is a known cause of an inadvertent activation; smoke from cooking is another cause of unnecessary nuisance alarms. Berger and Kuklinski[45] strongly recommend that smoke alarm distribution programs switch from ionization smoke alarms to photoelectric smoke detectors which are far less prone to nuisance alarming. In addition, research findings are pointing to the need for developing longer lasting power sources for alarms.[46] Lithium batteries generally last 10 years compared to the six-month life span of 9-volt batteries. Finally, in order to ensure universal protection, research support is mounting for national legislation requiring smoke alarms in all new and existing dwellings. According to Safe Kids, seven states have no comprehensive smoke alarm laws and another 11 states have laws that cover only new dwellings or multi-occupancy units. Research is also needed to determine the impact of interventions designed to teach fire prevention skills to young children.

Advocacy Efforts

Diane Denton, a nurse at the Kosair Children's Hospital in Louisville, Kentucky appealed to the CPSC in 1985 to require that disposable cigarette lighters be child resistant.[47] Nurse Denton's request came after seeing numerous children suffering from burns, talking to their parents about the incidents, and identifying a common culprit—disposable cigarette lighters.[48] Together with members of the burn prevention community, Ms. Denton compiled sufficient evidence to prompt the CPSC to further study the matter. Through their own epidemiological study of the issue during 1986–87, the CPSC estimated that such lighters could be found in 30 million households and that children under the age of 5 years old playing with them caused more than 5000 residential fires, approximately 150 deaths and 1000 injuries.[11] On July 12, 1994, a decade after being prompted by the actions of one nurse, the CPSC issued a product safety standard requiring disposable and novelty cigarette lighters to have a child-resistant mechanism that makes the lighters difficult to operate for children under the age of 5. The passion of a few individuals, coupled with solid data, brought about policy change to keep children safer from one consumer product. This change has been effective in saving lives. Researchers compiled data from 1997–99 about residential fires caused by children younger than 5 playing with cigarette lighters and compared it to similar data from 1985–87 and found a statistically significant reduction (OR = 0.42, p<0.01) that could be attributed to the child resistant lighter standard.[49]

Poisoning

Section Goals

Poisonings and poisoning exposures to children will be explored in this section, including a review of the major causes of poisonings, risk factors, and prevention strategies. As in other sections, research and advocacy efforts will be highlighted. Not addressed in this section are lead poisoning or poisoning resulting from an animal bite (evenomations).

Problem Description

Why are poisonings and poisoning exposures important?

Each year, poison control centers throughout the United States receive emergency calls of suspected and actual poisoning incidents. More than half of these incidents occur among children under the age of 6.[50] Luckily, most calls to poison control centers do not result in a hospital or emergency department visit. In fact, 75% of such calls are managed at the site of the exposure.[51] Nevertheless, the costs related to poisoning deaths and injury are staggering, nearly $21.8 billion for children under the age of 15 alone.[51] The Safe Kids Worldwide campaign also reports that the average cost of hospital treatment for one poisoning exposure is almost $9000.

Unfortunately, poisonings can be fatal. Take for instance the scenario described below:

> A ... father and his 3-year-old daughter died earlier today—and another person was hospitalized—after inhaling carbon monoxide fumes from a portable generator being used to power their home darkened by Hurricane Isabel... Firefighters ... found "high levels" of the odorless gas – more than 1000 parts per million. The gasoline powered portable generator was found in [their] basement...It was turned off but it had been used all night.[52]

What is a poisoning?

A poison exposure is defined as an ingestion of or contact with a substance that can produce toxic effects.[50] And, despite the fact that there is no universally agreed upon definition of a poisoning from either a clinical or epidemiological perspective,[53] we will define a poisoning as the result of "either a brief or long term exposure to a chemical agent" that results in physical harm.[50] Physical harm can range in severity from mild to fatal, and the physical effects of non-fatal injuries caused by poisonings can be temporary in nature or can result in lifelong disability.

This section focuses primarily on acute poisonings in children and will therefore not address the issue of lead poisoning. While an acute condition, foodborne illnesses are not typically considered a form of poisoning and also will not be addressed here.

How do children get poisoned?

When one considers the variety of products found in a typical home, it is quite easy to identify at least one potentially poisonous product likely to be in each room of the house. Just consider these common household items found throughout various rooms in a typical home: oven cleaner in the kitchen; nail polish remover in the bathroom; adult medications in the bedroom; plants in the living room, etc. What follows is a brief review of some of the most common poisonous products encountered by children.

Non-pharmaceutical products. The most frequently reported poison exposures involve non-pharmaceutical products. In a review of the American Association of Poison Control Centers Toxic Exposure Surveillance System (AAPCC TESS), McGuigan[54] identified "cosmetic/personal care products (eg, perfume, cologne and aftershave) (12%), household substances (eg, bleach and alkaline corrosives) (11%), and analgesics (acetaminophen) (8%) as the most frequently cited substances among calls to poison control centers from 1993 to 1997 involving children under the age of 6. Accounting for approximately another one-third of the calls were exposures involving plants (7%), cold and cough medications (7%), topical preparations (5%), antimicrobials (4%), vitamins (3%), gastrointestinal preparations (3%), and insecticides/pesticides (3%). It is important to remember that reported exposures may include both actual incidents as well as suspected ingestions. Regardless, due to the moderate degree of toxicity of these substances, the overwhelming majority of calls (98%) resulted in no or only minor clinical effects.

Unique differences among substances within the same class or category can yield very different clinical outcomes. For instance, while child pediatric multivitamins containing iron rarely result in fatalities due to their low toxicity, adult use multivitamins with iron can result in serious and sometimes fatal iron poisoning in young children.[55]

Pharmaceutical products. Using the AAPCC TESS data set for a different time period, 1990–2000, and for children less than two years of age, Bar-Oz, Levichek and Koren[56] identified medicines that are responsible for *fatal poisonings*. They reviewed all available drugs in North America and identified medicinal preparations that can be fatal for a 10kg toddler (about 22 pounds) upon ingestion of a one-dose unit of the drug (1–2 teaspoons). Included among their top ten fatal drug products were prescription medications for asthma, heart disease, and psychiatric problems. These drugs were responsible for 72% of fatal cases reported to AAPCC TESS from 1990–2000. Iron was implicated in the remaining fatal cases (38%) among children under the age of two.

Categorizing Substances

Solids: medicines, plants, powders, granular pesticides and fertilizers
Liquids: lotions, liquid laundry soap, furniture polish, lighter fluid, and syrup medicines
Sprays: insecticides, spray paint and some cleaning products
Invisibles: gases and vapors, including carbon monoxide

Pesticides. The use of pesticides, insecticides and yard chemicals are ubiquitous in the United States. The Environmental Protection Agency (EPA) identifies 900 pesticides that may be used in the home including insecticides, herbicides, rodenticides and fungicides; 150 of these products were implicated in calls to poison control centers in a two-year period.[57] For children in urban environments, they may be exposed to insecticides that are used to control insects and other infestations in the housing units where they live.[58] Children in rural areas may be exposed to chemicals that are applied in agricultural settings. The need for seasonal applications of pesticides raises concern about the cumulative nature of such exposures to children in these situations.[59] Children can be exposed by the air they breathe, the food they eat, the water they drink, or through other means of contamination.

Carbon monoxide. Carbon monoxide (CO) is a colorless, odorless gas produced from the incomplete combustion of carbon-containing substances. Common sources of CO include wood-burning or gas fire places that are improperly vented, car exhaust, and malfunctioning furnaces, gas space heaters, and stoves.[54] CO is absorbed through the lungs and displaces oxygen in the body. Depending upon the amount and duration of exposure to CO, symptoms can range from headache and dizziness to convulsions and loss of consciousness. Of the more than 16 000 exposures reported to poison control centers in the United States in 2003, 2038 involved children under the age of 6 and 2555 involved children ages 6–19 years.[60]

Morbidity and mortality data

The death toll from unintentional poisoning among young children has dropped dramatically over the last 30 years and is identified as one of the signature successes of the field of injury prevention and control.[61] According to the Poison Prevention Week Council,[62] 216 children under 5 years old died in 1972 while 28 children in this age group died in 2000 from unintentional poisonings, an 87% decrease in fatal childhood poisonings. Between 1992–1999, poisoning deaths among children less than 15 years of age ranked as the fifth leading cause of unintentional injury; 72 deaths were recorded during this time period.[63]

As with all injuries, deaths represent just a small proportion of the problem. Children between the ages of 1 and 4 have the highest rates of nonfatal poisonings (1189 per 100 000) and poisonings requiring an emergency department visit (508.1 per 100 000) compared to all other age groups.[63]

Child characteristics linked to poisoning exposures and injuries

More than half of all poison exposures occur among children under the age of 6. What is it that makes young children so susceptible to poisoning exposures and their resultant injuries?

Developmental characteristics. Children under the age of 5 are most vulnerable to accidental poisoning because they are in the growth and development stages that focus on exploration of their environment.[63] Young children often rely on touch and taste to learn about new things and this increases their risk of ingesting poisons.

Physical characteristics. Size is an important factor in the risk of poisoning, not only weight but height. Compare the ingestion of a single drug tablet in a child who weighs 20 pounds to an adult who weighs 150 pounds. Clearly the concentration of the substance in the child's body is higher than it will be for the heavier adult. Height is important in certain poisoning scenarios, particularly related to poisonous gases. Being lower to the ground may increase a child's exposure to vapor (particularly those that are heavier than air) compared to a taller adult.[59]

Compared to adults, children generally have faster rates of respiration, heartbeats, and metabolism. These developmental features may increase a child's exposure to certain poisons by facilitating their absorption into the child's body.

Other risk factors for poisoning injuries

Other variables come into play and must be considered when addressing the issue of poison prevention among young children.

Supervision of child. Children need adult care and supervision until they are mature enough to navigate the world safely. Parents and caretakers of children may store dangerous products safely but fail to supervise the child adequately when the product is being used.[64] Many children are exposed to harmful substances when those substances are in use by adults (eg, floor cleaner). Children must rely on the assistance of an adult for administration of medications. Research suggests that less than a third of caregivers are able to accurately measure a correct dosage when dispensing over-the-counter medications to their children, which could lead to unintentional poisoning.[65]

Characteristics of product packaging. The United States Poison Prevention Packaging Act of 1970[66] requires certain household chemicals and medicines to be packaged in such a way that it will be difficult for children less than 5 years old to open. Such "child resistant caps" do not guarantee that a child cannot access the contents; however, they do serve as a deterrent and increase the amount of time that it takes a child to open such a container.

When first adopted, the Poison Prevention Packaging Act was limited to aspirin.[67] Other prescription medicines,[68] over-the-counter drug products,[69] and household chemicals[70] have been added to the list of products over the years, broadening the reach and strengthening the impact of the Poison Prevention Packaging Act.

Amount of product available. Once a container with a child-resistant cap is open, the child could potentially access all the contents of the container, creating conditions for a fatal ingestion. The amount of product available in the container is a risk factor for a poisoning injury if the quantity is sufficient to cause harm.

Characteristics of the product. Different substances have different levels of toxicity and need to be taken into consideration when brought into a home with young children. In the event of a poisoning exposure, poorer medical outcomes are associated with higher levels of toxicity.[57] Similarly, products in concentrated form are more likely to cause serious harm to young children.

Other characteristics of a product, namely appearance, taste and smell, can be manipulated to minimize the product's "attractiveness" to a child, possibly minimizing the risk of its unintentional use or ingestion by young children. For instance, one study posited that young children being treated for rat poison ingestion could have mistaken it for a breakfast cereal because the product itself resembled corn meal.[71] Others have noted similarities between candy and various drug products, including iron.[56] In the same vein as adding a smell to improve the detection of natural gas, drug and product manufacturers should be encouraged to add flavors and scents to make products less attractive to young children.

Prevention Strategies

Cabinet locks. As with many injury areas, primary prevention is an important focus and a variety of countermeasures are available for averting poisoning exposures and poisonings. Many countermeasures require action and vigilance on the part of adult caretakers of children. Safety advocacy groups consistently recommend, for instance, that household poisons be stored in cabinets and drawers that close with locks or latches.[65] However, a recent survey of homes where children younger than 6 live or visit, medicines were easily accessible to children; respondents reported keeping medicines out in the open (33%), in an unlocked drawer or cabinet (82%) and in their purse (43%).[72]

Packaging. Another important step adults can take to minimize a child's risk of unintentional poisoning is to request the use of child-resistant containers on all their prescription medications. Numerous studies indicate that the Poison Prevention Packaging Act of 1970 and child-resistant packaging significantly reduce the morbidity and mortality of childhood poisonings.[67,73] Similarly, when adults buy any hazardous products that will be used in the home (eg, household cleaners, over-the-counter preparations), they should carefully consider the toxicity and packaging of the product.

Packaging is an important prevention consideration. Unit-dose packaging,[74] also known as unit-of-use packaging, encases one pill or unit of medication in a see-through plastic blister. To access the pill, the consumer simply pushes it through the paper or foil backing. Child resistant features can be integrated into such packaging by increasing the toughness of the backing material. The potential for fatal ingestions is minimized because access to fatal amounts of the medicine is limited.

An aspect of packaging that is less clear in protecting children is warning labels that are directed to children, commonly referred to as "Mr. Yuk." First created by the National Poison Control Center in Pittsburgh, "Mr. Yuk" is a bright green picture of a scowling face with a protruding tongue designed to be placed onto containers of harmful substances. "Mr. Yuk" stickers are well known among many parents and are frequently perceived as an effective countermeasure to protecting children from hazardous substances. However, one study of 2-year-olds showed no effect in reducing poisonings with the use of "Mr. Yuk" stickers.[75] A second study of children age 12 to 30 months showed an actual increase in the children's handling of medicines labeled with "Mr. Yuk" stickers.[76] Children at these young ages appear to be attracted to the colorful stickers, thus potentially increasing their risk of poisoning.

Syrup of ipecac. Once previously recommended by pediatric and poison control groups, syrup of ipecac, a pharmaceutical agent that induces vomiting, is now contraindicated for home use.[77] This change in policy and practice was brought about by several factors, including the dramatic decrease in childhood poisonings over the last 40 years and recent research evidence that failed to show a benefit for children who were treated with it.[78]

CO detectors. Proper maintenance of potential sources of carbon monoxide in the home is perhaps the best way to avoid carbon monoxide poisoning. Designed as an early warning device, carbon monoxide alarms offer another layer of protection by sounding a loud warning when carbon monoxide surpasses a safe threshold. Two studies reviewed deaths classified as unintentional carbon monoxide poisoning and estimated the number of deaths that could have been saved had a carbon monoxide alarm been in use[79,80]; however, no studies exist that examine the effectiveness of carbon monoxide alarms.[81]

Poison control centers. In the United States, poison control center staff are available 24-hours per day at an emergency hotline to dispense information and treatment advice. In 2002 alone poison control centers fielded more than 2.38 million such calls.[82] Poison control centers have been identified as the "lead agencies in the pursuit of poisoning control and prevention" and are well positioned to provide specialized services to both the general public and health professionals alike.[82] Among the other non-emergency services performed by poison control centers are public education, professional education, data collection and management and information and referral resources. Miller and Lestina[83] found that the average public call to a poison control center prevented $175 in other medical spending.

Until recently, access to the nation's 70 poison control centers was "hampered by a confusing array of telephone numbers and disjointed local prevention efforts."[50] Today, due to recent legislation, there is one nationwide toll-free number—1(800) 222-1222—that routes people to their closest regional center.

Recent Research Findings

While recent legislation is streamlining some aspects of poison control centers in the United States, a recent report by the Institute of Medicine (IOM)[84] outlines significant additional steps that are needed to create a truly coordinated and comprehensive national system for poison control and prevention. Included among the 12 specific recommendations are that all poison control centers should perform a core set of functions, be better integrated into the public health system, and be supported by sufficient and stable funding to fulfill their mission. The IOM report also identifies new realities of the 21st century including public health preparedness needs, especially those related to bioterrorism and chemical terrorism.

Another challenge for poison control centers across the country is to provide services to non-English speaking populations.[85] Creating awareness of poison control centers within non-native English speaking groups will likely be enhanced through culturally appropriate education, outreach efforts, and innovative use of technology. Kelly and colleagues[86] created a 9-minute videotape (available in both English and Spanish) that described general information about the poison control centers' hours and staff and depicts a poisoning scenario with an Hispanic family and one with an African American family. The study improved the knowledge, attitudes, behaviors and behavioral intentions regarding the use of poison control centers among low-income and Spanish-speaking parents.

An area that could benefit from additional investigation is the effectiveness of community-based models for injury prevention to compliment the educational,[81] regulatory,[69] and legislative[66] efforts that have contributed greatly to the reduction in poisonings among children. Nixon and colleagues[87] characterize community-based models as having shared ownership of the injury problem and its solution by members of the community and injury prevention experts. These researchers argue that "successful implementation of a poisoning prevention program in communities depends upon embedding the countermeasures in the contextual practices of social structures and that a multi-strategy program for preventing childhood poisoning is essential." A comprehensive review of the literature by these authors yielded no examples of such work.

Advocacy Efforts

The role of data has been central to reducing the death toll from unintentional poisoning among young children by contributing to the identification of the problem as well as to the creation and dissemination of effective solutions. Few people know the name Homer A. George, a Missouri pharmacist whose concern about the lack of pharmaceutical information in the 1950s is credited with the national public awareness campaign, Poison Prevention Week, which still exists today.[88] Troubled by missing or misleading information about pharmaceutical products, George convinced his town's mayor (1958) and later his state's governor to proclaim a Poison Prevention Week (PPW) to bring attention to preventable deaths and injuries caused by poisonings. By 1961, President John F. Kennedy signed legislation creating the Poison Prevention Week Council. By 1966, almost every state had some type of campaign to improve the public's understanding of childhood poisonings, which continues today to educate parents and caretakers of young children.

The establishment of the first poison control center in Chicago, Illinois in 1953 began a chain of events that has lead to the current system of regional poison control centers across the entire United States. Toward the end of the 1950s, another critical information need was beginning to be met—textbooks on emergency advice and treatment for poisoning victims became available,[89] in part because of the experience and data being collected in poison control centers around the country. Four decades later, the passage of the 1970 Poison Prevention Packaging Act—which ultimately has resulted in numerous hazardous pharmaceutical and other household products being in child-resistant containers—has been credited with the clear declines in poisonings and with preventing poisoning exposures.[90]

Falls

Section Goals

This section focuses on falls in the home, which can have dire consequences for children. Many serious fall injuries among young people occur on playgrounds and during sports and recreational activities, and these topics are discussed in other chapters. Here we focus on the most common causes of fall injuries to children in the home—stairs, furniture, and windows. As will be described, there are different risks for different age children, but there are effective and promising prevention strategies for all of these sources of fall injuries.

Problem Description

Why are falls important?

In 2001, falls caused 209 deaths and 2 944 395 emergency department visits among children and teens (birth to 19 years).[91] The enormous costs associated with fall injuries include those associated with the millions of emergency department visits as well as the additional burden of long hospital stays and rehabilitation for survivors, but, more importantly the burden of human suffering must be considered, as these real life examples suggest.

Eric Clapton wrote the famous song "Tears in Heaven" after the death of his son, Conor Clapton, who died at the age of 4 on March 20, 1991. He fell from a 53rd floor window in New York City, landing on the adjacent roof of a 4-story building. Although high rise apartments were required by a 1984 law to have window guards, condominium buildings, such as the one Conor Clapton lived in were exempt.[92]

In 1998, a happy 4 and one half-year-old by the name of Julie Rein was at home looking out a second-story window with her brother. They were watching their sister playing outdoors when Julie stepped up on the windowsill to get a better view. When she pressed against the screen, it suddenly came loose causing her to fall onto the driveway below. She suffered serious brain injury and was in a pediatric intensive care unit on a ventilator, partially paralyzed and in a coma for 13 days. Following months of intensive physical, occupational, speech and language therapy, Julie fully recovered and was able to enroll in kindergarten with her friends.[93]

What is a fall injury?

A fall is an event that results in a person coming to rest inadvertently on the ground or floor or other lower level.[94] Falls can occur on the same level as when a child trips or loses his balance, or falls can occur from one level to another as when a child falls from a window, down the stairs, or off furniture. When these events result in seeking medical care or are fatal, they are coded as fall injuries.

How do children get injured by falls?

The degree to which an injury results from a fall depends upon many factors. Most important to consider are the distance of the fall and the type of landing surface. The shorter the distance and the greater the energy-absorbing surface, the less severe the injury is likely to be. Individual differences in anatomy also affect fall injuries. Bone structure and fat composition affect injury severity and depend in part on the individual's age. Because an infants' heads are proportionally larger relative to their bodies and because their bones are still soft, they are particularly susceptible to both falling over and to suffering serious head injuries as a result.[95-97]

Morbidity and mortality data

Although falls represented only 1.7% of all unintentional injury deaths among children from birth to 19 years in 2001, they represented 30.4% of all non-fatal unintentional injuries and they are the leading cause of non-fatal injury for children up to 15 years.[91] The largest proportion of deaths (42%) occurred among teens 15–19, followed by 0–4 year olds (26%). The largest proportion of emergency department visits occurred among 0–4 year olds (35%), with teens accounting for the lowest proportion (15%). Fall death rates per 100 000 population were 0.43 for teens 15-19 and 0.28 for 0–4 year olds. The opposite pattern is seen for emergency visits, where the rate for teens is 2182 compared to 5367 for 0–4 year olds. According to an analysis of data on children younger than 15 by Ballesteros and colleagues,[98] for every child injury death due to falls, there are 19 000 non-fatal fall injuries seen in an emergency department.

Fall injuries that occur in the child's home and require medical attention are estimated to be 1.5 million annually among children younger than 15.[99] Interestingly, this number is 2.5 times larger than the next leading cause of home injury (which is being struck). According to the Safe Kids Worldwide, more than 80% of fall injuries to children younger than 4 years old occur in the home environment.[100] In an analysis specifically focused on unintentional home injuries from 1993–2000, the Home Safety Council found that among all children the rate of falls seen in emergency departments is highest for children younger than 5 (3756/ 100 000 for boys; 3001/100 000 for girls). In fact, this age group experiences non-fatal fall injuries in the home at a rate that is second only to that observed in the elderly population.[101]

Risk factors for fall injuries

Characteristics of both the child and the environment have been identified as risk factors for fall injuries in the home. In this section, we highlight some of the most prominent ones.

Child's age and development. The data presented above demonstrate the increased fall risk among children younger than 5. In fact, there are many developmental stages that children go through from birth to five, each of which confers its own unique risks.

In the first year of life, babies go from being reflexive and unable to control their body to becoming mobile but having generally poor balance. In these early stages, infants are at risk of wiggling off a changing table or other surfaces, and as they learn to walk and run they are naturally prone to falling. From about one year to three years, children's balance improves, they learn to climb and run, and they assert their independence while at the same time being able to follow only simple directions. This combination of attributes can be particularly hazardous as children try things that are beyond their skill level, such as climbing on furniture or running on uneven pavement, both of which pose serious fall risks.

Preschoolers and young children become increasingly independent, develop the ability to understand relationships between objects and begin to understand danger as well as warnings. They typically can understand a specific risk but may not be able to generalize to new situations. Children at these ages are still susceptible to fall injuries from their increased independence and the amount of time at play in or around the home.

Environmental risk factors. The physical environment is particularly relevant for fall injuries. In an analysis of the ten leading products ranked by percentage of nonfatal home injury costs in the United States in 2000, Zaloshnja and colleagues[102] identified beds as the leading product for children younger than 5, followed closely by stairs, floors, and tables. Bicycles were number one for children 5–14; interestingly trampolines also rated highly for this age group. While these analyses focused on all causes of nonfatal injuries, the nature of the products is strongly suggestive that falls would be the cause of many of them.

Products specifically made for children can also be hazards. Baby walkers, commonly used to provide ambulation for children before they learn to walk, have been found to account for more injuries among young children than any other nursery product.[103] Between 1973 and 1998, 34 infant walker-related deaths were reported.[103] The CPSC estimated that in a single year, 1997, walkers were involved in 14 300 emergency department visits due to injuries among children younger than 15 months. Caregivers often think that walkers help their baby learn to walk earlier and that they can properly supervise their child in the walker. In reality, baby walkers have no known developmental benefit and at least one study found a detrimental effect in terms of developmental delays.[96,104,105] Moreover, in a study by Chiaviello and others,[95] 69% of children injured in walkers were being supervised by an adult at the time, which is not surprising because babies in walkers can move at a speed of 3 feet/second making it very difficult to provide adequate supervision.

Other important fall hazards in the home environment include stairways and windows above ground level. Handrails on stairs offer some protection, yet a recent national survey found that 43% of homes with young children and stairs did not have banisters or handrails.[101] Stair gates are recommended for homes with infants and toddlers, yet their use does not appear to be widespread. Two studies of households in low-income urban environments found that one-quarter to one-third of families with young children were observed to be using stair gates.[106,107]

In a recent surveillance study in Dallas County, Texas, Istre and colleagues[108] studied falls from apartment balconies and windows among 98 children younger than 15. The two important environmental hazards identified were balcony railings more than 4 inches apart and windows that were within 2 feet of the floor. Window locks or safety guards are recommended for homes with floors above ground level, yet a national survey recently found that 73% of households in which children live or visit did not have such devices installed.[101]

The placement and type of furniture in the home is also relevant for fall injuries. For example, beds or other furniture placed under a window can be an enticement to young children that allows them access to an open window. Furniture with sharp edges can increase the risk of serious injury when children fall. There is an increased risk of injury and more serious injury from bunk beds relative to conventional beds.[109,110] The Consumer Product Safety Commission recommends that they not be used with children younger than 6 years of age.[111]

Prevention Strategies

There are myriad prevention strategies for fall injuries consistent with the vast array of risk factors. These include: eliminating the use of dangerous products, caregiver supervision and increased use of safety products, and modification of the living environment.

Banning the manufacture of mobile baby walkers and eliminating their use as supported by the American Academy of Pediatrics[105] is an example of the first strategy. Issuing regulations for safer product design as was done by the Consumer Product Safety Commission for bunk beds[112] and baby walkers[113] is another. Making caregivers aware of the fall risks and what they can do to prevent them—using age appropriate and safe products, using safety devices, and close supervision—is also an essential prevention strategy. It is worth noting that even when safer products have been introduced to the market, there is typically a lag time in which many of the unsafe products are still in use, and available at second-hand retail outlets. Modifying the living environment could happen through manufacturing redesign (eg, more energy absorbing flooring in homes, counters with rounded corners), but more typically the consumer must re-design their own living environment by making safety-conscious choices when furnishing their homes or by installing safety products (eg, well padded non-skid rugs, padded furniture corner guards).

Recent Research Findings

New research on how to protect children from fall injuries is emerging through studies that seek to understand the psychological determinants of parental safety practices[114] as well as intervention trial results.[115] Research by Morrongiello and Major[116] found that risk compensation does occur, in that parents report being more permissive with risk taking (including during climbing, jumping, and running activities) when in safer environments, when wearing safety gear and when they are perceived to be more experienced. The Cochrane Library contains a systematic review of interventions that attempted to modify the home environment,[115] which included fall related injuries among other topics. While the majority of studies with fall related outcomes were focused on older adults, several focused on children. Clamp and others[117] did find significant effects for "safe practices for windows" and our study[106] found significant increases in use of stair gates as a result of our interventions that included safety counseling by a pediatrician and use of a Children's Safety Center in the clinic setting where low cost safety products are available for purchase.

Advocacy Efforts

Two particularly noteworthy advocacy efforts to reduce children's in-home fall injuries are the window guard legislation in New York City and the baby walker ban in Canada. The role of solid data in stimulating a policy change is clear in these two examples.

Data available in 1976 demonstrated that window falls accounted for 12% of unintentional childhood injury deaths among children younger than 15. A pilot program that included distribution of free window guards and education about their importance resulted in a 35% reduction in deaths due to window falls and a 50% reduction in fall incidents.[118] In response to the data on the injury problem and the effectiveness of window guards, the New York City Board of Health passed a law requiring owners of multi-story buildings to provide window guards in apartments where children 10 years and younger lived. A reduction of up to 96% in admissions to local hospitals for window fall injury followed, making this combination of legislation, education, and free products a remarkable success in protecting children.[119] A voluntary program in Boston achieved significant reductions in fall injuries,[120] but generally, few other ordinances have been passed.[97]

On April 7, 2004, the Minister of Health Pierre Pettigrew announced that Canada would be the first country in the world to ban the sale, advertisement and importation of baby walkers in Canada. A voluntary retail industry ban on baby walkers had been in place since 1989, but recent years had seen an increase in the number of these products and injuries to children. Safe Kids Canada estimated that as many as 1000 Canadian children were injured each year using baby walkers, and in response they launched a successful letter-writing campaign in support of a ban.[121]

Choking/Suffocation Injuries

Section Goals

In this section we describe the variety of airway injuries that children experience from events and products in their homes. Three types of airway injuries are at issue—choking on objects or foods such that the airway is internally obstructed; suffocation, in which there is an external obstruction such as an object that covers the mouth and nose; and strangulation, in which external compression such as from strings around the neck or head entrapment causes the injury. All three of these are included under the typically used rubric of "choking/suffocation."

Section Goals

Why are choking/suffocation injuries important?

Airway obstruction injury is the leading cause of unintentional injury death among infants under age 1, and it remains among the 10 leading causes of injury deaths throughout childhood.[122] Stories like the following are, sadly, not uncommon.

'The baby's dying! He's dying! He's choking!' Family trip to the movies turns tragic when 3-year-old chokes to death on his popcorn. The article in the New York Daily News went on to report:

> The movie was only a few minutes old when Jody Green knew something was horribly wrong. Her 3-year-old son started gasping for air, choking to death on a mouthful of popcorn.... Despite the heroic efforts of a nurse, cops and paramedics, little Robert Green died minutes later.[123]

In August 2000, the Consumer Product Safety Commission announced that Kentucky Fried Chicken was voluntarily recalling 425 000 Tabled Treeples toys included with their kids' meals when a 19-month old girl nearly suffocated on the toy's container. The bottom of the plastic container was stuck over the child's nose and mouth causing her distress. Luckily, her mother was able to remove it, but the container was recalled because it posed a suffocation hazard to children younger than three.[124]

What is a choking/suffocation injury?

There are three types of airway injuries of concern for children. Suffocation occurs when an object covers the child's nose and mouth. Strangulation occurs when something compresses the child's neck making him unable to breathe, which can happen from cords being wrapped around the neck or from a head entrapment. Choking occurs when a small object gets lodged in the child's throat or windpipe. In each of these types of airway injuries, breathing is partially or completely obstructed. When the airway is completely blocked oxygen is prevented from getting to the lungs and the brain. When the brain is deprived of oxygen for more than four minutes brain damage or death may occur.[125–127]

How do choking/suffocation occur in children?

Many activities and products that are a normal part of every child's daily life can pose a hazard for airway obstruction injury. For example, 60% of infant suffocation occurs in the sleeping environment—infants can suffocate when their faces become wedged against something soft in the crib or if someone they are sleeping with rolls over on them.[128]

The most commonly cited strangulation hazards include cords on children's clothing or on window blinds that infants or toddlers have access to, as well as cribs with improperly spaced slats and toy chests with improper latching mechanisms. Product modification and caregiver vigilance can reduce these risks in the child's environment.

Foods are the most common choking hazard for young children, and include small round foods such as hot dogs, candies, nuts, grapes, carrots, raisins and popcorn. Toys and other small objects are also commonly encountered choking hazards, and round objects like coins and marbles or those that conform to the shape of the windpipe like balloons are particularly hazardous.

In a national study of nonfatal choking episodes treated in emergency departments among children younger than 14, 59.5% were due to food products, 12.7% were due to coins and 18.7% were due to other non-food products.[129] Toy balloons were the product most frequently responsible for deaths in a 10-year study of fatal aspirations among children younger than 14 in Cook County Illinois.[130]

When an object partially blocks the windpipe, the child's cough or gag reflex will usually clear it without any intervention. However, immediate action is required if the child stops breathing or crying; has a weakening cough that becomes wheezing or gasping; or starts turning blue in the face. Knowing the proper emergency response to an airway injury event is critical for caregivers of young children.[126]

Morbidity and mortality data

In 2001, unintentional choking/strangulation injuries killed 614 infants and an additional 250 children ages 1–14.[91] There were also an estimated

17 537 children aged less than or equal to 14 years who were treated in emergency departments just for choking-related episodes.[131]

Airway obstruction incidents are particularly lethal. Ballesteros and colleagues[98] found that the ratio of emergency department visits to deaths for these types of injuries was 14:1 for children from 0-14 years old, making airway obstruction injuries the second most lethal type of childhood injury, just behind drowning which had a ratio of 6:1.

The Home Safety Council's recently published analysis of injuries in the home provides the most current information on the national scope of the problem.[101] When location of the airway injury death was recorded (which is true for only 40% of all such deaths), 65% occurred in the home. When location of non-fatal airway injuries that required emergency department treatment was recorded (in 43% of the cases), the vast majority—94%—occurred in the home. While these data are for all age groups, children (especially those younger than five years) tend to spend much of their time in and around their homes. On average, the annual total number of home choking/suffocation deaths among 0–14 year olds is 496, with 24 131 non-fatal events occurring and resulting in an emergency department visit.

In addition, children ages 0–5 years old experience the highest rate of both fatal and non-fatal choking/suffocation injuries in the home. For boys the death rate is 2.6 and for girls it is 1.9 per 100 000 population. The rate of non-fatal choking/suffocation injuries that required an emergency department visit among boys is 100.3 and among girls it is 92.9 per 100 000 population.[101]

Risk factors for choking/suffocation

Characteristics of both the child and his/her environment are linked to the occurrence of choking/suffocation injuries.

Child characteristics. Infants from birth to one year have a large head relative to the size of their body, and they have limited ability to control their body movements. These characteristics combine to put them at risk for getting into deadly situations from which they cannot extricate themselves. For example, infants can go feet first through a small opening and strangle; this could happen in an older crib with slats that are too far apart (i.e., > 2 ⅜ inches). Infants can also suffocate by becoming wedged into a tight space or rolling face down onto a soft surface and being unable to move.

Mouthing and teething behaviors in infancy also put children at risk for choking, and as their curiosity and mobility increase as toddlers their exposure to choking/strangulation hazards increases. At these early ages, children have small airways as well, which makes them easy to block but difficult to resuscitate. Foods that can choke a small child include many widely available products such as grapes, hot dogs, and popcorn.

Hazardous features on products such as cribs, adult beds and bunk beds, window cords, toy chests, and clothing with drawstrings have been documented to cause serious strangulation injury or death to children. Only a few pounds of force on the blood vessels of a small child's neck can cause strangulation. Most young children cannot untwist a cord or strap, nor can they extricate themselves if they become entrapped.[132]

Combining the increased exploratory behavior and growing independence as toddlers become preschoolers with a lack of ability to assess risk and understand danger makes the years from birth to five extremely hazardous for choking/strangulation.

Older children have more independence, play with other children, and often engage in make-believe play. Yet their cognitive abilities are still limited with regard to awareness of risk and danger, and being able to generalize from one risky situation to a new one. Playtime activities can easily become dangerous because so many products that are part of the adult home environment may be attractive but hazardous for child play (eg, coins, cords such as window blinds).

Environmental risk factors. As the above discussion suggests, the characteristics of the child's environment are critical determinants of choking/strangulation risk. Foods that are served, household products and toys that are accessible and availability of adult supervision are all elements of the environment that influence risk. Some of the most commonly cited hazards are described in this section.

Foods. The size, consistency and shape of food influence its likelihood of being a choking hazard. A landmark 1984 study published in *JAMA*[133] reported on an analysis of national data on child choking deaths over a three-year period and identified the hazards of round foods including hot dogs, candy, nuts, and grapes. Morley and colleagues[134] analyzed data from 51 children younger than 3 who were treated for a foreign body aspiration and found that nuts, raw carrots and popcorn accounted for 64% of the aspirations. These authors note that before 2 years of age, children are poorly equipped to grind and swallow hard, crunchy food because they lack second molars and are still adjusting to the descent of the larynx.

Toys and Household Products. Myriad products in the home environment can be choking/suffocation hazards to children. To assess which are particularly risky, Rimell and colleagues[135] conducted a review of 165 children who underwent endoscopy for foreign body aspiration or ingestion and 449 deaths due to choking. Foods and coins were the most commonly removed objects in the nonfatal cases. Among those children who died, balloons caused 29% of the deaths overall, 33% of the deaths among children younger than 3 years, but 60% of the deaths among children older than 3 years. Lifshultz and Donoghue[136] analyzed 10 years of cases at the Cook County Medical Examiner's Office in which deaths in children 0–14 years were due to aspiration of foreign objects. Toy balloons were responsible for more fatal aspirations than any other product. Data from autopsy examination of a series of 5 children who died from aspirating a balloon indicated that the common scenario is the child playing with an un-inflated balloon, sucking or mouthing it.[137] Other products identified as choking hazards include marbles and small balls, toys with small parts or toys that can compress to fit entirely into a child's mouth, pen and marker caps, small batteries, and medicine syringes.[138]

Other types of products pose suffocation and strangulation risks. The Consumer Product Safety Commission is the primary source for information on hazardous products. Here are some of the most relevant products related to the discussion of suffocation and strangulation in children. All information about these products is fully described on the CPSC website (www.cpsc.gov)

Bedding. From January 1, 1999, to December 31, 2001, the CPSC learned of more than 100 deaths of children younger than 2 who suffocated in adult beds. Nearly all of the children, 98%, were babies under 1 year old. In 1992, the CPSC banned infant cushions (soft, loosely fitted with a granular material that conform to the face or body of an infant) that were involved in 36 infant suffocations.

Strings and cords. The CPSC has received reports of two to three deaths annually to children under two years old who were strangled by strings, cords, ribbons, or necklaces around their necks. Most of the deaths involved pacifiers tied around the child's neck. From 1985–1999, CPSC received reports of 22 deaths and 48 nonfatal incidents involving the entanglement of the drawstrings on the child's clothing. From 1991 to 2000, CPSC received reports of 160 strangulations involving cords on window blinds: 140 strangulations involved the outer pull cords, and 20 involved the inner cords that run through the blind slats.

Toy Chests. The CPSC knows of 45 children who died when lids of containers used for toy storage fell on their heads or necks; there have been at least three incidents of permanent brain damage.

Accordion-Style Baby Gates. The CPSC warns of an entrapment and strangulation hazard that exists with accordion style baby gates manufactured prior to February 1985. V-shaped openings along the top edge and diamond shaped openings in the sides can entrap a child's head. CPSC knows of 9 deaths and 25 "near misses."

Prevention Strategies

Small, round or hard foods are to be avoided. For example, hot dogs can be difficult to chew and they are the perfect shape to form a plug in the child's throat. Soft, smooth textured foods that are easy to chew are best for young children. The American Academy of Pediatrics recommends cutting foods for infants and young children into pieces no larger than one-half inch. Round foods like hot dogs and grapes should be cut lengthwise to reduce their plug-like qualities. See the table for a list of foods to avoid; these items are generally agreed to be dangerous for young children. However, the recommended age for being able to serve them varies: The American Academy of Pediatrics recommends age 4, whereas the Safe Kids Worldwide recommends age 6.

Warning labels on toys and household products should be read and treated seriously. Toys labeled as choking hazards for children younger than 3 years should be kept away from infants and toddlers. As older siblings begin to understand directions, they should be taught to participate on keeping the environment safe for their younger brothers

---

Foods Considered Choking Hazards for Young Children

Hot dogs
Nuts and seeds
Whole grapes
Hard, gooey, or sticky candy
Popcorn
Raw vegetables
Chunks of meat or cheese
Chunks of peanut butter
Raisins
Chewing gum

American Academy of Pediatrics, www. medem.com/medlb/article_ detaillb_for_ printer.cfm?article_ID= ZZZ8QH03B7C

and sisters. Warnings and instructions on other household products (eg, cribs, bunk beds, toy chests) should be inspected and followed as well. Older models of dangerous products (eg, toy chests with self closing lids, infant cushions) should be removed and destroyed. Purchases made at second hand shops or yard sales need to be carefully inspected to make sure that the product has not been recalled or identified as dangerous (eg, jackets with drawstrings). The CPSC website (www.cpsc.gov) or help line [800-638-2772, (TTY 800-638-8270)] can be very helpful in determining the safety of children's products.

Because of the immediacy of the risk when a child is choking, prompt intervention can be lifesaving. Therefore, adult caregivers should be trained in infant/child CPR.

Beyond what individuals can do to protect their children, everyone can be encouraged to become involved in promoting safer products. If there is an incident (a death or near miss) or a concern about a dangerous product, it should be reported to the CPSC. Local community groups can organize events to collect and destroy old unsafe products. Groups that have access to parents of young children (eg, childbirth classes, parenting groups, pediatric care providers) should take whatever steps available to them to alert families to the dangers of choking/strangulation in young children and instruct them in ways to avoid the risks. Increased access to CPR training could also help reduce the risk to children.

Recent Research Findings

Childhood suffocation/choking is a complex topic because of the myriad ways in which these injuries occur and the variation in underlying causes as children age. Moreover, limited research appears in the standard medical/public health databases like Medline. Two issues stand out in the recent research. First, new hazards are continually being identified. Second, there is some controversy over safety issues in the sleep environment for infants.

First, a recent report in Forensic Science International, detailed the death of a 2-year-old girl who asphyxiated when she swallowed a bitten-off piece of her pacifier while napping.[139] Another example comes from the Cook County Medical Examiner's Office, which reported on a 10-year-old boy who was accidentally hanged by the lanyard key chain he was wearing when it got caught on the bedpost of the bed he was jumping on.[140] Teenagers are at risk as well. For example, a case report published in Annals of Emergency Medicine in 2003 describes a new game played by adolescents, "suffocation roulette" in which a child takes a deep breath and holds it while friends hug him strongly from behind until he passes out.[141] The Consumer Product Safety Commission and Child Fatality Review Teams operating in all the States[142] are essential organizations in future efforts to synthesize seemingly disparate reports of accidental child deaths so that similar patterns of risk and protective factors can be identified and addressed.

The second noteworthy finding to emerge from a scan of the recent research literature has to do with where and how infants should sleep. The "Back to Sleep Campaign" to reduce the risk of Sudden Infant Death Syndrome has received widespread attention and has demonstrated success.[143] It is widely accepted that putting an infant to sleep on his/her back is the recommended safe practice. However, epidemiological studies of large numbers of infant suffocation deaths[144] and SIDS cases[145] have not resolved the debate over the possibility for safe co-sleeping or bedsharing. The debate centers on whether safe co-sleeping can exist, promote bonding and breastfeeding, or if all co-sleeping is unsafe. Risk factors for unsafe co-sleeping include sleeping with an adult smoker or one who is intoxicated, in a bed with soft, fluffy bedding or a water bed, and "wedging" hazards (eg, a mattress up against a wall); overlying is also a concern when an adult and infant share the same bed.[146] While research will likely continue, the SIDS Alliance, the Consumer Product Safety Commission, and the American Academy of Pediatrics all have registered concerns about allowing infants to sleep in adult beds.[147] The AAP suggests placing the infant's crib near the adults' bed to allow for more convenient contact.[147]

Advocacy Efforts

An example of an important advocacy effort is the establishment of the Danny Foundation (www.dannyfoundation.org). It was formed in 1986, two years after 23-month-old Danny Linewear suffered permanent brain damage and incapacitation when his shirt became entangled on the corner post extension of his crib. Danny died after nine years of difficult therapy. According to the Foundation, in the last 10 years, 540 children died from crib injuries, a rate of 54 children each year. Among all juvenile products, baby cribs are involved in more infant and toddler deaths than any other. As the Foundation notes, "cribs are the only piece of baby furniture manufactured expressly for leaving a child unattended. Therefore, every necessary measure should be taken to ensure that the crib is the safest possible environment." Although there are now voluntary safety standards for new cribs, many second-hand cribs exist and are responsible for most of the deaths. The Danny Foundation was working to promote passage of the Infant Crib Safety Act to assure that unsafe cribs are prohibited from sale, resale, lease, use in lodging facilities, and day care centers.*

Animal Bites

Section Goals

This section will focus primarily on dog bites, since that is the biting animal that children are mostly likely to encounter at home. Studies of animal bites reported to Animal Control authorities, for example, show a ratio of dog to cat bites of 6:1.[148] Due to their larger size, dogs also have the potential to cause more severe injuries than cats.

Most dog bites occur in or around the home of the victim.[149] That may surprise parents who have cautioned young children about the dangers of "stranger dogs." This problem is complex, because unlike other home hazards (ie unsafe products), dogs do not sit by passively in reaction to children's exploration. They can initiate contact on their own, and change their behaviors based upon both internal and external stimuli. There is

---

* In 2005, the Danny Foundation closed its doors. When the foundation started its program in 1986, there were an estimated 100 to 200 baby deaths per year involving cribs. Today, that number has been reduced to about 15 per year nationwide.

considerable epidemiologic data available about how dog bites occur, however. These will be reviewed for their relevance to prevention. Since the primary focus of this volume is prevention, we won't discuss how animal bites should be treated. Our discussion will also exclude injuries that result from attempted dog bites (eg a bicycle accident triggered by someone attempting to evade an aggressive canine).

Problem Description

Why are animal bites important?

Half of the 800 000 Americans who seek medical attention for dog bites each year are children.[150] One retrospective study of children aged 4 to 18 years old indicated that 45% had been bitten by dogs in their lifetimes.[151] Most such incidents are minor and self-treated, but the serious dog bites that do occur can be devastating.

In many respects, Jason Moore's experience was typical of such victims. The seven year old boy had certainly played with "Boo Boo" before, and his neighbor's six year old Akita was known to "love children." But when Jason slid into the chained dog one summer morning, Boo Boo locked his jaws around the boy's throat. The dog's owner was shocked at the bloody scene that awaited her when she responded to screams from her yard. She hit "Boo Boo" until he loosened his grip on Jason, but the dog then turned on the boy's mother as she pulled her son to safety. Jason was airlifted to the hospital in critical condition, suffering from a torn windpipe and esophagus. A week after the attack, he was off a ventilator and moved from intensive care, where Jason could only mouth "I love you" to his mother.[152] After a month, the young boy was back home with his family. He had to use a tracheotomy tube to communicate, however, and a feeding tube to eat. At last report, Jason was scheduled for more surgery and continued to suffer from post-traumatic stress disorder.[153]

Many features of this sad story are illustrative of what is known about the epidemiology of animal bites. Domestic pets, most notably dogs, are responsible for most animal bites.[154] And children, boys in particular, are their most frequent victims. Almost two-thirds of the injuries suffered by children under the age of five are to the head or neck,[148] which may explain why 80% of the people killed by dog attacks in the United States from 1995–1996 were children.[155]

This public health problem also produces considerable financial loss. It is estimated that one-third of all liability claims associated with home owners are dog-bite related, and that US insurance companies pay out more than $1 billion dollars a year on claims related to dog bite injuries.[156]

What are animal bites?

A bite has been defined as "any break in the skin caused by an animal's teeth, regardless of the intention."[151] Our discussion will focus primarily on dog bites, since they cause the majority of injuries among American children. During a three year period in Philadelphia, for example, 86% of animal "attacks" reported to authorities involved dogs, followed by cats (10%), rats and squirrels (<1% each).[157] This is not surprising since so many US families "include" a canine member. Most households with children also have pets, and dogs make up more than half of the animals in those homes.[158]

How do children get bitten?

Eighty percent of dog bites inflicted on people who are 18 years of age or younger are attributed to the family's own pet or a neighbor's dog.[151] Children are more likely to be bitten during the spring or summer,[157,159] in the late afternoon or early evening.[160] Cat bites do not appear to share these patterns of occurrence.[148]

While children are most likely to be bitten by dogs, cats favor adult victims. One Texas study which compared biting dog and cats, found that implicated felines were more likely to be less than three months of age, unrestrained, off their owner's property, and unvaccinated for rabies.[148] Unlike dogs, they were also more likely to have bitten a female than a male. Dog bites were also distributed all over the body, whereas 79% of cat bites were inflicted to the hands or arms. In particular, dog bites are 3–4 times more likely to affect the head, neck or face than cat bites.[161] Cat bites were also much less likely than dog bites to be characterized as "unprovoked."

Morbidity and mortality

Animal bites are grossly under-reported. For example, one study found that the actual dog bite rate among children aged 4 to 18 was 36 times the reported rate.[151] This is likely due to the fact that most bites are perceived as minor and are not called to the attention of a medical professional. Reporting bias favors more vicious attacks, brought on by large or wild animals, and those which occur in non-rural locations.[159]

National data on dog-bite-related fatalities, defined as "a death caused by acute trauma from a dog attack," are tracked by the Humane Society of the United States.[155] A supplemented review of their registry indicated that from 1995 to 1996, at least twenty children (<12 years of age) died as a result of dog attacks—three within their first month of life.[155] Three-quarters of fatal dog bites overall are inflicted upon household members of the attacking canine, or guests on the family's property.[162]

For every fatality attributed to dog bites, it is estimated that there are 670 hospitalizations, and 16,000 emergency department visits.[163] In 1994, it is estimated that almost 2% of all Americans (4.7 million people) sustained a dog bite. It is estimated that 585 000 Americans a year suffer dog bites that require medical attention, or resulted in restricted activity. This makes dog bites the 12th leading cause of nonfatal injury in the United States.[155] Children who suffer multiple and/or deep dog bites are at documented risk for post-traumatic stress disorder.[164]

Although cats are less likely to bite than dogs, cat bites are more likely to cause infection.[154] It has been reported that 20–50% of cat bites become infected. Stray cats more than pet cats are more likely to be involved in biting incidents. Since cats are less likely to be vaccinated against rabies, and more likely to be exposed to bats, cat bites may pose a greater threat of rabies than dog bites.[148] Not surprisingly, cat victims are more likely than dog victims to be subjected to prophylaxis treatment for rabies, an expensive and potentially unpleasant ordeal.[161] Bites from non-immunized domestic animals do carry a risk of rabies, but bites from wild animals such as raccoons, skunks, bats and foxes are more likely to transmit the disease.[154]

Risk factors for dog bites

Risk factors for dog bites include characteristics of the animal, the child and other environmental factors, as reviewed in this section.

Animal factors

Breed of dog. Listing "breed of dog" as a risk factor is controversial, in part because previous studies have been criticized for lacking accurate denominator data. Also dog owners do not always know their dog's breed, and most household pets are a product of cross breeding. There are also many confounding factors that make researching this question a challenge.[165] Keeping those caveats in mind, we can report that between 1997 and 1998, Rottweillers and "pit bull type" dogs were responsible for 67% of dog-bite-related fatalities in the United States.[162] Other studies of dog bites have also implicated these breeds along with German Shepherds and Chow Chows.[148,157,166] Chows, German Shepherds, Pit bulls and Rottweillers have also been identified as being at much higher risk for unprovoked attacks than other dogs.[148,167]

Other animal characteristics. It stands to reason generally, that larger dogs/breeds tend to inflict the most serious injuries to children.[159] Despite this, a survey of Arizona parents found that 20% of families with children aged 0 to 1 years old had large dogs in their homes.[158] Male and un-neutered dogs are more likely to bite.[154] Dogs with a history of exhibiting aggressive behavior are also at higher risk for biting children.[149]

Child factors

Age. Children are at least 3 times more likely to suffer an injury-producing dog bite than adults.[165] The incidence of dog bites peaks among 5 to 9 year olds.[150,159] One- to 4-year-olds, however, may be at higher risk for incurring a dog bite that requires hospitalization.[168]

In the US, 70–80% of fatal dog bite victims are children.[155] Infants under three months of age appear to experience the highest rate of fatal dog bites[155]—once calculated as 370 times that of adults aged 30 to 49.[169]

Children's increased vulnerability stems, undoubtedly, from cognitive and physical limitations imposed by their phase of development. For example, while most adult victims are bitten on the extremities, greater than 70% of child victims receive an injury to the head, neck or face.[165] Very young children (≤5) are also more likely to have provoked their attack.[167]

Gender. Studies have shown consistently that boys are more likely to be bitten by dogs than are girls.[165] There is some suggestion that this disparity is related to different play patterns, because it appears to be more common among dogs other than the family pet,[159] and is more true of older boys who may be permitted to play farther from home.[165] Males are also overrepresented among fatal dog bite victims.

Personality. Cruelty to animals is a symptom of certain types of personality disorders, which may provoke an animal to bite.[159] It should be noted, however, that many behaviors common to healthy children (eg, yelling, grabbing, making darting movements) can trigger dog bites.[170]

Adult supervision. For minor bites, the relationship between adult presence and dog bite occurrence are mixed. Observers point out, however, that being present and monitoring are not necessarily the same behavior.

With regard to fatal dog bites, it has been reported that most child-victims are alone with a dog at the time of the attack.[149]

Other Environmental Factors. Due to issues of exposure, it is not surprising that dog ownership by household has emerged repeatedly as a risk factor for dog bites. Most children are bitten by dogs at home, rather than in public places.[168] Exposure is probably at play again, when we observe that younger children are more likely to be bitten at home than older children.[149] It has been reported that poor children are at higher risk of dog bite than are children of higher socioeconomic status.[149] Urban dwellers also appear to be at higher risk than rural or small town residents for experiencing an animal bite.[159]

In 1995-6, approximately two-thirds of fatal dog attacks involved more than one dog. About half of deaths involved an unrestrained dog on the owner's property, and 30% involved unrestrained dogs off the owner's property.[155] Despite these findings, a number of studies have reported that chained dogs are overrepresented in biting incidents generally.[166]

Prevention Strategies

Prior to acquiring a pet, parents should be informed about which breeds of dog are suitable for households with children, and to be cautious about bringing a dog into a home with infants or toddlers. (In the three neonate deaths mentioned previously, all occurred on the dog owner's property, and involved a sleeping child.) Adults should socialize family pets, and seek immediate professional help if their dog exhibits aggressive behaviors. Finally, they should understand that young children should not be left alone with any dog.[150] The Arizona study cited earlier[158] found that 63% of dog owners with children aged 0 to 5 believed that a 4-year-old would be safe if left unsupervised with their dog(s). The CDC[150] also recommends that children be taught some basic safety tips, like not to approach unfamiliar dogs, how to approach dogs they know, and how to react if they are knocked over or bitten by a dog. Canines should also be spayed or neutered. By taking these measures, families can enjoy the benefits of dog ownership while minimizing the likelihood that their child will be harmed in the process. The acquisition of wildlife as pets should be discouraged.[159] This is particularly true of raccoons, which represent an important reservoir for human and domestic pet exposure to rabies.[161]

At present, most pediatricians do not appear to discuss pet-related injuries with parents, despite the fact that they believe such counseling to be worthwhile.[158] Additional communication channels that might be considered include pet store personnel, veterinarians, local dog clubs and trainers, and the media.[158,170] It has been recommended that such counseling begin before a dog is acquired, and evolve in response to the behavior of individual animals and the developmental stage of the children in the home. A number of resources have been developed to guide providers through such sessions.[171,172] The importance of maintaining rabies vaccination is another message that should be stressed to parents. Educational resources geared towards adults, as well as children, can be accessed via the American Veterinary Medical Association's (AVMA) web page at http://www.avma. org/pubhlth/dogbite/default.asp. Schools should clearly be involved in dissemination campaigns, since children in grades K–4 are at highest risk of dog bites.

At the community level, animal control programs should be supported, along with strict regulation of vicious dogs.[155] Feral cat populations should also be controlled, and owners should be discouraged from allowing their cats to roam freely.[148] Better surveillance of animal bites, and the circumstances under which they occurred, would also facilitate preventive efforts. Finally, to prevent medical treatment and morbidity secondary to animal bites, municipalities should consider linking the ability to obtain a pet license with the requirement for documenting that the pet has a current rabies vaccination.[161]

Recent Research Findings

While numerous recommendations are advanced for reducing dog bite incidence, few are based upon empirical evidence. We did identify one intervention that fared well under fairly rigorous scrutiny. "Prevent-a-Bite" is an Australian program that was designed to instill precautionary behaviors in children when they are around dogs. In a randomized controlled trial, Chapman and colleagues[173] showed that 7–8 year old students who were exposed to a half hour instructional program were significantly less likely to pet a "strange" dog on the playground 10 days after the intervention. Long-term effects of the program, and its effect on injury rates, were not studied. One U.S. study, of a different program, documented increases in student awareness but did not assess behavior changes or injury rates.[174] Finally, there is evidence to indicate that dog training can reduce biting behaviors.[168] Obviously, more resources should be devoted to formal evaluation of dog bite prevention programs.

Advocacy Efforts

The American Veterinary Medical Association's Task Force on Canine Aggression and Human-Canine Interactions has developed a comprehensive set of recommendations[170] that could guide community-based prevention efforts while a more solid scientific foundation is being built. They advise advocates to promote this issue in collaboration with public officials and other community leaders, veterinarians and allied personnel, animal behaviorists, responsible dog breeders and trainers, physicians and nurses, animal control personnel, members of the judicial and educational systems, public health professionals, law enforcement representatives, business leaders (eg, pet stores, insurance companies), groups with occupational safety interests (eg, meter readers and postal workers), voluntary/non profit organizations (eg, Safe Kids, 4-H clubs), members of the animal welfare community (ie, the Humane Society, animal shelter/rescue personnel), recreational groups, and the media. The AVMA has itself partnered with the State Farm Insurance Company on a major education campaign designed to reduce dog bites.

Conclusion

Home injuries remain, unfortunately, all too common. This is especially true during the earliest years of children's lives, before they venture out into the world much on their own. Parents who are informed of potential sources of risk within the home environment can remove or modify them. Even when such steps have been taken, however, children's levels of physical and cognitive development pose inherent dangers. That is why vigilance is required of those responsible for protecting young children. Such advice can be hard to follow, however, in a household where siblings need attention, phones are ringing and chores must be completed. Up to now, our field has not helped parents determine what constitutes "adequate supervision." Recently, however, important research has been undertaken to define and measure supervision.[175] These efforts will enable us to understand which styles of caretaking are associated with injury risk, providing a basis for parental advice that is more specific and useful. In many cases, safety products already exist such as smoke alarms and cabinet locks, and the challenge is finding effective ways to promote their use. Evaluation studies of programs designed to prevent specific types of home injuries are needed.

Improved surveillance is also a critical need. As noted here, we do not even know how many U.S. children are killed or injured in their homes each year. Surveillance data on home injuries per se are not routinely collected. However, since 1971 a nationally representative sample of hospital emergency departments has provided the Consumer Product Safety Commission with data on consumer product related injuries, many of which affect children.[176] This system is known as the NEISS (National Electronic Injury Surveillance System). In 2000, the CPSC and the National Center for Injury Prevention and Control at CDC began jointly funding the NEISS-AIP ("All Injury Program," meaning that data are now provided routinely on all injuries, not just those that are product related). This more comprehensive data source has substantially strengthened our ability to document the burden of injury and new reports from this dataset have appeared in the published literature.[99] Improved data collection processes should be put in place, and organizations that carry out related work (eg, the Consumer Product Safety Commission, poison control centers) should be provided with adequate and secure funding.

An important new resource in the efforts to prevent home injury is the Home Safety Council. This national non-profit organization, based in Washington DC, is dedicated to advancing the state of home safety (www.homesafetycouncil.org). Using currently available data sources, the Home Safety Council has produced two "first of their kind" reports on home safety in the United States[177,178] as well as a special issue of the American Journal of Preventive Medicine[179] based on data analyzed for these reports. One of the Home Safety Council's strategies is to partner with people and organizations that share this goal. As the successful advocacy campaigns described in this chapter demonstrate, such alliances are key to moving public health agendas forward. That the American Public Health Association is publishing this text bodes well for our collective ability to make progress on the public health goal of preventing home injuries and reducing their impact on families and society.

References

1. Runyan CW, Casteel C. Nonfatal home injuries. In: Runyan CW, Casteel C, eds. *The State of Home Safety in America: Facts about Unintentional Injuries in the Home,* 2nd ed. Washington, DC: Home Safety Council, 2004: 25-32.

2. Runyan CW, Casteel C. Unintentional home injury deaths. In: Runyan CW, Casteel C, eds. *The State of Home Safety in America: Facts about Unintentional Injuries in the Home*, 2nd ed. Washington, DC: Home Safety Council, 2004: 21-24.

3. Casteel C, Runyan CW. Leading causes of unintentional home injury in high-risk groups. In: Runyan CW, Casteel C, eds. *The State of Home Safety in America: Facts about Unintentional Injuries in the Home*, 2nd ed. Washington, DC: Home Safety Council, 2004: 61-68.

4. Weiss HB, Friedman DI, Coben JH. Incidence of dog bite injuries treated in emergency departments. *JAMA*. 1998; 279:51-53.

5. Garage door openers: Friend or foe? Available at: www.criterium-engineers.com/residential/articles/garaged.html. Accessed October 13, 2004.

6. Garage door openers. Available at: www.cbc.ca/consumers/market/mp30/garage_doors.html. Accessed October 13, 2004.

7. O'Donnell GW, Mickalide AD. *SAFE KIDS At Home, At Play & On the Way: A Report to the Nation on Unintentional Childhood Injury*. Washington, DC: National SAFE KIDS Campaign. May, 1998. pg 32

8. National Center for Injury Prevention and Control (NCIPC), Centers for Disease Control and Prevention. Fire deaths and injuries: Fact Sheet. Available at: www.cdc.gov/ncipc/factsheets/fire.htm. Accessed August 15, 2004.

9. Karter MJ. *Fire Loss in the United States during 2002*. Quincy, Mass: National Fire Protection Association, Fire Analysis and Research Division; 2003.

10. Barrillo DJ, Goode R. Fire fatality study: Demographics of fire victims. *Burns*. 1996;22:85-88.

11. Consumer Product Safety Commission (CPSC). Child-resistant lighters protect young children. Available at: www.cpsc.gov. Accessed October 24, 2004.

12. Leistikow BN, Martin DC, Milano CE. Fire injuries, disasters, and costs from cigarettes and cigarette lights: A global overview. *Preventive Med.* 2000;31:91-99.

13. Dunst CM, Scott EC, Kraatz JJ, Anderson PM, Twomey JA, Pelter GL. Contact palm burns in toddlers from glass enclosed fireplaces. *J Burn Care Rehabil*. 2004; 25(1): 67-70.

14. CPSC. Consumer product safety alert: Young children and teens burned by hair curling irons. Available at: www.cpsc.gov. Accessed August 15, 2004.

15. Fiebiger B, Whitmire F, Law E, Still JM. Causes and treatment of burns from grease. *J Burn Care Rehabil*. 2004; 25(4): 374-376.

16. Feldman KW, Schaller RT, Feldman JA et al. Tap water scald burns in children. *Pediatrics*. 1978;62:1-7.

17. Barrow RE, Spies M, Barrow LN, Herndon DN. Influence of demographics and inhalation injury on burn mortality in children. *Burns*. 2004;30(1):72-77.

18. Maguina P, Palmieri TL, Greenhalgh DG. Treadmills: a preventable source of pediatric friction burn injuries. *J Burn Care Rehabil*. 2004;25(2):201-204.

19. Lee JW, Jang YC, Oh SJ. Pediatric electrical burn: outlet injury caused by steel chopstick misuse. *Burn*. 2004; 30(3):244-247.

20. CPSC. Consumer product safety alert: Household batteries can cause chemical burns. Available at: www.cpsc.gov Accessed August 15, 2004.

21. Greene MA, Race PM. *2003 Fireworks Annual Report: Fireworks Related Deaths, Emergency Department Treated Injuries, and Enforcement Activities During 2003*. Available at: http://www.cpsc.gov/LIBRARY/2001fwreport.pdf. Accessed September 15, 2004.

22. Casteel C, Runyan CW. Leading causes of unintentional home injury death. In: Runyan CW, Casteel C, eds. *The State of Home Safety in America: Facts about Unintentional Injuries in the Home*, 2nd ed. Washington, DC: Home Safety Council, 2004: 33-60.

23. SAFE KIDS. Injury Facts: Fire Injury (Residential). Available at: http://www.safe

kids.org. Accessed August 15, 2004.

24. Federal Interagency Forum on Child and Family Statistics. Table HEALTH7.A Child mortality: Death rates for children ages 1 to 4 by gender, race, Hispanic origin, and cause of death, 1980-2001. Available at: http://childstats.gov/ac2004/tables/health7a.asp. Accessed August 15, 2004.

25. NCIPC, CDC. WISQARS. 2001, United States Unintentional Fire/burn deaths and rates per 100,000. Available at: www.cdc.gov/ncipc/wisqars. Accessed August 15, 2004.

26. CDC. Deaths resulting from residential fires and the prevalence of smoke alarms—United States 1991-1995. *JAMA.* 1998;280 (16):1395.

27. Warda L, Tenenbein M. Moffatt, MEK. House fire injury prevention update. Part I. A review of risk factors for fatal and non-fatal house fire injury. *Injury Prevention.* 1999;5:145-150.

28. Istre GR, McCoy M, Carlin DK, McClain J. Residential fire related deaths and injuries among children: fireplay, smoke alarms, and prevention. *Injury Prevention.* 2002;8:128-132.

29. Mangus RS, Bergman D, Zieger M, Coleman JJ. Burn injuries in children with attention-deficit/hyperactivity disorder. *Burns.* 2004;30(2):148-150.

30. Katcher ML. Scald burns from hot tap water. *Pediatrics.* 1983;71:145-146.

31. Joseph KE, Adams CD, Goldfarb IW, Slater H. Parental correlates of unintentional burn injuries in infancy and early childhood. *Burns.* 2002;28(5):455-463.

32. Levy DT, Mallonnee S, Miller TR, et al. Alcohol involvement in burn, submersion, spinal cord, and brain injuries. *Med Sci Monit.* 2004;10(1):CR17-24.

33. Smith GS, Branas CC, Miller TR. Fatal non-traffic injuries involving alcohol: A metaanalysis. *Ann Emerg Med.* 1999;33(6):659-68.

34. U.S. Fire Administration. *Establishing a Relationship between Alcohol and Casualties of Fire.* Emmitsburg, Md: U.S. Fire Administration, July 2003.

35. Istre GR, McCoy MA, Osborn L, Barnard JJ, Bolton A. Deaths and injuries from house fires. *NEJM.* 2001;344: 1911-1916.

36. Shenassa Ed, Stubbendick A, Brown MJ. Social disparities in housing and related pediatric injury; a multilevel study. *Am J Public Health.* 2004;94(4): 633-639.

37. National Fire Protection Association (NFPA). NFPA Fact Sheets: Smoke alarms: Make them work for your safety. Available at: http://www.nfpa.org/Research/NFPAFactSheets/Alarms/Alarms.asp. Accessed August 20, 2004.

38. Runyan CW, Bangdiwala SI, Linzer MA, Sacks JJ, Butts J. Risk factors for fatal residential fires. *NEJM.* 1992; 37(12):859-863

39. Marshall S, Runyan CW, Bangdiwala SI, et al. Fatal residential fires: who dies and who survives. *JAMA.* 1998;279:1633-1637.

40. Thompson NH, Waterman MS, Sleet DA. Using behavioral science to improve fire escape behaviors in response to a smoke alarm. *J Burn Care Rehabil.* 2004; 25(2):179-188.

41. Holmes GA, Jones RT. Fire evacuation skills: cognitive behavior versus computer-mediated instruction. *Fire Technology.* 1996; First Quarter: 51-64.

42. Hillman HS. Memory processing and overlearning in the acquisition and maintenance of fire-safety skills. University of Pittsburgh, 1983.

43. Corrarino JE, Walsh PJ, Nadel E. Does teaching scald burn prevention to families of young children make a difference? A pilot study. *J Pediatr Nur.* 2001; 16(4):256-262.

44. Erdmann TC, Feldman KW, Rivara FP, et al. Tap water burn prevention: the effect of legislation. *Pediatrics.* 1991;88:572-7.

45. Berger LR, Kuklinski DM. When smoke alarms are a nuisance. *Arch Pediatr Adolesc Med.* 2001;155(8): 875-876.

46. Rowland D, DiGuiseppi C, Roberts I, et al. Prevalence of working smoke alarms

in local authority inner city housing: randomized controlled trial. *BMJ.* 2002; 325:998-1001.

47. CPSC. CPSC initiates rulemaking for cigarette lighters. Press release #880001. Washington, DC: Consumer Product Safety Commission, January 7, 1988.

48. Sleet DA, Gielen AC. Injury Prevention (Chapter 10). In: Gorin SS and Arnold A (Eds.), *Health Promotion Handbook,* Chapter 10: 247-275. 1998, St. Louis, Mosby.

49. Smith LE, Greene MA, Singh HA. Study of the effectiveness of the US safety standard for child resistant cigarette lighters. *Injury Prevention.* 2002;8:192-196.

50. NCIPC. Injury Fact Book 2001-2002. Atlanta, Ga: Centers for Disease Control and Prevention; 2001

51. National SAFE Kids Campaign. (2004). Injury facts: Poisoning. Available at: http://www.safekids.org/tier3_printable.cfm?content_item_id=1152&folder_id+540. Accessed September 2, 2004.

52. Beamon T. 2 dead from generator fumes. *The Baltimore Sun.* (Maryland) 2003, September 20.

53. Institute of Medicine. *Forging a Poison Prevention and Control System.* New York: The National Academy of Sciences; 2004.

54. McGuigan MA. Common culprits in childhood poisoning: Epidemiology, treatment and parental advice for prevention. *Paediatr Drugs;* 1999;1(4):313-324.

55. McGuigan MA. Acute iron poisoning. *Pediatr Ann.* 1996;25(1):33-8.

56. Bar-Oz B, Levichek Z, and Koren G. Medications that can be fatal for a toddler with one tablet or teaspoon: a 2004 update. *Paediatr Drugs.* 2004;6(2):123-126.

57. Spann MF, Blondell JM, Hunting KL. Acute hazards to young children from residential pesticide exposures. *Am J Public Health.* 2000; 90(6): 971-973.

58. Landrigan PJ, Claudio L, Markowitz SB, et al. Pesticides and inner city children: exposures, risks, and prevention. *Environ Health Perspect.* 1999;107(Suppl 3): 431-437.

59. Garry VF, Harkins ME, Erickson LL, et al. Birth defects, season of conception, and sex of children born to pesticide applicators living in the Red River Valley of Minnesota, USA. *Environ Health Perspect.* 2002;110(Suppl 3):441-449.

60. Watson WA, Litovitz LT, Klein-Schwartz W, et al. 2003 annual report of the American Association of Poison Control Centers Toxic Exposure Surveillance System. *Am J Emerg Med.* 2004;222(5):335-404.

61. Sleet DA, Schieber RA, Gilchrist J. Health promotion policy and politics: Lessons from childhood injury prevention. *Health Promot Prac.* 2003;4(2):103-108.

62. Poison Prevention Week Council. 2003 Report on National Poison Prevention Week. Available from: PPWC, PO Box 1543, Washington, DC, 20013.

63. Runyan CW, Casteel C (eds.) *The State of Home Safety in America: Facts about Unintentional Injuries in the Home,* 2nd edition. Washington, DC: Home Safety Council, 2004.

64. American Association of Poison Control Centers. Poison prevention tips to keep our children safe. Available at: http://www.aapcc.org/children.htm. Accessed August 29, 2004.

65. National SAFE Kids Campaign. (2004). Injury facts: Poisoning. Available at: http://www.safekids.org/tier3_printable.cfm?content_item_id=1152&folder_i d+540. Accessed September 2, 2004.

66. Technical Advisory Committee. Poison prevention packaging act of 1970. *Bull Natl Clgh Poison Control Cent.* 1971; May-June:1-2.

67. Walton WW. An evaluation of the Poison Prevention Packaging Act. *Pediatrics.* 1982;69(3):363-70.

68. CPSC. Poison prevention packaging requirements; exemption of hormone replacement therapy products. *Fed Regist.* 2002; 67(212):66550-2.

69. CPSC. Child-resistant packaging for certain over-the-counter drug products.

Final rule. *Fed Regist.* 2001;6(149):40111-6.

70. Blumenthal D. Artificial nail remover poses poisoning risk. *FDA Consumer.* 1989;23(5):26-33.

71. Schum TR, Lachman BS. Effect of packaging and appearance on childhood poisoning: Vacor Rat Poison. *Clinical Ped.* 1982;21(5): 282-285.

72. Coyne-Beasley T, Runyan CW, Baccaglini L, Perkis D, Johnson RM. Storage of poisonous substances and firearms in homes with young children visitors and older adults. *Am J Prevent Med* 2005;28(10):109-115.

73. Dole EJ, Czajka PA, Rivara FP. Evaluation of pharmacists' compliance with the Poison Prevention Packaging Act. *Am J Public Health.* 1986;76(11):1335-1336.

74. Hingley AT. Preventing childhood poisoning. *FDA Consumer Magazine.* 1997;30 (2): 1-7.

75. Fergusson DM, Horwood LJ, Beautrais AL, Shannon FT. A controlled field trial of a poisoning prevention method. *Pediatrics.* 1982;69(5):515-520.

76. Vernberg K, Culver-Dickinson P, Spyker DA. The deterrent effect of poison-warning stickers. *Am J Dis Children.* 1984;138(11):1018-1020.

77. Committee on Injury, Violence and Poison Prevention. Poison treatment in the home. *Pediatrics.* 2003;112(5):1182-1185.

78. Bond GR. Home syrup of ipecac use does not reduce emergency department use or improve outcome. *Pediatrics.* 2003;112(5):1061-1064.

79. Yoon SS, Macdonald SC, Parrish RG. Deaths from unintentional carbon monoxide poisoning and potential for prevention with carbon monoxide detectors. *JAMA.* 1998;279(9): 685-687.

80. CDC. Use of carbon monoxide alarms to prevent poisonings during a power outage—North Carolina, December 2002. *MMWR.* 2004;53(9):189-192.

81. Harborview Injury Prevention and Research Center. Poisoning interventions: Carbon monoxide alarms. Available at: http://depts.washington.edu/hiprc/practices/topic/poisoning/coalarms.html. Accessed September 15, 2004.

82. Woolf A. Challenge and promise: the future of poison control services. *Toxicology.* 2004;198:285-289.

83. Miller TR, Lestina DC. Costs of poisoning in the United States and savings from poison control centers: a benefit-cost analysis. *Ann Emerg Med.* 1997; 29(2):246-7.

84. Institute of Medicine. *The Future of Poison Prevention and Control Services.* New York: Institute of Medicine of the National Academies, 2004.

85. Shepherd G, Larkin GL, Velez LI, Huddleston, L. Language preferences among callers to a regional Poison Center. *Vet Hum Toxicol.* 2004; 46(2):100-101.

86. Kelly NR, Huffman LC, Mendoza FS, Robinson TN. Effects of a videotape to increase use of poison control centers by low-income and Spanish-speaking families: a randomized, controlled trial. *Pediatrics.* 2003;111(1):21-6.

87. Nixon J, Spinks A. Turner C, McClure R. Community based programs to prevent poisoning in children 0-15 years. *Injury Prevention.* 2004;10:43-46.

88. CDC. Perspectives in disease prevention and health promotion National Poison Prevention Week: 25th anniversary observance. *MMWR.* 1986;35(10):149-152.

89. Fisher L. Prevention and control: National poison prevention week 2004: March 21-27, 2004. American Public Health Association's Injury Control and Emergency Health Services Section Electronic New, March 2004. Available at: members only website. Accessed on October 25, 2004.

90. Harborview Injury Prevention and Research Center. Poisoning interventions: Child resistant packaging and the Poison Prevention Packaging Act. Available at: http://depts.washington.edu/hiprc/practices/topic/poisoning/packaging.html. Assessed September 15, 2004.

91. CDC, NCIPC, WISQARS Injury Mortality and Non-fatal Injury Reports, 8/15/2004

92. Tears in Heaven. Available at: http://www.snopes.com/music/songs/tears. htm. Accessed on September 15, 2004.

93. Kate Barry. Available at: http://www.chp.edu/besafe/adults/02onechildsstory. php. Accessed September 15, 2004.

94. World Health Organization. Injuries and violence prevention. Available at: http://www.who.int/violence_injury_prevention/unintentional_injuries/falls/ falls1/en/. Accessed September 15, 2004.

95. Chiaviello CT, Christof RA, Bond GR,, Infant walker-related injuries: a prospective study of severity and incidence. *Pediatrics* 93(6):974-976, 1994.

96. Wilson MEH, Baker SP, Teret SP, et al. *Saving Children: A Guide to Injury Prevention.* New York, NY: Oxford University Press, Chapter 9, 1991.

97. American Academy of Pediatrics, Committee on Injury and Poison Prevention. Falls from Heights: Windows, Roofs, and Balconies. *Pediatrics.* 2001; 107(5): 1188-1191.

98. Ballesteros MF, Schieber RA, Gilchrist J, Holmgreen P, and Annest JL. Differential ranking of causes of fatal versus non-fatal injuries among US children. *Injury Prevention.* 2003; 9:173-176.

99. Runyan CW, Perkis D, Marshall SW, Johnson RM, Coyne-Beasley T, Waller AE, Black C, Baccaglini L, Unintentional injuries in the home in the United States—Part 11: Morbidity. *Am J Prev Med,* in press, 2004.

100. National SAFE Kids Campaign. Injury Facts—Falls. Available at: http://www. safekids.org/tier3_cd.cfm?folder_id=540&content_item_id=1050. Accessed September 15, 2004.

101. Casteel C and Runyan CW, Leading causes of unintentional home injury in high-risk age groups, Chapter 4 in Runyan CW and Casteel C (eds) *The State of Home Safety in America,* 2nd Edition, Washington, DC: Home Safety Council, pages 61-68.

102. Zaloshnja E, Miller TR, Lawrence BA, Romano E, The costs of unintentional home injuries, *Am J Prev Med,* in press, 2004.

103. U.S. Consumer Product Safety Commission. CPSC Gets New, Safer Baby Walkers on the Market, http://www.cpsc.gov/CPSCPUB/PUBS/5086.pdf.

104. Siegel AC, Burton RV. Effects of baby walkers on motor and mental development in human infants. *J Dev Behav Pediatr.* 1999;20(5):355-61.

105. Committee on Injury and Poison Prevention. Injuries associated with infant walkers. *Pediatrics.* 2001;108(3):790-792.

106. Gielen AC, McDonald EM, Wilson MEH, et al. Effects of improved access to safety counseling, products, and home visits on parents' safety practices. *Arch Pediatr Adolesc Med.* 2002;156:33-40.

107. Gielen AC, Wilson MEH, McDonald EM, et al. Randomized trial of enhanced anticipatory guidance for injury prevention. *Arch Pediatr Adolesc Med.* 2001;155: 42-49.

108. Istre GR, McCoy MA, Stowe M, et al. Childhood injuries due to falls from apartment balconies and windows. *Injury Prevention.* 2003;9:349-352.

109. Belechri M, Petridou E, Trichopoulos D. Bunk versus conventional beds: a comparative assessment of fall injury risk. *J Epidemiol Community Health.* 2002; 56:413-417.

110. Macgregor, DM. Injuries associated with falls from beds. *Injury Prevention.* 2000;6;291-292.

111. CPSC. Just the facts: Bunk beds. Available at: http://www.cpsc.gov/CPSCPUB/ PUBS/071.html. Accessed September 15, 2004.

112. CPSC. Requirements for Bunk Beds, 16 C.F.R. Part 1213, 1500, and 1513. Washington, DC: U.S. Consumer Product Safety Commission Office of Compliance, January, 2001.

113. CPSC. CPSC gets newer, safer baby walker on the market. Available at: http://www.cpsc.gov/CPSCPUB/PUBS/5086.pdf. Accessed September 15, 2004.

114. Morrongiello BA, Kiriakou S. Mothers' home safety practices for preventing six types of childhood injuries: What do they do and why? *J Pediatr Psychol.* 2004;29(4):285-297.

115. Lyons RA, Sander LV, Weightman AL, et al. Modification of the home environment for the reduction of injuries (Cochrane Review). In: The Cochrane Library, Issue 3, 2004. Chichester, UK: John Wiley & Sons, Ltd.

116. Morrongeillo BA, Major K. Influence of safety gear on parental perceptions of injury risk and tolerance for children's risk taking. *Injury Prevention.* 2002; 8:27-31.

117. Clamp M, Kendrick D, A randomized controlled trial of general practitioner safety advice for families with children under 5 years. *BMJ,* 316: 1575-1579, 1998.

118. Spiegel CN, Lindaman FC. Children can't fly: A program to prevent childhood morbidity and morality from window falls. *Am J Public Health.* 1977;67:1143-1147.

119. Barlow B, Niemirska M, Gandhi R, Leblane W. Ten years of experience with falls from a height in children. *J Pediatr Surg.* 1983; 18:509-511.

120. Vinci RJ, Freedman E, Wolski K. Preventing falls from windows: The efficacy of the Boston window fall prevention program. *Arch Pediatr Adolesc Med.* 1996; 150:32.

121. Safe Kids Thrilled by Government's Ban on Baby Walkers: Asks parents to take action and wipe out walkers. Available at: http://www.safekidscanada.ca/ENGLISH/Media/Media_babywalkersbanned.html. Accessed September 15, 2004.

122. Vyrostek SB, Annest JL, Ryan GW, Surveillance for fatal and nonfatal injuries—United States, 2001, *MMWR,* 53(SS07);1-57

123. Weir R. "The baby's dying! He's dying! He's choking!" Available at: www.nydailynews.com/front/story/222938p-191512c.html. Accessed September 15, 2004.

124. CPSC. CPSC, KFC Corporation announce recall of toy included with KFC kids meal. Available at: http://www.recall-warnings.com/cpsc-content-00-00162.html. Accessed September 15, 2004.

125. Tarrago SB. Prevention of choking, strangulation, and suffocation in childhood. *WMJ.* 2000;99(9):43-6.

126. Mayo Foundation for Medical Education and Research, Choking and other airway emergencies in babies: Recognition, first aid and prevention, Available at: http://www.mayoclinic.com/invoke.cfm?id=PR00042. Accessed November 13, 2004.

127. American Academy of Pediatrics, Choking: Common Dangers for Children, Information Sheet, 2001.

128. SAFE Kids. Injury Facts: Airway obstruction. Available at: http://www.safekids.org/tier3_cd.cfm?folder_id=540&content_item_id=991. Accessed September 15, 2004.

129. Centers for Disease Control and Prevention, Nonfatal choking-related episodes among children—United States, 2001, MMWR, 51(42):945-948.

130. Lifschultz BD, Donoghue ER. Deaths due to foreign body aspiration in children: the continuing hazard of toy balloons, *J Forensic Sci,* 41(2):247-51, 1996.

131. CDC. Nonfatal choking-related episodes among children—United States, 2001. *MMWR.* 2002;51(42):945-948.

132. CPSC. Strings and straps on toys can strangle young children. Available at: http://www.cpsc.gov/cpscpub/pubs/5100.html. Accessed September 15, 2004.

133. Harris CD, Baker SP, Smith GA, Harris RM. Childhood asphyxiation by food: A national analysis and overview. *JAMA*. 1984;251(17):2231-2235.

134. Morely RE, Ludemann JP, Moxham JP, Kozak FK, Riding KH. Foreign body aspiration in infants and toddlers: recent trends in British Columbia. *J Otolaryngol*. 2004;33(1):37-41.

135. Rimell FL, Thome A, Stool S, et al. Characteristics of objects that cause choking in children. *JAMA*. 1995;13;274(22):1763-6.

136. Lifschultz BD, Donoghue ER. Deaths due to foreign body aspiration in children: the continuing hazard of toy balloons. *J Forensic Sci*. 1996;41(2):247-251.

137. Abdel-Rahman HA. Fatal suffocation by rubber balloons in children: mechanism and prevention. *Forensic Sci Int*. 2000;108(2):97-105

138. American Academy of Pediatrics, Choking Prevention, Information Sheet, 2001.

139. Wehner F, Martin DD, Wehner HD. Asphyxia due to pacifier—case report and review of the literature. *Forensic Sci Int*. 2004;141:73-75.

140. Denton JS. Fatal accidental hanging from a lanyard key chain in a 10-year-old boy. *J Forensic Sci*. 2002;47(6):1345-6.

141. Shlamovitz GZ, Assia A, Ben-Sira L, Rachmel A. "Suffocation routlette": A case of recurrent syncope in an adolescent boy. *Ann Emerg Med*. 2003;41;223-226.

142. Langstaff J, Sleeper T. The National Center on Child Fatality Review. OJJDP Fact Sheet #12, April 2001, US Department of Justice.

143. Task Force on Infant Sleep Position and Sudden Infant Death Syndrome. Changing concepts of sudden infant death syndrome: Implications for infant sleeping environment and sleep position. *Pediatrics*. 2000;105(3):650-656.

144. Drago DA, Dannenberg AL. Infant mechanical suffocation deaths in the United States, 1980-1997. *Pediatrics*. 1999;103(5):e59.

145. Carpenter RG, IRgens LM, Blair PS, et al. Sudden unexplained infant death in 20 regions in Europe: case control study. *Lancet*. 2004;363(9404):185-191.

146. O'Hara M, Harruff R, Smialek JE, et al. Sleep location and suffocation: How good is the evidence. *Pediatrics*. 2000;105; 915-920.

147. CPSC. Babies in adult beds. Article published in *Consumer Project Safety Review*. Winter 2000, 4(3):5.

148. Patrick GR, O'Rourke KM. Dog and cat bites: epidemiologic analyses suggest different prevention strategies. *Public Health Reports*. 1998;113(3):252-257.

149. Mathews JR, Lattal KA. A behavioral analysis of dog bites to children. *Develop Behav Pediatr*. 1994;15(1):44-52.

150. NCIPC, CDC. National Dog Bite Prevention Week, 2004. Available at: http://www.cdc.gov/ncipc/duip/biteprevention.html. Accessed July 8, 2004.

151. Beck AM, Jones B. Unreported dog bites in children. *Public Health Reports*. 1985;100:315-321.

152. Townsend A. Former owner: Dog bit before. Available at: www.shelbystar.com/portal/ASP/article.asp?ID=9954. Accessed July 8, 2004.

153. Morehouse B. Road to recovery is tough after attack. Available at: www.news14Charlotte.com/content/local_news/?ArID=67436&SecID=2. Accessed November 28, 2004.

154. Mayo Clinic. Animal bites. Available at: http://www.mayoclinic.com/invoke.cfm?id=FA00044. Accessed November 28, 2004.

155. NCIPC, CDC. Dog-bite-related fatalities-United States, 1995-6. *MMWR*. 1997; 46(21):463-467.

156. Overall KL, Love M. Dog bites to humans—demography, epidemiology, injury and risk. *J Am Vet Med Assoc*. 2001;218(12):1923-1934.

157. Stull JW, Hodge RR. An analysis of reported dog bites: reporting issues and the

impact of unowned dogs. *J Environ Health.* 2000;62(8):17.

158. Villar RG, Connick M, Barton et al. Parent and pediatrician knowledge, attitudes, and practices regarding pet-associated hazards. *Arch Pediat Adolesc Med.* 1998;152(10):1035-1037.

159. Sinclair CL, Zhou C. Descriptive epidemiology of animal bites in Indiana, 1990-92-a rationale for intervention. *Public Health Reports.* 1995;110(1):64-67.

160. Bernardo LM,, Gardner MJ, O'Connor JO, Amon N. Dog bites in children treated in a pediatric emergency department. *J Soc Pediatr Nurses.* 2000;5(2):87.

161. Moore DA, Sischo WM, Hunter A, Miles T. Animal bite epidemiology and surveillance for rabies postexposure prophylaxis. *J Am Vet Med Assoc.* 2000;217(2): 190-194.

162. Sacks JJ, Sinclair L, Gilchrist J, Golab GC, Lockwood R. Breeds of dogs involved in fatal human attacks in the United States between 1979 and 1998. *J Am Vet Med Assoc.* 2000;217(6):836-840.

163. Weiss HB, Friedman DI, Coben JH. Incidence of dog bite injuries treated in emergency departments. *JAMA.* 1998;279:51-53.

164. Peters V, Sottiaux M, Appelboom J, Kahn A. Posttraumatic stress disorder after dog bites in children. *J Pediatrics.* 2004;January:121-122.

165. Overall KL, Love M. Dog bites to humans—demography, epidemiology, injury and risk. *J Am Vet Med Assoc.* 2001; 218(12):1923-1934.

166. Gershman KA, Sacks JJ, Wright JC. Which dogs bite? A case-control study of risk factors. *Pediatrics.* 1994;93(6):913-917.

167. Avner JR, Baker MD. Dog bites in urban children. Pediatrics. 1991;88:55-57.

168. Ozanne-Smith J. Ashby K, Stathakis VZ. Dog bite and injury prevention—analysis, critical review and research agenda. *Injury Prevention.* 2001;7(4):321-326.

169. Sacks JL, Sattin RW, Bonzo SE. Dog bite-related fatalities from 1979 to 1988. *JAMA.* 1989;262(11):1489-1492.

170. American Veterinary Medical Association (AVMA), Task Force on Canine Aggression and Human-Canine Interactions. A community approach to dog bite prevention. *J Am Vet Med Assoc.* 2001; 218(11):1732-1746.

171. Love M, Overall KL. How anticipating relationships between dogs and children can prevent disasters. *J Am Vet Med Assoc.* 2001;219(4):446-453.

172. Hart BL. Selecting, raising and caring for dogs to avoid problem aggression. *J Am Vet Med Assoc.* 1997;210:1129-1134.

173. Chapman S, Cornwall J, Righetti J, Sung L. Preventing dog bites in children: randomized controlled trial of an educational intervention. *BMJ.* 2000;320 (7248):1512.

174. Spiegel B. A Pilot Study to evaluate an elementary school-based dog bite prevention program. *ANTHROZOÖS.* 2000;13(3):164-173.

175. Morrongiello BA, House K. Measuring parent attributes and supervision behaviors relevant to child injury risk: examining the usefulness of questionnaire measures. *Injury Prevention.* 2004;10:114-118.

176. CPSC. The National Electronic Injury Surveillance System: A Tool for Researchers. Available at: http://www.cpsc.gov/Neiss/2000d015.pdf. Accessed September 15, 2004.

177. Home Safety Council. *The State of Home Safety in America: The Facts About Unintentional Injuries in the Home.* 2002 Edition. Wilkesboro, NC.

178. Runyan CW and Casteel C (Eds) *The State of Home Safety in America,* 2nd Edition, Washington, DC: Home Safety Council, 2004.

179. Gielen, AC (Editor), Home Injuries in America, A Special Issue of the *American Journal of Preventive Medicine,* in press, 2004.

CHAPTER 6

Adolescent Employment: Relationships to Injury and Violence

Carol W. Runyan, MPH, PhD,[1]
Michael Schulman, PhD,[2]
and Myduc Ta, MPH[3]

W orking for pay, either after school or during the summer, is a usual part of teenage life in the United States. Though most teens work in the retail or service sectors, others are employed in manufacturing, construction, and agriculture. Despite the presence of child labor laws, many of the situations in which teens work are in violation of these laws. Even those in conformance with the laws may be dangerous. Teens are exposed to a variety of workplace hazards, including operating dangerous tools, machinery, and vehicles and handling cash in situations prone to robbery. Training is sometimes minimal and adult supervision limited.

Work can be an important component of adolescent development, helping teens develop skills, exercise autonomy, and achieve a greater degree of competence and control. But, in their quest to demonstrate that they are good workers with adult-like skills, they may not question the safety of their working conditions as often or as forcefully as they should. Likewise, employers may not fully understand the laws or be motivated to comply with them or they may not realize that these inexperienced workers need special training and supervision. Parents may also assume that teen jobs are safe and may not question their son or daughter about work until a major incident occurs, especially if the child's job is obtained through family or friend networks. Those charged with enforcement may not have

1   The University of North Carolina: Injury Prevention Research Center, Department of Health Behavior and Health Education, Department of Pediatrics, and Department of Epidemiology.
2   The University of North Carolina: Injury Prevention Research Center and Department of Health Behavior and Health Education; and North Carolina State University, Department of Sociology and Anthropology.
3   The University of North Carolina: Injury Prevention Research Center and Department of Epidemiology.

sufficient support to carry out their duties, in part because the public and policymakers are unaware of the importance of the issue.

The vignettes below about real teens and their work injury experiences reveal some of the important hidden aspects of teen work and injury. We then follow with a discussion about what is known about the risks and benefits of teen work, the epidemiology of injuries among working teenagers, and a discussion of strategies for preventing injuries. Because there is another chapter on agricultural injury, we will focus here only on the non-agricultural settings in which teens work.

Vignettes of real working teenagers: The December 17, 2004 broadcast of the Montel Williams daytime TV show featured four working teenagers who were injured on the job. These are their stories.[1]

- On his first day of work at a metal stamping plant, Brad lost half of his right arm and his left hand when the press stamped down while he was trying to make sure that the metal part was situated correctly in the machine.
- Mallory, aged fourteen, had her hands caught in the auger of an ice packing machine while trying to retrieve a bag that was caught in the machinery.
- John, aged sixteen, was operating a forklift without a license. When he tried to move the forklift without being seated in the driver's seat (something he had seen older workers do), he slipped on some oil on the floor and the forklift ran over him crushing his back.
- Jennifer lost three fingers while operating a dough machine at a pizza restaurant.

Other stories of teen injuries and workplace death are readily available. The CDC/NIOSH Fatality Assessment and Control Evaluation (FACE) Program website[2] lists approximately 85 fatality investigation reports of cases where young workers under the age of eighteen were killed at work. For example, in March 2004, a 16-year old Hispanic construction laborer on a framing crew died from head injuries after falling ten feet from a scaffold onto to a concrete slab. The teen was working with his father and four uncles for a subcontractor who employed a crew leader responsible for finding and paying (in cash) Hispanic workers. The fatality investigation[3] revealed that the teen had been working on the framing crew for approximately two weeks. He, and the other Hispanic workers, were Mexican nationals who spoke little or no English, and that there was no documentation of training for any of the workers who were performing framing work. Another fatality report[4] details the cases of a 17-year old warehouse worker who died after the forklift he was operating overturned and crushed him. The youth was participating in a work-based learning program through his high school and had worked at the warehouse for approximately 3 months. Yet, under the Hazardous Order provisions of the Fair Labor Standards Act (FLSA), persons below the age of 18 are prohibited from operating forklifts.

Teen Work Experience

Numbers and types of teen work experiences: In 2000, the estimated labor force participation rates for adolescents was 68.5% for those age 16-17 and 68.2%

for 18-19 year olds.[5] But many teens begin working before their 16th birthdays. Once adolescents enter the labor market, they usually continue working, though they change jobs frequently.[6] Most working adolescents are employed during both the school year and the summer, with the proportions working during both periods increasing from 60% among 16 year olds to 68% of 17 year olds, and 77% of 18 year olds.[7,8] By the time they graduate from high school, approximately 80% of teens have had job experience.

Though most research has focused on teens age 14-17 years, the ages covered by child labor laws, a recent study in Wisconsin reported that 58% of teens in a study group of more than 5000 youth aged 10-14 surveyed in school reported working, with approximately 16% of working youth indicating they were "self-employed" (eg, babysitting, lawn mowing).[9] The National Longitudinal Survey of Youth 1997 (NLSY97), a nationally representative annual survey of youths as young as 12 years of age, provides further insight into the work activities of youth under 14 years of age. Estimates from the NLSY97 suggest that over half (52.5%) of the 12- and 13-year olds surveyed had held a job; primarily a freelance job whereby tasks are performed without a specific "boss."[10]

The largest proportion (approximately 60%) of adolescents work in retail places, of which half are eating and drinking establishments. The second largest number work in the service industry.[7] Occupations of these adolescents vary by sex, with the most common occupations for 16 year old males being cooks, stock handlers, baggers, cashiers, and food counter operators; while females most often work as cashiers, food counter operators, sales workers, wait persons, supervisors of food preparation and in service occupations.[7,8]

Teens also work long hours. One study showed that 39% work 20 or more hours per week in a typical week during the school year and that 25% work some or part of the day without an adult supervisor at the worksite.[11] Among the teens in the 10-14 age group surveyed by Zierold et al[9] fifty-four percent reported having more than one job and 30% reported working more than ten hours a week.

While estimates of illegal child labor are difficult to find because of the lack of high-quality data, there is some evidence showing that it is substantial. Using the 1980s Current Population Survey datasets and the 1979 and 1997 National Longitudinal Survey datasets, Kruse and Mahony[12] estimate that 153 600 children under 18 work illegally in the United States in an average week. The estimated number of teen workers under age 18 working illegally sometime during the year is 300 900, of whom 295 800 work in non-agricultural industries. Employer's cost savings from illegal child labor are calculated to be approximately $136 million per year. Kruse and Mahony[12] conclude that illegal employment cuts across all demographic and geographic segments of the population.

Social context of teen work: Labor sociologists study the way work is actually done within different organizational contexts; for example, the tools, technology, division of labor and organization of work and the extent to which workers control the way work is done versus the way managers control workers to increase productivity and efficiency. Scholars argue that work in the 20th century has been "deskilled"; that is, broken down into component parts. In addition, workers in this environment have lost control over the pace of their work.[13]

Although jobs may be broken down into a series of tasks with very formal safety procedures, workers may have a variety of reasons for not adhering to safety rules. In situations where speed and efficiency are at a premium, or if wages are determined by piece rate, following safety procedures may slow down production and be a disincentive. Experienced workers may teach younger workers ways to facilitate getting the jobs done quickly, but not necessarily safely. Furthermore, in this environment inexperienced workers, like teenagers, can do jobs that used to require expertise based on careful training and job tasks are organized so that managers and machines control their timing and execution. Mechanization and automation are assumed to make tasks easier and safer, but this may be a false assumption, especially given workplace demands for speed which may make teens rushed in their work, a factor that has been documented to relate to injury.[14] In addition, teen workers may realize that they are easily replaceable, and fear loss of employment.[15] As a result, concerns about injury prevention may take a backseat to keeping their jobs.[16]

In addition, safety equipment may be too hot or too cumbersome. In many industries, teens start working at low level jobs and may attempt to "earn" respect by demonstrating their ability to do dirty, hard, and dangerous work, especially since older teens or adult co-workers started in the same positions. In some large and complex workplaces (ie, a construction site), adolescent workers may not have the opportunity to learn how their particular job is linked or connected with others in the work site. In smaller firms where work group cohesion exists, co-workers keep each other's safety in mind, and they share in knowledge of both safe and unsafe practices.[16] Efforts to curb costs to the employers have increased the use of lesser qualified and inexperienced workers.[16] Poorly trained workers often will not have the necessary knowledge to deal with problematic workplace hazards.

According to Scharf et al,[17] constant change is a core feature of the most hazardous work environments such as agriculture, construction, and transport. Related to this is the observation that workplace hazards vary by the degree of control that the worker has over the labor process and the predictability, visibility, movement, speed and force of the tools, equipment, and exposures that are specific to the work environment.[18] Agriculture, transportation, and construction are inherently dangerous work environments because of the complex interactions of environment, job tasks, tools, and other workers: farm fields or construction sites may be hot, cold, wet, or sandy; workers are alone, in small groups, or with many other crews; machinery is large and complex; and raw materials, from lumber to soil is not uniform. The combination of inexperienced teen workers looking to demonstrate competence at work and the constantly changing hazards in dangerous work environments creates especially high risk situations for young workers in these settings.

Benefits and Risks of Teen Work

Teen Work and Employment as a Stage in the Life Course: The life course perspective emphasizes stages and transitions that individuals experience in the social context of normal development and aging. This perspective reflects the interaction of social and historical factors with personal biography.

Transitions (changes in status that are discrete and bounded in duration) and trajectories (long term patterns of stability and change) are key parts of the life course perspective.[19] A life course perspective views work and employment for pay outside of the home as a key stage in adolescent development.

Whether work has a positive or negative impact on adolescent life course development is a topic of debate about both methodology and findings of the research.[20] For example, there is literature suggesting that work is beneficial in reducing violent behaviors with working teens, developing improved job skills, including time management, and improved self-esteem, future time perspective and social consciousness.[6,21] Call and Mortimer[20] emphasize the benefits of work, arguing that work is an "arena of comfort" that can provide a safe haven for adolescents who experience stress from family, school, and/or peers. Using survey data from the Youth Development Study conducted in Minnesota, Finch et al[22] argue that the vast majority of teens find work to be satisfying and low stress and that positive support from supervisors can buffer family-based distress for working teens. They also find few significant differences between working and non-working teens except for an association between working long hours and alcohol abuse.

Many of the studies addressing the impact of working or not working on teen violence emphasize the impact of work intensity (ie, working 20 or more hours a week during the school year).[23-28] Some researchers argue for the importance of considering aspects of the work other than intensity.[26] Staff and Uggen[29] have reported that adolescents with more autonomy at work, with jobs that raise their status among peer groups, and with high paying jobs are more likely to engage in substance use. However, adolescents with jobs that are compatible with their schoolwork or that provide opportunities for useful learning are less likely to engage in substance use. Work settings provide opportunities for teens to learn and model behaviors, either positive or negative, from co-workers and supervisors.

The Descriptive Epidemiology of Injuries to Teen Workers

Data to understand the epidemiology of teen worker injury are limited. Likewise, because of differences in reporting injuries to teens vs. adults, comparisons must be made with caution. Though the literature on risk factors for injuries to young workers is growing, it still remains extremely limited at present. Few analytic epidemiologic studies exist; that is, case control or cohort studies assessing the relative influence of different risk factors. Several cross sectional studies, however, have identified risk factors that appear to be associated with increased risks of injuries in teen workers. In this section, we review the burden of injuries (fatal and nonfatal) among young workers and what is known about risk factors associated with an increased risk of injury within the teen workforce.

Fatal Injuries: Despite its potential benefits, employment has serious negative consequences for many adolescents. Several studies in the last decade have documented the magnitude of fatal injuries to young workers.[30-39] Between 1992 and 1997, more than 400 U.S. workers under age 18 died from occupational injuries.[38] Using actual hours worked converted to full time equivalency (since youth work part-time or for limited time periods), results in estimated fatality rates of 3.4 per 100 000 workers for 16 year olds and 3.7

per 100 000 for 17 year olds which were below the rate for all workers (5.0) while the rate of 5.1 per 100 000 for 15 year olds was slightly higher.[40]

Statistics on work-related fatalities among youth, age 17 and younger, are compiled by the Bureau of Labor Statistics (BLS) Census of Fatal Occupational Injuries (CFOI), an annual census covering all sectors of the United States economy. Based on CFOI data for 1992 through 1998, an average of 67 workplace deaths occurred annually among youths under 18, approximately one tenth of all worker deaths.[7] A review of pooled CFOI data for the 10-year period, 1993-2002, conducted by NIOSH appears in Table 1. Declines, over the time period, in fatal occupational injury rates are indicated for employed workers aged 16-17 (from 2 to 1.1 per 100 000) as well as for workers aged 18-19 (from 3 to 2.2 per 100 000). Fatal injury rates for workers younger than 16 years of age were not reported.

According to the CFOI data from 1992–2002, 89% of fatally injured youths were male; 73.6% were White, non-Hispanic and 60.5% were ages 16 or 17. Young Hispanic workers experienced the second highest proportion (16.1%) of the reported occupational injury fatalities during this 11-year period, though they represent a much smaller proportion of the working population in the age group. Based on estimates from the National Longitudinal Survey of Youth 1997 (NLSY 1997), 41% of Hispanic youths had worked by age 14 (compared to 64% of 14 year old White youths); by age 15, 48% of Hispanic and 71.8% of White youths had worked.[41] Though the majority of deaths were among working youths aged 16 and 17, youths 12 and under also incurred 13.3% of the deaths in the under 18 age group during this period. Approximately half of all youths interviewed in the NLSY 1997 engaged in a work activity when they were 12 years of age.[41]

Contrasting sharply with the industry distribution of fatalities for older workers, about three-fourths of the deaths of youth workers under 18 were

Table 1

Numbers and rates of fatal occupational injuries among workers aged 16–17 and 18–19, 1993–2002

Year	Number		Rate*	
	Age 16–17	Age 18–19	Age 16–17	Age 18–19
1993	39	102	2	3
1994	42	114	2	3
1995	42	130	2	3
1996	43	125	1.6	3.1
1997	41	113	1.5	2.8
1998	32	137	1.2	3.1
1999	46	122	1.6	2.7
2000	44	127	1.6	2.7
2001	33	122	1.3	2.8
2002	25	92	1.1	2.2

* Rate per 100,000 workers.

NOTE: BLS rounded the CFOI rates for 1992-95 to whole numbers, and to 1 decimal place beginning with the 1996 data.

Source: NIOSH Worker Health Chartbook, 2004

concentrated in three industries: agriculture (includes forestry and fishing), construction and retail trade (Table 2). Fatal injuries to teen workers were distributed as follows: 43.3% in agriculture, 19.2% in retail, and 16.1% in construction (Table 2). Separate analyses by BLS reveal that the burden of youth fatalities in agriculture is disproportionately borne by the youngest workers, approximately three-quarters of all deaths to workers under 15 years of age, and commonly involves farm machinery,[7] usually tractors.[40]

Computed rate ratios based on 1994-98 employment data, reported by the Department of Labor[7] suggest that the risk of a fatality, per hour worked, in an agriculture wage and salary job was over 4 times greater than the average risk for all working youths. For this same 4-year period, the Department of Labor's Report on the Youth Labor Force[7] identified youths working in family businesses as having an especially high fatality risk, irrespective of whether or not these jobs were inside (relative risk index of 5.28) or outside (relative risk index of 4.31) of agriculture.

Jobs in the retail trade industry comprise the largest share of youth employment and two thirds of fatalities among youth in retail trade between 1992 and 1998 were homicides.[7] Robberies accounted for one-quarter to one-half of all youth fatalities in retail trades.[39] Interestingly, the proportion of occupational fatalities among retail workers that are homicides is identical for both younger (under 18) and older (18 and over) workers—about two-thirds of all fatalities in each group.[39] In construction work, falls and electrocutions were the leading causes of youth fatalities.[40]

Events (manner in which fatal injuries were inflicted or produced) or exposures commonly responsible for the reported fatal occupational injuries during the 1992–2002 period involved transportation incidents (Table 3). Incidents on highways, farms or industrial premises taken together made up 75% of all transportation incidents. Contact with objects and equipment, followed by assaults and violent acts round out the top 3 leading events or exposures associated with youth occupational injury fatalities.

Comparisons with adult workers: It is hard to compare fatal injury risks for teen and adult workers because teens typically work part-time. Even computing based on hours worked is difficult; because hours worked data are often not readily available for young workers, especially those under 15 years of age. In a recent study of fatal teen injuries in the U.S. construction industry, Suruda et al[42] noted that although the rate of fatalities was lower for teens than adults using standard employment denominators, the adolescent rate may actually be greater than for adults on an hour-worked basis. This research also indicated that teenage workers killed while doing construction work were more likely than their adult counterparts to be working in non-union firms, smaller firms, and to be employed by employers with more safety citations from the US Department of Labor Occupational Safety and Health Administration (OSHA). In fact, about half the teen workers killed were in apparent violation of child labor regulations.[42]

Despite the difficulties and limitations in the estimation of youth hours-based employment, analysts using data from the 1994–98 Current Population Surveys at the Bureau of Labor Statistics[7] estimated that 88% of all youth work time was spent in wage and salary jobs in the private sector while agricultural jobs comprise 6.3% of all work hours.

Table 2

Distribution and number of fatal occupational injuries among workers aged 17 and younger by industry, 1992–2002

Private industry	1992	1993	1994	1995	1996	1997	1998	1999	2000	2001	2002	1992–2002 Number	1992–2002 Percent
Agriculture, forestry, and fishing	28	25	24	30	31	24	38	31	24	16	16	287	43.3%
Mining	—	—	—	—	—	—	—	—	—	—	—	—	—
Construction	5	9	9	7	11	12	11	9	11	18	5	107	16.1%
Manufacturing	—	—	—	5	—	—	—	—	8	—	—	40	6.0%
Transportation and public utilities	—	5	5	—	—	—	—	—	—	—	—	17	2.6%
Wholesale trade	—	5	—	13	5	15	—	—	—	—	—	15	2.3%
Retail trade	15	16	15	13	13	15	—	16	11	5	5	127	19.2%
Finance, insurance, and real estate	—	—	—	—	—	—	—	—	—	—	—	—	—
Services	7	7	5	—	—	5	6	9	8	9	6	70	10.6%
Total	66	66	64	65	68	62	63	71	63	52	38	678	

NOTE: Dashes (—) indicate no data reported or data do not meet BLS publication criteria.

NOTE: Sum of column entries may not add to total due to BLS publication criteria.

Source: NIOSH Worker Health Chartbook, 2004.

When compared to adults age 25–44, with the same sector and class-of-worker status, youths with wage and salary jobs outside agriculture had substantially less risk of a fatality (relative risk index of 0.62) than their adult counterparts.[7] However the risks of a fatality occurring to youths working in agriculture are very close to the corresponding risks to adults working in agriculture (relative risk indices of 0.95 for agricultural wage and salary worker, and 1.05 for all agricultural workers).[7]

Among industries outside of agriculture, the construction industry is particularly hazardous. One-fifth of all job-related fatalities among both youths and adults aged 25–44, over the time period 1994–98, occurred in construction although only 2.8% of youths' total work hours were spent in construction employment.[7] Despite youths' much smaller share of all hours worked in the construction industry than the corresponding share for adults, the risk of an occupational fatality per hour worked was about twice as high for youths as it was for adults working in construction over the 1994–98 period.[7]

The profile of fatal work injuries among youths (age <18 years) generally mirrors those incurred by adult workers. Using national data, Windau et al, revealed that, among youths, homicides were slightly higher than highway incidents as the leading cause of deaths at work.[39] Although highway incidents continue to be the leading cause of occupational death for adult workers, a larger proportion of vehicle-related incidents occurring on farms, industrial premises or in parking lots were among youth workers.[39] Other noticeable differences reported by Windau et al[39] involve fatalities resulting from falls, which were higher for all workers, and contact with objects and equipment, a greater number of which occurred among youth workers.

As previously noted 89% of the fatal occupational injuries among youths 17 and younger were male workers.[43] For all workers, males also

Table 3

Distribution and number of fatal occupational injuries among workers age 17 years old and younger, 1992–2002.

Event or Exposure	Number	Percent
Transportation incidents	320	45.3%
Highway	137	
Farm, industrial premises	101	
Struck by vehicle, mobile equipment	52	
Water vehicle	15	
Railway	8	
Other	7	
Assaults and violent acts	126	17.8%
Contact with objects and equipment	132	18.7%
Falls	48	6.8%
Exposure to harmful environments	68	9.6%
Fires and Explosions	11	1.6%
Other	2	0.3%
Total	707	

Source: NIOSH Worker Health Chartbook, 2004.

incurred the majority of fatal occupational injuries. Male workers generally work in more high risk industries and male youths are no exception. Though eating and drinking places were the most common employer of both male and female 14–15 year old youths, the construction industry was the second most prominent employer of 14–15 year old male youths and male 14 year old workers were 3 times as likely to work in construction as their female counterparts.[7] By age 15, construction remained a substantial employer of male youth workers but was not among the top 15 industries for female workers of the same age.[7]

Nonfatal injuries among working youth: Though teens have a rate per population of fatal work injury slightly less than that of adults,[30] the number of injuries per hour worked may be greater for youth. Layne et al[44] estimated that 64 100 youths between the ages of 14–17 were treated in emergency departments for occupational injuries in 1992 while NIOSH estimates that nearly 200 000 adolescents are injured at work every year.[45] Several studies have examined workers' compensation data to determine the incidence of nonfatal injuries to teen workers,[32,46-52] while others have examined first report of injury records[53] or used surveys of adolescents.[53-59] For example, a Washington State study using four years of workers' compensation data estimated the injury rate among 16–17 year-olds to be more than three times that for adult workers.[51] This is particularly troubling since child labor laws prohibit teens from working in occupations of highest risk, such as mining and manufacturing. Evidence from Canada suggests that the lost time claims for workers in their first month on the job are as much as five to seven times greater than those in the second or subsequent months.[60] Interestingly, this is true for both teens and older workers. However, given that young workers change jobs frequently, the overall impact of increased risk in the first month on the job may be greater for teenagers.[60]

Annual national data on nonfatal injuries and illnesses come from the BLS program: Survey of Occupational Injuries and Illnesses (SOII), which provides annual numbers of workplace injuries and illnesses in private industries and the frequency of these incidents. These data are not without limitations with respect to measurement of work injuries to youth. The exclusion of agriculture and family businesses omits an important source of jobs for youths; while the threshold for case inclusion (not being able to return to work on the "next regular workday") may be higher for younger workers since they tend to work part time compared to the majority of the labor force. Thus the estimates derived from these data are more likely to undercount the magnitude of nonfatal injuries to working youth.

Trend analyses of SOII data, 1992–2001, reported by NIOSH (Table 4) found nonfatal injuries and illnesses involving days away from work to be rare for workers younger than 14, with no cases reported for the 1997–2001 period and a comparably small number of cases for 1992–96. Among 14 and 15 year old workers, reported cases of nonfatal occupational injury and illness involving days away from work ranged from a low of 276 in 1998 to a high of 1476 in 1996. Workers in the age group 16–19 experienced a decreasing trend in reported cases for the time period 1992–2001.

Even though the rates are declining and may be small relative to all workers, the numbers of teens injured at work is substantial. The most recent data reported by NIOSH,[43] reflecting injuries in 2001, indicate that an estimated

44 249 cases of occupational injury and illness involving days away from work among workers aged 16–19 years old. By industry, the majority of nonfatal occupational injury and illness cases involving days away from work (n = 44 535) were in wholesale (45.6%) and retail trade (21.2%).

Injury severity and type: Muscle sprain, strain, or tear is the most frequent injury resulting in lost work time among youths under 18 years of age.[7] The cause of this injury is most often overexertion in lifting a heavy or bulky object.[39] These musculoskeletal injuries often do not result in medical care and are in sharp contrast to the more common work-related cuts and laceration injuries based on emergency room statistics reported for youths.[7] Data from a Massachusetts State surveillance program of adolescent occupational injuries using emergency department and workers' compensation data found strains and sprains to predominate among workers' compensation cases; while cuts, lacerations, and punctures were more common in emergency department cases.[7]

A New York State study[47] found that 44% of teens injured at work who filed workers' compensation claims suffered a permanent disability. Another study[57] revealed that 25% of teens treated in Emergency Departments for work injuries experienced limitations in their activities for more than a week. In our 1995 survey of working teens in North Carolina,[56] we discovered that 12% of injured youth reported missing school or work for a day and 16% required medical care. The majority of these reported working in retail trade and service; over half were injured at least once while ever working a paid job, most often from being cut or burned.

There are noteworthy gender differences with respect to frequency and type of nonfatal injury. Male workers represent two-thirds (62.5%) of adolescent injuries tracked in Massachusetts.[43] For 1997, sprains, strains and tears occurred more often during female youths' work time (37%) than during that of male youths (22%) while cuts and lacerations were more common among male youths.[43]

Table 4

Number of nonfatal occupational injuries and illnesses involving days away from work among young workers in private industry, 1992–2001.

Year	<14 years	14–15 years	16–19 years
1992	91	1,247	96,008
1993	23	889	95,790
1994	55	1,181	97,262
1995	17	865	83,512
1996	34	1,476	73,817
1997	(—)	284	59,737
1998	(—)	276	60,415
1999	(—)	866	58,206
2000	(—)	573	54,134
2001	(—)	908	44,535

NOTE: Dashes (—) indicate data are not available.

Source: NIOSH Worker Health Chartbook, 2004.

A commonly used measure for injury severity involves median number of workdays away from work. Using this metric, young workers overall have less severe injuries than all other workers combined; four days for young workers compared to five days for all other workers.[7] Comparing workers of the same age group, the median number of lost workdays in 1992 for young women (≤18 years of age) was 3 days; compared to 4 days for men of the same age group. By 1997, both male and female injured youths experienced about 4 median days of lost work time.[7]

The most current available information on lost work days reported by NIOSH (Table 5) is based on 2001 data and support the observation that work loss experienced by young workers tends to be short term. About two-thirds (62.3%) of cases among workers aged 14–15 lost 1–2 days of work and a similar proportion (60.1%) of cases among workers aged 16–19 involved 5 or fewer days of lost work. The median number of loss workdays was 2 for workers aged 14–15 and 4 days for workers aged 16–19. For comparative purposes, the median number of days away from work for all private sector cases was 6 days.[43]

Lost work time injuries to youths aged 16–17 were distributed across the six industries where youth employment is most concentrated: eating and drinking places, food stores, general merchandise stores, health services, amusement and recreation, and business services.[7] Analyses conducted by the U.S. Department of Labor indicate that the risk of an injury resulting in lost work time in health services was on average about 3 times greater than the risk in eating and drink, food stores, or general merchandise industries, respectively.[7] A higher number of median lost workdays, suggestive of more injuries, were also found in health services. In contrast, youths employed in amusement and recreation had on average about half the risk of a lost work time injury in comparison to their counterparts in other industries and these injuries also tended to be less severe, resulting in a median of 2 lost workdays.[7]

Though more severe nonfatal work injuries are relatively uncommon, it is important to have information on these injury types in order to monitor job safety among young workers. A BLS analysis[7] of data for 1992 through 1997 identified falls from ladders that resulted in bruises and contusions (median of 20 lost workdays) and fractures resulting from being caught or compressed by equipment or objects (median lost workdays of 14 days) as important contributors of morbidity among working youths.

Table 5

Percent distribution of occupational injuries and illnesses involving days away from work among workers aged 14–19 in private industry by number of days away from work, 2001.

Age Group	1 day	2 days	3–5 days	6–10 days	11–20 days	21–30 days	31 days or more
			Days away from work				
14–15	10.2%	52.1%	18.6%	8.5%	8.4%	0.4%	1.8%
16–19	18.1%	17.1%	24.9%	14.4%	9.4%	5.6%	10.5%

Source: NIOSH Worker Health Chartbook, 2004.

Comparisons with adult workers: Comparisons of the distribution of lost workdays between adults and youths suggest that injured adult workers lose more workdays than injured youth. For example, in 1997, roughly 25% of all workers with lost workdays were away from work for more than 20 days (4 weeks or more on a full-time schedule) while only about 10% of employed youths experienced this same amount of lost workdays. A 2004 study by Ehrlich et al[61] examined worker's compensation data for West Virginia and noted that the rate of injuries requiring surgical intervention among workers under age 19 (9.3% per year) was slightly higher than that for adults (8.9% per year). Of particular note was the nearly four times higher incidence of amputations among teen vs. adult workers.[61]

It is important to note that the use of lost work days as an indicator of injury severity may over-emphasize the relative severity of adult work injuries since youths are more likely to hold short duration jobs or work intermittent schedules than adults. Twenty or more lost workdays reflect a longer recuperation period for workers on intermittent schedules. Similarly, workers with short duration jobs often do not have the opportunity to work additional days. It is conceivable that recuperation time for youths includes non-scheduled work time, which would not be included in counts of days away from work thereby underestimating the severity of youth injuries.

Industry and job-related characteristics: Some industries and their associated job related conditions present high injury risk settings for teen workers.[15,62-64] Absence of safety devices and being rushed also constitute potential risk factors. Certain industries are more dangerous simply due to the types of jobs they offer. For example, the majority of young worker fatalities occur in agricultural settings,[31,34] mostly associated with operating tractors and other machinery.[36,37,64-66] Retail establishments involve exchange of cash, a known risk factor for robbery and worker assaults[67-71] and for which potentially modifiable cash handling practices appear to be influential in the level of risk experiences.[70,71] Analyses of data from the National Electronic Injury Surveillance System for adolescents aged 14 through 17 showed that the highest number of work-related injuries to youth under 18 were in eating and drinking establishments and food stores,[72] with the fast food industry being the source of a large proportion of occupational injuries to adolescents.[73] Hendricks et al[73] identified the specific safety practices of fast food restaurants that are associated with teens' increased risks of burns and falls in those settings, including the floor surfacing and how fryers are operated and maintained. Likewise, there is evidence that the types of cutting instruments provided in grocery stores influence the incidence of cut injuries among teen workers.[46] Similarly, youth working in construction are exposed to various types of hazardous equipment (eg, electrical equipment, machinery) as well as working conditions (eg, heights, extreme weather) that are associated with injury[42,74,75] while those working in jobs involving transportation are subjected to other hazard associated with operating, riding in, or working near motor vehicles.[35]

Preventing Teen Worker Injury

A huge gap exists in the understanding of factors that might contribute to prevention of teen worker injury and in evaluating the effectiveness of specific preventive interventions. As with most types of injuries, the prevention of injuries at work requires broad thinking and multiple types of strategies. Unlike some other areas of injury control, there is very limited evidence about successful approaches to prevention of teen worker injuries or other negative outcomes that may be associated with teen work.

Training: Though data on worker training are scant, the lack of training appears to place workers at increased risk.[6,62,76-79] Several recent studies[44,57,80] have documented that youth receive little training about workplace safety. There is little information on training and its effects on teen worker safety, though one recent study[79] suggests that trained teens working in construction experienced a 42% reduction in workers' compensation claims compared to those not trained.

However, training is often not available. In a survey of teen workers in sites within Massachusetts, California, Pennsylvania and throughout North Carolina, few teens reported having been trained about safety procedures related to their specific job tasks.[54,63,68,81] Work by Knight et al[57] reported 54% of the injured adolescent workers had not received safety training. Several studies[15,82,83] suggest teens may not distinguish between training on "how to do their jobs" and "how to do their jobs safely" and what their rights as workers are. Focus group discussions with teen workers have surfaced their concerns about the quality of training they have received.[15] Others have noted that training is very often not offered at all, or on a very limited basis[9,11,75,82,83] and may not be in a language appropriate to the workers.[75]

Supervision: Given this lack of training, the fact that many teens work alone, without adult supervision, and/or after dark is particularly troublesome.[11,84] For example, in one study, more than one fifth of teens reported working alone after dark, yet only 55% had been trained on how to deal with robberies, and fewer than a fifth had training on sexual harassment; while 65% reported having training on dealing with angry customers.[68]

This lack of adequate supervision has been linked to injury risks.[6,77] For example, nearly a fourth of the teens interviewed by Knight et al[57] had been alone at the time of their injury event, and 80% had no supervisor present. Several studies indicate teens routinely work without supervision and alone. One study found the average young worker spent only 12 percent of his or her time in the presence of a supervisor.[85]

Regulatory approaches: In 1938, the Federal government included child labor provisions in the Fair Labor Standards Act (FLSA). Most states have since passed laws to supplement the FLSA. These Federal and state laws, commonly known as child labor laws (CLLs) are designed to protect youth under age 18 from hazardous work conditions. They specify minimum ages for general and specific types of employment, prohibit work during night hours ("night work restrictions"), prohibit certain kinds of employment ("hazardous orders"), and dictate maximum daily and weekly hours of work. The Labor Department's Occupational Safety and Health Administration (OSHA), which establishes and enforces mandatory safety and health standards for workers of all ages, also protects teen workers.

Forty-one states have laws that require young workers (age 14–17) to obtain a work permit, with the intent that these procedures will ensure greater compliance with worker safety standards and teen labor laws. The effectiveness of the work permit system is currently being studied (J. Dal

Santo, oral communication, January 2005) but has not yet been examined in detail. However, there is some suggestion that work permits appear to be effective in limiting certain types of hazardous practices.[82]

Also important is enforcement of existing laws. For example, several studies report that large proportions of teens killed at work had been employed in situations in, or appearing to be in violation of the Fair Labor Standards Act (FLSA) or involving youth working in unregulated settings.[35,38] Nationally, it is estimated that 19% of teens treated in emergency departments for work-related injuries had been hurt while doing jobs prohibited by child labor laws.[57] The Department of Labor found 1475 serious injuries of illegally employed children between 1983–1990, 85% of which were associated with "hazardous order" violations.[86] More recent research examined youths employed in construction and noted that in at least 49% of the deaths of teen workers, there were apparent violations.[42] Some specific tasks appear to be responsible for a large number of the injuries to youth, despite the fact that they are not prohibited by the FLSA. These tasks include: handling hot liquids and grease,[53,87] using cutting tools,[46,52,88] using non-powered hand tools,[89] using power machinery,[57] lifting or moving heavy objects,[53,57] operating tractors,[90-92] and working late at night and/or alone.[57,93]

Recent efforts have been proposed to strengthen the laws subsequent to a careful review of Federal policy about hazardous work and prohibited occupations.[94] This effort has suggested that attention needs to be paid to specific areas of concern: working on roofs and in confined spaces; use of power-driven equipment, meat slicers, and various types of construction work. In addition, the need for more attention to workplace violence risks, bloodborne pathogen exposures, firefighting, youth peddling, and weight restrictions for lifting[94] was cited.

To the extent regulation is effective, it requires careful enforcement. In addition, education to help ensure that employers, health and educational professionals, parents and working teens are aware of the laws and their requirements is potentially important to increase adherence. Child labor laws, though useful in reducing many risks to teen workers, do not protect teens from all injuries. Federal reports have called for employers to "strive to implement available prevention strategies for hazards that are not covered by existing standards."[95,96]

Worksite safety interventions: Other than regulatory measures, there is little published evidence about the implementation or effectiveness of specific intervention strategies to improve teen worker safety in the United States. In Canada, a variety of teen worker safety projects are underway and evidence may emerge in the coming years.

One set of projects in the United States involved the development of school-based curricula for teaching teens about safe work practices.[73,83] However, data on program effectiveness have not been published. Other curricula have been developed within the US and Canada, though evaluation of effectiveness has not yet been documented in the peer-reviewed literature.

Even with these new efforts to produce curricula, there is not consistent exposure to these programs. In our national study of teens conducted in 2003, we asked teens about the training they had received to do their jobs. Approximately two-thirds reported having received some sort of training, mostly by demonstration at the workplace. Fewer than 10% reported having received worker safety training at school.[11] Despite the fact many teens report having received training at work, the content of that training is widely variable and may or may not be well matched to their job duties or the fact that they are inexperienced workers. Issues associated with workers for whom English is not their first language pose even greater challenges.[75]

Only one study[97] has been found in the literature assessing the implementation of a worker safety program designed to reduce risks for teen workers—a randomized trial that examined the effects of worker safety training and changes in the types of box cutters used by grocery store workers. Their results indicate that the greatest decrease in case-cutting injuries were in stores that introduced both new safety cutters and worker safety education, though stores with just an education program also had decreases in case-cutting injuries. However, the study was small and may not be generalizable to other settings or risks.

Studies show that parents of teen workers usually express approval and pride when teens enter the workforce[21,98] and that both teens and parents evaluate their own early work experiences as favorable.[99] Structural changes in the labor market, including the growth of the service sector and the extended hours of service establishments, have changed parents' role in teen job acquisition. These changes in the youth labor market mean that parental involvement, at least in states that do not require parent signatures on work permits, is no longer absolutely necessary for a teen to find a job. However, parents still play a vital role in helping teens develop better understandings of the world of work and in using their personal and social resources to help find desirable jobs.[100] Little is known about parental roles in assisting teens in learning about child labor laws and developing workplace safety behaviors and attitudes, though our own research has demonstrated that parents report involvement in helping their adolescents find jobs and consider work hours.[11] They are, however, less involved in helping teens learn about worker rights and workplace safety. This is consistent with the low level of concern they express about worker safety, indicating a need for efforts to increase their awareness both of workplace safety hazards as well as protective strategies, including child labor laws in their respective States. If parents are to become a resource for injury control, more information is needed about their knowledge and attitudes concerning youth labor and their interactions with their working teenage children. Yet, parents have received limited attention in efforts to prevent teen occupational injury.

Though parents have not been a frequent target of teen occupational injury prevention efforts, a few resources targeting parents do exist. The National Consumer's League web site[101] has a detailed "Parents Primer" about teen work which recommends that parents set limits, talk frequently with their son/daughter about work, visit their teenager's workplace, meet the boss, and check on the employer's history of labor law violations. Likewise, NIOSH's publication[102]: *Promoting Safe Work for Young Workers* encourages young worker safety projects to partner with parents in the effort to promote safety.

Conclusion

Summary: Employment of teens, while highly variable in nature, is a common and important element of this phase of development, as teens learn independence and develop new skills. Teens work for a variety of reasons and derive varied benefits from their employment. At the same time, work experiences vary widely with respect to the type of work, hours worked, duration of employment and quality of the experience. As a result the positive and negative effects of adolescent employment differ.

Measuring and quantifying the effects of teen labor is difficult. Furthermore, making assessments of the risks and benefits are complex and comparisons to adult workers especially challenging. Unlike adults, most teen workers work part time, change jobs frequently, and in a given position may perform a wide variety of tasks. For example, those working in service and retail settings do such diverse tasks as cleaning, lifting, handling cash, working at heights, using knives, ovens, and operating fryers. Even where data on young workers exist, there are variations in how information is recorded and which age groups are included.

Despite the difficulties in understanding the work patterns and experiences of teens, a fair amount is known. In the US, the majority of teen workers are employed in the retail and trade industries, with smaller proportions working in agriculture, construction, and manufacturing. Within these work environments they are exposed to a large array of hazards including working alone, late at night, handling cash, and dealing with potentially angry customers as well as working with dangerous equipment, and chemicals or in other dangerous conditions (eg, heights), despite legal requirements designed to protect young workers. Employers often provide very limited training and supervision to these young employees.

While both child labor and worker safety laws are designed to protect these young workers from many hazards, they are not fully enforced and gaps exist. In addition, many teens are not aware of the laws or of their rights as workers, so they may not always raise questions when they are asked to perform dangerous tasks. Likewise, their parents may be unaware of the laws or of safety issues in the places their adolescents work.

A common tendency in the social sciences and public health is to examine a problem in terms of a limited set of organizing categories (eg, black versus white; rural versus urban). These categories are useful for discovering and analyzing disparities in health, but they can also lead to divisions among scholars and health professionals. The state of research and intervention on health consequences of adolescent employment is indicative of this type of division. The *work is good versus work is bad* debate is only one part of the division. Different groups of scholars and health professionals deal with violence and delinquency, school achievement and occupational attainment, and occupational injury and fatality outcomes. This is not surprising given the complexity of adolescent development and the necessity of examining a variety of background variables, occupational exposures, and health beliefs in accounting for the consequences of teen employment. However, it is time to begin to integrate the empirical work and prevention efforts.

Implications for future research and prevention efforts: Little evidence exists about successful interventions to protect young workers from injury on-the-job. While increasing attention has been paid to development of worker safety training programs for youth, no one knows what elements of these programs are successful and how to deliver them in the most effective manner. Furthermore, to focus the majority of intervention energy on education directed at the teen employees, while it may be helpful, has only limited potential effect. New efforts are needed that bring together diverse expertise to design interventions that address not only the knowledge, attitudes, skills and behaviors of the teen workers, but that also address the need for changes in the social and physical environments in which work takes place. The Haddon Matrix is a useful model for generating ideas about multiple approaches to interventions.[103-105] Using the matrix in a multidisciplinary group has great benefit in identifying options that derive from varied areas of expertise and that speak to the pros and cons of teen employment experiences.

Once interventions of any type are developed, they need to be carefully designed so as to allow sound evaluations. This will enable good decision-making about continuing strategies that work and abandoning interventions which have no effect or which may, in fact, be harmful. Those conducting evaluations must not only do them well, but must make efforts to disseminate the findings of their work, both positive and negative, so that others can learn from the experience and replicate the high quality interventions in new locales and either modify or avoid interventions that have proven to be unsuccessful.

Part of what is needed is to examine adolescent work within a life course perspective that recognizes the important role work plays in adolescent development. This calls our attention not just to the exposures in the workplace, but to the interaction of parents, teens, and employers in the labor process. Teens, wanting to demonstrate competence may not ask questions about workplace safety. Employers may assume that teens understand the workplace or may place responsibility for training and safety on older workers. Parents, especially those who help teens find jobs through their personal networks, assume that the workplace is safe. There is great need to understand these interactions more fully and to develop intervention strategies that address the complexity of the contexts in which teens work. In taking this approach, there needs to be close involvement of professionals involved in youth development such as teachers, pediatricians, and school counselors as well as parents, employers, and the adolescents themselves.

Finally, careful work needs to examine the nature, implementation and enforcement of policies both that are designed to protect young workers as well as those that may have unintended effects (positive or negative) on the employment prospects and experiences of teen workers.

While further scientific evidence about the problem and about interventions is being developed, we suggest that efforts be made to continue to engage parents, teens, employers and teachers in developing and implementing strategies to improve awareness of workplace safety issues. Efforts should incorporate education, regulation, legislation and, as necessary, litigation.

Youth advocacy and worker's rights organizations should take advantage of their abilities to advance teen worker safety as they advocate with decision makers in schools, health care providers, and government bodies. Every working teen and his/her parents should receive clear, understandable information about the policies that affect teen work in their locale as well as information about workers rights and safety measures, whether covered by existing law or not. They should have guidance with regard to hazards in specific types of workplaces and suggestions for how to assess the safety of a particular job, questions to ask employers, and where to get help if safety is in question. Much of this information can be obtained from sources listed in Figure 1. Advocacy should also focus on ensuring that worker safety policies, whether general or specific to teens, are properly disseminated to employers with clear expectations and assistance for achieving compliance. Advocacy groups should also monitor the regulatory process and promote clear and complete enforcement of measures designed to protect young workers.

Figure 1

Selected resources for further information

CDC National Center for Injury Prevention and Control
  www.cdc.gov/ncipc/

Children's Safety Network
National Injury and Violence Prevention Resource Center
  www.edc.org/HHD/csn
National Children's Center for Rural and Agricultural Health and Safety
  http://research.marshfieldclinic.org/children
Economics and Insurance Resource Center
  http://www.csneric.org
National Injury Data Technical Assistance Center
  http://www.nidtac.org

These are four national resource centers that provide information, training, and technical assistance for injury and violence prevention programs for state and local health departments. Also provided are publications and resource guides for professionals to assist them with injury control and violence prevention programs for adolescents.

FEDNET: Federal Network for Young Workers Safety and Health
  http://www.cdc.gov/niosh/fedNET/

Website gateway to nine federal agencies.

Labor Occupational Health Program, UC Berkeley, Young Workers' Health and Safety Website
  http://socrates.berkeley.edu/^safejobs

Information for teens, parents, employers and teachers.

National Consumer's League: Child Labor Coalition
  http://nclnet.org/childlabor

A private non-profit organization that is a major advocate for youth safety at work, both for teens working in traditional jobs and especially for teens working in traveling sales crews.

National COSH: The National Council for Occupational Safety and Health
  http://www.coshnetwork.org/english_resources.htm

Network of non-profit organizations working on workers' rights, health and safety.

continued

Educators should incorporate basic information about worker safety into standard health and safety curricula at schools so as to help raise teen awareness of the issues and encourage a culture of safety. Curricula should target all teens, not just those in work-based learning programs.

Parents should engage with advocacy groups and support their efforts to monitor and enhance regulatory measures and their enforcement. They should also discuss workplace safety with their teen workers and help them

Figure 1

continued

New York Committee for Occupational Safety and Health (NYCOSH)
http://www.nycosh.org

Non-profit provider of occupational safety and information training and information to workers and unions in the New York metropolitan area.

Occupational Health Surveillance Program, Massachusetts Department of Public Health, Teens at Work Surveillance and Prevention Project
www.state.ma.us/dph/bhsre/ohsp

Collects information on work-related injuries to teens under 18 in Massachusetts and recommendations for targeted interventions and prevention activities.

University of Illinois, Urbana School of Social Work, Child Labor Resource Office
http://childlabor.social.uiuc.edu/childlabor_files/home.html

Mission of the Child Labor Resource Office is to end the worst forms of child labor worldwide. Provides resources on the causes and consequences of child labor. Website includes online resource guide.

US Department of Labor, Bureau of Labor Statistics, Injuries, Illnesses and Fatalities Home Page
http://www.bls.gov/iif

Provides data on illnesses and injuries on the job and data on worker fatalities.

U.S. Department of Labor, OSHA, Teen Workers Safety and Health Page
http://www.youth2wprk.gov

Designed to educate teen workers, parents, employers and educators about workplace safety. Provides fact sheets on job hazards, rights and responsibilities, ways to prevent injuries, child labor laws, and links to state resources.

WCB Worksafe BC Young Workers Health and Safety Centre
http://youngwworker.healthandsafetycentre.org/s/Home.asp

Workman's Compensation Board of British Columbia with online resources for workers, employers, parents and educators.

Young Worker Safety and Health Network
http://www.osha.gov/SLTC/teenworkers/networkmembers.html

Network of researchers, educators, physicians, and other professionals working to ensure the safety of youth in the workplace.

assess the safety of jobs they are considering and monitor safety conditions and exercise their rights as workers once employed.

Health care professionals, particularly pediatricians who care for adolescents, should become familiar with worker safety issues, regulations and strategies for providing guidance to their teen patients. They should become advocates for worker safety regulatory measures and assist parents in providing guidance to teens.

Employers need to assume the major burden for ensuring a safe workplace for teens by developing their own and their managers' knowledge and awareness of safety issues, including ensuring full compliance with workplace safety and youth labor regulations. They should implement carefully considered training and supervision practices, based on sound evidence and should monitor safety regularly, inform young workers of their rights and encourage and reward safety consciousness among teen workers and their supervisors.

Government officials at the Federal and State level should maintain high standards for businesses and enforce existing laws to the full extent, while providing employers with assistance in finding ways to make work safer for teen workers. They should collect surveillance data and use it to monitor teen worker safety issues so as to make appropriate adjustments in policies, enforcement, educational and assistive efforts. In addition, the Federal government should ensure sufficient funding for research on teen labor safety as well as support mechanisms for periodical exchange of information both within the US and with international colleagues so as to enhance dissemination of evidence-based and best practices for reducing teen worker injury. Furthermore, support for a national resource center on teen worker safety, similar to what has been developed at the National Children's Center for Rural and Agricultural Health and Safety to address agricultural safety issues, would be one mechanism for synthesizing information from research and practice so as to enhance adoption of innovations that encourage best practices within businesses.

The *media* should continue to give coverage to the issue of occupational health and safety through both news and feature stories, helping to reinforce that injury at work is aberrant and should not be considered just "the cost of doing business" and noting that teen workers are a group requiring special attention. This, hopefully, will help establish a social norm that reinforces the importance of a culture of safety at work.

Finally, all the various groups and activities identified will work best if there is clear communication and networking among them and commonality in the message. Advocacy groups and health professionals should take a leadership role in developing a community-based social marketing programs for teenage occupational injury. This approach would engage parents, teens, and employers in choosing a package of health promotion and information tools to reduce the risks of teen occupational injury in their community. Ultimately, through these various means, we may be able to find the "tipping point"[106] by which safety of young workers is highly valued and considered normative as something that is not left to a few safety professionals to advocate.

References

1. Montel Williams Talk Show. Working Teens: Dangerous Jobs. Available at: http://www.montelshow.com/show/past_detail_11_17_2004.htm. Accessed January 13, 2005.

2. National Institute for Occupational Safety and Health FACE program. Youth Fatality Investigation Reports [Available online at: http://www.cdc.gov/niosh/injury/traumayouthface.html]. Accessed January 25, 2005.

3. National Institute for Occupational Safety and Health FACE Investigations of Young Worker Incidents 2004. Sixteen-Year-Old Hispanic Youth Dies After Falling From A Job-Made Elevated Work Platform During Construction—South Carolina [online document: http://www.cdc.gov/niosh/face/In-house/full 200406.html]. Accessed January 25, 2005.

4. National Institute for Occupational Safety and Health FACE Investigations of Young Worker Incidents 2004. Seventeen-Year-Old High School Student Working as a Warehouse Laborer in Work-Based Learning Program Dies After Forklift Tips Over and Crushes Him—Tennessee [online document: http://www.cdc.gov/niosh/face/In-house/full200403.html]. Accessed January 25, 2005.

5. Szafran R. Age-adjusted labor force participation rates, 1960-2045. *Mon Labor Rev.* 2002;125:46.

6. Committee on the Health and Safety Implications of Child Labor—National Research Council and Institute of Medicine. *Protecting Youth at Work: Health, Safety, and Development of Working Children and Adolescents in the United States.* Washington, DC: National Academy Press; 1998.

7. Herman AM. *Report on the Youth Labor Force.* Washington, D. C.: Office of Publications and Special Studies, U.S. Department of Labor, Bureau of Labor Statistics; November 2000.

8. Bureau of Labor Statistics. Youth Employment, Unemployment Both Rise in the Summer. *Bureau of Labor Statistics, United States Department of Labor.* Available at: http://stats.bls.gov/opub/ted/2001/aug/wk3/art03.htm. Accessed 2003, October.

9. Zierold KM, Garman S, Anderson H. Summer work and injury among middle school students, aged 10-14 years. *Occup Environ Med.* Jun 2004;61(6):518-522.

10. Huang L, Pergamit M, Shlolnik J. Youth initiation into the labor market. *Mon Labor Rev.* 2001;124(8):18-24.

11. Runyan CW, Bowling JM, Schulman MD, et al. *Safety of Youth Employment: A National Study of Parents and Teens. Final Grant Report to the National Institute for Occupational Safety and Health.* Chapel Hill, NC: The University of North Carolina Injury Prevention Research Center; 2004. Grant-Number-R01-OH-003530.

12. Kruse DL, Mahony D. Illegal child labor in the United States: prevalence and characteristics. *Ind Labor Relat Rev.* 2000;54(1):17-40.

13. Bravermann H. *Labor and Monopoly Capital.* New York, NY: Monthly Review Press; 1974.

14. Evenson CT, Schulman MD, Runyan CW, Zakocs RC, Dunn KA. The downside of adolescent employment: hazards and injuries among working teens in North Carolina. *J Adolesc.* 2000;23(5):545-560.

15. Zakocs R, Runyan CW, Schulman MD, Dunn KA, Evenson C. Improving safety for teens working in the retail trade sector: opportunities and obstacles. *Am J Ind Med.* 1998;34:342-350.

16. Dwyer T. *Life and Death at Work: Industrial Accidents as a Case of Socially Produced Error.* New York, NY: Plenum Press; 1991.

17. Scharf T, Vaught C, Kidd P, et al. Toward a typology of dynamic and hazardous work environments. *Human Ecol Risk Assess.* 2001;7(7):1827-1842.

18. Schulman MD, Slesinger DP. Health hazards of rural extractive industries and occupations. In: Glasgow N, Morton LW, Johnson NE, eds. *Critical Issues in Rural Health*. Ames, IA: Blackwell; 2004:49-60.

19. George LK. Sociological perspectives on life transitions. *Ann Rev Sociol.* 1993; 19:353-373.

20. Call KT, Mortimer JT. *Arenas of Comfort in Adolescence: A Study of Adjustment in Context*. Mahwah, NJ: Lawrence Erlbaum Associates; 2001.

21. Phillips S, Sandstrom KL. Parental attitudes toward youth work. *Youth Soc.* 1990;22:160-183.

22. Finch MD, Mortimer JT, Ryu S. Transition in part-time work: health risks and opportunities. In: Schulenberg J, Maggs JL, Hurrelmann K, eds. *Health Risks and Developmental Transitions During Adolescence*. New York, NY: Cambridge University Press; 1997.

23. Heimer K. Gender, race and the pathways to delinquency: an interactionist analysis. In: Hagan J, Peterson RD, eds. *Crime and Inequality*. Stanford, CA: Stanford University Press; 1995.

24. Wofford M, Elliott S, Elliott D. Short- and long-term consequences of adolescent work. *Youth Soc.* 1997;28:464-509.

25. Miller WJ, Matthews RA. Youth employment, differential association, and juvenile delinquency. *Sociol Focus.* 2001;34:251-268.

26. Wright JP, Cullen FT, Williams N. Working while in school and delinquent involvement: implications for social policy. *Crime Delinq.* 1997;43:203-221.

27. Safron DJ, Schulenberg J, Bachman JG. Part-time work and hurried adolescence: the links among work intensity, social activities, health behaviors, and substance use. *J Health Soc Behav.* 2001;42:425-449.

28. Ploeger M. Youth employment and delinquency: reconsidering a problematic relationship. *Criminology.* 1997;35:659-675.

29. Staff J, Uggen C. The fruits of good work: early work experiences and adolescent deviance. *J Res Crime Delinq.* 2003;40:263-290.

30. Castillo DN, Malit BD. Occupational injury deaths of 16 and 17 year olds in the US: trends and comparisons with older workers. *Inj Prev.* Dec 1997;3(4):277-281.

31. Castillo DN, Landen DD, Layne LA. Occupational injury deaths of 16- and 17-year-olds in the United States. *Am J Public Health.* Apr 1994;84(4):646-649.

32. Cooper SP, Rothstein MA. Health hazards among working children in Texas. *South Med J.* May 1995;88(5):550-554.

33. The hazards of child labor. Committee on Environmental Health, American Academy of Pediatrics. *Pediatrics.* Feb 1995;95(2):311-313.

34. Derstine B. The hazards of child labor. *Compens Work Con.* 1996;Dec:40-42.

35. Dunn KA, Runyan CW. Deaths at work among children and adolescents. *Am J Dis Child.* 1993;147:1044-1047.

36. Rivara FP. Fatal and non-fatal farm injuries to children and adolescents in the United States, 1990-3. *Inj Prev.* Sep 1997;3(3):190-194.

37. Schenker MB, Lopez R, Wintemute G. Farm-related fatalities among children in California, 1980 to 1989. *Am J Public Health.* Jan 1995;85(1):89-92.

38. Suruda A, Halperin W. Work-related deaths in children. *Am J Ind Med.* 1991; 19(6):739-745.

39. Windau J, Sygnatur E, Toscano G. Profile of work injuries incurred by young workers. *Mon Labor Rev.* 1999;122(6):3-10.

40. Cimini MH. Research summary: fatal injuries and young workers. *Compens Work Cond.* 1999;Summer:27-29.

41. Rothstein DS. Youth employment in the United States. *Mon Labor Rev.* 2001; 124(8):6-17.

42. Suruda A, Philips P, Lillquist D, Sesek R. Fatal injuries to teenage construction workers in the US. *Am J Ind Med.* Nov 2003;44(5):510-514.

43. National Institute for Occupational Safety and Health. *Worker Health Chartbook, 2004.* Cincinnati, OH: NIOSH Publications; 2004. Publication 2004-146.

44. Layne LA, Castillo DN, Stout N, Cutlip P. Adolescent occupational injuries requiring hospital emergency department treatment: a nationally representative sample. *Am J Public Health.* Apr 1994;84(4):657-660.

45. National Institute for Occupational Safety and Health. *NIOSH Alert: Request for assistance in preventing deaths and injuries of adolescent workers.* Washington, DC: US Department of Health and Human Services; 1995. Publication 95-125.

46. Banco L, Lapidus G, Braddock M. Work-related injury among Connecticut minors. *Pediatrics.* May 1992;89(5 Pt 1):957-960.

47. Belville R, Pollack SH, Godbold JH, Landrigan PJ. Occupational injuries among working adolescents in New York State. *JAMA.* Jun 2 1993;269(21):2754-2759.

48. Brooks DR, Davis LK. Work-related injuries to Massachusetts teens, 1987-1990. *Am J Ind Med.* Feb 1996;29(2):153-160.

49. Cooper SP, Burau KD, Robison TB, Richardson S, Schnitzer PG, Fraser JJ, Jr. Adolescent occupational injuries: Texas, 1990-1996. *Am J Ind Med.* Jan 1999;35(1):43-50.

50. Heyer NJ, Franklin G, Rivara FP, Parker P, Haug JA. Occupational injuries among minors doing farm work in Washington State: 1986 to 1989. *Am J Public Health.* Apr 1992;82(4):557-560.

51. Miller ME, Kaufman JD. Occupational injuries among adolescents in Washington State, 1988-1991. *Am J Ind Med.* Aug 1998;34(2):121-132.

52. Schober SE, Handke JL, Halperin WE, Moll MB, Thun MJ. Work-related injuries in minors. *Am J Ind Med.* 1988;14(5):585-595.

53. Parker DL, Carl WR, French LR, Martin FB. Characteristics of adolescent work injuries reported to the Minnesota Department of Labor and Industry. *Am J Public Health.* Apr 1994;84(4):606-611.

54. Bowling JM, Runyan CW, Miara C, et al. Teenage workers' occupational safety: results of a four-school study. Paper presented at: The Fourth World Conference on Injury Prevention and Control; May 1998, Amsterdam, The Netherlands.

55. Cohen LR, Runyan CW, Dunn KA, Schulman MD. Work patterns and occupational hazard exposures of North Carolina adolescents in 4-H clubs. *Inj Prev.* 1996;2:274-277.

56. Dunn KA, Runyan CW, Cohen LR, Schulman MD. Teens at work: a statewide study of jobs, hazards, and injuries. *J Adolesc Health.* 1996;22(1):274-277.

57. Knight EB, Castillo DN, Layne LA. A detailed analysis of work-related injury among youth treated in emergency departments. *Am J Ind Med.* Jun 1995;27(6):793-805.

58. Parker DL, Carl WR, French LR, Martin FB. Nature and incidence of self-reported adolescent work injury in Minnesota. *Am J Ind Med.* Oct 1994;26(4):529-541.

59. Schulman MD, Evenson C, Runyan CW, Cohen LR, Dunn KA. Farm work is dangerous for teens: agricultural hazards and injuries. *J Rural Health.* 1997;13:295-305.

60. Chapeskie K, Breslin F. Securing a safe and healthy future: The road to injury prevention for Ontario's Young Workers. *In Focus: Current workplace research—a supplement to at work.* 2003;Fall 2003(34a).

61. Ehrlich PF, McClellan WT, Hemkamp JC, Islam SS, Ducatman AM. Understanding work-related injuries in children: a perspective in West Virginia using

the state-managed workers' compensation system. *J Pediatr Surg.* May 2004; 39(5):768-772.

62. National Institute for Occupational Safety and Health. *Violence in the Workplace: Risk Factors and Prevention Strategies.* Cincinnati, OH: Publications Dissemination, EID; 1996. Publication No. 96-100.

63. Runyan CW, Zakocs R, Dunn KA, Schulman MD, Evenson CT. Teen workers' training and concerns about safety. Paper presented at: 125th Annual Meeting of the American Public Health Association; November 9-12, 1997; Indianapolis, IN.

64. Stueland DT, Lee BC, Nordstrom DL, Layde PM, Wittman LM. A population based case-control study of agricultural injuries in children. *Inj Prev.* Sep 1996;2(3):192-196.

65. Centers for Disease Control and Prevention. Youth agricultural work-related injuries treated in emergency departments: United States, October 1995-September 1997. *MMWR Morbid Mortal Wkly Rep.* 1998;47(35):733-739.

66. Swanson JA, Sachs MI, Dahlgren KA, Tinguely SJ. Accidental farm injuries in children. *Am J Dis Child.* Dec 1987;141(12):1276-1279.

67. Moracco KE, Runyan CW, Loomis DP, Wolf SH, Napp D, Butts JD. Killed on the clock: a population-based study of workplace homicide, 1977-1991. *Am J Ind Med.* Jun 2000;37(6):629-636.

68. Runyan CW, Schulman M, Hoffman C. Understanding and preventing violence against adolescent workers: what is known and what is missing? *Clin Occup Environ Med.* 2003;3:711-720.

69. Peek-Asa C, Erickson R, Kraus JF. Traumatic occupational fatalities in the retail industry, United States 1992-1996. *Am J Ind Med.* Feb 1999;35(2):186-191.

70. Loomis D, Marshall SW, Wolf SH, Runyan CW, Butts JD. Effectiveness of safety measures recommended for prevention of workplace homicide. *JAMA.* Feb 27 2002;287(8):1011-1017.

71. Loomis D, Wolf SH, Runyan CW, Marshall SW, Butts JD. Homicide on the job: workplace and community determinants. *Am J Epidemiol.* Sep 1 2001; 154(5):410-417.

72. Mardis AL, Pratt SG. Nonfatal injuries to young workers in the retail trades and services industries in 1998. *J Occup Environ Med.* Mar 2003;45(3):316-323.

73. Hendricks KJ, Layne LA. Adolescent occupational injuries in fast food restaurants: an examination of the problem from a national perspective. *J Occup Environ Med.* Dec 1999;41(12):1146-1153.

74. Lipscomb HJ, Li L. Injuries among teens employed in the homebuilding industry in North Carolina. *Inj Prev.* Sep 2001;7(3):205-209.

75. O'Connor T LD, Runyan C, Dal Santo J, Schulman M. Adequacy of health and safety training among young Latino construction workers. *Am J Public Health.* In press.

76. Goldenhar LM, Schulte PA. Intervention research in occupational health and safety. *J Occup Med.* Jul 1994;36(7):763-775.

77. National Institute for Occupational Safety and Health Child Labor Working Team. *NIOSH Special Hazard Review-Child Labor Research Needs: Recommendations from the NIOSH Child Labor Working Team.* Washington, DC: US Department of Health and Human Services; 1997. Publication 97-143.

78. Office of Technology Assessment (OTA). *Preventing illness and injury in the workplace.* Washington, DC: US Government Printing Office; 1985. Publication OAT-H-256.

79. Dong X, Entzel P, Men Y, Chowdhury R, Schneider S. Effects of safety and health training on work-related injury among construction laborers. *J Occup Environ Med.* Dec 2004;46(12):1222-1228.

80. Bush D, Baker R. *Young Workers at Risk: Health and Safety Education and the Schools.* Berkeley, CA: Labor Occupational Health Program, University of California; 1994.

81. Runyan CW, Bowling JM, Schulman M, Gallagher SS. Potential for Violence Against Adolescent Workers in the U.S. *J Adolesc Health.* In Press.

82. Delp L, Runyan CW, Brown M, Bowling JM, Jahan SA. Role of work permits in teen workers' experiences. *Am J Ind Med.* Jun 2002;41(6):477-482.

83. Miara C, Gallagher S, Bush D, Dewey R. Developing an effective tool for teaching teens about workplace safety. *Am J Health Educ.* 2003;35(5, Supplement):30-34.

84. Runyan CW, Zakocs R. Epidemiology and prevention of injuries among adolescent workers in the US. *Ann Rev Public Health.* 2000;21:247-269.

85. Greenberger E, Steinberg L. *When Teenagers Work: The Psychological and Social Costs of Adolescent Employment.* New York, NY: Basic Books Inc. Publishers; 1986.

86. U.S. General Accounting Office. *Child Labor: Characteristics of Working Children.* Washington, DC: US General Accounting Office; 1998. Report No. GAO/HRD-91-83BR.

87. Hayes-Lundy C, Ward RS, Saffle JR, Reddy R, Warden GD, Schnebly WA. Grease burns at fast-food restaurants. Adolescents at risk. *J Burn Care Rehabil.* Mar-Apr 1991;12(2):203-208.

88. Brooks DR, Davis LK, Gallagher SS. Work-related injuries among Massachusetts children: a study based on emergency department data. *Am J Ind Med.* Sep 1993;24(3):313-324.

89. National Center for Health Statistics. *Healthy People 2000 Review, 1993.* Hyattsville, MD: US Public Health Service; 1994.

90. Children's Safety Network. *Injury Prevention Outlook: An Assessment of Injury Prevention in State MCH Agencies.* Newton, MA: Education Development Center, Inc.; 1992.

91. Kerr G, Fowler B. The relationship between psychological factors and sports injuries. *Sports Med.* Sep 1988;6(3):127-134.

92. Rivara FP. Fatal and nonfatal farm injuries to children and adolescents in the United States. *Pediatrics.* Oct 1985;76(4):567-573.

93. National Consumers League for the Child Labor Coalition. Late night hours can be killers. *Child Labor Monit.* 1993 (summer);3(2):1-2,8.

94. Miller ME, Bush D. Review of the Federal child labor regulations: updating hazardous and prohibited occupations. *Am J Ind Med.* Feb 2004;45(2):218-221.

95. Centers for Disease Control and Prevention. *Injury Control in the 1990s: A National Plan for Action. A report to the Second World Conference on Injury Control.* Atlanta, GA: National Center for Injury Prevention and Control, Centers for Disease Control and Prevention; 1993.

96. Wegman DH, Davis LK. Protecting youth at work. *Am J Ind Med.* Nov 1999; 36(5):579-583.

97. Banco L, Lapidus G, Monopoli J, Zavoski R. The Safe Teen Work Project: a study to reduce cutting injuries among young and inexperienced workers. *Am J Ind Med.* May 1997;31(5):619-622.

98. Lescohier I, Gallager SS. Unintentional injury. In: DiClement RJ, Hansen WB, Ponton LE, eds. *Handbook of Adolescent Risk Behavior.* New York, NY: Plenum Press; 1996:225-258.

99. Aronson PJ, Mortimer JT, Zierman C, Hacker M. Generational differences in early work experiences and evaluations. In: Mortimer JT, Finch MD, eds. *Adolescents, Work and Family.* Thousand Oaks, CA: Sage Publications; 1996:25-62.

100. Schneider B, Stevenson D. *The Ambitious Generation.* New Haven, CT: Yale University Press; 1999.

101. National Consumers League Child Labor Coalition. Working the Smart Shift: Helping Parents Help their Teens Avoid Dangerous Jobs [online document: http://www.stopchildlabor.org/USchildlabor/kidprime.htm]. Accessed January 25, 2005.

102. National Institute for Occupational Safety and Health. Promoting Safe Work for Young Workers: A Community Based Approach. Available at: http://www.cdc.gov/niosh/99-141.html. Accessed January 25, 2005.

103. Haddon W, Jr. Advances in the epidemiology of injuries as a basis for public policy. *Public Health Rep.* Sep-Oct 1980;95(5):411-421.

104. Haddon W, Jr. Options for the prevention of motor vehicle crash injury. *Israeli Med J.* 1980;16:45-65.

105. Runyan CW. Using the Haddon matrix: introducing the third dimension. *Inj Prev.* Dec 1998;4(4):302-307.

106. Gladwell M. *The Tipping Point: How Little Things Can Make a Big Difference.* Boston, MA: Little Brown and Company; 2002.

CHAPTER 7

Injuries in the School Environment

Ellen R. Schmidt,[1] Abbey Mahady,[2] and Stephanie Bryn[3]

Schools that are unable to protect students from injury and violence while on school grounds or involved in school-sponsored activities ignore a basic responsibility (Posner, 2000). It is estimated that up to 25 percent of all child and adolescent injuries occur on school grounds (Danseco, Miller, and Spicer, 2000). As injuries remain the leading cause of death and disability for school-aged children, public health and safety professionals must align themselves with school personnel to address the needs of this population.

Injuries in the school environment range from minor cuts and bruises from a playground fall to fatal acts of violence or school bus crashes. Many of these injuries can be prevented with strong policy development, implementation, and enforcement; comprehensive health education programs; environmental changes; and other components of a coordinated school health program.

Stories from Students and Their Families

Although all of the stories below are true, names and locations have been changed to protect the privacy of the individual.

Mark

Mark, a 15-year-old high school sophomore, was using the table saw in shop class when he lost control of the board he was cutting. In an attempt to stabilize the board, he used his hands to push the wood down. As he did this, his hand landed on the saw blade, and as a result he lost most of the flesh in his left thumb. Mark underwent a fusion of joints in his index and middle finger following the incident, and now has little feeling and no fine motor coordination in his left hand. The school staff person responsible for

1   Children's Safety Network at the Education Development Center.
2   Education Development Center.
3   HRSA/Maternal and Child Health Bureau.

technical education had removed the saw guard and neglected to replace the important safety precaution (Children's Safety Network, 1997).

Brian

Brian was a 15-year-old freshman who went on a shooting spree in his high school. Brian took a .22 caliber handgun from his father's gun cabinet to school and proceeded to open fire on his classmates. Brian killed two students and wounded 13 others in a six-minute time span.

After the incident, details surfaced that Brian's rash of violence was a response to being picked on and bullied by other students and neighborhood kids. Brian was a smaller kid and always remarked that people thought he was dumb. The bullying led to depression, and there are numerous reports that Brian was considering suicide. Brian said that he never intended to kill anyone, but rather wanted to get caught with a gun on school premises so the school bullies would know that he was a tough guy too. Brian had shared his intentions to bring a gun to school with some of his friends and his mother's boyfriend, but nobody believed him.

Brian was tried as an adult for his crime and was sentenced to 50 years to life in prison for two counts of murder and 13 counts of attempted murder. Brian will not be eligible for parole until 2051 when he will be 65 years old (Reaves, 2001).

Rachel

Rachel, a six-year old elementary-school student, took the bus home from school everyday. One Tuesday afternoon, Rachel got off the bus and, while crossing the busy street in front of her house, was struck by the driver's side-view mirror of a passing car. Rachel sustained serious damage to her optic nerve and is now totally blind. The reasons for this event are two-fold; the bus stop was determined to be in an unsafe location and the bus driver had not used flashing lights to stop oncoming traffic for a sufficient period of time (Children's Safety Network, 1997).

Overview

Schools have a responsibility to prevent injuries from occurring on school property and at school-sponsored events. Schools have always been involved in injury and violence prevention. Policies that prohibit running in the hallways, fire drills, and helmet and mouth guard requirements for sports are staples of school life. However, in most cases, injury and violence prevention in schools has been done on an ad hoc basis as opposed to a coordinated injury and violence prevention effort (Posner, 2000). The application of the public health model to school injuries suggests that injuries occur in the context of the interaction between students and their environment and that interventions can focus on changing these interactions (Posner, 2000). This chapter will review prevalence and incidence data for injuries common on school grounds and at school events, and will offer recommendations for how schools can develop and implement a coordinated injury prevention initiative.

As mentioned in other chapters, unintentional injuries and violence represent the leading causes of death and disability for school-aged children. Schools are well positioned to teach students the skills needed to promote safety and prevent unintentional injury, violence, and suicide while at home, at work, at play, in the community, and throughout their lives. Schools are where our youth learn to become productive members of society and where both students and staff spend a significant portion of their weekdays. While this chapter will focus on injuries and violence occurring at school and school events, school-based curricula for general injury and violence prevention are important and will be discussed as well.

Despite the prevalence and importance of injuries and violence, many schools are not equipped to focus on prevention. A lack of resources and time, coupled with increasing pressure to achieve higher academic test scores, can make it difficult for schools to address injury and violence prevention in a coordinated manner. Without enthusiasm among school staff and collaboration with parents and community partners, a coordinated approach to injury and violence prevention is unlikely. This chapter will offer recommendations for how public health and safety professionals can and should work with schools to develop collaborations and make injury and violence prevention an institutional priority. Recommendations will be discussed within the framework of five key programmatic components: infrastructure, data collection and analysis, interventions, training and technical assistance, and public policy and advocacy.

The impact of injury and violence on academic success, cost, and liability are other factors that make prevention a priority. Annual medical spending on school injuries has been estimated at $3.2 billion (Miller and Spicer, 1998). Nonfatal school-related injuries to children result in an additional $10 billion in lost future work and $34 billion in lessened quality of life (Danseco, Miller, and Spicer, 2000). But these are societal costs. Schools have paid awards in injury liability suits as high as $15 million, with an average award of more than half a million dollars (Barrios, Jones, and Gallagher, in press). According to the National School Boards Association, "parents of student victims of bullies are increasingly turning to the courts. The number of personal protection orders issued by Michigan courts in cases involving minors increased from 600 in 2002 to approximately 700 in 2003" (NSBA, 2004). Awareness of expenses and lost time associated with injuries can be a great motivator for administrators to take actions for prevention (McIlveen, 2001). Many states are beginning to realize that money saved through injury prevention goes directly back to districts and helps keep liability insurance premiums down.

At first glance it would seem that the education system, responsible for the social cognitive development and academic achievement of students, and the public health system, responsible for protecting the health of the population, would have different goals and objectives. However, when it comes to the issue of injuries and violence in the school environment, it becomes clear that the objectives are not mutually exclusive, but rather dependent upon one another.

In Healthy People 2010, the US Department of Health and Human Services outlines an agenda for health promotion and disease prevention. Healthy People 2010 recognizes injury, violence, and mental health among the ten leading public health concerns for the nation and outlines a comprehensive set of objectives to address these issues. Objectives relevant to school injuries and violence include:

- Increase the proportion of schools that provide health education to prevent injury, violence, and suicide.
- Increase the proportion of schools that require use of appropriate head, face, eye, and mouth protection for students participating in school-sponsored physical activities.
- Reduce physical assaults and physical fighting among adolescents and reduce weapon carrying by adolescents on school property.
- Reduce the suicide rate and the number of suicide attempts made by students.

An additional Healthy People 2010 objective may be surprising. It is to increase high school completion to 90 percent (USDHHS, 2000). Dropping out of school is associated with multiple social and health problems, including substance abuse, delinquency, intentional and unintentional injury, and unintended pregnancy. For the public health community, high school completion is an important step in preventing poor health outcomes.

This objective of high school completion is consistent with national education goals. For the education community, high school completion is a mark of academic success and achievement. Students who are unable to attend school because of poor health, fear of violence, or sustained injuries will have a difficult time achieving academic success and face numerous barriers in attempting to reach graduation.

Healthy People 2010 offers national public health goals. Schools, school districts, and state education departments have their own goals and objectives. Public health professionals should be mindful of such goals as they cultivate relationships with schools. Any successful partnership will begin by understanding the needs, goals, and measures to which the school is held accountable. Schools differ from one another and school systems in one state might be governed very differently than those in another.

Understanding the differences between the public health system and the education system will make it easier for public health professionals to identify key decision makers for the purposes of partnerships and/or advocacy. The US does not have a national education system; constitutionally, state governments are responsible for public education and thus, school districts and school are technically agents of the state. The governance structure varies for each state and is usually defined in the state constitution or education code adopted by the legislature. The education structure of governance differs greatly from the public health structure and these differences are present at the federal, state, and local levels. Differences also can be seen in how these services are funded. Unlike public health funding which comes from federal and state budgets, the majority of funds for K-12 public schools is raised through local taxes on private property. State funds account for less than half and federal funds account for only about seven percent of the money spent for schools nationwide.

Most educational reforms and decisions are made at the state level. Educational reforms are an important issue for many state legislatures and governors. Policy responsibility in the state is shared between the governor, the legislature, and the state board of education (SBE). SBEs are typically responsible for establishing education goals and standards, setting graduation requirements, establishing teacher certification requirements, approving textbooks, and developing or implementing assessment programs.

Also operating at the state level is the Chief State School Officer and the State Education Agency (SEA). The SEA is at the same level as the State Health Department (SHD), and the agency lead may be called the State School Superintendent, Chief State School Officer, or State Secretary of Education. These state officials establish academic standards, provide financial resources to school districts, manage information and reporting systems, develop the public education infrastructure, and hold districts accountable for student performance and achievement.

The Local Educational Agency (LEA), also referred to as the School District, is located within a county, city, or township. The LEA establishes district-wide standards, monitors and reports on school performance, provides leadership, engages parents and community members, and creates partnerships with local organizations.

At the school level, the principal is usually the most important decision maker (National Association of State Boards of Education, 1993). The principal is responsible for academic programs, teachers, staff, students, budget, and resource allocation, and is expected to enforce federal, state, and district rules, policies, and laws. The principal is usually viewed as the leader of the school and is the school's primary representative to parents and the community.

Schools may have a school health program coordinator or appoint a physical education or health educator to this position. Some schools establish a school health council, including community members and parents, to assist in the oversight, management, planning, and evaluation of school health and safety programs and policies. Other key stakeholders within the school who may serve as a point of entry for public health and safety professionals include school nurses or school health center staff, teachers, guidance counselors, school psychologists and/or social workers.

Unlike the public health system of governance, schools operating on the local level have more autonomy and are more likely to make independent policy and program decisions. While federal policy is an important means to create change in the education system, working at the state and local level may be more advantageous for those seeking to implement changes in injury and violence prevention.

At a 2001 American School Health Association (ASHA) conference, school superintendents offered the following suggestions for strengthening the working relationships between school administrators and health and safety professionals:

- Link health and safety education and programs to:
  - academic performance;
  - attendance;
  - holistic education; and,
  - the budget.
- Approach administration with an offer of what you can do for the school, rather than asking the school to do something for you. The benefit to the school, students, and staff should be clearly identified when you propose a project or policy.

- Pay attention to your language—terminology can have different meanings in an education environment than in a public health setting. For example, the term 'surveillance' commonly used by public health professionals to mean data collection and trend analysis might infer the use of security cameras when talking with school administrators.
- Use a team approach that involves staff, parents, students, and community members.
- Make presentations at school administrator conferences and invite administrators to present at school health and safety conferences. Joint presentations can be especially effective (Education Development Center, Inc., 2002).

Morbidity, Mortality, and Risk Factors

Every year approximately four million children and adolescents are injured at school (Danseco, Miller, and Spicer, 2000). It is estimated that close to 25 percent of all child and adolescent injuries occur on school grounds (Danseco, Miller, and Spicer, 2000), and school nurses would agree that injuries are the most common health problem they address among students (CDC, 2001). However, most of the injuries that occur on school grounds are unintentional and minor. Serious injuries are more likely to occur at home or in the community, and fatalities due to injuries sustained on school grounds are rare. Schools are where students gain knowledge and skills to use throughout their life span.

Older students are more likely to be injured; middle school and high school students represent 58 percent of the student population, but account for 72 percent of all school injuries (Miller and Spicer, 1998). Each year, 11 percent of high school students, eight percent of middle school students, and five percent of elementary school students are injured at school (Miller and Spicer, 1998).

Injuries occur more frequently among males. The school injury rate for high school males is nine per 100, whereas the rate for high school females is six per 100 (Miller and Spicer, 1998). Injuries are most likely to occur on playgrounds, athletic fields, and in gymnasiums. The most frequent causes of school-associated injuries resulting in hospitalization are falls (43 percent), sports activities (34 percent) and assaults (10 percent) (DiScala, Gallagher, and Schneps, 1997).

Children with special health care needs are also at higher risk for suicide, victimization, and unintentional injury. It should be noted that injury patterns differ across disabilities. A study of 6769 Los Angeles schoolchildren with disabilities who were followed for four years showed that physically disabled children had a modest increase of odds of injury, but those with multiple disabilities had a 70 percent increased odds of injury compared with the developmentally disabled (Ramirez, Peek-Asa, and Kraus, 2004).

Data about common school-related injuries are provided below. However, because there is not a national reporting system for school-associated injuries and violence, these data may not accurately reflect what is happening in our nation's schools (US Congress, Office of Technology Assessment, 1995). In 31 percent of states and 90 percent of districts, schools are required to write an injury report when a student is seriously injured on school property (CDC,

2001). However, among the states that require such reporting, only two require districts or schools to submit injury report data to the state health department (CDC, 2001).

Unintentional Injuries at School

The School Environment

The physical environment of a school, including walkways and grounds, playgrounds, sports fields, parking lots, school vehicles, gymnasiums, classrooms, shop and vocational education classrooms, cafeterias, corridors, and bathrooms, as well as the equipment used in these places, can affect unintentional injuries and violence.

Playgrounds and Sports Activities

Each year in the US, more than 200 000 children age 14 and under are treated in emergency departments for playground-related injuries (Tinsworth and McDonald, 2001). Approximately 15 children in this age group die from playground-related injuries; one-half of these deaths are due to strangulation and one quarter due to falls to the playground surface (Tinsworth and McDonald, 2001). Seventy-five percent of non-fatal playground injuries occur at public playgrounds, including schools and daycare centers (Phelan, Khoury, Kalkwarf, and Lanphear, 2001). Of non-fatal playground injuries, 45 percent are considered severe and may include fractures, internal injuries, concussions, and dislocations (Phelan, Khoury, Kalkwarf, and Lanphear, 2001).

All children who use playgrounds are at risk for injury. However there are some factors that increase the susceptibility to injury. Children ages five to nine have a higher rate of emergency department visits for playground injuries than any other age group. On public playgrounds, more injuries occur on climbers than any other equipment (Tinsworth and McDonald, 2001). Due to the high number of playground-related injuries that occur on school property, some studies suggest that an intervention focused on school playgrounds has the potential to most significantly reduce the number of school-based injuries for elementary school students (Phelan, Khoury, Kalkwarf, and Lanphear, 2001).

Thirty-four percent of school-related injuries are sustained during sports (CDC, 2001). Approximately eight million high school students participate in organized school- or community- sponsored sports annually (CDC, 2002). Close to one million serious sports-related injuries (ie, resulting in hospitalization, surgical treatment, missed school, or one half day or more in bed) occur annually to adolescents aged 10–17 (Bijur, 1995).

Many sports injuries are the result of re-injury. Recurring knee or ankle injuries commonly fall into this category. A more serious case of re-injury is called second impact syndrome. This is a result of repeated mild brain concussions over a short time. Second impact syndrome may lead to severe traumatic brain injuries and death (CDC, 1997).

Transportation

An average of 22 school-age children die in school transportation-related crashes every year. This includes six occupants of school transportation vehicles (ie, school busses) and 16 pedestrians (National Highway Traffic Safety Administration (NHTSA, 2004). From 1993 to 2003, more than one-half of the school-age children killed in school transportation-related crashes were between five and seven years old (NHTSA, 2004).

Since 1993, 1,488 people have died in school bus-related crashes; an average of 135 fatalities a year. Of those crashes 69 percent of those killed were occupants of other vehicles (eg, in the car that collided with the school bus), 23 percent of those killed were non-occupants (eg, pedestrians, bicyclists, etc.), and eight percent of those killed were occupants of school transportation vehicles (NHTSA, 2004). Approximately 8600 students are non-fatally injured each year in school bus-related incidents and 90 percent of those students were bus occupants while 10 percent were injured pedestrians (Miller and Spicer, 1998).

Bicycle- and pedestrian-related injuries are also important to consider. In 1998, among children and adolescents aged 5–19 years, a total of 260 deaths occurred among those riding a bicycle and 778 deaths occurred among pedestrians (CDC, 2001). Among bicycle-related deaths, 90 percent were the result of a collision with a motor-vehicle. It is also known that 86 percent of high school students rarely or never wear bicycle helmets (CDC, 2004). While these figures do not represent incidences solely on school property, or in route to school, they illustrate the need to keep children safe on the roads and address risk behaviors such as not wearing a helmet while biking.

The risk for motor-vehicle crashes is higher among 16–19 year olds than any other age group (NHTSA, 2004). In 2001, more than 4700 teens, aged 16 to 19 years old, died of injuries caused by a motor-vehicle crash (CDC, 2003). The crash risk is particularly high during the first years that teenagers are eligible to drive (Insurance Institute for Highway Safety, 2003), and the presence of teen passengers increases the crash risk (Chen, Baker, Braver, and Guohua, 2000). Some of this is due to inexperience, but it can also be attributed to the fact that teens are more likely than older drivers to: underestimate dangers in a hazardous situation, speed, run red lights, make illegal turns, ride with an intoxicated driver, drive under the influence of drugs or alcohol, and not wear seat belts (Jonah and Dawson, 1997).

Intentional Injuries and Violence at School

Bullying and Fighting

Bullying is far too often seen as an inevitable part of schoolyard culture, but the consequences of bullying can be serious. Bullying is intentional and persistent aggressive behavior and can include physical violence, teasing and name calling, intimidation, and social exclusion. Bullying can also be related to the harassment of racial and ethnic minorities and gay, lesbian, and bisexual youth (CSN, 2004).

Survey results have shown that 11 percent of American schoolchildren in the sixth through tenth grades have been bullied, 13 percent have engaged in bullying, and six percent have been both perpetrators and victims of bullying (Nansel, Overpeck, Pilla, Ruan, Simons-Morton, and Scheidt, 2001). Bullies tend to be physically larger than their peers; they are aggressive, quick to anger, impulsive, lack empathy, and have lower self-esteem. Victims of bullying are often socially isolated, lack social skills, and are physically smaller than their peers (National Youth Violence Prevention Resource Center, 2005). Students who are repeatedly bullied are at increased risk for mental health problems, suicidal ideation, and bullying can lead to more violence.

According to the Youth Risk Behavior Survey (YRBS), a third of all high school students were in a physical fight during the previous year (Grunbaum, Kann, et al, 2004). While this figure remains high, it has significantly declined from 42.4 percent in 1991 (Grunbaum, Kann, et al, 2004). Physical fighting on school property also decreased from 16.2 percent in 1993 to 12.8 percent in 2003 and this trend was seen across all subgroups (Grunbaum, Kann, et al, 2004). In 2003, 4.2 percent of high school students reported being injured while in a physical fight and 5.4 percent of students reported not attending school because of safety concerns (Grunbaum, Kann, et al, 2004).

Homicide and Suicide

Although shootings in US schools have captured media and public attention, homicides are rarely associated with schools. Less than one percent of homicides and suicides among children and adolescents are school-related (Anderson, Kaufman, et al, 2001). Between 1994 and 1999, 172 school-associated violent deaths occurred in the US, including 146 homicides and 24 suicides (Anderson, Kaufman, et al, 2001). These deaths occurred in 25 states, in both primary and secondary schools, and in communities of all sizes. Firearms were the method of injury in 74.5 percent of the fatalities (Anderson, Kaufman, et al, 2001).

While suicide is the third leading cause of death among young people aged 15 to 24, it is also rarely school-related. In 2000, 3,971 suicides were reported among this age group, but only 24 suicides were school-associated between 1994 and 1999 (Anderson, Kaufman, et al, 2001). In 2001, firearms were used in 54 percent of youth suicides (Anderson, Kaufman, et al, 2003).

The 2003 YRBS found that 17 percent of high school students carried a weapon (eg, gun, knife, or club) to school; six percent carried a gun. Males are significantly more likely than females to carry a weapon to school (Grunbaum, Kann, et al 2004).

Dating and Sexual Violence

Dating and sexual violence are forms of violence to which middle and high school personnel must pay close attention. Twenty percent of female high school students have been physically or sexually abused by a dating partner (CDC, 2001). Twenty-five percent of male and female students in eighth and ninth grade have been victims of non-sexual dating violence, and eight percent have been victims of sexual dating violence (eg, non-consensual sexual contact, attempted or completed rape, or abusive sexual contact) (CDC, 2001).

Current Research Findings and Prevention Practices

The State and Territorial Injury Prevention Directors Association (STIPDA) developed the *Safe States* document (STIPDA, 2003) to help public health agencies develop injury and violence prevention programs. The core components of a state injury and violence prevention program are identified as: Collecting and Analyzing Injury Data; Designing, Implementing and Evaluating Interventions; Building a Solid Infrastructure for Injury Prevention; Providing Technical Support and Training; and Affecting Public Policy. These core components are also essential to school-based injury and violence prevention programs and will be discussed in this section.

Two sets of nationally developed guidelines illustrate how public health and safety professionals can best address the issues of injury and violence in schools. These guidelines reflect current research findings and recognized 'best practice' approaches to school-related injury and violence prevention.

School Health Guidelines to Prevent Unintentional Injuries and Violence (CDC, 2001). The School Health Guidelines were developed by the Centers for Disease Control and Prevention (CDC) and published in 2001. The guidelines are based on a comprehensive review of published literature on strategies for the prevention of unintentional injuries, violence, and suicide in the school environment. Recommendations address school environment, education, services, and staff and community members (USDHHS, 2000).

Health, Mental Health and Safety Guidelines for Schools. The Health, Mental Health and Safety Guidelines for Schools were developed by more than 300 health, education, and safety professionals from more than 30 different national organizations. The American Academy of Pediatrics (AAP), the National Association of School Nurses (NASN), and the Health Resource Services Administration's Maternal and Child Health Bureau (MCHB) were the lead organizations on this project. The goal of the guidelines is to help school administrators, staff, and those working with schools address important health, mental health, and safety issues (Duncan, Luckenbill, Robinson, Wheeler, and Wooley, 2004).

Data Collection, Analysis, and Dissemination

Data are the fundamental building blocks of all public health programs and policies, and this holds true for school-based interventions. Understanding trends and prevalence of injury and violence guides policymakers, school administrators, and public health professionals in making decisions to implement a program or utilize resources to address a problem.

The lack of comprehensive national or state data collection systems creates a significant deficit in providing schools with information on injuries in the school environment. However, four states do maintain some type of school-related injury database. Arizona, Hawaii, South Carolina, and Utah collect school-based injury data through voluntary reporting (Kaldahl and Blair, 2005).

The Utah Student Injury Reporting System (SIRS) was initiated by state health department nurses in 1984 to monitor injuries in students in grades K-12. The nurses found there was not a standardized form used to record student injuries. In response, they developed such a form and had it endorsed by the Utah Office of Education.

There are 40 public school districts in Utah and all of them voluntarily participate in the program (Spicer, Cazier, Keller, and Miller, 2002). The Department of Health manages all of the data collection, analysis, and report generation. School districts send the forms to the Utah State prison where inmates code and enter the data into a database. The inmates' accuracy in entering the data has been researched and reported to be 99.9% accurate. The project is funded by the Utah Department of Health's Title V MCH Block Grant through the Violence and Injury Prevention Program (VIPP). The system costs the state approximately $35,000 - $40,000 per year, and most of the cost covers the salary of a part-time surveillance system technician (Spicer, Cazier, Keller, and Miller, 2002).

Utah has found the system to be very successful. In 1987, health officials began to track the severity and magnitude of playground injuries among elementary school students. As a result, the state received federal funding to implement a pilot playground program in 17 schools. The data collected over the next few years showed that the pilot was successful in decreasing rates and the program was expanded statewide (Spicer, Cazier, Keller, and Miller, 2002).

Intervention Design, Implementation, and Evaluation

For data collection to be truly useful, information gathered must be put into action. Comprehensive school-focused injury and violence prevention programs could include policies and procedures addressing environmental modifications, student behavior interventions, injury and violence prevention training for faculty and staff, and increased supervision during student activities (Kaldahl and Blair, 2005). These interventions fall into one of three categories, often referred to as the three E's:

- Environmental Modifications
- Education Programs
- Enforcement of Policies

Determining which interventions to implement is a complex decision and should involve multiple partners. In deciding to implement a program, it is important to develop a strategic plan of action with timed and measurable goals and objectives and include an evaluation plan. Other important considerations include:

- Do the data indicate a need?
- Is the timing right for this program?
- Is there political support for the program?
- Are there resources for the program?
- Is the program effective in similar settings?

There are a number of educational programs that have been designed and implemented in the schools to reduce injuries and violence. Some have been evaluated, but many have not and without evaluation it is difficult to know whether the program was effective. Some researchers are making efforts to evaluate injury prevention programs in local school settings. For example, Liller and colleagues have developed, implemented, and evaluated firearm safety, agricultural injuries, poison prevention, and bicycle helmet injury prevention programs in elementary school settings in Florida (Liller and Pintado, 2005; Liller, Perrin, Nearns, Crane, Pesce, and Gonzalez, 2003; Liller, Craig, Crane, and McDermott, 1998; Liller, Smorynski,

McDermott, Crane, and Weibley, 1997; Liller, and McDermott 1996; Liller, Smorynski, McDermott, Crane, and Weibley, 1995).

In addition, many of the curricula of these studies above have been described in the *American Journal of Health Education* or the *Journal of School Health* as teaching ideas or techniques. The efficacy of these programs has usually been determined by pre- and post-test studies, although the bicycle helmet study was also evaluated through school and community observations of children's helmet use. More of these types of evaluations need to be conducted and published. In addition, the use of more sophisticated study designs is also needed. Unfortunately, there are many limitations that preclude the use of controlled experimental designs in schools. One such limiting factor is time. Schools are often inundated with requests to have special studies or special programs implemented. There is limited time and resources for these types of activities, including those efforts related to conducting lengthy and complicated evaluations.

An important area for prevention is school violence. This is a challenge for teachers, administrators, and other school personnel. As school shootings captured national attention in the 1990s, schools increasingly used policy, technological changes, staffing increases, and environmental changes to decrease the presence of weapons on school grounds. Schools have also been able to address these serious issues of violence through educational programs, policies for student identification and referral, and mental health counseling.

Environmental Modifications

A safe school environment includes both the physical and social environments. Ensuring that the school building and campus are in proper condition is as important as ensuring positive and healthy relationships between students, faculty, and staff. Schools have implemented a range of actions to ensure that the physical environment helps prevent unintentional injuries. Ensuring that flooring surfaces are slip-resistant and stairwells have sturdy handrails are important ways to reduce the number of falls (CDC, 2001). Regular safety and hazard assessments coupled with routine maintenance of school structures and equipment are essential.

There are a number of tools that schools are using and could use to improve the safety of their playground. The US Consumer Product Safety Commission (CPSC), the National Program for Playground Safety, and the Consumer Federation of America have all developed safety checklists and equipment guidelines to maximize the safety of playground design and maintenance. Supervision is a key element to ensuring playground safety. Staff members responsible for playground and recreational supervision should be trained in first aid and cardiopulmonary resuscitation (CPR) (CDC, 2001). Similar guidelines for school bus and traffic safety are available from the National Highway Traffic Safety Administration (NHTSA).

Interventions addressing physical environmental modifications include:

- installing and maintaining playgrounds to meet CPSC guidelines;
- inspecting playground equipment and athletic fields regularly;
- creating pedestrian crossing areas protected from bus and auto traffic;
- ensuring proper lighting and low shrubbery at blind corners of buildings;

- removing glass from doors;
- ensuring the presence of working smoking alarms, fire extinguishers and sprinklers;
- locking roof doors and limiting access to maintenance areas;
- providing storage for student backpacks; and
- installing and maintaining railing along stairwells.

The social environment encompasses the formal and informal policies, norms, climate, and mechanisms through which students, faculty, and staff members interact daily. A social environment can promote safety or contribute to increased risk for unintentional injuries, violence, and suicide. Schools can implement strategies to improve the social environment and create a climate of caring and respect. One strategy is to encourage students' feeling of connectedness to school; students are more likely to feel connected to the school if they believe they are treated fairly, feel safe, and believe that their teachers are supportive (Samdal, Nutbeam, Wold, and Kannas, 1998). School norms for teachers, staff members, and students can support positive, pro-social, helping behaviors and discourage bullying, discrimination, intimidation, violence, or aggression. For example, adult supervision on playgrounds and in hallways can express disapproval of pushing, shoving, or sexual harassment (CDC, 2001).

Interventions addressing social environmental modifications include:

- implementing a bullying prevention program;
- implementing a conflict resolution program;
- establishing school-wide policies for mutual respect;
- involving youth and parents in the planning and implementation of programs; and
- implementing an anonymous student incident reporting system.

School-Based Educational Programs

According to the Council of Chief State School Officers, *"Schools are society's vehicle for providing young people with the tools for successful adulthood. Perhaps no tool is more essential than good health"* (Council of Chief State School Officers, 1991). More than 53 million young people attend over 119 000 schools every day. Including adults, one-fifth of the US population can be found in schools on any given day (CDC, 2001). Children spend seven to nine waking hours five days per week, eight months per year, in school or on school property. Thus, school-based programs are an efficient way to reach the nation's children and adolescents, as well as a large population of adults (CDC, 2001).

It is essential to implement injury and violence prevention programs in schools not only because that is where children and adolescents spend most of there time, but because health and academic success are reciprocal (National Governors' Association, 2000). Individuals with more years of education experience better health than those with fewer years of education (Ross and Mirowsky, 1999). Similarly, persons who engage in health-promoting behaviors during adolescence achieve higher levels of education in adulthood (Koivusilta, Rimpela, and Rimpela, 1998). Sometimes the association between safety and achievement is obvious (eg, an injury that causes absence from school). At other times the association between student achievement and health and safety is not easily observed (eg, when a student's anxiety about a real or perceived threat of violence affects his/her attention to class work, such as in bullying situations).

The supervisory nature and structure of a school district are reasons that schools are cost-effective venues for injury and violence prevention programs (Miller and Spicer, 1998). Schools can teach students the skills needed to promote safety and violence prevention in their families and communities. These skills might include: problem solving, communication, decision making, impulse control, conflict resolution, stress management, and anger management. Likewise, the community, including local universities, fire departments, police departments, and health care professionals, can partner with the school to help develop or implement safety precautions or real-world experiences as part of a safety or violence education curriculum.

Education programs can address injury and violence prevention on school property or general skills for prevention outside the classroom. Many schools have found it valuable to include safety lessons within the context of other classroom work, for example physical education, technical education, home economics, and sciences classes are all conducive to including safety lessons as part of the regular curriculum. Additional education programs to reduce injury and violence on school property or at school events include:

- teaching children safe playground behavior;
- teaching pedestrian safety in the classroom at the beginning of the year;
- conflict-resolution and peer mediation training;
- instructing teachers and other staff gatekeeper training (for suicide prevention); and
- teaching children about the physics of protective equipment.

Risk Watch is a safety education curriculum for preschool through grade eight students developed by the National Fire Protection Association. It is one of only a few evaluated school-based safety curricula. The evaluation covered three years of implementation and showed a statistically significant improvement in student knowledge from pre- to post-test in most grades as compared to a control group. In addition, teacher surveys indicated that teachers found the program easy to use and that their students enjoyed and learned important messages from the program (National Fire Protection Association, 2001).

Police Enforcement as an Intervention

Written policies provide formal rules that guide schools in planning, implementing, and evaluating unintentional injury, violence, and suicide prevention activities. School policies should comply with federal, state, and local laws (Amundson, 1993). Additionally, schools should consider recommendations and standards provided by national, state, and local agencies and organizations when establishing policies. For example, the American Academy of Pediatrics has a number of policy recommendations related to injury and violence prevention. Schools should also consider the needs of their students, staff, and community members in developing policy. Those potentially affected by the policies (ie, students, parents, teachers, and community members) and those responsible for implementing the policies should be active participants in their development. In order to be effective, schools must clearly state their policies, implement them consistently and evaluate their effectiveness.

Examples of school policies include:

- establishing and enforcing weight and age requirements for sports.
- canceling sports activities in bad weather.
- developing appropriate bus pick-up and drop-off policies.
- Mandating identification cards to access school building and school events.
- Requiring protective equipment for sports.

Model school health and safety policies have been developed or compiled by the following organizations:

- Center for Health and Health Care in Schools (www.healthinschools. org)
- Council of Chief State School Officers (www.ccsso.org)
- Health Policy Coach (www.healthpolicycoach.org)
- National Association of State Boards of Education (www.nasbe.org)
- National School Boards Association (www.nsba.org)

Organizational Infrastructure

Three aspects of infrastructure are organizational strength, staffing, and funding (STIPDA, 2003). In schools, infrastructure is closely linked with planning, coordination with partners, and collaboration with parents, administrators, students, staff, and other community members.

In most schools, injury and violence prevention is done on an ad hoc basis, fire drills are conducted on a routine basis and there are strict policies about participation in sports. However, in order to comprehensively address injuries and violence, a coordinated approach must be implemented. School administrators, public health and safety professionals, teachers and other staff, parents, students, and community members must all be engaged in the process. Increasingly, school districts are implementing school health councils. In many cases, these councils are made up of parents, students, business and community leaders, and school staff, with the goal of supporting and guiding school health and safety practices, programs, and policies. The council, which may not be part of the administrative school district structure, can offer assistance in program planning, curriculum review, advocacy, fiscal planning, evaluation, accountability, and identifying resources (Shirer and Miller, 2003).

Other examples of infrastructure-building activities include:

- allocating resources for data collection and analysis;
- providing mental health services;
- developing a system for identifying, counseling, and referring high-risk students.

- increasing security or police presence;
- providing resources to implement programs and evaluate their effectiveness;
- assigning staff to lead injury and violence prevention efforts;
- developing safety rules;
- increasing staff presence to improve supervision of students during recess and recreation.

Training and Technical Assistance

Trained staff members are essential to implementing a coordinated school injury and violence prevention program. Staff members who understand how to prevent unintentional injury, violence, and suicide are a valuable asset as they can assist students in need and also educate them. Staff members who act to prevent unintentional injuries and violence can be positive role models for students. Staff attendance can also be improved by preventing injuries outside of school.

Schools should consider the training needs of their faculty and staff. Teachers could receive professional staff development on developing and maintaining a safe learning environment. Effective educational techniques for creating a safe learning environment include proactive classroom management, cooperative learning methods, social skills training, promoting interactive learning, and environmental modifications (CDC, 2001). Schools may want to include bus drivers, security personnel, grounds and custodial staff members, and food service staff in educational sessions as well.

Other training activities include:

- hazard identification;
- hazard elimination;
- completion of injury report forms and the usefulness of prevention;
- use and proper fit of safety gear;
- training coaches, gym teachers, and other school personnel in emergency first aid and CPR;
- training coaches to enforce safe play guidelines and to identify warning signs of injury;
- training staff in the use of peer mediation, and conflict resolution.

A survey of Virginia public school personnel (Department of Criminal Justice Services, 2002) found that staff wanted training in many safety topics, including:

- identifying students in need of special services or assistance;
- methods for diffusing disruptive students;
- identifying students at risk for violent behavior;
- identifying and preventing at-risk situations;
- intervening with angry and/or abusive families; and
- methods for improving personal safety.

Trainings should review school policies, identify best practices, be provided to all staff, with special attention to new school personnel, and aim to improve communication among school personnel (Department of Criminal Justice Services, 2002).

In order to prevent youth suicides, many schools have implemented gatekeeper training programs. Gatekeeper training provides teachers, aides, and other staff with basic suicide prevention and intervention skills. Trainings enable these individuals to recognize at-risk students and warning signs, and make appropriate interventions or referrals.

Policy and Advocacy

Policy and advocacy are essential in creating a school environment that is safe and fosters the development of safe and productive students. It is important to recognize the role that policy and advocacy play in the individual school, but it is equally important to understand how local, state and federal policy affect the individual school or school district. Public health and safety professionals can advocate for local, state, and federal policy to ensure the safety of their students and staff.

While in a perfect world, policy is data-driven, it is sometimes true that policy is made by anecdote. As a result, public health and school officials must be aware of what is happening in homes, in school, and around the community as events in these arenas can play a significant role in the creation and implementation of new policies. Timing can be everything and public health and safety advocates must be prepared to activate networks and partnerships when an appropriate opportunity presents itself. This necessitates that partnerships and coalitions founded upon the same objectives, goals, and priorities be established and ready for action.

While schools are governed by federal and state laws, most school safety practices and policies are developed and implemented at the SEA and LEA levels. This means that LEAs, school health and safety councils, public health professionals, parents, student, and community members can be active in advocating for change. Parents might advocate for more lights around the school, the school health and safety council might advocate for needed facility repair and maintenance, and community members might want to increase enforcement of bicycle helmet laws. These are all examples of advocacy on the local level.

An example of advocacy on the state level is the recent efforts to implement policies and programs to prevent bullying. As of 2003, at least 15 states have passed laws addressing bullying among school children and many others have considered legislation (Limber, 2003). The content and purpose of the laws vary. Some legislation encourages schools to develop policies against bullying, some legislation mandates reporting bullying behavior to the authorities, and other legislation aims to encourage the implementation of bullying prevention programs for both student and staff (Limber, 2003).

Most bullying-related laws have been in effect since 2001. Their passage was motivated, in part, by tragic shootings at several US high schools in the late 1990s. Advocates for public health and safe schools continue to push for state legislation on bullying. Public health and safety professionals also have an important role to play in evaluating current state policies, as these evaluations will help guide policy makers and school administrators in the future (USDHHS, 2004).

Another type of policy is regulatory action. For example, in Rhode Island, the state health department and the education department collaborated to develop two regulations. One regulation required schools to develop and implement a school transportation safety plan and the other required schools to implement the Consumer Product Safety Commission Guidelines for Playground Safety.

Future Research, Practices, and Advocacy Directions

Overall, the future can be directed by the multiple sets of guidelines developed to provide guidance to schools and their partners to define, plan, intervene and advocate for reducing injuries and violence among school-aged children and youth.

Data Collection, Analysis, and Dissemination

Data are essential to evaluate the effectiveness and cost effectiveness of injury or violence prevention programs. Public health and safety professionals can make an important contribution to the prevention of injuries and violence by helping to establish data collection systems in schools. These systems should collect data on all school-related incidents of injury and violence. Reports should include all information pertinent to the event, including: the nature, extent, location, and cause of the incident, in addition to relevant information about the victim including age, grade, and sex. (CDC, 2001). Confidentiality is an important consideration in any form of data collection and safeguards should be implemented in any surveillance program to protect victims and the school (CDC, 2001).

Public health and safety professionals can play a large role in analyzing data and making recommendations to school officials and policy makers as to programs or policies that could be implemented, revised, and evaluated to address issues raised. Public health and safety professionals can contribute epidemiological expertise and the public health perspective to refine the evidence available on the causes, consequences, and prevention of injuries and violence. Moreover, they can collaborate with state and federal departments of education and justice to educate school staff about mandatory reporting of injuries, violence, and hate-related incidents and support efforts to increase school-related incident data collection.

Every school may have a different system for collecting and recording data. However, it is important to have as consistent a database as possible for programming across more than one school and to influence policies and programs at the district and state level. Who should collect the information may also vary from school to school. Often school nurses are in a position to collect incident information, but it requires cooperation from students and staff to share relevant data.

Intervention Design, Implementation, and Evaluation

Public health and safety professionals can partner with education professionals to design and implement public education campaigns, incorporate injury and violence prevention activities in health or other school curricula, and advocate for evaluation of injury and violence prevention programs. Local public health and safety professionals can recruit schools as partners in community-based prevention initiatives and conduct joint training and planning activities.

Public health and safety professionals should also play a role in the development of a school-based injury and violence prevention council and help the school create a comprehensive and coordinated safety plan. In addition to program and policy changes, public health and safety professionals can aid in the identification and implementation of environmental changes to increase safety on playgrounds, school grounds, and in transportation areas (ie, bus stops, student drop-off areas).

Public health and safety professionals can contribute evaluation expertise in determining the most effective methods to use to address injuries and violence for children and youth. Given appropriate resources, public health and education could partner to conduct evaluations. Collaboration with community colleges and universities for evaluation planning and implementation can be very helpful. It is also important that mechanisms for appropriate distribution of findings be included in evaluation planning.

Technical Support and Training

Public health and safety professionals can play a major role in technical support and training activities to prevent school injuries and violence by:

- advocating to include school injury and violence prevention in state injury prevention conferences and department of education trainings and conferences.
- providing training and resources to local health department staff.
- teaching school nurses, teachers, guidance counselors, coaches, and parents to ask students about their relationships with peers, their experiences with violence, bullying, and harassment.
- training school staff to recognize the signs of victimization in children and what to do when they identify a child that has been victimized.

State public health and safety professionals can provide their local counterparts with ideas from other states and updates on federal initiatives related to injury prevention, bullying, and other school violence issues.

Policy and Advocacy

Public health and safety professionals can encourage the development of policies that incorporate injury and violence prevention into curricula and school-based programs. They can advocate for legislation that supports safer playground standards, after-school recreation programs, and dating violence prevention programs. School health councils can serve as advocates and work to ensure that sufficient resources are allotted to support school health and health education programs. Advocacy efforts can also help to develop understanding and communication channels between the school and other community resources. In considering injury and violence prevention, the school health council may want to ensure strong relationships with the fire and police department, mental health counselors, environmental designers, and transportation officials and planners.

Many resources are available to assist public health and safety professionals as they begin to work on school-related injury and violence problems. A partial list of resources follows. Through partnering, public health and the schools can make great strides in the reduction of injuries and violence among children and adolescents.

Resources and Organizations

- The American Academy of Pediatrics (AAP) School Health Resources
  www.schoolhealth.org
- American Association for Health Education
  www.aahperd.org/aahe
- American Association of School Administrators (AASA)
  www.aasa.org
- The American School Counselor Association (ASCA)
  www.schoolcounselor.org
- American School Health Association (ASHA)
  www.ashaweb.org
- Center for Health and Health Care in Schools
  www.healthinschools.org
- Center for School Mental Health Assistance
  http://csmha.umaryland.edu
- Council of Chief State School Officers (CCSSO)
  www.ccsso.org
  * National Health Education Standards, Education Development Center
    www.edc.org
- National Assembly on School-Based Health Care
  www.nasbhc.org
- National Association of Elementary School Principals
  www.naesp.org
- National Association of School Nurses (NASN)
  www.nasn.org
- The National Association of School Psychologists (NASP)
  www.nasponline.org
- National Association of School Resource Officers (NASRO)
  www.nasro.org
- National Association of Secondary School Principals
  www.nassp.org
- National Association of State Boards of Education
  www.nasbe.org
- National Association of Student Personnel Administrators
  www.naspa.org
- National Fire Protection Association (NFPA)
  www.nfpa.org
  * Risk Watch Curriculum

- National Organizations for Youth Safety
  www.noys.org
- National PTA
  www.pta.org
- National School Boards Association
  www.nsba.org
- National School Safety Center
  www.nssc.org
- National School Transportation Association (NSTA)
  www.schooltrans.com
- Safe Schools Now Network
  www.nea.org/echostar/safeschools/index.html
- Society of State Directors of Health, Physical Education, and
  Recreation
  www.thesociety.org

References

1. Amundson, K. (1993). *Violence in Schools: How America's School Boards are Safeguarding our Children.* Alexandria, VA: National School Boards Association.
2. Anderson, M., Kaufman J., Simon, T.R., Barrios, L., Paulozzi, L., Ryan, G., Hammond, R., Modzeleski, W., Feucht, T., Potter, L., and the School-Associated Violent Deaths Study Group. (2001). School-Associated Violent Deaths in the United States, 1994–1999. *JAMA,* 286 (21), 2695-2702.
3. Bijur, P. (1995). Sports and recreation injuries in US children and adolescents. *Archives of Pediatric and Adolescent Medicine* 149, 1009-1016.
4. Centers for Disease Control and Prevention (CDC). (1997) Sports-related recurrent brain injuries—United States. *Morbidity and Mortality Weekly Report* 46, 224-227.
5. Centers for Disease Control and Prevention (CDC). (2001). School health guidelines to prevent unintentional injuries and violence. *Morbidity and Mortality Weekly Report,* 50 (RR-22).
6. Centers for Disease Control and Prevention (CDC). (2002). Youth Risk Behavior Surveillance—United States, 2001. *Morbidity and Mortality Weekly Report* 51, 1–64.
7. Centers for Disease Control and Prevention (CDC), National Center for Injury Prevention and Control, Office of Statistics and Programming. (2003) *Web-based Injury Statistics Query and Reporting System (WISQARS).* Retrieved January 31, 2005, from http://www.cdc.gov/ncipc/wisqars.
8. Centers for Disease Control and Prevention (CDC). (2004). Violence-Related Behavior among High School Students. *Morbidity and Mortality Weekly Report,* 53 (29), 651-655.
9. Chen, L., Baker, S., Braver, E., Guohua, L. (2000). Carrying passengers as a risk factor for crashes fatal to 16- and 17-year old drivers. *JAMA,* 283 (12), 1578–1582.
10. Children's Safety Network (CSN). (1997). *Injuries in the School Environment: A Resource Guide (Second Edition).* Newton, MA: Education Development Center, Inc.
11. Children's Safety Network (CSN). (2004) *Bullying Prevention: The Role of the Public Health Professional.* Retrieved January 12, 2005, from http://www.childrens safety network.org.
12. Council of Chief State School Officers. (1991). *Beyond the Health Room.* Washington, DC: Council of Chief State School Officers.

13. Danseco, E., Miller, T., and Spicer, R. (2000). Incidence and cost of 1987-1994 childhood injuries: demographic breakdowns. *Pediatrics* 105 (2).

14. Department of Criminal Justice Services, Criminal Justice Research Center, Evaluation Unit. (2002). *School Safety Training Needs Assessment: Report on Findings.* Retrieved on June 16, 2005 from: www.dcjs.state.va.us

15. Di Scala, C., Gallagher, S.S., and Schneps, S.E. (1997). Causes and Outcomes of Pediatric Injuries Occurring at School. *J School Health;* 67 (9).

16. Duncan P., Luckenbill D., Robinson J., Wheeler L., and Wooley S. (Eds.) (2004). *Health, Mental Health and Safety Guidelines for Schools.* Retrieved February 16, 2005, from http://www.schoolhealth.org.

17. Education Development Center, Inc. (2002). *School Health News.*

18. Grunbaum, J.A., Kann, L., Kinchen, S., Williams, B., Ross, J.G., Lowry, R., and Kolbe, L. Youth Risk Behavior Surveillance—United States, 2003 *Morbidity and Mortality Weekly Report* 2004;53(SS-2):1–29.

19. Insurance Institute for Highway Safety. (2003). *Fatality Facts: Teenagers. Arlington, VA: The Institute for Highway Safety.* Retrieved February 16, 2005, from: http://www. iihs.org/safety_facts/teens.htm.

20. Jonah, B., Dawson, N.E. (1997). Youth and risk: age differences in risky driving, risk perception, and risk utility. *Alcohol, Drugs and Driving* 3, 13–29.

21. Kaldahl, M.A., Blair, E.H. (2005). Student Injury Rates in Public Schools. *J School Health;* 75 (1): 38-40.

22. Koivusilta, L., Rimpela, A., Rimpela, M. (1998). Health related lifestyle in adolescents predicts educational level: a longitudinal study from Finland. *J Epidemiology Community Health,* 52, 794-801.

23. Liller, K.D., and Pintado, I. (2005). Kids and Communities Count: Reaching migrant children and families with the North American Guidelines for Children's Agricultural Tasks (NAGCAT), *J Agricultural Safety Health,* in press.

24. Liller, K.D., Perrin, K., Nearns, J., Crane, N., Pesce, K., and Gonzalez, R. (2003). Evaluation of the "Respect Not Risk" firearm safety lesson for third graders. *J School Nursing,* 19, 338-343.

25. Liller, K.D., Craig, J., Crane, N., and McDermott, R.J. (1998). Evaluation of a poison prevention lesson for kindergarten and third grade students. *Injury Prev,* 4, 218-221.

26. Liller, K.D., Smorynski, A., McDermott, R.J., Crane, N.B.,and Weibley, R.E. (1997). Effects of the MORE HEALTH Bicycle Safety Project on children's helmet use. *Am J Health Studies,* 13, 57-64.

27. Liller, K.D., and McDermott, R.J. (1996). Increasing children's bicycle helmet use through a school-based intervention. *The Health Education Monograph Series,* 14, 26-29.

28. Liller, K.D., Smorynski, A., McDermott, R.J., Crane, N.B., and Weibley, R.E. (1995). The MORE HEALTH Bicycle Safety Project. *J School Health,* 65, 87-90.

29. Limber, S. (2003) State laws and policies to address bullying in US schools. *School Psychology Review* 32 (3), 445-455.

30. McIlveen, J. (Ed.). (2001). *Limiting Your School's Exposure to Negligent Supervision and Safety Claims.* Horsham, PA: LRP Publications.

31. Miller, T., Spicer, R.(1998). How safe are our schools? *Am J Public Health,* 88 (3), 413-418.

32. Nansel, T., Overpeck, M., Pilla, R., Ruan, W., Simons-Morton, B., Scheidt, P. (2001). Bullying behaviors among youth: Prevalence and association with psychosocial adjustment. *JAMA,* 285.,16, 2094-2100.

33. National Association of State Boards of Education. (1993). *How Schools Work & How to Work with Schools: A Primer for Professionals Who Serve Children and Youth.* Washington, DC: National Association of School Board of Education

34. National Fire Protection Agency (NFPA). (2001). Final Report of the Three-Year Evaluation of Risk Watch. Retrieved on January 12, 2005, from www.nfpa.org

35. National Governors' Association. (2000). *Improving academic performance by meeting student health needs.* Washington, DC: National Governors' Association.

36. National Highway Traffic Safety Administration (NHTSA). (2004). *Traffic safety facts 2003: School Transportation-Related Crashes.* Washington, DC: US Department of Transportation, National Highway Safety Administration.

37. National School Boards Association. (2004). *Legal Clips: Parents of student victims of bullies increasingly are turning to the courts.* Retrieved January 12, 2005, from http://www.nsba.org.

38. National Youth Violence Prevention Resource Center. (n.d) *Frequently Asked Questions for Educators: Bullying.* Retrieved January 12, 2005, from http://www.safeyouth.org

39. Phelan, K.J., Khoury, J., Kalkwarf, H.J., and Lamphear, B.P. (2001). Trends and patterns of playground injuries in United States children and adolescents. *Ambulatory Pediatrics* 1, (4):227–233.

40. Posner, M. (2000). *Preventing School Injuries.* New Brunswick: Rutgers University Press.

41. Ramirez, M., Peek-Asa, C., Kraus, J.K. (2004). Disability and risk of school related injury. *Injury Prevention,* 10:21-26.

42. Reaves, J. (2001, March). Charles 'Andy' Williams. *Time.*

43. Ross, C.E., Mirowsky, J. (1999). Refining the association between education and health: the effects of quantity, credential, and selectivity. *Demography,* 36, 445-460.

44. Samdal, O., Nutbeam, D., Wold, B., Kannas, L. (1998). Achieving health and education goals through schools—a study of importance of the school climate and students' satisfaction with school. *Health Education Research;* 13:338-397.

45. Shirer, K. and Miller, P.P. (2003). *Promoting Health Youth, Schools, and Communities: A Guide to Community-School Health Councils.* The American Cancer Society.

46. Spicer, R.S., Cazier, C., Keller, P., Miller, T.R. (2002). Evaluation of the Utah Student Injury Reporting System. *Journal of School Health* 72, (2): 47-50.

47. State and Territorial Injury Prevention Directors Association (STIPDA). (2003). Safe States, 2003 Edition. Atlanta (GA): State and Territorial Injury Prevention Directors Association.

48. Tinsworth, D., McDonald, J.E. (2001). *Special Study: Injuries and Deaths Associated with Children's Playground Equipment.* Washington DC: US Consumer Product Safety Commission, 2001.

49. United States Congress, Office of Technology Assessment. (1995). *Risks to Students in School.* Washington, DC: GPO. 1995.

50. United States Department of Health and Human Services (USDHHS). (2000). *Healthy People 2010.* 2nd ed. With Understanding and Improving Health and Objectives for Improving Health. Washington, DC: GPO.

51. United States Department of Health and Human Services (USDHHS), Health Resources and Services Administration (HRSA). (2004) *Stop Bullying Now: State Laws Related to Bullying Among Children and Youth.* Retrieved on February 12, 2005, from www.stopbullyingnow.hrsa.gov]

CHAPTER 8

Childhood Agricultural Injuries

Barbara C. Lee
and Barbara Marlenga

Children and Agriculture:
Searching Beyond the News Clippings

June 29, 2002, Demolition on Farm Takes Area Teen's Life.[1] "Silo collapse killed a rural boy. At 6:23 pm, the County Communications Center was notified of a 14-year old youth seriously injured by falling debris from a building. First responders transported James from the farm scene to the area Medical Center where he died as a result of massive head and chest injuries. The Sheriff's investigation indicates the youth and his 16-year-old brother were demolishing a 30-foot-high concrete stave silo when it collapsed unexpectedly. James sought shelter from the falling silo in the adjacent barn, which was also in the process of being dismantled. The collapsing silo fell against the end of the barn, breaking a large hand hewn oak beam that fell on him. James had recently completed 8th grade at Webb Middle School. He enjoyed soccer, hunting, and biking. He is survived by his parents and one brother; as well as grandparents, many aunts, uncles and cousins."

September 18, 2002, Boy Killed in Tractor Accident.[2] "An 11-year-old boy was killed when a tractor he was operating flipped over and pinned him underneath, according to local deputies. The accident occurred about 7:45 pm. An ambulance and medical helicopter was called to the scene. Steven was discovered pinned under the tractor by his 15-year-old brother who had come to check on him. Medical personnel were unable to revive the boy at the scene and he was later pronounced dead. It appeared as though the boy was driving the tractor on a steep incline when it flipped over, the sheriff's official said."

Grief over a preventable death of a child often follows, as in a tragic sequela to the previous event: *November 5, 2002, Man Kills Self in Hospital.*[3]

National Children's Center for Rural and Agricultural Health and Safety, National Farm Medicine Center, Marshfield Clinic Research Foundation, Marshfield, Wisconsin.

"Officers were called to Sacred Heart Hospital after a shooting on a mental health ward. Police haven't determined how a handgun got into a patient's room. A 43-year old man had been under treatment for mental strain and took his own life. His 11-year old son had died two months earlier when a tractor flipped over and pinned him beneath."

March 19, 2003, Farm Accident Claims Life of Three-Year-Old.[4] "The North Dakota County Deputy Sheriff was called to a farm accident on Saturday evening. Three-year-old Alexander had been accidentally run over, crushed by a Bobcat skidsteer loader, operated by his older brother. The juvenile was cleaning the dairy farm yard with the Bobcat and he did not know the toddler was behind him. Alexander was pronounced dead on the scene. Survivors include his parents, four brothers, maternal grandparents, several aunts, uncles and cousins."

April 23, 2003, Local Teen Dies in Tractor Rollover.[5] "A 15-year old boy, was killed Monday when the tractor he was driving apparently pinned him underneath, according to the Sheriff's Department. A preliminary investigation indicates Kevin was trying to use a tractor to move a trailer that was stuck in a field. As Kevin tried to move the trailer, the tractor he was driving flipped over backward. He was found pinned under the machine by a friend who went looking for him after he didn't return before dark. Fire and rescue personnel responded to the scene and extricated him."

October 14, 2004, Child Killed in Accident on Farm.[6] "A 3-year-old child was killed in a farm-related accident Wednesday morning in south central Wisconsin. Preliminary autopsy results state the child died of multiple trauma. He became entangled in the apron gear of a forage wagon, a large self-unloading wagon with multiple moving parts. Upon arrival, emergency workers discovered that the child had become entangled in the equipment. The County Medical Examiner pronounced the child dead at the scene. Parents later explained the child had been with his uncle at the time of the accident."

October 15, 2004, Amish Girl Dies in Accident on Family Farm.[7] "A 5-year-old Amish girl died of injuries suffered in an accident on her family's farm in Iowa on Friday. Karlene was playing outside when a piece of metal her father uses in welding fell on her, according to the County Sheriff's detective. The farm is also the site of the family Welding & Equipment business. The detective described a 7-foot-tall, T-shaped frame used to hang metal pieces on when they're being welded. 'It was standing upright by his shop, it fell over. I assume the kids were probably playing and for whatever reason, it fell over.' The child died at the scene."

These actual cases, all reported in public newspapers, are just a sampling of the tragedies that occur on farms and ranches across the US. The fatalities have striking similarities, such as siblings working together, inadequate adult supervision, and farm machinery designed for adults who willingly choose to work in one of our nation's most dangerous occupation.[8] Beyond the news clippings, is the unreported psychological, social and financial toll that often reaps a devastating impact on survivors, especially parents.

In addition to the annual toll of child fatalities that occur once every three to four days on US farms,[9] data reveal that each day, about 62 children are injured on farms.[10] No other occupation in the US can claim this toll on children.

This chapter provides an overview of the epidemiology of childhood agricultural fatal and non-fatal injuries (work-related and non-work-related), including data sources and limitations of data. We then describe common injury risk factors among children involved in agricultural work as well as children who are not working, but are victims of agricultural injuries. This is followed by a description of injury prevention strategies for working as well as non-working children. Advocacy efforts for children on farms were formally introduced two decades ago, trailing behind those of other child safety concerns. The major advocacy initiatives are described, followed by recommendations for action.

Epidemiology of Injuries

Population at Risk. In 2001, there were approximately 1.1 million children living on farms in the United States.[11] More than half these children worked on the farm, with the highest proportion of youth workers between the ages of 10 and 15 years.[11] In addition, more than 400 000 youth were hired to work on these farms in 2001.[12]

Fatalities. There is no comprehensive national database of childhood agricultural fatalities in the United States and descriptions of agricultural injury events are somewhat limited.[13,14] Based on the National Center for Health Statistics Mortality Files, it is estimated that more than 100 children die each year on farms and ranches,[9,15] however, there are no estimates on the proportion of these deaths that are work-related. Farm machinery is the leading source of fatal injury, followed by drowning.[9,15] Males account for nearly 90% of the fatal injuries on farms.[9,15] Youth 15–19 years experience the most fatal injuries (34%) followed by children less than 5 years of age (25%).[9,15] The greatest proportion of deaths occurs in the Midwest and the Southern United States.[9,15]

There is no surveillance system to monitor youth worker fatalities in agriculture on an annual basis at either the national or state level. Several studies have tried to identify the scope of the problem using typical occupational fatality databases, but have recognized the fact that agricultural youth fatalities are poorly captured.[16-18] The Census of Fatal Occupational Injuries (CFOI) managed by the Bureau of Labor Statistics (BLS) is a multiple record based census of occupational fatalities covering all industries, occupations, and ages of workers.[19] The National Traumatic Occupational Fatalities (NTOF) is a death certificate based census of occupational fatalities maintained by the National Institute for Occupational Safety and Health (NIOSH) that includes workers 16 years and older.[20] Both CFOI and NTOF show that the risk for fatal injury for young agricultural workers is three to four times that of young workers in other workplaces.[17,21] Agricultural youth worker fatalities also differ from other work place fatalities in that half the workers fatally injured in agricultural production are younger than 15 years and are working on the family farm/ranch.[22] Tractors are the leading source of death for youth working in agriculture and male workers account for nearly all the fatalities.[17]

Castillo and colleagues conducted a comprehensive analysis of the CFOI data for fatal injuries to youth workers by agricultural sector.[16] Nearly half the fatally injured youth were working in a family business. Crop production was the agricultural sector that accounted for the most deaths

(52%) followed by livestock production (31%).[16] Tractors were the leading source of fatalities and males accounted for nearly all the fatalities. Similar to other data sources, nearly half the fatalities occurred in the Midwest (46%) followed by the South (22.3%).[16]

Emergency Department Visits. National estimates of non-fatal youth agricultural injuries requiring emergency room visits are limited. Two studies examined emergency department visits using the National Electronic Injury Surveillance System (NEISS).[9,23] NEISS is a surveillance system operated by the US Consumer Product Safety Commission for the primary purpose of monitoring consumer product related injuries.[24] The data are collected from a probability sample of hospitals with emergency departments and do not necessarily represent rural hospitals.

Based on the NEISS data, it is estimated that around 22 000 children were treated in emergency departments annually and that approximately 5400 were work-related injuries.[9,23] Males sustained the overwhelming majority of injuries and tractors were the leading consumer product involved in farm injuries.[9] The 15–19 year age group had the highest rate of farm injuries requiring emergency department treatment, followed by the 10–14 year age group.[9]

Restricted Activity Injuries. There is no comprehensive national database of childhood injuries that captures injuries of varying severity. However, as a part of the *Childhood Agricultural Injury Prevention Initiative*,[25] the National Agricultural Statistics Service conducted a national childhood agricultural injury survey for NIOSH to assemble a cross-sectional picture of injuries that occur to youth less than 20 years of age.[10] The telephone survey was conducted with a stratified random sample of 50 000 farms and ranches in the United States. Farm operators were asked about injuries that occurred on the farm operation in 2001 that result in at least 4 hours of restricted activity.[10]

An estimated 22 648 childhood agricultural-related injuries occurred on farms in 2001, a decline of about 11 000 injuries compared to the finding from the previous survey in 1998.[10,26] The number of farms declined over that same time period, so the resultant injury rate was virtually unchanged.[10,26] In 2001, 75% of the injuries were sustained by youth who lived on the farm.[10,26] Thirty-seven percent of the youth were injured while performing farm work, with the remainder classified as non-work injuries.[10] Males comprised the largest proportion of injured youth (62%), as did the age group 10–15 years (46%). The Midwest and the South accounted for 79% of the non-fatal childhood farm injuries.[10]

Risk Factors for Childhood Agricultural Injuries

The classic Haddon matrix of agent, host, and environment,[27] and modifications of its use as proposed by Runyan[28] and Rivara[29] depict risk factors and their underlying etiology in the pre-event, event, and post-event phase of any injury. Studying injury events from this public health framework offers insights that can guide injury prevention interventions. In this chapter's first agricultural case report, the agent of injury was the energy from the force of a collapsing farm silo and adjacent building structure, the host was a 14-year old boy, untrained in demolition mechanics, and the environment was an unsupervised, dangerous work site.

Stallones and Gunderson[30] were the first to apply the Haddon theoretical framework to childhood agricultural injuries when they pieced together available data sources and demonstrated how the matrix of agent, host and environment could identify prevention strategies. Yet, applicability of this matrix for proposing agricultural injury prevention strategies is limited for two primary reasons. First, there is a wide spectrum of agricultural conditions, many of which have no control mechanisms (eg, weather). Second, a parent or other adult bears accountability for a minor's presence in a hazardous work setting, thus, the principle intervention is to modify underlying adult decisions, rather than address modification of the agent, host, or environment. A brief description of those risk factors most amenable to interventions for preventing childhood agricultural injuries are described in the context of children involved in agricultural work, followed by children exposed to agricultural work hazards while not actively engaged in work.

Working Children and Adolescents

Worldwide, agriculture is the occupation most likely to involve children.[31] Unlike most occupational settings, it can be difficult to separate bona fide work from non-work activities. A traditional farmstead in the US includes the home contiguous with the worksite where children have open access to both. To make matters more complex, there can be problems distinguishing when and where labor regulations and safety standards apply. These factors complicate injury data collection as well as the design and implementation of injury prevention strategies.

Vehicles of Injury among Working Youth

Data from several sources consistently depict the most common vehicles of injuries and fatalities on farms. Farm machinery, including tractor rollovers (victim is on the tractor when it tips over) and runovers (victim is stationary on the ground or falls off a moving tractor, then is crushed underneath a tractor wheel), account for more than one-third of deaths to youth less than 20 years.[15] Many engineering designs for improving tractor and machinery safety on farms have been introduced by manufacturers over the past 50 years. Rollover protective structures (ROPS), combined with seatbelts are recommended for all tractors, but are mandatory in only a few situations in the US.[32] Likewise, safety guards for rotating machinery parts are provided by manufacturers and recommended for safety, but unlike industry settings, there are few mandates to enforce these standard safety features.

Since 1968 when the Hazardous Occupations Order for Agriculture specified restrictions to children's work, the US Department of Agriculture (USDA) has been authorized to address youth farm safety education and certification.[33] Local programs have been coordinated by state Cooperative Extension Service or high school agriculture instructors.[33] Tractor and machinery training and certification programs, consisting of about 20 hours of lecture and driving experience, are intended to improve the safety of youth at risk of tractor-related injuries. However, these training and certification programs have not been consistently implemented. Further, program evaluations have shown mixed results.[34–36] While engineering improvements and labor laws might be effective interventions, a more basic issue is the adult decision (ie, work assignment to youth) that preceded the child/adolescent being on or near farm machinery and the effectiveness of training and supervision when such work is assigned.

Non-fatal work injuries among children often include livestock and horses.[11,37] Risk factors leading to animal injuries include inadequate fencing or other barriers, inappropriate access of children to animals, and the unpredictable and unmanageable nature of the animals themselves. Addressing these risk factors requires modification of the work setting by the farm owner in addition to training and supervision of the young worker.

Host Characteristics. In looking at risk factors associated with the injury host (ie the child on the farm), data sources highlight basic demographic characteristics of age, gender, farm residency status, geographic location and agricultural commodity. Research has demonstrated that children working on their family farm are at notably greater risk of injury than hired youth. Indeed, of all injuries to all youth on farms, only 8% occur to youth hired to work on non-family farms.[10] There are often different expectations of youth working on family farms versus those hired on non-resident farms. Farm parents sometimes perceive that growing up on a farm lends itself to being more cognizant of inherent dangers, and more capable of handling risky tasks at an earlier age.[38] In addition, children strive to please their parents and willingly perform tasks that exceed their abilities.[39,40]

Hours of work, fatigue, training and supervision are other host factors that put a child at risk of agricultural injury.[41,42] Interventions for addressing these host characteristics include parent and work supervisor training regarding child and youth development as well as revised regulations that would mandate limited work hours, certified training and apprenticeships.

Host risk factors also include culture, ethnicity, and assimilation into the "culture of agriculture." The past two decades have witnessed a demographic shift in agricultural workers that is not well captured in injury surveillance data. Recently, NIOSH surveillance identified 47 700 farms, or 2% of all US farms that were owned and operated by minority populations.[43] As the industry of agriculture opens new opportunities for niche products, minority populations have become increasingly involved in agriculture, including Hispanic/Latino immigrants, Hmong, and Anabaptist (eg, Amish, Mennonite). Children of this new workforce are engaging in work on family and non-family farms. Issues such as language barriers, basic safety and hygiene principles, housing, and transportation introduce new challenges for professionals dealing with agricultural health and safety. Behind the reported demographic risk factors specific to agriculture, are a myriad of general factors related to child development, including physical strength and psychological state, which prevail in any child safety situation.

Environmental Factors. A variety of factors associated with the physical and social environment of an agricultural site have been associated with childhood agricultural injuries.[26,41,42] Environmental factors include the agricultural commodity, geographic features such as terrain or climate, economic conditions, and training and supervision standards for workers. Awareness of the inherent risks of childhood injuries associated with different agricultural enterprises can be helpful. For example, crop production accounts for more than half of all work-related fatalities to children, including hired youth.[10,16] When looking solely at youth residing on farms, livestock operations are slightly more hazardous than other enterprises.[26]

Training and supervision of youth working in agriculture differs from occupations such as quick service restaurants. Many industries have safety standards and compliance expectations for all employees, including young workers. This is not the case in agriculture. A recent survey of agricultural employers found that about half do not currently hire teen workers because of concern over labor regulations and requirements for monitoring and supervision.[44] Among those employers that do hire teen workers, the majority were interested in improving their practices related to training and supervision.[44] For the many youth working on family farms, supervision and training is strictly the prerogative of the parent or farm owner.

Ideally, adolescents would be hired to conduct safe, appropriate agricultural work. Training programs modeled on effective programs in other industries should be considered for agricultural settings where youth are legally hired, including seasonal jobs that fill employment needs of young workers.[45]

Labor Policy. The 2002 Census of Agriculture identified 2.1 million farms in the US[46] and an estimated 90% of these are exempt from enforcement of OSHA standards because they employ fewer than 11 employees.[47,48] It is important to note that the Department of Labor's Fair Labor Standards Act with Child Labor regulations has two primary distinctions: agricultural work and all other work.[49,50] Further, the Hazardous Occupations Order for Agriculture that attempts to protect youth by limiting their employment activities to non-hazardous agricultural work, has many exemptions applicable to family farms.[14,49,50] Thus, unlike conditions for youth employed in non-agricultural jobs, regulations and safety standards are primarily voluntary, except where youth are hired to work on non-family farms.

Non-Working Children

Similar to conditions of youth who are working, tractors and machinery are often involved in deaths and injuries of non-working children. Young children are likely to fall from and/or be run over by tractors or farm equipment. Safety specialists strongly promote the "No Extra Rider" rule to keep young children off tractors, however, the practice of children riding on tractors or playing near tractor pathways remains common on many farms.

Following machinery and vehicles, drowning is a major cause of childhood agricultural fatalities,[15] and on minority farm operations, drowning is the leading cause of death to children.[43] Unlike urban drownings, the agricultural water source can be an irrigation ditch, farm pond for animals and wildlife, or a livestock-watering trough. Prevention strategies to minimize on-farm drownings include secure fencing or other barriers as well as close supervision around water hazards.

Falls occur frequently among children on farms, and these events are associated with high structures, tall machinery, climate, and slippery surfaces. Interventions should first address removal of children from these work settings; then address safety hazards for adults as well as children. A recent case illustrates the need for a two-step intervention. A 12-year-old girl suffered a severe head injury after falling from a hayloft. The girl was playing basketball with her siblings in a makeshift upper hayloft court. A hay shoot floor latch broke open, resulting in her fall through the hole, crashing to a concrete floor 13 feet below. To prevent future injuries the strategy is first to prohibit children from playing in the loft and then repair the dysfunctional shoot latch to protect adults working in the area.

Supervision. Safety professionals state that young children injured in agricultural settings are in the "wrong place...all of the time."[51] Research has shown that parents justify children's presence in hazardous work settings based upon specific attitudes and subjective norms.[52] For example, busy farm parents allow children in the worksite so they can spend time together, supervise a child while getting work done, help a child gain a strong work ethic, and provide an opportunity for fun. The same study reported that the people most likely to influence parents' decisions are grandparents and spouse, while health professionals have little influence on such decisions. Another study, which specifically analyzed the effect of supervision on childhood agricultural injuries, noted that about half of all injured children were being "supervised" by an adult who was actively conducting farm work at the same time.[53]

The availability or absence of affordable, high quality childcare services is a key determinant affecting the presence of young children in agricultural work sites. Previously, farm enterprises were generational in nature, increasing the likelihood that children could be cared for by non-working family members or neighbors. Contemporary farms typically have one or both parents employed off the farm to augment income. Thus, dependable childcare services are needed in farming communities to the same extent as their urban counterparts, yet few options exist.

Interventions and Their Effectiveness

Concern over children being injured while living, working, or visiting farms has always been present, but a targeted effort to address these concerns was not undertaken as a national public health initiative until recently. In 1991, a Surgeon General's Conference on Agricultural Safety and Health was held in Des Moines, Iowa. During this conference, a session entitled *Intervention: Safe Behaviors Among Adults and Children* highlighted the risks faced by people, both youth and adult, involved with production agriculture.[54] This was followed in 1992 by a Childhood Agricultural Injury Prevention Symposium held in Marshfield, Wisconsin. The symposium was sponsored by the National Farm Medicine Center and sought to understand key issues from the different perspectives of farm parents, pediatricians, researchers, educators, engineers and the media. Participants formulated discussion points, identified areas for further consideration, and published their proceedings.[55]

As a follow up to the 1992 Symposium, a core of 42 individuals formed the National Committee for Childhood Agricultural Injury Prevention.[13] Over a 16-month period, members of the committee finalized a National Action Plan that was released in 1996 for addressing the childhood agricultural injury problem.[13] The National Action Plan, endorsed by more than 80 professional organizations and agricultural groups, recommended leadership, surveillance, research, education, and public policy. Committee members advocated for formal adoption of the plan and in October 1996 the US Congress endorsed the plan and targeted funding for its implementation.

The 1996 National Action Plan recommended that NIOSH serve as the lead federal agency in preventing childhood agricultural injury. In late 1996, NIOSH rolled out its National Childhood Agricultural Injury Prevention Initiative with goals to fill critical data needs; establish an infrastructure which facilitates the use of data to develop and improve upon prevention efforts; and encourage the use of effective prevention strategies by the private and public sectors.[25] To date, NIOSH has undertaken a number of activities to address the recommendations in the National Action Plan.[56] It is through this NIOSH-led initiative that the majority of intervention research and injury surveillance has been funded.

A team of Canadian scientists recently conducted a systematic review of interventions for preventing childhood agricultural injuries.[57] Their findings, based on a comprehensive assessment of controlled research trials and observational studies, provide valuable insights into strengths and weaknesses of some of the most prominent interventions currently in place. For example, they found that school-based programs appear to be effective at increasing short-term knowledge gain among children, especially when interactive learning methods are employed; and the popular one-day farm safety day camps demonstrate children's ability to retain selected safety messages. There were mixed results from evaluations of tractor safety training and general farm safety community-based initiatives.[57]

Interventions to Prevent Agricultural Work-Related Injuries

In 1999, the North American Guidelines for Children's Agricultural Tasks (NAGCAT) were released as a new resource to help adults match a child's physical, mental and psychosocial abilities with the requirements of agricultural jobs.[58] The NAGCAT enable children ages 7–16 years to have safe, meaningful work experiences in agriculture. It is important to note that the NAGCAT were developed for use in family farm settings, so they do not match up with child labor regulations or conditions where youth are employed in non-family settings.[59] Using the job hazard analysis framework, detailed information for 62 agricultural jobs commonly performed by children is provided in a professional resource manual along with illustrated posters for parent use.[60] These resources can be downloaded from a dedicated website, www.nagcat.org.

NIOSH-funded evaluation studies have demonstrated that parents' use of NAGCAT improves if dissemination is accompanied by a farm visit from a safety specialist or if child development principles are provided and promoted along with the print guidelines.[61,62] Further, a review of injury cases highlighted that if NAGCAT recommendations had been applied, 70% to 80% of the most serious work-related injuries could have been prevented.[63] The NAGCAT resources and modifications are used in the US, Canada, Scandinavia and Australia. In some cases, the NAGCAT have been tested with underserved populations, including Hispanic and Asian farmworker families.[64,65]

In 2001, under the direction of the USDA, a multi-faceted program was implemented to improve tractor and machinery safety training and certification for youth. The Hazardous Occupations Safety Training in Agriculture (HOSTA) initiative is currently refining a formal training program (including low-literacy resources) with a national tracking and recording system for use where employers need verification of training by minor employees.[33] Refer to http://hosta.nsc.org for more information.

Other interventions for youth working in agriculture include information dissemination from the state Cooperative Extension Service, non-government agencies, or the Department of Labor (DOL). For example, the DOL works with OSHA to regularly update the *Youth Rules!* website at http://www.youthrules.dol.gov/, providing guidance to teens, parents, educators and employers.[66] The site includes specific information for youth working in agriculture including OSHA safety standards, pertinent labor laws, and safety tips for jobs such as tractor operations and working in confined spaces.[67]

Non-Work-Related Research and Interventions

The strategy of relying on educational interventions to protect non-working children on farms is controversial. Because the farm is an occupational worksite, children who are not engaged in formal work would ideally be separated from the work setting, thus, there would be no need to educate them regarding injury prevention. Indeed, parents or responsible adults should be knowledgeable of the rationale for separating non-working children from farm worksites. While many current interventions focus on education for young children, most safety professionals promote removing young children from the worksite altogether. However, the perspective that it is inappropriate for children to be in the worksite directly conflicts with populations that practice traditional agriculture.

Off-site childcare for non-working children of farm owners and farmworkers is an ideal injury prevention option. Attempts have been made to implement rural childcare cooperative programs for farm families with mixed results. Childcare services for farm families must have flexible hours to match farmers' variable, often unscheduled, work activities. Additionally, childcare services for an agricultural population must accommodate cultural values and economic limitations of parents and guardians who depend on these services. The Redlands Christian Migrant Association (RCMA) of Immokalee, Florida, is a successful cooperative venture between growers, migrant farmworker women, and churches that provides graduated levels of programming and services for children of various ages.[68] After three decades of trial and error, RCMA now serves more than 5000 individuals from programs in 17 Florida counties and it is endorsed by major farm organizations such as the American Farm Bureau.

When off-site childcare is not an option for non-working children, designated safe play areas on farms are recommended.[69] A safe play area on a farm is a carefully planned, designated location with limited exposure to hazards such as traffic, agricultural production and environmental concerns. In 2003, Australia adopted a national child farm safety plan that included "safe play areas on farms" as a major national theme, promoting fencing and supervision in a manner consistent with their national swimming pool safety campaign.[70] In 2003, a US team of agricultural safety and playground safety specialists generated a detailed guide, based on playground safety and child development principles, to be used by farm owners.[71] *Creating Safe Play Areas on Farms* serves as a guidance document to facilitate action by farm owners when off-site childcare is not a viable option.[71]

The document can be downloaded from the internet at http://www2.marshfieldclinic.org/research/children/safePlay.

Community-based interventions, including initiatives such as Farm Safety 4 Just Kids (FS4JK) chapters where rural mothers introduce safety education for children, have been popular in many areas of the US and Canada.[72] While these programs are presumed to have benefits for parents and children, and many have demonstrated short-term knowledge gain, there is not definitive research to demonstrate they reduce the toll of childhood agricultural injuries.[57,73,74]

Advocacy

In the early 1990s the primary advocacy efforts toward child safety on farms involved the development, endorsement, and the implementation of the National Action Plan for Childhood Agricultural Injury Prevention.[13,25] In order to assess the extent to which progress was being made on the National Action Plan, an in-depth assessment of activities was facilitated by the National Children's Center for Rural and Agricultural Health and Safety.[75]

Assessment summaries were discussed at length among 100 individuals participating in the 2001 Summit on Childhood Agricultural Injury Prevention with proceedings published one year later.[69] The initial 1996 plan, combined with the 2001 follow up report, have served as the primary communication tools for advocacy. NIOSH uses these reports to solicit research proposals while individuals use the reports to justify grant requests to private foundations.

Advocacy efforts have also occurred within professional organizations and non-profit groups. For example, the American Academy of Pediatrics (AAP) developed and disseminated its policy statement on Childhood Agricultural Injuries.[76] The AAP also published guidelines for the care of migrant farmworkers' children.[77] The National Institute for Farm Safety (NIFS) is the professional organization of agricultural safety practitioners, including Cooperative Extension safety specialists and insurance company safety representatives. NIFS convenes annual conferences and publishes technical papers that include research and practical applications for child safety on farms. NIFS does not have formal lobbying efforts but endorses position papers and action plans. The American Society of Agricultural Engineers (ASAE) has a primary focus on engineering solutions to agricultural hazards. Like NIFS, the ASAE develops and endorses position papers on issues such as "buddy seats" in tractors, but does not have an official advocacy arm to the organization. The American Public Health Association (APHA) indirectly addresses childhood agricultural injury prevention through two special interest group sections: Injury Control and Emergency Health Services and the Occupational Health and Safety group. APHA also supports a Young Worker Network that, if called upon, would propose and endorse policy changes to protect youth working on farms.

In the private sector, non-government organizations such as FS4JK have raised the profile of the injury problem by gaining regional and national coverage in the general media and farm press. In 2004, the Founder and President of FS4JK, Marilyn Adams, was named one of the 25 outstanding "Faces of Public Health" for her grass-roots efforts to bring national attention to the problem of children being injured and killed on farms across the US.[78] Advocacy groups and coalitions can learn much from this and other like organizations on how to unite professionals and lay persons together to combat children's injuries.

Future Directions

Although progress has been made on preventing childhood agricultural injuries in the past two decades, more can be done. Action plans for general as well as child-specific agricultural safety have been developed through consensus methods involving agricultural stakeholders. The various plans include general and detailed recommendations for minimizing injuries to children on farms.

National agricultural health and safety recommendations that address child and adolescent safety are:

- *Agriculture at Risk: A Report to the Nation*[79]
- *Children and Agriculture: Opportunities for Safety and Health. A National Action Plan*[13]
- *Migrant and Seasonal Hired Adolescent Farmworkers: A Plan to Improve Working Conditions*[45]
- *Childhood Agricultural Injury Prevention: Progress Report and Updated National Action Plan from the 2001 Summit*[69]
- *National Agenda for Action: National Land Grant Research and Extension Agenda for Agricultural Safety and Health*[80]
- *Using History and Accomplishments to Plan for the Future: A Summary of 15 Years in Agricultural Safety and Health, and Action Steps for Future Directions*[81]
- *Looking Beneath the Surface of Agricultural Safety and Health: Chapter 7, Challenges, Opportunities and Ideas for the Future*[82]
- *National Agricultural Tractor and Safety Initiative: A Plan of the NIOSH Agricultural Safety and Health Centers*[32]

There is no shortage of suggestions for improving the safety of children and adults on our nation's farms and ranches. Where we fall short is in leadership and ability to enact recommendations. For a number of reasons, individuals and organizations find it difficult to implement desired strategies for childhood agricultural injury prevention. Factors such as economic farm policy, the independent nature of farming and farmers, resistance to change, and limitations in rural services prevail. For example, farm policies in the US have primarily focused on global trade, product safety, and environmental preservation, not on worker health and safety. In those cases where worker safety policy is addressed, it rarely incorporates issues of children living and working on family farms where the majority of childhood injuries occur.

Resistance to safety interventions can be compared to other areas of injury prevention such as motorcycle helmet use, where the irony is that resistance is greatest among the population with the most at stake. Another limiting factor is the obvious dissonance between safety professionals and the general farm community regarding an acceptable degree of risk in agricultural work settings. Indeed, farm owners seem to have lower expectations for occupational safety conditions than do the public health and agricultural safety professionals serving them.

Initial Action. In the near future, attention should be given to the young, non-working children at risk of injuries. Having affordable, accessible childcare options available and used by farm owners and parents would remove the most vulnerable children from the immediate risk of injury. Government or private-sector incentives for increasing the number and quality of rural childcare programs should be encouraged.[83] Parents and farm owners should be held accountable for child protection, consistent with urban parents. Finally, insurance companies should offer incentives to farm owners that physically separate children from the occupational worksite.

Long-Term Action. In the long run, organizational policy, public policy and regulatory changes are warranted on several fronts. Some of these policy changes include:

- National, state and organizational policies should provide financial incentives to farm owners for improving the safety environment and practices in their agricultural enterprise, especially as they affect children. Farm subsidies should be contingent upon safe working conditions. Such policies could mimic other government programs that reward agricultural producers for environmental practices; or they could be filtered through property insurers.
- Policy recommendations of the 1996 National Action Plan should be addressed. These include: mandating the restriction of youth under 18 years from operating tractors without seat belts and ROPS and restricting tractor operations on public roads to youth of 16 years or older who have a valid drivers license.[13]
- The Hazardous Occupations Order for Agriculture that affect youth working on farms should be updated and enforced.[84] Particular attention should be given to agricultural work that is highly associated with childhood morbidity and mortality.
- OSHA's regulation of farm safety equipment should be strengthened to increase the likelihood that working conditions for adults and youth meet minimum safety standards.

While we have focused heavily on the adverse outcomes of children's presence in agricultural worksites, it is important to maintain a balanced perspective. Agriculture offers many positive benefits for children. The largest youth serving organization in the US, the National FFA (formerly Future Farmers of America), was chartered by the US Congress on the principle that agriculture provides unique opportunities for young people to develop "premier leadership, personal growth, and career success."[85] Future research should enhance our knowledge regarding the benefits and risks of living and working on farms so that injury prevention strategies, such as stricter child labor regulations, are based on scientific findings that will stand the test of time.

References

1. Anonymous. (2002, June 29). Demolition accident takes area teen's life. *Reedsburg Times Press.*

2. Anonymous. (2002, September 18). Boy killed in tractor accident. *The Country Today.*

3. Olson, N. (2002, November 5). Man shoots, kills self in hospital. *Marshfield News-Herald.* p. A3.

4. Priebe, P. (2003, February 24). Farm accident claims life of three-year-old. *Central Dakota Times.* p.1.

5. Anonymous. (2003, April 23). Stanley teen dies in tractor rollover. *Marshfield News-Herald.* Retrieved April 23, 2003, from http://www.wisinfo.com/news herald/mnhlocal/277543772013871.shtml

6. Kottke, C. (2004, October 14). Child killed in accident on farm. *The Reporter.* p. A8.

7. Anonymous. (2004, October 15). Amish girl dies in accident on family farm. *WI State Farmer.* p. 5A.

8. National Safety Council (2004). *Injury Facts, 2004 Edition.* Itasca, IL: National Safety Council.

9. Rivara, F.P. (1997). Fatal and non-fatal injuries to children and adolescents in the United States, 1990-3. *Inj Prev, 3,* 190-194.

10. National Agricultural Statistics Service. (2004, January 8). *2001 Childhood agricultural-related injuries.* Retrieved January 2, 2005, from http://usda.mannlib.cornell. edu/reports/nassr/other/injury/injr0104.pdf

11. Hendricks, K.J., Layne, L.A., Goldcamp, E. M., and Myers, J.R. (2004). *Injuries among youth living on farms in the United States, 2001* (RIP No. 06). Paper presented at the meeting of the National Institute of Farm Safety, Keystone, CO.

12. Goldcamp, M., Myers, J., Hendricks, K., Layne, L. (2004) *Non-fatal all-terrain vehicle injuries to youth on farms in the United States, 2001* (RIP No. 03). Paper presented at the meeting of the National Institute of Farm Safety, Keystone, CO.

13. National Committee for Childhood Agricultural Injury Prevention. (1996). *Children and agriculture: Opportunities for safety and health.* Marshfield, WI: Marshfield Clinic.

14. US General Account Office (1998). *Child labor in agriculture.* (GAO/HEHS Publication No. 98-193). Washington, DC.

15. Adekoya, N., and Pratt, S. G. (2001). *Fatal unintentional farm injuries among persons less than 20 years of age in the United States: Geographic profiles* (DHHS/NIOSH Publication No. 2001-131). Cincinnati, OH.

16. Castillo, D.N., Adekoya, N., and Myers, J.R. (1999). Fatal work-related injuries in the agricultural production and services sectors among youth in the United States, 1992-96. *J Agromedicine,* 6(3), 27-41.

17. Hard, D., Myers, J., Snyder, K., Casini, V., Morton, L., Cianfrocco, R., et al. (1999). Young workers at risk when working in agricultural production [Supplement]. *Am J Ind Med,* 1, 31-33.

18. Windau, J., Sygnatur, E., and Toscano, G. (1999). *Profile of work injuries incurred by young workers.* Retrieved January 5, 2005, from http://www.bls.gov/opub/mlr/1999/06/art1full.pdf

19. US Department of Labor. (2004). *Census of fatal occupational injuries summary, 2003.* Retrieved December 31, 2004, from http://www.bls.gov/news.release/cfoi.nr0.htm

20. National Institute for Occupation Safety and Health (NIOSH). (1993). *Summary of traumatic occupational fatalities in the United States, 1980-1989: A decade of surveillance.* (DHHS, NIOSH Publication no. 93-108S). Cincinnati, OH.

21. Bureau of Labor Statistics. (2000). *Report on the youth labor force.* Washington, DC: US Department of Labor.

22. Centers for Disease Control and Prevention. (2003). *NIOSH alert: Preventing deaths, injuries, and illnesses of young workers.* (DHHS/NIOSH Publication No. 2003-128). Cincinnati, OH.

23. Centers for Disease Control and Prevention. (1998, September 11). Youth agricultural work-related injuries treated in emergency departments—United States, October 1995–September 1997. *Morbidity Mortality Weekly Report.* Retrieved January 5, 2005, from http://www.cdc.gov/mmwr/preview/mmwrhtml/00054662.htm

24. Consumer Product Safety Commission. (n.d.) *National Electronic Injury Surveillance System* (CPSC Doc. No. 3002). Retrieved January 1, 2005, from http://www.cpsc.gov/cpscpub/pubs/3002.html

25. Castillo, D., Hard, D., Myers, J., Pizatella, T., and Stout, N. (1998). A national childhood agricultural injury prevention initiative [Special issue]. *J Agricultural Safety Health,* (1), 183-191.

26. Myers, J.R., and Hendricks, K.J. (2001, June) *Injuries among youth on farms in the United States 1998.* (DHHS NIOSH Publication No. 2001-154). Washington, DC.

27. Haddon, W. (1972). A logical framework for categorizing highway safety phenomena and activity. *J Trauma,* 12(3), 193-207.

28. Runyan, C.W. (1998). Using the Haddon matrix: Introducing the third dimension. *Inj Prev,* (4), 302-307.

29. Rivara, F.P. (2002). Prevention of injuries to children and adolescents. *Inj Prev,* 8(Suppl IV): iv5-iv8.

30. Stallones, L., and Gunderson, P. (1994). Epidemiological perspectives on childhood agricultural injuries within the United States. *J Agromedicine,* 1(4), 3-18.

31. Forastieri, V. (2002). *Children at work health and safety risks.* (second edition) Geneva, Switzerland: International Labour Organization.

32. Swenson, E. (Ed.)(2004). *National Agricultural Tractor and Safety Initiative: A plan of the NIOSH Agricultural Safety and Health Centers.* Seattle, WA: University of Washington.

33. National Safety Council. (2004, November). *Hazardous Occupations Safety Training in Agriculture (HOSTA) Steering Committee Program Manual.* Itasca, IL: National Safety Council.

34. Schuler, R.T., Skjolaas, C.A. Purschwitz, M.A., and Wilkinson, T.L. (1994). Wisconsin youth tractor and machinery certification programs evaluation. ASAE Paper No. 94-5503. St. Joseph Michigan: American Society of Agricultural Engineers.

35. Carrabba, J.J., Field, W.E., Tormoehlen, R.L., and Talbert, B.A. (2000). Effectiveness of the Indiana 4-H tractor program at instillint safe tractor operating behaviors and attitudes in youth. *J Agricultural Safety and Health,* 6: 179-189.

36. Heaney, C.A. (2001). Reducing tractor-related injuries among youth: Impact of a tractor certification program. American Public Health Association 129th Annual Meeting, proceedings. 4060.0. October 23, 2001.

37. Hendricks, K.J., and Adekoya, N. (2001) Non-fatal animal related injuries to youth occurring on farms in the United States. *Inj Prev,* 7(4):307-311.

38. Neufeld, S., Wright, S. M., and Gaut, J. (2002). Not raising a "bubble kid": Farm parents' attitudes and practices regarding the employment, training and supervision of their children. *J Rural Health,* 18(1), 57-66.

39. Darraugh, A.R., Stallones, L. Sample, P.L., and Sweitzer, K. (1998). Perceptions of farm hazards and personal safety behavior among adolescent farmers. *J Agricultural Safety and Health* [special issue]. 1: 159-169.

40. Kidd, P., Townley, K., Cole, H., McKnight, R., and Piercy, L. (1997). The process of chore teaching: Implications for farm youth injury. *Family Community Health,* 19(4): 78-89.

41. Stueland, D.T., Lee, B.C., Nordstrom, D.L., Layde, P.M., and Wittman, L.M. (1996). A population based case-control study of agricultural injuries in children. *Inj Prev,* 2: 192-196.

42. Gerberich, S.G., Gibson, R.W., French, L.R., Renier, C.M., Lee, T.Y, Carr, W.P., and Shutske, J. (2001). Injuries among children and youth in farm households: Regional Rural Injury Study-I. *Inj Prev,* 7:117-122.

43. Centers for Disease Control and Prevention. (2004). *Injuries to youth on minority farm operations.* (NIOSH Publication No. 2004-117). Retrieved January 16, 2005, from http://www.cdc.gov/niosh/docs/2004-117/

44. Lee, B., Westaby, J. Benetti, L. Chyou, P., Peters, M. and Purschwitz, M. (2004). *Benchmarking report: Hiring and safety practices for adolescent workers in agriculture.* Marshfield, WI: Marshfield Clinic.

45. Vela Acosta, M.S., and Lee, B. (Eds.)(2001). *Migrant and seasonal hired adolescent farmworkers: A plan to improve working conditions.* Marshfield, WI: Marshfield Clinic.

46. National Agricultural Statistics Service. (2002) Census of Agriculture. Retrieved from http://www.naas.usda.gov/census/

47. US Department of Labor. (1975). *Occupational safety and health standards for agriculture.* Retrieved from http://www.osha.gov/pls/oshaweb/owadisp.show_document?p_table=STANDARDS&p_id=10954

48. Murphy, D.J. (1992). *Safety and health for production agriculture.* St. Joseph, MI: American Society of Agricultural Engineers.

49. US Department of Labor. (1991). *The fair labor stands act of 1938, as amended.* (WH Publication No. 1318). Washington, DC: US Government Printing Office.

50. US Department of Labor. (2004). *Child labor requirements in agricultural occupations under the fair labor standards act.* Child labor bulletin 102. (WH Publication No. 1295). Washington, DC: US Government Printing Office.

51. Esser, N. (2001, April). In the wrong place-all of the time. *Dairy Today.* p. 44.

52. Lee, B., Jenkins L., and Westaby, J. (1997). Factors influencing exposure of children to major hazards on family farms. *J Rural Health,* 13(3), 206-215.

53. Pryor, S.K., Caruth, A.K., and McCoy, C.A. (2002). Children's injuries in agriculture related events: the effect of supervision on the injury experience. *Issues Comprehensive Pediatric Nursing,* 25(3):189-205.

54. Armbruster, W.J. (1991). Intervention—Safe behaviors among adults and children. In *Papers and Proceedings of the Surgeon General's Conference on Agricultural Safety and Health.* Washington DC: USDHHS. p. 462-465.

55. Lee, B.C. and Gunderson, P.D. (Eds.). (1992, April). Childhood agricultural injury prevention: Issues and interventions from multiple perspectives. *Proceedings from the Childhood Agricultural Injury Prevention Symposium,* Marshfield, WI: Marshfield Clinic, National Farm Medicine Center.

56. Centers for Disease Control and Prevention. *NIOSH safety and health topic: Childhood agricultural injury prevention initiative.* Retrieved February 9, 2005, from http://www.cdc.gov/niosh/childag/.

57. Hartling, L., Brison, R.J., Crumley, E.T., Klassen, T. P., and Pickett, W. (2004). A systematic review of interventions to prevent childhood farm injures. *Pediatrics,* 114, 483-496.

58. Lee, B., and Marlenga, B. (Eds.) (1999). *Professional Resource Manual: North American Guidelines for Children's Agricultural Tasks.* Marshfield, WI: Marshfield Clinic.

59. Cohen, A. (2002). *North American Guidelines for Children's Agricultural Tasks and Child labor Regulations.* NIOSH report. Available at http://www.cdc.gov/niosh/childag/.

60. National Children's Center for Rural and Agricultural Health and Safety. *North American Guidelines for Children's Agricultural Tasks.* Retrieved February 9, 2005, from http://www.nagcat.org/

61. Gadomski, A., Burdick, P., Jenkins, P., Ackerman, S., and May, J. (2003). Randomized field trial to evaluate the effectiveness of the North American Guide-

lines for Childhood Agricultural Injury Prevention (NAGCAT). (American Public Health Association Abstract No. 64051). Abstract retrieved January 27, 2005, from http://apha.confex.com/apha/131am/techprogram/paper_64051.htm

62. Marlenga, B., Pickett, W., and Berg, R. L. (2002). Evaluation of an enhanced approach to the dissemination of the North American Guidelines for Children's Agricultural Tasks: A randomized controlled trial. *Preventive Medicine, 35*, 150-159.

63. Marlenga, B., Brison, R.J., Berg, R.L., Zentner, J., Linneman, J., and Pickett, W. (2004). Evaluation of the North American Guidelines for Children's Agricultural Tasks using a case series of injuries. *Inj Prev,* 10(6): 350-357.

64. Liller, K.D., Noland, V., Rijal, P., Pesce, K., and Gonzalez, R. (2002). Development and Evaluation of the Kids Count Farm Safety Lesson. *J Agricultural Safety and Health,* 8(4), 411-421.

65. Rasmussen, R.C., Schermann, M.A., Shutske, J.M., and Olson, D.K. (2003). Use of the North American Guidelines for Children's Agricultural Tasks with Hmong Farm Families. *J Agricultural Safety and Health,* 9(4):265-274.

66. US Department of Labor. (2004). *Youth Rules.* Retrieved February 9, 2005 from http://www.youthrules.dol.gov/

67. US Department of Labor. *Youth in Agriculture.* Retrieved February 9, 2005 from http://www.osha.gov/SLTC/youth/agriculture/index.html

68. Redlands Christian Migrant Associatoin (RCMA), (n.d.). *Groups that change communities.* Retrieved January 19, 2005, from http://www.grass-roots.org/usa/redlands.shtml

69. Lee, B., Gallagher, S., Marlenga, B., and Hard, D. (Eds.). (2002). *Childhood agricultural injury prevention: Progress report and updated national action plan from the 2001 summit.* Marshfield, WI: Marshfield Clinic.

70. Farmsafe Australia (2003). *Safe Play Areas on Farms. A Resource Package.* New South Wales: Farm Safe Australia, Inc.

71. Esser, N., Heiberger, S., and Lee, B. (Eds.) (2004). Creating safe play areas on farms. (second edition). Marshfield, WI: Marshfield Clinic. Available at http://www2.marshfieldclinic.org/research/children/safePlay/

72. Farm Safety 4 Just Kids. Retrieved February 9, 2005, from http://www.fs4jk.org/about.html

73. Reed, D. B., and Claunch, D.T. (2000). Nonfatal farm injury incidence and disability to children. A systematic review. *Am J Preventive Medicine,* 18(4S) 70-79.

74. DeRoo, L.A., and Rautianen, R. (2000). A systematic review of farm safety interventions. *Am J Preventive Medicine,* 18: 51-62.

75. National Children's Center for Rural and Agricultural Health and Safety. Retrieved February 9, 2005, from http://research.marshfieldclinic.org/children/

76. Committee on Injury and Poison Prevention and Committee on Community Health Services. (2001, October). American Academy of Pediatrics: Prevention of agricultural injuries among children and adolescents [Electronic version]. *Pediatrics,* 108(4), 1016-1019.

77. McLaurin, J. (Ed.) (2000). *Guidelines for the care of migrant farmworkers' children.* AAP Committee on Community Health Services and Migrant Clinicians Network. Elm Grove Village: IL: American Academy of Pediatrics.

78. Pfizer Global Pharmaceuticals, Pfizer Inc. (2004) Farm safety awareness in *The Faces of Public Health.* (pp. 6-11). New York.

79. Merchant, J.A., Kross, B., Donham, K., and Pratt, D. (Eds.). (1989). *A report to the nation: Agricultural Occupational and Environmental Health: Policy Strategies for the Future.* Iowa City, IA: The National Coalition for Agricultural Safety and Health.

80. Committee NCR-197 (2003). *National agenda for action: National land grant re-*

search and extension agenda for agricultural safety and health. Washington DC: USDA.

81. Petrea, R.E. (Ed.). (2003). *Using history and accomplishments to plan for the future: A summary of 15 years in agricultural safety and health and action steps for future directions.* Urbana, IL: Agricultural Safety and Health Network.

82. Murphy, D. (2003). *Looking beneath the surface of agricultural safety and health.* St. Joseph, MI: American Society of Agricultural Engineers.

83. Children's Defense Fund. (2001). A Fragile Foundation: State Childcare Assistance policies. Washington DC: Children's Defense Fund.

84. Miller, M., and Bush, D. (2004). Review of the federal child labor regulations: Updating hazardous and prohibited occupations. *Am J Ind Med, 45,* 218-221.

85. National FFA Organization. Retrieved February 9, 2005 from http://www.ffa.org/.

CHAPTER 9

Sports and Recreational Injuries

Gitanjali Saluja,[1] Stephen W. Marshall,[2]
Julie Gilchrist,[3] and Tom Schroeder[4]

B randon Schultz had just turned 16 when he played in a football game that would forever change his life. He was a member of the junior varsity football team of his high school in Washington State. On October 25, 1993, he made a tackle that appeared harmless to spectators, including his parents who were videotaping the game. Right after making the tackle, Brandon slowly got up and did not appear to lose consciousness. In the minutes following that tackle he complained that his head hurt, but he was still able to walk and talk. He walked to the end zone and ten minutes later he collapsed, had a series of seizures and lost consciousness. His brain had swelled and hemorrhaged.

Since the tackle did not appear to be extraordinarily forceful and it was not apparent that there had been head to head contact, this reaction was a surprise. However, Brandon had been removed from play one week earlier after he suffered a concussion in which he momentarily lost consciousness. During that week, he was removed from practice and he complained of headaches, but he never visited a doctor.

Brandon suffered what is known as Second Impact Syndrome (SIS). Although his injury was not fatal, as of 2000 he was still living in a neurological facility and he was unable to walk without the help of a brace. His cognitive functions were severely compromised and he required constant supervision. Physicians were not optimistic about his development.[1]

Injuries related to sports and recreation seem like a contradiction of sorts. When people think of recreation, they typically associate it with fun and relaxation. Two young brothers were probably seeking fun on a summer afternoon in June, 2004, when they were riding on an all-terrain vehicle on a paved, public road in their rural town. On this particular day, the 6 year old brother was driving, and the 8 year old was a passenger. As they

---

1   National Institutes of Health.
2   University of North Carolina at Chapel Hill.
3   Centers for Disease Control and Prevention.
4   US Consumer Product Safety Commission.

approached a driveway and slowed down to turn into it, their front tire entered a ditch, which resulted in the vehicle being pulled into the ditch, and both boys being thrown. Neither boy was wearing a helmet. The six year old boy sustained minor cuts and bruises and the eight year old boy died as a result of serious head injuries.[2]

Both of the above stories involve catastrophic injuries that could have been prevented. Although death and disability are fortunately not common outcomes of sports and recreational injuries, injuries due to sports and recreational activities have a significant public health impact. According to data collected by the National Health Interview Survey, which is an annual face to face survey of over 37 000 households in the United States, nearly 7 million Americans each year sought medical care for a sports or recreational injury between 1997–99. This translates to a rate of 26 injury episodes per 1000 persons per year. More than half of these injuries were sustained by youth between the ages of 5–24.[3] According to another estimate, more than 3.5 million children ages 14 and under suffer from sports- and recreation-related injuries each year.[4] Furthermore, injuries associated with participation in sports and recreational activities account for 21 percent of all traumatic brain injuries among children in the United States.[4] In boys ages 15–19 years, 52% of all unintentional injury visits to the Emergency Department are for sports- and recreation-related injuries; for girls in this age group, it is 38%.[5]

Sports injuries are considered by some as "just part of the game," and some athletes wear their scars as if they are "badges of honor." However, similar to other injuries, sports injuries are preventable. Further, the economic costs associated with sports and recreational injuries are remarkable. The medical costs of sports and recreational injuries to children under age 18 were over $11 billion in 2003. If you include parents' work losses, pain and suffering, and product liability and legal fees, this societal cost spirals to over $121 billion in 2003.[6,7] Although much of the morbidity does not ultimately result in hospitalization, children often have to miss school for treatment and/or recovery. According to one study, 20% of injured school children lost one or more days per year from school due to their injury.[3] Thus, caregivers have to arrange care for them.

Historically, sports/recreational injury prevention research has been limited—possibly because many of these injuries tend to be less severe than injuries from other causes. Most people don't die from sports and recreation injuries, and most of these injuries are not catastrophic in nature. There are also many challenges associated with conducting research on sports and recreational injury. For one, since the outcome of most of these injuries is rarely death, counting these injuries becomes less concrete. A great number of sports and recreational injuries are not reported and the injured don't seek medical care. In cases where victims undergo medical treatment, the manner in which their injuries are classified is limited by which codes are available from the International Classification of Diseases (ICD) manuals. Although these codes have become more refined with each revision, even the most recent version, ICD-10, fails to capture most sports and recreational activities. For example, bicycling-related deaths are captured in this coding system; however, team sports such as basketball and football, are not. Although fatalities associated with these activities are rare, the lack of codes is a limiting factor in accurately determining the number of sports and recreational injuries associated with specific activities.

Even if it were possible to count all sports and recreational injuries, calculating the risk of injury would still be difficult, as we lack the data needed to determine population exposure. The National Center for Catastrophic Sport Injury Research (http://www.unc.edu/depts/nccsi) collects data on fatal and serious non-fatal injuries among high school and college athletes participating in school sponsored teams. By determining the number of individuals who participate in team sports, they are able to calculate injury rates for these activities; however, since many injuries occur in less formal, unstructured and unregulated settings, these rates only provide a partial picture of the sports injury problem.

Given the steadily increasing number of sedentary people in the US, the Surgeon General has recommended that Americans engage in more physical activity and exercise in order to prevent obesity related disease.[8] According to some estimates, there has been an increase in the number of children participating in organized sports in the last several years.[9] Children seem to be involved in organized training at younger ages than before as well, and there are training programs available for preschool aged children and children younger than preschool age.[9,10] Increased participation in sports and recreational activities, which results in increased exposure, leads to an increased risk for injury. Thus, it is critical that as we look toward a nation of potentially more active youth, we look forward with an eye toward the risks associated with these activities as well as the manner in which to prevent them.

Morbidity and Mortality Related to the Most Common Injuries

Injuries due to participation in organized sports are in many ways categorically different than recreational injuries. Organized sports are generally governed by certain rules that are developed to ensure fair play and safety. Further, in contrast to play in less structured settings, organized sports have coaches and referees present to enforce rules and encourage players to use the required protective gear. Unstructured play and recreational activities leave the responsibility of safe play up to the individual (or in young children, their caregivers). For these reasons, as we address the specific injuries related to sports and recreation activities, we will consider them individually. Additionally, we will separate common injuries, which are generally not life threatening, and catastrophic injuries, which are less common, but warrant examination as they are devastating but preventable.

According to data collected by the Consumer Product Safety Commission in 2000, the eight sports and recreational activities resulting in the highest number of injuries to children ages 5–14 were as follows: baseball/softball, basketball, bicycling, football, playgrounds, roller sports, soccer, and trampolines.[11] These activities have high numbers of injuries as compared to other activities, but not necessarily high rates of injuries. When considering these injuries, it is important to keep in mind that we have limited exposure data for sports and recreational activities. Thus, we are usually unable to calculate rates (or risk) of injury, unless we limit our analysis to injuries as a result of participation in organized, registered sports (large numbers of injuries in one sport over another may simply reflect a larger number of participants in that sport). Similarly, low numbers of injuries in a sport does not indicate that the sport is safer than other sports. For example, cheerleading and gymnastics have low numbers of injuries overall; however, the rate of catastrophic injury due to these sports is high, compared to other sports.[11]

The National Center for Catastrophic Sport Injury Research classifies fatal sports injuries as direct or indirect. Direct injuries refer to those which result directly from participation in the skills of the sport (eg, direct head trauma or spinal cord injury). Indirect injuries are those that are caused as a result of exertion while participating in a sport, or a secondary complication to a non-fatal injury (eg, heat-related illness).[12] Deaths due to sports and recreation are usually a result of head injuries, heat stroke, or cardiac arrest.[11] In very rare cases, a sudden impact to the chest wall, such as from a baseball or a hockey puck, can trigger cardiac arrest.[13,14]

Although fatal events are rare, they have great social significance because they engender enormous grief in the community. The inherent tragedy of a child who dies playing organized sport makes these injuries highly unacceptable to society. Furthermore, fatal sports injuries sometimes serve as springboards for community-driven prevention activities that may safeguard against similar tragedies in the future. Prevention activities for these types of events include allowing extra water breaks at football practice when the weather is hot; ensuring that adequate face and head protection is worn; and removing concussed athletes from competition.

In the following section, we will focus on the activities that have a high number of injuries, as well as the activities that have a high rate of catastrophic injuries in youth.

Team Sports Injuries

Basketball

Basketball is one of the most common activities among youth in the United States, and perhaps the most popular youth team sport. Although basketball has traditionally been considered a non-contact sport, the sport has evolved such that contact between players has become common.[15] Among high school and college basketball players, basketball injuries result in a high number of indirect fatalities compared to other sports.[12] It is also the team sport associated with the most injuries.[3,7] This might be partially explained by the large numbers of people who participate in the sport, rather than an innate danger in the sport itself. Nonetheless, there are ways to make the sport safer, and certain measures have already been shown to effectively decrease the number of injuries.

High school players are more likely to become injured during practice, whereas college athletes are more likely to become injured during competition.[15] Canadian data have shown that the most common types of basketball injuries are sprains, fractures and dislocations.[16] Hands and fingers are commonly injured, as are knees and ankles.[11,15,16] Eye injuries are common, but most can be prevented with proper eye protection.[15] Head and spinal cord injuries are rare.

Randomized controlled trials in college-age military cadets indicate that ankle braces have some effectiveness in preventing injuries in basketball.[17] Whether these interventions have efficacy in younger populations is still unknown. Mouth guards have been shown to be effective in preventing dental injuries in the college game and there is every reason to assume they are also effective in younger athletes.[18] Dentist-fitted mouth guards are recommended and they need to be replaced when damaged or when children might out-grow them.

Football

Of the sports that are widely played in the United States, football has the distinction of having the greatest risk of injury. In the early part of the 20th century, when the game was still evolving, the number of deaths and injuries in college football was a matter of national concern. The modern game retains the sport's early emphasis on vigorous body contact, body mass, and athletic acceleration, but has invested heavily in protective equipment as a means of controlling injury. Pioneering research during the 1960s demonstrated that cleat length had an impact on the risk of knee injury, with shorter cleats reducing the risk of injury. Further, maintenance of the playing field was also important to reducing injury risk.[19]

As a general recommendation, all protective equipment should be in good condition and provide a good fit to the young athlete. In addition, youth need to be trained to use equipment correctly. This is particularly true of the helmet. When the modern hard-shell helmet was first introduced into the sport in 1970s, it was initially used by some as a battering ram, resulting in an upswing in the incidence of paralysis and other catastrophic injuries. Educational campaigns and rules prohibiting making initial contact with the opponent using the head were introduced to correct this situation.[20]

Concussion in football (which players sometimes playfully refer to as "getting dinged"), as in all sports, poses special risks, since the management of this injury is problematic and requires trained professionals. Any youth athlete showing signs of concussion should be removed from the field of play and should not be allowed to return to the sport until some time after the symptoms have resolved, even if that is a matter of weeks or months.[21] Careful evaluation by a sports medicine professional and/or a neurologist is required. Signs and symptoms of concussion include (but are not limited to) long-term and short-term memory loss, delays in cognitive processing, dizziness and balance problems, nausea and vomiting, visual disturbances, neck pain, and headache. Loss of consciousness, long considered to be the hallmark sign of concussion, is actually rare.[22] The cumulative effects of multiple concussions are poorly understood at this time but there is evidence that youth athletes with a past history of concussion are at increased risk for further concussions.[22] In addition, if a second blow to the head occurs while the athlete is still suffering from the first concussion, the consequences can be severe or even fatal. This is a serious condition known as second-impact syndrome and can be fatal 50% of the time.[23]

Baseball/softball

Baseball enjoys a special place in American culture. The sport has historically claimed to epitomize American values and dominated the sports landscape in the US during much of the 20th century.[24] Modern baseball is largely a youth sport. Nearly two-thirds of baseball participants are less than 18 years of age; older participants tend to transition into recreational softball leagues.[25]

Because of the popularity among youth, there has been long-standing interest in reducing the risk of injury to children and adolescents playing these sports.[26] Breakaway bases have demonstrated effectiveness in youth and recreational adult baseball and softball, and their use should be encouraged throughout baseball and softball at all levels.[27–28] Studies of protective eyewear indicate that polycarbonate lenses provide excellent protection for batters from the risk of being hit in the eye by a pitched ball.[29–30] Faceguards are strongly recommended for batters. Two independent studies have indicated that faceguards reduce the risk of facial injury by 23% to 35%.[31–32]

Uncontrolled contact with the ball is the single most frequent proximate cause of injury for youth participants and thus use of safety balls also has the potential to considerably reduce the overall risk of injury.[33–35] Two studies indicate a protective effect for use of safety balls, ranging from 13% to 23%.[32,34] There are a wide range of safety balls used in youth baseball, including tennis balls, rubber balls, cloth balls, and specialized reduced impact balls (also known as RIF balls). One study has indicated the reduced impact balls may be the most effective type of safety ball.[32] Reduced impact balls have polyurethane core (in contrast to the traditional wool yarn wound around a cork core), and they flatten out and deform more than the traditional ball when they hit a child. This helps to dissipate the force of impact.

Pitching a baseball is an ergonomically stressful activity, and youth pitchers that throw a large number of pitches in a short span of time run the risk of incurring repetitive overuse syndrome.[36,37] Care should be taken to monitor the number and frequency of pitches thrown by a child or adolescent and restrict the amount of pitching if pain, swelling, or other overuse symptoms appear in the arm, particularly the elbow, or shoulder. USA Baseball recommends that pitchers who are 9–10 years old should be limited to no more than 75 pitches per week and no more than 50 pitches in any one game. For 11–12 year old pitchers, the limits are 100 pitches per week and no more than 75 pitches per game, and for 13–14 year old pitchers it is 125 pitches per week and 75 pitches per game. Further recommendations for youth pitchers are available from USA Baseball (http://www.usabaseball. com/med_position_statement.html).

Soccer

Soccer is the most popular sport in the world, for adults and youth. Of the 18 million people who compete in organized soccer in the US, 75% are under 18 years of age. Driven in part by the competitive success of the US women's soccer team, and in part by the arrival of soccer superstar Mia Hamm, participation in soccer at the high school level for both girls and boys jumped during the 1980s and 1990s (increased 73% overall between 1989 and 1999).[38] The intensity and standard of competition has also risen.

As in many sports, games are far riskier than practices and females have a greater risk of injury than males. Over half of the injuries to females occur from the knee to the foot, while males add injuries to the head to this list. From a practical standpoint, playing fields should be well-maintained and in good condition. Goalposts can be padded to limit the risk of injury from goalpost collisions. If movable goals are used, they must be correctly anchored, since death can result if the goals tip over during play.[39]

The detection of deficits in cognitive processing in professional European soccer stars[40] has lead to great concern about the potential for heading of the ball to adversely affect academic performance in youth players. In fact, similar deficits do not seem to exist in collegiate players in the US, and it is highly doubtful that they would exist in youth players.[41] Nevertheless, a product designed to absorb impact forces has been marketed in the US. It resembles a padded headband, but it's effectiveness has not been proven. The neurological deficits observed in professional soccer players may not in fact be the result of heading the ball, but rather they may stem from repeated concussions due to impacts with other players or the ground.[42] This suggest that a "fair head rule"—allowing a player who is well-positioned to take a header uncontested—would do much to address the safety issues associated with heading.

It has been suggested that training in movement techniques—known as neuromuscular, pylometric, or proprioceptive training—can reduce the risk of ankle and knee injury in soccer and other sports that involve landing and jumping.[43–44] These training programs typically target prevention of tears and rupture of the anterior cruciate ligament (ACL), a ligament within the knee that is more prone to rupture in girls than in boys. Although the cause of ACL injury is probably multi-factorial in nature, neuromuscular training programs provide the most promising opportunity for prevention.[45-46]

Ice hockey

Hockey has a high risk of oro-facial and dental injury.[47] Approximately 1/3 of collegiate players have previously suffered a dental injury.[48] This injury is preventable if a face guard that completely covers the lower and upper face, is worn. However, the standard helmet face guard has an opening in the lower face that permits the intrusion of the hockey stick. In addition, the face guard is hinged, and players sometimes skate with the face guard in the up position. This alters the impact dynamics of the helmet by re-positioning the mass of the helmet on the player's head; thus, it greatly increases the loading on the cervical spine and places the player at risk for spinal cord injury.[49]

The game is fast-paced, involves body checking, and is played on a slippery surface. As a result, it has a high rate of injury. Play should not commence if the ice is not in good condition. Furthermore, parents, officials, administrators, and officials should collaborate to ensure that fighting is strongly discouraged. Players who become overly aggressive should be removed from the game.

Cheerleading

Over the past 2 decades, cheerleading has evolved from support-orientated dance routines on the sidelines of the high school football game into a sport in its own right.[50] Modern cheerleading teams (or, more formally, competitive spirit squads) compete against one another in standalone competitions. They perform aerobic routines and gymnastic stunts that sometimes involve high-risk formations such as 3-level pyramids. At the high school level, it is the ninth most popular sport for girls nationally, with nearly 90 000 participants.[51] There is also a burgeoning private gym industry devoted to cheerleading.

As the athletic demands of the sport have increased, so have concerns about safety. As a result, the American Association of Cheerleading Coaches and Advisors (AACCA) has published a comprehensive cheerleading safety manual. They urge that teams work slowly towards the more demanding athletic stunts and that adequate numbers of spotters should be present in both competitions and practices. Aerial tumbling moves and pyramid formations should only be attempted with adequate preparation and under close supervision. Further, high school cheerleading teams are restricted to pyramids no higher than two levels. Poor quality coaching has been identified as a risk factor for cheerleading injury at the high school level. Thus, school officials should ensure that coaching staff are experienced and qualified.[52]

Individual Sports/Recreational Injuries

Playground Injuries

Injuries related to playground activities account for many of the injuries to youth aged 0-9.[5] Although the mortality associated with these activities is not high (4 playground deaths in 2001),[53] morbidity is significant with more than 200 000 children visiting emergency departments for treatment of a playground injury each year.[54] Most injuries on playgrounds are due to falls, and obviously falls from higher elevations generally result in more serious injuries than falls from lower surfaces. Fractures to upper limbs are the most common type of injury.[55] Although less frequent than falls, children can also become injured by colliding with swings or other moving equipment and coming into contact with sharp surfaces or pinch points. From January 1990 through August 2000, the US Consumer Product Safety Commission received reports of 147 deaths to children involving playground equipment. Seventy percent of these occurred in home locations. Over one-half of all playground equipment-related deaths involved hanging, primarily from ropes, shoestrings, cords, leashes, clothing strings, and other items tied to, or entangled on the equipment.[56]

The introduction of softer, impact absorbing surfaces under playground equipment combined with ensuring that equipment meets height and maintenance standards[54] has decreased the number of serious injuries due to falls. The number of head injuries due to falls on playgrounds has also decreased with the implementation of softer surfaces.[55] Generally speaking, children should be limited to playing on playgrounds that follow guidelines set forth by the US Consumer Product Safety Commission. This includes ensuring that there are adequate spaces between equipment items so that the flow of children around the equipment does not become congested, creating the potential for falls and collisions. Children are guaranteed to use equipment in ways that were not initially intended for them. For example, they will jump off of swings and merry-go-rounds while they are still in motion; thus, it is important that there is adequate space for them to land safely. Few children slide down a slides while facing forward and sitting upright. Thus, it is critical that there is adequate space for them to land and a soft surface upon which to fall.

Impact-absorbing surfaces reduce the risk of injury on playgrounds, but these surfaces do require maintenance on a regular basis. Wood or bark chips tend to migrate away from high-traffic area and must be regularly redistributed to ensure a uniform depth across the whole playground. They may also be prone to run-off following a heavy thunderstorm. Synthetic mats can erode over time. Caregivers should walk around the playground, inspect the surfacing, and arrange for repairs if needed.

In 2001 the US Consumer Product Safety Commission released results of a playground special study done using 1999 injury data. Approximately 75% of playground injuries occur on equipment designed for public use while the rest occur on equipment designed for home use or home-made equipment. In locations where injuries occurred on public equipment, almost 80% had some kind of protective surface under the equipment such as bark mulch or wood chips. In contrast, only about nine percent of injuries occurring at home had a protective surfacing, most often sand.[56]

Young children grow rapidly and playground equipment varies in size in order to accommodate children of all ages. It is important that caregivers are aware of the physical and developmental capabilities of their children and allow them to only play on equipment that is safe and age/size appropriate.

Bicycle Injuries

Bicycling is one of the most popular recreational activities among children, with an estimated 44.3 million youth under 21 riding bicycles in the US.[57] In addition to recreation, many youth use bicycles as a means of transportation to school or other activities. Unfortunately, bicycle injuries are one of the most common types of sports and recreation injuries for youth,[5] and the most common for children aged 5–14 years.[3] In 2001, a total of 185 children ages 0–18 died in 2001 of bicycle-related deaths.[58] Of these 185 deaths, 122 suffered a head injury, 14 suffered a neck injury and 10 suffered both a head and neck injury. Further, the US Consumer Product Safety Commission estimated 415 000 children experienced a musculoskeletal injury due to cycling in 2000.[11] Bicycle related injuries account for more emergency department visits for children and adolescents as compared to other sports/recreation injuries, and two-thirds of all bicycle related fatalities are due to traumatic brain injuries.[59]

The most common bicycle injuries result from falls and collisions with immovable objects, but the more serious bicycle crashes typically involve collisions with motor vehicles. One way of preventing bicycles from colliding with motor-vehicle traffic is to separate the cyclists from the drivers. Bicycle lanes and paths have become more common, but studies that have been able to measure their effectiveness are scarce. According to the American Academy of Pediatrics Committee on Injury and Poison Prevention, wearing a bicycle helmet is one of the most effective safety measures that a child can take to prevent injury.[60] The percentage of cyclists who wear helmets has steadily increased over the years; however, many children and most adolescents still do not wear helmets regularly or at all.[61] Educational campaigns, helmet subsidies and local and state legislation have all been proven effective in increasing helmet use and decreasing the number of bicycle injuries.[63] Many states have laws in place requiring youth under age 16 to wear helmets. Other states have different age requirements, and several localities require all ages to wear helmets. At this point in time, there are no states that require people of all ages to wear helmets and only about half of America's children under the age of 15 are covered by a helmet law.[62-63]

Winter sports: Skiing and Snowboarding

Skiing and snowboarding are popular winter sports for children and adolescents, with snowboarding gaining in popularity. Fifty-two-thousand children and adolescents are seen in US hospital emergency departments each year for injuries from winter sports.[7] However, these sports have distinct injury patterns with snowboarding responsible for a larger proportion of head injuries, neck and spinal injuries, upper limb fractures and foot/ankle injuries than skiing. Skiers commonly experience knee, thumb and shoulder injuries from falling.

Head injuries account for the majority of deaths and serious injuries in both skiing and snowboarding. The rates of head and spinal injuries in these sports have been on the rise with the advent of increased jumping in both sports.[64] Evidence suggests a potential benefit of helmets in skiing and snowboarding.[65] However, others suggest that helmets may increase the rate of neck injuries[64] or may lead to an increase in risk taking behavior.[66] However, a similar argument has been used and refuted regarding helmets in cycling, football, and hockey. Evidence based recommendations are not yet available; however, for those who choose to wear a helmet, it should be one that conforms to a performance standard such as the Snell Foundation's RS98.

Knee injuries are common among skiers, but less so among snowboarders. With the advent of the bindings that reliably release, lower leg and ankle fracture rates have decreased. Leather alpine boots have been replaced by stiff plastic boots that protect the ankle and lower leg. However, this redistributes forces up to the knee with a dramatic increase in ligamentous injuries to the knee (particularly the ACL). Conventional binding systems release in response to twisting or a forward lean. Newer "multi-release" bindings may also release with a lateral twist at the heel or a backward lean, however, no decrease in ACL injuries in association with these newer bindings has yet been demonstrated.

Another key injury prevention area in winter sports includes the adjustment of bindings to set what force is necessary to release the boot from the ski. Standards have been developed and a device to measure release values is available. Unfortunately, these are not routinely used in ski shops. Inappropriately adjusted bindings have been associated with increased rates of injury in children.[67-68] While knee injuries are less common in snowboarding, the rates of wrist, ankle, and spinal injuries are more common in snowboarders. There is strong evidence to support the use of wrist guards to prevent injuries in snowboarding.[69]

Finally, novice skiers and snowboarders tend to have higher rates of injuries than more experienced participants. Two studies of lessons have been unable to demonstrate a decreased risk of injury in those who participated in lessons. However, inexperienced or novice skiers should consider participating in lessons, and should be supervised until they can reliably perform basic skills. All participants should ski within their ability levels, always maintain control and adhere to the National Ski Patrol's Responsibility Code (Figure 1).

Trampolines

Trampolines, though not commonly used, have a high rate of injury. There are an estimated 3 million backyard trampolines in use today.[70] The US Consumer Product Safety Commission estimates that over 209,000 trampoline-related injuries received medical attention in 2003 for children ages 18 and under of which 96% occurred at home. Sprains and strains along with fractures accounted for 60% of the injuries. Injuries to the lower extremities, head and neck, and upper extremities accounted for 36%, 22%, and 30% of the injury estimates, respectively.[7,71] The resulting medical costs alone for these injuries was over $260 million.[6] Because of the high rate of serious or fatal head or neck injuries, the American Academy of Pediatrics recommends that trampolines not be used in the home, outdoor playgrounds or in routine physical education programs.[72]

All terrain vehicles

All-terrain vehicles (ATVs) are three or four wheeled vehicles that were initially intended for use in rural environments where off-road travel was necessary for activities such as farming and logging. Since then, their popularity has gained and they are used widely for recreational purposes. They are marketed toward young adults and children as young as 4 years of age. The US Consumer Product Safety Commission estimates that over 1700 deaths and over 284 000 emergency department treated injuries have occurred related to ATVs from 1999-2001. Ninety-four-thousand (33%) of these injuries occurred to children under the age of 16.[73]

Figure 1

National Ski Patrol's Responsibility Code

- Always stay in control, and be able to stop or avoid other people or objects.
- People ahead of you have the right of way; it is your responsibility to avoid them.
- You must not stop where you obstruct a trail or are not visible from above.
- When starting downhill or merging into a trail, look uphill and yield to others.
- Always use devices to help prevent runaway equipment.
- Observe all posted warning signs; keep off closed trails and out of closed areas.
- Before using any lift, you must have the knowledge and ability to load, ride and unload safely.

Youth are often hurt while riding ATVs on their own; however, incidents involving very young children who are riding ATVs as passengers are not unusual. Legislation requiring helmet use on ATVs is lacking in most places. Enforcement of these laws is another challenge, as ATV use often occurs on private property, that is unlikely to be patrolled.

In the late 1980s ATV manufactures entered into consent decrees with the US Consumer Product Safety Commission. Among other things, the consent decrees stopped the sale by dealers of three-wheel ATVs, placed engine size restrictions on sales intended for children, and implemented driver-training programs. The consent decrees expired in 1998; however, features are still in place voluntarily by major manufacturers. The major ATV manufacturers agreed in consent decrees in 1988 and in subsequent voluntary action plans that engine size restrictions would be placed on ATVs sold for use by children less than 16 years of age. Despite the recommended engine size of ≤ 90 cubic centimeters for children under 16 years of age, 87% of all emergency department treated injuries in 2001 were related to ATVs of a larger engine size for this age group.[74] In addition to the restriction on engine size, the US Consumer Product Safety Commission has other safety recommendations for operating ATVs (See Figure 2).[75]

In recent years, ATV injury estimates have been at or have approached injury levels seen prior to the consent decrees. From 1997 to 2001, the esti-mated number of ATV-related injuries treated in hospital emergency departments have more than doubled. Increases in the number of ATV rid-ers, hours of ATV riding, and number of ATVs in use have also increased during this time. The increase in exposure to ATVs does not completely account for the rise in injuries over this time period.[74]

In-line skating/roller sports

Many children and adolescents participate in roller sports, including skate-boarding, riding scooters, roller skating and in-line skating. Much of this activity is recreational in nature, but some is conducted in a team situation, such as in the case of roller hockey. In recent years, in-line skating has gained popularity among people of all ages, as it can be a good form of aer-obic exercise as well as a convenient mode of transportation. Skateboarding and riding scooters have recently re-gained popularity. As with many other sports and recreational activities, the rise in participation has come with a

---

Figure 2

Consumer Product Safety Commission recommendations for operating ATVs

- Take a hands-on safety training course.
- Always wear a helmet while on an ATV.
- Never drive an ATV on paved roads.
- Never drive under the influence of drugs or alcohol.
- Never drive an ATV with a passenger, and never ride as a passenger.
- Use the ATV in a responsible and controlled manner at all times.

rise in injuries. Scooter and in-line skate injuries tend to occur more often to youth between the ages of 5 and 12, whereas skateboarding injuries occur more often to teenage youth.[77]

Some of the injury patterns for roller sports mirror those of bicycling injuries, due to the fact that both activities involve the possibility of traveling at high speeds. Both activities come with the possibility of falling as well as colliding with other objects, either stationary or moving. Deaths due to in-line skating are rare, and similar to bicycling fatalities, the majority are due to collisions with motor-vehicles.[76] Separating the skaters from traffic is an obvious step in reducing fatalities and serious injuries. With regard to scooters, a study at a Pittsburgh hospital found that most non-motorized scooter injuries were due to falls and 26% were due to collisions with motor vehicles.[78] More recently, motorized scooters, which are similar to un-powered scooters but sport a small gasoline engine or electric motor and a battery, have been gaining in popularity. Although most injury data on scooters focuses on non-powered scooters, the Consumer Product Safety Commission estimates that in 2000, there were over 4000 emergency room visits as a result of motorized scooters. They recommend that children under 12 should not ride motorized scooters.[77]

As with other sports and recreational injuries, the majority of injuries due to roller sports are not fatal. Wrists are most commonly injured, although knees and elbows are common injury sites as well. Wrist guards, knee pads and elbow pads have proven effective in protecting in-line skaters against injuries[80] and are recommended for all roller activities. The importance of helmets cannot be underestimated.

Risk and Protective Factors

What places some youth at greater risk of injury than others? In general, risk factors for sports and recreation injuries can be classified as intrinsic or extrinsic. Intrinsic risk factors refer to the characteristics that individual athletes bring with them to the situation. Characteristics such as age and gender are intrinsic since they define the individual, but these characteristics, if identified as risk factors, are not modifiable. Other intrinsic factors, such as level of conditioning and history of previous injury, if identified as risk factors, can be altered. For example, programs to improve athlete conditioning or prevent injury may decrease the risk for subsequent injury. Extrinsic risk factors can be explained as those factors outside the individual, such as the risks inherent in the activity, the environment in which the activity is performed, and the equipment used in specific activities. For example, an uneven playing field is a condition that creates an injury-prone environment for all players; thus, it is classified as an extrinsic risk factor.

Intrinsic risk and protective factors

Due to physical, cognitive and behavioral differences, children are more susceptible to certain kinds of injury than adults. Prior to puberty, children have a lower sweat rate and a higher threshold for sweating—since they do not adjust to heat as well, they are at greater risk for heat-related injuries.[10-11] Growing cartilage in young children may be more vulnerable to stresses (such as overuse injuries). Children have proportionately bigger heads than adults with a higher center of gravity and possibly immature balance and coordination, which can lead to more head injuries.[10] Younger children tend to sustain more head injuries and more frequent injuries to upper extremities in general than older children or adults,[11] perhaps due to their higher center of gravity. On a positive note, children tend to fare better from traumatic brain injuries than adults because the developing brain is able to adapt better post-injury. Also, given their smaller size/mass, children generate less force than adults in a fall. As children grow stronger and heavier, they generate greater acceleration and thus greater forces. This, combined with the increased competitiveness that often comes with higher levels of play, puts older children at greater risk for contact injuries. Further, children do not grow in uniform amounts at predetermined ages; thus, appropriate matching of competitors so that children of similar size, strength, and skill are competitors may help reduce injuries in contact sports.[81]

In general, children younger than age 10 have less developed motor skills than older children.[10] This, combined with less developed cognitive and perceptive skills also puts children at greater risk than adults. Children might be less capable than adults perceiving risks (eg, less attention to inputs from peripheral vision[82]) and assessing those risks in certain situations. Young children may not be capable of fully understanding the need for certain rules and skills of a sport, regardless of the fact that they are being taught by a coach.[9]

Studies in adults demonstrate a relationship between lower levels of physical fitness and injury.[83] Although this has not been thoroughly examined in children, similar findings have been documented in studies of sports such as football and soccer which demonstrated that pre-season and off-season conditioning and training programs reduced in-season injuries, and that warm-ups prior to the start of the third quarter of football games reduced injuries in the second half.[84]

In many activities, improved skill sets may be protective. For instance, appropriate tackling technique is important in preventing injuries in football and soccer. Correct biomechanics also play a role in baseball, softball and many other activities. However, in several limited studies of bicycle safety education and skiing lessons, there was no demonstrated effect on injury rates. However, all participants should make use of available resources to learn the necessary skills and to ensure appropriate biomechanics before undertaking activities independently.

Overall, boys have higher rates of injury than girls. Children aged 0–4 have the lowest rate of injuries due to sports and recreation, as compared to all other age groups.[5] This is likely due to minimal exposure to such activities. In contrast, the majority of sports and recreation injuries affect those aged 5–24. Among boys, those aged 15–24 are at highest risk, whereas 5–14 year old females are most likely to get injured as a result of a sports and recreational injury.[5] Overall, unlike other causes of injury, White youth seem to get injured (or seek medical attention) as a result of sports and recreational injuries more often than Black youth.[3,85] Additionally, children from non-poor households have a higher rate of injuries than children from near-poor and poor households.[85] Both of these may be due to increased participation among White youth and children from non-poor households.

Finally, intrinsic characteristics of the individual (risk taking, sensation seeking) may contribute to injury risk. Those prone to engaging in risky behaviors, such as extreme sports, might be more likely to place themselves in situations which expose them to higher risks. Recreational and sporting activities certainly allow participants to push their physical limits; the amount that each participant is willing to push forward may contribute to injury risk.

Extrinsic risk and protective factors

A previously-developed Haddon Matrix for youth sports injury demonstrates the importance of extrinsic factors (Table 1). Injury risks can often be reduced through the provision of good quality equipment and facilities. This could include providing areas for children to ride bicycles and skateboards, safety bases for youth baseball, adequate lighting for evening and night events, good quality playing surfaces (removing lumpy or pitted areas), and personal use of protective equipment such as bicycle helmets, reflective clothing, eyewear, or faceguards. In organized sports, use of protective equipment needs to be regulated if it is to be universally implemented—that it is, part of the rules of the game, and it has to be requirement of the administrators and coaches. Simply making the equipment available typically does not work, since social pressure inhibits the voluntary usage of protective equipment in sports and recreation. Further, children should be properly fitted for protective gear. Some children may be too small for certain equipment. If the gear does not fit properly or is uncomfortable, children will be less likely to wear it at all or consistently. Also, poor-fitting equipment might not offer the proper protection.[10]

Parents can play an important role by ensuring that protective equipment is available, in good condition, fits well, and is used consistently. In organized sports, coaching quality and behavioral characteristics are widely assumed to be important. Coaches at the youth level should emphasize building the skills of the sport and enjoyment of participation over winning. Teamwork and sportsmanship are important lessons that will serve participants well in other areas of their lives.[86] Most organized sports have training and certification programs for coaches.

Interventions to Reduce Injuries, including Research Endeavors

Interventions can fall into behavioral, environmental, or policy categories. Behavioral interventions are those that involve a participant making a change to decrease risk of injury such as improving conditioning, wearing protective gear appropriately and consistently, or choosing activities or locations to minimize risk of injury (eg, riding on a bicycle path rather than in the road with traffic). Environmental interventions are those which alter the environment in which athletes participate. Examples include building bike paths, improving field conditions and padding or removing obstacles near the area of play. Finally, policy changes can have broad effects in encouraging changes to reduce injury risks. Policy changes may be limited to a particular team or group (eg, all bike club members must wear helmets on club rides), or may include legislation which includes all members of the population (eg, state or local bike helmet laws).

Table I

Haddon Matrix for Youth Recreational and Sports Injury (Adapted from Weaver et al. 2002)

	Host (athlete)	Agent/vehicle (energy)	Physical environment (playing field)	Social environment (team/coach/school/parents)
Pre-event (before the injury)	Appropriateness of the activity to the skills of the child Recognition of injury risk factors	Sports equipment to be more energy absorbing Visibility of child (reflective materials)	Layout of playground equipment (uncluttered, allows for flow around equipment items) Condition and lighting of playing surfaces	Support for defined play areas for children (skateboard parks, playgrounds) Attitudes towards healthy competition Restriction of dangerous play or movement Neuromuscular training programs
Event (during the injury event)	Physical characteristics (joint laxity, physique) Response time during the event	Energy absorbing balls (baseball) and surfaces (playgrounds) Protective equipment that is appropriate to the activity and fits the child	Surfacing (artificial or natural) Padding (eg. on goalposts)	Monitoring of children by parents and others Financial support for on site athletic trainers at all sporting events
Post-event (after the injury)	Conditioning, adherence to rehabilitation Parental management of rehabilitation compliance	Reporting faulty equipment to Consumer Product Safety Commission	Ensure that emergency medical personnel have access to environment	Quick and appropriate response Access to appropriate clinicians trained in sports and recreational injuries (Team Physician, Certified Athletic Trainer) Recognition of the dangers and careful management of concussions and availability of complete information to make return to play decisions Parental support of an injured athlete

Weaver NL, Marshall SW, Miller MD. Preventing Sports Injuries: Opportunities for intervention in youth athletics. Patient Education and Counseling 2002:46:3:199-204.

Behavioral Interventions

Behavioral interventions occur at the level of the individual. These are interventions that each participant can choose whether or not to adopt. Appropriate decision-making can be influenced by parents, coaches, social norms, educational campaigns, policies and legislation. For instance, research in football and soccer shows that strengthening, conditioning and balance training can reduce injuries.[87] Additionally, research in military basic trainees demonstrates that those with higher levels of aerobic physical fitness are less likely to be injured compared with those who are less fit.[83] This is likely generalizable to many activities.

Other proven behavioral interventions include the use of certain protective equipment. This is particularly relevant in recreational activities or unorganized sporting activities where policies and regulations may not be present to require the appropriate use of gear. For instance, bicycle helmets are extremely effective in preventing head and brain injuries.[61] This evidence has led to state laws covering many or most of the children in 19 states and the District of Columbia and many other cities and counties (http://www.bhsi.org/mandator.htm). However, in all other areas, riders are left to choose. Other gear such as elbow pads and wrist guards are recommended for those participating in small wheeled sports such as roller skating, in-line skating, and skateboarding.[88-89] Most sports with an organized component have recommended or required protective gear which participants, even in unorganized settings, should be encouraged to wear. Gear should be appropriate to the sport and player position, maintained in good condition, fit the player correctly, and be used consistently.

Skills training is another behavioral intervention which can be important in the prevention of injuries. However, studies to assess the injury prevention effects of skills training in various sports have had mixed results. Ski lessons and bicycle skills education have not been associated with a decrease in injury risk in research studies.[87] However, football coaches who instruct in proper technique, are older, have advanced degrees, have collegiate playing experience, and utilize assistant coaches had teams with lower injury rates.[87,90]

Finally, participants should take personal responsibility to learn the appropriate skills necessary to participate safely in their chosen activities. For instance, as shown earlier, the National Ski Patrol has a Responsibility Code which is posted on most ski and snowboarding slopes (Figure 1). This delineates the tenets that participants must abide by to decrease injury risk for all participants.

Environmental Interventions

Environmental interventions decrease injuries by altering how a participant encounters their surroundings. Many of the serious and fatal injuries suffered by recreational cyclists and pedestrians (such as walkers, joggers, and participants in small-wheeled sports) occur when they encounter motor vehicle traffic. Separation of these participants from the traffic through the use of bike lanes, sidewalks, and walking trails is effective in decreasing injury rates.[91]

In organized sports, environmental interventions can also reduce injuries. Break-away bases are effective in reducing sliding injuries in male and female athletes at the recreational, collegiate and professional levels.[94-95]

Other simple interventions include ensuring that the playing fields and courts are free from holes, obstacles, or other tripping hazards; ensuring that goal posts are padded and secured; and providing a space between the legal field of play and seats, bleachers, fences, walls and other obstacles. Strict refereeing to ensure compliance with rules developed to decrease injuries is important. Studies in football demonstrate the benefit of rules preventing spearing, face tackling, and butt blocking,[94-96] and in hockey, prevention of checking from behind.[97] Players, coaches and spectators should encourage strict adherence to rules of fair play.

Other interventions are effective in the prevention of heat-related illnesses when the play environment is hot or humid. Among US high school athletes, heat illness is the third leading cause of death.[98] Gradual acclimation to hot or humid environments can minimize effects. Close attention to hydration and appropriate dress is critical. Finally, consideration of altering or canceling practice or participation in high risk conditions is important. Organized sporting groups and organizations should develop guidelines for practices and competitions under high-risk conditions.

Policy/Legislation Interventions

Policies and legislation can help ensure that covered groups conform to injury prevention recommendations. These can occur at a variety of levels from rules and policies required to participate with recreational teams and activities to comprehensive legislation mandating certain behaviors under penalty of law. Injury prevention policies and legislation are powerful tools to change the social norm regarding injury prevention behaviors.

The most commonly studied injury prevention policy is bicycle helmet legislation. Following studies demonstrating the benefit of helmet use, local and state officials began mandating helmet use in some groups through legislative action. The first mandatory helmet use law was passed in 1990 in Victoria, Australia. During the previous decade, safety advocates had conducted multifaceted school and community based education programs to encourage helmet use, resulting in observed helmet use of 31%. One year after enacting the legislation, observed helmet use increased to 75%; however, bicycle use in children and teens decreased.[99] This experience, and others to follow, suggested several tenets of successful injury prevention programs. Policy and legislative actions should be accompanied by education and enforcement. If these are overlooked, understanding of the necessity of the policy/rule/legislation and the consequences of inaction will be lacking and may result in less than optimal compliance.

In addition to state and local legislative mandates, school and community policies are also important. Currently, 97% of middle schools and 99% of high schools have policies in place regarding the appropriate use of gear in interscholastic sports and activities; however, only 79% of middle schools and 86% of high schools have similar policies covering these same sports when played in a physical education class.[100] Increasingly, children are participating in sports and recreational activities outside of the school setting and appropriate policies are necessary to protect the participants.

Examination of sports injury data is useful in identifying common injury circumstances. Many of these have been addressed successfully through rules changes and age-appropriate limitations (eg, elimination of spearing, clipping, and grabbing the facemask in football, rear checking in hockey, age limitations on heading in soccer and checking in hockey, and restrictions on pyramid height and certain stunts in competitive cheerleading). Consistent and rigorous examination of injury information and research into circumstances of common and severe injuries is critical in informing future decisions regarding rules changes.

Research studies to examine the effectiveness of behavioral, environmental, and policy changes in youth sports and recreation can be challenging. Randomization of athletes is not always possible. Further, even if randomization is possible, ensuring compliance with the equipment or application under study may prove to be difficult. Often environmental changes, policies and legislation, and community education programs are evaluated in a non-randomized fashion using observational trials because the decision about what group or area receives the intervention is often out of the investigator's control. However, such research in critically important to ensure that promising interventions are evaluated, current practices are streamlined, and ineffective devices, policies and programs are identified.

Advocating for Safer Sports and Recreational Activities

Given the steadily increasing number of sedentary people in the US, the Surgeon General has recommended that Americans engage in more physical activity and exercise in order to prevent obesity-related diseases.[8] As Americans attempt to become more active, they should become more cognizant of the risks associated with the activities in which they choose to engage. They should also be given guidance as to what activities would benefit them the most while minimizing the risk for injury. Injury is a major barrier to the maintenance of physical activity, so it makes sense not just to promote physical activity, but to promote safe physical activity. The public health message should be to exercise safely, not just to exercise. This is true among young children as well. A serious childhood injury can later impact overall health and fitness through adulthood, both through discouraging maintenance of regular physical activity, and through long-term sequelae of injury such as osteoarthritis.

As we have noted throughout the chapter, many interventions geared at sports and recreational safety have been successfully implemented, which has resulted in safer play for youth and countless saved lives. Football athletes have been outfitted from head to toe, with helmets on their heads and shorter cleats on their shoes. Baseball fields now have break-away bases and soccer fields have padded and anchored movable goal posts. Many public playgrounds all over the country now have softer surfaces underneath equipment. All of these interventions began with efforts by individuals who advocated for safety.

For example, in 1990, Howard County, Maryland became the first jurisdiction in the United States to mandate the use of bicycle helmets for bicyclists younger than 16 years old. This was prompted by the death of two individuals who were students at the same school and were killed as a result of bicycle crashes in two separate incidents. Neither of the victims was wearing a helmet.[101] After the deaths of their students and classmates, students and teachers at the school became committed to improving bicycle safety in

Howard County. They met with law makers in their community who worked to draft a bill that required that all youth under 16 to wear an approved bicycle helmet while riding in county. Those who failed to follow the law would be fined. With great support of the community, the bill was passed.[101] Prior to the law being passed, law enforcement officers worked to educate youth about safety and the importance of helmet use.[102] The community worked together to enact legislation that has led to Howard County having the highest rate of bicycle helmet use in the United States.[102]

Youth can be extremely effective at advocating for their own safety. In 1994, five-year-old Andrew Kidd was injured after falling from a climber on a playground. His injuries were severe, and after 15 surgeries he has become a leading advocate for playground safety. He and his brother travel around the country and talk to children and parents about the importance of playground safety. They have taught playground safety classes to other youth and have talked to legislators as well. They have been the recipients of many awards and have appeared on national television.[103]

Parents of children are often very concerned about the risk of recreational and sports activities. No single uniform agency exists for distributing risk information on sports and recreational activities to parents. In addition, parents of injured children have generally been neither vocal nor organized in lobbying for increased resources for prevention of sports and recreational injury. Thus, there is a need for professionals in the community to connect the many disparate threads in this area. Advocacy groups such as the Consumer Federation of America are currently lobbying on a ban on youth ATV use and stricter safety standards at playgrounds. The National Program for Playground Safety (NPPS) is an example of one organization which is dedicated to advocating for children's playground safety. Change often begins with grassroots efforts and a few committed citizens.

There is an urgent need to build the advocate base for youth sports and recreational injury. Parents should be cognizant of their children's activities and seek out information from reputable sources to help their children participate safely. In addition, parents, injury prevention professionals, and other interested parties can work at the local level to encourage local schools, parks, clubs leagues, and other groups to provide the safest possible environment for all participants. Finally, these parties can encourage agencies and organizations at the local, state, and national level to support further prevention research and dissemination efforts.

Building a climate of safety around youth recreation and sports is a delicate balancing act. On the one hand, we want to encourage and promote physical activity in youth. On the other hand, it must be recognized that there are inherent risks in all physical activity, but that these can be minimized through the use of injury control strategies. In addition to the NPPS, there are a large number of organizations that actively work to promote safety in youth sports and recreational activity. Many of these target injury prevention (see Table 2). These organizations often do not have the opportunity to include input from injury prevention professionals and would welcome involvement from this community. Injury prevention professionals can assist advocates in locating and using data to support the need for change and to evaluate the effects of changes. Additionally, advocates may need guidance to ensure that promoted efforts are scientifically supported.

Table 2

Organizations that actively promote youth sports safety

Organization	Website	What's There?
National Athletic Trainers Association	www.nata.org (under "Public Information")	Information on: • Minimizing the Risk of Injury in High School Athletics • Management of Spinal Injury • What Happens if Your Child is Injured on the Sports Field? • Suggested Safety Items Parents Should Look for in a High School Athletic Program • Heat Illness • Lighting Safety • Concussion Management
National Center for Catastrophic Sports Injury Research	http://www.unc.edu/depts/nccsi/	Data on sports injuries resulting in death and permanent disability.
American Academy of Pediatrics: Committee on Sports Medicine and Fitness and Committee on Injury, Violence and Poison Prevention	www.aap.org/policy	Policies and Recommendations on: • Injuries in Youth Soccer: A Subject Review • Climatic Heat Stress and the Exercising Child and Adolescent • Guidelines for Emergency Medical Care in School • Trampolines at Home, School, and Recreational Centers • Safety in Youth Ice Hockey: The Effects of Body Checking • In-line Skating Injuries in Children and Adolescents • Participation in Boxing by Children, Adolescents, and Young Adults • Risk of Injury From Baseball and Softball in Children • Horseback Riding and Head Injuries • Protective Eyewear for Young Athletes • Knee Brace Use in the Young Athlete
National Youth Sports Safety Foundation	www.nyssf.org	Subscribe to their newsletter, SIDELINES. Purchase fact sheets and guidelines. Post a question for an expert.

continued

Table 2 continued

Organization	Website	What's There?
American College of Sports Medicine Under "Newsroom and Publications"	www.acsm.org	Order publications on sports medicine Current Comments, free downloadable 2 page fact sheets on: • Alcohol and Athletic Performance • Football Helmet Removal • Plyometric Training for Children and Adolescents • Posterior Cruciate Ligament Injuries • Pre-participation Physical Examinations • Preseason Conditioning for Young Athletes • Resistance Training and Injury Prevention • Skiing Injuries • Tennis Elbow • Youth Strength Training
American Orthopedic Society for Sports Medicine	www.sportsmed.org Under "AOSSM library"	Sports Medicine Updates: a free downloadable bi-monthly newsletter featuring articles on sports medicine Post a question for an expert. Order publications on sports medicine
Consumer Product Safety Commission	www.cpsc.gov Under "CPSC Publications"	Safety Alerts and Guidelines on: • ATVs • Baseball • Bicycles and bicycle helmets • Playgrounds • Scooters • Skateboards • Soccer goals • Trampolines
National Safe Kids Campaign	www.safekids.org Under "safety tips"	Information on childhood injuries, including sports, playground, and bicycle injuries.
National Federation of State High Schools Associations	www.nfhs.org Under "Survey Resources"	Data on the numbers of participants in High School sports, by sport and state Summary of research regarding benefits of extracurricular activities
National Program for Playground Safety	http://www.uni.edu/playground/home.html	Information on safety tips, educational materials, equipment distributors and standards.

In the 21st century, it is more important than ever to promote sports and recreational physical activities for youth and children. Through the incorporation of safety messages and injury control measures into these activities, much can be done to ensure that children truly enjoy sports and recreational pastimes and continue to participate in physically active recreational pursuits as they mature into adults.

References

1. Tyler, Jeffrey H., and Michael E. Nelson. Second Impact Syndrome: Sports Confront Consequences of Concussions. *USA Today* (Magazine) May, 2000.

2. United States Consumer Product Safety Commission. Epidemiologic Investigation Report # 040629HCN0739. Washington D.C.: US Consumer Product Safety Commission, 2004.

3. Conn J.M., J.L. Annest, J. Gilchrist. Sports and recreation related injury episodes in the US population, 1997-99. *Injury Prevention* 9 (2003): 117-23.

4. Children's Safety Network National Injury and Violence Prevention Resource Center. Recreational Injury. January 5, 2005. <http://www.childrenssafetynetwork.org/Recreational%20Safety.pdf>.

5. Gotsch K., J.L. Annest, P. Homlgreen, J. Gilchrist. Nonfatal Sports- and Recreation-Related Injuries Treated in Emergency Departments, United States, July 2000-June 2001. *MMWR* 51.53 (2002): 736-740.

6. United States Consumer Product Safety Commission, Directorate for Economic Analysis. *The Consumer Product Safety Commission's Revised Injury Cost Model.* Washington D.C.: US Consumer Product Safety Commission, 2000.

7. United States Consumer Product Safety Commission. *NEISS Coding Manual, 2003: National Electronic Injury Surveillance System.* Washington DC: US Consumer Product Safety Commission, 2003.

8. Surgeon General's Report on Physical Activity and Health, 1996. Centers for Disease Control's National Center for Chronic Disease Prevention and Health Promotion. January 5, 2005. <http://www.cdc.gov/nccdphp/sgr/sgr.htm>.

9. American Academy of Pediatrics Committee on Sports Medicine and Fitness and Committee on School Health. Organized Sport for Children and Pre-adolescents. *Pediatrics* 107.6 (2001): 1459-1462.

10. Adirim T.A., T.L. Cheng. Overview of Injuries in the Young Athlete. *Sports Medicine* 33.1 (2003): 75-81.

11. Purvis J.M., R.G. Burke. Recreational Injuries in Children: Incidence and Prevention. *J Am Academy of Orthopedic Surgeons* 9.6 (2001): 365-374.

12. National Center for Catastrophic Sport Injury Research. *National Center for Catastrophic Sport Injury Research 21st Annual Report.* January 5, 2005. <http://www.unc.edu/depts/nccsi/AllSport.htm>.

13. Link M.S. et al. An experimental model of sudden death due to low-energy chest-wall impact (Comotio Cordis). *N Engl J Med* 339 (1998): 1805-1811.

14. Maron BJ, L.C. Poliac, J.A. Kaplan, F.O. Mueller. Blunt impact to the chest leading to sudden death from cardiac arrest during sports activities. *N Engl J Med* 333 (1995): 337-342.

15. Zvijac J., W. Thompson. Basketball. *Epidemiology of Sports Injuries.* Ed. D.J. Caine, C.G. Caine, and K.J. Lindner. Champaign, IL: Human Kinetics Publishers, Inc., 1996.

16. Scanlan A, et al. *Sports and Recreation Injury Prevention Strategies.* November 2001. November 29, 2004. <http://www.injuryresearch.bc.ca/Publications/ Reports/ SportSystematicReport.pdf>

17. Sitler M, et al. The efficacy of a semirigid ankle stabilizer to reduce acute ankle injuries in basketball. A randomized clinical study at West Point. *Am J Sports Medicine* 22.4 (1994): 454-61.

18. Labella C.R., B.W. Smith, A. Sigurdsson. Effect of mouthguards on dental injuries and concussions in college basketball. *Medicine and Science in Sports and Exercise.* 34.1 (2002): 41-4.

19. Robey J.M., C.S. Blyth, F.O. Mueller. Athletic injuries: application of epidemiologic methods. *JAMA* 217 (1971): 184-189.

20. Mueller F.O., C.S. Blyth. Fatalities from head and cervical spine injuries occurring in tackle football: 40 years' experience. *Clinics in Sports Medicine* 6 (1987): 185-196.

21. Cantu R.C. Cerebral concussion in sport, management and prevention. *Sports Medicine* 14 (1992): 64-74.

22. Guskiewicz K.M. et al. Cumulative consequences of recurrent concussion in collegiate football players: the NCAA concussion study. *JAMA* 290.19 (2003): 2549-2555.

23. Cantu R.C., R. Voy. Second impact syndrome: a risk in any contact sport. *Physician and Sports Medicine* 23 (1995): 27-34.

24. Rader B.G. *Baseball: A history of America's Game.* Urbana, IL: University of Illinois Press, 1992.

25. Baseball and Softball Council. *Baseball: A Report on Participation in America's National Pastime, 1996.* North Palm Beach, FL: Sporting Goods Manufacturers Association, 1996.

26. American Academy of Pediatrics, Committee on Sports Medicine and Fitness. Risk of injury from baseball and softball in children 5 to 14 years of age. *Pediatrics.* 93 (1994): 690-692.

27. Janda D.H., E.M. Wojtys, F.M. Hankin, M.E. Benedict. Softball sliding injuries. A prospective study comparing standard and non-traditional bases. *JAMA* 259 (1988): 1848-1850.

28. Sendre R.A., T.M. Keating, J.E. Hornak, P.A. Newitt. Use of the Hollywood Impact Base and standard stationary base to reduce sliding and base-running injuries in baseball and softball. *Am J Sports Medicine* 22 (1994): 450-453.

29. Vinger P.F., P. Leonard, D.V. Alfaro, T. Woods, B.S. Abrams. Shatter Resistance of Spectacle Lenses. *JAMA* 277.2 (1997): 142-144.

30. American Academy of Pediatrics (1996). Protective Eyewear for Young Athletes. *Pediatrics* 98 (1996): 311-313.

31. Danis R.P., K. Hu, M. Bell. Acceptability of baseball faceguards and reduction of oculofacial injury in receptive youth league players. *Injury Prevention* 6 (2000): 232-234.

32. Marshall S.W., F.O. Mueller, D.T. Kirby, J. Yang. Evaluation of safety balls and face guards to prevent injury in youth baseball. *JAMA* 289 (2003): 568-574.

33. Kyle S.B. *Consumer Product Safety Commission Youth Baseball Protective Equipment Project Final Report.* Washington, DC: US Consumer Product Safety Commission, Office of Information and Public Affairs, 1996.

34. Pasternack J.S., K.R. Veenema, C.M. Callahan. Baseball injuries: a Little League survey. *Pediatrics* 98 (1996): 445-448.

35. Mueller FO, Marshall SW, Kirby D. Injuries in Little League Baseball 1987-1996. *Physician and Sports Medicine* 29 (2001): 41-48.

36. Andrews J.R., G.S. Fleisig. Preventing throwing injuries. *J Orthopedic and Sports Physical Therapy* 27 (1998): 187-188.

37. Fleisig G.S., J.R. Andrews, C.J. Dillman, R.F. Escamilla. Kinetics of baseball pitching with implications about injury mechanisms. *Am J Sports Medicine* 23 (1995): 233-239.

38. National Federation of State High School Associations. *NFHS 2003-04 High School Athletics Participation Survey*. Indianapolis: National Federation of State High School Associations, 2000.

39. United States Consumer Product Safety Commission. *Guidelines for Movable Soccer Goal Safety*. Washington DC: US Consumer Product Safety Commission, 1995.

40. Matser E.J., A.G. Kessels, M.D. Lezak, B.D. Jordan, J. Troost. Neuropsychological impairment in amateur soccer players. *JAMA* 282.10 (1999): 971-3.

41. Guskiewicz K.M., S.W. Marshall, S.P. Broglio, R.C. Cantu, D.T. Kirkendell. No evidence of impaired neurocognitive performance in collegiate soccer players. *Am J Sports Medicine* 30.2 (2002): 157-162.

42. Kirkendall DT, Garrett WE Jr. Heading in Soccer: Integral Skill or Grounds for Cognitive Dysfunction? *J Athletic Training* 36.3 (2001): 328-333.

43. Myklebust G, et al. Prevention of Anterior Cruciate Ligament Injuries in Female Team Handball Players: A Prospective Intervention Study Over Three Seasons. *Clinical Journal of Sports Medicine: Official Journal of the Canadian Academy of Sports Medicine*. 13 (2003): 71–78.

44. Junge A., J. Dvorak. Soccer injuries: A review on incidence and prevention. *Sports Medicine* 34 (2004): 929-938.

45. Griffin L. (ed) *Prevention of Noncontact ACL Injuries*. Rosemont Il: American Academy of Orthopedic Surgeons, 2001.

46. Griffin L. Noncontact anterior cruciate ligament injuries: risk factors and prevention strategies. *J Am Academy of Orthopedic Surgeons* 8 (2000): 141-150.

47. Gerberich S.G., R. Finke, M. Madden, J.D. Priest, G. Aamoth, K. Murray. An epidemiological study of high school ice hockey injuries. *Child's Nervous System* 3 (1987): 59-64.

48. Sane J., P. Ylipaavalniemi, H. Leppanen. Maxillofacial and dental ice hockey injuries. *Medicine and Science in Sports and Exercise* 20 (1988): 202-207.

49. Reynen P.D., J.G. Clancy. Cervical spine injury, hockey helmets, and face masks. *Am J Sports Medicine* 22 (1994): 167-170.

50. Hutchinson M.R. Cheerleading injuries: patterns, prevention, case reports. *Physician and Sports Medicine* 25 (1997): 83-90.

51. National Federation of State High School Associations. *NFHS 2001 High School Athletics Participation Survey*. Kansas City, Missouri: National Federation of State High School Associations, 2001.

52. Schulz M.R. et al. A prospective cohort study of injury incidence and risk factors in North Carolina high school competitive cheerleaders. *Am J Sports Medicine* 32.2 (2004): 396-405.

53. Division of Public Health Surveillance and Informatics, Epidemiology Program Office, Centers for Disease Control and Prevention. CDC Wonder. August 20, 2004 <http://wonder.cdc.gov>.

54. United States Consumer Product Safety Commission. Handbook for Public Playground Safety. Washington D.C.: US Consumer Product Safety Commission, 2003.

55. Norton C., J. Nixon, J.R. Sibert. Playground injuries to children. *Archives of Disease in Childhood* 89 (2004): 103-108.

56. Tinsworth Deborah K., Joyce E. McDonald. *Special Study: Injuries and Deaths Associated with Children's Playground Equipment. April 2001*. Washington, D.C.: US Consumer Product Safety Commission, 2001.

57. Rodgers G.B. Bicycle and bicycle helmet use patterns in the United States in 1998. *J Safety Research* 31 (2000): 149-158.

58. National Center for Health Statistics, *2001 Multiple Cause-of-Death File*. Hyattsville, MD: United States Department of Health and Human Services, Centers

for Disease Control and Prevention, National Center for Health Statistics, 2003.

59. Centers for Disease Control and Prevention. Injury-control recommendations: bicycle helmets. MMWR 44.RR-1 (1995): 1-17.

60. AAP Committee on Injury and Poison Prevention. Bicycle Helmets. *Pediatrics* 108.4 (2001): 1030-1032.

61. Rivara F.P., D.C. Thompson, M.Q. Patterson, R.S. Thompson. Prevention of bicycle related injuries: helmets, legislation and education. *Ann Rev Public Health* 19 (1998): 293-318.

62. Bicycle Helmet Safety Institute. *Helmet Laws for Bicycle Riders.* October 16, 2004. <http://www.helmets.org/mandator.htm>.

63. Schieber R.A., J. Gilchrist, D.A. Sleet. Legislative and Regulatory Strategies to Reduce Childhood Unintentional Injuries. *Future of Children,* Eds. F.P. Rivara, R.E. Berman. 10.1 (2000): 111-36.

64. Koehle M.S., R. Lloyd-Smith, J.E. Taunton. Alpine ski injuries and their prevention. *Sports Medicine* 32.12 (2002): 785-793.

65. United States Consumer Product Safety Commission. *Skiing Helmets: an Evaluation of the Potential to Reduce Head Injury.* Washington, DC: US Consumer Product Safety Commission, 1999.

66. Rees-Jones A. Skiing helmets. *British J Sports Medicine* 33.1 (1999): 3.

67. Finch C.F., H.L. Kelsall. The effectiveness of ski bindings and their professional adjustment for preventing alpine skiing injuries. *Sports Medicine* 25.6 (1998): 407-16.

68. Goulet C., et al. Risk factors associated with alpine skiing injuries in children: a case-control study. *Am J Sports Medicine* 27.5 (1999): 644-50.

69. Machold W., et al. Reduction of severe wrist injuries in snowboarding by an optimized wrist protection device: a prospective randomized trial. *J Trauma* 52.3 (2002): 517-20.

70. United States Consumer Product Safety Commission. Trampolines. Washington DC: US Consumer Product Safety Commission, 2000.

71. Schroeder T. *The NEISS Sample (Design and Implementation) From 1997 to the Present.* Washington D.C.: US Consumer Product Safety Commission, 2001.

72. American Academy of Pediatrics Committee on Injury and Poison Prevention and Committee on Sports Medicine and Fitness. Trampolines at Home, School, and Recreational Centers. *Pediatrics* 103.5 (1999): 1053-1056.

73. Ingle, R. 2002. *Annual Report of ATV Deaths and Injuries.* Washington D.C.: US Consumer Product Safety Commission, 2003.

74. Levenson, M. *All-Terrain Vehicle 2001 Injury and Exposure Studies.* Washington D.C.: US Consumer Product Safety Commission, 2003.

75. United States Consumer Product Safety Commission. *All-Terrain Vehicle Safety.* Washington D.C.: US Consumer Product Safety Commission, 2004.

76. American Academy of Pediatrics Committee on Injury and Poison Prevention and Committee on Sports Medicine and Fitness. In-line Skating Injuries in Children and Adolescents. *Pediatrics* 101.4 (1998): 720-722.

77. Powell E.C., R.R. Tanz. Incidence and description of scooter-related injuries among children. *Ambulatory Pediatrics* 4.6 (2004): 495-9.

78. Gaines B.A., B.L. Shultz, H.R. Ford. Nonmotorized scooters: a source of significant morbidity in children. *J Trauma* 57.1 (2004): 111-3.

79. Office of Information and Public Affairs, United States Consumer Product Safety Commission. Motorized Scooter Use Increases and Injuries Climb. *News from CPSC.* Washington, D.C.

80. Schieber R.A., et al. Risk factors for injuries from in-line skating and the effectiveness of safety gear. *N Engl J Med* 28.335.22 (1996): 1680-2.

81. Dyment P.G. (ed) *Sports Medicine: Health Care for Young Athletes*, 2nd edition. Elk Grove Village IL: American Academy of Pediatrics, 1991.

82. Gilchrist J., B.H. Jones, D.A. Sleet, C. Dexter Kimsey. Exercise-related injuries among women: Strategies for prevention from civilian and military studies. *MMWR* 49.RR-2 (2000): 15-34.

83. Bixler B, R.L. Jones. High school football injuries: effects of a post-halftime warm-up and stretching routine. *Family Practice Research J* 12.2 (1992): 131-9.

84. Gilchrist J., K. Gotsch, G. Ryan. Nonfatal and Fatal Drownings in Recreational Water Settings—United States, 2001–2002. *MMWR* 53.21 (2004): 447-452.

85. Ni H, Barnes P, Hardy AM. Recreational injury and it's relation to socioeconomic status among school aged children in the US. *Injury Prevention* 8 (2002): 60-65.

86. National Federation of State High School Associations. The Case for High School Activities. November 16, 2004 <http://www.nfhs.org/scriptcontent/ Va_custom/va_cm/contentpagedisplay.cfm?content_ID=163>

87. MacKay M. et al. Looking for the evidence: a systematic review of prevention strategies addressing sport and recreational injury among children and youth. *J Science and Medicine in Sport* 7.1 (2004): 58-73.

88. Schieber R.A. et al. Risk factors for injuries from in-line skating and the effectiveness of safety gear. *N Engl J Med* 335.22 (1996): 1630-5.

89. Schieber R.A., C.M. Branche-Dorsey, G.W. Ryan. Comparison of in-line skating injuries with roller-skating and skateboarding injuries. *JAMA* 271.23 (1994): 1856-8.

90. Blythe C.S., F.O. Mueller. Football injury survey 3. Injury rates vary with coaching. *Physician and Sports Medicine* 2.11 (1974): 45-50.

91. Retting R.A., S.A. Ferguson, A.T. McCartt. A review of evidence-based traffic engineering measures designed to reduce pedestrian-motor vehicle crashes. *Am J Public Health* 23.9 (2003): 1456-63.

92. Janda D.H. E.M. Wojtys, F.M. Hankin, M.E. Benedict, R.N. Hensinger. A three-phase analysis of the prevention of recreational softball injuries. *Am J Sports Medicine* 18.6 (1990): 632-5.

93. Sendre R.A., T.M. Keating, J.E. Hornak, P.A. Newitt. Use of the Hollywood Impact Base and standard stationary base to reduce sliding and base-running injuries in baseball and softball. *Am J Sports Medicine* 22.4 (1994): 450-3.

94. Mueller F.O., C.S. Blyth. Fatalities from head and cervical spine injuries occurring in tackle football: 40 years' experience. *Clinics in Sports Medicine* 6.1 (1987): 185-96.

95. Torg J.S., et al. The National Football Head and Neck Injury Registry. Report and conclusions 1978. *JAMA* 241.14 (1979): 1477-9.

96. Torg J.S., J.J. Vegso, B. Sennett. The National Football Head and Neck Injury Registry: 14-year report on cervical quadriplegia (1971-1984). *Clinics in Sports Medicine* 6.1 (1987): 61-72.

97. Watson R.C., C.D. Singer, J.R. Sproule. Checking from behind in ice hockey: a study of injury and penalty data in the Ontario University Athletic Association Hockey League. *Clinical J Sport Medicine* 6.2 (1996): 108-11.

98. Coris E.E., A.M. Ramirez, D.J. Van Durme. Heat illness in athletes: the dangerous combination of heat, humidity and exercise. *Sports Medicine* 34.1 (2004): 9-16.

99. United States Centers for Disease Control and Prevention. Mandatory Bicycle Helmet Use—Victoria, Australia. *MMWR* 14.42.18 (1993): 359-63.

100. Kolbe L.J., L. Kann, N.D. Brener. Overview and summary of findings: School Health Policies and Programs Study 2000. *J School Health* 71.7 (2001): 253-9.

101. Scheidt P.C., M.H. Wilson, M.S. Stern. Bicycle helmet law for children: a case study of activism in injury control. *Pediatrics* 89.6 (1992): 1248-50.

102. Cote T.R., J.J. Sacks, D.A. Lambert-Huber, A.L. Dannenberg, M.J. Kresnow, C.M. Lipsitz, E.R., Schmidt ER. Bicycle helmet use among Maryland children: effect of legislation and education. *Pediatrics* 89.6 (1992): 1216-20.
103. National Program for Playground Safety. Playground Safety for Kids: Kidd Brothers' Biography. January 13, 2005 <http://www.kidchecker.org/story.htm>.

CHAPTER 10

Water-Related Injuries of Children and Adolescents

Linda Quan, MD,[1] Karen D. Liller, PhD,[2]
and Elizabeth Bennett, MPH, CHES[3]

**The tragedy that befell Preston Thomas de Ibern,
as told by his mother, Carole Y. de Ibern.**

Of all the unexpected twists and turns that life presents, none could have been more amazing, more thrilling or more unexpected than finding out I was pregnant for the first time (after 18 years of marriage)! We named our precious son Preston Thomas de Ibern.

Preston grew from a cute little baby into an adorable, precocious little boy full of curiosity, antics, laughter and wonder. His most favorite toy of all was his man-sized construction helmet. At the age of 4, he could read and write his name and the alphabet, he could count in Spanish and English, and was going to own his very own construction company when he grew up, so that he could be the boss.

Now it was time for Preston to start kindergarten and for me to return to the work place to begin a new career. As much as he was looking forward to school, he was also insecure about leaving his family. With tenderness and sincerity, he advised me to go up to my boss and tell him "I'm fired!" and then just turn around and walk away. He said, "Don't look back mommy, just come here and get me!" Oh, how I wish I had listened to him.

Although I was new to the department, I was invited, along with everyone else, to a co-worker's barbeque party on July 4th weekend, 1995. What could be better than a dip in the pool, a fresh grilled burger and making new friends, on a sultry Florida day like this? Who would have thought that everything in our lives was about to change.

Soon everyone was leaving. The lady of the house invited me for a tour of their new home before we left. I told my boys to go change their clothes so off they went, along with the owner's children. Normally I would have gone to help Preston change but he was 5 years old and I knew that he could do it all

---

1   University of Washington
2   USF College of Public Health
3   Children's Hospital and Regional Medical Center, Seattle, WA

by himself. Besides, I would only be a few minutes and then I would help him finish up. Everyone had come inside; no one was outside by the pool. The husbands sat, chatting, at the dinning room table while the kids were in the bathroom changing their clothes. The lady of the house showed me the bedroom furniture and their new roman tub, then we walked across the house, past the husbands who were still chatting, and over to the kids room. My older son Josh and the owner's little boy were getting ready to play a Nintendo game. I didn't see Preston with the boys. Immediately, I called…. "where is Preston?" Suddenly, I felt panicky and started to scan the surroundings, calling frantically. In horror and total dismay, my eyes fell upon what appeared to be something floating out in the pool. I screamed and Preston's dad leaped from the chair, lunged into the pool and handed up our son. His eyes and lips were blue and his little body was limp and lifeless. The neighbors all heard my screams and someone called 911. Preston's father and a nurse who lived nearby performed CPR, to no avail. The paramedics were there within minutes. Everyone peered at the paramedics as they worked feverishly. Frozen in place, I watched the oxygen mask go on, needles injected into his arms and legs and finally he was shocked with paddles several times. Minutes became an eternity until…finally…they had a breath!

By now there were people everywhere as the stretcher was rushed to the waiting helicopter. Stunned, I stood glaring as the helicopter lifted off. I was not allowed to ride with my baby. The world seemed to move in slow motion as we made the long trek to the children's hospital. Like robots in motion, our bodies moved but no words were spoken. Suddenly, everything that was important in life no longer mattered. All the materialistic things that we so highly regarded; the house, the mortgage, the car, our jobs, suddenly didn't matter. I felt as if I were in a long, dark, empty tunnel with a million of my own thoughts rushing through my mind. How did this happen? Why did this happen? Would Preston survive…would he be normal?

We arrived at the hospital to find Preston in a cold, lonely room with machines beeping, which were attached by wires to his body. He lay there motionless, eyes closed. I had to remind myself to breathe. We were informed that he was in a coma and was not expected to live more than 72 hours. The doctors tried their best to encourage us to shut off the machines but I could not. I promised God that if He allowed Preston to live, I would do everything possible to help him have the best life he could have. I would love him unconditionally and I would find a way to give his life purpose and meaning.

At the age of 5, Preston had a whole world of opportunities ahead of him. All of that changed in the 3–5 minutes that doctors estimate he was under water. There was a swollen, bruised area above his left eyebrow. It appears that he ran out to put a toy in the toy box, where he slipped and fell, bumped his head and rolled into the water, unconscious. Preston survived but his brain was devastated. He would never walk again nor would he utter a single word for the rest of his life. He would never again eat by mouth. It took nearly 6 months of therapy for vision to return though he eventually could see well enough to enjoy watching movies on TV. His body was racked with posturing, seizures, severe respiratory problems and a multitude of other complex problems. He required total care around the clock. I quit my job to stay at his side and care for him. The little boy who, at age 4, knew the names of all the planets, no longer knew the difference between night and day. The one thing he did understand was love. In spite of all that he had gone through, all that he had suffered, having lost all the abilities we all take so much for granted, Preston remained a happy little boy. In most every picture, both before and after his accident, he wears an incredible smile! Preston was my joy…the light of my life! Having endured seven and a half years of numerous hospitalizations, as many as 21 medications daily, constant therapies and 15 pneumonias, his tired weak body could no longer fight. On December 2, 2000, the angels carried Preston to Heaven. He was 12 years old.

I never forgot the promise I made to God that day. It wasn't long after Preston's accident that I started finding out that there were many other near drowning victims, all of them profoundly handicapped. I discovered that an average of 75 perfectly healthy, normal children, under the age of five, were drowning and nearly four times that many were near drowning victims every year. I realized that there was no turning back or changing what happened. All I could do was to try to stop it from happening to other children and spare their families the suffering and grief that my family knew so intimately. I could not believe that Florida could have well over a million back yard pools and no statewide legislation to protect our children. In 1996, with Preston by my side, I started to research and pursue legislation. I had never been involved in politics and had no clue that there could possibly be such adversity in trying to save the lives of little children. Appalled at the apathy I had encountered, I became driven. In 1997 I was introduced to Representative Debbie Wasserman Schultz, a Florida congresswoman who was working on pool safety legislation. Together, we began lobbying the legislature to adopt a bill that would address pool safety. The controversial bill met with a great deal of adversity and was almost immediately diluted. With perseverance and determination, Representative Wasserman Schultz, Preston and I, Kathy Ward (whose only grandchild, MacKenzie Merriam, drowned at age 1), and others worked diligently to finally get the bill passed on May 5, 2000. Each time that I testified before the House and/or Senate, Preston was by my side. The bill was given the name: The Preston de Ibern, MacKenzie Merriam, Residential Pool Safety Act.

Now that you have had a glimpse into the personal life of Preston and his family, my hope is that you will walk away and never forget his story. I want you to realize that this can happen to anyone wherever there are unprotected swimming pools. The fact is that until and unless we have constant and continuing awareness programs, more stringent legislation which addresses all pools and spas (including those built before Oct, 2000) and until we change the attitudes of consumers, we will continue to lose our most precious resources…our children. Please do all that you can to keep our children safe!

Morbidity/Mortality Information and Pertinent Risk Factors

Mortality

Worldwide, drowning is the major cause of injury death to children.[1] In the United States, it is the second major cause of unintentional death in children less than 15 years, third in unintentional deaths in those 15 to 34 years, and remains in the top 10 causes of unintentional deaths of those over 35 years (www.cdc.gov/ncipc/wisqars).

Death rates from drowning are highest in those 1 to 4 years of age in all countries except those in Africa. Drowning death rates are second highest in 15–24-year-olds.[2] In 2001, 1265 persons less than 19 years drowned in the U.S. with the highest drowning rate (2.95) in those <5 years, and the second highest rate (1.71) in those 15–19 years. (www.cdc.gov/ncipc/ wisqars) The lowest drowning rates occur in school-aged children.

Drowning as a method of suicide or homicide is also a cause of intentional deaths. When it is difficult to determine whether some drownings were intentional they are classified as "undetermined." In addition, in small communities, coroners are often unwilling to label such deaths because of the stigma of intentional death. Thus, intentional drowning deaths are probably underestimated.[3]

Morbidity

It is estimated that for each drowning death, there are 1 to 4 nonfatal submersions serious enough to result in hospitalization. Most of those who survive a drowning event that involved medical care survive intact. Pearn initially noted young pediatric survivors had an average IQ of 114 and no other abnormalities.[4] However, there is probably a bias to medically evaluate and hospitalize younger children with minor drowning incidents. However, approximately 7–13% of drowning victims[2,5] and most of those who survive a cardiac arrest following a drowning are devastated neurologically by the hypoxia incurred during the submersion and subsequent cardiac arrest.[6]

Unable to ambulate and respond in a purposeful manner, or in a persistent vegetative state, the economic and emotional toll they represent are enormous. In fact, analyses for some communities have shown positive benefit in terms of cost ratios for prevention programs by reducing medical and public program expenses, lost productivity, and quality adjusted life years saved.[7]

E coding of hospital discharges has allowed determination of the ratio of children surviving hospitalization to those who died following drowning. While the ratios vary by state, they consistently vary by age group, with high survival to death ratios in those <5 years and inversely low ratios in adolescents and adults.[8,9] Among injuries, drowning has the highest fatality ratios reported.

Risk factors

Host or victim related risk factors include age, gender, ethnicity, seizure history, and use of alcohol.

As with most other injuries, males drown more commonly than females. Once admitted to a hospital following a drowning, are were more likely to die.[10]

The remarkable preponderance of males greater than age 1 year, especially among those 15–24 years, involved in drowning incidents may in part be explained by behaviors. Men report more water activities than women and are more likely than women to consume alcohol when engaging in these activities.[11,12] Howland attributed the higher alcohol use by males as a major contributor to increased drowning risk.[12] In addition, when surveyed, men reported less likely use of injury prevention practices than women.[17] Studies in Montreal, New York and Washington confirmed that females were more likely than men in powered watercrafts to use life jackets (RR 1.5, 95% confidence limits 1.3, 1.6).[14-16] Thus, male behaviors of increased exposure, risk taking, and decreased use of safe practices may explain their greater risk for drowning death.[17]

Ethnicity

In the United States, non-whites also have higher drowning rates than whites[9,18] but the explanation for this finding has not been elucidated. In the United States, African-American children have the highest drowning rates.[18] In Washington state, Asian/Pacific Islanders have the highest drowning death rates, accounting for 18% of drowning deaths although they represent only 7% of the state's population.[19] Exposure to water activities and/or water safety awareness may differ. African Americans reported less swimming ability than whites.[20]

Other conditions

The risk factors that have been clearly shown to increase risk for drowning are those that impair the victim's abilities, a history of seizure disorder, and alcohol use.

Drownings are the most common cause of injury death among epileptics.[21] Epilepsy-related drownings accounted for 5–7% of drowning deaths in Canada and King County, WA.[9,22] Studying a population based cohort, Diekema demonstrated greatly increased relative risks for both injury (9.9) and death from drowning (10.4) in children and adolescents with epilepsy and no other disability compared to those without epilepsy.[23] Relative risks for drowning and death among children with epilepsy were highest for children 5 to 19 years and those in bathtubs where the event was unwitnessed.

Alcohol increases the risk for drowning death. Blood alcohol levels are positive among 20–30% of adolescent drowning deaths.[24] Alcohol use is very prevalent in water activities.[12] In a case controlled study of alcohol related drowning, Smith demonstrated that a positive blood alcohol level increased the risk of boater drowning death and the risk of drowning death increases with increasing blood alcohol levels.[25]

The Vehicle: Water

The most common vehicle involved in drownings is water. In a review of 496 unintentional childhood drowning deaths submitted to the National SAFE KIDS Campaign,* 39% occurred in pools, 37% occurred in open bodies of water (such as lakes, rivers and ponds) and 18% occurred in an around the home, in places such as bathtubs, buckets and spas. In a review of child deaths in Washington State, 32% of drownings among children and teens, birth to 17 years, occurred while playing near the water and 19% were on boats, rafts or inner tubes. Twenty-eight percent were swimming right before they drowned and 19% were playing in the water.[26]

Drowning rates vary in different bodies of water. This variance may be attributable to the age, gender, predrowning activity, and supervision of the victim in that setting. Bathtub drowning death rates are highest in those less than 1 year of age. Drowning death rates are highest in swimming pools in those less than 5 years of age. Drowning death rates are highest in rivers,

---

* Now clled Safe Kids Worldwide.

lakes, and salt water for those over 5 through age 65 years.[9],[18] However, confounders such as water clarity, current and temperature of different bodies of water may also affect rescue and thus outcome.

Bath tubs, Swimming pools, and Open Bodies of Water

Bathtub drownings involve three different groups of victims; the inadequately supervised infant or toddler, the child or adolescent with a seizure disorder, and the victims of homicide. Neglect or child abuse should always be considered in bathtub drownings.[27] The great majority of children are often placed in the bathtub by a caregiver, and over half of these children were in the bath with another child.[28] Bath tub rings and seats have been associated with drownings of infants <1 year who have been left unattended in the bathtub. Their use may increase the likelihood that the parent will leave the infant unsupervised.[29] What is clear is that they should not be used as a substitute for at hand supervision.

In a review of child deaths nationally, 39% occurred in pools (14% residential, 7% community and 18% of unknown type). Swimming pools were the site for 44% of the drownings among 1–4 year olds. In reviewed deaths where barriers were breached, 63% of victims entered through an open or unlocked gate. Of victims whose supervision was known, 39% were alone.[26]

Open water is the most likely drowning site for people over age 4 years in most countries.[2,18] Most victims are males who were swimming or boating prior to the drowning event. Child death reviews in Washington State found that 36% of drownings occurred in a lake or pond, 28% in rivers and 4% in the ocean or sound.[19] In a coastal community in Florida, drownings involving children over 11 years of age were most likely to occur in natural bodies of saltwater.[30] Weather and water conditions may contribute to the risk.

Current Research Findings and Prevention Efforts (Including Behavioral Interventions)

Recommendations for the prevention of child and adolescent drownings have been developed by the American Academy of Pediatrics, the National SAFE KIDS Campaign, Consumer Product Safety Commission and the World Congress on Drowning. Prevention has focused on four-sided fencing, pool alarms and covers, swimming instruction, supervision and lifeguards, and use of life jackets.

Pool Barriers

While drowning ranks second or third behind motor vehicles and fires as a leading cause of unintentional injury death to children less than 15, drowning in residential pools is the leading cause of death for children between the ages of 1–4 years in Florida. Drowning rates in 2001 for Florida's children <4 years were 6.7. (www.cdc.gov/ncipc/wisqars) To address this specific problem and prevent children's unsupervised access to water, the prevention tactic has been to modify the environment with barriers. Most fencing laws require public and semipublic pools, such as motels or swim clubs, to have 4-sided fencing. However, the approach to residential pools has differed, allowing the house to be the fourth side of the fence. To be effective barriers, pool fences need to be at least 4 feet high, unclimbable, with spacing no more than 4 inches so small children cannot squeeze through. Gates need to be self-closing and self-latching. Thus, pool fencing is passive-environmental to the point that the self-latching gate is appropriately used.

The latest Cochrane Collaboration review included published studies that evaluated pool fencing in a defined population and provided relevant and interpretable data that objectively measured the risk of drowning or near drowning or provided rates of these outcomes in fenced and unfenced pools.[32] Three published studies from different countries met the selection criteria and all were of the case control design. They showed that pool fencing significantly reduced the risk of drowning. The odds ratio for drowning or near drowning risk in a fenced pool compared to an unfenced pool was 0.27 (95% CI: 0.16–0.47). Isolation fencing (four-sided) was superior to perimeter fencing because perimeter or property fencing allows access to the pool from the house. The odds ratio for pools with isolation fencing in comparison to three-sided fencing was 0.17 (95% CI: 0.07–0.44). Based on these findings, the report concluded: Pool fences should have a dynamic and secure gate and isolate (ie, four-sided fencing) the pool from the house. Legislation should require isolation fencing with secure, self-latching gates for all pools, public, semi-public and private.

Evaluations of pediatric drowning deaths have determined that 80–90% of backyard pool drownings could have been prevented with four-sided isolation fencing.[33],[34] However, limitations in the laws, enforcement, and use have limited the laws' impact on pool related deaths.

Life Jackets

Life jackets (also known as personal flotation devices, PFDs or life vests) have been made of various materials and used for centuries to enhance flotation. The United States Coast Guard developed standards for varying types of use. Only life jackets designated "U.S. Coast Guard approved" should be considered effective. The US Coast Guard, boating organizations, and the American Academy of Pediatrics recommend wearing life jackets when on a boat.[6]

Despite these longstanding recommendations, while life jacket use is high among young children, use remains low among teen and adult boaters. In Washington State, observation studies of life jacket use in passengers in small boats in 1995 showed only 25% of boaters wore life jackets. However, there was wide variation in use by gender, age, and boat type. Males, persons over 14 years of age, and motor boaters, were the highest nonusers of life jackets. Children <15 years were more likely to wear a life jacket if an adult in the boat was wearing one.[14] Following statewide efforts to increase life jacket use, repeat observation studies in 2000 showed a 21% increase in use among children. The media promotes these unsafe behaviors; in a study of G-rated and PG-rated movies, only 17% of boaters wore life jackets.[35] In a national review of child drowning deaths, 97% of children who drowned in pools or open bodies of water were not wearing a life jacket at the time of drowning.[26]

Effectiveness of life jackets

All evaluations of life jacket use are purely descriptive; most show that 85% or more of persons who died of drowning in boating related incidents were not wearing life jackets.[36] One study, evaluating personal watercraft crash data, surmised that life jackets saved lives of persons who were ejected from the personal watercraft (PWC)[37] Though a more formal evaluation of life jacket effectiveness does not exist, use of life jackets is likely to decrease drowning among children when boating or playing in or near the water.[38]

Barriers to use

Barriers such as cost and availability of life jackets may affect use. Changes in these may affect the cost benefit ratio for use. Barriers to wearing life jackets on boats fall into five broad categories based on boater perception that: there is a low risk of drowning; wearing a life jacket restricts movement and interferes with performance of activities; wearing a life jacket is uncomfortable; life jackets are unattractive or unfashionable; and wearing a life jacket is a sign of fear.[39]

Effectiveness of life jacket loan programs

Many communities have implemented life jacket loan programs to make life jackets available to boaters, swimmers, and for other types of water recreation. Loaner programs may increase use; in Alaska, 75% of children under 18 used them at loaner sites compared to 50% at non-loaner sites. [40] Loaner programs in Washington State have resulted in at least four documented saves and loan anywhere from a few dozen to over 500 jackets.[41] Boat US Foundation reported at least three documented saves with their loaner program.

Parents of children who do not always wear life jackets on boats commonly cite reasons for non-use. These include how close they are to the child, having a life jacket available nearby if needed, and the child's swimming ability. Children 8–12 years old reported they did not wear life jackets because they could swim, they could grab the life jacket easily if needed, or there was no life jacket available. In addition, 23% of parents reported that they themselves don't wear life jackets on a boat. Parents mistake the effectiveness of swimming aids; 19% believed that water wings protect children.[26]

Parents' confidence in their ability to choose and fit a life jacket, life jacket ownership, and perception that child could not swim well were also factors that influenced reported life jacket use.[42] In other research, teen males were particularly concerned that a life jacket might negatively affect their desire to present an image of fearlessness and believe that life jackets are a sign of being afraid.[43]

Campaigns to increase the use of life jackets must focus on adult life jacket use in addition to use by children since adult role modeling affects use. As found with seat belts and bike helmets, life jacket use was significantly higher among children in boats if at least one accompanying adult was also wearing a life jacket.[14,44] More colorful, lightweight, and less bulky life jackets have been developed to address the issue of bulk and discomfort and the perceived 'ugly' factor. Coast Guard standards have been changed to allow for approved use of inflatable life jackets. It is not clear whether the change in standards has increased life jacket use. Changes to further lessen the bulk of life jackets might also be needed.[39]

Behavioral Interventions

Supervision

Inadequate supervision is cited as a primary contributing factor in most drowning studies.[31,33,45] In a national child death review, 88% of deaths occurred while the child was being supervised.[26] However supervision has not been well defined, using Saluja's three domains of proximity, continuity, and attention, for drowning situations.[13] Many parents believe the cinematic portrayal of drowning as a noisy event and allow themselves to be distracted or out of sight of the child, expecting to be warned of sounds of distress. Some families report leaving their infants and toddlers for periods of time in the bathtub.[46,47] Parents may be more likely to allow their child to swim without supervision if the child is perceived to be an excellent swimmer, if the child swims with a buddy, or if the child has had several years of swimming lessons.[26] Drownings can occur when an older sibling, usually <4 years of age, is left to provide supervision.[46] Parents become overconfident about their children's safety and abilities around water. In one study, 55% of parents say that they do not worry much or at all about their child drowning.[26]

Adult supervision, at hand, and being continuously present is needed for children bathing and in open water. Young children should be within an arm's length providing "touch supervision." Attention should be focused on the child and the adult should not be engaged in other distracting activities.[6]

Nowhere has the role of supervision been more contentious than in swimming pools. The fact that 80% of toddler swimming pool drownings occur in residential homes, usually their own, has been interpreted differently. Many believe this illustrates the failure of reliance on supervision, an active intervention since no one could be more invested in their child's safety than a parent. Others believe parental supervision should be improved.

Adolescent Risk and Assets Model

Supervision is a more difficult prevention tactic among adolescents. The majority of adolescent drownings occur while swimming, playing, or boating with peers in open water such as lakes and rivers. Using a conceptual framework for adolescent risk behavior, adolescent drowning prevention must consider both risks and protective factors that take into account a combination of biology/genetics, social environment, perceived environment, personality and behavior.[48] For example, social risk factors might include lack of adult supervision or a party with alcohol that precedes water activity. Protective factors might include adult role models for life jacket use and family life with clear rules and consequences. Making good decisions about where and when to swim are important factors.[49]

The Developmental Asset framework, developed by the Search Institute, should be considered in designing adolescent drowning prevention interventions.[50] The framework acknowledges the research-based associations of 40 qualities, attitudes and behaviors—called 'developmental assets'—with success and safety among young people. The assets are categorized into two groups. External assets identify important roles that families and communities play in promoting healthy development. Internal assets identify those characteristics and behaviors that reflect positive internal growth and development of young people. The internal assets help young people make thoughtful and positive choices and, in turn, be better prepared for challenging situations. Several assets are directly applicable to drowning risk and prevention:

- Adult role models who demonstrate positive responsible behavior
- Positive peer influence
- Responsibility for choices
- Planning and decision making
- Resistance skills
- Youth programs such as teen swimming lessons

Development of these assets may help protect adolescents from drowning and also establish a foundation for other kinds of success.

Lifeguarding

Lifeguards provide classic prevention in that they can prevent drownings from occurring and may be able to prevent a drowning in progress from being deadly.[51] Lifeguard presence has been shown to decrease activities and behaviors among pool goers that would probably increase risk of drowning.[52] In King County, WA, drownings at public and semi-public pools decreased dramatically when lifeguard supervision was improved.[53] No study has conclusively proven that lifeguard presence decreases drowning.

Swimming Lessons

Swimming lessons remain a questionable drowning prevention intervention.[54] Studies show that swimming lessons improved the swimming abilities of preschool children.[55, 56] However, the concern remains that swimming lessons might induce a false sense of security leading parents to supervise their child less around water or allow children to take more risks around water.[57] All studies report that up to 20–50% of those who died of drowning were known swimmers.[58] Thus, the swimmer's perceived ability may not match the water conditions.

The American Academy of Pediatrics recommended that children are not developmentally ready for formal swimming lessons until after their fourth birthday, aquatic programs should not be promoted as a means to prevent drownings, and parents must continually supervise infants and toddlers around water regardless of past or present swimming instruction.[59] Recommendations include that parents should practice "touch supervision" whereby an adult should be within arm's length of the child and all aquatic programs should include information on the cognitive and motor limitations of infants and toddlers, the inherent risks of water, the strategies for drowning prevention, and the role of adults in supervision and monitoring of the safety of children in and around water.

Role of Advocacy and Legislation

Australia and New Zealand have pioneered drowning prevention to address their high toddler pool drowning rates. Their data, legislative approach, and efforts to maintain their laws to address obstacles and evaluate the effect over 20 years provide many useful lessons.

Pool Fencing Laws

Unfortunately, residential pool fencing laws have not been the panacea for toddler pool drownings. Estimates of the impact of pool fencing laws suggested the number of pool drowning deaths would decrease by only 40 to 67% in New Zealand and by 19% in the USA if all pools were adequately fenced.[60, 61] Early reports of a 50% decrease in the numbers of pool drownings following pool fencing laws in Arizona were encouraging; however, toddler drowning death rates have not changed in New Zealand, Australia, and the USA.[31,62] Some of the lack of change in rates may be explained by increased exposure as the number of pools has increased.[61,63] Exposure data [ie, Pearn's Swimming Pool Drowning Index, SPDI = (Number of pool fatalities/Number of children at risk) × (No. of private pools/No. of private dwellings)] are needed to better evaluate the effects of the laws.[63]

The content of the laws have been part of the problem. Most laws apply only to newly constructed pools since they are primarily building code ordinances that involve permits enforced by building code inspectors at the time of construction. Preexisting residential pools have been included only occasionally. For example, in 2000, Florida amended its originally proposed pool barrier legislation that required a child resistant fence 5 feet high surrounding residential swimming pools on any new residential swimming pool built after October 1, 1998 and on any private swimming pool before the act when the dwelling was sold, leased, or rented after October 1, 1998 (Chapter 515, F.S., November 25, 1997). The bill was subsequently changed in 2000 so that it applied to only new residential pools, spas, and hot tubs and requires pool owners to have one of four safety features to supplement and complement the requirement for constant adult supervision of young children and medically frail elderly persons around such aquatic environments. These safety features included a pool barrier (4 ft. high) that isolates the pool from the home, the use of an approved safety pool cover, all doors and windows providing direct access from the home to the pool must be equipped with an exit alarm that has a minimum sound pressure rating of 85 dB A at 10 feet or all doors providing direct access from the home to the pool must be equipped with a self-closing, self-latching device with a release mechanism placed no lower than 54 inches above the floor. While four-sided fencing is most likely the best barrier method, states have adapted legislation to include other options as well.

Inevitably, the incomplete success of pool fencing laws lies with care providers. Unfortunately, pool fencing, primarily a passive intervention, requires some active participation by care providers to maintain the fence and gate and ensure the gate is closed. Indepth reviews of child drownings show failure to properly use barriers and gates.[64,65] This is not surprising, for when surveyed, Australian pool owners did not perceive that the pool was a hazard and that a childproof fence was important. This belief was not affected by whether or not they had children.[66] In California, a state with a very high toddler drowning rate, only 35% of those who endorsed 4 sided fencing around pools actually had a fence surrounding their own pool.[67] This phenomenon, called the knowledge-user gap, is a well-described hurdle in changing human behaviors.

The failure of the pool fencing laws to greatly reduce toddler deaths primarily lies in failure to implement or enforce the laws. In New Zealand, a country with one of the longest standing national pool fencing laws, only 44% of authorities reported complying with the law.[68] In the US, most fencing laws are county based ordinances; only a few state wide laws exist. A national law is needed coupled with a commitment to enforcement.

The disturbing complacencies among pool owners show that caregivers alone will not provide adequate prevention of toddler drownings. While better pool fencing laws and their enforcement are needed, care provider compliance must be won. Care provider disbelief and the failure of pool fencing to protect children highlight the need for new behavioral approaches to preventing pool drownings.

Life jacket laws

Life jacket use is mandated for children on boats in the United States. In 2004, 40 states had state laws as well as a federal statute. State laws vary by age of child, boat length, and boating activities such as being underway or not. The Federal rule requires any child under 13 to wear a life jacket when on any type and size of recreational boating vessel. However it does not replace state legislation. Another Federal rule requires appropriately sized life jackets for anyone riding in a boat.[69] However, there has not been a clear mandate for life jacket use among adolescents and adults, the victims of most boating related drownings. Observation data show that life jacket use decreases as a child gets older. Whereas use among those <5 years was 90%, among those >14 years, use was 13%. Efforts to increase use should target parents as adult life jacket use increases the likelihood of child use.[14]

Not surprisingly, it is difficult to demonstrate an association between life jacket laws and significant decreases in drowning deaths. In Washington state, prior to a state law requiring <13 year olds to wear life jackets, 63% of those <15 years were already wearing life jackets in small boats; after the law, 77% were wearing them.[70] Although this reflected a 22% increase, it was not statistically significant.

Alcohol use

Many states have boating while intoxicated (BWI) legislation. A study conducted by the National Association of State Boating Law Administrators in 1990 found that there was a higher percent decline in boating fatalities in states with more stringent BWI laws.[71]

The Role of Physician Advocacy

Health care providers are in a powerful role for advising parents. However, a national survey of 560 pediatricians selected from the Fellows of the American Academy of Pediatrics showed that very few (4.1%) were involved in community and/or legislative efforts to prevent childhood drownings and less than half provided written materials about drowning prevention to their patients (40.5%). Even more disturbing was the fact that only 17.9% of pediatricians received formal education on drowning prevention during their pediatric residency training.[72] A later study of Los Angeles County pediatricians, family physicians, and pediatric nurse practitioners showed that about two-thirds of the sample did not know that drowning deaths were more common than deaths due to toxic ingestions or firearm injuries for young children. Also, only one-third of clinicians said they counseled on injury prevention.[73] Studies consistently show that female clinicians are more likely to counsel about drowning prevention than male clinicians. Emergency departments provide an opportunity to reach large numbers of patients and families. Surprisingly, parents of children visiting a pediatric emergency department valued drowning prevention messages included in their written discharge instructions. In fact, 35% said they would consider buying a life jacket because of the messages.[74] Distribution of safety equipment can also be successful in the emergency department setting.

Physician counseling should address: identification of risks, such as pool, pond, waterfront ownership, boating, and seizure disorder; use of life jackets for water related activities including playing near water and swimming; AAP recommendations; and level of supervision.

Seizure patients deserve and need special counseling. The Epilepsy Foundation recommends: not swimming when anticonvulsant medications have not been taken, wearing a life jacket, informing lifeguards and teachers of the seizure risk, swimming with someone who could provide rescue, and never leaving a child unattended. (www.epilepsyfoundation.org) However, patients of all ages with seizure disorders should be encouraged to shower, and not bathe since their drowning risk continues through adulthood.[9]

Recommendations for Research, Practice, Advocacy

Research needs abound in the epidemiology, behavioral aspects, and intervention of drowning. Denominator data is needed for exposure to water activities, swimming ability, and supervision using Saluja's criteria.[13] Furthermore, research needs to address various ethnic groups to explain their increased risk and ways to address it. The attitudes of and barriers to safe practice around water activities need to be explored in high risk groups such as adolescent males, motor boaters, and in non-white communities. Ways to improve supervision, safe bathing and swimming practices among those listed previously and those with epilepsy, need exploration. A water safety awareness/risk perception schema needs development to identify and prioritize high risk groups and the effects of interventions to increase awareness. Among the intervention studies needed, the efficacy of life jackets, swimming lessons, lifeguard presence, and boating safety education should be prioritized.

While drowning prevention must be perceived by the individual, advocacy for drowning prevention requires multiple levels and types of involvement. Christoffel has provided a conceptual framework for understanding the advocacy process that includes stages of gathering information, developing strategies, and taking action.[75] Although the stages are sequential they are also simultaneous so that adjustments based on findings from each stage are continually made. Successful advocacy efforts require involvement of many participants, including drowning prevention coalitions, community groups, health service providers, health provider organizations, journal editors, legal experts, legislators, the private sector, researchers and academicians, research funding agencies, and victims' families.[75] The leaders of the advocacy effort need to identify participating individuals whose skills will differ and develop complementary, interacting, and distinct roles for each of them.

Existing laws need to be reviewed for content and enforcement. Pool fencing laws need to apply to all pools, public and private, established and new, and be enforced. A national law is needed.

Another example of the need for enforcement addresses the role of alcohol. An evaluation of drowning rate trends suggested that the observed decreasing prevalence of positive blood alcohol levels among drowning victims might explain some of the decrease in drowning rates in some regions.[76] While the contribution of alcohol to drowning has been recognized, efforts should be directed to decreasing alcohol use around water. Boating while intoxicated laws apply to boaters in all 50 U.S. states. However, they are not often enforced. This may help explain why lowering the drinking age did not affect the drowning rate of teenagers.[77]

Given that the majority of adolescents and adults drownings occur in open water, prevention of open water drownings needs emphasis. Efforts should address the underestimation of the risk of water, of combining alcohol with water, and the use of life jackets.[78]

Efforts to decrease boat related drownings center around increasing life jacket use and safe boating practices. Mandatory life jacket use must be considered for all age groups. Over half the states have in place laws requiring boating safety courses for boaters. The effectiveness of these courses needs evaluation.

In some states, such as Idaho and Washington, state budget cuts ended lifeguarding in state parks. The effect of the lack of supervised swim areas warrants evaluation. A decrease in swimming opportunities could increase drownings if swimmers swim unsupervised or could decrease drownings if exposure decreases.

How can we apply all of this information to practice? Awareness of risks and prevention strategies as well as supervisory and rescue skills for drowning prevention are needed. Risk perception plays a major role in drowning prevention. The public underestimates the risk and overestimates treatment outcomes.[79] Issues such as protective hypothermia, the dive reflex, and resuscitation convey a sense of good outcome that is not supported by fact. Practitioners and educators need to better inform the public of the risks and prevention opportunities. Drowning prevention history shows clearly that success cannot be achieved without individual compliance. Important messages to impart include the following:

- Improve and increase supervision around water using lifeguards and parents who constantly watch their children and are prepared for an emergency.
- Change the culture of life jacket use. Life jackets should be introduced where and when children learn to swim. Local pools need to welcome life jacket use in the pool.
- Include water survival as part of swim lesson instruction. Swimming lessons should address use of life jackets, discussion of the differences between pool and open water swimming including identifying some of the dangers of open water, and provide advice on safe swimming practices as well.
- Educate families who have children with seizures about ongoing risks. Children and adolescents with seizure disorders need to recognize the

lifetime risk of drowning, especially in a bathtub. Changing to a lifestyle of showering, not bathing should be encouraged by health care practitioners.

- Provide adolescents with safe swimming environments and skills to make appropriate decisions around the water. Being able to identify water risks, stand up to peer pressure, plan ahead for going out on the water, take personal responsibility and be able to apply resistance skills may be useful strategies to prevent adolescent drowning.[80] Changing current norms around adult life jacket use and alcohol will impact adolescent behavior.
- Target messages to high risk populations such as adolescents and young adults, fishermen, and motor boaters to influence their risk perception and behaviors around use of prevention technology like life jackets.
- Develop comprehensive community efforts to increase life jacket using behavioral theories and by adapting campaigns that have increased the use of booster seats and bicycle helmets.[42] Social marketing campaigns may be very useful to explore.
- Increase the number of pool owners trained in CPR and water rescue as bystander cardiopulmonary resuscitation increases the likelihood of survival following a drowning event.[81]

In addition to drowning, other water injuries can be very serious. However, a recent review study of non-submersion injuries in aquatic sporting and recreational activities showed that adequate descriptive studies for the activities of swimming, diving, boating, surf sports, fishing, water polo, and water sliding are lacking.[82] There is much inconsistency in inclusion criteria and reporting of incidence rates. Although the incidence rates for these injuries overall are low (ie. fractures, wounds, dislocations, etc.), severe disabling injuries occurred with diving (spinal cord injuries) and amputation from boat propeller strikes. There is a need for well-designed studies that accurately describe the injuries and their incidence with risk factor information. Several large retrospective studies showed that traumatic injuries were rare in children and adolescents who drowned; cervical spine injury was the most prominent of these injuries, related to a history of diving or motor vehicle related drowning, and occurred mostly in adolescent males.[83,84]

For children and adolescents, serious diving injuries occur when striking one's head on the bottom of the pool or other body of water following miscalculation of water depth. Recreational diving spinal cord injuries occur more frequently in males younger that 25 years of age with the highest incidence in males between the ages of 11–15 years. Most of these injuries occur in private residential pools.[85] Diving injuries are likely to be underestimated due to the victim's drowning and the report of death being drowning only.[86]

To prevent diving-related spinal cord injuries, water depth, the angle of the dive entry, and the diver's velocity are very important.[85] Recommended water depths for recreational diving are not less than 1.52m and pools that are deep at one end and quickly and suddenly decline in depth in the shallow end should be avoided. Reports suggest that the best time to teach safe diving is when one is learning how to swim. This instruction should include not only the dangers of diving in shallow water but also how to position the arms and head before entering the water, steering up to the water surface after the dive, and jumping in feet first instead of diving or sliding into the water.[86]

A Final Note: Personal Watercraft (PWC) Injuries

The authors believe that personal watercraft injuries, though generally not causing drowning, were important to report as a unique set of water related injuries. A PWC is a watercraft that is designed to be operated by a person or persons sitting, standing, or kneeling on the craft, rather than the conventional manner of sitting or standing inside. It is also designed to carry between one and three persons. There are currently 1.2 million PWC owned by Americans.[87] National sales average 189 000 per year over the last three years, more than one-third of the new recreational boat sales in the US. While PWCs account for 11% of all registered watercrafts, they are involved with 35% of watercraft "accidents." Since 1990 more than 30 000 Americans have been injured on PWC and in 2002 there were 71 PWC fatalities, the second leading category following open motorboat. (See US Department of Homeland Security-United States Coast Guard, 2002). Age of PWC operators is a major risk factor. US Coast Guard statistics (www.uscgboating.org) show that in 2002, 38% (532/1362) of PWC related deaths were to persons <20 years of age compared to approximately 13% of the 750 boating related deaths.

PWCs are the ONLY type of recreational watercraft where the leading cause of death is not drowning but blunt trauma. Injuries of children in Florida admitted to a local trauma center for jet ski injuries were more serious than those that occur in small boats.[88] Built to go faster, today's PWCs have greater than 120–135 horsepower engines, reaching top speeds of 65–70 miles per hour[37] thereby increasing the risk for injuries. A ten-year retrospective review of PWC injuries from the National Pediatric Trauma Registry showed that of 66 children between the ages of 5-19 hospitalized for PWC injuries, 4 died and 28 incurred disabilities.[89] The most common injury mechanism was collision with another PWC, boat, or fixed object. Most injury diagnoses involved the head, face, and/or neck (55.1%) and included lacerations, contusions, fractures, maxillofacial, arterial, and brain injuries.[90,91]

Improved technology represents a major injury prevention opportunity as jet skis are maneuverable only when the throttle is open.[92] They can avoid an obstacle, not by slowing and changing direction as other vehicles do, but by increasing speed and turning direction. Also, stopping is only achieved by cutting the throttle—this leads to coasting and loss of steering ability. While newer models now incorporate off-throttle steering capacity, many older models will continue to be used for years.

Legislation has been passed to mitigate some of the risk factors. In Florida, rental personal watercraft in 2003 were involved in 49% of PWC "accidents" statewide and 31% of PWC injury victims were age 13–19 years. (2003 Florida Boating Accident Statistical Report) Therefore, to operate a PWC in Florida in 2004, one must be > 14 years of age; to rent a PWC, one must be 18 years of age. Four states, Alabama, Connecticut, Florida and New Jersey, require every PWC operator to take an educational course. However, efficacy of these courses has not been evaluated.

Areas for safety promotion include having safety equipment, educational training requirements, a citizen complaint provision, and at least a minimum of prohibited operations. To improve safety for children the American Academy of Pediatrics recommends: 1) no one younger than 16 should operate a PWC; 2) the operator and passengers should wear US Coast-Guard-approved personal flotation devices; 3) Alcohol and other drug use should be avoided before and while operating a PWC; 4) operators should participate in a safe boating course; 5) safe operating practices should always be followed; 6) PWCs should not be operated when swimmers are in the water if a PWC is used to tow another person on skis, knee boards, tubes, or other devices; 7) a second person must face the rear to monitor the person being towed; 8) all persons who rent PWCs should comply with all recommendations; and 9) protective equipment such as wet suits, gloves, boots, eyewear, and helmets may be important to wear.[92]

Personal water-craft injuries treated in US emergency departments increased four-fold from 1990 (N=2860) to 1995 (N>12, 000).[90] It is likely that without the support of better regulations and related legislation PWC injuries will increase. The speeds of these crafts continue to increase as does their overall use. The AAP recommended additional PWC safety research, work within communities to pass legislation that support the recommendations, and funding to support enforcement of all regulations.[92]

In conclusion, a resonating theme throughout this chapter has been not only the importance of water-related injuries but the need for better research, practice, and advocacy, involving active and passive measures. It is hypothesized that research, practice, and advocacy working in concert will prevent needless water-related injuries and deaths among children and adolescents. Preston's story certainly illustrates that no more time can be wasted in pursuing the answers.

References

1. Peden, M.M. and K. McGee, The epidemiology of drowning worldwide. *Injury Control and Safety Promotion, 2003.* 10(4): p. 195–9.
2. Bierens, J.J., J.T. Knape, and H.P. Gelissen, Drowning. *Current Opinion in Critical Care,* 2002. 8(6): p. 578–86.
3. Smith, G.S. and J. Howland, Declines in drowning: exploring the epidemiology of favorable trends.[comment]. *JAMA,* 1999. 281(23): p. 2245–7.
4. Pearn, J., Neurological and phychometric studies in children surviving freshwater immersion accidents. *Lancet,* 1977. 1(8001): p. 7–9.
5. Quan, L., et al., Ten-year study of pediatric drownings and near-drownings in King County, Washington: lessons in injury prevention. *Pediatrics,* 1989. 83(6): p. 1035–40.
6. American Academy of Pediatrics Committee on Injury, V. and P. Poison, Prevention of drowning in infants, children, and adolescents. *Pediatrics.,* 2003. 112(2): p. 437–9.
7. Zaloshnja, E., et al., Reducing injuries among Native Americans: five cost-outcome analyses. *Accident Analysis and Prevention,* 2003. 35(5): p. 631–9.
8. Centers for Disease Control and Prevention, Nonfatal and fatal drownings in recreational water settings—United States, 2001–2002. *MMWR,* 2004. 53(21): p. 447–52.

9. Quan, L. and P. Cummings, Characteristics of drowning by different age groups. *Injury Prevention.*, 2003. 9(2): p. 163–8.

10. Graf, W.D., et al., Predicting outcome in pediatric submersion victims. *Ann Emerg Med*, 1995. 26(3): p. 312–9.

11. Howland, J., et al., A pilot survey of aquatic activities and related consumption of alcohol, with implications for drowning. *Public Health Rep*, 1990. 105(4): p. 415–9.

12. Howland, J., et al., Alcohol Use and Aquatiac Activities—United States, 1991. *MMWR*, 1993. 42(35): p. 675–82.

13. Saluja, G., et al., The role of supervision in child injury risk: definition, conceptual and measurement issues. *Injury Control and Safety Promotion*, 2004. 11(1): p. 17–22.

14. Quan, L., et al., Are life vests worn? A multiregional observational study of personal flotation device use in small boats. *Injury Prevention*, 1998. 4(3): p. 203–5.

15. Browne, M.L., E.L. Lewis-Michl, and A.D. Stark, Watercraft-related drownings among New York State residents, 1988–1994. *Public Health Reports*, 2003. 118(5): p. 459–63.

16. Nguyen, M.N., et al., Comportements et croyances des amateurs d'activites nautiques et de plein air. Etude sur les comportements et les perceptions des risques a la sante. Canadian Journal of Public Health. *Revue Canadienne de Sante Publique*, 2002. 93(3): p. 208–12.

17. Howland, J., et al., Why are most drowning victims men? Sex differences in aquatic skills and behaviors. *AJPH*, 1996. 86(1): p. 93–6.

18. Brenner, R.A., et al., Where children drown, United States, 1995. *Pediatrics*, 2001. 108(1): p. 85–89.

19. Health, W.S.D.o., Child death review state committee recommendations on child drowning prevention. 2004, Washington State Department of Health: Community and Family Health: Olympia, WA.

20. Gilchrist, J., J.J. Sacks, and C.M. Branche, Self-reported swimming ability in US adults, 1994. *Public Health Reports*, 2000. 115(2-3): p. 110–1.

21. Jansson, B. and N. Ahmed, Epilepsy and injury mortality in Sweden—the importance of changes in coding practice. *Seizure*, 2002. 11(6): p. 361–70.

22. Ryan, C.A. and G. Dowling, Drowning deaths in people with epilepsy. *Canadian Medical Association Journal*, 1993. 148(5): p. 781–4.

23. Diekema, D.S., L. Quan, and V.L. Holt, Epilepsy as a risk factor for submersion injury in children. *Pediatrics*, 1993. 91(3): p. 612–6.

24. Howland, J. and R. Hingson, Alcohol as a risk factor for drownings: a review of the literature (1950–1985). *Accid Anal Prev*, 1988. 20(1): p. 19–25.

25. Smith, G.S., et al., Drinking and recreational boating fatalities: a population-based case-control study. *JAMA*, 2001. 286(23): p. 2974–80.

26. Cody, B., et al., Clear danger: A national study of childhood drowning and related attitudes and behaviors. 2004, National Safe Kids Campaign: Washington DC.

27. Lavelle, J.M., et al., Ten-year review of pediatric bathtub near-drownings: evaluation for child abuse and neglect. *Annals of Emergency Medicine*, 1995. 25(3): p. 344–8.

28. Sweet, D., Memorandum: Fatality Information for the "In-Home Drowning Prevention Campaign", M. Ross, Editor. 2002, United States Consumer Product Safety Commission: Washington DC. p. Memorandum.

29. Rauchschwalbe, R., R.A. Brenner, and G.S. Smith, The role of bathtub seats and rings in infant drowning deaths. *Pediatrics*, 1997. 100(4): p. E1.

30. Nichter, M.A. and P.B. Everett, Profile of drowning victims in a coastal community. *Journal of the Florida Medical Association*, 1989. 76(2): p. 253–6.

31. Brenner, R.A., Prevention of drowning in infants, children, and adolescents. *Pediatrics.*, 2003. 112(2): p. 440–5.

32. Thompson, D.C. and F.P. Rivara, Pool fencing for preventing drowning in children. *Cochrane Database of Systematic Reviews*, 2000(2): p. CD001047.

33. Rimsza, M.E., et al., Can child deaths be prevented? The Arizona Child Fatality Review Program experience. *Pediatrics*, 2002. 110(1 Pt 1): p. e11.

34. Hassall, I.B., Thirty-six consecutive under 5 year old domestic swimming pool drownings. *Australian Paediatric Journal*, 1989. 25(3): p. 143–6.

35. Pelletier, A.R., et al., Injury prevention practices as depicted in G-rated and PG-rated movies. *Archives of Pediatrics and Adolescent Medicine*, 2000. 154(3): p. 283–6.

36. U.S. Department of Transportation United States Coast Guard, Boating Statistics 1994. 1995: Washington, DC.

37. Jones, C.S., Drowning among personal watercraft passengers: the ability of personal flotation devices to preserve life on Arkansas waterways, 1994–1997. *Journal of the Arkansas Medical Society*, 1999. 96(3): p. 97–8.

38. Langley, J., Review of literature on available strategies for drowning prevention, Task Force on the Epidemiology of Drowning, World Congress on Drowning: Prevention, Rescue and Treatment. Available at: http://www.drowning.nl/csi/drowning.nsf/index/home/$file/index.htm.

39. Groff, P. and J. Ghadiali, Will it float? Mandatory PFD legislation: A background research paper, in Presented to The Canadian Safe Boating Council. 2003, SMARTRISK: Toronto, ON. p. 1–287.

40. Delaney, M., Loaner life jackets saving Alaskan children's lives, in Coast Guard Public Affairs. 2002, United States Coast Guard 17th District: Kodiak, Alaska.

41. Bennett, E. and T. Bernthal, Life vest loan program guide. 2001, Children's Hospital and Regional Medical Center: Seattle, WA.

42. Bennett, E., et al., Evaluation of a drowning prevention campaign in King County, Washington. *Injury Prevention*, 1999. 5(2): p. 109–13.

43. Consulting, I.-L.R., Water safety study: Full results. 1994, Royal Life Saving Society, Canada: Ontario Branch: Toronto, ON.

44. Treser, C.D., M.N. Trusty, and P.P. Yang, Personal flotation device usage: do educational efforts have an impact? *Journal of Public Health Policy*, 1997. 18(3): p. 346–56.

45. Landen, M.G., U. Bauer, and M. Kohn, Inadequate supervision as a cause of injury deaths among young children in Alaska and Louisiana. *Pediatrics*, 2003. 111(2): p. 328–31.

46. Byard, R., et al., Shared bathing and drowning in infants and young children. *Journal of Paediatrics and Child Health*, 2001. 37(6): p. 542–4.

47. Simon, H.K., T. Tamura, and K. Colton, Reported level of supervision of young children while in the bathtub. *Ambulatory Pediatrics*, 2003. 3(2): p. 106–8.

48. Jessor, R., Risk behavior in adolescence: a psychosocial framework for understanding and action. *Journal of Adolescent Health*, 1991. 12(8): p. 597–605.

49. Baker, S.P., B. O'Neill, and S. Karpf, The injury fact book. 2nd edition ed. 1992, New York: Oxford University Press.

50. Benson PL, S.P., Leffert N, Roehlkepartain EC., A fragile foundation: The state of developmental assets among American youth. 1999, Minneapolis: Search Institute.

51. Branche, C., S. Stewart (Editors), Lifeguard effectiveness: A report of the working group. 2001, Centers for Disease Control and Prevention, National Center for Injury Prevention and Control: Atlanta, GA.

52. Harrell, W.A., Does supervision by a lifeguard make a difference in rule violations? Effects of lifeguards' scanning. *Psychological Reports*, 2001. 89(2): p. 327–30.

53. Quan, L. and A. Gomez, Swimming pool safety—An effective submersion prevention program. *J Env Health*, 1990. 52: p. 344–346.

54. Brenner, R.A., G. Saluja, and G.S. Smith, Swimming lessons, swimming ability, and the risk of drowning. *Injury Control and Safety Promotion*, 2003. 10(4): p. 211–6.

55. Asher, K.N., et al., Water safety training as a potential means of reducing risk of young children's drowning. *Injury Prevention*, 1995. 1(4): p. 228–33.

56. Parker, H.E. and B.A. Blanksby, Starting age and aquatic skill learning in young children: mastery of prerequisite water confidence and basic aquatic locomotion skills. *Australian Journal of Science and Medicine in Sport*, 1997. 29(3): p. 83–7.

57. Barss, P., Cautionary notes on teaching water safety skills. *Injury Prevention*, 1995. 1(4): p. 218–9.

58. Cross, C.R., Visual Surveillance Report, in National Drowning Report. 2000, The Canadian Red Cross Society: Ottawa, ON.

59. Anonymous, Swimming programs for infants and toddlers. Committee on Sports Medicine and Fitness and Committee on Injury and Poison Prevention. American Academy of Pediatrics. *Pediatrics*, 2000. 105(4 Pt 1): p. 868–70.

60. Logan, P., et al., Childhood drownings and fencing of outdoor pools in the United States, 1994. *Pediatrics*, 1998. 101(6): p. E3.

61. Fergusson, D.M., L.J. Horwood, and F.T. Shannon, The safety standards of domestic swimming pools 1980–1982. *New Zealand Medical Journal*, 1983. 96(725): p. 93–5.

62. Fenner, P.J., Patterns of drowning in Australia, 1992–1997. [letter; comment.]. *Medical Journal of Australia*, 1999. 171(11-12): p. 587–90.

63. Langley, J., International comparisons: we need to know a lot more. *Injury Prevention*, 2001. 7(4): p. 267–9.

64. Morgenstern, H., T. Bingham, and A. Reza, Effects of pool-fencing ordinances and other factors on childhood drowning in Los Angeles County, 1990–1995. *AJPH*, 2000. 90(4): p. 595–601.

65. Browne, M.L., E.L. Lewis-Michl, and A.D. Stark, Unintentional drownings among New York State residents, 1988–1994. *Public Health Reports*, 2003. 118(5): p. 448–58.

66. Fisher, K.J. and K.P. Balanda, Caregiver factors and pool fencing: an exploratory analysis.[see comment]. *Injury Prevention*, 1997. 3(4): p. 257–61.

67. Wintemute, G.J. and M.A. Wright, The attitude-practice gap revisited: risk reduction beliefs and behaviors among owners of residential swimming pools. *Pediatrics*, 1991. 88(6): p. 1168–71.

68. Morrison, L., et al., Achieving compliance with pool fencing legislation in New Zealand: a survey of regulatory authorities. *Injury Prevention*, 1999. 5(2): p. 114–8.

69. DOT, U.S.C.G., Wearing of personal flotation devices (PFD) by certain children aboard recreational vessels, in Federal Register. 2002, United States Coast Guard, Department of Transportation.

70. Quan, L., et al., Washington state drowning prevention project PFD observation results. 2000: Seattle, WA.

71. National Transportation Safety Board, Recreational boating safety. 1993, Washington, DC: National Transportation Safety Board.

72. O'Flaherty, J. and P. Pirie, Prevention of Pediatric Drowning and Near-Drowning: A Survey of Members of the American Academy of Pediatrics. *Pediatrics*, 1996. 99(2): p. 169–174.

73. Barkin, S. and L. Gelberg, Sink or swim—clinicians don't often counsel on drowning prevention. *Pediatrics*, 1999. 104(5 Pt 2): p. 1217–9.

74. Quan, L., et al., Do parents value drowning prevention information at discharge from the emergency department? *Annals of Emergency Medicine*, 2001. 37(4): p. 382–5.

75. Christoffel, K.K., Public health advocacy: process and product. *AJPH*, 2000. 90(5): p. 722–6.

76. Cummings, P. and L. Quan, Trends in unintentional drowning: the role of alcohol and medical care. *JAMA*, 1999. 281(23): p. 2198–202.

77. Howland, J., et al., Did changes in minimum age drinking laws affect adolescent drowning (1970–90)? *Injury Prevention*, 1998. 4(4): p. 288–91.

78. Howland, J., et al., Missing the boat on drinking and boating. *JAMA*, 1993. 270(1): p. 91–2.

79. Michalsen, A., Risk assessment and perception. *Injury Control and Safety Promotion*, 2003. 10(4): p. 201–4.

80. Institute, S., The Asset Approach. 2002, Search Institute: Minneapolis, MN. p. 1–8.

81. Kyriacou, D.N., et al., Effect of immediate resuscitation on children with submersion injury. *Pediatrics*, 1994. 94(2 Pt 1): p. 137–42.

82. Chalmers, D. and L. Morrison, Epidemiology of non-submersion injuries in aquatic sporting and recreational activities. *Sports Medicine*, 2003. 33(10): p. 745–70.

83. Hwang, V., et al., Prevalence of traumatic injuries in drowning and near drowning in children and adolescents. *Archives of Pediatrics and Adolescent Medicine*, 2003. 157(1): p. 50–3.

84. Watson, R.S., et al., Cervical spine injuries among submersion victims. *Journal of Trauma-Injury Infection and Critical Care*, 2001. 51(4): p. 658–62.

85. Blanksby, B.A., et al., Aetiology and occurrence of diving injuries. A review of diving safety. *Sports Medicine*, 1997. 23(4): p. 228–46.

86. Kluger, Y., et al., Diving injuries: a preventable catastrophe. *Journal of Trauma-Injury Infection and Critical Care*, 1994. 36(3): p. 349–51.

87. Splett, J., Watercraft use: A nationwide problem requiring local regulation. *Journal of Environmental Law and Litigation*, 1999.

88. Beierle, E.A., et al., Small watercraft injuries in children. *American Surgeon*, 2002. 68(6): p. 535–8; discussion 538.

89. Rubin, L.E., et al., Pediatric trauma due to personal watercraft: a ten-year retrospective. *Journal of Pediatric Surgery*, 10/2003.

90. Branche, C.M., J.M. Conn, and J.L. Annest, Personal watercraft-related injuries. A growing public health concern. *JAMA*, 1997. 278(8): p. 663–5.

91. Shatz, D.V., et al., Personal watercraft crash injuries: an emerging problem. *Journal of Trauma*, 1998. 44(1): p. 198–201.

92. Anonymous, Personal watercraft use by children and adolescents. American Academy of Pediatrics. Committee on Injury and Poison Prevention. *Pediatrics*, 2000. 105(2): p. 452–3.

CHAPTER 11

Child Abuse and Neglect

David DiLillo, Michelle A. Fortier,
and Andrea R. Perry

Putting a Face on Injury:
The True Case of Little Diana N. Molina[*]

In June of 2003, Germai Molina traveled from his residence in Grand Island, Nebraska, to El Salvador to pick up his two-year-old daughter, Diana N. Molina (referred to henceforth as Little Diana), who had been staying with her maternal grandmother. Approximately a month later on July 23, 2003, in the early morning hours, Little Diana died of blunt head trauma in the emergency room at St. Francis Medical Center in Grand Island, Nebraska. Although the medical staff attempted to resuscitate the child, her body was lifeless, bruised, and lacerated upon arrival at the hospital. Initially, her biological parents, Germai Molina, 22, and Diana C. Molina, 25, indicated that the child had fallen down three flights of stairs. However, medical examinations and subsequent testimony from the girl's mother would reveal that two-year-old Diana had likely been beaten to death. Based largely on the testimony of Diana C. Molina, who agreed to testify against her husband in exchange for receiving a lesser charge of felony permitting child abuse, Germai Molina was convicted and sentenced to 80 years to life in prison for both second-degree murder and felony child abuse resulting in death.

During the trial, which began in August, 2004, an emotional Diana C. Molina recounted, through a Spanish-language interpreter, the harrowing events that led to her daughter's death. Mrs. Molina testified that the severe physical and psychological punishment inflicted upon Little Diana was a consequence of the child urinating in her crib the day before her death and failing to alert her parents of the accident. She reported that, in response to the bedwetting, her husband had forced Little Diana to stand on top of a

---

University of Nebraska-Lincoln
* The case presented herein is an actual occurrence of severe child abuse. The facts described are drawn from various local, regional, and national media accounts of this case appearing between July 2003 and September 2004.

bucket-type platform for a period of approximately three hours. During this time, Mrs. Molina recounted that her husband sat opposite, on the edge of a bed, and beat the child with one of her own belts. If the child fell asleep, Mr. Molina reportedly awoke her and struck her again. Mrs. Molina estimated that Little Diana was belted between 60 and 100 times. Mrs. Molina also testified that Mr. Molina had either picked up Little Diana repeatedly and dropped her on her head or kicked her numerous times in the head.

According to Mrs. Molina, when she asked her husband to stop the abuse, he stated that he was "tired of talking to [Little Diana] and that if he hit her she would understand because it would hurt her." Mrs. Molina admitted that she made no further attempts to intervene because she was terrified at the repercussions she might face from her husband, who had threatened to kill Little Diana, their 10-month-old, her, and himself. She also claimed that she felt powerless in her relationship with her husband. Driven by fear and helplessness, Mrs. Molina reported that she retreated to the bedroom and tried to sleep. However, she stated that she could hear her daughter being beaten and was awake when, at approximately 3:00 a.m., Mr. Molina carried an unresponsive Little Diana into the couple's bedroom. It was at this time that Mr. Molina alerted Mrs. Molina of Little Diana's unconsciousness, and they agreed to take the child to the hospital. On the way to the hospital, Mrs. Molina reported that her husband expressed fear of going to jail and instructed her to tell hospital staff that the child had fallen down the stairs.

Consistent with Mrs. Molina's accounts of severe child abuse, Dr. Jerry Jones of Omaha, Nebraska, a forensic pathologist who performed Little Diana's autopsy, testified that the child's injuries were the "result of a horrific beating" and were highly inconsistent with an accidental death, such as the child falling down the stairs. Accompanied by graphic photos of the deceased child, Dr. Jones illuminated the severity of Little Diana's injuries, which included full body bruising, abrasions and lacerations on her back, blackened eyes, and brain hemorrhaging and swelling. In one of the most disturbing moments of the trial, the forensic pathologist stated that the nature and positioning of some of the marks on Little Diana suggested that she had attempted to defend herself from her father's blows. He concluded that two-year-old Diana's body succumbed to the impact of the trauma, with brain damage causing critical body functions in her heart and lungs to fail. DNA evidence also suggested that Little Diana had not fallen down the stairs.

Putting It into Context: Advocacy

Although all child abuse is disturbing, the story of Little Diana represents a particularly horrific example—one involving extreme cruelty that resulted the death of a young child. While death is not the most common consequence of abuse, it is the most tragic and unacceptable outcome. What can be gleaned from this case that might prove useful in preventing similar incidents of abuse in the future? In considering this question, two factors emerge that may shed light on important directions for child abuse advocacy. These factors center around the unique challenges faced by immigrant families, and the need for increased perpetrator intervention and rehabilitation efforts within the correctional system.

As an immigrant family from El Salvador, Mr. and Mrs. Molina relied on work visas to maintain legal residency in the US. However, reports that Mrs. Molina quit her job to stay at home following the birth of their second child suggest that fear of deportation may have discouraged her from reaching out for help during the stressful events leading up to Little Diana's death. For immigrant families, fear of deportation—in addition to other cultural and linguistic barriers associated with the transition to life in another country—may accompany and exacerbate more broadly recognized risk factors for abuse. In the case of Little Diana, Mrs. Molina may have feared that discovery by authorities would threaten her status as a US resident. It is also reasonable to wonder whether other common risk factors were present in the Molina household, including substance abuse, domestic violence, social isolation, parental views of punishment and developmental expectations, and psychopathology. Unfortunately, Little Diana's family appeared to have no contact with agencies that could have initiated interventions to address such issues. How can professionals and groups work together to provide services to immigrant families who may fear deportation, yet also be at risk for child maltreatment? Can family violence coalitions provide support to families who fear being identified or cannot easily access services because of linguistic or cultural barriers? Although the answers to these questions are complex, it seems vital for child abuse advocates to increase efforts to provide at-risk families, regardless of ethnic or citizenship status, access to social services. These collaborative efforts may be particularly crucial in cases where there is a presence of multiple risk factors for abuse.

A second area in which increased advocacy is needed concerns the rehabilitation and treatment of convicted child abuse perpetrators. Currently, the majority of psychosocial interventions are aimed at ensuring the physical safety of children in the aftermath of abuse and, occasionally, providing psychological interventions to victimized children and non-offending parents. As important as these efforts are, the "other side of the coin" (ie, perpetrator treatment) has too often been overlooked as a potential point of intervention to prevent the recurrence of abuse. Although the primary offender in Little Diana's case is likely to remain incarcerated for life, most abusers are eventually re-integrated into society without having experienced remedial services during their imprisonment. Indeed, the period of confinement represents an opportune time to attempt treatment and rehabilitation of child abuse offenders. Unfortunately, although inmates occasionally receive services for select issues such as alcohol and drug problems, rehabilitation for physical child abusers is practically unheard of within the US corrections system. Especially concerning is the likelihood that Mrs. Molina, who will be released within a few years, will not receive abuse-specific education or intervention to reduce the risk of subsequently repeating her patterns of neglectful parenting. In Mrs. Molina's case, imprisonment provides an opportunity to provide education regarding the need for appropriate protective supervision and developmental expectations of children, as well as individual therapy to address issues that maintained her abusive relationship with her husband. Although criminal punishment may be the primary societal motivation behind incarceration, confinement also presents a unique opportunity to implement remedial steps to reduce the perpetration of future abuse.

Morbidity/Mortality and Risk Factor Information

Conceptual Issues

Child maltreatment is not a new phenomenon. However, research, practice, and advocacy efforts in this field have been relatively slow to develop.[1] Child physical abuse and neglect began to receive increased attention in the early 1960s, following the efforts of pediatrician Henry Kempe and his colleagues, who coined the term "battered child syndrome" to describe traumatic injury inflicted upon children by parents.[2] Kempe and his colleagues directed much of their efforts at describing the syndrome of child abuse in terms of the injury and physical impairments caused to children, and focused on parental factors (eg, psychopathology) as contributing factors. The efforts of Kempe and colleagues sparked an interest in the topic of child physical abuse and neglect that continues today, although professionals still struggle with how to define these phenomena. In fact, as noted by the National Research Council,[1] little progress has been made in generating a clear and consistent definition of child abuse and neglect in the past several decades. Some researchers have further observed that investigators may shape their definitions to fit the agenda of inquiry.[3] For example, a researcher's definition may be based on his or her theoretical orientation, whereas legal professionals may focus on documentation of abusive acts.[3] Regardless of one's definitional goal, researchers acknowledge that child maltreatment is a complex and heterogeneous problem[4-6] that is difficult to define.[7,8]

Many experts have noted that determining whether an act is abusive involves consideration of a variety of factors surrounding the behavior. Regarding physical abuse, for example, Zuravin[6] acknowledged the importance of taking into account the potential for severe consequences of an act (eg, slapping versus scalding). Other important factors deserving consideration include prevalence, severity, chronicity, duration, and age of onset of abuse[6,7,9,10] as well as the impact of cultural and community values on parents' socialization practices.[7] Moreover, although data suggest that almost all children in the United States have experienced corporal punishment (eg, spanking, slapping) at some point,[11-13] there is lack of consensus regarding whether this form of discipline should be considered abusive. Views among even prominent child abuse experts vary on this issue, with some proposing that corporal punishment has harmful effects for children (eg, antisocial behavior) and that discipline should never involve spanking,[14,15] while others question the link between spanking and detrimental effects, and suggest that corporal punishment may be as effective as other means of discipline.[16] Thus, distinguishing between acts that constitute an extreme form of physical discipline and those that qualify as abuse is quite problematic.[17,18]

Not only is it difficult to establish a consistent operational definition of child physical abuse, some researchers propose that the current conceptual divide between unintentional child injury and intentional injury to children is a false dichotomy.[19,20] More specifically, these researchers argue that the two areas of research are likely part of a larger, multifaceted phenomenon, noting that both fields have much in common.[20] For example, Peterson and Brown[20] note that virtually all serious injuries to children could be prevented, thus, the label of neglect becomes "meaningless" (p. 297).

Moreover, although some make the distinction that unintentional injuries are "accidental" and that intentional injuries involve an intent to harm, investigators have reported that the risk factors for both categories of injury are similar, regardless of intent.[19] Consequently, as noted by Liller,[19] the continued distinction between these types of injury to children may preclude collaborative prevention and intervention efforts that may apply to the broader field of violence to children. Thus, it has been argued that rather than classifying abuse as unintentional or nonaccidental, both child physical abuse and neglect are better conceptualized as a violation of standards of care for children.[21]

Although some consider neglect to be "the central feature of all maltreatment,"[22] this form of abuse has been the focus of far fewer investigative efforts than has physical abuse. The many difficulties encountered in trying to operationalize neglect may be one reason why this form of abuse has received less attention. First, and possibly most problematic, is the difficulty in determining which parental behaviors constitute minimum standards of care. This task is challenging because it involves placing a subjective judgment on what "adequate" parenting/caregiver behavior involves.[23] Further, the detrimental effects of neglect may be difficult to observe, particularly in the short-term. Thus, many professionals have suggested that definitions of neglect should not be contingent upon the presence of short-term sequelae because, in many cases, the effects of neglect do not emerge in the immediate aftermath of maltreatment.[22]

Definitions of Child Physical Abuse and Neglect

Despite difficulties in formulating cohesive definitions of child physical abuse and neglect, several concepts have converged in the literature to provide some conceptual consistency. As cited by Peterson and Brown,[20] a common definition of child abuse and neglect includes intentional harm to a child's development as a result of contact with a caregiver.[24] States are mandated by the federal government to incorporate the following into determinations of child maltreatment: 1) "Any recent act or failure to act on the part of a parent or caretaker which results in death, serious physical or emotional harm, sexual abuse or exploitation" or 2) "An act or failure to act which presents an imminent risk or serious harm."[25,26] Further, physical abuse is often conceptualized as encompassing act(s) of commission in which a caregiver intentionally inflicts physical pain or injury upon a child.[6,17,27] Conversely, neglect is thought of as encompassing act(s) of omission, or failure to provide for a child in a manner that promotes healthy growth and development.[6,23,27]

Consistent with these perspectives, the National Center for Child Abuse and Neglect (NCCAN)[26] defined child physical abuse as "physical injury (ranging from minor bruises to severe fractures or death) as a result of punching, beating, kicking, biting, shaking, throwing, stabbing, choking, hitting (with a hand, stick, strap, or other object), burning, or otherwise harming a child" (p. 2). Moreover, any behavior that results in injury to a child qualifies as abuse, regardless of the caregiver's intent. In addition, NCCAN defines neglect as a "failure to provide for a child's basic needs" in one or more of the following areas: physical, medical, educational, and emotional (p. 1). Supplementary categories of neglect have been proposed, such as mental health neglect,[22] supervisory neglect,[1] and abandonment.[28] Thus, in determining neglectful behaviors, areas of providing proper nutrition and shelter, protection from harm, appropriate medical, mental health, and educational services for children, and attention to a child's physical, psychological, and emotional needs must be considered.[22,28]

Physical Injury and Death

According to the National Research Council,[1] the increase in reported cases of child maltreatment has caused some to label the phenomenon an "epidemic." Data from the National Incidence Study of Child Abuse and Neglect (NIS-3) suggest that between 1993 and 1994, 614 100 children were deemed at-risk for harm from physical abuse, 1 335 100 from physical neglect, and 585 100 from emotional neglect.[29] Similarly, an investigation of maltreatment cases reported to Child Protective Services indicates a national victimization rate of 12.3 per every 1000 children (18.6% physically abused; 60.5% neglected[26]). However, databases that include only reported incidents of abuse underestimate the actual prevalence of child maltreatment. Surveys including non-reported abuse incidents suggest an estimated 110 incidents of parental assault per 1000 children occur in a one-year period.[30]

Injuries sustained from acts of abuse range from minor physical injuries (eg, bruises) to serious disfigurement and disability. Obviously, the most severe consequence of child abuse is death. According to Daro,[31] deaths related to child abuse are a leading cause of both infant and child mortality. It has been reported that an estimated 1400 children died from some form of child abuse or neglect in 2002.[26] Approximately two-thirds of all maltreatment deaths are related to child physical abuse.[32] Furthermore, it has been suggested that many injuries classified as unintentional were in fact due to child abuse or neglect and that as many as 50% to 60% of deaths that are a result of abuse or neglect are not recorded.[33] Thus, it is likely that mortality rates may be higher than estimated.[34] Children who sustain physical force or violent shaking often suffer head injuries, which are one of the most life-threatening injuries related to maltreatment.[35] In fact, head injuries are the most common cause of death in maltreated children and it has been estimated that approximately 20% to 25% of infants who suffer from shaken-baby syndrome die as a result of their injuries.[36] Other common injuries sustained by abused children are burns, chest and abdominal injuries, and fractures.[9,37] Finally, neglect may result in growth and developmental delays, lead poisoning, and failure to thrive.[9,38]

Short- and Long-Term Psychological Consequences

In general, maltreated children may experience a variety of detrimental abuse-related outcomes, including intellectual difficulties, and impaired physical, social, and psychological development. In particular, abuse and neglect are associated with poorer long-term physical health among children (eg, cancer, heart disease[26]). Moreover, child physical abuse has been linked to emotional difficulties such as depression, anxiety, and suicide attempts,[39,40] impaired language and cognitive development, as well as poor academic achievement,[26] and externalizing behaviors (eg, heightened oppositionality and aggression).[41] Research specifically examining neglect has suggested that neglected children experience disruptions in attachment and various psychological factors such as self-esteem[42,43] as well as cognitive deficits, particularly when coupled with a child's failure to thrive.[44] Additionally, it has been found that neglected children exhibit impaired social interactions and are seen as dependent and distractible in classroom settings.[45]

Not only do maltreated children experience short-term cognitive, emotional, and behavioral difficulties, but the detrimental effects of abuse and neglect have been shown to extend beyond childhood. For example, research has demonstrated that internalizing symptoms are seen not only in abused children, but also adolescents[46] and that physical abuse is associated with many internalizing as well as externalizing mental health diagnoses in both children and adolescents.[47] In fact, adolescence may be a particularly troublesome time for physically abused and neglected children, as maltreatment is associated with higher rates of delinquency among youth.[48,49] Even beyond adolescence, the effects of child maltreatment have also been found to extend into adulthood. For example, physical abuse is associated with an increased likelihood of violence in subsequent dating relationships as well as greater rates of perpetrating abuse against one's children.[28] Widom[51] has also documented associations with child physical abuse and adult violence. Further, adults abused as children also display greater rates of substance abuse[50] and have been found to be four times more likely to experience personality disorders during early adulthood.[52]

Costs

Although children bear the overwhelming personal costs of physical abuse and neglect, the financial toll of maltreatment extends far beyond the boundaries of the child and family. For example, child physical abuse exacts an indirect toll on society through its relationship to violent crime, symptoms of antisocial personality disorder, prostitution, and lower I.Q.[52] Abuse-related costs can also be seen in loss of job productivity by adults with a history of abuse and neglect, and such costs have been estimated at more than $69 million per year.[53] Direct costs to society include those incurred through the child welfare system, which investigates potential incidents of abuse and neglect, as well as costs to mental health, legal, healthcare, and judicial systems.[26] The cost of providing services to maltreated families has been estimated to be $24 billion per year.[53]

Risk Factors

Child

Investigations to determine individual child risk factors for abuse and neglect often produce inconsistent and contradictory results.[1] Difficulties in such research include disentangling those factors that truly serve as risk variables, and those that are consequences of abuse. However, such research efforts have provided insight into potential child-related factors that may place children at increased risk for physical abuse and neglect. For example, data suggest that child fatalities are more common among young children, particularly those under the age of three.[26] Further, health status (eg, physical and emotional disabilities) and difficult temperament/behavior (eg, increased oppositionality) have also been linked to an increased risk for maltreatment.[18,26] NCCAN[45] suggests that childhood trauma, birth-related difficulties (eg, premature birth, exposure to toxins), and involvement with antisocial peer groups are risk factors for child abuse and neglect. However, it is important to note that investigators have suggested that child risk factors may play a greater role in the maintenance of abusive and neglectful behaviors, rather than their onset.[54,55]

Parent

A number of factors related to caregivers place children at an increased risk for physical abuse and neglect. With regard to fatalities, those related to child physical abuse are more often caused by male caregivers, including fathers, and those associated with neglect tend to be due to mothers.[26] Furthermore, data suggest that younger parents are more likely to physically abuse their children[56] and that abusive mothers report decreased social support networks.[57] Kolko[18] summarizes a number of parental factors associated with child maltreatment, including those with a history of abuse, increased stress, maladaptive coping strategies (eg, anger management difficulties, emotion-focused coping) and psychological factors (eg, depression). Additionally, parental substance abuse and parenting styles that are inconsistent or overly controlling or critical have been linked to physical abuse and neglect.[18] Caregivers who have inappropriate developmental expectations of their children and those who demonstrate negative attributions about their children's behaviors are also at an increased risk for maltreatment.[26]

Family

Ecologically-based models of child maltreatment suggest that abuse is a product not only of the immediate family context, but also of the relationship of the family with the surrounding environmental influences.[58] Indeed, although maltreatment occurs within the context of the parent-child relationship, it is a complex phenomenon that results from an interaction of child, parent, and larger societal factors.[38] Thus, a number of family variables, including family interactions with the broader community and societal contexts, may place a child at increased risk of abuse and neglect. More specifically, coercive parent-child interactions and poor family relationships (eg, limited cohesion and satisfaction), unemployment, poverty, marital discord, exposure to domestic violence, and lack of social support have all been suggested as risk factors for maltreatment.[18] Furthermore, NCCAN[26] reported that low socioeconomic status, homelessness, community violence, poor schools, life stressors, divorce, and domestic violence are all family variables that increase the probability that maltreatment will occur. According to researchers, poverty, substance abuse, maternal depression, social isolation, and negative life events (eg, family stress) have been identified as risk factors that have been predictive of neglect specifically.[59]

Up-To-Date Research Findings and Recommendations for Practice

Prevention of Abuse

Due to the potential risk factors associated with abuse and neglect, as well as the deleterious sequelae of maltreatment, efforts at preventing child maltreatment are of enormous importance. Typically, prevention efforts are organized using a primary, secondary, and tertiary framework[60] or the more recent basis for organization, universal, selected, and indicated prevention.[61,62] The majority of treatment approaches can be classified as tertiary/indicated, and sometimes secondary/selected prevention attempts. Thus, this section will largely focus on primary/universal prevention efforts.

As acknowledged by Wekerle and Wolfe,[63] there has been a shift away from the pathological view of abusive and neglectful families toward efforts that attempt to target parenting skills and education, as well as reduce parenting related stress. Thus, the identification of families at-risk for abuse is crucial in prevention efforts. Consequently, similar to many treatment approaches, specific prevention efforts are aimed at assisting and supporting parents. Home visitation programs are one such approach, and often involve targeting new parents to provide education and mold early parent-child interactions.[64] Specific in-home approaches often involve nurse visitation programs, which have demonstrated efficacy in improving caregiving behaviors (ie, reduced rates of maltreatment, as well as medical encounters related to injury), and maternal health care.[65-67] In addition, these programs provide both support and education for parents[28,68] and are recommended in the prevention of child physical abuse.[28]

Related interventions, such as Project SafeCare,[69] target families at-risk for abuse or neglect, and may be classified 'as a secondary/selected effort. This in-home approach has been shown to improve child health care, home safety, and strengthen the parent-child relationship.[69] Alternative universal prevention approaches are group interventions, which provide parents with the opportunity to gain support and knowledge from one another, and are often successful in providing motivation to commit to services due to the support network inherent in the group.[64] Such interventions may be provided by local schools or community-based programs (eg, Head Start) and have been linked to positive outcomes such as increased parental functioning, positive parent-child interactions, and a strengthened social support network.[64]

Rather than target parents specifically, some prevention efforts adopt a broader focus by targeting society in an attempt to prevent child maltreatment. The argument behind this approach is that maltreatment is a product not just of parenting deficits or child behavior problems, but of various social factors (eg, poverty, unemployment) that exert influence on the occurrence of abuse and neglect.[3,70] Examples are efforts at public education, which often utilize the media to publicize child abuse awareness campaigns. Several organizations, both nationwide and at state and local levels have attempted to increase public awareness regarding the problem of child abuse for several decades. For example, Prevent Child Abuse America (PCAA) promoted public service announcements depicting the horrors of abuse beginning in the 1970s.[64] Such efforts have been associated with increased public awareness, as well as an increase in reports of child abuse.[71] Various other efforts, including the Blue Ribbon Campaign to Prevent Child Abuse in Virginia and the Nebraska Health and Human Services public awareness campaign entitled, "You Have the Power to Protect a Child" represent state-wide approaches to alert society to the tragedy of child abuse. The former campaign includes television and radio spots highlighting child maltreatment as well as newspaper advertisements.

Treatment Approaches

Once physical abuse has occurred, interventions include those that target the individual child, those that focus on the parent, family treatment, and multisystemic approaches. For neglectful families, interventions primarily focus on caregivers' parenting behaviors. Such interventions are typically time intensive and involve multiple providers. What follows is a brief overview of some of the main treatment approaches for child physical abuse and neglect.

Child-focused interventions

The treatment of abused and neglected children can be challenging because there is no consistent clinical picture of an abused child. Thus, as noted by Wurtele,[72] there are several potential domains of intervention (eg, physical, cognitive, behavioral, socioemotional); effective treatment must involve comprehensive assessment across these domains to determine the necessary targets for intervention. Interventions directed at physically abused children may initially involve medical practitioners to treat physical injury, as well as set the foundation for later psychological, psychosocial, and legal intervention.[38] For neglected children, initial intervention will likely also involve medical intervention to establish a stable environment and determine the developmental, educational, and medical and emotional health status of the child.[38] Psychological interventions for maltreated children are designed to assist them in managing the emotional and behavioral sequelae of physical abuse and neglect. Such interventions include day treatment programs, individual therapy, and play therapy sessions.[28] Although studies have demonstrated the effectiveness of child-focused interventions,[73,74] continued research in this area is necessary, as most of these investigations have involved young children and have not differentiated between types of abuse.

Despite some limitations in the literature, the National Crime Victims Research and Treatment Center (NCVRTC) recently prepared a report synthesizing current knowledge about the effectiveness of interventions for abuse and neglect and with goals involving organizing treatment approaches with empirical support of both efficacy and effectiveness (*Child Physical and Sexual Abuse: Guidelines for Treatment [Revised Report: April 26, 2004]*).[75] Although some treatments in the report receive the highest rating, indicating an empirically-supported, efficacious treatment, the majority of the treatments were classified only as "supported and acceptable" (see Chambless and Ollendick[76] for details of effective and efficacious classification criteria). The majority of interventions for abused and neglected children are tertiary approaches.

One approach noted in the NCVRTC report is cognitive behavioral therapy (CBT), which involves helping children identify and alter abuse-related cognitions, teaching new coping skills to manage the emotional and behavioral symptoms related to abuse, and increasing social competence[77] in an effort to decrease the interpersonal outcomes related to maltreatment. Several CBT approaches have demonstrated empirical support and are considered acceptable treatments for maltreated children, including an individual child physical abuse-focused CBT protocol by Kolko and Swenson[78] that consists of child components that involve addressing views of family violence, coping strategies, interpersonal skills and the use of role-plays, feedback, and homework exercises. CBT approaches for children may also target trauma-related symptoms of abuse, including Cognitive Processing Therapy (CPT)[79] and trauma-focused models of CBT.[80,81] Such interventions are designed to reduce the emotional outcomes related to abuse, as well as address cognitive distortions and negative, abuse-related schemas. Neglected children may evidence a variety of developmental delays; thus, intervention efforts may include therapeutic school settings that focus on addressing cognitive, motor, and social delays, or in the case of severe neglect, hospitalization and medical management.[70]

Parent-focused interventions

As noted, child physical abuse may stem, in part, from increasingly coercive parent-child interactions.[82] More specifically, abusive parents often demonstrate negative conceptualizations of their children (eg, seeing innocuous behaviors as defiant) and perceive that the only effective discipline techniques are those involving physical punishment.[82] Interventions have been used to help maltreating caregivers alter these perceptions and interrupt the coercive patterns that develop with their children. In general, these interventions target children who display behavioral problems and involve teaching parents skills to increase child compliance, decrease disruptive behaviors, and increase positive parent-child interactions.[83]

One model that is widely used with physically abusive parents is Parent Child Interaction Therapy (PCIT),[84] which has received support as an acceptable treatment. When applied to physical abuse, PCIT targets deficits in the dysfunctional parent-child relationship that can lead to violence.[85] PCIT has been shown to reduce child behavior problems and increase positive parent-child interactions.[86] It has also been shown to reduce the incidence of future child abuse reports.[82] Furthermore, PCIT has demonstrated effectiveness across a variety of populations,[84] with treatment gains having been shown to generalize across time,[87] settings,[88] and even to untreated siblings.[89] Several other parent training interventions used with maltreating families include Patterson and Gullion's[90] Living With Children, Forehand's[91] Social Learning Parent Training, and Barkley's[92] Defiant Children.

Family-focused and multisystemic interventions

Family focused interventions not only address individual child (eg, disruptive behavior) and parent (eg, anger management) variables, they also target the parent-child relationship and various family issues (eg, boundaries).[93] For example, intensive family preservation programs (IFPP) provide interventions that may be tailored to a family's needs, and may involve crisis intervention and behavior modification to address a variety of family risk factors.[18,94] Such interventions are designed to prevent the out-of-home placement of abused and neglected children[28] and have not only been shown to prevent children from being placed out-of-home,[95] but have demonstrated improvements in family functioning (eg, communication, behavior problems[96]). An additional family treatment program is the

Parent-Child Education Program,[97] which targets the use of power in discipline and aims to establish positive parent-child interactions. This program involves the use of effective parenting strategies, increasing compliance, strengthening the parent-child relationship, and learning new coping strategies to deal with parenting stress.[98] Another family-focused intervention is Physical Abuse-Informed Family Therapy,[99] which includes each family member and addresses understanding of coercive behavior, problemsolving, and communication skills. This treatment has been shown to improve child outcomes related to abuse and reduce violence when compared to traditional community services.[99]

According to the perspective of multisystemic approaches, abusive behaviors are maintained through interactions between a variety of factors within the systems (eg, family, school, peer, society) surrounding the behavior.[100] Therefore, these treatment approaches are aimed at a number of factors, including systemic problems, which may aid families in maintaining motivation to change,[101] as well as reducing the stress level of abusive parents so that therapeutic concerns can be addressed.[28] Abusive families may display a wide variety of dysfunction that requires the provision of multiple services, and multisystemic and societal approaches emphasize this need.[18] A well-known approach for abusive and neglectful families is Multisystemic Therapy (MST).[102] Although created to target antisocial behavior in youth, MST has been used with maltreating and neglectful families and has been shown to improve parent-child interactions when compared to parent training approaches.[103]

Role and Importance of Advocacy

Advocacy has been defined as the pursuit of influencing outcomes—including public policy and resource allocation decisions within political, economic and social systems and institutions—that directly affect people's lives.[104] Much like those with severe mental illnesses, children, as a constituency, are lacking in the ability to advocate for themselves. They must instead depend upon others to work on their behalf toward the prevention of abuse and neglect, and to serve as a voice for their interests when maltreatment does occur. As noted previously, child abuse advocacy might be said to have started with Kempe and colleagues' exposure of the battered child syndrome over 40 years ago. It was this exposure that brought attention to what had previously been considered private family matters, and precipitated scientific and public interest in the physical abuse of children. Today, child abuse advocacy is not a highly organized or integrated movement. Rather, it is a conglomeration of various entities, including specialized organizations, professional associations, and legal and policy groups that work in various ways to reduce the prevalence and impact of child abuse and neglect. Discussed here will be some of the most visible entities representing these groups. To aid readers in learning about child abuse advocacy, Web addresses for relevant organizations are provided.

Specialized Organizations

A fundamental belief of many advocacy groups is that increased societal awareness of abuse can help reduce its prevalence. Along these lines, there are several national organizations that focus on public education campaigns about specific abuse issues. The National Center on Shaken Baby Syndrome (www.dontshake.com), for example, has a mission of educating parents and childcare providers about the dangers of shaking babies and promoting research on the prevention of shaken baby syndrome. The Center also works to train professionals to prevent and identify cases of shaken baby syndrome. Similarly, the National Organization on Fetal Alcohol Syndrome (www. nofas.org) works through communities to help local advocates evaluate and address the prevalence of fetal alcohol syndrome.

There are also organizations with broader objectives that subsume issues related to abuse and neglect. The Child Welfare League of America (www.cwla.org), for example, is a membership organization, dedicated to the overall well-being of children. This organization's advocacy agenda is broad, dealing with a host of interrelated issues, ranging from childcare, to teen pregnancy, to youth substance abuse issues. Child abuse and neglect are also included in this agenda. Within this realm, the League supports community based approaches to preventing abuse and neglect by strengthening families, as well as improving Child Protective Service's ability to address maltreatment. The League also draws attention to specific abuse-related issues, such as baby abandonment. Like the Child Welfare League, the Children's Defense Fund (CDF) (www.childrensdefense.org) pursues a broad child-oriented agenda that includes the problems of under-education, poverty, and illness. Their efforts in the area of maltreatment are based on the belief that partnerships between public child protection agencies, other agencies and organizations serving children, and families themselves, can be most effective in combating abuse. The CDF works at national, state, and local levels. A third organization, Prevent Child Abuse America (www.preventchildabuse.org), also works to advocate for children on multiple levels. This organization serves to influence the legislative process, build awareness, and provide education regarding child abuse and neglect. The organization is also involved in ongoing research efforts to track patterns of child abuse prevention and fatalities.

Professional Membership Associations

Membership associations are multidisciplinary groups consisting of professionals who have a vested interest in reducing the incidence or effects of child abuse and neglect. These nonprofit groups contain members of various fields that span the areas of research, treatment, and policy related to child maltreatment. The American Professional Society on the Abuse of Children (APSAC) (www.apsac.org) is one such group, dedicated to identifying, treating, and preventing child abuse. The group also seeks to educate the public and impact policy on multiple levels. Part of APSAC's mission is fulfilled by local chapters in several states. The International Society for the Prevention of Child Abuse and Neglect (www.ispcan.org) is another prominent organization that promotes the exchange of information related to child maltreatment, with an explicitly global focus. Both of these professional organizations facilitate communication through the publication of newsletters, official society journals that provide outlets for empirical research, and regular conferences to facilitate exchange information and ideas relevant to maltreatment.

Legal and Policy Groups

The Court Appointed Special Advocate (CASA) (www.nationalcasa.org) program represents a significant and growing source of advocacy for abused children within the legal system. Although CASA operates with several different models, the essence of the program consists of volunteers serving as advocates for child abuse and neglect victims who are involved in judicial proceedings. These volunteers (70 000 nationally) are appointed by the court to familiarize themselves with the facts of a case (through interviews with the child, parents, and involved professionals), to develop a relationship with the child victim, and to advocate for that child during legal proceedings. CASAs are able to make official reports to the court regarding recommendations for placing children in permanent, safe living situations. One strength of the CASA program is that data supporting its effectiveness are starting to emerge. For example, there is evidence that CASAs are at least as effective as attorney guardian ad litems in achieving several goals, including: being more likely to make face-to-face contact with children, more likely to file written briefs with the court, and most importantly, having more cases that result in adoption and fewer that involve repeated stints in foster care.[105]

Other law and policy related groups are also involved in child abuse advocacy, at both the national and local levels. The American Bar Association Center for Children and the Law (www.abanet.org/child/home.html) was formed in the late 1970s exclusively to focus on issues of child abuse and neglect. Although its purview has expanded, the Center remains involved in abuse and neglect issues, ranging from improving the judicial processes related to abuse and neglect, to developing alternative techniques for the forensic interviewing of child victims, and influencing public policy that impacts the well-being of children.

On more of a state than national level are law and policy centers that seek to monitor legal and policy matters related to abuse and neglect, and to empirically evaluate their implementation and effectiveness. Staffed primarily by attorneys and behavioral and social scientists, these centers attempt to link research to the legislative and policy issues that affect families, such as poverty, domestic violence, unwanted pregnancy, and matters related to abuse and neglect, including child welfare reform, the foster care system, and juvenile justice. One such center is the Center for Children, Families, and the Law at the University of Nebraska-Lincoln (ccfl.unl.edu). Established in 1987, the Center fulfills it mission through a combination of research, outreach, and training activities, which include competency-based case management training for child protection and safety workers in the state of Nebraska.

Critics of Child Advocacy

Advocacy groups are in the vanguard of efforts to reduce and prevent child abuse and neglect. Despite the seemingly indisputable merit of their goals, the abuse advocacy movement is not without detractors. Some opposition groups have coalesced around the notion that individuals are sometimes accused falsely of child abuse. A quick search of the Web uncovers sites such as the Resource Center to Help the Falsely Accused (www.accused.com), which claims that extreme cases of abuse involving severe injuries are rare yet often used by advocate groups to promote their legislative agendas. This group also attempts to focus attention on cases of accidental injury that are wrongly prosecuted as abuse, as well as to highlight a supposed blurring of boundaries between science and advocacy in the field (eg, trained scientists testifying more like advocates). Although the skepticism brought about by these groups may have been useful in drawing attention to issues such as the possible overzealous prosecution of child molesters based on adult memories of childhood sexual abuse, advocates may feel that these organizations introduce an unnecessarily adversarial element to issues of child physical abuse and neglect. Of course, just as children have a need for advocacy, so too do opposing interest groups have a right to express their views. Ultimately, it would seem beneficial for child advocates and their critics to engage in more direct dialogue in order to identify common ground and establish consensus about issues such as the scientific validity of adult recollections of abuse and the admissibility of child testimony. After all, both parties would agree that those who are guilty of abuse (and not others) should be prosecuted.

Future Research, Practice, and Advocacy Directions

Research

Researchers have typically divided child maltreatment into different subtypes, including child physical abuse, sexual abuse, neglect, psychological abuse, and exposure to domestic violence. Traditionally, research has been conducted independently in each of these realms. To a large degree, however, the traditional divisions between abuse types—and those who research them—may be false. Households in which one type of abuse occurs are often fraught with other forms as well.[106] Consider, for example, the interrelated nature of physical mistreatment and accompanying emotional and verbal abuse. The failure to examine the overlapping features of different forms of maltreatment has been a limitation in previous research, particularly when looking at the long-term consequences of such acts. Rather than examining the ill effects of isolated abuse types, a more realistic picture of child maltreatment may come from examining the range of outcomes (eg, social, cognitive, occupational) associated with the co-occurrences of multiple abuse types.

A related issue is the need to develop more comprehensive etiological models of child abuse and neglect, and to examine the mechanisms by which they have their impact. Most studies to date have investigated single factor theories of the causes and effects of abuse. However, the complex nature of maltreatment calls for models that take into account multiple contributing factors. Conceptual models that consider transactions among various levels of risk factors have been proposed.[107] However, from both a methodological and resource standpoint, it is difficult to account for the many factors—societal, cultural, family, individual—that play a role in the development of abuse. Longitudinal studies, which follow abused and matched nonabused controls prospectively to evaluate adjustment across time, hold promise for illuminating the complex nature of abuse and neglect. Although a few such studies are in existence, greater use of longitudinal approaches would shed light on important questions about the etiology, consequences, and mechanisms of abuse.

Finally, definitional inconsistencies have long plagued this area of research, limiting generalization of findings and making comparisons across studies difficult. Neglect, in particular, has been difficult to define, probably because of the inherent challenges in measuring the absence of parental behaviors, rather than the more salient acts of commission that constitute physical abuse. The field would benefit from greater consensus regarding what constitutes various abuse types.

Practice

There are several directions in which the prevention and treatment of abuse issues could go in the future. Most importantly, perhaps, is the need for interventionists to utilize current scientific knowledge in the course of practice with maltreated children. As noted previously, prevention and treatment approaches for abused and neglected youth are still in the early stages of development. As more randomized controlled trials are conducted, it will be incumbent upon practitioners to stay abreast of the current findings in order to employ the most empirically supported approaches in their practice. Too often there has been a disconnect between those producing the empirical research on abuse and neglect and the practitioners for whom those findings are most relevant. It will be important for both researchers and practitioners to reach across this divide to offer more coordinated services to those in need.

To date, most empirically supported interventions are aimed at younger children, often preschool age. There is need, however, to extend treatment gains made with younger populations to older victims. Many victims are in late childhood or early adolescence when abuse occurs, or there is a delay in the emergence of symptoms.

Advocacy

Advocates have long led the way in increasing awareness about cutting edge issues related to abuse and neglect. From this standpoint, the advocacy movement is in an excellent position to keep child maltreatment on the "radar" of policy makers and the public at large. Topics such as shaken baby syndrome have come into the public's consciousness largely through advocacy efforts. Advocacy organizations also strive to keep maltreatment issues at the top of policy makers' agendas, so that their cause is not adversely affected by the usual dips in political attention that affect so many social issues. It will be important for the movement to continue to spotlight the topic of abuse and neglect, for not only do traditional problems in the area persist, but new issues emerge all the time (for example, recent awareness of Munchausen's Syndrome by proxy).

There are certain challenges that face the advocacy movement as well. One issue involves the need to remain vigilant about the accurate use of research findings. Whereas the research enterprise is based upon a premise of remaining values-neutral, this is not necessarily the case in the world of advocacy, where—because of passion and ardent beliefs—proponents of a specific viewpoint may sometimes be tempted to pick, choose, or occasionally distort so called "facts" to support a particular cause. Although this may be less of an issue in the field of abuse, which is less politically charged than others (eg, abortion, the environment), it will nevertheless be beneficial for advocates to make continued yet careful use of research findings when supporting their cause. Arguments that are derived from empirical data rather than emotions may help bridge the gap between child abuse advocates and those groups who oppose such causes. After all, it is by basing intervention and policy on sound scientific evidence that children will best be served in the long run.

References

1. National Research Council. *Understanding Child Abuse and Neglect.* Washington, DC: National Academy Press; 1993.

2. Kempe CH, Silverman FN, Steele BF, Droegemueller W, Silver HK. The battered child syndrome. *JAMA.* 1962;181:17–24.

3. Miller-Perrin CL, Perrin RD. *Child Maltreatment: An Introduction.* Thousand Oaks: Sage Publications; 1999.

4. Cicchetti D. The organization and coherence of socioemotional, cognitive, and representational development: Illustrations through a developmental psychopathology perspective on Down syndrome and child maltreatment. In: Thompson RA, ed. *36th Annual Nebraska Symposium on Motivation: Socioemotional development.* Lincoln, NE: University of Nebraska Press; 1990:259–366.

5. Wolfe DA, McGee R. Assessment of emotional status among maltreated children. In: R. H. Starr J, Wolfe DA, eds. *The Effects of Child Abuse and Neglect: Issues and Research.* New York: Guilford; 1991:257–277.

6. Zuravin SJ. Research definitions of child physical abuse and neglect: Current problems. In: R. H. Starr J, Wolfe DA, eds. *The Effects of Child Abuse and Neglect: Issues and Research.* New York: Guilford; 1991:100–128.

7. Wolfe DA. *Child Abuse: Implications for Child Development and Psychopathology.* Newbury Park: Sage Publications; 1987.

8. Wolfe DA. *Child Abuse: Implications for Child Development and Psychopathology (2nd ed.).* Thousand Oaks, CA: Sage Publications; 1999.

9. Hecht DB, Hansen DJ. The environment of child maltreatment: contextual factors and the development of psychopathology. *Aggression and Violent Behavior.* 2001;6:433–457.

10. Widom CS. Motivation and mechanisms in the "cycle of violence". In: Hansen DJ, ed. *Motivation and Child Maltreatment.* Vol 46. Lincoln, NE: University of Nebraska Press; 2000:1–37.

11. Bryan JW, Freed FW. Corporal punishment: Normative data and sociological and psychological correlates in a community college population. *J. of Youth and Adolescence.* 1982;11:77–87.

12. Holden GW, Coleman SM, Schmidt KL. Why 3-year-old children get spanked: Parent and child determinants as reported by college-educated mothers. *Merrill-Palmer Quarterly.* 1995;41:431–452.

13. Straus MA. Corporal punishment, child abuse, and wife-beating: What do they have in common? In: Finkelhor D, Gelles RJ, Hotaling GT, Straus MA, eds. *The Dark Side of Families: Current Family Violence Research.* Newbury Park, CA: Sage; 1983.

14. Straus MA. Corporal punishment and primary prevention of physical abuse. *Child Abuse and Neglect.* 2000;24(9):1109–1114.

15. Straus MA, Stewart JH. Corporal punishment by American parents: National data on prevalence, chronicity, severity, and duration, in relation to child and family characteristics. *Clinical Child and Family Psychology Rev.* 1999;2(2):55–70.

16. Larzelere RE. Child outcomes of nonabusive and customary physical punishment by parents: An updated literature review. *Clinical Child and Family Psychology Rev.* 2000;3(4):199–221.

17. Hansen DJ, Sedlar G, Warner-Rogers JE. Child physical abuse. In: Ammerman RT, Hersen M, eds. *Assessment of Family Violence: A Clinical and Legal Sourcebook.* New York: Wiley; 1999:127–156.

18. Kolko DJ. Child physical abuse. In: Myers JEB, Berliner L, Briere J, Hendrix CT, Jenny C, Reid TA, eds. *The APSAC Handbook on Child Maltreatment (2nd ed.).* Thousand Oaks, CA: Sage; 2002:21–54.

19. Liller KD. The importance of integrating approaches in child abuse/neglect and unintentional injury prevention efforts: Implications for health educators. *The International Electronic J. of Hlth. Educ.* 2001;4:283–289.

20. Peterson L, Brown D. Integrating child injury and abuse-neglect research: Common histories, etiologies, and solutions. *Psychological Bull..* 1994;116(2): 293–315.

21. Garbarino J, Guttmann E, Seeley JW. *The Psychologically Battered Child: Strategies for Identification, Assessment, and Intervention.* San Francisco: Jossey-Bass; 1986.

22. Erickson MF, Egeland B. Child neglect. In: Myers JEB, Berliner L, Briere J, Hendrix CT, Jenny C, Reid TA, eds. *The APSAC Handbook on Child Maltreatment.* Thousand Oaks: Sage Publications; 2002.

23. National Clearinghouse on Child Abuse and Neglect. *Acts of omission: An Overview of Child Neglect.* Washington, DC: US Department of Health and Human Services.; 2001.

24. Helfer RE. A review of the literature on the prevention of child abuse and neglect. *Child Abuse and Neglect.* 1982;6:251–261.

25. National Clearinghouse on Child Abuse and Neglect. *2003 Child Abuse and Neglect State Statute Series Statutes-at-a-Glance: Definitions of Child Abuse and Neglect.* Washington, DC: US Department of Health and Human Services; 2003.

26. National Clearinghouse on Child Abuse and Neglect. *What is Child Abuse and Neglect?* Washington, DC: US Department of Health and Human Services; 2004.

27. Warner-Rogers JE, Hansen, D.J., and Hecht, D.B. Child physical abuse and neglect. In: Van Hasselt H, ed. *Handbook of Psychological Approaches with Violent Offenders: Contemporary Strategies and Issues.* New York: Kluwer Academic/Plenum Publishers; 1999.

28. Barnett OW, Miller-Perrin, C.L., and Perrin, R.D. *Family Violence Across the Lifespan: An Introduction.* Thousand Oaks: Sage; 1997.

29. Sedlak AJ, Broadhurst DD. *Executive Summary of The Third National Incidence Study of Child Abuse and Neglect.* Washington, DC: US Department of Health and Human Services; 1996.

30. Straus MA, Smith C. Violence in Hispanic families in the United States: Incidence rates and structural interpretations. In: Straus MA, Gelles RJ, eds. *Physical Violence in American Families.* New Brunswick, NJ: Transaction Publishers; 1990:341–367.

31. Daro D. *Confronting Child Abuse Research for Effective Program Design.* New York: Free Press; 1988.

32. United States Department of Health and Human Services. *Administration on Children, Youth, and Families. National Child Abuse and Neglect Data System (NCANDS) Glossary.* Washington, DC: US Government Printing Office; 2000.

33. Crume T, DiGuiseppi C, Byers T, Sirotnak A, Garrett C. Underascertainment of child maltreatment fatalities by death certificates, 1990–1998. *Pediatrics.* 2002;110(2):1–6.

34. Wiese D, Daro D. *Current Trends in Child Abuse Reporting and Fatalities: The Results of the 1994 Annual Fifty State Survey.* Chicago: National Committee to Prevent Child Abuse; 1995.

35. Committee on Child Abuse and Neglect. Shaken-baby syndrome: Rotational cranial injuries technical report. *Pediatrics.* 2001;108:206–210.

36. United States Advisory Board on Child Abuse and Neglect *A Nation's Shame: Fatal Child Abuse and Neglect in the United States.* Washington, DC: US Department of Health and Human Services; 1995.

37. Myers JEB. *Legal Issues in Child Abuse and Neglect.* Thousand Oaks, CA: Sage; 1992.

38. Ricci LR. Initial medical treatment of the physically abused child. In: Reece RM, ed. *Treatment of Child Abuse: Common Ground for Mental Health, Medical, and Legal Practitioners.* Baltimore: The Johns Hopkins University Press; 2000:81–94.

39. Johnson RM, Kotch JB, Catellier DJ, Winsor JR, Dufort V, Hunter W. Adverse behavioral and emotional outcomes from child abuse and witnessed violence. *Child Maltreatment.* 2002;7:179–186.

40. Silverman AB, Reinherz HZ, Giaconia RM. The long-term sequelae of child and adolescent abuse: A longitudinal community study. *Child Abuse and Neglect.* 1996;20:709–723.

41. Trickett PK, Kuczynski L. Children's misbehaviors and parental discipline strategies in abusive and nonabusive families. *Developmental Psychology.* 1986;22(1):115–123.

42. Egeland B. A longitudinal study of high-risk families: Issues and findings. In: R. H. Starr J, Wolfe DA, eds. *The Effects of Child Abuse and Neglect: Issues and Research.* New York: Guilford; 1991:33–56.

43. Kaufman J, Cicchetti D. Effects of maltreatment on school-age children's socio-emotional development: Assessments in a day-camp setting. *Developmental Psychology.* 1989;25(4):516–524.

44. Mackner LM, Starr RH, Black MM. The cumulative effect of neglect and failure to thrive on cognitive functioning. *Child Abuse and Neglect.* 1997;21: 691–700.

45. National Clearinghouse on Child Abuse and Neglect . *Recognizing Child Abuse and Neglect: Signs and Symptoms.* Washington, DC: US Department of Health and Human Services; 2003.

46. Pelcovitz D, Kaplan S, Goldenberg B, Mandel F. Posttraumatic stress disorder in physically abused adolescents. *J. of the American Academy of Child and Adolescent Psychiatry.* 1994;33(3):305–312.

47. Flisher AJ, Kramer RA, Hoven CW, et al. Psychosocial characteristics of physically abused children and adolescents. *J. of the American Academy of Child and Adolescent Psychiatry.* 1997;36(1):123–131.

48. Kelley BT, Thornberry TP, Smith CA. *In the Wake of Childhood Maltreatment.* Washington, DC: National Institute of Justice; 1997.

49. Widom CS. Child abuse, neglect and adult behavior: Research design and findings on criminality, violence, and child abuse. *American J. of Orthopsychiatry.* 1989;58:260–270.

50. Malinosky-Rummell R, Hansen DJ. Long-term consequences of childhood physical abuse. *Psychological Bull.* 1993;114(1):68–79.

51. Widom CS. Does violence beget violence? A critical examination of the literature. *Psychological Bull.* 1989;106(1):3–28.

52. Johnson J, Cohen P, Brown J, Smailes EM, Bernstein DP. Childhood maltreatment increases risk for personality disorders during early adulthood. *Archives of General Psychiatry.* 1999;56:600–606.

53. Prevent Child Abuse America. Total estimated cost of child abuse and neglect in the United States [Online:www.preventchildabuse.org/learn_more/research_docs/cost_analysis.pdf]. Accessed July, 2003.

54. Ammerman RT. The role of the child in physical abuse: A reappraisal. *Violence and Victims.* 1991;6(2):87–101.

55. Wolfe DA. Child-abusive parents: An empirical review and analysis. *Psychological Bull.* 1985;97(3):462–482.

56. Brown J, Cohen P, Johnson J, Salzinger S. A longitudinal analysis of risk factors for child maltreatment: Findings of a prospective study of officially recorded and self-reported child abuse and neglect. *Child Abuse and Neglect.* 1998;22:1065–1079.

57. Bishop SJ, Leadbeater BJ. Maternal social support patterns and child maltreatment: Comparison of maltreating and nonmaltreating mothers. *American J. of Orthopsychiatry.* 1999;69(2):172–181.

58. Belsky J. Etiology of child maltreatment: A developmental-ecological analysis. *Psychological Bull.* 1993;114(3):413–434.

59. Ondersma SJ. Predictors of neglect within low-SES families: The importance of substance abuse. *American J. of Orthopsychiatry.* 2002;72(3):383–391.

60. Commission on Chronic Illness. *Chronic Illness in the United States, Vol. 1.* Cambridge, MA: Harvard University Press; 1957.

61. Mrazek PJ, Haggerty RJ. *Reducing Risks for Mental Disorders.* Washington, DC: National Academy Press; 1994.

62. Guterman NB. Advancing prevention research on child abuse, youth violence, and domestic violence: Emerging strategies and issues. *J. of Interpersonal Violence.* 2004;19(3):299–321.

63. Wekerle C, Wolfe DA. The role of child maltreatment and attachment style in adolescent relationship violence. *Development and Psychopathology.* 1998;10:571–586.

64. Daro D, Donnelly AC. Child abuse prevention: Accomplishments and challenges. In: Myers JEB, Berliner L, Briere J, Hendrix CT, Jenny C, Reid TA, eds. *The APSAC Handbook on Child Maltreatment, 2nd ed.* Thousand Oaks, CA: Sage; 2002.

65. Eckenrode J, Zielinski D, Smith E, et al. Child maltreatment and the early onset of problem behaviors: Can a program of nurse home visitation break the link? *Development and Psychopathology.* 2001;13:873–890.

66. Korfmacher J, Kitzman H, Olds DL. Intervention processes as predictors of outcomes in a preventive home-visitation program. *Journal of Community Psychology, Special issue: Home Visitation II.* 1998;26(1):49–64.

67. Olds DL, Henderson CR, Kitzman H, Eckenrode J, Cole R, Tatelbaum R. The promise of home visitation: Results of two randomized trials. *J. of Community Psychology.* 1998;26(1):5–21.

68. Roberts RN, Wasik BH, Casto G, Ramey CT. Family support in the home: Programs, policy, and social change. *American Psychologist.* 1991;46:131–137.

69. Gershater-Molko RM, Lutzker JR, Wesch D. Project SafeCare: Improving health, safety, and parenting skills in families reported for, and at-risk for child maltreatment. *J. of Family Violence.* 2003;18(6):377–389.

70. Gelles RJ, Straus MA. *Intimate Violence.* New York: Simon and Schuster; 1988.

71. McCurdy K, Daro D. Current trends in child abuse reporting and fatalities. *Journal of Interpersonal Violence.* 1994;9:75–94.

72. Wurtele S. Victims of Child Maltreatment. In: Singh N, ed. *Applications in Diverse Populations.* Vol 9. 1 ed: Elsevier; 1998:341–358.

73. Oates RK, Bross DC. What have we learned about treating child physical abuse? A literature review of the last decade. *Child Abuse and Neglect.* 1995;19: 463–473.

74. Wolfe DA, Wekerle C. Treatment strategies for child physical abuse and neglect: A critical progress report. *Clinical Psychology Rev.* 1993;13:473–500.

75. Saunders BE, Berliner L, Hanson RFE. *Child Physical and Sexual Abuse: Guidelines for Treatment (Revised Report: April 26, 2004).* Charleston, SC: National Crime Victims Research and Treatment Center; 2004.

76. Chambless DL, Ollendick TH. Empirically supported psychological interventions: Controversies and evidence. *Annual Rev. of Psychology.* 2000;52:685–716.

77. Bonner B. Cognitive-behavioral and Dynamic Play Therapy for children with sexual behavior problems and their caregivers. In: Saunders BE, Berliner L, Hanson RF, eds. *Child Physical and Sexual Abuse: Guidelines for Treatment (Revised Report: April 26, 2004)*. Charleston, SC: National Crime Victims Research and Treatment Center; 2004.

78. Kolko DJ, Swenson CC. *Assessing and Treating Physically Abused Children and Their Families: A Cognitive-Behavioral Approach*. Thousand Oaks, CA: Sage; 2002.

79. Resick PA, Schnicke MK. *Cognitive Processing Therapy for Rape Victims: A Treatment Manual*. Newbury Park, CA: Sage; 1993.

80. Deblinger E, Heflin AH. *Treatment for Sexually Abused Children and Their Non-Offending Parents: A Cognitive-Behavioral Approach*. Thousand Oaks, CA: Sage; 1996.

81. Cohen JA, Mannarino AP. A treatment model of sexually abused preschoolers. *Journal of Interpersonal Violence*. 1993;8:115–131.

82. Chaffin M, Silovsky JF, Funderburk B, Valle LA, Brestan EV, Balachova T. Parent-child interaction therapy with physically abusive parents: Efficacy for reducing future abuse reports. *J. of Consulting and Clinical Psychology*. 2004;72: 500-510.

83. Brestan E, Payne H. Behavioral parent training interventions for conduct-disordered children. In: Saunders BE, Berliner L, Hanson RF, eds. *Child Physical and Sexual Abuse: Guidelines for Treatment (Revised Report: April 26, 2004)*. Charleston, SC: National Crime Victims Research and Treatment Center; 2004.

84. Hembree-Kigin TL, McNeil CB. *Parent-Child Interaction Therapy*. New York: Plenum Press; 1995.

85. Urquiza A. Parent-child interaction therapy (PCIT). In: Saunders BE, Berliner L, Hanson RF, eds. *Child Physical and Sexual Abuse: Guidelines for Treatment (Revised Report: April 26, 2004)*. Charleston, SC: National Crime Victims Research and Treatment Center; 2004.

86. Borrego J, Urquiza A, Rasmussen R, Zebell N. Parent-child interaction therapy with a family at high risk for physical abuse. *Child Maltreatment*. 1999;4: 331–342.

87. Eyberg SM, Funderburk BW, Hembree-Kigin TL, McNeil CB, Querido JG, Hood KK. Parent-child interaction therapy with behavior problem children: One and two year maintenance of treatment effects in the family. *Child and Family Behavior Therapy*. 2001;23:1–20.

88. McNeil CB, Eyberg SM, Eisenstadt TH, Newcomb K, Funderburk B. Parent-child interaction therapy with behavior problem children: Generalization of treatment effects to the school setting. *J. of Child Clinical Psychology*. 1991;20: 140–151.

89. Brestan EV, Eyberg SM, Boggs SR, Algina J. Parent-child interaction therapy: Parents' perceptions of untreated siblings. *Child and Family Behavior Therapy*. 1997;19:13–28.

90. Patterson GR, Gullion ME. *Living with Children: New Methods for Parents and Teachers*. Champaign, IL: Research Press; 1968.

91. Forehand R, McMahon R. *Helping the Noncompliant Child: A Clinician's Guide to Parent Training*. New York: Guilford; 1981.

92. Barkley RA. *Defiant children: A Clinician's Manual for Assessment and Parent Training*. New York: Guilford; 1997.

93. Ralston ME, Sosnowski PB. Family focused, child centered treatment interventions in child maltreatment. In: Saunders BE, Berliner L, Hanson RF, eds. *Child Physical and Sexual Abuse: Guidelines for Treatment (Revised Report: April 26, 2004)*. Charleston, SC: National Crime Victims Research and Treatment Center; 2004.

94. Haapala DA, Kinney JM. Avoiding out-of-home placement of high-risk status offenders through the use of intensive family preservation services. *Criminal Justice and Behavior.* 1988;15:334–348.

95. Bath HI, Haapala DA. Intensive family preservation services with abused and neglected children: An examination of group differences. *Child Abuse and Neglect.* 1993;17:213–225.

96. Blythe BJ, Jiordano MJ, Kelly SA. Family preservation with substance abusing families: Help that works. *Child, Youth, and Family Services Quarterly.* 1991;14: 12–13.

97. Wolfe DA. *Preventing Physical and Emotional Abuse of Children.* New York: Guilford; 1991.

98. Wolfe DA. Parent-child education program for physically abusive parents. In: Saunders BE, Berliner L, Hanson RF, eds. *Child Physical and Sexual Abuse: Guidelines for Treatment (Revised Report: April 26, 2004).* Charleston, SC: National Crime Victims Research and Treatment Center; 2004.

99. Kolko DJ. Individual cognitive behavioral therapy and family therapy for physically abused children and their offending parents: A comparison of clinical outcomes. *Child Maltreatment.* 1996;1:322–342.

100. Bronfenbrenner U. *The ecology of human development: Experiments by Nature and Design.* Cambridge, MA: Harvard University Press; 1979.

101. Ayoub C, Willett JB, Robinson DS. Families at risk of child maltreatment: Entry-level characteristics and growth in family functioning during treatment. *Child Abuse and Neglect.* 1992;16:495-511.

102. Henggeler SW, Schoenwald SK, Borduin CM, Rowland MD, Cunningham PB. *Multisystemic Treatment of Antisocial Behavior in Children and Adolescents.* New York: Guilford; 1998.

103. Brunk M, Henggeler SW, Whelan JP. A comparison of multisystemic therapy and parent training in the brief treatment of child abuse and neglect. *J. of Consulting and Clinical Psychology.* 1987;55:311–318.

104. Advocacy Institute page. Available at: www.advocacy.org. Accessed August 10, 2004.

105. Youngclarke D, Ramos KD, Granger-Merkle L. A Systematic Review of the Impact of Court Appointed Special Advocates. *The Journal of the Center for Families, Children and the Courts.* in press.

106. Clemmons JC, DiLillo D, Martinez IG, DeGue S, Jeffcott M. Co-occurring forms of child maltreatment and adult adjustment reported by Latina college students. *Child Abuse and Neglect.* 2003;27:751-767.

107. Cicchetti D, Lynch M. Toward an ecological/transactional model of community violence and child maltreatment: consequences for children's development. *Psychiatry.* 1993;56:96-118.

CHAPTER 12

Firearm Injuries

Shannon Frattaroli, PhD, MPH,[1] Sara B. Johnson, PhD, MPH,[1] and Stephen P. Teret, JD, MPH[2]

A nthony, at age 13, had little reason to believe that his father's semi-automatic pistol was loaded when he pointed it at his best friend, Eric, age 14, and pulled the trigger.

Earlier that afternoon, when the two boys left school, they went to Anthony's house for a snack and to play. Anthony's mother had an appointment that took her away from home, so the boys fended for themselves. After eating, Anthony said to Eric "Come with me. I want to show you something." They went upstairs to Anthony's parent's bedroom, where Anthony opened the door to his father's closet, reached up to the shelf, and pulled down the loaded pistol that his father kept there for protection. Anthony removed from the pistol the magazine or clip that held the ammunition, and thinking that the gun was then unloaded, took it downstairs and outside the home where he and Eric could play with it. In the yard, Anthony pointed the gun at Eric's head, saying "BAM!" as he pulled the trigger. The pistol discharged the round that had remained in the chamber, and the bullet entered Eric's face to the left of his nose. Eric fell to the ground, unconscious; Anthony ran back into the house, replaced the gun in his father's closet, and called 911. By the time the first responders got to Anthony's home, Eric had died.*

The story of Anthony and Eric represents a common tragedy that underscores the need to apply effective injury prevention strategies to the firearm injury problem. Over the past few decades, researchers, advocates, and practitioners have advanced the science and practice of injury prevention principles to address the needs of gun violence prevention. In this chapter, we summarize the lessons learned from this work, and suggest directions for advancing the accomplishments to date. While the complex nature of firearm injury presents a formidable challenge for the injury prevention field, it is a challenge that we are well-equipped to face.

---

1 The Johns Hopkins Bloomberg School of Public Health.
2 Professor of Health Policy and Management and Director of the Johns Hopkins Center for Law and the Public's Health.
* The names used in this story are fictional, and the facts are an amalgam taken from actual, similar incidents.

The Nature of Firearm Injury in the United States

Mortality

In 2001, 2937 youth 19 years of age and younger died from firearm injuries. Of these deaths, 60% were homicides, 32% were suicides, 6% were unintentionally inflicted, and 2% were caused by undetermined intent. Eighty-seven percent of young people who were killed by gunfire were male. The disproportionate burden of gun death falls on adolescents between the ages of 15 and 19, who accounted for 86% of people under 20 who died in 2001 as a result of firearm injuries.

While 58% of those who died were white, black youth were disproportionately affected. Considering mortality per 100 000 population, black youth were 3.4 times more likely than white youth to die by gunfire. For violent injuries, the racial differences in gun deaths are even more alarming: black youth are 6.6 times more likely than white youth to die from gun homicide, a figure that grows to 7.7 times among 15–19 year olds.[1]

Youth gun violence began to increase rapidly in the mid-1980s, and reached a peak in the early 1990s. In 1993, young people were killed by guns at a rate of 8 per 100 000; more than twice the 2001 rate (3.64/ 100 000). In recent years the number and rate of gun deaths among youth has declined, but remains high, especially for teenage minority youth.[1,2]

Morbidity

Firearm injuries are among the most lethal types of injury, so the ratio of fatal to non-fatal injuries is smaller in comparison to many other mechanisms of childhood injury. Nonetheless, for every youth killed by gunfire, more than four others are injured. In total, 13 053 children and adolescents under age 20 survived gunshot injuries in 2001 at a rate of 16/ 100 000. Sixty-four percent of these non-fatal injuries resulted from assault, 32% resulted from unintended gunfire, and 3% were a result of suicide attempts. The small proportion of non-fatal firearm suicide attempts reflects the lethality of the method; if one intends to kill himself using a firearm, death will likely result. As with fatal gun injuries, the majority of victims of non-fatal injuries are male (88%) and between the ages of 15 and 19 (90%).[3]

Costs of Gun Violence

Using 1994 data, Cook et al. estimated the lifetime medical cost of gunshot injuries at $2.3 billion annually, approximately half of which is paid for with tax dollars. Nearly three-quarters of the gun-related hospitalizations examined were due to assaults.[4] However, the direct medical costs of gun violence are only a fraction of their total cost to society. Other costs include lost productivity, reduced quality of life, and other intangible costs. Based on a "willingness to pay" analysis, Cook and Ludwig estimated that gun violence costs society approximately $100 billion per year. They attribute $15 billion of these costs to youth gun violence.[5,6] The authors also found that gun violence reduces the quality of life for all children in the US by influencing housing choices and mobility, instilling fear, and restricting freedom of movement.[6]

Risk Factors

Consideration of the risk factors associated with firearm injuries reveals important differences between guns and other injury causing vehicles. Unlike other consumer products for which injury is an unintended consequence, firearms are designed to inflict harm. The ease with which a shooter can discharge a force that is destructive to humans is one important reason that firearms are the most lethal method of suicide and homicide. Despite their danger, the Consumer Product Safety Commission (CPSC) has no jurisdiction over firearms due to a decision by Congress in which the CPSC was explicitly forbidden from regulating guns.[7] As a result, unlike every other consumer product that is legally sold in the United States, the federal government does not regulate the design of guns to protect the public's health and safety.

Firearms are dangerous products to have in the home. Researchers have documented associations between rates of household firearm ownership and firearm homicide, suicide, and unintentional firearm deaths,[8-10] and established that the presence of a gun in the home increases the risk of injury to household residents.[11,12] One study described the burden of living in a gun-owning home by tracing the source of guns used in unintentional or self-inflicted injuries to children and youth. Fifty-seven percent of the self-inflicted gun injuries and 19% of the unintentional gun injuries examined were caused by guns from the victims' parents' homes. Those numbers increased to 90% and 72% when the researchers expanded the gun sources to include the homes of relatives and friends, in addition to parents.[13]

The risk to children associated with guns in the home is modified by many factors, including gun storage. Approximately one-third of homes with children in the United States have a gun.[14,15] In 43% of these homes, parents store their guns unlocked; in 9% parents store their guns unlocked and loaded.[15] Anecdotal evidence and experimental research findings offer vivid evidence of children's curiosity with regard to guns. Researchers who observed young boys playing in a room with a planted, hidden gun documented that when the boys found the gun, 76% of the time they handled it, and in almost half those instances, they pulled the trigger.[16] The American Academy of Pediatrics (AAP) recommends that parents keep homes with children gun-free. However, for parents who choose to bring a gun into the home, AAP advises parents to lock the gun unloaded and store ammunition separately.[17]

The home is a place where too many children and youth can access guns, but the presence of a gun in the home is a risk that parents can eliminate or control. Parents' decisions to keep their homes gun-free do not affect the risks to their children associated with guns accessible outside the home. In a society where guns are plentiful[†] and subject to minimal regulation, that youth report obtaining firearms through corrupt licensed dealers, straw purchasers, unlicensed street dealers, friends, family, acquaintances, and through theft should come as no surprise.[19-22] How best to address these risks in light of available research is the focus of the remainder of this chapter.

---

† Cook and Ludwig estimate that the United States is home to at least 200 million privately owned firearms.[18]

Application of Research to Practice and Advocacy

Strategies for Changing Individual Behavior—Education

Given the dangerous nature of firearms, their prevalence in society, and the many opportunities for children and youth to access guns, strategies that aim to change individuals' behavior in order to minimize or eliminate the risks previously described offer a seemingly logical approach to preventing gun injuries among youth. Several programs designed to teach children to avoid guns they may encounter during play exist, and their sponsoring organizations promote these curricula as effective. An evaluation measuring the impact of firearm safety education programs on children's knowledge gain showed promising results.[23] However, most evaluations that assess whether such programs confer the gun avoidance skills children need to avoid injury demonstrate that such behavior change does not result from completing the programs.[24-26] These findings may not represent the potential of all firearm safety education programs for all children. One evaluation assessed the efficacy of a behavioral skills training program and found that the 6 and 7 year old participants were able to demonstrate the gun avoidance behaviors they were taught when tested in a simulated real world setting. The study's authors note that Himle, et al. did not find the same intervention to be effective with a sample of younger children, and that their own efficacy test was limited both by a lack of long term follow-up and the challenges associated with simulating a real world environment.[27] These findings should be interpreted with caution. Given the allure of guns to naturally curious children, the cognitive limitations that characterize childhood, and the established challenges associated with teaching gun safety to children, there are good reasons to pursue alternative strategies to those that seek to gun-proof children.[28,29]

Parent-oriented educational interventions provide an appealing alternative to those aimed at children. However, evaluations of clinic-based educational programs fail to show an adequately positive impact on gun storage practices among patients of a primary care pediatrics practice[30] or on parents' decisions to remove firearms from the homes of suicidal adolescents.[31] The disappointing results of parent-focused educational programs are not surprising in light of the evidence that parents tend to overestimate their children's ability to act safely in the presence of guns.[32-34] In addition, the viability of pediatrician firearm counseling models is questionable. While pediatricians and pediatric residents express high levels of support for counseling parents about the risk of firearms in the home, a majority failed to report providing such counseling.[35,36]

Clinic-based educational interventions aimed at parents have not translated into the safe storage behaviors intended by the interventions' developers. Findings from North Carolina suggest that a safe storage message alone is insufficient to prompt the desired behavior change. Following a community intervention that included firearm safety counseling and free gun locks, researchers reported increases in self-reported safe firearm storage practices among a cohort of participating gun owners.[37] An Alaskan program that provided gun safes and trigger locks to gun owning families demonstrated an increase in the use of safes on follow-up.[38] This strategy of providing information and products to facilitate safer gun storage builds upon the self-reported behavior change of patients who were offered low or no cost safety products in combination with injury prevention messages in clinical settings.[39] While evaluations of these message/product distribution interventions are promising, the long-term effect on behavior change remains untested. Furthermore, the question of whether these interventions result in the repeated safe behaviors (replacing a trigger lock after every gun use, for example) needed for safe storage practices to affect firearm injury rates is also unanswered.

Educational strategies for preventing firearm injuries are plentiful. As is the case for other areas of injury prevention, the logic and seeming simplicity of strategies that aim to teach people to act safely is a powerful lure. However, evaluations of several educational interventions reveal that attempts to teach children gun avoidance skills may only be effective among certain ages of children, and may require more skill focused training than exists with the most commonly used programs. Furthermore, the tendency of parents to underestimate the risks to their children associated with guns in the home also calls into question the value of parental education and counseling to reduce firearm injury among children. Programs that provide access to the safety products referenced in educational messages do show promise, and any future parent-focused educational efforts should invest the resources needed to provide parents with the information and *means* to reduce the risks posed to their children by keeping guns in the home. The disappointing impact of interventions designed to gun-proof children suggests that real progress on this issue will only result when interventions cease relying on children to keep themselves safe from weapons intended for use by adults.

Strategies for Changing Individual Behavior—Reducing Demand

For adolescents, strategies that aim to reduce the demand for guns offer an alternative behavior change strategy that doesn't rely on the safe behavior messages previously described. Youth report that fear of arrest and incarceration influences their decision-making about whether to acquire and carry guns.[40] How, and the extent to which such fears impact youth gun *behaviors* is not known. The literature concerning adult fear of incarceration and guns suggests harsh sentencing policies do not deter criminal gun activity. An evaluation of the effect of enhanced penalties for felons charged with illegal gun possession concluded that one program, Project Exile, failed to accomplish reductions in gun homicide.[41] Interventions that seek to capitalize on adolescent fear of incarceration, such as the Scared Straight program, have also failed to demonstrate a positive impact on youth criminal behavior.[42]

While programs that rely solely on punishment and incarceration as a strategy for deterring youth gun involvement are ineffective, interventions that threaten punishment in the context of more comprehensive, community-based campaigns are encouraging. In Boston, a community gun violence prevention initiative that included participation from law enforcement (police, prosecutors, parole and probation, the federal Bureau of Alcohol, Tobacco, Firearms and Explosives), the faith community, and gang outreach street workers resulted in dramatic declines in youth gun homicides.[43] The intervention included strategies to reduce the supply of guns to Boston youth in targeted neighborhoods, and Boston youth's demand for guns. Several other communities have experimented with variations on the law enforcement-community partnerships approach to identify, deter, and punish youth gun violence.[44]

The Role of Advocacy and Practice

Evaluations of individual behavior change interventions are instructive with regard to how best to use prevention resources. Interventions that rely solely on educational messages to teach children safe gun behavior, or fear tactics to discourage juvenile delinquency have not been demonstrated effective. There is a need for advocates and practitioners to discourage efforts that rely solely on children's ability to make safe decisions about guns in order to reduce firearm violence. This is a heavy burden that children are ill-equipped to bear.

The individual education model is similarly disappointing when applied to parents. However, more comprehensive approaches that deliver individual behavior change messages in combination with safe storage products have led to changes in gun storage practices. And while fear-based admonitions aimed at dissuading children from engaging in criminal gun behaviors alone are unlikely to affect their decision-making, penalties for gun involvement that are certain and swift, and supported by a community-based infrastructure have yielded impressive results. The challenge for advocates and practitioners therefore is to resist the surface appeal associated with individual behavior change strategies in favor of more comprehensive models that target both individual behavior and the settings in which children make decisions about guns.

Strategies for Designing Safer Guns

Guns are designed to inflict serious or fatal injury. Perhaps it is this fact that has delayed progress on safer gun designs. In 2001, 182 gun deaths and 4136 gun injuries involving children and youth resulted from unintentionally fired guns. These injuries, often referred to by the media as "accidents," are in fact events that occur regularly, with a strikingly similar fact pattern: A child finds an unlocked gun, and in the course of play, the gun discharges, injuring (often fatally) a sibling or playmate.[45,46] The injury profile that began this chapter is a more detailed example of such incidents.

Why guns are operable by children is a question without a reasonable answer. Beginning in the 1970s, injury prevention researchers began advocating for changes in the design of guns that would render them inoperable in a child's hand.[47] "Childproof" gun designs actually date back to the late 1800s when, in response to a child's injury as a result of unintentional gun fire, legend has it that D.B. Wesson of Smith & Wesson fame charged one of his designers to develop a gun that could not be fired by a child.[48] Early designs relied on mechanical impediments to prevent unintended gunfire. As this design strategy evolved, the preference for personalized guns, or guns that could only be fired by an authorized user, took hold. High-technology radio frequency transponders, fingerprint recognition systems, and computer chips became the technologies of choice for the modern personalized gun. The realization that technology could offer the public a gun that is both inoperable by children and operable only by authorized users expanded the potential impact of personalized guns. The availability of such a gun has implications for adolescent suicide prevention, as well as the prevention of assaults and homicides committed with stolen guns.[49-51]

As of this writing, personalized gun technology is not generally available to consumers. Two less sophisticated safety devices, the magazine safety and the loaded chamber indicator,‡ have long been available on select gun models. While the preventive potential of these devices is more modest than personalized gun technology, their life-saving potential is well-documented.[52,53] Had the gun that fired the fatal bullet to Eric's head included either a magazine safety or a loaded chamber indicator, the play of Anthony and Eric described at the start of this chapter would have been a reckless footnote to an otherwise typical day in the lives of two adolescent boys.

The Role of Advocacy and Practice

To date, progress toward increasing the availability of safer guns has been realized through advocacy and practice efforts. In California, advocates organized in support of State Senator Jack Scott's bill requiring that new semi-automatic handguns sold in the state be equipped with a magazine safety and a loaded chamber indicator. The law will be fully in effect in 2007.[54] The Massachusetts legislature enacted into law a bill that requires all handguns sold in the state to meet certain childproofing standards.[55] Under Maryland's Responsible Gun Safety Act of 2000, only handguns with an approved integrated locking mechanism can be sold new in the state. The law also mandates that the state's Handgun Roster Board produce an annual report on the status of personalized gun technology.[56] In 2002, New Jersey passed a law that will permit only personalized guns to be sold in the state once their Attorney General deems the technology ready for public use.[57] Several other state and local governments, as well as the US Congress have considered variations of these safer gun design bills. Continued advances on designing safer guns and assuring their availability to consumers will likely occur only with support and action from advocates and practitioners.§

Regulatory strategies to encourage safer gun design offer an alternative to the legislative approaches previously described. In 1997, Massachusetts Attorney General Scott Harshbarger promulgated the nation's first consumer protection regulations for handguns. This application of executive power established a precedent for translating the consumer safety responsibility of Attorneys General into design safety standards for firearms. While the reach of consumer protection authority by Attorneys General varies among the states, a report issued by a national gun violence prevention organization identifies twenty states with the apparent legal authority needed to regulate gun design using consumer protection powers.[59] This strate-

---

‡ A magazine safety is a built-in feature on some pistols that prevents the gun from firing once the magazine is removed. This feature is important because people often incorrectly believe that a gun has no ammunition when the magazine has been removed. A loaded chamber indicator is a device designed to indicate whether the gun is loaded and ready to fire.
§ A model personalized gun bill, developed by The Johns Hopkins Center for Gun Policy and Research, is available for advocates' and legislators' use.[58]

gy is an important, yet underutilized approach to influencing the safety design features available to gun purchasers.

Efforts to bring safer gun designs to consumers include the use of litigation.[60-64] Whereas legislators may be more susceptible to the influence of the powerful lobbies that oppose calls to mandate safer gun designs, the courts are generally viewed as more independent. Lawsuits initiated by victims of tragedies similar to Anthony and Eric's story may seek monetary damages from gun manufacturers in order to raise the cost of ignoring safety technology and encourage the investment needed to bring safer gun designs to the market. The ultimate success of litigation as a strategy to influence gun manufacturers' design decisions with regard to safety remains to be seen. As of this writing, several cases were pending in courts throughout the country.¶

Strategies for Changing the Environment

Firearm injuries to children and youth are a byproduct of individuals and guns mixing in a particular setting. Interventions aimed at reducing these injuries by adjusting individuals' behaviors, and those that focus on gun design grapple with the human and product factors. Interventions aimed at changing the environment in which firearm injury occurs offer another approach. With an estimated 200 million privately owned guns[18] and a timid regulatory system for minimizing the foreseeable harms that are likely to result from this massive civilian arms stockpile, the United States provides an environment where children and guns too often collide.

Federal oversight of the gun industry and gun sales is perpetually underfunded, under-valued, and in recent decades, under threat of elimination.[65] The weak system of federal oversight contributes to the availability and accessibility of guns to youth.[22,66] In response to the shortcomings at the federal level, some states have enacted laws to control gun commerce within their borders.[67] Evaluations of state policies that: require licensing of gun owners and registration of guns; place limits on the number of guns that can be purchased by an individual; and ban the sale of Saturday night special guns, all demonstrate positive impacts on measures of illegal gun trafficking and easy accessibility.[68-70]

Other strategies seeking to change the environment in which firearm injuries occur focus directly on gun possession. In response to citizen reports or law enforcement intelligence, St. Louis police officers visited the homes of youth allegedly in possession of firearms. Police asked parents for permission to search for and remove firearms believed to be in their child's possession. In order to encourage participation, police removed firearms from the home without pressing charges. The program resulted in police seizing more than 1300 guns in three years.[71] In Kansas City, police identified areas where concentrated, high rates of violent crime were occurring, and targeted people in these "hot spots" for aggressive weapons searches. The effect of working with the community to develop this intervention that targeted law enforcement resources on a violent part of the City was to gain

---

¶ In October 2005, President Bush signed into law the Protection of Lawful Commerce in Arms Act, which grants the firearm industry immunity from most civil lawsuits involving injuries and deaths caused by guns, such as those described in this chapter.

the support of the community and reduce gun crime and homicide during the intervention period.[72]

In an attempt to encourage safer gun storage, eighteen states have enacted child access prevention (CAP) laws that specify criminal penalties for adults whose guns are accessible to youth. Such laws are enforceable only after an incident resulting from a child's access to firearms occurs. This post-hoc threat of criminal prosecution is based on the notion that such penalties will raise the stakes associated with keeping an unlocked gun accessible to children, increase the proportion of gun owners who safely store their guns, and reduce youth access to guns. Evaluations of such laws have yielded mixed results with regard to the impact on unintentional firearm deaths,[73,70] and a modest positive effect on suicide.[74]

The Role of Advocacy and Practice

Legislative initiatives to control the illicit market that supplies guns to youth is a focus of several gun violence prevention advocacy organizations. Licensing and registration, and one gun a month laws are two examples of such policies.[75] Creative use of executive authority by one local health commissioner led to the temporary closure of a hardware store known to sell ammunition to youth illegally, suggesting that in some jurisdictions, executive authority to address the environmental conditions that support and profit from youth gun violence can be addressed through public health agencies.[76]

The courts are providing a testing ground for the power of lawsuits to influence the gun industry's decision to design safer guns, as previously described. Plaintiffs seeking to change the way guns are distributed and sold aim to affect the environment in order to reduce youth access to guns.

The ASK (Asking Saves Kids) Campaign of the PAX organization is based on the idea that changes in social norms regarding guns are needed to achieve reductions in youth gun violence prevention. The Campaign encourages parents to "ASK" other parents if a gun is present in their home before sending their children to play. By establishing the ASK norm, PAX intends to increase awareness and action concerning the dangers associated with keeping guns in homes where children play. Perhaps such a discussion would have motivated Anthony's parents to lock away the pistol that fired the fatal shot to Eric's head in the injury profile that began this chapter.

Future Research, Advocacy and Practice

Research

Social Norms

Several public health campaigns have sought to change individual behavior by changing collective attitudes and the social acceptability of health risk behaviors. "Social norms" campaigns have been applied, with varying degrees of success, to such injury risk factors as seat belt use and binge drinking.[77-81] The ASK Campaign is one example of a social norms approach to gun violence prevention. By enlisting parents to inquire about guns and gun storage in the homes where their children play, the Campaign may influence gun storage norms. Research is needed to establish how social norms approaches can best be applied to youth gun violence prevention efforts, and to evaluate the impact of such interventions.

Whereas some programs target broader social norms, there is evidence of the need for more focused social norms change in communities where youth gun violence is pervasive. For example, Rich and Stone identified a widespread sentiment among young men in urban Boston. Specifically, these men felt pressure to engage in retaliatory violence in response to their own victimization to avoid being labeled "suckers." This norm fueled cycles of shootings and stabbings.[82] Thus, prevention programs can be used to their best advantage by acknowledging and addressing social norms supportive of gun violence in various communities.

Organizing and Advocating for Gun Violence Prevention

Gun violence prevention efforts are heavily dependent on advocates to help mobilize the grassroots, encourage research funding, and focus the political debate about firearms. The field would benefit from more systematic study of how to effectively organize and advocate for gun violence prevention. During the 1990s, the number of gun violence prevention advocacy groups increased and the issue gained visibility. There are many lessons to be learned from the experiences of advocacy organizations in the gun violence prevention community, and in other issue areas that face similar challenges.

Adolescent Development Research

Understanding youth development, and the particular developmental vulnerabilities to injury that exist throughout childhood and adolescence, is critical to crafting effective youth gun violence prevention strategies. Knowledge of early childhood development has been used to promote age appropriate interventions designed to prevent unintentional injuries in young children. For example, childproof caps for medicines are now recognized as an effective strategy for preventing curious youngsters from accidental poisoning.[83] This kind of developmental approach to prevention should be extended into adolescence.

Adolescents' access to firearms in their homes, communities and through their peer networks comes at a time when they are particularly developmentally vulnerable to injury. In the last several years, the process of brain development has received increased attention in the research literature. Adolescence is a time when the brain undergoes a wave of major development and remodeling. "Executive functions" of the brain which govern impulse control, planning, foresight, and emotional regulation are still developing until the early 20s.[84-87] That adolescents' brains may not yet be capable of fully processing and evaluating the consequences of their decisions has implications for education and policy strategies related to youth gun violence prevention, as adolescents' ability to resist firearms and other potentially seductive items is questionable. The allure of guns for adolescents has been documented in the literature. For adolescent boys left in a room with a gun but instructed not to touch it, the majority found the allure of the gun too strong to comply with the admonition.[29]

Since adolescents may not be able to act unfailingly in accordance with health education messages, environmental modification may provide a "safety net" for adolescents who make poor decisions.[88] Remembering that adolescence is a time of increasing autonomy (and decreasing supervision), the high prevalence of guns in the United States means that youth are gaining their independence in an environment where guns are accessible to them and when they are developmentally ill-equipped to consider the consequences of misusing a gun. This research is in its infancy, but should be further explored in the context of youth violence prevention.

Policy Implementation

Policies that prevent access to firearms, alter the way they are sold or marketed, or mandate safer designs are among the most potentially effective tools for preventing youth violence.[66] However, research demonstrates that gun violence prevention policies are not always implemented, or implemented in a way that fails to achieve the greatest public health gain.[89] Additional attention to the implementation phase of the policy process is needed, particularly in the area of gun violence prevention where policies are subject to passionate social and political debate. By understanding how best to translate written policies into effective preventive actions, gun violence prevention researchers can provide advocates and practitioners with the tools needed to assure the life-saving impact policy-makers intend.

Surveillance

The need for systematic collection of firearm injury data has long been advocated to better understand the nature of the problem, and to craft appropriate prevention strategies.[90-92] Unlike motor vehicle crashes and other unintentional injury issues, until recently there have been few detailed data on firearm deaths. In response to this need, an increasing number of state and local violent injury reporting systems are being developed.[93] The National Violent Injury Statistics System (NVISS) at the Harvard School of Public Health is coordinating these efforts.[93,94] The NVISS system, modeled in part on the National Highway Traffic Safety Administration's Fatality Analysis Reporting System, is designed to inform violence prevention research and policy.

Advocacy and Practice

Several high-profile school shootings in the late 1990s have brought gun violence "closer to home" for many Americans. This, coupled with the broader public concern that gun violence has disproportionately affected the nation's youth, have contributed to a proliferation of gun violence prevention and advocacy organizations in the last decade.[95] In 2000, several hundred thousand people gathered in Washington, D.C. to take part in the "Million Mom March," arguably the nation's most successful public gun control advocacy event.[96] The March aimed to promote "sensible gun laws," demonstrate the political counterpoint to gun-rights organizations, and hold Congress accountable for gun violence prevention legislation.[96]

Despite the success of the Million Mom March, advocacy groups have struggled to harness the power of their grassroots supporters in a sustained way.[95,96] There are several strategies that could help advocates maximize the impact of their resources. Gun violence prevention advocates tend to focus their policy efforts on enacting legislation. However, greater attention also should be paid to how the policies they support are implemented. Policies with poor (or no) implementation threaten to squander both the hard-won gains of the movement and the political will necessary to achieve them.

Gun violence prevention advocates would benefit from expanding to include groups of people who have traditionally not been active on the issue, but may be disproportionately affected by guns, such as people of color. By expanding the field and focusing on diversity, advocacy organizations can build broader appeal. In addition, the effectiveness of gun violence prevention advocates is somewhat hindered by a lack of cooperation within the field. Strategies to increase cooperation would likely prove beneficial. Finally, partnerships with officials in health departments and law enforcement would likely strengthen existing advocacy efforts, and provide valuable insight into the government systems responsible for preventing, treating, and controlling youth gun violence.[95] To best advocate for prevention, the youth gun violence prevention movement needs to keep the "grassroots" involved and energized, promote unity within the movement, foster diversity, and identify political opportunities to effect change and promote careful policy implementation.

Conclusion

The combined efforts of researchers, practitioners, and advocates working in the field of injury prevention hold great promise for reducing the toll of unnecessary deaths from trauma. Hundreds of thousands of lives have already been saved by modifying products such as automobiles. The greatest savings of lives lost by gunfire remain in our future. While changes in violent or careless behaviors need to occur, and methods for achieving those behavioral changes should be perfected, we can also save lives in the immediate future by modifying the design and availability of guns. These injury prevention strategies are within our technological grasp; the critical question, however, is whether they are within our political grasp. It is for this reason that injury prevention researchers, practitioners, and advocates need to work collaboratively at the federal, state, and local levels to translate promising ideas into life-saving reality.

References

1. National Center for Injury Prevention and Control. WISQARS fatal injury reports 2001. WISQARS. 1–19-2004.
2. Fingerhut LA, Christoffel KK. Firearm-related death and injury among children and adolescents. *Future Child.* 2002;12:24–37.
3. National Center for Injury Prevention and Control. WISQARS nonfatal injury reports 2001. WISQARS. 1–19-2004.
4. Cook PJ, Lawrence BA, Ludwig J, Miller TR. The medical costs of gunshot injuries in the United States. *JAMA.* 1999;282:447–454.
5. Cook PJ, Ludwig J. *Gun violence: the real costs.* New York: Oxford Univ. Press; 2000.
6. Cook PJ, Ludwig J. The costs of gun violence against children. *Future Child.* 2002;12:86–99.
7. 15 U.S.C.Sec.2052(a)(1)(E). 1982.
8. Miller M, Azrael D, Hemenway D. Rates of household firearm ownership and homicide across US regions and states, 1988–1997. *Am J Public Health.* 2002;92: 1988–1993.

9. Miller M, Azrael D, Hemenway D. Household firearm ownership and suicide rates in the United States. *Epidemiology.* 2002;13:517–524.

10. Miller M, Azrael D, Hemenway D. Firearm availability and unintentional firearm deaths. *Accident Analysis and Prevention.* 2001;33:477–484.

11. Kellermann AL, Rivara FP, Somes G et al. Suicide in the home in relation to gun ownership. *N Engl J Med.* 1992;327:467–472.

12. Kellermann AL, Rivara FP, Rushforth NB et al. Gun ownership as a risk factor for homicide in the home. *N Engl J Med.* 1993;329:1084–1091.

13. Grossman DC, Reay DT, Baker SA. Self-inflicted and unintentional firearm injuries among children and adolescents: The source of the firearm. *Arch Pediatr Adolesc Med.* 1999;153:875–878.

14. Smith, TW. 2001 national gun policy survey of the National Opinion Research Center: Research findings. 2001. Chicago, National Opinion Research Center.

15. Schuster MA, Franke TM, Bastian AM, Sor S, Halfon N. Firearm storage patterns in US homes with children. *Am J Public Health.* 2000;90:588–594.

16. Jackman GA, Farah MM, Kellermann AL, Simon HK. Seeing is believing: What do boys do when they find a real gun? *Pediatrics.* 2001;107:1247.

17. Committee on Injury and Poison Prevention. Firearm-Related Injuries Affecting the Pediatric Population. *Pediatrics.* 2000;105:888–895.

18. Cook PJ, Ludwig J. Guns in America: Results of a comprehensive survey of gun ownership and use. 1996. Washington, D.C., Police Foundation.

19. Braga A, Kennedy D. The illicit acquisition of firearms by youth and juveniles. *Journal of Criminal Justice.* 2001;29:379–388.

20. Ash P, Kellermann AL, Fuqua-Whitley D, Johnson A. Gun acquisition and use by juvenile offenders. *JAMA.* 1996;275:1754–1758.

21. Webster DW, Freed LH, Frattaroli S, Wilson MH. How delinquent youths acquire guns: Initial versus most recent gun acquisitions. *J Urban Health.* 2002; 79:60–69.

22. Cook PJ, Molliconi S, Cole T. Regulating gun markets. *Journal of Criminal Law and Criminology.* 1995;86:59–92.

23. Liller KD, Perrin K, Nearns J, Pesce K, Crane NB, Gonzalez RR. Evaluation of the "Respect Not Risk" firearm safety lesson for 3rd-graders. *J Sch Nurs.* 2003; 19:338–343.

24. Hardy MS, Armstrong FD, Martin BL, Strawn KN. A firearm safety program for children: They just can't say no. *J Dev Behav Pediatr.* 1996;17:216–221.

25. Hardy MS. Teaching firearm safety to children: Failure of a program. *J Dev Behav Pediatr.* 2002;23:71–76.

26. Himle MB, Miltenberger RG, Gatheridge BJ, Flessner CA. An evaluation of two procedures for training skills to prevent gun play in children. *Pediatrics.* 2004;113:70–77.

27. Gatheridge BJ, Miltenberger RG, Huneke DF, et al. Comparison of two programs to teach firearm injury prevention skills to 6- and 7-year-old children. *Pediatrics.* 2004;114:e294–e299.

28. Hardy MS. Behavior-oriented approaches to reducing youth gun violence. *Future Child.* 2002;12:100–117.

29. Hardy MS. Effects of gun admonitions on the behaviors and attitudes of school-aged boys. *J Dev Behav Pediatr.* 2003;24:352–358.

30. Grossman DC, Cummings P, Koepsell TD, et al. Firearm safety counseling in primary care pediatrics: A randomized, controlled trial. *Pediatrics.* 2000;106: 22–26.

31. Brent DA, Baugher M, Birmaher B, Kolko DJ, Bridge J. Compliance with recommendations to remove firearms in families participating in a clinical trial for adolescent depression. *J Am Acad Child Adolesc Psychiatry.* 2000;39:1220–1226.

32. Connor SM, Wesolowski KL. "They're too smart for that": Predicting what children would do in the presence of guns. *Pediatrics.* 2003;111:E109–E114.

33. Webster DW, Wilson ME, Duggan AK, Pakula LC. Parents' beliefs about preventing gun injuries to children. *Pediatrics.* 1992;89:908–914.

34. Farah MM, Simon HK, Kellermann AL. Firearms in the home: Parental perceptions. *Pediatrics.* 1999;104:1059.

35. Webster DW, Wilson ME, Duggan AK, Pakula LC. Firearm injury prevention counseling: A study of pediatricians' beliefs and practices. *Pediatrics.* 1992;89: 902–907.

36. Solomon BS, Duggan AK, Webster D, Serwint JR. Pediatric residents' attitudes and behaviors related to counseling adolescents and their parents about firearm safety. *Arch Pediatr Adolesc Med.* 2002;156:769–775.

37. Coyne-Beasley T, Schoenbach VJ, Johnson RM. "Love our kids, lock your guns": A community-based firearm safety counseling and gun lock distribution program. *Arch Pediatr Adolesc Med.* 2001;155:659–664.

38. Horn A, Grossman DC, Jones W, Berger LR. Community based program to improve firearm storage practices in rural Alaska. *Inj Prev.* 2003;9:231–234.

39. Gielen AC, McDonald EM, Wilson MEH, et al. Effects of improved access to safety counseling, products, and home visits on parents' safety practices: Results of a randomized trial. *Arch Pediatr Adolesc Med.* 2002;156:33–40.

40. Freed LH, Webster DW, Longwell JJ, Carrese J, Wilson MEH. Factors preventing gun acquisition and carrying among incarcerated adolescent males. *Arch Pediatr Adolesc Med.* 2001;155:335–341.

41. Raphael S, Ludwig J. Prison sentence enhancements: The case of Project Exile. In: Ludwig J, Cook PJ, eds. *Evaluating Gun Policy: Effects on Crime and Violence.* Washington, D.C.: The Brookings Institution Press; 2003:251–86.

42. Finckenauer JO, Gavin PW. *Scared Straight: The Panacea Phenomenon Revisited.* Prospect Heights: Waveland Press; 1999.

43. Kennedy D, Piehl A, Braga A. Youth violence in Boston: Gun markets, serious youth offenders, and a use reduction strategy. *Law and Contemporary Problems.* 1996;59:147–198.

44. Fagan J. Policing guns and gun violence. *Future Child.* 2002;12:133–151.

45. Wintemute GJ, Teret SP, Kraus JF, Wright MA, Bradfield G. When children shoot children: 88 unintended deaths in California. *JAMA.* 1987;257:3107–3109.

46. Ismach RB, Reza A, Ary R, Sampson TR, Bartolomeos K, Kellermann AL. Unintended shootings in a large metropolitan area: An incident-based analysis. *Ann Emerg Med.* 2003;41:10–17.

47. Baker SP, Teret SP, Dietz PE. Firearms and the public health. *J Public Health Policy.* 1980;1:224–229.

48. Jinks RG. *History of Smith & Wesson: Nothing of Importance Will Come without Effort.* Beinfeld Publishing Company; 1977.

49. Teret SP, Wintemute GJ. Policies to prevent firearm injuries. *Health Affairs.* 1993; 12:96–108.

50. Teret SP, DeFrancesco S, Hargarten SW, Robinson K. Making guns safer. *Issues in Science and Technology.* 1998;Summer:37–40.

51. Freed LH, Vernick JS, Hargarten SW. Prevention of firearm-related injuries and deaths among youth. A product-oriented approach. *Pediatr Clin North Am.* 1998; 45:427–438.

52. General Accounting Office. Accidental Shooting: Many Deaths and Injuries Caused by Firearms could be Prevented. 1991. Washington, DC, US General Accounting Office.

53. Vernick JS, O'Brien M, Hepburn LM, Johnson SB, Webster DW, Hargarten SW. Unintentional and undetermined firearm related deaths: A preventable death analysis for three safety devices. *Inj Prev.* 2003;9:307–311.

54. Cal.Penal Code. 12130. 2003.

55. Massachusetts Gen.Laws. ch. 140 sec. 12130. 2000.

56. Md.Public Safety Code. sec. 5-132(d)(1). 2000.

57. New Jersey Rev.Stat. 2C:39-1dd. 2002.

58. DeFrancesco S, Lester KJ, Teret SP, Vernick JS. A Model Handgun Safety Standard Act. 1-26. 2000. Baltimore, The Johns Hopkins Center for Gun Policy and Research.

59. Center to Prevent Handgun Violence. Targeting Safety: How State Attorneys General Can Act Now to Save Lives. 1-29. 2001. Washington, D.C., Center to Prevent Handgun Violence.

60. Teret SP, Wintemute GJ. Handgun injuries: The epidemiologic evidence for assessing legal responsibility. *Hamline Law Review.* 1983;6:341–350.

61. Association of Trial Lawyers of America and the Johns Hopkins Center for Gun Policy and Research. Conference Report: Guns, A Public Health Approach. 5–23–1995.

62. Vernick JS, Teret SP. New courtroom strategies regarding firearms: Tort litigation against firearm manufacturers and constitutional challenges to gun laws. *Houston Law Review.* 1999;36:1713–1753.

63. Vernick JS, Teret SP. A public health approach to regulating firearms as consumer products. *University of Pennsylvania Law Review.* 2000;148:1192–1211.

64. Mair JS, Teret SP, Frattaroli S. A public health perspective on gun violence prevention. In: Lytton TD, ed. *Suing the Firearms Industry: A Legal Battle at the Crossroads of Gun Control and Mass Torts.* Ann Arbor: University of Michigan Press; 2005; *in press.*

65. Vizzard WJ. *In the Cross Fire: A Political History of the Bureau of Alcohol, Tobacco and Firearms.* Boulder: Lynne Rienner Publishers; 1997.

66. Wintemute G. Where the guns come from: The gun industry and gun commerce. *Future Child.* 2002;12:54–71.

67. Vernick JS, Hepburn L. Examining state and federal gun laws: Trends for 1970–1999. In: Cook PJ, Ludwig J, eds. *Evaluating Gun Policy.* Washington, DC: Brookings Institution Press; 2003.

68. Webster DW, Vernick JS, Hepburn LM. Relationship between licensing, registration, and other gun sales laws and the source state of crime guns. *Inj Prev.* 2001;7:184–189.

69. Weil DS, Knox RC. Effects of limiting handgun purchases on interstate transfer of firearms. *JAMA.* 1996;275:1759–1761.

70. Webster DW, Starnes M. Reexamining the association between child access prevention gun laws and unintentional shooting deaths of children. *Pediatrics.* 2000;106:1466–1469.

71. Office of Juvenile Justice and Delinquency Prevention. Promising Strategies to Reduce Gun Violence. 1999. Washington, DC, National Institute of Justice.

72. Sherman L, Shaw JW, Rogan DP. The Kansas City Gun Experiment. 1–11. 1995. Washington, D.C., National Institute of Justice. Research in Brief.

73. Cummings P, Grossman DC, Rivara FP, Koepsell TD. State gun safe storage laws and child mortality due to firearms. *JAMA.* 1997;278:1084–1086.

74. Webster DW, Vernick JS, Zeioli AM, Manganello JA. Association between youth focused firearm laws and youth suicide. *JAMA.* 2004;292:594–601.

75. DeMarco V, Schneider GE. Elections and public health. *Am J Public Health.* 2000;90:1513–1514.

76. Lewin NL, Vernick JS, Beilenson PL, et al. Using local public health powers as a tool for gun violence prevention: The Baltimore youth ammunition initiative. *Am J Public Health.* 2005;95:72-5.

77. Glider P, Midyett SJ, Mills-Novoa B, Johannessen K, Collins C. Challenging the

collegiate rite of passage: A campus-wide social marketing media campaign to reduce binge drinking. *J Drug Educ.* 2001;31:207–220.

78. Wechsler H, Nelson TE, Lee JE, Seibring M, Lewis C, Keeling RP. Perception and reality: A national evaluation of social norms marketing interventions to reduce college students' heavy alcohol use. *J Stud Alcohol.* 2003;64:484–494.

79. Haines M, Spear SF. Changing the perception of the norm: A strategy to decrease binge drinking among college students. *J Am Coll Health.* 1996;45: 134–140.

80. Cohn LD, Hernandez D, Byrd T, Cortes M. A program to increase seat belt use along the Texas-Mexico border. *Am J Public Health.* 2002;92:1918–1920.

81. Wechsler H, Seibring M, Liu IC, Ahl M. Colleges respond to student binge drinking: Reducing student demand or limiting access. *J Am Coll Health.* 2004;52:159–168.

82. Rich JA, Stone DA. The experience of violent injury for young African-American men: The meaning of being a "sucker." *Journal of General Internal Medicine.* 1996;11:77–82.

83. Christoffel T, Gallagher SS. *Injury Prevention and Public Health: Practical Knowledge, Skills, and Strategies.* Jones and Bartlett Publishers; 1999.

84. Giedd J, Blumenthal J, Jeffries NO, et al. Brain development during childhood and adolescence: A longitudinal MRI study. *Nat Neurosci.* 1999;2:861–863.

85. Sowell ER, Thompson PM, Holmes CJ, Jernigan TL, Toga AW. In vivo evidence for post-adolescent brain maturation in frontal and striatal regions. *Nature Neuroscience.* 1999;2:859–861.

86. Sowell ER, Thompson PM, Holmes CJ, Batth R, Jernigan TL, Toga A. Localizing age-related changes in brain structure between childhood and adolescence using statistical parametric mapping. *NeuroImage.* 1999;9:587–597.

87. Sowell ER, Thompson PM, Tessner KD, Toga AW. Mapping continued brain growth and gray matter density reduction in dorsal frontal cortex: Inverse relationships during post-adolescent brain maturation. *The Journal of Neuroscience.* 2001;21:8819–8829.

88. Johnson SB, Frattaroli S. The adolescent brain as a work in progress: A new way of thinking about kids and guns. Poster presented at the 9th Annual Citizens' Conference to Stop Gun Violence. 2003. Arlington, VA.

89. Frattaroli S. *The Implementation of the 1996 Maryland Gun Violence Act: A Case Study.* The Johns Hopkins School of Hygiene and Public Health, 1999.

90. Rosenberg M, Hammond W. Surveillance: The key to firearm injury prevention. *Am J Prev Med.* 1995;15:1.

91. Teret SP, Wintemute GJ, Beilenson PL. The Firearm Fatality Reporting System. A proposal. *JAMA.* 1992;267:3073–3074.

92. Mercy JA, Ikeda R, Powell KE. Firearm-related injury surveillance. An overview of progress and the challenges ahead. *Am J Prev Med.* 1998;15:6–16.

93. Barber C, Hemenway D, Hargarten S, Kellermann A, Azrael D, Wilt S. A "call to arms" for a national reporting system on firearm injuries. *Am J Public Health.* 2000;90:1191–1193.

94. Harvard Injury Control Research Center. National Violent Injury Statistics System homepage. Harvard Injury Control Research Center. 2004;6-14-2004.

95. Frattaroli S. Grassroots advocacy for gun violence prevention: A status report on mobilizing a movement. *J Public Health Policy.* 2003;24:332–354.

96. Wallack L, Winett L, Nettekoven L. The Million Mom March: Engaging the public on gun policy. *J Public Health Policy.* 2003;24:355–379.

CHAPTER 13

Youth Suicide

Lloyd B.Potter[1]

James

James's father describes the day he thought that his world had ended as the day he lost his once vibrant 13 year-old son who had hanged himself. James was a kind child who would always stop and talk with people and would say pleasant things to make them happy. Seventh grade had been a hard year for him at school. He struggled with a few of his classes, a few kids bullied him, and his best friend moved to another state. James' family was concerned about his lack of energy and loss of interest in school so they took him to their HMO. According to his father, the doctors who had seen him appeared to be "more interested in saving money than in saving James." James had come within one week of surviving that school year. His father reflects on the opportunities missed to help his dear son at home, at his school, and at his HMO. His father now works tirelessly on efforts to raise awareness in the hope that his profound loss can somehow contribute to preventing the loss of others.

Introduction

In the United States, 71.7% of all deaths among youth and young adults aged 10–24 years result from only four causes: motor-vehicle crashes (32.6%), other unintentional injuries (13%), homicide (14.6%), and suicide (11.5%) in 2002 (Centers for Disease Control and Prevention, 2005). Thus suicide is the fourth leading cause of death in this age group. While many communities and schools recognized that youth suicide is a significant problem, most struggle with how they can effectively address suicide prevention. The consequences of self-inflicted injuries among youth and losing youth to suicide are serious to individuals, families and the broader society. In addition to causing injury and death, youth suicide poses a substantial burden on communities, health care and other service systems.

A public health approach brings emphasis and commitment to identifying policies and programs to prevent youth suicide. It derives from a tradi-

---

1   PhD, MPH, Education Development Center, Inc.

tion of collaboration among a broad spectrum of scientific disciplines, organizations, and communities to solve the problem of suicide. In particular, the health sector, including emergency departments and community health agencies, plays a prominent role as a source of data and a potential site for interventions to prevent future suicidal behavior. The public health approach also highlights the potential utility of applying a variety of scientific tools (eg, the tools of epidemiology, behavioral and social sciences, and engineering). explicitly toward identifying effective prevention strategies. In these key ways, the perspective and methods of public health complement those of criminal justice and other sectors in understanding and responding to suicide.

Significant advances have been made in understanding suicide as a public health issue. In 1996, the World Health Organization (WHO) issued the *Prevention of Suicide: Guidelines for the Formulation and Implementation of National Strategies*, (WHO 1996). Recognizing the growing problem of suicide worldwide, WHO urged member nations to address this issue. In the US, an innovative public/private partnership to seek a national strategy for the United States was established, including agencies in the US Department of Health and Human Services, encompassing the Centers for Disease Control and Prevention (CDC), the Health Resources and Services Administration (HRSA), the Indian Health Service (IHS), the National Institute of Mental Health (NIMH), the Office of the Surgeon General, the Substance Abuse and Mental Health Services Administration (SAMHSA) and the Suicide Prevention Advocacy Network (SPAN), a public grassroots advocacy organization made up of suicide survivors (persons close to someone who completed suicide), attempters of suicide, community activists, and health and mental health clinicians. In 1999, the US Surgeon General's office issued a brief report, *The Surgeon General's Call to Action to Prevent Suicide*, (US PHS 1999) and the Institute of Medicine in 2002 published a report on the causes of suicide and to recommend prevention strategies (Goldsmith et al, 2002). The 2001 release of the National Strategy for Suicide Prevention, developed with public and private sector partners with leadership and support from the Surgeon General, created a framework with specific goals and objectives that has guided the development of many state plans. (US, PHS 2001)

Mortality & Morbidity Information

Despite the declining rates in recent years, suicide continues to be one of the leading cause of death among youth 15–24 years of age. (Centers for Disease Control and Prevention, 2005). With 4270 suicide deaths in this age group, suicide was the third leading cause of death among youth in 2002. Since 1995, the suicide rate among those aged 10 to 24 years declined 25%, from 9.07 to 6.84 per 100 000. A recent report highlighted a change in methods of suicide among those aged 10–19. Between 1992 and 2001 rates of suicide using firearms and poisoning declined, while suicides by suffocation increased.

Suicide rates vary substantially by sex and across racial/ethnic groups. Suicide is substantially more likely for males. In 2002, the suicide rate for young males (11.44 per 100 000) was 5.35 times higher than the rate for females (2.14 per 100 000) (Centers for Disease Control and Prevention, 2005). Suicide rates are highest among American Indian/Alaskan Native (15.51 per 100 000) and Non-Hispanic White youth (7.95 per 100 000) and lower among Non-Hispanic Black (4.66 per 100 000), Hispanic (4.61 per 100 000) and Asian (3.81 per 100 000) youth.

Most incidents of self-directed violence do not result in death. Many young survivors become severely and often permanently injured.

Data from a nationally representative sample of US emergency departments collected by the National Electronic Injury Surveillance System provide an estimate of the number of nonfatal injuries due to self-directed violence that are treated in US emergency departments. An estimated 124 409 injuries among youth aged 10–24 years were attributed to self-directed violence (Centers for Disease Control and Prevention, 2005). Females (75 214) were more likely to be treated for injuries due to self-directed violence than males (49 172). Given that males are far more likely to die from suicide than females, the ratio of nonfatal injuries to suicides is far lower in males (13.6 to 1) than in females (117.2 to 1).

To fully understand the prevalence of youth suicide it is necessary to look beyond incidents that are brought to the attention of a coroner, or emergency departments. Self-report data allow us to estimate the proportion of youth who engage in a variety of behaviors that put them or others at risk for violence-related injury. For example, data from CDC's Youth Risk Behavior Survey are collected every other year from a large nationally representative sample of high school students. Data from the sample of 15 240 students surveyed in 2003 allow us to estimate the proportion of high school students in the US who experienced suicidal behavior. These data indicate that approximately 1 in 10 female high school students (11.5%) attempted suicide at least once in the past 12 months (Grunbaum et al, 2004). About half as many males (5.4%) reported attempting suicide. Suicidal ideation was far more common, with 21.3% of females and 12.8% of males reporting having seriously considered suicide in the past 12 months.

Risk and Protective Factors

An ecological systems model of human development provides a useful framework for understanding the risk and protective factors for suicidal behavior as well as potentially identifying opportunities for intervention. A simplified version of this model has the individual existing and developing within the context of close interpersonal relationships (family and peers). Individuals, family, and peers exist and develop in the context of their community, and all of these exist within a broader social, cultural, economic, macrosystem. Each level influences and is influenced by other levels. There are several implications of this ecological model for understanding suicidal behavior. First it allows for the direct influence of environmental factors (familial, societal, and physical) on behavior. The model also explicitly acknowledges the multilevel determinants of behavior. Fitting the model to suicidal behavior, it is not just family or community or societal factors but all of these that contribute to the development of suicidal behavior. Moreover these factors interact with one another to influence whether or not individuals engage in suicidal behavior.

Most etiologic research into suicidal behavior occurs at one level of analysis. Studies that are limited to one level of analysis are easier to conduct although, at higher levels of aggregation, they suffer from potential interpretation problems when attempting across-level interpretation (Glick and Roberts, 1994; Iversen, 1991; Richards, Gottfredson, and Gottfredson, 1990). A classic example of an ecological analysis is that of Emile Durkheim's (1951) study of suicide. He explored ecological associations between suicide rates and population characteristics (eg, religion and marital status). While Durkheim was able to say there was an association between suicide rates of a population and population characteristics, he was not able to make statements of causation at the individual level of analysis. The discussion that follows utilizes the basic framework of the ecological model (individual, family and peers, community, macro system) as the basis for discussing research at each level.

At the individual level, there are biological and behavioral characteristics that have been associated with suicide. A number of studies have implicated hereditary factors and biological factors influencing the propensity for suicidal behavior (Arana and Hyman, 1989; Mann, 1987; Rainer, 1984; Roy, 1993). Substantial evidence has suggested that deficiencies in the serotonergic system are associated with suicidal behavior (Baldwin, Bullock, Montgomery, and Montgomery, 1991; Lowther et al, 1997; Mann, Arango, and Underwood, 1990; Ohmori, Arora, and Meltzer, 1992; Van Praag, 1991). A feeling of hopelessness is one characteristic that has been generally associated with suicidal behavior (Beck, Brown, and Steer, 1997; Beck, Steer, Beck, and Nwan, 1993; Beck, Steer, Kovacs, and Garrson, 1985; Hill, Gallagher, Thompson and Ishida, 1988; Keller and Wolfersdorf, 1993; Nimeus, Traskman-Bendz, and Alsen, 1997; Rotheram-Borus and Trautman, 1988; Shaffer et al, 1996; Weishaar and Beck, 1992). A number of psychiatric disorders have been associated with suicidal behavior such as depression (Adolescent suicide, 1996; Beck, Steer, Kovacs, and Garrison, 1985; Berglund, 1984; Brent, 1995; Brent et al, 1988; Brent, Kolko, Allan, and Brown, 1990; Brent, Perper, Moritz, Allman et al, 1993a; Harrington et al, 1994; Lewinsohn, Rohed, and Seeley, 1994; Osgood, 1992; Porsteinsson et al, 1997; Roy, 1986; Wolk and Weissman, 1996; Young, Fogg, Scheftner, and Fawcett, 1994), bipolar affective disorder (Ahrens, Grof, Moller, Muller-Oerlinghausen, and Wolf, 1995; Krupinski et al, 1998; Mueller-Oerlinghausen, Mueser-Causemann, and Volk, 1992; Tondo, Jamison, and Baldessarini, 1997; Tondo et al, 1998), conduct disorder (Apter, Bleich, Plutchik, Mendolsohn, and Tyano, 1988; Brent, Perper, Moritz, Baugher et al, 1993; Shaffer et al, 1996; Shafii et al, 1988), and alcoholism and substance abuse (Bryant, Garrison, Valois, Rivard, and Hinkle, 1995; Burge, Felts, Chenier, and Parrillo, 1995; Garrison, McKeown, Valois, and Vincent, 1993; Marzuketal., 1992; Rossow and Amundsen, 1995; Roy, Dejong, Lamparski, Adinoff et al, 1991; Roy, Dejong, Lamparski, George et al, 1991; Shaffer et al, 1996; Shafii et al, 1988; Stack and Wasserman, 1995; Vilhjalmsson, Kristjansdotti, and Sueibjarnardottir, 1998; Windle and Windle, 1997) among others.

Family and Close Relationships

Characteristics of and behavior within the family environment profoundly influence the development of individuals. A number of family environment characteristics have been associated with suicide and suicidal behavior including family conflict or discord (Brent, 1995; Brent et al, 1994; Campbell, Milling, Laughlin, and Bush, 1993; Wright, 1985), parental attachment (Dejong, 1992), poor family functioning (Adams, Overholser, and Lehnert, 1994), childhood separation from parents (Bagley and Ramsay, 1985), child abuse and neglect (Bergman and Brismar, 1991; Brent et al, 1994; Briere and Runtz, 1986; Bryant and Range, 1997; Deykin, Alpert, and McNamara, 1985; Grossman, Milligan, and Deyo, 1991; Molnar, Shade, Kral, Booth, and Watters, 1998; Straus and Kantor, 1994), being a victim of intimate partner abuse/conflict (Deykin, Alpert, and McNamara, 1985) and loss of a peer (Brent, Perper, Moritz, Friend et al, 1993; Brent, Perper, Moritz, Liotus et al, 1993; Brent et al, 1995; Brent, Moritz, Bridge, Perper, and Canobbio, 1996).

Another factor that may operate at the level of family and peers, although it is clearly linked to community characteristics, is access to means. A number of studies have indicated with varying degrees of rigor that access to firearms increases risk of completed suicide (Beautrais, Joyce, and Mulder, 1996; Boor and Bair, 1990; Brent et al, 1991; Brent, Perper, Moritz, Baugher et al, 1993b; Cummings, Koepsell, Grossman, Savarino, and Thompson, 1997; Medoff and Magaddino, 1983; Sloan, Rivaran, Reay, Ferris, and Kellerman, 1990).

Community and Societal

Internationally, suicide rates vary substantially (Krug, Dahlberg, and Powell, 1996) suggesting cultural differences in suicidal behavior. These cultural differences appear to result in variation of method selected (Adityanjee, 1986; Burvill, 1995; Canetto and Lester, 1995; Ko and Kua, 1995). Various indicators of economic factors have been explored in relation to suicide rates (Adityanjee, 1986; Araki and Murata, 1987; Burvill, 1995; Canetto and Lester, 1995; Cormier and Klerman, 1985; Ko and Kua, 1995; Ragland and Berman, 1990-1991; Reinfurt, Stewart, and Weaver, 1991; Yang, 1995; Yang and Lester. 1990). Studies generally support an association between economic factors and suicide, although several have not found an association.

There are a number of key concepts at several levels of aggregation (individual, family/peer, community, and macrosystem) that appear to be central for understanding the causes suicide. Unfortunately, there are no research findings that have been able to simultaneously link all these levels together to provide an understanding of the causes of suicide that would allow us to develop and implement highly effective multi-systemic interventions for the prevention of suicidal behavior. This highlights the issue of taxonomy. In reviewing the literature on suicide, very few studies use the same definitions. Variables and constructs that we use as predictors occupy a vast range as do variables and constructs that actually measure some form of suicidal behavior. Thus while there have been limited efforts to articulate taxonomy of suicide (O'Caroll et al, 1996) we are left with a rapidly developing field of research that is struggling for both a more refined taxonomy and a more developed framework for understanding the causes of suicide.

Current Research, Prevention and Intervention Strategies

CDC has reviewed and summarized a range of strategies intended to prevent suicidal behavior (Centers for Disease Control and Prevention, 1992). A review of suicide prevention efforts listed in the guide suggests that most suicide prevention programs embrace the high-risk model of prevention where the goal is case finding and referral (Rose, 1985). Screening and referral, crisis centers, and community organization are common examples of this high-risk approach. Suicide awareness or education activities, media guidelines, and means restriction are examples of population-based interventions. Currently, neither the high risk nor the population prevention approach can be said to be more effective than the other. However, it is reasonable to expect that a combination of these approaches would be a more effective way to affect suicide rates and suicide related morbidity than only one approach. By implementing efforts to reduce suicide risk with a focus on a population or a population segment combined with more intensive efforts to identify and provide services for those at greatest risk should lead to more positive outcomes.

There are a number of programmatic strategies for suicide prevention that schools and communities might consider to implement. Regardless of the strategies a school may employ, it is important that the school develop a [b comprehensive plan b] for preventing suicide, for safely managing a student who may be suicidal, and for responding appropriately and effectively after a suicide occurs. Other strategies include gatekeeper training, prevention education, screening, peer support programs, crisis intervention, restricting access to means, providing aftercare to those who experience significant loss, and educating families.

Gatekeeper training in schools is a type of program designed to help school staff (eg, teachers, counselors, and coaches) identify and refer students at risk for suicide. These programs teach staff how to respond to suicide or other crises in the school. This is a commonly implemented strategy and it makes sense to ensure that key school staff know how to respond to someone in crisis or someone who is thinking about suicide. There are a number of different programs available and some communities have developed their own programs. Most gatekeeper models tend to include training individuals to ask if someone they have concerns about is thinking about suicide. They also tend to emphasize listening, being supportive, and transferring care of persons who are considering suicide to an appropriate professional. The logic of the gatekeeper model is that adults who come in contact with youth should know clearly what they should do if they encounter a youth whom they think might be suicidal. There are several assumptions inherent in the model that should be considered. It assumes that appropriate services are available and that a system is in place to enable the gatekeeper to make an appropriate referral and transfer care. The gatekeeper model assumes that youth who are at risk for suicide will be more likely to be identified and more likely to receive effective care if a person trained as a gatekeeper has contact with them.

Results from evaluations of gatekeeper training programs indicate that persons trained are more likely to: (1) believe they would act to prevent youth suicide, (2) demonstrate greater confidence in suicide assessment and intervention knowledge, and (3) report higher levels of comfort, competence, and confidence in helping at-risk youth. Youth who participated in a 2-day gatekeeper training were significantly more likely to know warning signs for suicide and more likely to respond with effective suicide prevention steps than non-participating peers (University of Washington, 1999). Gatekeeper training programs in Colorado and New Jersey have shown similar results (Barrett, 1985). Currently, there is no evidence from experimental or quasi-experimental evaluation studies that provide information on suicide related outcomes for this strategy. However the logic and rational of gatekeeper training make it a compelling strategy for schools to employ.

The concept behind the **suicide prevention education** is that students learn about suicide, its warning signs, and how to seek help for themselves or others. These programs often incorporate a variety of activities that develop self-esteem and social competency. An educational approach is relatively popular. Substantial numbers of people can be reached and the programs are usually delivered with limited duration and exposure. Studies indicate that an educational approach can increase knowledge of warning signs and sources of help and referral. There is little evidence to suggest that an educational strategy will result in changing attitudes toward suicide or willingness to seek help. There is evidence from one study that youth who had attempted suicide in the past had negative reactions to an education program (Shaffer, Garland, Vieland, Underwood, Busner, 1991). Thus caution should be taken in implementing this strategy and resources should be in place to recognize persons who may be at risk and to provide appropriate care and referrals. As with any curricula being considered, suicide prevention education programs should be evaluated in terms of the practicality of the content and duration for achieving intended outcomes. If the content and duration are limited, achieving desired outcomes may be limited as well.

Screening programs usually involve administering a questionnaire or other screening instrument to identify high-risk adolescents and young adults and provide further assessment and treatment. Repeated assessment can be used to measure changes in attitudes or behaviors over time, to test the effectiveness of a prevention strategy, and to detect potential suicidal behavior.

Screening strategies are focused on identifying underlying characteristics associated with suicidal behavior. Behaviors and symptoms associated with major depression are usually the factors that are focused upon. Not all persons who attempt or complete suicide exhibit behaviors or symptoms consistent with diagnosis of major depression. Though there is a fair amount of evidence that many, if not most, persons exhibiting suicidal behavior have some form of diagnosable mood disorder. Screening only for indicators of mood disorder will miss some percentage of persons who will go on to attempt or complete suicide. This may be a small number.

In one study, the Diagnostic Interview Schedule for Children (DISC) had a very high rate of sensitivity (identified all cases) for major depression, and had specificity of less than 1 (.88 which is, by most standards, good) (Lucas et al, 2001). The result of lack of specificity in a screening program is that more youth with low risk would need to be seen by a clinician. This increases the cost of screening.

Another issue in screening is that not all persons who are depressed or have a psychiatric disorder will attempt or complete suicide. In many ways, a strategy of screening for psychiatric disorders and case management through treatment is expected to result in reducing suicide rates. The logic is sound but there does not appear to be experimental or quasi-experimental evaluations conducted to conclude that this strategy will reduce suicidal behavior.

The American Academy of Pediatrics (AAP) recommends screening for suicide risk. They recommend asking all adolescents about suicidal thoughts when taking a routine medical history. The American Medical Association in their Guidelines For Adolescent Preventive Services (GAPS) (Elster and Kuznets, 1994) and Bright Futures (Green, 1994) recommend that providers screen adolescents annually to identify those at risk for suicide. The Guide to Clinical Preventive Services, Second Edition (US Preventive Services Task Force, 1996) does not recommend screening for suicide because there were no valid or reliable instruments for suicide risk at the time the guide was written.

Mental health screening should probably be part of any school health program. This may be a resource intensive endeavor however because it requires that the system is prepared to provide and manage services for those identified. In any effort to provide services across agencies and organizations, coordination is essential. Coordination must occur among the youth, school, referral agency and the home. It is also essential that all youth know to whom they can go if they or a friend needs help. Having a designated coordinator for youth mental health services would facilitate coordination of services and follow-up with at risk youth. A coordinator could also provide leadership in the event of a suicide within the school's population.

Identifying and treating depression has long been at the foundation of efforts to prevent suicide. Millions of Americans have relied upon **selective serotonin reuptake inhibitors** (SSRIs) to treat depression or anxiety. For most adults, SSRIs effectively treat these symptoms though the Federal Drug Administration (FDA) has recently released and advisory regarding the risk of suicide in adults taking SSRIs. There is also some debate about research suggesting that in some patients, and youth in particular, SSRIs are associated with increases in suicidal ideation and behavior. This debate has culminated in the review of evidence on this topic by the FDA. The FDA reviewed clinical trials of SSRIs and found that no completed suicides occurred among nearly 2200 children treated with SSRI medications. However, the rate of suicidal thinking or behavior, including actual suicidal attempts, was 4 percent for those on SSRI medications, twice the rate of those on inert placebo pills. This led the FDA to adopt a "black box" label warning that antidepressants were found to increase the risk of suicidal thinking and behavior in children and adolescents with major depressive disorder. A black-box warning is the most serious type of warning in prescription drug labeling.

The black-box warning states that children and adolescents who are started on SSRI medications should be closely monitored for any worsening in depression, emergence of suicidal thinking or behavior, and in general for any unusual changes in behavior—such as sleeplessness, agitation, or withdraw from normal social situations. Monitoring for these behaviors and symptoms is especially important during the first four weeks of treatment. The publicity associated with the FDA review and action has resulted in concern by some that persons diagnosed with depression will be less likely to treat their symptoms with SSRI medications which conceivably may lead to overall increases in suicidal ideation and behavior.

Peer support programs can be conducted in or outside of school and are designed to foster peer relationships and competency in social skills among high-risk adolescents and young adults. Peer support programs attempt to provide a setting in which young people who may be at risk for suicide can receive support of their peers and develop positive interpersonal relationships.

One of the most extensively evaluated peer-support programs is Reconnecting Youth (Eggert, Thompson, Herting, Nicholas, 1995; Eggert, Thompson, Herting, and Randell, 2001; Eggert, Thompson, Herting, and Nicholas, 1994). The program incorporates social support and life skills training with the following components: a semester-long, daily class designed to enhance self-esteem, decision-making, personal control, and interpersonal communication; social activities and school bonding, drug-free social activities and friendships, as well as improve a teenager's relationship to school; and a school system crisis response plan, for addressing suicide prevention approaches. Another program that employs a peer support model is called Natural Helpers. This program was implemented in a Native American community and was associated with a decline in suicide rates (Centers for Disease Control and Prevention, 1998). The peer support model is one to consider for primary prevention of suicide and, if implemented well, may actually result in positive outcomes for a number of health issues affecting youth.

In **crisis centers and on hotlines** trained volunteers and paid staff provide telephone counseling and other services for suicidal persons. Such programs also may offer a "drop-in" crisis center and referral to mental health services. The function of these services relies on the presumption that suicide attempts are often impulsive and contemplated with ambivalence. Hotlines are designed to deter the caller from self-destructive behaviors until the immediate crisis has passed. The anonymity afforded by hotline calls allows the caller to feel secure and in control. Many hotlines are linked to schools and to mental health services.

Earlier studies indicate that crisis centers and hotlines may reduce the rate of suicide among young women (Centers for Disease Control and Prevention, 1992). Emerging and currently unpublished research is indicating that crisis centers and hotlines may be beneficial toward reducing suicidality of most suicidal callers. The effectiveness of hotlines and crisis centers might be improved by increasing outreach to at risk groups, requiring consistent training of volunteer staff, and taking steps to improve follow-through with those who call.

Restriction of access to lethal means. Activities are designed to restrict access to handguns, drugs, and other common means of suicide. Impulsiveness and ambivalence are important factors in suicidal behaviors among young people (Simon et al, 2001). Therefore, means restriction has the potential for preventing suicides. At least some portion of impulsive decisions to attempt suicide might never be acted on if substantial efforts were needed to arrange for a method of suicide. Means restriction has proven to be a controversial approach to prevention. This is mostly true for firearms, but efforts to promote constructing barriers on bridges, to modify the design of automobiles, and imposing restrictions on dispensing of medication have also resulted in controversy. Efforts to educate parents of youth about risks associated with access to firearms and lethal doses of drugs may be one way that schools can employ this strategy for prevention. Also, when a youth is considered to be at risk for suicide, some assessment of their access to means may be called for and some effort to restrict access to means should be implemented.

Intervention after a suicide. These programs focus on friends and relatives of persons who have committed suicide. They are partially designed to help prevent or contain suicide clusters and to help adolescents and young adults cope effectively with the feelings of loss that follow the sudden death or suicide of a peer. As part of their crisis response plan, schools should have a concerted effort to identify persons who witness a traumatic event or who experienced significant loss as a result of the event. This plan should include provision of appropriated counseling and means to refer and follow-up with those affected.

Family education and involvement. Parents and caregivers of youth are important to consider when developing and implementing a suicide prevention effort. Family members are often most aware of the mood states and issues troubling children. All too frequently, family members are not aware of signs and symptoms of mood disorders or of suicide until the situation of a child has evolved into a crisis. Educating parents and caregivers about how to recognize possible symptoms and what to do when they are concerned may be an effective strategy to prevent suicide.

Future Research, Practice, and Advocacy

Identifying and implementing effective interventions with the goal of reducing the incidence of suicidal behavior is an important and resource intensive step in addressing youth suicide.

The research on risk and protective factors suggests that one promising prevention strategy is to promote overall mental health among school-aged children by reducing early risk factors for depression, substance abuse and aggressive behaviors and building resiliency. In addition to the potential for saving lives, youths benefit from an overall enhancement of academic performance and a reduction in peer and family conflict. A second positive approach is to detect youth most likely to be suicidal by confidentially screening for depression, substance abuse, and suicidal ideation. If a youth reports any of these, further evaluation of the youth can take place by professionals, followed by referral for treatment as needed. Efforts should be made to develop and implement strategies to reduce the stigma associated with accessing mental health, substance abuse, and suicide prevention treatments. Adequate treatment of mental disorders among youth, whether they are suicidal or not, has important academic, peer and family relationship benefits.

Additionally, efforts to limit young people's access to lethal agents—including firearms and medications—may hold great suicide prevention value. Media education is also important, as the risk for suicide contagion as a result of media reporting can be minimized by limited, factual and concise media reports of suicide. Finally, following exposure to suicide or suicidal behaviors within one's family or peer group, suicide risk can be minimized by having family members, friends, peers, and colleagues of the victim evaluated by a mental health professional. Persons deemed at risk for suicide should then be referred for additional mental health services.

Caution should be used in the development of suicide prevention programs for youth, because researchers have found that some types of suicide prevention efforts may be counterproductive. For example, some school-based youth suicide awareness and prevention programs have had unintended negative effects. Because of the tremendous effort and cost involved in starting and maintaining programs, we should be certain that they are safe and effective before they are further used or promoted.

While progress is being made toward developing a knowledge base from which we can make programmatic decisions, the need for outcome evaluation of interventions is imperative. There is simply insufficient quality, scientifically based information that we can use to make decisions about where to spend precious intervention resources. The balance between service delivery and research involves difficult choices but it is important to note that effective service delivery often lies on a foundation of well planned and executed interventions that have been carefully evaluated.

Advocacy on the part of survivors (those who have lost loved ones to suicide) has been an essential element to moving the field of suicide prevention ahead. The Surgeon General's Call to Action to Prevent Suicide (US PHS 1999) came about, in part, in response to work of survivors advocating for public health to take on and address suicide as a public health issue. This led to development of the National Strategy to Prevent Suicide (US, PHS 2001) that had been one of the major intermediary outcomes for which advocates had pressed. Clinicians, researchers, persons who care for persons with mental illness, persons who attempted suicide, among others, have also made significant advocacy efforts. Over the past 8-10 years, national, state and local advocacy efforts have grown much more strong and have influenced the resolve of public officials to begin or expand efforts to address suicide prevention. Recently, the US Congress passed and funded the Garrett Lee Smith Memorial Act, which provides support to states and colleges and universities to develop and deliver suicide prevention program efforts. Advocacy efforts most certainly supported advancing this legislation and are pressing efforts toward additional suicide prevention legislation. The future of suicide prevention in the United States is largely dependent on the ability and resolve of advocates to continue and expand efforts to convince public officials that suicide is a true public health issue.

Developing an Integrated Research, Practice, and Advocacy Agenda

Nascent efforts involving researchers, policymakers and practitioners about how to study and prevent the co-occurrence of varied forms of violence are occurring (Daro, Edleson, and Pinderhughes, 2004). Gaps in our understanding of how different types of violent behaviors are interrelated and whether they share common risk factors have limited the ability to design more cost-effective violence prevention and intervention efforts that could address multiple types of violence among youth. Efficiency and efficacy of prevention efforts might enhance our ability to reduce perpetration of multiple types of violence impacting youth while other prevention strategies may need to focus on a particular type of violence and the groups at greatest risk.

Research has begun to describe youth involvement in multiple forms of violent behavior, documenting the involvement in varied forms of peer violence and suicidal behaviors. One of the few studies that have specifically examined the overlap between physical peer violence and suicidal behaviors was based on the 1997 New York State Youth Risk Behavior Survey. This study found that 11% of high school students reported both suicidal and violent behavior in the past year (Cleary, 2000). Research based on the 2001 National Youth Risk Behavior Survey found that adolescents who report suicidal behavior are more likely to report involvement in physical fighting (Swahn, Lubell, Simon, 2004). More specifically, high school students who reported attempting suicide were more likely to have been in a physical fight than students who reported not attempting suicide (61.5% versus 30.3%) (Swahn, Lubell, Simon, 2004). Higher proportions of both boys and girls who had attempted suicide (77.8% and 54.0%, respectively) reported fighting than those boys and girls who had not attempted suicide (41.2% and 19.8%, respectively). Moreover, among those students who reported attempting suicide, the proportion that reported fighting was highest among 9th graders (64.5%) and decreased with each subsequent grade.

Research has also found that youth who have attacked others with a weapon (Evans, Marte, Betts, and Silliman, 2001; Flannery, Singer, and Wester, 2001), engaged in dating violence (particularly for males; Coker, McKeown, and Sanderson et al, 2000), or perpetrated sexual violence (Borowsky, Hogan, and Ireland, 1997) have been shown to be at higher risk for suicidal behavior.

Research with adults suggests that peer violence and suicide are strongly linked, however the strength of this association among adolescents and the degree to which it changes by age remain unclear. Also, the extent to which risk for participation in single versus multiple types of violence varies for adolescent boys and girls is generally not well understood. In particular, we have a very limited understanding of the role that gender, age or developmental stage or race and ethnicity may have on the associations of different violent behaviors. Additional information on the linkages among forms of youth violence and how these linkages differ by gender and age is needed to guide the selection, timing, and focus of prevention strategies.

Etiologic research has provided extensive information about the risk factors for youth interpersonal violence. Given the strong evidence that these factors contribute to risk for involvement in youth peer violence and that they are integral components of effective prevention programs, it is important for etiologic research to determine whether they also are relevant to suicidal behavior and other forms of youth violence (such as gang and dating violence). Researchers need to integrate the findings and lessons learned from the different disciplines involved in violence related research (Guterman, 2004) and provide an overarching framework that guides future research (Daro, Edleson and Pinderhughes, 2004). Comprehensive views of violence at different stages in development and in different contexts are needed to provide better prevention strategies.

Advancing a complementary ecological model to think more clearly about how to create communities with a rich network of nurturing supportive relationships has been advocated by some neuroscientists, research scholars, pediatricians, and youth service professionals (Eccles 2002). Reviewing new research on the brain, human behavior, and social trends, networks of enduring, nurturing relationships have been shown to significantly strengthen brain development and diminishing the likelihood of aggression, depression, and substance abuse. The characteristics of social groups—whether of families or other social groups that will produce good outcomes for children have begun to be identified and can be incorporated into community programs (Eccles, 2002). This approach does not replace the focus on preventing problems, but provides a broader view of helping youth, and undergirds a wide array of activities such as community-service, school to work transition programs, parenting, mentoring, arts and recreation activities, among others. A few of these have been identified as effective in preventing delinquency, drug and alcohol use, high-risk sexual behavior, aggressive behavior, violence, truancy and smoking, as well as increasing psychological and social assets among youth in high quality comprehensive experimental and quasi experimental evaluations (Catalano, 1999; Catalano 2000). Much more collaborative comprehensive and longitudinal research is needed to evaluate which features of community programs influence development, which processes within each activity are related to these outcomes, and which combination of features are best for which outcomes to supplement family based, school setting prevention efforts.

The greater public health community can play an important role in helping to advance a broad suicide prevention and mental health promotion policy. At a national level, relevant associations and institutions can promote collective, educational, scholarly and dissemination activities among their members and allied groups, through a broad range of research, program and policy development, teaching and other activities that synthesize expertise from multiple disciplines, settings and perspectives. Efforts to build bridges between communities and those sectors that work directly with children and youth at risk can further the coordination of findings, address specific youth suicide prevention issues, and develop a more inclusive suicide prevention agenda. Public health professionals can strengthen ongoing efforts to foster community level change by working with local and national youth development communities and organizations.

Important research, practice and advocacy lessons for national public health efforts can be learned from other countries working to reduce and prevent self-inflicted injuries among youth. The publication of The World Report on Violence and Health, published by the World Health Organization (WHO) in 2002 (Krug et al, 2002), offers examples of increasingly coordinated preventive action and research across types of violence. Also included are efforts to address social, economic and policy factors that transcend national boundaries and initiatives that are focused upon suicide and violence prevention efforts on a regional or global scale. The Report offers evidence of the prevention of suicide and violence from micro-level individual and community efforts to broader national policy initiatives. In sum, the report charges injury and prevention professionals and their constituent and allied groups to think globally even as they act locally, exchanging information, ideas, approaches and experiences.

Resources

- American Association of Suicidology
  www.suicidology.org
- American Foundation for Suicide Prevention
  www.afsp.org
- NAMI
  www.nami.org
- National Registry of Effective Programs and Practices (NREPP)
  www.modelprograms.samhsa.gov
- National Suicide Prevention Resource Center
  www.sprc.org
- National Youth Violence Prevention Resource Center
  www.safeyouth.org
- Suicide Prevention Action Network
  www.spanusa.org
- Children's Safety Network
  www. ChildrensSafetyNetwork.org

References

1. Adams, D. M., Overholser, J. C., and Lehnert, K. L. (1994). Perceived family functioning and adolescent suicidal behavior. journal of the *American Academy of Child & Adolescent Psychiatry*, 33, 498-507.
2. Adityanjee, D. (1986). Suicide attempts and suicides in India. *International Journal of Social Psychiatry*, 32, 64-73.
3. *Adolescent Suicide*. (1996). Group for the Advancement of Psychiatry, 140, 1-184.
4. Ahrens, B., Grof, P., Moller, H. J., Muller-Oerlinghausen, B., and Wolf, T. (1995). Extended survival of patients on long-term lithium treatment. *Canadian journal of Psychiatry*, 40, 241- 246.
5. Apter, A., Bleich, A., Plutchik, R., Mendelsohn, S., and Tyano, S. (1988). Suicidal behavior, depression, and conduct disorder in hospitalized adolescents. *Journal of the American Academy of Child and Adolescent Psychiatry*, 27; 696-699.
6. Araki, S., and Murata, K. (1987). Suicide in Japan. *Suicide and Life-Threatening Behavior*, 17; 64-71.
7. Arana, G. W., and Hyman, S. (1989). Biological contributions to suicide. In D. Jacobs and H. N.
8. Bagley, C., and Ramsay, R. (1985). Psychosocial correlates of suicidal behaviors in an urban population. *Crisis*, 6, 63-77.
9. Baldwin, D., Bullock, T., Montgomery, D., and Montgomery, S. (1991). 5-HT reuptake inhibitors, tricyclic antidepressants and suicidal behaviour. *International Clinical Psychopharmacology*, 6(Suppl. 3); 49-56.
10. Barrett. T. *Youth in Crisis: Seeking Solutions to Self-Destructive Behavior*. Longmont, CO: Sopris West, 1985.
11. Beautrais, A. t., Joyce, P. R., and Mulder, R. T. (1996). Access to firearms and the risk of suicide. *Australian and New Zealand Journal of Psychiatry*, 3D, 741-748.

12. Beck, A. T., Brown, G. K., and Steer, R. A. (1997). Psychometric characteristics of the Scale for Suicide Ideation with psychiatric outpatients. *Behaviour Research and Therapy*, 35, 1039-1046.

13. Beck, A. T., Steer, R. A., Beck, J. S., and Newman, C. F. (1993). Hopelessness, depression, suicidal ideation, and clinical diagnosis of depression. *Suicide and Life-Threatening Behavior*, 23, 139- 145.

14. Beck, A. T., Steer, R. A., Kovacs, M., and Garrison, B. (1985). Hopelessness and eventual suicide. *American Journal of Psychiatry*, 142, 559-563.

15. Berglund, M. (1984). Suicide in alcoholism. *Archives of General Psychiatry*, 41, 888-891.

16. Bergman, B., and Brismar, B. (1991). Suicide attempts by battered wives. *Acta Psychiatrica Scandinavica*, 83, 380-384.

17. Boor, M., and Bair, J. H. (1990). Suicide rates, handgun control laws, and sociodemographic variables. *Psychological Reports*, 66, 923-930.

18. Borowsky, I.W., Hogan, M., Ireland, M. (1997). Adolescent sexual aggression: risk and protective factors. *Pediatrics, 100*(6).

19. Briere, J., and Runtz, M. (1986). Suicidal lhoughts and behaviours in former sexual abuse victims. *Canadian Journal of Behavioural Science*, 18, 413-423.

20. Brent, D. A. (1995). Risk factors for adolescent suicide and suicidal behavior. *Suicide and Life- Threatening Behavior*, 25(Suppl.), 52-63.

21. Brent, D. A., Kolko, D. J., Allan, M. J., and Brown, R. V. (1990). Suicidality in affectively disordered adolescent inpatients. *Journal of the American Academy of Child and Adolescent Psychiatry*, 29, 586-593.

22. Brent, D. A., Moritz, G., Bridge, J., Perper, J., and Canobbio, R. (1996). The impact of adolescent suicide on siblings and parents. *Suicide and Life-Threatening Behavior*, 26, 253-259.

23. Brent, D. A., Perper, J. A., Goldstein, C. E., Kolko, D. J., Allan, M. J., Allman, C. J., and Zelenak, J. P. (1988). Risk factors for adolescent suicide. *Archives of General Psychiatry*, 45, 581-588.

24. Brent, D. A., Perper, J. A., Moritz, G., Allman, C., Friend, A., Roth, C., Schweers, J., Balach, T., and Baugher, M. (1993). Psychiatric risk factors for adolescent suicide. *Journal of the American Academy of Child and Adolescent Psychiatry*, 32, 521-529.

25. Brent, D. A., Perper, J. A., Moritz, G., Baugher, M., Schweers, J., and Roth, C. (1993). Firearms and adolescent suicide. *American Journal of Diseases of Children*, 147; 1066-1071.

26. Brent, D. A., Perper, J. A., Moritz, G., Friend, A., Schweers, J., Allman, C., McQuiston, T., Boylan, M., Roth, C., and Balach, t. (1993). Adolescent witnesses to a peer suicide. *Journal of the American Academy of Child and Adolescent Psychiatry*, 32, 1184-1188.

27. Brent, D. A., Perper, J. A., Moritz, G., Liotus, t., Schweers, J., Balach, t., and Roth, C. (1994). Familial risk factors for adolescent suicide. *Acta Psychiatrica Scandinavica*, 89, 52-58.

28. Brent, D. A., Perper, J. A., Moritz, G., Liotus, t., Schweers, J., Roth, C., Balach, t., and Allman, C. (1993). Psychiatric impact of the loss of an adolescent sibling to suicide. *Journal of Affective Disorders*, 28, 249-256.

29. Bryant, E. S., Garrison, C. Z., Valois, R. F., Rivard, J. C., and Hinkle, K. T. (1995). Suicidal behavior among youth with severe emotional disturbance. *Journal of Child and Family Studies*, 4, 429-443.

30. Bryant, S. L., and Range, L. M. (1997). Type and severity of child abuse and college students' lifetime suicidality. *Child Abuse and Neglect*, 21, 1169-1176.

31. Burge, V., Felts, M., Chenier, T., and Parrillo, A. V. (1995). Drug use, sexual activity, and suicidal behavior in U.S. high school students. *Journal of School Health*, 65, 222-227.

32. Burvill, P. W. (1995). Suicide in the multiethnic elderly population of Australia, 1979-1990. *International Psychogeriatrics,* 7; 319-333.

33. Campbell, N. B., Milling, L., Laughlin, A., and Bush, E. (1993). The psychosocial climate of families with suicidal preadolescent children. *American Journal of Orthopsychiatry,* 63, 142-145.

34. Canetto, S. S., and Lester, D. (1995). Gender and the primary prevention of suicide mortality. *Suicide and Life-Threatening Behavior,* 25,58-69.

35. Catalano, R.F., Hawkins, J.D., Berglund, L., Pollard, J., Arthur, M. (2002). Prevention science and positive youth development: Competitive or cooperative frameworks? *Journal of Adolescent Health,* 31(6 Suppl. 1), 230-239.

36. Catalano, R., Berglund, M.L., Ryan, J.A.M., Lonczak, H.S., Hawkins, J.D. (2002) Positive Youth Development in the United States: Research findings on evaluations of positive youth development programs. *Prevention and Treatment,* 5, article 15.

37. Centers for Disease Control and Prevention. "Suicide Prevention Evaluation in a Western Athabaskan American Indian Tribe -New Mexico, 1988-1997." *MMWR* 47.13 (1998): 257-61.

38. Centers for Disease Control and Prevention. *Youth Suicide Prevention Programs: A Resource Guide.* Atlanta, GA: Centers for Disease Control and Prevention, 1992.

39. Centers for Disease Control and Prevention. Web-based Injury Statistics Query and Reporting System (WISQARS) [online]. (2005) {11-5-05}. Available from: www.cdc.gov/ncipc/wisqars

40. Cleary, S. D. (2000). Adolescent victimization and associated suicidal and violent behaviors. *Adolescence* 2000;35:671-82.

41. Coker, A. L., and et al. "Severe Dating Violence and Quality of Life Among South Carolina High School Students." *American Journal of Preventive Medicine* 19 (2000): 220-27.

42. Cormier, H. J., and KIerman, G. L. (1985). Unemployment and male-female labor force participation as determinants of changing suicide rates of males and females in Quebec. *Social Psychiatry,* 20, 109-114.

43. Cummings, P., Koepsell, T. D., Grossman, D. C., Savarino, J., and Thompson, R. S. (1997). The association between the purchase of a handgun and homicide or suicide. *American journal of Public Health,* 87; 974-978.

44. Daro D., Edleson, J. L., Pinderhughes, H. (2004). Finding common ground in the study of Dorwart, R. A., and L. Chartock. "Suicide: A Public Health Perspective." *Suicide: Understanding and Responding: Harvard Medical School Perspectives.* Madison, CT: International Universities Press, Inc., 1989. 31-55.

45. DeJong, M. L. (1992). Attachment, individuation, and risk of suicide in late adolescence. *Journal of Youth and Adolescence,* 21, 357-373.

46. Deykin, E. Y., Alpert, J. J., and McNamara, J. J. (1985). A pilot study of the effect of exposure to child abuse or neglect on adolescent suicidal behavior. *American Journal of Psychiatry,* 142, 1299-1303.

47. Durkheim, E. (1951). *Suicide: A Study in Sociology.* New York: The Free Press.

48. Eccles, J and J.A. Gootman, National Research Council and Institute of Medicine (eds.), *Community Programs to Promote Youth Development* (Washington, DC: National Academies Press, 2002).

49. Eggert, L. L., et al. "Prevention Research Program: Reconnecting at-Risk Youth." *Issues in Mental Health Nursing* 15.2 (1994): 107-35. Notes: Taylor and Francis, US, Http://Www.Taylorandfrancis.Com.

50. ___"Reducing Suicide Potential Among High-Risk Youth: Tests of a School-Based Prevention Program." *Suicide and Life-Threatening Behavior* 25.2 (1995): 276-96 Notes: Guilford Publications, US, http://www.Guilford.Com.

51. Eggert, L. L., et al. "Reconnecting Youth to Prevent Drug Abuse, School Dropout and Suicidal Behaviors Among High-Risk Youth." *Innovations in Adolescent Substance Abuse Interventions.* Ed. Eric F. Wagner and Holly B. Waldron. Amsterdam, Netherlands: Pergamon/Elsevier Science Inc., 2001. 51-84.

52. Elster, A., and Kuznets, N.J., *AMA Guidelines for Adolescent Preventive Services (GAPS): Recommendations and Rationale.* Ed. Kuznets N.J., Elster,A.B. Baltimore: Williams and Wilkins, 1994. 131-43.

53. Evans, W. P., Marte, R. M., Betts, S., Silliman, B. (2001). Adolescent suicide risk and peer-related violent behaviors and victimization. *Journal of Interpersonal Violence.* Vol 16(12). Dec 2001, 1330-1348.

54. Flannery, D.J., Singer, M.I., and Wester, K. (2001). Violence exposure, psychological trauma, and suicide risk in a community sample of dangerously violence adolescents. *Journal of the American Academy of Child and Adolescent Psychiatry.* Vol 40(4) April, 2001, 435-442.

55. Garrison, C. Z., McKeown, R. E., Valois, R. F., and Vincent, M. L. (1993). Aggression, substance use, and suicidal behaviors in high school students. *American journal of Public Health,* 83, 179-184.

56. Glick, W. H., and Roberts, K. H. (1994). Hypothesized interdependence, assumed independence. *Academy of Management Review,* 9, 722-735.

57. Goldsmith, S.K.,et al. (2002). Reducing Suicide: A National Imperative. Committee on Pathophysiology and Prevention of Adolescent and Adult Suicide, Board on Neuroscience and Behavioral Health, Institute of Medicine.

58. Green, M. *Bright Futures: Guidelines for Health Supervision of Infants, Children, and Adolescents.* Arlington, VA: National Center for Education in Maternal and Child Health, 1994.

59. Grossman, D. C., Milligan, B. C., and Deyo, R. A. (1991). Risk factors for suicide attempts among Navajo adolescents. *American Journal of Public Health,* 81, 870-874.

60. Grunbaum, JA, Kann, L., Kichen, S, Ross, J, et al, (2004). Youth Risk Behavior Surveillance—United States, 2003. *MMWR,* May 21, 2004 / 53(SS02);1-96

61. Guterman, N. B. (2004). Advancing prevention research on child abuse, youth violence, and domestic violence. *Journal of Interpersonal Violence, 19.*299-321.

62. Harrington, R., Bredenkamp, D., Groothues, C., Rutter, M., Fudge, H., and Pickles, A. (1994). Adult outcomes of childhood and adolescent depression. *Journal of Child Psychology and Psychiatry and Allied Disciplines,* 35, 1309-1319.

63. Hill, R. D., Gallagher, D., Thompson, L. W., and Ishida, T. (1988). Hopelessness as a measure of suicidal intent in the depressed elderly. *Psychology and Aging,* 3, 230-232.

64. Iversen, G. R. (1991). *Contextual Analysis.* Newbury Park, CA: Sage.

65. Keller, F., and Wolfersdorf, M. (1993). Hopelessness and the tendency to commit suicide in the course of depressive disorders. *Crisis,* 14, 173-177.

66. Ko, S. M., and Kua, E. H. (1995). Ethnicity and elderly suicide in Singapore. *International Psychogeriatrics,* 7; 309-317.

67. Krug, E.G. et al., eds. *World Report on Violence and Health.* Geneva, World Health Organization, 2002.

68. Krug, E. G., Dahlberg, L. L., and Powell, K. E. (1996). Childhood homicide, suicide, and firearm deaths. *World Health Statistics Quarterly,* 49(3-4), 230-235.

69. Krupinski, M., Fischer, A., Grohmann, R., Engel, R. R., Hollweg, M., and Moeller, H. J. (1998). Psychopharmacological therapy and suicide of inpatients with depressive psychoses. *Archives of Suicide Research,* 4, 143-155.

70. Lewinsohn, P. M., Rohde, P., and Seeley, J. R. (1994). Psychosocial risk factors for future adolescent suicide attempts. *Journal of Consulting and Clinical Psychology,* 62, 297-305.

71. Lowther, S., De Paermentier, F., Cheetham, S. C., Crompton, M. R., Katona, C. L., and Horton, R. W. (1997). 5-HT1A receptor binding sites in post-mortem brain samples from depressed suicides and controls. *Journal of Affective Disorders*, 42, 199-207.

72. Lucas, C. P., et al. "The DISC Predictive Scales (DPS): Efficiently Screening for Diagnoses." *Journal of the American Academy of Child and Adolescent Psychiatry* 40.4 (2001): 443-49.

73. Mann, J. J. (1987). Psychobiologic predictors of suicide. *Journal of Clinical Psychiatry*, 48(December Suppl.), 39-43.

74. Mann, J. J., Arango, V., and Underwood, M. D. (1990). Serotonin and suicidal behavior. *Annals of the New York Academy of Sciences*, 600, 476-485.

75. Marzuk, P. M., Tardiff, K., Leon, A. C., Stajic, M., Morgan, E. B., and Mann, J. J. (1992). Prevalence of cocaine use among residents of New York City who committed suicide during a one-year period. *American Journal of Psychiatry*, 149, 371-375.

76. Medoff, M. H., and Magaddino, J. P. (1983). Suicides and firearm control laws. *Evaluation Review,* 7; 357-372.

77. Molnar, B. E., Shade, S. B., Kral, A. H., Booth, R. E., and Watters, J. K. (1998). Suicidal behavior and sexual/physical abuse among street youth. *Child Abuse and Neglect*, 22, 213-222.

78. Mueller-Oerlinghausen, B., Mueser-Causemann, B., and Volk, J. (1992). Suicides and parasuicides in a high-risk patient group on and off lithium long-term medication. *Journal of Affective Disorders*, 25, 261-269.

79. Nimeus, A., Traskman-Bendz, L., and Alsen, M. (1997). Hopelessness and suicidal behavior. *Journal of Affective Disorders*, 42, 137-144.

80. O'Carroll, P. W., Berman, A. L., Maris, R. W., Moscicki, E. K., Tanney, B. L., and Silverman, M. M. (1996). *Beyond the Tower of Babel. Suicide and Life-Threatening Behavior,* 26, 237-252.

81. Ohmori, T., Arora, R. C., and Meltzer, H. Y. (1992). Serotonergic measures in suicide brain. *Biological Psychiatry*, 32, 57-71 .

82. Osgood, N. J. (1992). Suicide in the elderly. International Review of Psychiatry, 4, 217-223.

83. Peck, D. L., and Warner, K. (1995). Accident or suicide? *Adolescence*, 30, 463-472.

84. Porsteinsson, A., Duberstein, P. R., Conwell, Y., Cox, C., Forbes, N., and Caine, E. D. (1997). Suicide and alcoholism. *American Journal on Addictions*, 6, 304-310.

85. Ragland, J. D., and Berman, A. L. (1990-1991). Farm crisis and suicide. *Omega*, 22,173-185.

86. Rainer, J. D. (1984). Genetic factors in depression and suicide. *American Journal of Psychotherapy*, 38, 329-340.

87. Reinfurt, D. W., Stewart, J. R., and Weaver, N. L. (1991). The economy as a factor in motor vehicle fatalities, suicides, and homicides. *Accident Analysis and Prevention*, 23, 453-462.

88. Richards, J. M., Gottfredson, D. C., and Gottfredson, G. D. (1990). Units of analysis and item statistics for environmental assessment scales. Current Psychology, 9,407-413.

89. Rose, G. "Sick Individuals and Sick Populations." *International Journal of Epidemiology* 14.1 (1985): 32-38.

90. Rossow, I., and Amundsen, A. (1995). Alcohol abuse and suicide. *Addiction*, 90, 685-691.

91. Rotheram-Borus, M. J., and Trautman, P. D. (1988). Hopelessness, depression, and suicidal intent among adolescent suicide attempters. *Journal of the American Academy of Child and Adolescent Psychiatry*, 27; 700-704.

92. Roy, A. (1986). Depression, attempted suicide, and suicide in patients with chronic schizophrenia. *Psychiatric Clinics of North America*, 9(1), 193-206.

93. Roy, A. (1993). Genetic and biologic risk factors for suicide in depressive disorders. *Psychiatric Quarterly*, 64, 345-358.

94. Roy, A., Dejong, J., Lamparski, D., Adinoff, B., George, T., Moore, V., Garnett, D., Kerich, M., and Linnoila, M. (1991). Mental disorders among alcoholics. *Archives of General Psychiatry*, 48, 423-427.

95. Roy, A., Dejong, J., Lamparski, D., George, T., and Linnoila, M. (1991). Depression among alcoholics. *Archives of General Psychiatry*, 48, 428-432.

96. Shaffer, D., et al. "The Impact of Curriculum-Based Suicide Prevention Programs for Teenagers." *Journal of the American Academy of Child and Adolescent Psychiatry* 30.4 (1991): 588-96.

97. Shaffer, D., Fisher, P., Trautman, P., Moreau, D., Kleinman, M., and Flory, M. (1996). Psychiatric diagnosis in child and adolescent suicide. *Archives of General Psychiatry*, 53, 339-348.

98. Shafii, M., Steltz-Lenarsky, J., Derrick, A. M., Beckner, C., et al. (1988). Comorbidity of mental disorders in the postmortem diagnosis of completed suicide in children and adolescents. *Journal of Affective Disorders*, 15,227-233.

99. Simon, Thomas R., et al. "Characteristics of Impulsive Suicide Attempts and Attempters." *Suicide and Life-Threatening Behavior* 32.Suppl (2001): 49-59.

100. Sloan,J. H., Rivara, F. P., Reay, D. T., Ferris,J. A., and Kellerman, A. L. (1990). Firearm regulations and rates of suicide. *New England Journal of Medicine*, 322, 369-373.

101. Stack, S., and Wasserman, I. M. (1995). Marital status, alcohol abuse and attempted suicide. *Journal of Addictive Diseases*, 14(2),43-51.

102. Strauss, M. A., and Kantor, G. K. (1994). Corporal punishment of adolescents by parents. *Adolescence*, 29, 543-561.

103. Swahn, M. H., Lubell, K. M., Simon T. R. (2004). Suicide Attempt and Physical Fighting Among High School Students—United States, 2001. *MMWR*, June 11 (53(22);474-476.

104. Tondo, L., Baldessarini, R. J., Hennen, J., Floris, G., Silvetti, F., and Tohen, M. (1998). Lithium treatment and risk of suicidal behavior in bipolar disorder patients. *Journal of Clinical Psychiatry*, 59, 405-414.

105. Tondo, L., Jamison, K. R., and Baldessarini, R. J. (1997). Effect of lithium maintenance on suicidal behavior in major mood disorders. *Annals of the New York Academy of Sciences*, 836, 339- 351.

106. U.S. Preventive Services Task Force. *Guide to Clinical Preventive Services, 2nd Edition*. Washington, DC: U.S. Department of Health and Human Services, Office of Disease Prevention and Health Promotion, 1996.

107. U.S. Public Health Service, The Surgeon General's Call To Action To Prevent Suicide. Washington, DC: 1999.

108. U.S. Public Health Service. The National Strategy for Suicide Prevention. 2001

109. University of Washington, School of Nursing 1999 Washington State Youth Suicide Prevention Program. Report of Activities 1997-1999. Seattle Washington.

110. Van Praag, H. M. (1991). Serotonergic dysfunction and aggression control. *Psychological Medicine*, 21, 15-19.

111. Vilhjalmsson, R., Kristjansdottir, G., and Sveinbjarnardottir, E. (1998). Factors associated with suicide ideation in adults. Social Psychiatry and Psychiatric Epidemiology, 33, 97-103.

112. Weishaar, M. E., and Beck, A. T. (1992). Hopelessness and suicide. *International Review of Psychiatry*, 4, 177-184.

113. Windle, R. C., and Windle, M. (1997). An investigation of adolescents' sub-

stance use behaviors, depressed affect, and suicidal behaviors. *Journal of Child Psychology and Psychiatry and Allied Disciplines,* 38, 921-929.

114. World Health Organization. Prevention of Suicide: *Guidelines for the Formulation and Implementation of National Strategies.* Geneva: World Health Organization, 1996.

115. Wolk, S. I., and Weissman, M. M. (1996). Suicidal behavior in depressed children grown up. *Psychiatric Annals,* 26, 331-335.

116. Wright, L. S. (1985). Suicidal thoughts and their relationship to family stress and personal problems among high school seniors and college undergraduates. *Adolescence,* 20, 575-580

117. Webster, D.W., Gainer, P.S., and Champion, H.R. (1993). Weapon carrying among inner-city junior high school students: Defensive behavior versus aggressive delinquency. *American Journal of Public Health,* 83, 1604-1608.

118. Yang, B. (1995). The differential impact of the economy on suicide in the young and the elderly. *Archives of Suicide Research,* 1, 111-120.

119. Yang, B., and Lester. D. (1990). Time-series analyses of the American suicide rate. *Social Psychiatry and Psychiatric Epidemiology,* 25, 274-275.

120. Young, M. A., Fogg, L. F., Scheftner, W. A., and Fawcett, J. A. (1994). Interactions of risk factors in predicting suicide. *American Journal of Psychiatry,* 151, 434-435.

CHAPTER 14

Conclusions and Recommendations for the Future

Karen D. Liller, PhD*

While this book was not meant to be an exhaustive review of child and adolescent injuries, it was designed to inform academicians, students, and practitioners of up-to-date research, practice, and advocacy efforts, and what is needed for the future.

There was a need to look comprehensively at injury prevention efforts for children and adolescents. An important reason for this is that research alone will not solve the problem, nor will practice, nor will advocacy, but when these elements work in synergy, a tremendous impact can be made. We have seen the successful incorporation of all of these areas in child and adolescent injury prevention already, such as in the use of child safety seats, seatbelts, and the prevention of poisonings. But more can be done, and innovative approaches need to take place with motor vehicle injuries, recreational injuries, residential injuries, school injuries, agricultural injuries, workplace injuries, youth violence, child abuse and neglect, and injuries related to firearms, to name a few.

What questions need to be pursued and answered in the future pertaining to children's injuries? For research, a common theme across injury topics is the need for better surveillance data (especially for morbidity). Data systems have improved such as with the National Electronic Injury Surveillance System's All Injury Program and the National Violent Death Reporting System, but much more needs to be done. For example, all hospitals and emergency departments need to report injuries and their etiologies in a uniform manner that is useful for research and practice.

Research needs to continue on the most appropriate role of education in child and adolescent injury prevention and the role of parental supervision. Parental advocacy of safety continues to be important as children age. This is seen in many areas, including motor vehicle injury prevention and safe work environments for adolescents. Comprehensive evaluations of

* University of South Florida, College of Public Health

interventions need to be developed and implemented utilizing more sophisticated research designs. Research in children's and adolescent injury prevention needs to be developmentally-based and incorporate as much as possible the community participatory research model where communities are directly involved with research endeavors.

In terms of practice, it is very important that practitioners and researchers work in concert. Representatives from education, media, advocacy groups, business, engineering, law enforcement, and others should be at the table. As child and adolescent unintentional injury and violence researchers and practitioners pursue prevention efforts together, injuries will need to be analyzed through multilevel explanations (individual, interpersonal, organizational, community, and societal factors) and not by using a risk factor only approach. Much emphasis has been placed on the environment in the past, leading to less effort being expended on behavioral factors related to injury. According to Sleet and Gielen,[1] there is rarely an environmental change that does not require some type of human adaptation. For example, how could child safety seats prevent injuries if they were not installed by parents? Or how can pool fencing lead to less drowning and near-drownings if the gates are not functional and always closed? This points to the need for strong theoretically-designed behavioral interventions that are appropriately evaluated for efficacy. Practitioners need to collaborate with researchers and their students often located in universities and academic settings to strategically work together to build plans for prevention strategies.

In addition, knowledge of the costs related to injury is extremely important to incorporate in our prevention efforts. Legislative committees often want to know how much money interventions will cost the state and/or community and what exactly are the cost benefits to society as whole. What will society be willing to pay for these efforts? Focusing only on those injuries that lead to death will not lead to the most effective use of resources for prevention strategies.

A most important role for child and adolescent injury prevention is advocacy. Knowing how to work with the media, legislators and understanding the role of coalitions is vital. The American Public Health Association provides several helpful educational materials on these topics. Being known to legislators and testifying on legislative committees, writing editorials and press releases, conducting press conferences, utilizing media advocacy to promote injury policies, and joining community coalitions are just a few of the ways that injury prevention advocates can make their voices heard.

Injury prevention education needs to continue and be included in grades pre-K–12 and in higher learning. Injury and violence competencies have been developed for leaders, practitioners, and partners. The school system and other educational institutions have vital roles here as important community leaders in injury prevention efforts. With education, reinforcement, and environmental change, injury prevention will become more normative in society.

The National Center for Injury Prevention and Control has been very important to the growth of injury prevention efforts throughout the country. Their current research agenda includes many of the research, practice, and advocacy measures already described in the text. In fact, the overall research priorities include evaluating the most effective methods for translating research findings into public health programs and policies; evaluating the effectiveness of interventions to improve parenting skills and reduce risky use of alcohol; identifying the costs and consequences of injury; and building the research infrastructure.[2]

Finally, there now is a real need to pursue intervention efforts in developing countries. Road injuries alone pose major threats to life across the globe. As efforts continue with the World Health Organization pertaining to children's injuries, researchers and practitioners will need to become active partners.

This book began with a discussion about the importance of child and adolescent injury prevention and putting a "face" on each injury statistic. I hope that this has been accomplished and you as readers have been inspired to begin and/or continue in your tireless prevention efforts. With all of us working together those needless injuries that rob our children and adolescents of their future should become a part of the past.

References

1. Sleet DA, Gielen AC. Developing injury interventions: the role of behavioural science. In McClure R, Stevenson M, McEvoy S.eds. *The Scientific Basis of Injury Prevention and Control.* Victoria, Australia: IP Communications; 2004.
2. National Center for Injury Prevention and Control. Available at http://www.cdc.gov/ncipc. Assessed December 28, 2004.

Selected Historic Time Line
for Injury Prevention and Control

Les Fisher[1]

T he Time Line shows the dynamic growth of our field. At www.icehs. org there are newsletters and other information including discussions, archival historical critical analyses and archival references on the events below as well as many other timeline leadership milestones in injury prevention and control. The events listed along this timetable are only a few of the seminal events that have shaped the history of injury prevention and control and offer guidance and strength for the future.

Bold Items in the Time Line, below, represent key happenings in road safety in America. Those **bold *and italicized*** are from a broader time line in Reducing the Burden of Injury.

Historic Time Line

1924   **Cadillac offers first car with safety windshield glass equipment as a standard.**

1913   **US Congress charters National Safety Council.**

1932   **Maryland is first US State to introduce mandatory car inspections.**

1937   **Godfrey publishes one of the first U.S. statements on the need for public health involvement in "accident" prevention, in AJPH.**

1943   APHA Committee on Administrative Practice appoints a subcommittee on "accident" prevention.

1945   **APHA Subcommittee on "Accident" Prevention develops program guidelines for accident prevention.**

1950   **American Academy of Pediatrics forms Committee on "Accident" Prevention and Poison Control.**

1955   **McFarland publishes "Epidemiological Principles Applicable to the Study and Prevention of Child Accidents" in AJPH.**

1956   **First annual Stapp conference on the biomechanics of crashes.**

---

1. Archivisit, Injury Control and Emergency Health Services Section of the American Public Health Association and Safety/Management Consultant

1957   APHA policy statement urges health agencies to assume an active role in all types of "accident" prevention programs.

1959   **Insurance Institute for Highway Safety founded.**

1960   **APHA publishes public policy statement recommending that "accident" prevention be recognized as a major public health problem.**

1961   **APHA publishes Accident Prevention: The Role of Physicians and Public Health Workers. Journal of Trauma begins.**

1963   **Haddon publishes "injury matrix" concept paper.**

1964   Injury Prevention training offered in 11 schools of public health.

1965   **Ralph Nader publishes "Unsafe at Any Speed."**

1966   **National Highway Safety Bureau (later National Highway Traffic Safety Administration, NHTSA) established to set car safety standards in 1968.**

1966   **National Research Council report: Accidental Death and Disability: The Neglected Disease of Modern Society in published.**

1968   The Federal Gun Control Act passed by Congress

        American Trauma Association established

        Lap belts in all seated occupants are installed by the four major manufacturers of US automobiles.

1969   **Accident Analysis and Prevention and also, the Journal of Safety Research began publication.**

1970   The Federal Poison Prevention Packaging Act passed.

        National Institutes on Alcohol Abuse and Alcoholism established.

        National Institute for Occupational Safety and Health established.

1972   The Federal Flammable Clothing Act passed.

        Consumer Product Safety Commission established.

1973   **EMS Act passes U.S. Congress.**

        National Center on Child Abuse and Neglect established.

1974   General Motors produces first air bag.

        Congress mandates 55 mph national maximum speed limit.

        National Association of Governor's Highway Traffic Safety Representatives established.

1976   National EMS/PCC law passed with limited funding.

1978   **US state of Tennessee first worldwide to mandate child passenger safety law.**

        US RID (Remove Intoxicated Drivers) established.

1979   Federal Division of Maternal and Child Health (DMCH) of the US Department of Health and Human Services established (designated as a Bureau later).

        Promoting Health/Preventing Disease: Objectives for the Nation published.

        Center for Disease Control (CDC) establishes a violence epidemiology branch to track incidence of interpersonal violence.

1980   First population-based and emergency room based injury surveillance system implemented in two states.

Mothers Against Drunk Driving (MADD) established.

1981   **First National Conference on Injury Control, sponsored by the Johns Hopkins University and CDC.**

1982   CDC publishes *Injury Control Implementation Plan for State and Local Governments.*

1983   **MCHB publishes *Developing Childhood Injury Prevention Programs: An Administrative Guide for Maternal and Child Health (Title V) Programs.***

1984   **Congress establishes the Emergency Medical Services for Children program.**

New York State enacts first U.S. seat belt law.

1985   **Every state has passed legislation requiring the use of child safety seats.**

***Injury in America: A Continuing Public Health Problem* published by the Committee on Trauma Research.**

Surgeon General's workshop on "Violence and Public Health."

1986   **CDC awards five academic centers $2 million to address research on injuries.**

MCHB awards demonstration funding to address violence prevention.

Minimum Drinking Age passed by Congress.

1987   **Launch of the National Safe Kids Campaign.**

First *Injury in America* Conference (as partnership with CDC and NHTSA).

1988   ***Injury Control*, a follow-up to *Injury in America* published.**

CDC established the National Center for Injury Prevention and Control.

Surgeon General's workshop on drunk driving.

***The Future of Public Health* released by the Institute of Medicine.**

1989   **Release of *Cost of Injury*, a report to Congress.**

***Injury Prevention: Meeting the Challenge* published as a supplement to the American Journal of Preventive Medicine.**

1990   ***Healthy People 2000—National Health Promotion and Disease Prevention Objectives* report published.**

E-coding mandated by six states.

1991   WHO Helmet initiative begins.

Rosenberg JL, Fenley MA. *Violence in America-A Public Health Approach.* Oxford University Press: New York.

1992   California Wellness Foundation begins a 5-year Violence Prevention Initiative.

1993   President Clinton declares violence to be a public health emergency.

1995   **Injury Prevention begins publication.**

1997   **E-coding mandated in 17 states.**

Institute of Medicine National Committee on Injury Prevention and Control holds public meeting in Washington, DC.

1998   Centers for Disease Control and Prevention's Tenth Anniversary of the National Center for Injury Prevention and Control (with a timeline)

1999   Bonnie RJ, Fulco CE, Liverman CT (eds.). *Reducing the burder of injury: Advancing prevention and treatment.* Committee on Injury Prevention and Control, Division of Health Promotion and Disease Prevention, Institute of Medicine.

2001   Funding of National Poison Control Center Enhancement Act

National Strategies for Suicide Prevention. Goals and Objectives for Action, US Department of Health and Human Services

School Health Guidelines to Prevent Unintentional Injuries and Violence *MMWR.* Dec 7, 2001, No. RR-22

2002   Goldsmith et al. *Reducing Suicide. Committee on Pathophysiology & Prevention of Adolescent Suicides. A National Imperative.* Institute of Medicine of the National Academy of Sciences.

World Report on Violence and Health. WHO, Geneva

2003   Baldessarini RJ and Tondo, L. Suicide Risk and Treatments for Patients with Bipolar Disorder. *JAMA* 290:1467-1473; Editorial, Ibid, 1517-1519.

Linkage between Rx drugs and intentional injury.

2004   *Forging a Poison Prevention and Control System.* Committee on Poison Prevention and Control. Board on Health Promotion and Disease Prevention. Institute of Medicine of the National Academies of Sciences, Washington DC

Suicide Prevention Law signed by President Bush, Nov. 2004

Firearms and Violence, National Academy of Sciences, Washington, DC

World report on road traffic injury prevention, WHO, Geneva

2005   Asia's tsunamis and follow up public health/injury control responses

---

Credits Note: Above **bold italics are items published in**: Reducing the Burden of Injury: Advancing Prevention and Treatment. Richard C.J. Bonnie, Carolyn E. Fulco, Catharyn T. Liverman, editors; Committee on Injury Prevention and Control, Division of Health Promotion and Disease Prevention, Institute of Medicine, 1999. That publication used the other listings in the above original chart as prepared by Les Fisher, Archivist, Injury Control and Emergency Health Services Section, American Public Health Association, 1990, Safety/Management Consultant, 97 Union Avenue, South. Delmar, New York, 12054. fisher166@juno.com.

Resources

The Resources listed in Appendix II were derived from many sources and while not meant to be exhaustive, they should assist in learning more about injury prevention resources and materials.

I. Funding Resources

A variety of funding opportunities are available to help support the planning, implementation, and evaluation of injury prevention and control research and programs. Visit these sites to learn more about different funding opportunities.

- CDC Funding Opportunities
  www.cdc.gov/od/pgo/funding/funding.htm
- CDC's National Center for Injury Prevention and Control
  www.cdc.gov/ncipc/ncipchm.htm
- Children's Safety Network Finding Funding for Injury and Violence Prevention—These fact sheets include information on Federal and State funding, finding corporate sponsors, private foundations, etc.
  www.childrenssafetynetwork.org/FUNDING.pdf
- Community of Science, Inc.
  www.cos.com/
- Directory of Charitable Grantmakers
  www.foundations.org
- Federal Money Retriever
  www.idimagic.com/fedspending2.html
- Federal Funding Opportunities and Agencies
  http://ocga2.ucsd.edu/agencies/federal.html
- Fundsnet Services Online
  http://fundsnetservices.com/main.htm

Thanks to Irene Pintado, Doctoral Student, University of South Florida College of Public Health, who was instrumental in the preparation of this Appendix.

- The Foundation Center
    www.fdncenter.org
- NIH Grants Database
    www.nih.gov/grants/oer.htm
- RAMS-FIE
    www.rams-fie.com/
- Small Business Innovative Research
    www.sbaonline.sba.gov/hotlist/sbir.html

In addition to sites listed above, several Federal agencies (Department of Transportation, Department of Justice, and the Department of Health and Human Services) offer state funding for impaired driving prevention and intervention programs. Find out more at http://www.nhtsa.dot.gov/people/injury/alcohol/StopImpaired/funding.html. Additional funding sources are also discussed at http://www.nhtsa.dot.gov/people/perform/Pages/funding.htm

II. Research Centers and Organizations of Interest

(Note: information for many of the organizations was found on their website).
    The CDC National Center for Injury Prevention and Control funds ten Injury Control Research Centers around the country to conduct research and serve as both training centers for public health professionals and information centers for the public.

- Colorado Injury Control Research Center.
    http://psy.psych.colostate.edu/CICRC
- Harborview Injury Prevention Research Center.
    http://depts.washington.edu/hiprc
- Harvard Injury Prevention Research Center.
    www.hsph.harvard.edu/hicrc
- The John Hopkins Center for Injury Research and Policy.
    www.jhsph.edu/InjuryCenter
- Southern California Injury Prevention Research Center.
    www.ph.ucla.edu/sciprc
- Birmingham Injury Control Research Center.
    www.uab.edu/icrc
- San Francisco Injury Center.
    www.surgery.ucsf.edu/sfic
- University of Iowa Injury Prevention Research Center.
    www.public-health.uiowa.edu/IPRC
- University of North Carolina Injury Prevention Research Center.
    www.iprc.unc.edu
- University of Pittsburgh Center for Injury Research and Control.
    www.circl.pitt.edu/home

- **American Association of Poison Control Centers**
    www.aapcc.org
    The American Association of Poison Control Centers (AAPCC) is a nationwide organization of poison centers and interested individuals. Its

objectives are to provide a forum for poison centers and interested individuals to promote the reduction of morbidity and mortality from poisonings through public and professional education and scientific research and to set voluntary standards for poison center operations.

- **American Burn Association**
  www.ameriburn.org
  The American Burn Association and its members dedicate their efforts and resources to promoting and supporting burn-related research, education, care, rehabilitation, and prevention. The ABA has more than 3,500 members in the United States, Canada, Europe, Asia, and Latin America. Members include physicians, nurses, occupational and physical therapists, researchers, social workers, firefighters, and hospitals with burn centers. The multidisciplinary membership enhances the ability to work toward common goals with other organizations on educational/prevention programs.

- **American Public Health Association—Injury Control and Emergency Health Services Section**, formed in 1972, addresses violence, unintentional injuries, and all types of emergency public health for persons of all ages.
  www.icehs.org

- **American Spinal Injury Association (ASIA)**
  http://www.asia-spinalinjury.org/home/index.html
  The American Spinal Injury Association has developed an Internet website to provide information and education about Spinal Cord Injury (SCI) to ASIA members and to the general public. Among its objectives ASIA aims to foster research which aims at preventing spinal cord injury, improving care, reducing consequent disability, and finding a cure for both acute and chronic SCI.

- **Arizona Rape Prevention and Education Project**
  www.azrapeprevention.org
  The site is designed to provide information about currently funded rape prevention and education programs in Arizona, share rape and sexual assault statistics, provide citations for evaluation tools, offer an overview of research materials for more than 30 rape-related topics, and provide information on books and films related to sexual violence and prevention. The links section provides Internet, or phone and email information for all state coalitions focusing on sexual assault and other links that provide information to the public.

- **Association for the Advancement of Automotive Medicine (AAAM)**
  www.carcrash.org
  The Association for the Advancement of Automotive Medicine (AAAM) is a professional multidisciplinary organization dedicated entirely to motor vehicle crash injury prevention and control.

- **Bike Helmet Safety Institute**
    www.bhsi.org
    The Bike Helmet Safety Institute is a small, active, non-profit consumer-funded program acting as a clearinghouse and a technical resource for bicycle helmet information. Through their Web site the Bike Helmet Safety Institute tries to explain the technology of helmets to consumers, and promote better helmets through improved standards.

- **The Burn and Shock Trauma Institute**
    www.luhs.org/depts/bsti/index.html
    The Burn and Shock Trauma Institute of Loyola University is a unique community of scientists and clinicians devoted to the study of traumatic injury. This is a multidisciplinary research institute, whose programs include both clinical and laboratory research relevant to trauma injury and burns. In the laboratories, scientists investigate the body's reaction to injury and infection, with the hope that their research findings may someday lead to innovative therapies for trauma and burn patients.

- **Canadian Hospitals Injury Reporting and Prevention Program, Child Injury Division**
    www.phac-aspc.gc.ca/injury-bles
    This Web site will provide you with the most current injury statistics in Canada. You will be able to look at injury mortality and hospital separations by province and territory, by age group, and over time. You will also be able look at injuries and the circumstances of injuries treated in the emergency departments of the Canadian Hospitals Injury Reporting and Prevention Program (CHIRPP).

- **The Center for Injury Prevention Policy and Practice** was formed in 1986 and serves as a resource center on child, adolescent, and older adult injury prevention strategies. Among the many resources available at this site is a link to tips for writing proposals.
    www.cippp.org

- **Center for the Prevention of School Violence**
    www.ncdjjdp.org/cpsv
    Established in 1993 as one of the nation's first state school safety centers, the North Carolina Department of Juvenile Justice and Delinquency Prevention—Center for the Prevention of School Violence serves as a resource center and "think tank" for efforts that promote safer schools and foster positive youth development. The Center's efforts in support of safer schools are directed at understanding the problems of school violence and developing solutions to them.

- **Center for Violence Prevention and Control (CVPC)**
    www1.umn.edu/cvpc
    The Center for Violence Prevention and Control is an academic research center dedicated to the development and facilitation of interdisciplinary collaboration in research and graduate education efforts that can ultimately affect the prevention and control of violence.

- **Children's Safety Network**
    www.childrenssafetynetwork.org
    The Children's Safety Network is composed of several resource centers
    funded by the Maternal and Child Health Bureau (MCHB) of the U.S.
    Department of Health and Human Services. CSN provides technical
    assistance, training, and resources to MCH and other injury prevention
    professionals in an extensive effort to reduce the burden of injury and
    violence to our nation's children and adolescents.

- **Crash Analysis and Reporting System (CARE)**
    http://care.cs.ua.edu
    CARE Research & Development Laboratory (CRDL) is a rapidly
    expanding operation with a growing staff. Associated with the
    University of Alabama, CRDL uses leading edge technologies to offer
    products and specialized software development services in a variety of
    areas, particularly traffic safety and law enforcement.

- **Emory Center for Injury Control**
    www.sph.emory.edu/CIC
    Jointly supported by Emory University's Rollins School of Public Health
    and the Department of Emergency Medicine, School of Medicine, the
    Emory Center for Injury Control is dedicated to reducing the health
    and economic impact of injuries in Atlanta, throughout Georgia, and
    worldwide.

- **European Consumer Safety Association (ECOSA)**
    www.ecosa.org
    ECOSA was established in 1985 as a non-profit organization to promote
    safety. The founding members were senior representatives of govern-
    mental and non-governmental organizations with expertise in the field
    of consumer safety and the promotion of home and leisure safety. Over
    the years ECOSA has developed into an organization that is concerned
    about safety in all settings and risk areas. Its European Child Safety
    Alliance is, for instance, dedicated to the prevention of injuries at home
    as well as those caused by motor vehicle crashes.

- **Family Violence Prevention Fund**
    http://endabuse.org
    The Family Violence Prevention Fund works to prevent violence within
    the home, and in the community, to help those whose lives are devas-
    tated by violence because everyone has the right to live free of violence.

- **Foundation for Spinal Cord Injury Prevention, Care & Cure (FSCIPCC)**
    www.fscip.org
    The Foundation for Spinal Cord Injury Prevention, Care & Cure
    (FSCIPCC) is a non-profit educational group dedicated to the preven-
    tion, care and cure of spinal cord injuries through public awareness,
    education and funding research.

- **Injury Free Coalition for Kids**
  www.injuryfree.org
  The Injury Free Coalition for Kids is a National Program of the Robert Wood Johnson Foundation comprised of hospital-based, community-oriented programs, whose efforts are anchored in research, education, and advocacy. Currently, the coalition includes 40 sites located in 37 cities, each housed in the trauma centers of their participating institutions.

- **Injury Control Resource Information Network**
  www.injurycontrol.com/icrin
  This Web site provides a list of key Internet accessible resources related to the field of injury research and control. The resources are in the form of annotated clickable hyperlinks to other Internet sources and documents.

- Many of the U.S. states have joined together within their health regions to form **Injury Prevention Networks.** Generally, these networks were formed within the boundaries of the US-DHHS or NHTSA federal administrative regions. Most regional networks involve those working in several disciplines. Members come from the fields of public health, traffic safety, consumer product safety, building codes and standards, and health care. News and information are posted to their Web sites. The **Region 4** (AL, FL, GA, KY, MS, NC, SC, TN) Injury Prevention Network is known as the **Southeastern Regional Injury Control Network (SERICN).** Since 1990, the University of North Carolina's Injury Prevention Research Center (UNC IPRC) has jointly sponsored the Southeastern Regional Injury Control Network (SERICN) with the University of Alabama at Birmingham Injury Control Research Center (UAB ICRC). Besides these two regional Injury Centers, the Network includes the lead state public health agency injury prevention program, and selected traffic safety, child-centered, and emergency medical services programs in each of the states. This organization, with financial support from both Centers, meets three times a year to exchange program ideas and develop a range of expertise. Over the years, several joint projects have emanated from the group. A recent example of the power of this partnership occurred in April 2003, when the Network hosted a pilot training session on child safety in agriculture. More information can be found at www.iprc.unc.edu/pages/sericn. The **Region 1** (CT, ME, MA, NH, NJ, NY, RI, VT) Injury Prevention Network is known as the **Northeast Injury Prevention Network (NEIPN).** NEIPN, along with partner organizations, has been very involved in youth suicide prevention research and poisoning prevention. Although no one website is dedicated to release information regarding NEIPN activities, information about this Injury Prevention Network can be found in the department of health websites of the participating states. Information regarding the **Region 9** (AZ, CA, NV, HI) Injury Prevention Network activities can be found in the California Emergency Medical Services Authority Website at www.emsa.ca.gov/emsdivision/injprev.asp. More information on Regional Injury Prevention Networks can be found at the Children's

Safety Network (CSN) Website at www.childrenssafetynetwork.org/calendar.asp

- **Injury Prevention Web**
  www.injuryprevention.org
  The Injury Prevention Web hosts the Web sites of several agencies and organizations working to prevent injuries. This site contains a weekly literature update of recent journal articles and agency reports, injury data for every U.S. state, and more than 1400 links to government and non-profit injury prevention sites worldwide.

- **Institute for Preventative Sports Medicine (IPSM)**
  www.ipsm.org
  The Institute for Preventative Sports Medicine is a non-profit research organization dedicated to the prevention of sports-related injuries and health care cost containment. Its research focuses on finding effective and practical ways to reduce sports related injuries and speed the rehabilitation of injured athletes. The Institute also seeks ways to disseminate its research findings to benefit the public at large.

- **Insurance Institute for Highway Safety**
  www.highwaysafety.org
  The Insurance Institute for Highway Safety is an independent, nonprofit, scientific and educational organization dedicated to reducing the losses—deaths, injuries, and property damage—from crashes on the nation's highways. The Institute is wholly supported by auto insurers.

- **International Society for Child and Adolescent Injury Prevention (ISCAIP)**
  www.iscaip.net
  During the Second World Conference on Injury Control in Atlanta, Georgia, the ISCAIP was created with a goal to promote a significant reduction in the number and severity of injuries to children and adolescents through international collaboration. Both unintentional injury and violence are addressed by the Society. The objectives of the Society are to: 1) Provide a multi-disciplinary forum; 2) Provide advocacy at national and international levels; 3) Foster national injury prevention initiatives; 4) Stimulate the translation of research findings into programs and policies; 5) Facilitate collaborative and inter-disciplinary international research; and 6) Liaise with relevant international organizations.

- **International Traffic Medicine Association** (ITMA) was founded in 1960 as the International Association for Accident and Traffic Medicine. The ITMA works to promote and develop the study of traffic medicine in all transport modes.
  www.trafficmedicine.org

- **National Alliance for Safe Schools (NASS)**
  www.safeschools.org
  Founded in 1977 by a group of school security directors, the National

Alliance for Safe Schools was established to provide training, technical assistance, and publications to school districts interested in reducing school based crime and violence. NASS is committed to the belief that no child should go to school in fear.

- **National Association of Governors' Highway Safety Representatives (NAGHSR)**
  www.naghsr.org
  The Governors Highway Safety Association (GHSA) is the states' voice on highway safety. A 501(c)(3) nonprofit association, GHSA represents the highway safety programs of states and territories on the human behavioral aspects of highway safety. Such areas include occupant protection, impaired driving, speed enforcement, aggressive driving, and pedestrian and bicycle safety, as well as highway safety issues relating to older and younger drivers, drowsy driving and distracted driving. In addition to the behaviorial aspects of driving, GHSA also represents other aspects of highway safety, such as traffic records and training. GHSA's mission is to provide leadership in the development of national policy to ensure effective highway safety programs.

- **National Center for Injury Prevention and Control (NCIPC)**
  www.cdc.gov/ncipc
  The National Center for Injury Prevention and Control works to reduce morbidity, disability, mortality, and costs associated with injuries.

- **National Center for Statistics and Analysis (NCSA) of the National Highway Traffic Safety Administration (NHTSA)—Crash Outcome Data Evaluation System (CODES)**
  www-nrd.nhtsa.dot.gov/departments/nrd-30/ncsa/codes.html
  CODES evolved from a congressional mandate to report on the benefits of safety belts and motorcycle helmets. The purpose of CODES is to prevent injuries resulting from motor vehicle crashes by better understanding their type, severity and cost in relation to the characteristics of the crash, vehicles, and persons involved. Crash data alone do not indicate the injury problem in terms of the medical and financial consequences. By linking crash, vehicle, and behavior characteristics to their specific medical and financial outcomes, CODES can identify prevention factors.

- **National Children's Center for Rural and Agricultural Health and Safety** strives to enhance the health and safety of all children exposed to hazards associated with agricultural work and rural environments.
  http://research.marshfieldclinic.org/children

- **National Highway Traffic Safety Administration (NHTSA)** was established by the Highway Safety Act of 1970, as the successor to the National Highway Safety Bureau, to carry out safety programs under the National Traffic and Motor Vehicle Safety Act of 1966 and the Highway Safety Act of 1966. NHTSA also carries out consumer programs established by the Motor Vehicle Information and Cost Savings Act of 1972,

which has been recodified in various Chapters under Title 49. NHTSA is responsible for reducing deaths, injuries and economic losses resulting from motor vehicle crashes. This is accomplished by setting and enforcing safety performance standards for motor vehicles and motor vehicle equipment, and through grants to state and local governments to enable them to conduct effective local highway safety programs.
    www.nhtsa.dot.gov

- **National Program for Playground Safety**
    www.uni.edu/playground/home.htm
    In 1995, the University of Northern Iowa established the National Program for Playground Safety (NPPS) with funding from the Centers for Disease Control and Injury Prevention (CDC) in Atlanta. NPPS serves as a national resource for the latest educational and research information on playground safety.

- **National Safety Council**
    www.nsc.org/insidensc.htm
    The National Safety Council's mission is to educate and influence society to adopt safety, health and environmental policies, practices and procedures that prevent and mitigate human suffering and economic losses arising from preventable causes.

- **National Youth Violence Prevention Resource Center**
    www.safeyouth.org/scripts/index.asp
    Developed by the Centers for Disease Control and Prevention and other Federal partners, the Resource Center provides current information developed by Federal agencies or with Federal support pertaining to youth violence. A gateway for professionals, parents, youth and other interested individuals, the Resource Center offers the latest tools to facilitate discussion with children, to resolve conflicts nonviolently, to stop bullying, to prevent teen suicide, and to end violence committed by and against young people. Resources include fact sheets, best practices documents, funding and conference announcements, statistics, research bulletins, surveillance reports, and profiles of promising programs.

- **National Youth Sports Safety Foundation** is a national non-profit, educational organization dedicated to reducing the number and severity of injuries youth sustain in sports and fitness activities.
    www.nyssf.org

- **Operation Lifesaver**
    www.oli.org
    Operation Lifesaver is a national, non-profit education and awareness program dedicated to ending tragic collisions, fatalities and injuries at highway-rail grade crossings and on railroad rights of way. To accomplish its mission, Operation Lifesaver promotes 3 Es: 1) Education; 2) Enforcement, and 3) Engineering.

- **Partnership Against Violence Network (PAVNET)**
  http://pavnet.org
  Partnerships Against Violence Network is a "virtual library" of information about violence and youth-at-risk, representing data from seven different Federal agencies.

- **SafeKids Worldwide**. Launched in 1987 the National SAFE KIDS Campaign is the first and only national non-profit organization dedicated solely to the prevention of unintentional childhood injury.
  www.safekids.org

- **SafetyBeltSafe U.S.A.**
  www.carseat.org
  SafetyBeltSafe is the national, non-profit organization dedicated to child passenger safety. Their mission is to help reduce the number of serious and fatal traffic injuries suffered by children by promoting the correct, consistent use of safety seats and safety belts.

- **SafetyLit.org** is the Web site of the Injury Prevention Resource Library at San Diego State University School of Public Health. Information about the occurrence and prevention of injuries is available from many sources and disciplines. SafetyLit staff and volunteers regularly examine more than 500 journals and scores of reports from government agencies and organizations.
  www.safetylit.org

- **SafetyPolicy.org** was created to present in simple and straightforward terms policies that are known to be effective in the prevention of injuries.
  www.safetypolicy.org

- **Safe Ride News**
  www.saferidenews.com
  The goals of Safe Ride News Publications are to help save lives and prevent injury to children in traffic. Safe Ride New does this primarily by developing accurate and up-to-date information on injury prevention for professionals, advocates, and parents. They also advocate for improved standards, laws, and programs related to childhood injury prevention by supporting and collaborating with other organizations and agencies working in this field.

- **Society for the Advancement of Violence and Injury Research (SAVIR) (formerly National Association of Injury Control Research Centers (NAICRC)) Member Research Data Bank**
  www.quickbase.com/db/6tejwf5t
  This Web site provides access to a dynamic database of current and recent research and education projects conducted by the NAICRC injury control research centers. Listed projects are funded by various internal and external sources. Please note that not all projects may be listed, time coverage may vary between Centers, Centers have had different

levels of support over time, and fiscal information may be incomplete. Therefore, comparisons between Centers may be limited. More information on SAVIR can be found at:

www.naicrc.org

- **State and Territorial Injury Prevention Directors' Association (STIPDA)** was formed in 1992. Its mission is to promote, sustain, and enhance the ability of state and territorial public health departments to reduce death and disability associated with injuries.

www.stipda.org

- **ThinkFirst National Injury Prevention Foundation (Formally known as the National Health and Spinal Cord Injury Prevention Program).** Today this organization offers a research-validated multi-level educational program that has reached over 8 million people nationally and internationally, has had major influences on policy initiatives, and continues to expand to reach those most vulnerable to traumatic injuries.

www.thinkfirst.org

- **Unintentional Injury: A Resource for Health Education and Health Promotion**

www.astdhpphe.org/injury/index.html

The Unintentional Injury Prevention Website was developed by the Society for Public Health Education (SOPHE) and the Directors of Health Promotion and Education (DHPE), with technical assistance from the CDC, National Center for Injury Prevention and Control. This site was designed to help strengthen the relationship between health education, behavioral science and unintentional injury prevention and includes a wide range of resources including general information, funding resources, and useful contacts.

- **U.S. Consumer Product Safety Commission** is charged with protecting the public from unreasonable risks of serious injury or death from more than 15,000 types of consumer products under the agency's jurisdiction.

www.cpsc.gov/about/about.html

- **Violence and Injury Control through Education, Networking and Training on the World Wide Web**

www.ibiblio.org/vincentweb

This is a free introductory course on injury prevention and control contains material from the June 6, 1997 videoconference, "Getting Started in Injury Control and Violence Prevention" presented in a web-based format that expands upon and supplements the televised program.

- **World Health Organization's Department of Violence and Injury Prevention (VIP)**

www.who.int/violence_injury_prevention/en

The World Health Organization's Department of Injuries and Violence Prevention works to prevent injuries and violence, to mitigate their consequences, and to enhance the quality of life for persons with disabilities irrespective of the causes.

- **World Health Organization's Helmet Initiative**
  www.whohelmets.org
  The World Health Organization Helmet Initiative promotes the use of helmets as a strategy for preventing head injuries caused by bicycle or motorcycle crash or fall.

- **Article—Internet Resources for Injury and Violence Prevention**
  Hopkins, K., Sleet, D.A., Mickalide, A., Gorcowski, S., Bryn, S., Balsey, T., & Mitchko, J. (2003). Internet resources for injury and violence prevention. *American Journal of Health Education, 34*(5), S62-S64.

  This article provides an overview and a list of internet resources on unintentional injury prevention, acute care and trauma, and violence prevention. Information on obtaining reprints of this article can be found at www.aahperd.org/aahe/template.cfm?template=ajhe_main. html. The authors include representatives from the CDC National Center for Injury Prevention and Control, the National SAFE KIDS Campaign (now known as Safe Kids Worldwide), the National Highway Traffic Safety Administration, and the Maternal and Child Health Bureau, Health Resources and Services Administration.

III. Data Sources of Interest

- **The National Electronic Injury Surveillance System (NEISS)**
  The system is comprised of a sample of hospitals that are statistically representative of hospital emergency rooms nationwide. From the data collected, estimates can be made of the numbers of injuries associated with consumer products and treated in hospital emergency departments. Data is collected on a broad range of injury-related issues, covering hundreds of product categories, and provides national estimates of the number and severity of product-related injuries.

- **Death Certificate File**
  Death certificates where consumer products are involved are provided to CPSC through state health departments. The Clearinghouse provides summaries of these, with victim information removed.

- **In-Depth Investigations (INDP) File**
  This file contains summaries of reports of investigations into events surrounding product-related injuries or incidents. Based on victim/witness interviews, the reports provide details about incident sequence, human behavior, and product involvement.

- **Injury/Potential Injury Incident File (IPII)**
  This file contains summaries, indexed by consumer product, of Hotline reports, product-related newspaper accounts, reports from medical examiners, and letters to CPSC.

- **CPSC's Injury Data Publication**
  In 1996, CPSC introduced the *Consumer Product Safety Review*. Included is national injury data from NEISS hospitals; studies of emerging and continuing hazards; technical articles on injury/death topics; and important recall and corrective action activities. Annual subscriptions are available for $18.00 ($25.20 foreign) from the Government Printing Office. Phone (202) 512-1800. Copies may also be obtained through CPSC's World Wide Web site at:
  www.cpsc.gov/cpscpub/pubs/cpsr.html.

- **National Center for Injury Prevention and Control**
  The National Center for Injury Prevention and Control (NCIPC) works to reduce morbidity, disability, mortality, and costs associated with injuries. The site offers links to injury data in a variety of formats (including WISQARS), including vital statistics, the National Electronic Injury Surveillance System All Injury Program (NEISS-AIP) that includes data on all emergency room injuries, not just those related to consumer products, and international data information.
  www.cdc.gov/ncipc/osp/data.htm

IV. Selected Journals of Interest

The journals listed in this section publish articles relating primarily to injury. However, there are many journals, whose focus is not on injury, but publish articles related to the field. A fairly comprehensive list is available at the SafetyLit Web site: www.safetylit.org/week/journals.htm.

- **Accident Analysis and Prevention**
  Elsevier Science—www.elsevier.com/wps/find/journaldescription.cws_home/336/description#description

- **Aggressive Behavior**
  Wiley-Liss—www3.interscience.wiley.com/cgi-bin/jhome/32356

- **Aggression & Violent Behavior**
  Elsevier Science—www3.interscience.wiley.com/cgi-bin/jhome/32356

- **Archives of Suicide Research**
  Taylor & Francis Group—www.tandf.co.uk/journals/titles/13811118.asp

  International Academy of Suicide Research
  Australasian Journal of Disaster and Trauma Studies
  Massey University, New Zealand—www.massey.ac.nz/~trauma

- **Brain Injury**
  Taylor & Francis Group—www.tandf.co.uk/journals/titles/02699052.asp

- **Burns**
  Elsevier Science—www.elsevier.com/wps/find/journaldescription.cws_home/30394 description#description

- **Child Abuse & Neglect**
  Elsevier Science—www.elsevier.com/wps/find/journaldescription.cws_
  home/586/description#description

- **Crime & Delinquency**
  Sage Publishing—www.sagepub.com/journal.aspx?pid=209

- **Crime Prevention & Community Safety**
  Perpetuity Press—www.perpetuitypress.com/acatalog/Perpetuity_Press_
  Crime_Prevention_and_Community_Safety_25.html

- **Disaster Management and Response**
  Mosby—http://gort.ucsd.edu/newjour/d/msg02587.html

- **Fire Safety Journal**
  Elsevier Science—www.elsevier.com/wps/find/journaldescription.cws_
  home/405896/description#description

- **Homicide Studies**
  Sage Publishing—www.sagepub.com/journal.aspx?pid=74

- **Injury: International Journal of the Care of the Injured**
  Elsevier Science—www.elsevier.com/wps/find/journaldescription.cws_
  home/30428/description#description

- **Injury Control and Safety Promotion**
  Taylor & Francis—www.tandf.co.uk/journals/titles/17457300.asp

- **Injury Prevention**
  BMJ Publishing Group—http://ip.bmjjournals.com

- **Journal of Burn Care & Rehabilitation**
  Lippincott, Williams & Wilkins—www.burncarerehab.com/pt/re/
  jburncr/ home.htm

- **Journal of Family Violence**
  Kluwer—http://gort.ucsd.edu/newjour/j/msg03207.html

- **Journal of Interpersonal Violence**
  Sage—www.sagepub.com/journal.aspx?pid=108

- **Journal of Safety Research**
  Elsevier Science—www.nsc.org/lrs/res/jsr.htm

- **Journal of School Violence**
  Haworth Press—www.haworthpressinc.com/web/JSV

- **National Safety**
  Safety First Association of South Africa—www.safety1st.org.za

- **Safety Science**
  Elsevier Science—www.elsevier.com/wps/find/journaldescription.cws_
  home/505657/description#description

- **Suicide and Life Threatening Behavior**
  Guilford Publishing—www.guilford.com/cgi-bin/cartscript.cgi?page=pr/
  jnsl.htm&dir=periodicals&cart_id

- **Traffic Injury Prevention**
  Taylor & Francis Group—www.tandf.co.uk/journals/titles/15389588.asp

- **Trauma Violence & Abuse**
  Sage—www.sagepub.com/journal.aspx?pid=39

- **Violence Against Women**
  Sage Publishing—www.sagepub.com/journal.aspx?pid=93

- **Violence and Victims**
  Springer Publishing—www.springerpub.com/journals/violence_&_
  victims.html

V. Related Books of Interest

Abrahamson, P., & Abrahamson, J. (1997) *Brain Injury: a Family Tragedy.* Houston, TX: HDI Publishers.

Aherin, R.A., Murphy, D.J., & Westaby, J.D. (1992). *Reducing Farm Injuries: Issues and Methods.* St. Joseph, MI: American Society of Agricultural Engineers.

Allen, NH. (1980). *Homicide: Perspectives on Prevention.* New York, NY: Human Sciences Press.

American Medical Association. (1984) *Guides to the Evaluation of Permanent Impairment.* Chicago, IL: American Medical Association.

American Public Health Association. (1981). *Public Swimming Pools: Recommended Regulations for Design and Construction, Operation And Maintenance.* Washington, DC: American Public Health Association.

Apple, D.F. (1994). *Prevention of Falls and Hip Fractures in the Elderly.* Rosemont, IL: American Academy of Orthopaedic Surgeons.

Archer, D. (1984). *Violence and Crime in Cross-National Perspective.* New Haven, CT:Yale University Press.

Ashley, M.J. (1995) *Traumatic Brain Injury Rehabilitation.* Boca Raton, FL: CRC Press.

Aspen Reference Group. (1996). *Brain Injury Survivor and Caregiver Education Manual.* Gaithersburg, MD: Aspen Publications.

Associates of Trial Lawyers of America. (1995). *Guns—A Public Health Approach: Making Changes in Making Guns.* Washington, DC: John Hopkins Center for Gun Policy and Research.

Athens, L. (1997). *Violent Criminal Acts and Actors Revisited.* Champaign, IL: University of Illinois Press.

Backaitis, S.H. (1993). *Biomechanics of Impact Injury and Injury Tolerances of the Head-Neck Complex.* Warrendale, PA: Society of Automotive Engineers.

Baker, S.P., Fingerhut, L.A., Higgins, L., Chen, L-H., & Braver, E.R. (1996). *Injury to Children and Teenagers-State-by-State Mortality Facts.* Baltimore: The Johns Hopkins Center for Injury Research and Policy.

Baker, S.P., Li, G., Fowler, C., & Dannenberg, A.L. (1993). *Injuries to Bicyclists: A National Perspective.* Baltimore: The Johns Hopkins Injury Prevention Center, The Johns Hopkins University School of Public Health.

Baker, S.P., O'Neill, B., Ginsburg, M.J., & Li, G. (1992). *The Injury Fact Book* (2nd ed). New York: Oxford University Press.

Baker, S.P., & Waller, A.E. (1989). *Childhood Injury Mortality—State-by-State Mortality Facts.* Baltimore: The Johns Hopkins Injury Prevention Center, The Johns Hopkins University School of Public Health.

Barss, P., Smith, G., Baker, S., & Mohan, D. (1998). *Injury Prevention: An International Perspective: Epidemiology, Surveillance and Policy.* New York, NY: Oxford University Press.

Begali, V. (1996). *Head Injury in Children and Adolescents: A Resource and Review for School and Allied Professionals.* New York, NY: John Wiley & Sons.

Berger, R., & Mohan, D. (1996). *Injury Control—A Global View.* Oxford: Oxford University Press.

Bergman, A.B. (1992). *Political Approaches to Injury Control at the State Level.* Seattle, WA: University of Washington Press.

Berman, A. (1990). *Suicide Prevention: Case Consultations.* New York, NY: Springer Publishing Company.

Berman, A.L., & Jobes, D.A. (1991). *Adolescent Suicide: Assessment and Intervention.* Washington, DC: American Psychological Association.

Bowker, L. H.(1997). *Masculinities and Violence.* Thousand Oaks, CA: Sage Publications.

Browne, K., & Herbert, M. (1996). *Preventing Family Violence.* New York, NY: John Wiley & Sons.

Burn Prevention Foundation. (1997). *Burn Prevention Foundation: Prevention Through Education [Preschool-3rd Grade Curriculum].* Allentown, PA: Burn Prevention Foundation.

Cabutan, R. R. (1996). *Sport of Bicycling—Helmet Laws, Head, and Body Injuries and Accident Prevention: Index and Reference Book of New Information.* Washington, DC: ABBE Publications.

Caine, D. (1996). *Epidemiology of Sports Injuries.* Champaign, IL: Human Kinetics.

Canada, G. (1995). *Fist, Stick, Knife, Gun: A Personal History of Violence in America.* Boston, MA: Beacon Press.

Canetto, S.S., & Lester, D. (1995). *Women and Suicidal Behavior.* New York, NY: Springer; 1995.

Center for Gun Policy and Research. (1997). *Firearm Violence: An Annotated Bibliography.* Baltimore, MD: Johns Hopkins University, School of Public Health, Center for Gun Policy and Research.

Chaiet, D. (1995). *Staying Safe at School.* New York, NY: Rosen Publishing Group; 1995.

Chalk, R., & King, P. (1998). *Violence in Families: Assessing Prevention and Treatment Programs.* Washington, DC: National Academy Press.

Chappell, D. (1975). *Violence and Criminal Justice.* Lexington, MA: Lexington Books.

Children's Safety Network. (1991). *A Data Book of Child and Adolescent Injury.*

Arlington, VA: National Center for Education in Maternal and Child Health.

Children's Safety Network. (1996). *Youth Violence: Locating and Using the Data*. Newton, MA: Children's Safety Network.

Children's Safety Network. (1997). *Injuries in the School Environment: A Resource Guide*. Newton, MA: Children's Safety Network.

Christoffel, T, & Gallagher, S. (1999) *Injury Prevention and Public Health: Practical Knowledge, Skills, and Strategies*. Gaitherburg, MD: Aspen.

Christoffel, K.K., & Runyan, C.W. (1995). *Adolescent Injuries: Epidemiology and Prevention*. Philadelphia, PA: Hanley & Belfus.

Costa, J. J. (1983). *Abuse of Women: Legislation, Reporting, and Prevention*. Lexington, MA: Lexington Books.

Cote, A.E., & Bugbee, P. (1988). *Principles of Fire Protection*. Quincy, MA: National Fire Protection Association.

Commission on Violence and Youth. (1993). *Violence and Youth: Psychology's Response*. Washington, DC: American Psychological Association.

Committee on Trauma Research, Commission on Life Sciences, National Research Council, Institute of Medicine. (1985). *Injury in America: A Continuing Public Health Problem*. Washington, DC: National Academy Press.

Cook P, & Ludwig J. (1996). *Guns in America: Results of a Comprehensive National Survey on Firearms Ownership and Use: A Summary Report*. Washington, DC: Police Foundation.

Courtney, L. J. (1994). *Integrating Community Resources*. Houston, TX: HDI Publishers.

Currie, D.G. (1993). *The Management of Head Injuries*. New York, NY: Oxford University Press.

Christoffel, T., & Teret, S.P. (1993). *Protecting the public—Legal Issues in Injury Prevention*. New York: Oxford University Press.

De Becker, G. (1997). *The Gift of Fear: Survival Signals that Protect us From Violence*. Boston, MA: Little, Brown and Company.

Devine, J. (1996). *Maximum Security: The Culture of Violence in Inner-City Schools*. Chicago, IL: University of Chicago Press.

Dobrin, A. (1996). *Statistical Handbook on Violence in America*. Phoenix, AZ: Oryx Press.

Donham, K.J. (1997). *Agricultural Health and Safety*. Binghamton, NY: Haworth Press.

Edleson, J.L. (1996). *Future Intervention with Battered Women and Their Families*. Thousand Oaks, CA: Sage Publications.

Eron, L. (1994). Reason *to hope: A Psychosocial Perspective on Violence and Youth*. Washington, DC: American Psychological Association.

Felcher, E.M. (2001). *It's No Accident-How Corporations Sell Dangerous Baby Products*. Monroe, ME: Common Courage Press.

Finger, S. (1988). *Brain Injury and Recovery: Theoretical and Controversial Issues*. New York, NY: Plenum.

Freeman, A., & Reinecke, M.A. (1993). *Cognitive Therapy of Suicidal Behavior: A Manual for Treatment*. New York, NY: Springer Publishing Company.

Fu, F.H., & Stone, D.A. (1994). *Sports Injuries: Mechanisms, Prevention, Treatment*. Baltimore, MD: Williams & Wilkins.

Gall, T. (1996). *Statistics on Weapons and Violence: A Selection of Statistical*

Charts, Graphs, and Tables About Weapons and Violence From a Variety of Published Sources. Detroit, MI: Gale Research.

Gaylin, W. (1981). *Violence and the Politics of Research.* New York, NY: Plenam Press.

Gilligan, J. (1997). *Violence: Our Deadly Epidemic and its Causes.* New York, NY: Putnam.

Goldstein, M. (1997). *Dealing with childhood Depression and Teen Suicide.* Plainview, NY: Bureau for At-Risk Youth.

Gonsiorek JC. *Male sexual abuse: A Trilogy of Intervention Strategies.* Thousand Oaks, CA: Sage Publications; 1994.

Graham, J.D. (1988). *Preventing Automobile Injury: New Findings from Evaluation Research.* Dover, MA: Auburn House Publishing Company.

Guard, A. (1997). *Violence and Teen Pregnancy.* Newton, MA: Children's Safety Network.

Hamberger, L.K, Burge, S.K., Graham, A.V., & Costa, A.J. (1996). *Violence Issues for Health Care Educators and Providers.* Binghamton, NY: Haworth Press.

Hamilton, J.R. (1982). *Dangerousness: Psychiatric Assessment and Management.* London: Gaskell.

Hemenway, D. (2004). *Private Guns Public Health.* Ann Arbor, MI: University of Michigan Press.

Henke, R., & Henke, J. (1996). *Injury Prevention: Teacher/Student Resource—Comprehensive Health for the Middle Grades.* Santa Cruz, CA: ETR Associates.

Herington, T.N. (1995). *Occupational Injuries: Evaluation, Management, and ·Prevention.* St. Louis, MO: Mosby.

Hicks, B.B. (1990). *Youth Suicide: A Comprehensive Manual for Prevention and Intervention.* Bloomington, IN: National Education Service.

Hoffman, A. (1996). *Schools, Violence, and Society.* Westport, CT: Greenwood Press.

Hyde, A.S. (1992). *Crash Injuries: How and Why They Happen: A Primer for Anyone Who Cares About People in Cars.* Key Biscayne, FL: Hyde Associates.

Institute of Medicine Committee on Injury Prevention and Control-Division of Health Promotion and Disease Prevention (1999). *Reducing the Burden of Injury-Advancing Prevention and Treatment.* Washington, DC: National Academy Press.

Jaros, K.J. (1992). Violence as a public health problem: Developing culturally appropriate prevention strategies for adolescents and children: *Proceedings of the Annual Public Health Social Work Maternal and Child Health Institute.* Arlington, VA: National Center for Education in Maternal and Child Health.

Johnson, U. (1993). *Gang Violence Prevention: A Curriculum and Discussion Guide.* Pleasantville, NY: Sunburst Communications.

Karlson, T., & Hargarten, S. (1997). *Reducing Firearm Injury and Death.* New Brunswick, NJ: Rutgers University Press.

Kirk, W.G. (1993). *Adolescent Suicide: A School-Based Approach to Assessment and Intervention.* Champaign, IL: Research Press.

Klein, M.W. (1995). *The American Street Gang: Its Nature, Prevalence and Control.* New York, NY: Oxford University Press.

Krantzler, N.J., & Miner, K.R. (1996). *Violence Health Facts.* Santa Cruz, CA: ETR Associates.

Lee, B., & Marlenga, B. (Eds.). (1999). *Professional Resource Manual: North American Guidelines for Children's Agricultural Tasks*. Marshfield, WI: Marshfield Clinic.

Leenaars, A.A., & Wenckstern, S. (1991). *Suicide Prevention in Schools*. New York, NY: Hemisphere Publishing.

Levy, B., & Sidel, V.W. (1996). *War and Public Health*. New York, NY: Oxford University Press.

MacLean, G. (1990). *Suicide in Children and Adolescents*. Kirkland, WA: Hogrefe & Huber Publishers.

Maltsberger, J.T., & Goldblatt, M.J. (1996). *Essential Papers on Suicide*. New York: New York University Press.

Mann, J.J., & Stanley, M. (1986). *Psychobiology of Suicidal Behavior*. New York, NY: New York Academy of Sciences.

Marge, M. (1998). *Violence as a Cause of Disability: Proceedings and Recommendations of the National Violence Prevention Conference*. Fayetteville, NY: American Disability Prevention and Wellness Association.

Mashaly, A.Y., Graiter, P.L., & Youssef, Z. M. (1993). *Injury in Egypt: Injuries as a Public Health Problem*. Cairo, Egypt: Rose El Youssef New Presses.

McClure R, Stevenson M, McEvoy S.eds. (2004). *The Scientific Basis of Injury Prevention and Control*. Victoria, Australia: IP Communications.

Mckee, P.W., Jones, R., Wayne, B., & Richard, H. (1993). *Suicide and the School: A Practical Guide to Suicide Prevention*. Horsham, PA: LRP Publications.

Meeks, L. (1995). *Violence Prevention: Totally Awesome Teaching Strategies for Safe and Drug-Free Schools*. San Diego, CA: Meeks Heit Publishing Company.

Miller, M. (1993). *Coping with Weapons and Violence in School and on Your Streets*. New York, NY: Rosen Publishing Group.

Miller, M. (1995). *Drugs and Gun Violence*. Plainview, NY: The Bureau for At-Risk Youth.

Miller, T.R., Pindus, N.M., Douglass, J.B., & Rossman, S.B. (1995). *Databook on Nonfatal Injury*. Washington, D.C.: Urban Institute Press.

Monsey, B.R. (1995). *What Works in Preventing Rural Violence: Strategies, Risk Factors, and Assessment Tools*. St. Paul, MN: Amherst H. Wilder Foundation.

Murphy, D. J. (1992). *Safety and Health for Production Agriculture*. St. Joseph, MI: American Society of Agricultural Engineers.

National Center for Injury Prevention and Control. (2001). *Injury Fact Book 2001-2002*. Atlanta: Centers for Disease Control and Prevention.

National Center for Injury Prevention and Control (2002). *CDC injury Research Agenda*. Atlanta: Centers for Disease Control and Prevention.

National Conference of State Legislatures. (1998). *Reducing Crashes, Casualties and Costs: Traffic Safety Challenges for State Legislatures*. Denver, CO: National Conference of State Legislatures.

National Pediatric Trauma Registry. (1996). *Children and Adolescents with Disability Due to Traumatic Injury: A Data Book*. Boston, MA: Research and Training Center in Rehabilitation and Childhood Trauma, Tufts University School of Medicine.

Nesbett, R.E. (1996). *Culture of Honor: The Psychology of Violence in the South*. Boulder, CO: Westview.

O'Donnell, L., Cohen, S., Hausman, A. (1990). *The Evaluation of Community-*

Based Violence Prevention Programs. Newton, MA: Education Development Center.

Oh, S. (1985). *Prevention of Head Injuries in Skiing: Mechanisms, Experimental Study, Prevention.* New York, NY: Karger.

Pecina, M. (1993). *Overuse Injuries of the Musculoskeletal System.* Boca Raton, FL: CRC Press.

Posner, M. (2000). *Preventing school Injuries.* Piscataway, NJ: Rutgers University Press.

Prothrow-Stith, D. (1991). *Deadly Consequences.* New York, NY: Harper-Collins.

Prothrow-Stith, D., & Spivak, H. (2003). *Murder is no accident: Understanding and Preventing Youth Violence in America.* John Wiley and Sons.

Reiss, A.J., & Roth, J.A. (1993). *Understanding and Preventing Violence.* Washington, DC: National Academy Press.

Ray, L., & Yuwiler, J. (1994). *A Data Book of Child and Adolescent Injury.* San Diego, CA: Children's Safety Network Injury Data Technical Assistance Center.

Rice, D.P., MacKenzie, E.J., & Associates. (1989). *Cost of Injury in the United States: A Report to Congress.* San Francisco, CA: Institute for Health & Aging, University of California and Injury Prevention Center, The Johns Hopkins University.

Rivara, F.P., Cummings, P., Koepsell, T.D., Grossman, D.C., & Maier, R.V. (2001). *Injury Control: A Guide to Research and Program Evaluation.* Cambridge, UK: Cambridge University Press.

Robertson, L.S. (1998). *Injury Epidemiology* (2nd ed.). New York: Oxford University Press.

Rose, T. (1969). *Violence in America: A Historical and Contemporary Reader.* New York, NY: Random House.

Schwartz, M.D., & DeKeseredy, W.S. (1997). *Sexual Assault on the College Campus: The Role of Male Peer Support.* Thousand Oaks, CA: Sage Publications.

Schmid, A.P. (1982). *Violence as Communication: Insurgent Terrorism and the Western News Media.* Thousand Oaks, CA: Sage Publications.

Sculli, J.G. (1997). *Dating Violence: Youth at Risk .* Plainview, NY: Bureau For At-Risk Youth.

Sipe, B., & Hall, E. (1996). *I am not Your Victim: Anatomy of Domestic Violence.* Thousand Oaks, CA: Sage Publications.

Southerland, M., Collins, P., & Scarborough, K. (1997). *Workplace Violence: A Continuum from Threat to Death.* Cincinnati, OH: Anderson Publishing.

Society of Automotive Engineers. (1993). *Child Occupant Protection.* Warrendale, PA: Society of Automotive Engineers.

Society of Automotive Engineers International. (1996). *Technologies for occupant Protection Assessment: SP-1174.* Warrendale, PA: Society of Automotive Engineers International.

Society of Automotive Engineers International. (1996). *Topics in Vehicle Safety Technology: SP-1139.* Warrendale, PA: Society of Automotive Engineers International.

Stang, L., & Miner, K. R. (1994). *Injury and Violence Prevention: Health Facts.* Santa Cruz, CA: ETR Associates.

Stephens, R.D. (1994). *Safe Schools: A Handbook for Violence Prevention.*

Bloomington, IN: National Educational Service.

Strauss, S, & Espeland, P. (1992). *Sexual Harassment and Teens: A Program for Positive Change.* Minneapolis, MN: Free Spirit Publishing.

Templer, D.I. (1992). *Preventable Brain Damage: Brain Vulnerability and Brain Health.* New York, NY: Springer.

The David and Lucille Packard Foundation (2002). *The Future of Children-Children, Youth, and Gun Violence.* Los Angeles: The David and Lucille Packard Foundation.

The David and Lucille Packard Foundation. (2000). *The Future of Children-Unintentional Injuries in Childhood.* Los Angeles: The David and Lucille Packard Foundation.

Thompson, C., & Cowen, P. (1993). *Violence: Basic and Clinical Science.* Boston, MA: Butterworth-Heinemann.

United States Department of Health & Human Services, Centers for Disease Control. (1991). *Injury Mortality Atlas for the United States, 1979-1987.* Atlanta, GA: Centers for Disease Control.

United States Department of Health & Human Services, Centers for Disease Control. (1991). *Position Papers from The Third National Injury Control Conference.* Atlanta, GA: Centers for Disease Control.

Waller, J.A. (1985). *Injury Control.* Lexington, MA: Lexington Books.

Weiner, N.A. (1990). *Violence: Patterns, Causes, Public Policy.* San Diego, CA: Harcourt Brace Jovanovich.

Whetsell-Mitchell, J. (1995). *Rape of the Innocent: Understanding and Preventing Child Sexual Abuse.* Washington, D.C.: Accelerated Development.

Whitaker, L.C., & Pollard, J.W. (1993). *Campus Violence: Kinds, Causes, and Cures.* Binghamton, NY: Haworth Press.

Whitham, R.A. (1994). *Making Sense out of Nonsense: Models of Head Injury Rehabilitation.* Houston, TX: HDI Publishers.

Williams, K., Guerra, N., & Elliot, D. (1996). *Human Development and Violence Prevention: A Focus on Youth.* Boulder, CO: Center for the Study and Prevention of Violence.

Wilson, M.H., Baker, S.P., Teret, S.P., Shock, S., & Garbarino, J. (1991). *Saving Children-A Guide to Injury Prevention.* New York: Oxford University Press.

Wright, J.D., Rossi, P.H., & Daly, K. (1983). *Under the Gun: Weapons, Crime, and Violence in America.* New York, NY: Aldine De Gruyter.

VI. Related Listservs

- **BIOMCH-L** is a list is intended for members of the International, European, American, Canadian and other Societies of Biomechanics, ISEK (International Society of Electrophysiological Kinesiology), and for all others with an interest in the general field of biomechanics and human or animal movement. For the scope of this list, see, e.g., the Journal of Biomechanics (Pergamon Press), the Journal of Biomechanical Engineering (ASME), or Human Movement Science (North-Holland). Biomch-L is operated under the Patronage of the International Society of Biomechanics.Technical help can be obtained by sending the command 'sendbiomch-l guide' to LISTSERV@HEARN or LISTSERV@NIC.SURF NET.NL, or by contacting one of the list owners.Contact: listserv@nic.

surfnet.nl (Ton van den Bogert). **LISTSERV@NIC.SURFNET.NL**

- **CPSCINFO-L.** CPSC List server application for automatic distribution of CPSC press releases and the CPSC Public Calendar. **LISTPROC@ CPSC.GOV**

- **EHS-INFO** has been created to sponsor and support peer discussions among individuals researching, developing or implementing informatics-related initiatives for prehospital and hospital emergency health services systems or organizations. The list is called EHS-INFO (Emergency Health Informatics and Information Systems). For more information, contact: Ronald Benoit (ron@aemrc.arizona.edu). **LISTPROC@ AEMRC.ARIZONA.EDU**

- **EJINTVIO**, the Electronic Journal of Intimate Violence, is published as a list. Topics include physical child abuse, sexual child abuse, child neglect, physical spouse abuse, sexual spouse abuse, psychological abuse, elder abuse, and dating violence, as well as other related topics subscribers may wish to explore. For more information contact Glenn Wolfner, Assistant Director of Family Violence Research Program at the University of Rhode Island. Send comments and questions to the editors (famviol@uri.acc.edu). **LISTSERV@URIACC.URI.EDU**

- **EMSNY-L** is a forum for discussion of issues affecting EMS providers. Although the focus is on New York State issues, often the discussion is far broader. For instance, a recent thread discussed the need for CPR certification by EMT's. When appropriate, questions are answered by State EMS staff. The listserv includes a number of files of interest, including New York State laws and rules related to EMS. List manager: John D. Lewis. Internet address: jdl02%albnydh2.bitnet@uacsc2.albany.edu. **LISTSERV@ALBNYDH@.BITNET**

- **INJURY-L** is a list for injury research, epidemiology and prevention maintained by the Center for Rural Emergency Medicine and the Injury Control Center of West Virginia University. Injury-L Listserv is a front end to Injury-L. The valuable Injury-L Archives can be found here as well. List manager: Paul M. (Mike) Furbee, Research Coordinator, Center for Rural Emergency Medicine, P.O. BOX 9151, Robert C. Byrd Health Sciences Center, Morgantown WV 26506, (304) 293-6682. E-mail address: furbee@wvu.edu. **LISTSERV@WVNVM.WVNET.EDU**

- **INTVIO-L** is devoted to all aspects of family violence. It is maintained by the Family Violence Research Team at the University of Rhode Island. The INTVIO-L list serves as a networking system devoted to all aspects of family violence. While various other lists may explore the topics of child abuse or violence within the family, the intimate violence list is unique in that it serves a wide range of areas that constitute the definition of intimate violence. This list is designed to encompass all areas of interest regarding family violence rather than limiting discussion to one interest. **LISTSERV@URIACC.URI.EDU**

- **SAFETY** list discusses safety issues, with a focus on educational institutions. **LISTSERV@UVMVM.UVM.EDU**

- **TBI-SPRT**. The St. Johns University Traumatic Brain Injury Support List was created for the exchange of information by survivors, supporters, and professionals concerned with traumatic brain injury and other neurological impairments. TBI-SPRT listserv archive contains the more substantial discussion threads that have occurred on TBI-SPRT since the list came on-line. They have been sorted by topic and date. Also see the related WEB site, TBI-SPRT (Traumatic Brain Injury Support List) Home Page. List owner: Len Burns (lburns@sasquatch.com).
  LISTSERV@SJUVM.STJOHNS.EDU

- **EPIDEMIOL-L**. Epidemiology list server.
  LISTPROC@CC.UMONTREAL.CA

- **TRAUMA-LIST** is a forum for professionals and interested laypersons for the discussion of trauma and burn injuries, including their prevention, treatment, and sequelae. It is maintained at Duquesne University, Pittsburgh, Pennsylvania, in cooperation with the Division of Multisystem Trauma at The Mercy Hospital of Pittsburgh. For information contact Victor L. Landry, Ph.D. (412) 232-8414; fax (412) 232-8096 Dept. of Biological Science, Mellon Hall, Duquesne University, Pittsburgh, PA 15282. **MAJORDOMO@DUQLISTS.DUQ.EDU**

* Members of ISCAIP can join the ISCAIP discussion group—see **ISCAIP@yahoogroups.com**

Data charts from the National Center for Injury Prevention and Control, Centers for Disease Control and Prevention

Table 1

10 Leading Causes of Death, United States, 2002, All Races, Both Sexes

Rank	<1	1–4	5–9	10–14	15–24	25–34	35–44	45–54	55–64	65+	All Ages
1	Congenital Anomalies 5623	Unint. Injury 1641	Unint. Injury 1176	Unint. Injury 1542	Unint. Injury 15 412	Unint. Injury 12 569	Unint. Injury 16 710	Malignant Neoplasms 49 637	Malignant Neoplasms 91 793	Heart Disease 576 301	Heart Disease 696 947
2	Short Gestation 4637	Congenital Anomalies 530	Malignant Neoplasms 537	Malignant Neoplasms 535	Homicide 5219	Suicide 5046	Malignant Neoplasms 16 085	Heart Disease 37 470	Heart Disease 64 234	Malignant Neoplasms 391 001	Malignant Neoplasms 557 271
3	SIDS 2295	Homicide 423	Congenital Anomalies 199	Suicide 260	Suicide 4010	Homicide 4489	Heart Disease 13 688	Unint. Injury 14 675	CLR Disease 11 280	Cerebro-Vascular 143 293	Cerebro-Vascular 162 672
4	Mat. Preg. Comp. 1708	Malignant Neoplasms 402	Homicide 140	Congenital Anomalies 218	Malignant Neoplasms 1730	Malignant Neoplasms 3872	Suicide 6851	Liver Disease 7216	Diabetes Mellitus 10 022	CLR Disease 108 313	CLR Disease 124 816
5	Placenta Cord Mem. 1028	Heart Disease 165	Heart Disease 92	Homicide 216	Heart Disease 1022	Heart Disease 3165	HIV 5707	Suicide 6308	Cerebro-vascular 9897	Influenza & Pneumonia 58 826	Unint. Injury 106 742
6	Unint. Injury 946	Influenza & Pneumonia 110	Benign Neoplasms 44	Heart Disease 163	Congenital Anomalies 492	HIV 1,839	Homicide 3239	Cerebro-Vascular 6055	Unint. Injury 8345	Alzheimer's Disease 58 289	Diabetes Mellitus 73 249
7	Respiratory Distress 943	Septicemia 79	Septicemia 42	CLR Disease 95	CLR Disease 192	Diabetes Mellitus 642	Liver Disease 3154	Diabetes Mellitus 5496	Liver Disease 6097	Diabetes Mellitus 54 715	Influenza & Pneumonia 65 681
8	Bacterial Sepsis 749	CLR Disease 65	CLR Disease 41	Cerebro-Vascular 58	HIV 178	Cerebro-Vascular 567	Cerebro-Vascular 2425	HIV 4474	Suicide 3618	Nephritis 35 636	Alzheimer's Disease 58 866
9	Circ. Syst. Disease 667	Perinatal Period 65	Influenza & Pneumonia 38	Influenza & Pneumonia 53	Cerebro-Vascular 171	Congenital Anomalies 475	Diabetes Mellitus 2164	CLR Disease 3475	Nephritis 3455	Unint. Injury 33 641	Nephritis 40 974
10	Intrauterine Hypoxia 583	Benign Neoplasms 60	Cerebro-Vascular 33	Septicemia 53	Diabetes Mellitus 171	Liver Disease 374	CLR Disease 1008	Viral Hepatitis 2331	Septicemia 3360	Septicemia 26 670	Septicemia 33 865

Circ. Syst. Disease = Circulatory System Disease; CLR Disease = Chronic Low Respiratory Disease; Mat. Preg. Comp. = Maternal Pregnancy Complications; Placenta Cord Mem. = Placenta Cord Membranes; Unint. Injury = Unintentional Injury.

Table 2

10 Leading Causes of Nonfatal Injury, United States, 2003, All Races, Both Sexes, Disposition: All Cases

Rank	<1	1–4	5–9	10–14	15–24	25–34	35–44	45–54	55–64	65+	All Ages
1	Unint. Fall 122 276	Unint. Fall 865 209	Unint. Fall 670 107	Unint. Fall 678 897	Unint.Struck by/Against 973 073	Unint. Fall 754 691	Unint. Fall 812 270	Unint. Fall 739 365	Unint. Fall 563 973	Unint. Fall 1 822 157	Unint. Fall 7 895 385
2	Unint. Struck by/Against 33 132	Unint. Struck by/Against 364 168	Unint. Struck by/Against 411 733	Unint. Struck by/Against 593 148	Unint. MV-Occupant 916 330	Unint. Overexertion 694 464	Unint. Overexertion 657 267	Unint. Overexertion 436 494	Unint. Overexertion 193 361	Unint. Struck by/Against 194 435	Unint. Struck by/Against 4 422 252
3	Unint. Fire/Burn 11 306	Unint. Other Bite/Sting 134 964	Unint. Cut/Pierce 125 350	Unint. Overexertion 278 182	Unint. Fall 866 078	Unint. Struck by/Against 675 770	Unint. Struck by/Against 594 628	Unint. Struck by/Against 390 563	Unint. Struck by/Against 191 370	Unint. MV-Occupant 186 278	Unint. Overexertion 3 324 641
4	Unint. Other Bite/Sting 11 141	Unint. Other Bite/Sting 108 037	Unint. Pedal Cyclist 113 513	Unint. Cut/Pierce 158 011	Unint. Overexertion 746 386	Unint. MV-Occupant 629 739	Unint. MV-Occupant 522 621	Unint. MV-Occupant 351 415	Unint. MV-Occupant 186 101	Unint. Overexertion 168 995	Unint. MV-Occupant 3 026 595
5	Unint. Cut/Pierce 7731	Unint. Cut/Pierce 85 140	Unint. Other Bite/Sting 91 662	Unint. Pedal Cyclist 141 252	Unint. Cut/Pierce 493 032	Unint. Cut/Pierce 441 956	Unint. Cut/Pierce 391 061	Unint. Cut/Pierce 273 232	Unint. Cut/Pierce 143 244	Unint. Cut/Pierce 116 915	Unint. Cut/Pierce 2 235 869
6	Unint. MV-Occupant 7713	Unint. Overexertion 67 227	Unint. Overexertion 76 045	Unint. Unk/Unspecified 117 463	Oth.Assault* Strk. by/Agnst. 436 395	Oth.Assault* Strk. by/Agnst. 270 689	Oth.Assault* Strk. by/Agnst. 218 136	Unint. Other Specified 141 179	Unint. Other Bite/Sting 65 417	Unint. Other Bite/Sting 77 191	Oth.Assault* Strk.by/Agnst. 1 247 857
7	Unint. Foreign Body 7465	Unint. Poisoning 62 661	Unint. MV-Occupant 71 653	Oth.Assault* Strk. by/Agnst. 116 873	Unint. Other Bite/Sting 164 502	Unint. Other Bite/Sting 141 176	Unint. Oth. Specified 175 356	Unint. Other Bite/Sting 106 604	Unint. Other Specified 51 566	Unint. Poisoning 46 581	Unint. Other Bite/Sting 998 451
8	Unint. Poisoning 6095	Unint. Fire/Burn 58 931	Unint. Other Transport 51 878	Unint. MV-Occupant 108 609	Unint. Unk/ Unspecified 164 325	Unint. Other Specified 138 591	Unint. Oth Bite/Sting 142 866	Oth.Assault* Strk. by/Agnst. 101 341	Unint. Poisoning 34 436	Unint. Other Transport 46 507	Unint. Other Specified 763 029
9	Unint. Overexertion 5975	Unint. Unk/ Unspecified 50 343	Unint. Dog Bite 49 285	Unint. Other Transport 64 821	Unint. Other Specified 148 112	Unint. Other Transport 102 373	Unint. Poisoning 106 914	Unint. Poisoning 86 187	Unint. Unk/ Unspecified 32 529	Unint. Unk/ Unspecified 45 837	Unint. Unk/ Unspecified 688 779
10	Unint. Unk/ Unspecified 5703	Unint. MV-Occupant 43 495	Unint. Foreign Body 48 816	Unint. Other Bite/Sting 62 926	Unint. Other Transport 137 327	Unint.Unk/ Unspecified 97 096	Unint. Foreign Body 89 692	Unint. Other Transport 63 781	Unint. Other Transport 32 097	Unint. Other Specified 36 156	Unint. Other Transport 619 544

Oth. = Other; Strk. by/Agnst. = Struck by/Against; Unint. = Unintentional; Unk. = Unknown

Produced by: Office of Statistics and Programming, National Center for Injury Prevention and Control, CDC

Data Source: NEISS All Injury Program operated by the Consumer Product Safety Commission (CPSC).

* The 'Other Assault' Category includes all assaults that are not classified as sexual assault. It represents the majority of assaults.

Table 3

10 Leading Causes of Nonfatal Violence-Related Injury, United States, 2003, All Races, Both Sexes, Disposition: All Cases

Rank	<1	1–4	5–9	10–14	15–24	25–34	35–44	45–54	55–64	65+	All Ages
1	Oth. Assault† Strk. by/Agnst. 2017	Oth. Assault† Strk. by/Agnst. 15 308	Oth. Assault† Strk. by/Agnst. 40 050	Oth. Assault† Strk. by/Agnst. 116 873	Oth. Assault† Strk. by/Agnst. 436 395	Oth. Assault† Strk. by/Agnst. 270 689	Oth. Assault† Strk. by/Agnst. 218 136	Oth. Assault† Strk. by/Agnst. 101 341	Oth. Assault† Strk. by/Agnst. 28 892	Oth. Assault† Strk. by/Agnst. 18 045	Oth. Assault† Strk. by/Agnst. 1 247 857
2	Oth. Assault† Oth. Bite/Sting 559*	Sexual Assault 9712	Sexual Assault 7727	Self-harm Poisoning 12 492	Self-harm Poisoning 79 212	Self-harm Poisoning 60 764	Self-harm Poisoning 65 133	Self-harm Poisoning 40 642	Self-harm Poisoning 10 738	Self-harm Poisoning 4611	Self-harm Poisoning 273 898
3	Oth. Assault† Fire/Burn 287*	Oth. Assault† Oth. Bite/Sting 2634	Oth. Assault† Cut/Pierce 2308*	Sexual Assault 11 323	Oth. Assault† Cut/Pierce 49 900	Oth. Assault† Cut/Pierce 34 667	Oth. Assault† Cut/Pierce 22 599	Oth. Assault† Cut/Pierce 8976	Oth. Assault† Cut/Pierce 2216	Oth. Assault† Cut/Pierce 766*	Oth. Assault† Cut/Pierce 126 720
4	Oth. Assault† Fall 274*	Oth. Assault† Fall 1326*	Oth. Assault† Fall 1676	Oth. Assault† Cut/Pierce 4403	Sexual Assault 27 354	Self-harm Cut/Pierce 17 429	Self-harm Cut/Pierce 13 409	Self-harm Oth. Specified 7703	Self-harm Cut/Pierce 1780	Self-harm Cut/Pierce 757*	Sexual Assault 73 834
5	Sexual Assault 254*	Oth. Assault† Cut/Pierce 850*	Oth. Assault† Oth. Bite/Sting 1489*	Oth. Assault† Oth. Bite/Sting 4359	Self-harm Cut/Pierce 25 675	Oth. Assault† Firearm/Gun. 13 301	Self-harm Oth. Specified 11 129	Self-harm Cut/Pierce 5729	Legal Int. Strk. by/Agnst. 1124*	Self-harm Oth. Specified 750*	Self-harm Cut/Pierce 68 910
6	Oth. Assault† Unk/Unspec. 170*	Oth. Assault† Fire/Burn 629*	Oth. Assault† Overexertion 639*	Oth. Assault† Fall 4314	Oth. Assault† Firearm/Gun. 18 998	Oth. Assault† Oth. Bite/Sting 12 591	Oth. Assault† Oth. Bite/Sting 8963	Oth. Assault† Oth. Bite/Sting 4545	Oth. Assault† Oth. Bite/Sting 915*	Oth. Assault† Oth. Bite/Sting 618*	Oth. Assault† Oth. Bite/Sting 54 963
7	Oth. Assault† Oth. Specified 50*	Oth. Assault† Poisoning 323*	Oth. Assault† Fire/Burn 538*	Self-harm Cut/Pierce 3500	Oth. Assault† Oth. Bite/Sting 18 291	Legal Int. Strk. by/Agnst. 11 179	Legal Int. Strk. by/Agnst. 7119	Legal Int. Strk. by/Agnst. 3762	Self-harm Oth. Specified 835*	Sexual Assault 524*	Self-harm Oth. Specified 43 154
8	Oth. Assault† Unk/Unspec. 29*	Oth. Assault† Overexertion 286*	Self-harm Cut/Pierce 478*	Self-harm Oth. Specified 1823	Legal Int. Strk. by/Agnst. 13 195	Self-harm Oth. Specified 10 023	Sexual Assault 6845	Oth. Assault† Firearm/Gun. 2490*	Oth. Assault† Oth. Specified 761*	Oth. Assault† Fall 346*	Oth. Assault† Firearm/Gun. 42 455
9	Legal Int. Strk. by/Agnst. 25*	Oth. Assault† Overexertion 273*	Self-harm Poisoning 280*	Legal Int. Strk. by/Agnst. 881*	Self-harm Oth. Specified 10 872	Sexual Assault 8194	Oth. Assault† Firearm/Gun. 5605	Oth. Assault† Oth. Specified 2311	Oth. Assault† Fall 741*	Oth. Assault† Firearm/Gun 339*	Legal Int. Strk. by/Agnst. 37 590
10	Two Tied 10*	Legal Int. Dog Bite 140*	Oth. Assault† Foreign Body 265*	Oth. Assault† Overexertion 861*	Oth. Assault† Fall 6873	Oth. Assault† Overexertion 6956	Oth. Assault† Fall 5352	Oth. Assault† Fall 1742	Oth. Assault† Firearm/Gun. 637*	Self-harm Firearm/Gun. 311*	Oth. Assault† Fall 27 816

Firearm/Gun. = Firearm/Gunshot; Oth. = Other; Strk. by/Agnst. = Struck by/Against; Unint. = Unintentional; Unk = Unknown; Unspec. = Unspecified.
Produced by: Office of Statistics and Programming, National Center for Injury Prevention and Control, CDC
Data Source: NEISS All Injury Program operated by the Consumer Product Safety Commission (CPSC).
† The 'Other Assault' Category includes all assaults that are not classified as sexual assault. It represents the majority of assaults.

Table 4

National Estimates of the 10 Leading Causes of Nonfatal Injuries, Treated in Hospital Emergency Departments, United States, 2002

Rank	<1	1–4	5–9	10–14	15–24	25–34	35–44	45–54	55–64	65+	All Ages
1	Unint. Fall 126 459	Unint. Fall 870 950	Unint. Fall 676 444	Unint. Fall 659 923	Unint. Strk. by/Agnst. 951 681	Unint. Fall 702 946	Unint. Fall 765 275	Unint. Fall 634 042	Unint. Fall 490 737	Unint. Fall 1 638 883	Unint. Fall 7 410 159
2	Unint. Strk. by/Agnst. 33 021	Unint. Strk. by/Agnst. 390 945	Unint. Strk. by/Agnst. 449 222	Unint. Strk. by/Agnst. 622 615	Unint. MV-Occupant 902 196	Unint. Overexertion 701 783	Unint. Overexertion 656 122	Unint. Overexertion 350 639	Unint. Strk. by/Agnst. 185 922	Unint. MV-Occupant 193 063	Unint. Strk. by/Agnst. 4 490 061
3	Unint. Fire/Burn 13 193	Unint. Oth. Bite/Sting 126 710	Unint. Cut/Pierce 135 098	Unint. Overexertion 268 074	Unint. Fall 794 263	Unint. Strk. by/Agnst. 671 811	Unint. Strk. by/Agnst. 609 021	Unint. Strk. by/Agnst. 385 139	Unint. MV-Occupant 179 527	Unint. Strk. by/Agnst. 190 501	Unint. Overexertion 3 286 856
4	Unint. Oth. Bite/Sting 10 926	Unint. Foreign Body 106 331	Unint. Pedal Cyclist 118 046	Unint. Cut/Pierce 170 062	Unint. Overexertion 758 312	Unint. MV-Occupant 609 656	Unint. MV-Occupant 515 768	Unint. MV-Occupant 332 260	Unint. Overexertion 175 009	Unint. Overexertion 156 231	Unint. MV-Occupant 2 933 054
5	Unint. MV-Occupant 9 336	Unint. Cut/Pierce 87 836	Unint. Oth. Bite/Sting 96 330	Unint. Pedal Cyclist 142 085	Unint. Cut/Pierce 492 172	Unint. Cut/Pierce 461 058	Unint. Cut/Pierce 394 133	Unint. Cut/Pierce 272 953	Unint. Cut/Pierce 142 911	Unint. Cut/Pierce 115 708	Unint. Cut/Pierce 2 278 105
6	Unint. Poisoning 8 814	Unint. Poisoning 76 238	Unint. MV-Occupant 79 531	Unint. MV-Occupant 115 920	Oth. Assault* Strk. by/Agnst. 445 965	Oth. Assault* Strk. by/Agnst. 271 774	Oth. Assault* Strk. by/Agnst. 226 208	Oth. Assault* Strk. by/Agnst. 102 941	Unint. Oth. Bite/Sting 57 805	Unint. Oth. Bite/Sting 70 093	Oth. Assault* Strk. by/Agnst. 1 270 224
7	Unint. Foreign Body 8 776	Unint. Overexertion 74 530	Unint. Overexertion 76 811	Oth. Assault* Strk. by/Agnst. 114 891	Unint. Oth. Bite/Sting 126 498	Unint. Oth. Bite/Sting 121 398	Unint. Oth. Specified 129 831	Unint. Oth. Bite/Sting 94 895	Unint. Oth. Specified 37 399	Unint. Unk/Unspec. 47 825	Unint. Oth. Bite/Sting 890 910
8	Unint. Unk/Unspec. 6 916	Unint. Fire/Burn 62 673	Unint. Foreign Body 54 164	Unint. Unk/Unspec. 129 355	Unint. Unk/Unspec. 174 572	Unint. Oth. Specified 110 163	Unint. Oth. Bite/Sting 115 409	Unint. Oth. Specified 93 356	Unint. Oth. Transport 34 315	Unint. Oth. Transport 44 759	Unint. Unk/Unspec. 742 185
9	Unint. Inhalation/Suff. 6 452	Unint. MV-Occupant 50 331	Unint. Oth. Bite/Sting 51 882	Unint. Oth. Transport 65 375	Unint. Oth. Transport 126 085	Unint. Unk/Unspec. 109 749	Unint. Poisoning 97 480	Unint. Poisoning 74 802	Unint. Unk/Unspec. 28 358	Unint. Poisoning 31 073	Unint. Oth. Transport 594 127
10	Unint. Overexertion 6 336	Unint. Unk/Unspec. 48 293	Unint. Unk/Unspec. 48 079	Unint. Oth. Bite/Sting 60 780	Unint. Oth. Specified 111 000	Unint. Oth. Transport 95 680	Unint. Unk/Unspec. 92 403	Unint. Foreign Body 57 803	Oth. Assault* Strk. by/Agnst. 26 989	Unint. Foreign Body 28 723	Unint. Foreign Body 577 622

Oth. = Other; Strk. by/Agnst. = Struck by/Against; Unint. = Unintentional; Unk. = Unknown; Unspec. = Unspecified.

Chart developed by the National Center for Injury Prevention and Control, CDC

Data Source: National Electronic Injury Surveillance System All Injury Program operated by the Consumer Product Safety Commission (CPSC).

* The 'Other Assault' Category includes all assaults that are not classified as sexual assault. It represents the majority of assaults.